Introduction to PSYCHOPATHOLOGY

LAWRENCE I. O'KELLY

Professor of Psychology
University of Illinois

FREDERICK A. MUCKLER

Human Factors Specialist
The Martin Company

Introduction to

PSYCHOPATHOLOGY

SECOND EDITION

PRENTICE-HALL, INC.
Englewood Cliffs, N.J.

FOURTH PRINTING.........AUGUST, 1959

L. C. Cat. Card No.: 55-10156

49379

Preface to the Second Edition

In the first edition of this book the fundamentals of psychopathology were presented in a manner readily understandable by the advanced undergraduate student and were organized to be consistent with the general tenor of contemporary biological and social science. In the present edition we have tried to preserve and strengthen the book on both fronts. To this end the present edition has an altered order of topics, both between and within chapters, the new order being based on the recommendations of others and our own experience in teaching the first edition. Some of the chapters have been shortened, some divided, and several completely recast. The entire book has been carefully re-examined in the light of accumulated publication since 1948, and where new material has warranted, changes have been made. The bibliographic notes have been completely reworked. We hope they will prove of value to the student who wishes to read more widely and to the instructor who wishes to assign additional reading.

Our list of obligations is long. In addition to those who helped with the first edition, we are materially indebted to all the students and teachers who gave us their comments and suggestions for improvement of the earlier work. Our gratitude is extended to Nancy and John Nygaard for valuable editorial assistance. And, as is usual in such enterprises, the whole project was made possible by the tolerance and active cooperation of our wives, who typed, filed, and read far beyond the call of duty.

LAWRENCE I. O'KELLY
FREDERICK A. MUCKLER

Table of Contents

Introduction to Basic Concepts

Abnormal Psychology . . . An introduction to the psychological aspects of the behavior disorders . . . Prerequisite: a course in elementary psychology.

—FROM A UNIVERSITY CATALOGUE

Introduction

Man in sooth is a marvellous vain, fickle, and unstable subject.
—MONTAIGNE

Before we start the rather difficult matter of defining psychopathology, let us talk for a moment in more general terms about the subject matter of this science. If we humans were always happy and contented, if we always learned rapidly and efficiently to perform all the tasks that life imposes, if we never forgot nor confused our memories, if we were shielded from accident and disease, if we never hurt nor were hurt by other people—if, in short, life were impossibly perfect, this book could not have been written, for there would be no such science as psychopathology. In this book we will be concerned with the causes, symptoms, and consequences of unhappiness, discontent, inefficiency, and with many of the ways that people's behavior and personalities are affected by injury and disease.

The reader might be tempted, and one could hardly blame him, to stop at this point and conclude that such a book would be indeed a gloomy and morbid production and that the authors of such a book could only be a variety of latter-day scientific hobgoblin. But there is a more hopeful aspect of the matter. Modern science studies disease with the motive of finding ways to remedy and control it. One of the necessary steps toward happiness and a more effective life, for the individual or society, is an understanding of unhappiness. Also, since everyone has his own season of unhappiness, his own sense of disparity between aspiration and accomplishment, this book is not just about other people, but is, here and there, about your problems and ours. In this sense, we can approach our subject in the same way we approach any part of psychology, knowing that one of the great personal motives for studying the science is the comfortable egocentric feeling that we are engaged in an effort to understand ourselves.

There is another preliminary point we should discuss. Let us state some ground rules and general admonitions culled from the experience of people who have explored this area before us. Some of these are of the most prosaic sort, somewhat equivalent to the inevitable lists of personal equipment one receives when going away to camp. Others are peculiar to the study of psychopathology. If all are followed, our journey will be pleasantly rewarding.

We start with the most obvious ones first:

1. *Psychopathology derives its way of expression from a conglomerate mass of special fields of learning.* Its data come from medicine, physiology, psychology, sociology, philosophy, theology, anthropology, and a dozen or so other disciplines. Consequently, its terminology dances madly through whole dictionaries of Latin and Greek roots, with a cosmopolitan representation of more modern tongues. Luckily there isn't a technical term that we employ that cannot be approximately defined in the combination of (a) a collegiate dictionary, (b) a medical dictionary, and (c) a psychological dictionary. Some useful dictionaries are mentioned in the Bibliographic Sources at the end of this chapter. Also, we will try to give specific definitions of terms as we go along. The rule is: *Understand the terms.*

2. *There is, at present, more of theory than of fact in psychopathology.* It is a *young science,* a *complicated science,* and *it is sometimes almost as difficult to attack experimentally as astronomy.* Yet it lives under the understandably human pressure of the need to help sick people get well. All this has encouraged a number of bold speculative approaches to explanation. In this book we shall try to distinguish between the varying degrees of certainty that exist over any specific aspect of the subject, but in supplementary reading and sometimes here also, the reader must assume the burden of evaluation. The rule is: *Distinguish theory from empirical evidence, and learn to withold judgment.*

3. Somewhat related is the matter of case studies as evidence. A number of short descriptions of the tribulations of individuals are cited in this book, and you will find similar cases in other such books. These case histories are to be used primarily as concrete illustrations of causes, symptoms, or treatments. For the most part, they are, in themselves,

very poor evidence for or against any theoretical point. They are, perhaps, fragments of data, but as single cases they establish nothing. The rule is: *Use the case as you would pictures, to see the appearance of phenomena, but not as competent arbiters of disputed issues.*

4. Because the subject matter of our study involves the hardships and perplexities that people have encountered in their everyday lives, it is almost certain that the student will perceive some fragment of himself in our descriptions of symptoms and causes. Indeed, it is very easy for a person to convince himself that he "has" the disorder about which he is studying. Much the same thing happens to medical students and the readers of the "home advice" type of medical essay in connection with somatic diseases whose symptoms are frequently a great deal more delimited and sharply defined than most of the disorders that we are about to study. This "suggestibility," to which humans seem peculiarly prone, can give us some bad moments if we are not aware of its operation. This leads to another helpful rule: *Before becoming alarmed about the seeming resemblance between the symptoms of some disorder discussed here and your own personal characteristics, do three things;* (a) *wait to see if other disorders are not equally suggestive,* (b) *ask yourself if the symptoms you seem to be experiencing are really constant and incapacitating, and* (c) *discuss your difficulties with your instructor or with some other competent counselors your instructor may recommend.*

5. The rule we have just given refers mostly to a process of "self-diagnosis," and it contains the implication that no person is competent to make such diagnoses on himself, particularly when his training has been confined to the partial subject matter of one course. Exactly these considerations apply to your judgments of other people. Although the study of psychopathology almost certainly will contribute to your knowledge and understanding of the actions of others, it is most dangerous to go around tagging your associates with diagnostic labels on the basis of superficial knowledge of both the person and psychopathology. The techniques needed for performing diagnostic examinations are specialized skills that can be acquired only after several years of closely supervised training in the medical speciality of psychiatry or in clinical psychology. Even the experts are not always sure of their diagnostic impressions. Therefore, let us suggest another rule: *If, on the basis of your observations and growing knowledge of maladjusted behavior, you believe a friend or associate is manifesting symptoms of disordered*

behavior, resist the temptation to label him, withhold judgment, and
if you are still concerned, discuss the matter with your instructor.
"A little knowledge is a dangerous thing" is a proverb worthy of your
meditation.

6. The last two rules require an escape clause. The subject matter of psychopathology lies all around us in the actions of ourselves and our fellows, and it would be poor learning policy if we confined ourselves just to a study of the textbook. On the other hand, it is difficult to provide a laboratory adjunct to a course of this kind. Sometimes it will be possible for your instructor to arrange trips to hospitals or clinics. If this is not possible, there is a very workable substitute that will help to make the course a worth-while experience for you. The daily papers report the whole gamut of distorted human behavior. Add to this incidents or depictions of personality in your fictional reading, your movie and television viewing, and your own personal reflections on these subjects. All this sounds suspiciously like extra labor, which it is, but the dividends of tolerance, understanding, and psychological sophistication make the investment of time attractive. We have found also that effort expended in this direction usually results in better grades. So the rule would be something like this: *Make an active effort to integrate your course content with the broad samples of behavior occurring in the world around you.*

7. This is the last rule; it may or may not be important for any particular person, but since in any class the problem sooner or later appears, it should be dealt with in a preliminary way now. This is the problem of scientific investigation and description versus moral, ethical, and aesthetic attitudes. More than a little of the content of this book is concerned with describing ways of behavior toward which our society or some parts of it have vigorously condemnatory attitudes. Also, some aspects of disordered behavior may be of negative aesthetic value. A necessary part of the scientific attitude is a vigorous attempt to maintain a steady objectivity toward the data which it is examining, and to minimize the ever-present danger of confusing the data by the distortions of subjective evaluation. For example, incestuous sexual relations are strongly forbidden in our culture, yet incestful behavior does occur, and as item of information must be impartially considered. The rule: *Maintain an objective attitude toward behavior, recognizing the importance of eliminating subjective moral, ethical, and aesthetic biases in your acceptance and interpretation of data.*

Definition of Psychopathology

Psychopathology may be tentatively defined as the branch of science that studies *defective, inefficient, or maladjustive behavior.* Interest is centered on the causes, symptoms, and consequences of such behavior. It is usual to call maladjustive behavior "abnormal," and much of the subject matter of psychopathology, as we are defining it, is frequently termed "abnormal" psychology.

As an introduction to the problems and content of what we will be studying in this book, let us start out by presenting brief abstracts of representative examples of maladjustive behavior. The first account gives a number of symptoms rather clearly but is vague about causation. The second account gives a superficial view of causes, only a little of symptoms, but quite directly reveals some of the possible consequences of maladjustment.

Case 1. Four young men came into the senior writer's office and announced that they were a committee from one of the campus fraternities. They said they wanted to consult me about one of their fraternity brothers. This boy, John, was behaving in ways that alarmed them, but they weren't certain what to do about it. He had seemed to be a likeable person when he was pledged and had withstood his neophyte period as well as any of the pledges, although they had noticed that he was somewhat shy and undertook tasks with an almost desperate intensity. During the present school year, however, John seemed to be developing a new personality. It started with a request John made for another roommate. When asked his reasons for wanting to make this change, John informed the committee that decided such things that his roommate had made homosexual advances and had also stolen some money. Circumstances were such that the accusations were taken lightly, and "to humor him," John was allowed to move to another room. A few weeks later John broke up a friendly game of bridge one evening by accusing his opponents of having a series of bidding signals and an extra deck of cards. He insisted on going through the cards they were using and placing small distinguishing marks on the face of every card. Only the intervention of bystanders prevented a fight. A short time later, the fraternity leader was summoned to the office of the Dean of Men, who showed him a letter, written by John, accusing the fraternity of requiring its members to participate in "sexual perversions" in order to maintain their active status. The Dean suggested that John be referred to the Student Health Service. However, when the leaders tried to do this, John submitted his resignation and moved out of the house. Matters had come to a head at the time the committee reported this, because John's father, who was a former "great" of the fraternity, was coming to visit and apparently knew nothing about the situation. Our advice, of course, was to tell the father that his son was sick and to put the responsibility for handling John in the hands of the psychiatrist at the Student Health Service.

Case 2. Jim was an electrician with three children and a wife who had social aspirations. He had an income that was above average but no more than was needed to support his family in moderate circumstances. His wife, whose parents occupied a position of some social prominence in their small town, frequently expressed the belief that she had "married below her station." Jim met these attacks on his self-respect by working harder and by going into debt to obtain the satisfactions his wife desired. Neither one faced the problems directly. One day, after a quarrel over money, Jim went out to the garage and ran a piece of garden hose from his truck's exhaust pipe into the cab, shut the doors, and started the motor. A neighbor discovered the situation, and Jim was rushed, still alive, to the hospital. He recovered to an extent, but psychological tests showed that he had incurred irreversible brain damage due to the asphyxiation he had experienced. No longer able to manage his contracting business, no longer able to think as well as his five-year-old child, he stumbled around town, an object of pity even to himself. His brain damage could be traced, not only to the action of carbon monoxide, but also to the series of refusals to face and to solve a serious personal and social problem.

You will find many more examples of disordered behavior in this book. As we said before, we want to introduce to you some of the names, causes, explanations, and treatments of this behavior.

First, however, it should be recognized that psychopathology, like any other branch of science, has implications beyond its own area. A few of these might be mentioned before we begin.

Applications and Values of Psychopathology

RELATIONSHIP TO GENERAL PSYCHOLOGY

Psychopathology is a part of the whole subject matter of general psychology. We will use the same basic concepts as working tools, and the laws or principles of general psychology will be equally applicable to psychopathology. Much of the research that has illuminated causes of maladjustment has been performed on subjects free of behavior disorder. The relationship is comparable to that obtaining between the general physiology of all living things and that special branch of the subject known as *cellular* or *tissue pathology*. The contributions are not unilaterally from general psychology to psychopathology, however. The very exaggerations of adaptive difficulties we see in the clinic and hospital often show the way to more adequate generalizations about the behavior of all people. Almost the first scientist to demonstrate the role of motivation in behavior was Sigmund Freud, a psychiatrist who observed the ways in which behavior was motivated in his patients. Much of what we know at present about thinking has come from studies of people who show disordered thought processes. Our knowledge of brain functions in humans has been materially advanced by observing patients with brain lesions.

More significantly, disordered behavior furnishes stringent tests for the validity of psychological hypotheses. Just because the behavior we are considering is so often unusual or exaggerated, a clearer check on the predictive value of our psychological laws can often be made. This relationship of psychopathology with general psychology has not, unfortunately, been exploited in a systematic manner. In the present state of development of psychological science, as we shall see in later chapters, many theories of behavior have had both their origin and their application exclusively in the frame of reference of disordered behavior, whereas other theories have been almost exclusively concerned with behavior that is considered "normal."

PSYCHOPATHOLOGY AND MEDICINE

There was a time, so recent as to be within the memory of most physicians now in practice, when psychiatry was a medical specialty primarily limited in its application to the custodial care of persons with "hopeless" mental disorders. Formal training for physicians in the psychological sciences was limited to a minor course in psychiatry offered during the junior or senior year of medical school. As Ebaugh and Rymer (1942) have shown in their history of psychiatric education, the average medical student of a few years ago might never have had the opportunity to learn anything about the evaluation of behavioral illness. No attempt was made to teach psychopathology in the medical schools, and most of the great contributions to this science came from individuals who worked privately or in nonacademic institutions.

To a large extent the responsibility for changes in this situation is attributable to the influence of two world wars. In both of these conflicts it was necessary to place great numbers of men in a distressful and difficult institutional environment and to maintain them in an effective state of mental and physical health. The responsibility for this task fell upon the medical and related professional groups. Most physicians saw, for the first time and on a scale that no medical school could approximate, the enormous variety that disordered behavior could assume. The inadequacies of medicine to deal with such problems became apparent. Military leaders were emphatic in their demands for efficient man power, and the extent to which medicine fell short of meeting these demands in World War I is indicated by the following cable received by the Surgeon General and written by General Pershing, commander of the American Expeditionary Forces in Europe:

Prevalence of mental disorders in replacement troops recently received suggests urgent importance of intensive efforts in eliminating mentally unfit from organization of new draft prior to departure from United States.[1]

After that war, interest in psychiatry increased, and the volume of writing and research in both psychiatry and psychopathology was accompanied by a greater emphasis on graduate training of psychiatrists and an increase in the number of physicians engaged in the private practice of psychiatry. World War II, more serious in all respects, brought even more problems of psychological medicine. The same need for careful selection of soldiers in the hope of eliminating the persons already mentally ill before they entered the service was present in both wars, and the task was better performed in the second war. Aside from this, however, the increase in complexity and variety of training, the increase in the severity of battle, and the much longer duration of the second war produced more problems of a psychiatric nature. The needs were so great that many physicians were given a three-month training course and then assigned to psychiatric services. The number of psychiatric casualties rose to over a million, and again it became apparent that disorders of behavior are among the most serious of human health problems.

During the Korean conflict, advances in the treatment of soldiers emotionally disturbed by exposure to combat were demonstrated. Psychiatric teams were located in the combat areas, and by prompt applica-

[1] P. Bailey, F. E. Williams, P. O. Komora, T. W. Salmon, and N. Fenton (1929), *The Medical Department of the United States Army in the World War,* Vol. X. Washington, D. C.: Government Printing Office. The great strides taken by psychiatry during World War I are well told in this official War Department account of the medical history of that conflict.

tion of therapy they were able to restore rapidly many soldiers to active duty.

Since World War II, the United States Public Health Service and the universities of the country have started a vast program of research on problems of disordered behavior and a training program designed to produce psychologists, psychiatrists, and social workers in quantities sufficient to meet the threats to happiness and efficiency posed by problems of pathological behavior. Psychopathology is now being taught in all levels of medical and pre-medical education, and the future physician will have a much more realistic idea of the role that psychological variables play in all problems of health and disease.

SOCIAL APPLICATIONS

War is only one of the social circumstances productive of mental illness. In times of peace our mental hospitals are crowded and have waiting lists. Physicians in general practice have made estimates that from 25 per cent to 75 per cent of their practice is devoted to people with less serious psychiatric problems. The physicians do not stand alone. Psychologists, social workers, personal counselors, vocational advisers, industrial personnel workers, ministers, and a host of other workers spend their time helping those who are falling short of successful adaptation. Table 1 presents some statistics on the current incidence of mental illness. These figures should be multiplied by many times to give an indication of how large a percentage of our population is experiencing psychological difficulties.

It has frequently been said during the last two decades of this troubled century that behavior disorders are on the increase, that more people are succumbing to the threats and anxieties of our frenetic civilization. Certainly the increase in the number of patients in mental hospitals is more than keeping pace with the general increase in our population. Although the general population has increased 14 per cent since 1939, 17 per cent more persons have been admitted to mental hospitals (Wortis, 1953). Another type of statistic is more startling. In 1880, the ratio of state mental hospital patients per 100,000 of population was 63.7 individuals. By 1948, however, the ratio had jumped to 324 individuals per 100,000 of the total United States population (Federal Security Agency, 1952).

It is difficult to say with any certainty, however, that this is due to an increase in the "true" rate or incidence of behavior disorders. There are an increasing number of people in the older age groups where the frequency of mental disorder is high. We are training people to be psychiatrists, clinical psychologists, and social workers at a faster rate also, and this means that the community at large is becoming more sensitive and discriminating of the mentally ill in their midst. As public education concerning matters of psychopathology becomes more general a great deal of the stigma once attached to a mental illness is no longer

TABLE 1

BEHAVIOR DISORDERS IN THE UNITED STATES

Type of Data	Number	Source of Data
Average census, hospitalized psychiatric patients, 1952	704,056	Arestad and McGovern (1953)
Individuals with behavior disorders in U.S.	9,000,000	Estimate by Felix (1953)
Number of men rejected from draft, 1941 to 1945, for psychiatric reasons	1,750,000	Appel (1946)
Number of psychiatric admissions to Army hospitals, 1941 to 1945	1,000,000	Appel (1946); Caldwell (1946)
Psychoneurotics	2,500,000	Estimate by Cobb (1943)
Alcoholics	1,600,000	Estimate by Cobb (1943)
Epileptics	1,500,000	Estimate by Forster (1953)
Number of hospitals, U.S., 1952	6,665	Arestad and McGovern (1953)
Number of mental hospitals, U.S., 1952	585	Arestad and McGovern (1953)
Total number of hospital beds in U.S.; all types of hospitals, 1952	1,541,615	Arestad and McGovern (1953)
Total number of psychiatric beds, U.S., 1952	732,929	Arestad and McGovern (1953)
Full-time employees, mental hospitals, U.S., 1949	100,040	Federal Security Agency (1952)
Total expenditure for care of all psychiatric cases in dollars, U.S., 1952	One billion dollars	Estimate by Felix (1953) and Wortis (1953)

present. More people actively seek out psychiatric care, and thus more people are counted in the statistics. Too, there has been a general trend away from home care of medical problems and toward institutional admittance. This has been true of obstetrical problems as well, and with the growth of institutional facilities families have given up much of the home care of their members with psychological problems. All these factors contribute to the difficulty of deciding whether, or how much of, an increase has really taken place in the incidence of mental illness. The personal opinion of the writers, for what it might be worth, is that there has been a real increase.

At any rate, there is no question that the behavior disorders present a tremendous problem. Note in Table 1 that the facilities necessary for and the cost of behavior disorders are alarming. Notice particularly that the total number of psychiatric beds is more than half the total number of hospital beds for all types of services in the United States. It should be clear from these data that maladjustment is a critical and chronic problem. Unfortunately, there is little general awareness of this fact.

Finally, not the least of the values of a study of psychopathology is the hope it gives us of understanding the deeply moving motives lying at the root of "man's inhumanity to man." All through history, and never more than at present, we see men torturing, persecuting, killing, and enslaving their fellows. War and its consequences seem to all reasoning persons to be acts of barbarism, yet we are powerless to help ourselves. Irony attends this spectacle of strife and aggression when we consider the magnificent and wonderful-sounding names that are given to the motives that drive us to behave so. In the social implications of psychopathology may lie the hope of escape from inhumanity and a release of the truly human values toward which *homo sapiens* has been struggling for so long.

DISCUSSION QUESTIONS

1. What are the roles of theory and experiment in science, with special reference to psychopathology?
2. Why are single case studies inadequate as conclusive evidence?
3. Have you seen examples of mental disorders?
4. What are the mental health facilities in your state?
5. Do you think that the incidence of mental disorders is increasing?
6. Can you suggest reasons for the study of psychopathology other than those given in this chapter?
7. What are some of the ways that abnormal behavior has been presented in literature? What attitudes toward mental illness do you find expressed there?
8. Is the attitude toward mental disorders different from the attitude toward other diseases?
9. What attitude should society have toward mental disorders?
10. Do you think, at this stage, that disordered behavior is always correctly identified or recognized when it occurs?

SUGGESTED READINGS

S. Cobb (1952), *Foundations of Neuropsychiatry* (Rev. Ed.). Baltimore: The Williams & Wilkins Company.

J. C. Coleman (1950), *Abnormal Psychology and Modern Life,* Chapters 1 and 2. Chicago: Scott, Foresman and Company.

A. Deutsch (1946), *The Mentally Ill in America: A History of Their Care and Treatment from Colonial Times.* New York: Columbia University Press.

K. Menninger (1937), *The Human Mind* (2nd Ed.), Chapter 1. New York: Alfred A. Knopf, Inc.

BIBLIOGRAPHIC SOURCES

The seven "rules" we gave in the beginning of this chapter are certainly not intended to be arbitrary dicta. We only hope that they make the time spent with this book more profitable and enjoyable.

The phrase, *abnormal psychology,* is more prevalent than *psychopathology,* and most books with purpose and content similar to this one use the former appellation. We have chosen the latter phrase in order to emphasize the subject matter more and the evaluation of the subject matter less.

Our definition of psychopathology rests on the concept of *adjustment-maladjustment,* treatments of which may be found in Shaffer (1936), Levine (1942), and Symonds (1946). In the next chapter we will relate this concept to the more general biological notion of *adaptation.* The student will find many different definitions of psychopathology in the various texts in this area.

To the student who does not have access to institutions caring for behavior disorders, contact with illustrative case material presents a problem. Two collections of case histories are available: Burton and Harris (1947) and Stone (1949). The *Journal of Abnormal and Social Psychology* contains an occasional case study in some detail. In addition, the periodical, *Case Reports in Clinical Psychology,* is devoted entirely to detailed case studies. If a particular type of case is desired, consult the index number of *Psychological Abstracts,* the abstracts, and then the article. A rich variety of illustrative material may be found in Menninger (1937). The daily newspaper stories of aberrant human behavior are at least substitutes for direct clinical presentations. Parenthetically, you will find that a great number of the case studies presented in this text have reference to military situations. This is a reflection of the impetus of war on the study of and knowledge about psychopathology.

That statistical data on mental ills are unreliable and incomplete is recognized by all authorities. For some of the methodological problems involved, see *Patients in Mental Institutions, 1949* (Federal Security Agency, 1952). Other suggested papers are Oedegaard (1952) and Felix and Cramer (1953). One study of interest is that of Egan, Jackson, and Eanes (1951). Of 2,054 neuropsychiatric draft rejectees who later entered military service, 1,630 or 79.4 per cent rendered satisfactory military service. If this result is valid and can be generalized, it may be seen from Table 1 that over one million men were lost to the service unnecessarily. However, see also the papers by Koontz (1948), Hunt and Wittson (1949), and Hunt, Wittson, and Hunt (1952) on just how well they serve. For further information on the incidence of mental disorders in old age consult Pollock's (1945) chapter in Kaplan (1945) and Himmler (1951). Incidentally, the figure shown in Table 1 on the cost of psychiatric care works out to about $2,000 per minute or $29,000,000 per day (Felix, 1953, p. 1087).

The effect of World War II upon British psychiatry is told in an excellent series of lectures by Rees (1945). For the experiences of American psychiatrists, see Menninger (1947). The problem of the behavior disorders in World War II as seen from the point of view of the military is told by Cooke (1946). That interest has not subsided may be seen from the recent book by Ginzberg, Herma, and Ginsburg (1953).

On the applications and uses of psychopathology, Richards (1946), Louttit (1947), Pennington and Berg (1948, 1954), Burtt (1948), Watson (1949, 1951), and G. W. Shaffer and Lazarus (1952) discuss the work of the clinical psychologist. Some idea of the varied tasks of clinical psychologists may be gained from various chapters in Fryer and Henry (1950) or Brower and Abt (1952). There are many fine psychiatric textbooks such as Noyes (1940), Muncie (1948), Strecker, Ebaugh, and Ewalt (1951), Alexander and Ross (1952), and Cobb (1952). A somewhat more popularized book by Strecker (1952) is delightful reading.

Good dictionaries in this and related areas are sometimes hard to find. For dictionaries of psychology, we suggest Harriman (1947) and Drever (1952). Since many terms in this book originated with psychoanalysis, we also suggest Fodor and Gaynor (1950) for psychoanalytic terms as defined in Freud's works. An immense and extremely handy medical dictionary is Hoerr, Osol, *et al.* (1952).

An excellent supplement to any text or lecture on the subject of psychopathology is the use of visual aids. Fortunately, there are many fine films on almost every topic covered in this book. On sources of films, *Psychological Abstracts* devotes a separate section to the abstracting of films. Producers and suppliers are, of course, numerous. We suggest you contact either (1) Encyclopaedia Britannica Films, 1150 Wilmette Avenue, Wilmette, Illinois, or (2) Psychological Cinema Register, Audio-Visual Aids Library, The Pennsylvania State University, State College, Pennsylvania. The Visual Aids Department of any university or college would probably have a large offering. If you wish to obtain detailed information about a particular film, we suggest the book by A. Nichtenhauser, Marie L. Coleman, and D. S. Ruhe (1953), which offers a description of 51 films and professional recommendations for their use.

✓ *Abnormal Behavior, Adaptation, and Adjustment*

> *Biological success is measured by the fitness of creatures for the lives they lead.*
>
> —JOHN HODGDON BRADLEY

You have heard two words probably more than any other in your previous contact with psychopathology. These are the words "normal" and "abnormal." In this section we will try to examine these words and see just what they signify.

Definition of Normal and Abnormal Behavior

How will we define "normal" and "abnormal" or "pathological"? This is the most troublesome question faced by any one who tries to be systematic in psychopathology, and the difficulty is reflected in the number of differing answers that have been given. In a day when science was young and when all questions of fact received an ethical orientation, the answer was simple: Any behavior that violated the ethical standards of the community was abnormal, or "unnatural," as it was often phrased. From a sheerly statistical point of view this resulted in some interesting divisions. In the early Christian communities the goal of behavior was attainment of utter perfection; most theological writers recognized how far men, in general, fell short of this mark. The deduction is plain: most men are, in this sense, abnormal. Calvin, among others, followed the implications to their limit in his stern and gloomy doctrine of predestination. Some queer incongruities with present-day views emerged; many mentally defective persons were called "God's innocents," and, by implication at least, were recognized as more "normal" than the people whose integrated efforts preserved the social group. Then, as is still true to some extent, many of the ablest scholars were regarded as excessively peculiar and lacking in the criterion traits of normality. The long list of martyrs to science is illustrative. One of the greatest of scientists, Galileo, escaped martyrdom only by a public recantation of what we would regard today as his sanity.

AN OVER-SIMPLIFIED DEFINITION DERIVED
FROM MEDICINE

As the science of medicine progressed and fundamental discoveries were made about disease processes, a new concept of "normal-abnormal" appeared. This consisted of a dichotomous division of people into the "healthy" and the "diseased." It seemed obvious to many thinkers that a state of health was in opposition to a state of disease, and that a person could not be both at the same time. This concept also persists, and we use it when we say of someone, "He's a sick man," or when we remark of another, "My, what a healthy youngster." Intellectually it probably represents only a more materialistic version of the preceding idea of the "good" and the "bad" being respectively normal and abnormal. Incongruities may be discovered within this concept also. In the first place there is the matter of setting limits. When shall we call a person "sick" and when is he "well"? A colleague boasts that he has never been sick a day in his life, yet he has a temper of such violent proportions that slight frustrations often disrupt his office staff for weeks at a time, and his output is lowered to a point far below that of another colleague who has had serious tubercular lesions and has spent months in bed in a sanitarium. The newspapers carried an account of a physician who knew for six months that he had an incurable cancer of the lung. During his last half-year of life, he was elected president of his national professional organization, he carried on an extensive practice, and he participated in a number of social enterprises. To one who did not know that he was fatally ill, his behavior would be classified as that of an extremely healthy person. The dichotomy of "sick-well" suffers the same fate that all narrow classifications must undergo—they are undermined and disqualified by the exceptions, by the border-line individuals who do not fit. It is also evident that poor adaptation with respect to one phase of life's activity does not inevitably imply that a person is equally handicapped in all other aspects of life.

A STATISTICAL DEFINITION

During the latter part of the nineteenth century, when statistics was developing as a powerful intellectual tool in the scientist's equipment, a

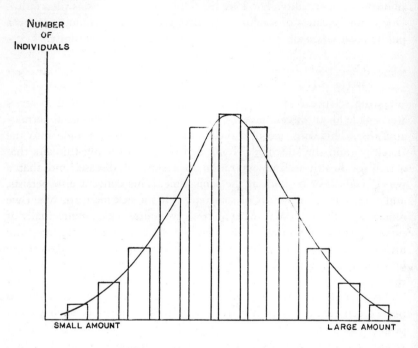

FIGURE 1. *Manner of distribution of many physical and psychological characteristics of living organisms.*

new concept of "normal-abnormal" appeared. Biological and social data, the statisticians observed, fell into orderly arrangements when properly treated. If the intensity or amount of any biological trait was measured in a large number of individuals, and if the number of individuals possessing each measurable degree of the trait were plotted against these various degrees of the trait, the resulting curve almost always assumed the shape shown in Figure 1, a symmetrical bell-shaped curve, having the maximal concentration of individuals in the center and showing fewer and fewer individuals as the curve went out to either extreme of the trait in question. Here seemed a perfectly objective way of distinguishing the normal from the abnormal. All that needed to be done was to equate "normal" with "usual," and "abnormal" with "rare" or "infrequent." Psychopathology, then, had as its subject matter the study of exaggerated or excessively minimized degrees of traits which, in some amount, everyone possessed.

For many types of problem this definition was the most satisfactory yet. Consider mental deficiency. The theologians had called it good, the physicians had called it bad. The statisticians said that everyone possesses some degree of intelligence, as shown by the various "intelligence tests," and the mental defectives were those relatively rare individuals whose small degree of intelligence separated them from the mean intelligence of the population by a recognizable degree. By the same devices, individuals of superior intelligence emerged at the opposite end of the curve. Abnormal psychology, then, would be concerned with quantitative differences, which could be measured, and not qualitative differences, which were so susceptible to errors of prejudice and subjective judgment. This concept has, in part, stood the test of time. We now recognize that everyone expresses to some degree the components of behavior disorder, and that the mentally ill person has symptoms that are directly related to the everyday behavior of all people. The reader will find that this text makes much implicit use of the statistical concept of abnormality.

The statistical approach to psychopathology is effective, but it fails to express sufficiently the problems with which we shall be dealing. The person whose behavior is disordered is not a simple arithmetical pattern of independent, quantitatively varying traits. People express their biosocial natures in many ways, behaving at many levels of adjustment. The relationships between all the variables that determine behavior are not uniformly and completely unitary. The feeble-minded person who is placed at a low position on the curve for distribution of intelligence may be higher than the average on the curve for blood pressure or for weight or for reaction time. Low or high ratings in one trait do not imply or predict similar ratings in other traits. This diversity of trait-degrees, which enter into the composition of all of us, is what makes for *individuals*. Each person is qualitatively as well as quantitatively different in his total make-up from every other person. This is not to say that the various traits do not exert influence on each other within the personality. Those influences, however, are not always in the same direction. High intelligence does not always increase the intensity of application to studies; suspicion of others does not invariably operate to make a person more aware of his environment. Trait interaction proceeds now in one way, now in another, and the resulting complexities go far beyond a simple statistical denotation of what is normal and what is abnormal. In the next section we will try to analyze the whole concept of adaptation and see what it implies for a definition of normality. We can anticipate to the extent, however, of pointing out that humans must adapt at many levels, and that the traits that operate in the direction of *statistical* abnormality at one level may have quite a different effect at another level.

SOCIAL RELATIVITY AS A FACTOR IN DEFINITION

One of the most recent attempts to define the abnormal has come in the past few years and is an outgrowth of the increased activity in social science. As anthropologists brought back descriptions of behavior in cultures other than our own, and as the sociologists secured a more inclusive and accurate picture of our contemporary social environment, it became apparent that human behavior was capable of extremely wide variability, and that many ways of acting, which we had regarded as rare (statistically abnormal), were actually the average way of doing things among other peoples. They also discovered the converse—many accepted and usual ways of behaving in our culture were equally as rare in other cultures and, from a statistical point of view, could only be labeled as abnormal if the other culture were taken as the reference point. This fact introduces something of a relativity into the controversy and shows an additional inadequacy in the purely statistical concept. The social science contribution emphasizes, as we shall see in future chapters, that abnormal behavior is not an inherent property of some few peculiar individuals, but is an outgrowth of the combined operations of a host of variables, some of which are internal and some external to all individuals.

Use of the socially accepted pattern of behavior as a principal criterion of normality is actually a refinement of the statistical method just discussed. Within any given cultural group the most usual behavior is called "normal" and the rare behavior is called "abnormal." The social concept does reflect a gain in our thinking, however. By describing the behaving individual in terms of a given cultural setting, we can see more readily the part played by social influences in determining his behavior, whether it be normal or abnormal. As a working hypothesis, this concept has stimulated a great deal of research on group behavior and has broadened our outlook on the range of variability the human organism manifests in its struggle for existence.

Because the social definition of abnormality is basically statistical, it is open to the same objections we raised earlier. To call any behavior normal because it is the most frequent would possibly be acceptable if the word "normal" were to be used solely as a synonym for "usual." But since we go further and equate "normal" with "well-adjusted," we make the tacit assumption that "normal" (usual) is "normal" (optimal or best). Nothing is easier than to show that the most frequent behavior in any social group is not necessarily the most desirable, either from the point of view of that group's biological needs or immediate social interests. To cite but one example, war as a social institution has increasingly involved larger and larger proportions of the world's population, yet no competent social scientist or biologist would claim that war was anything but a social and biological calamity. The usual is not necessarily the best nor is the usual always within the range of tolerable adjustment. The manner of conduct that receives general acceptance and approval in a social group may result in the total collapse of that group (for example, the general pattern of behavior in Nazi Germany). The same thing is true of sub-human aggregations. In northern Europe those small mammals, the lemmings, are occasionally observed to migrate by the thousands in a direct line to the sea. When they arrive at the shore, they plunge in and swim directly out into the ocean, to certain death. This is a behavioral policy in which a majority participate, but it is not adaptive behavior.

IS THE DISTINCTION BETWEEN "NORMAL" AND "ABNORMAL" NECESSARY?

So far, the various ways of thinking about this problem all have certain shortcomings that limit their precision. Dichotomous definitions break down because the lines are drawn too sharply and too many people fail to conform completely to one group or the other. Statistical or socio-statistical definitions replace the abrupt boundaries by the gradations of a normal distribution curve, but the dichotomy remains although the borders are blurred. None of these formulations is able to take care of the troublesome exceptions that unfortunately do not prove the rule. In the light of our discussion thus far, it seems legitimate to advance the possibility that the problem is a pseudo-problem, that we are being tricked by the words we use into asking a question to which there is not only no answer, but one which is not, from the scientific point of view, a question at all. The difficulty arises, possibly, because we have made the easy verbal transition from "normal" as *usual* to "normal" as *well adjusted* and then have tried to fit the "usual" to the demands of the "optimal," a definitely Procrustean task.

At first thought, it may seem somewhat unusual to start a discussion of abnormal psychology by denying any real distinction between the *abnormal* and *psychology* in general. Let us start our thinking about this by a fictitious, but possible, everyday happening.

Across the street from my office, a large new building was being erected. Among the sidewalk superintendents who gathered there daily were three distinctive characters named Tom, Dick, and Harry. They were acquainted with each other and exchanged frequent advisory comments about the progress of the building and the construction trade in general. From my office window I had seen them there day after day. On one particular day, while they were pursuing their observations, a tiger escaped from the zoo, which is less than a quarter of a mile north of our location. Angered by his keepers, who were in hot pursuit, the tiger ran roaring down the street. Harry chanced to look up, and although he had not heard the tiger over the din of the construction machinery, he saw this threatening animal coming directly toward him. With a loud but inarticulate cry, he too broke into a gallop and headed south down the street. Tom and Dick, distracted by the cry and sudden action of their companion, looked at each other, not seeing the tiger, and said, in the same breath, "Harry is certainly acting peculiarly today. Odd, he's never done anything like that before." As Tom looked at Dick to say this, he caught a glimpse of the tiger, and, being of a somewhat delicate constitution, he uttered a deep sigh and fainted. Dick, who still did not see the tiger, said to himself, "Tom is a mighty sick man. I'd better call the doctor." At this moment the tiger arrived on the scene and attacked Dick, who desperately picked up a piece of iron pipe and tried to defend himself. The construction foreman, separated by a high board fence from this scene, saw only the piece of company material being lifted and said to himself, "Who is trying to steal the pipe?" I, from my vantage point, saw all these events as I have reported them to you.

In this scientific parable several points relevant to our problem emerge. Except for myself, the scientific observer who could maintain a calm objectivity because I was not immediately involved in the situation, all the participants made evaluative judgments about the normality or abnormality of the behavior of the other people involved. Even Harry, as he desperately ran away, was thinking to himself that the tiger was certainly "mad." The tiger, if we may be allowed a certain liberty at guessing, almost certainly looked upon all human beings in its path as grave threats to its own safety and was responding to them in the variety of ways that come most naturally to tigers. Limited by their lack of an over-all point of view, they were all interpreting the situation in a way that did not develop the true cause-effect relationship; this was apparent only to me, because I could see the whole situation. Tom and Dick and the foreman all failed to see the tiger and did not take him into account when they were evaluating one another's behavior. The tiger, because of a lack of sophistication about the deep fear that humans have for such animals, also misconstrued the situation. Harry called the tiger "abnormal," Tom and Dick called Harry "abnormal," Dick called Tom "abnormal" in a slightly different sense, the foreman called Dick "abnormal" in a social sense, and the tiger acted as if all of them were "abnormal." When I talked to reporters after the incident, I did not find it necessary to call any of them "abnormal." As I told the reporters, *everyone acted in the only way he could be expected to act in his own particular situation.*

We have spent so much of your time on this story because it seems to emphasize the point of view we wish to express. In psychopathology we are interested in identifying and describing the factors that lead to lowered effectiveness of adaptation. In order to do so we must gain a view of behavior that is objective and detached enough to enable us to describe the larger setting in which the behavior occurs. When we gain this perspective, we begin to see, as in our story, that *every individual does what he does because that is the only possible thing he could do in his particular circumstances.* For our particular purpose, then, whether the behavior is labeled "normal" or "abnormal" is not the main point at issue. What we are chiefly interested in are the *circumstances* that make the person behave in such a way that he is *called* abnormal by his fellows and the factors that lower his adaptive efficiency.

Stated in another way, the controversy over what is to be called normal and what is to be called abnormal is pertinent to us only insofar as it calls our attention to problems of adaptation that people experience. This is a considerable interest, to be sure, since these labels serve to identify our *problems,* but that is as far as we need be concerned. Once the problem is identified, the psychopathologist becomes interested in the factors that produce the behavior and feels no further need for evaluative concepts. The situation is quite comparable to that which obtains in tissue pathology. The pathologist finds his problems arising from "illness"; a tubercular patient, for instance, is a problem. Once, however, the pathologist goes into his laboratory, he is concerned with an attempt to trace the reciprocal effects that the tubercle bacilli and the host tissues have on each other, and he finds that certain conditions produce certain reactions. His findings are neither added to nor subtracted from by the evaluations placed upon them by the physician, who is concerned with making sick people well.[1] The physician and the pathologist are concerned with different problems. In the same way, the psychopathologist is not immediately concerned with evaluations of behavior in the way that the psychiatrist and clinical psychologist are.

Adaptation

As psychologists, we are attempting to describe the behavior of living organisms; this endeavor places us firmly in the general scientific program of biology. Psychologists are biologists as well as social scientists. Our special problems in the field of biology may be better understood by overtly recognizing the basic biological concepts that we employ. Just as we believe there is an essential unity to the organism, there is also unity to the various aspects of science studying the organism. Our understanding of psychopathology is dependent upon an application of knowledge gained from many fields of biology and social science.

DEFINITION

The concept of *adaptation*[2] or *adjustment* is biologically fundamental. Living creatures are energy-consuming organizations and, to maintain

[1] Hammond (1948) has called attention to the fact that "perception of the abnormal . . . is held to be intuitive and judgmental" (p. 81), depending on many social or cultural factors acting on the person who makes the judgment of "abnormality" as potently as on the person who is so judged.

[2] Although we use these terms synonymously, some writers (cf. Mowrer and Kluckhohn, 1943) differentiate *adaptation* as the behavior best for the welfare of the animal and *adjustment* as the behavior directed toward tension reduction.

themselves, must secure and assimilate at least as much energy as they expend. They can exist only within rather narrow limits of pressure and temperature and under a limited variety of chemical conditions. Finally, they live in a natural community with other organisms, some aiding and some threatening or competing in any individual's effort at survival. This effort, with its particular and often precise demands, we term *adaptation.* At simple or direct physical and chemical levels this adjustment is obvious in its compelling necessity. The behavior involved in assuring correct concentrations of oxygen in our bloodstream is of immediate adaptive significance, as is the activity of eating as it relates to energy intake. At a somewhat more remote level are the activities of searching for the materials needed to maintain life or the activities connected with finding optimal environmental conditions. The periodic migrations of birds are an example of the latter, and the restless roving of the mammals of the Great Plains to find salt are examples of the former types of activity.

Adaptation at higher, more remote, or more complex levels does not always seem to have a great deal in common with the simpler and more direct activities we have just mentioned. The types of activity by means of which human beings assure their "bed and board" are most varied in character. Yet they all reduce to more or less effective ways of adapting to the problems of existing in a particular environment. *Ordered* or "normal" behavior usually means successful adaptation; *disordered* behavior is another way of labeling poor adaptation.

It seems obvious that the saving grace in this unabashedly evaluative concept of adaptation is the possibility of stating *objective criteria* of the "goodness" or "badness" of any given instance with which the scientist deals. There has been little difficulty in applying this evaluative system in most areas of biology. Evaluation is objective when reliable standards of reference are available; evaluation becomes difficult in proportion to their paucity. The kind and amount of vitamins needed by an individual if he is to maintain growth, the amount of oxygen needed for nerve cells to stay alive, the amount of damage to a lung by an infection with tubercle bacilli can all be quite reliably determined. For each there is known a number of *indicating variables* by which success or failure of adaptation may be measured. It is true that research has shown, even in these areas, a great complexity of the adjustmental mechanisms, and the interdependence of a multitude of factors makes understanding far from easy. In broad outline, however, we can be relatively sure of our facts, and thus of our evaluation of them, if we have objective criteria.

APPLICATION OF THE CONCEPT OF ADAPTATION TO SOCIAL BEHAVIOR

When we come to the behavior of human beings, in the social environment in which it takes place, the degree of adaptability is not so easily determined. All sorts of considerations arise. Much social behavior seems only remotely connected with the task of preserving the living system, and the application of our concept of adaptation, as used in a biological sense, may appear to oversimplify the problem. As has often been remarked, man has created his own environment and, we could add, he often has shown a striking inability to deal with his own creation. Psychopathology must recognize and account for the influence of social forces in the production of maladjustive behavior, and the first step in this task is a statement of standards of evaluating adaptation. What is *adaptive* social behavior, and how does it differ from defective or disordered social behavior? Where is the continuity between biological and social adjustment? The answer to these questions is a part of the goal of our science and a necessary first step in its systematization.

When the concept of adaptation, with its evaluative emphasis, is carried into the realm of human social behavior, a new danger to straight thinking emerges. "Good" and "bad" as applied to adaptive excellence and the same words applied to social standards of conduct in a given group are often erroneously assumed to have an identity of meaning. The major difference lies in the *testability* of adaptational "good" or "bad," with the consequence that all competent observers may reach agreement; this has never been possible with evaluative usages emerging from social taboos, mores, or ethical systems.

Thus, as Kinsey (1947, 1953) and his associates have so ably pointed out, writers have defined certain sex practices as "perversions" and labeled them, therefore, maladaptive, *without ever knowing how commonly such practices occurred, and whether or not the person who indulged in such practices was unsuccessful or ineffective in his adaptation.* In other words, social standards, "ideal guides to conduct," ethical goals, or just personal ideas of how people should behave may lead us to judge adaptation at a social level from a subjective point of view whose bias will distort our interpretation of the actual facts of behavior. We will try in this book to identify some of the social forces that influence adaptation, and, in doing so, will try to avoid the type of evaluative reaction we have described here.

STRESS

In psychopathology the term *stress* is used to label the wide variety of circumstances which render adaptation difficult or which call forth increased effort on the part of the organism. Generally, we can think of any factor as stressful which acts in such a way as to disturb a state of physical, physiological, or psychological equilibrium in the subject. Adjustment is necessary only because of the stresses that exist for the given organism. There must be, for example, a certain proportion of combined oxygen in the bloodstream of any mammal in order to sustain his vital processes. Theoretically, there is a certain optimal quantity of oxygen which, if never diminished or increased, would be sufficient. But the animal utilizes the oxygen in its blood as it circulates through the body, and the theoretically perfect equilibrium is never permanently attained. The animal is forced to adjust to the oxygen depletion by breathing. Oxygen lack is a stress on the organism. Usually, of course, it is a minor stress, and the animal resists it or adjusts to it adequately with little sense of effort. Only when he is placed in an environment with a low oxygen content, or when exercise increases the tissue demands for oxygen is there an increase in stress.

Stress may be applied to many different levels of the individual's economy. Oxygen lack is primarily a physiological or cellular stress. The same principle applies at other levels. Lesson assignments may be a constant source of psychological stress for a student, but adjustment is adequate if each day's tasks are performed in turn. If assignments pile up, however, the time may come when there are not enough hours remaining in the student's day for him to accomplish the tasks that have been required. The stress may then become very great, and even exceed his capacity for adjustment. The resulting behavior may then become disordered and pathological.

CATASTROPHIC RESPONSE AND THE ZONE OF TOLERANCE

Of great interest to the psychopathologist is the type of stress which is so great that the organism's normal repertoire of responses is not sufficient to the demands placed upon it. In such situations behavior appears to deteriorate and become disorganized. The usual adequacy of response disappears. To this stage of adjustive reaction the term *catastrophic response* has been applied (Goldstein, 1939).

The demands of human adjustment may be represented as a continuum, as in Figure 2. At the left are the minimal physical and chemical demands of all organic life; at the extreme right are the social and cultural conditions that must be met by every human individual. The base line of the continuum is enclosed, top and bottom, by

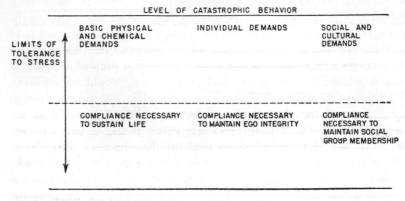

FIGURE 2. *The continuum of adjustmental demands in the life of every human.*

other lines, indicating that a certain range of imbalance or maladjustment can be tolerated by the organism. This "zone of tolerance" represents the limits within which the person normally operates in all aspects of his life.

The *zone of tolerance* is important. Living things are constantly meeting conditions that impair their equilibrium and call for adjustive behavior. For the most part, organisms are sufficiently flexible to meet the demands of day-to-day living. Even moderately intense hunger, for example, placing stress on the lower adaptive levels, need not interfere with the adequacy of behavior at higher levels. If the hunger becomes great enough to exceed the limits of tolerance for a particular organism, however, then the maladaptation will be felt at all parts of the hierarchy.

Case 3. A convincing example of the interrelationships between these various levels of adaptive stress is furnished by an occurrence during the California gold rush. A party of midwestern farmers, with their wives and children, set out for the West, traveling in an extensive caravan, complete with household goods and livestock. The leader of the little expedition, by whose name the party is now identified, was George Donner. Because of lack of pioneering experience and internal dissension, by late summer the group had progressed only as far as the east side of the Great Salt Desert, which lies between Wyoming and the eastern foothills of the Sierra Madre mountains. By following the misadvice of an unscrupulous "guide," and hampered by sporadic Indian raids on their livestock, the group was further delayed and completed their traverse of the desert in early autumn. As they started through the foothills, preparatory to crossing the high mountains ahead, further misfortune struck in the form of an unseasonal snowstorm of violent intensity. In the storm almost all the remaining cattle and horses were lost, and the rapidly mounting level of the snow made it apparent that they could not cross the mountains that winter. Because of the loss of horses and inadequacy of supplies, it was equally impossible for them to retrace their outward path the thousand miles or more to the nearest eastern settlements. They were thus forced to construct shelters and prepare to spend the winter where they were, at the foot of what is now called Donner Pass. The early storm was only the first of many that piled snow to a depth of fourteen feet on the level. Game was extremely scarce and, as food supplies diminished, their predicament became desperate. Some of the strongest men of the party set out for a midwinter crossing of the mountains to bring help from Sutter's Fort, far down on the western slope of the mountains. A few succeeded in crossing the pass, only to find it impossible to return because of the increasing depth of snow. About midway through the winter, with all supplies gone, with the leather of harnesses and boots converted into stew or baked crisp enough to eat, the stress of continued hunger overcame social and ego inhibitions. Some of the weaker members of the party had died, and their bodies, unburied because of the deep snow and hunger-inspired apathy of the survivors, furnished nutriment for some of those remaining alive.

To appreciate the extent to which this cannibalistic behavior represented a triumph of biological forces, we must take into account the social background of the Donner party. As George R. Stewart (1936) points out in his stirring book on the incident, *Ordeal by Hunger,* these people were respectable, conservative, middle-class folk. They all had behind them years of habitual conformity to the demands of social convention. Yet, in a situation of repeated and serious threat to their existence at a fundamental life level, the effort to reduce that threat resulted in violation of one of the strongest individual and social taboos.

It is of interest to note that those who lived through the long winter and were rescued returned to their former adequate level of social adjustment and became again solid respectable members of conventional social groups.

If social stresses are within the capacity of the organism, there will be little interference with cellular or individual psychological adjustment. As a matter of fact, the successful adaptive response to stresses within the zone of tolerance may actually have the effect of increasing the efficacy of adjustment at other levels. After a profitable day at the office a businessman may find his appetite stimulated and an increased confidence and self-assurance at the ego level of adjustment.

HABITUATION TO STRESS

But what if the organism, in meeting stresses that are outside its zone of tolerance, cannot find a way of directly reducing them? In such cases, if the stress does not exceed the *tolerance threshold* by too great an amount, and if its presence does not bring about immediate death or injury, the organism may become habituated to the changed conditions and extend its tolerance threshold. Studies of the adaptation of men to high altitudes (McFarland, 1946, Ullman, 1947) show that continued exposure to lowered oxygen content and pressure will gradually result in an habituation that permits them to perform work at a rate totally impossible when they were first introduced to the high altitude. The same habituation process may take place at higher levels of adaptation. After the Russian Revolution many members of the aristocracy became adjusted to menial labor and a standard of living that they would have termed "impossible" only a few years before. Prisoners may become so habituated to confinement as to be unable to readjust to freedom.

ADAPTATION A GENERALLY INCLUSIVE
CONCEPT

By now it should be apparent that the concept of adaptation includes all life phenomena. *Any manifestation of life is to some degree adaptive.* This is a significant guiding principle for psychopathology, since it provides a basis for evaluating any or all kinds of behavior in a way that is objective and free of ethical or moral bias. Further, this principle serves as a unification of all the multitudinous aspects of organic life, from the simplest cellular phenomena to the most complex social disorders. It provides a theme that runs through our whole consideration of psychopathological problems.

It has occurred repeatedly in the history of psychopathology that the appearance of abnormal behavior has been explained by an appeal to causes other than those commonly used for explaining so-called normal behavior. Consequently we have often had sets of mutually exclusive hypotheses for the normal and the abnormal. In the eighteenth century, for example, a rational explanation of normal behavior existed side by side with a demoniacal or supernatural explanation of many types of disordered behavior. By fully utilizing the implications of the concept of adaptation, in its fullest biological sense, such an unsatisfactory multiplicity of hypotheses is no longer tenable. *All behavior becomes to a greater or lesser degree adaptive.*

When we say a person is maladjusted we are usually evaluating that person's total adaptation to the whole range of adjustmental continuum. In a person with a bacterial infection, the physiological compensations that result in a fever are appropriate adaptations to a stressful physiological situation. Our judgment of his adaptive efficiency is based on the consequences of this reaction for his *total* adjustment. The effective or well-adjusted person is the one who is meeting adequately the demands at every level of adjustment, and the normal situation is one that does not present such severe demands at any one part of the continuum as to force the organism into a concentration of effort to restore equilibrium at that particular place to the detriment of his total adjustment. It is no exaggeration to say that the problem of adaptation is for the human being comparable to the situation facing a tight-rope walker who would be expected to walk his narrow wire across a chasm in a high wind while juggling eight or ten Indian clubs. A momentary overemphasis on one or another aspect of the total problem may lead to disastrous consequences in some other aspect. *Striving to adjust to de-* *mands at one level of adjustment may cause failure to adapt at another level.*

ADAPTATION AND SURVIVAL

Much of the specific subject matter of Darwin's discussion of evolution is now obsolete. Technical details of the exact way in which species of living things originated and changed are constantly being discovered, and a general theory of evolution at present is quite different from that contained in the *Origin of Species*. One of the biological principles of that time, however, still remains. *The organism must adapt or perish.* Adaptation is the price of survival. Adaptation, as Goldstein (1939) has emphasized, is the master drive, the dominant motive, from which all other drives and motives are derived. This fact has been stated perhaps most eloquently by Krecker (1934):[3]

The story of evolution has been the story of protoplasm's attempt to accommodate itself to its environment. It is as though in the beginning living material, protoplasm, was confronted with an environment which demanded obedience to its whims as the price of survival, and protoplasm, to live, has obeyed. It grovels in the slime as an Amoeba, it flies free through the air as a bird, it exists as a helpless parasite, it has risen to power as a man. Protoplasm has done everything, lived everywhere, assumed every conceivable form, has been humiliated and exalted, but it has lived.

SUMMARY: OUR BASIC WORKING ASSUMPTIONS

The position taken in this book grows out of a basic assumption that life processes have a fundamental underlying continuity of dynamic causation, best identified by the term "adaptation." It is further assumed that "abnormal" or "pathological" behavior occurs as a deviation from an optimum adjustmental pattern. There is, of course, nothing new in this. Almost all theorists in psychopathology have made a similar assumption. It is not always stated as definitely as it should be, particularly for the student just beginning his acquaintance with this fascinating field. So, although it may be thought a biological truism, the adaptation concept has been used as furnishing the best unifying principle we now possess for the organization of a group of facts of amazing surface diversity. As the field of comparative psychology demonstrates, the essential forms of behavior of thousands of species of differing degrees of complexity are understood most readily when this working principle is applied. It may be said that application of the idea of adaptive behavior and its deviants introduces a teleological flavor to our studies. The answer would appear to be that it does, but only to the extent that recognition of the relationship between motivation and behavior implies purpose in that behavior.

[3] Frederick H. Krecker (1934), *General Zoology*, pp. 574-575. New York: Henry Holt and Company.

DISCUSSION QUESTIONS

1. What other points of view or types of definitions of abnormality might have been added to the text?
2. Can you offer further criticisms of the various definitions of abnormality?
3. Which of these definitions, if any, do you believe to be the most correct?
4. Can you cite examples of adaptive and maladaptive behavior among subhuman animals?
5. Do you have any objections to our use of the concept of "adaptation" in psychopathology?
6. Is a biological approach necessary in psychopathology?
7. Is the distinction between "normal" and "abnormal" necessary?
8. How do our humanitarian efforts to protect the weak in our culture appear in the light of "survival of the fittest" slogans?
9. How are the criteria for "good" adaptation a function of the particular species for which you wish to make the evaluation?
10. Is it always advantageous for society to reduce the percentage of "abnormal" people by treatment and custodial protection?

SUGGESTED READINGS

O. H. Mowrer (1954), "What is normal behavior?" in L. A. Pennington and I. A. Berg, eds. (1954), *An Introduction to Clinical Psychology* (2nd Ed.), pp. 58-88. New York: The Ronald Press Company.

J. Romano, ed. (1949), *Adaptation*. Ithaca, N.Y.: Cornell University Press.

BIBLIOGRAPHIC SOURCES

For discussions of the various definitions of normal and abnormal behavior similar to the one given here, the student should consult the introductory chapters of the many excellent texts in this field: for example, Brown (1940), Morgan and Lovell (1948), Thorpe and Katz (1948), the chapters by Hanson and Higginson in Mikesell (1950), and Maslow and Mittleman (1951). Somewhat different, and particularly delightful, is the chapter by Mowrer (1954) in the text edited by Pennington and Berg (1954).

Mowrer constructs a hypothetical symposium between a statistician, a sociologist, an educator, a physician, a psychologist, a philosopher, an anthropologist, a theologian, a lawyer, a biologist, a psychoanalyst, a neurologist, and a layman on the topic, "What is normal behavior?" You will find that none of these disciplines is at a loss to supply well-solidified points of view. A reprint of the chapter may be found in Weider (1953).

Detailed criticisms of the many conceptions of normality and abnormality are numerous. A critique of the statistical concept of normality may be found in Morlan (1948). Both the statistical and the cultural conceptions are examined in a brilliant paper by Wegrocki (1939). Reider (1950) discusses clinical problems associated with patient's attitudes toward normality. The use of the concept of adaptation in this context has been judged by Kluckhohn (1949) and Martin (1952). One of the most frequently disapproved notions in this context is the equation of the usual and the adaptive. As McLaughlin (1950, p. 22) puts it: ". . . what is prevalent is not necessarily optimal." Finally, for a fascinating account of how the aboriginal views normality, read Berndt and Berndt (1951).

The existing empirically derived correlations of human characteristics are numerous. Pearl (1940, pp. 426-427) has collected 116 of these correlations into one table.

We have not included in this book any detailed material on the historical foundations of psychopathology. Either White (1948) or Thorpe and Katz (1948) are suggested.

There are many splendid discussions of adaptation. The unitary nature of the adaptive processes was first presented with full marshalling of the evidence by Ritter (1919) in two small volumes that may be read with interest today. Jennings' (1930) volume on the biological basis of human nature is still a good general introduction. Another broad aspect of adaptive struggle, the relationship of man to his climatic environment, is presented by Huntington (1924). The significance of our adaptive struggles for behavior in general is thoughtfully discussed by one of the greatest of physiologists, Sir Charles Sherrington (1953). For the implications of the adaptation concept for biology as a whole, a paper on "purpose" in biology by Agar (1938) is stimulating. The outline of a psychological theory based on the struggle of the organism to regain equilibria has been written by Raup (1926). For a contemporary restatement of some aspects of the "equilibrium" notion, see Stagner (1951). The operation of adaptation on the cellular level is discussed in Davies and Gale (1953). For the interaction of psychological and physiological variables in adaptation, Cleghorn (1952) is suggested. One of the best introductions to adaptation is a small but informative book edited by J. Romano (1949), entitled *Adaptation*. Five disciplines are represented: biology (P. Weiss), philosophy (H. W. Smith), psychology (H. S. Liddell), psychiatry (L. Kubie), and anthropology (C. Kluckhohn).

Basic to the concept of adaptation is the general theory of evolution. There are a number of excellent introductions to the theory of evolution. We suggest G. G. Simpson's (1949) *The Meaning of Evolution,* the same author's (1953) *The Major Features of Evolution,* or J. S. Huxley (1953), *Evolution in Action.*

The history of pioneering and exploration teems with examples of the reaction of humans to unusual stress. Among the best of these, because it was written by a biologist capable of making skilled observations, is Cherry-Gerard's (1930) account of Scott's Antarctic expedition of 1910-1913. On the Donner Party, Stewart's account has been cited in an attempt to show the interplay of motives under conditions of great stress and danger. Short but succulent discussions of these and other expeditions may be found in the second volume of Keys, *et al.* (1950).

Another fascinating account of individual adaptation to extreme stress is a paper by Bettelheim (1943). For a year he was a political prisoner in the German concentration camps at Dachau and Buchenwald. Under conditions of brutality and physical duress, individuals were forced to make radical changes in their basic attitudes in order to adapt to the incredible but true situation they faced. A careful reading of this paper and a paper by Nardini (1952), giving a firsthand account of the treatment of American prisoners of war by the Japanese in World War II, may lead the student to a better understanding of the hardships endured by American prisoners in Korea and the behavior which some of them displayed.

A monumental study to reactions to stress of semi-starvation is that of Keys (1950) and his associates at the Laboratory of Physiological Hygiene of the University of Minnesota. This two-volume work is the result of intensive morphological, biochemical, physiological, and psychological investigation of 36 volunteer conscientious objectors who were subjected to conditions of semi-starvation. No short summary can possibly do justice to this immense work, but a relatively brief account may be found in Franklin, *et al.* (1948).

Physiological changes resulting from stress situations have been studied in incredible amounts. For introductions to this literature, Selye (1950, 1953) and Selye and Fortier (1950) should be seen.

Recent military developments have brought increased concern about performance under stress. Much of this literature with its methodological and terminological difficulties is reviewed in a paper by Lazurus, Deese, and Osler (1952). For an outline of the type of problems involved in high altitude and high velocity flying see Webster (1950).

1-10-60

Some Basic Psychological Concepts
Used in Psychopathology

Order and simplification are the first steps toward the
mastery of a subject—the actual enemy is the unknown.
—THOMAS MANN, *The Magic Mountain*

Since psychopathology is but a part of the general science of psychology, the conceptual tools we will use are in no way different from those used in the science as a whole. The laws of behavior apply equally to the ordered and disordered psychological situation. Indeed, one of the values of psychopathology is the contribution it can make to discovery of the general laws of all behavior. Since the problems we are to consider are somewhat specialized, we will devote this chapter to a review of those aspects of psychology most immediately useful to our project.

Motivation

MOTIVATION GIVES DIRECTION TO BEHAVIOR

Out of the never-ending adaptive process at all its levels emerge those forces that give direction to a person's behavior, his motivation. Our understanding of any behavior, normal or abnormal, depends upon our knowledge of its direction, that is, upon knowing the needs that initiated it and the goals toward which it appears to be directed.

Motives obey common dynamic laws, although each motive is distinctive and individual. Motivation may be conceived as a force possessing vectorial characteristics of direction and magnitude. Behavior, as it occurs, is the resultant of all the motivational forces acting

36

upon the person at that time. Most of what we call the "why" of people's behavior and thus the key to predicting their future behavior lies in our knowledge of motivation.

PHYSIOLOGICAL NEEDS AND THEIR SOCIAL SETTING

Some features of motivational dynamics are of particular pertinence to psychopathology, since their effect on behavior frequently constitutes a source of stress for the organism. The first of these features is the *interrelation between physiological needs and their expression in a social environment.* Since all human behavior takes place in a social setting of one kind or another, it is inevitable that the basic physiological needs of the organism cannot always be met without encountering social friction. With the type of taboos and social regulation that surrounds expression of sexual functions in our society, sexual motives often meet resistance and the direction of behavior may become deflected into a variety of maladaptive channels. The structure of society and thus the type of social training its members receive is not always completely congruent with an easy and direct restoration of cellular disequilibria.

SOCIAL MOTIVES

If the problems of human behavior involved only the basic physiological drives, our task would be much simpler. Analysis of the individual behavior of lower animals, although technically difficult, is a relatively simple scientific problem. Most mammals have a minimum of social interaction. Their behavior takes place at a level of complexity almost free of symbolic communication. All this means that their motives seldom are directed higher than the basic tissue needs. There is relatively little of the elaboration of motivation we observe at the human level. Here we have emergence of motives that cannot be directly referred to the requirements of the body. *Social motives, developed as a consequence of growing up in a social world, are often as compelling and demand satisfaction as vigorously as do needs arising at the cellular level.* The desires for companionship, prestige, recognition, achievement, and intellectual stimulation are influential forces in determining our behavior. To the human being, "solitary confinement" is an extreme type of punishment—many lower animals know no other life.

DEVELOPMENT OF EGO NEEDS

In this connection it is useful to introduce another concept, one that has meaning only in terms of social motivation. Each person, in his relations with the social environment, gradually develops a conception of himself as an individual. This particular way of regarding ourselves, the meaning we attach to statements such as "*I am a junior in college*," "*I am disappointed*," and so forth, psychologists have termed *ego* functions. Ego functions apparently have great significance in a person's behavior. Situations, for the human, are defined in terms of the way they appear to him, the possible effect they will have on him. Actions are determined in the light of their possible ego-involvements.

This set of habits each of us acquires and which we term "ego functions" has a counterpart in another constellation of habits concerning ways of looking at and evaluating the various forms of behavior that may occur in our society. As a result of our experiences with other people, we acquire notions concerning the "goodness" and "badness" of actions. These moral codes, reflecting the ethical and religious thinking of the particular cultural groups that have influenced us, we may call *superego* functions. This "conscience" aspect of our habit patterns influences our approaches and avoidances in social situations. Superego is, in short, a type of social motivation.

Frustration and Conflict of Motives

DEFINITION OF FRUSTRATION

If motivated behavior always resulted in quick and easy attainment of goals, it is doubtful if there would be very much talk about psychopathology. Unfortunately, goal-directed behavior is complicated by many difficulties. In the first place we live in a physical setting where all movement through space is accomplished against the resistance of gravitation. Many other physical limitations of temperature, pressure, time, and distance also confront us. The attempts men have made to reach the North and South Poles, to climb Mt. Everest, to descend to the depths of the sea have tested these limits almost to their ultimate degree. Even thinking and problem-solving, goal-directed activities requiring very little actual movement, are influenced by physical factors.

Judgment deteriorates at high altitudes; consciousness is lost if oxygen need increases more rapidly than it can be compensated for.

Further limitations to goal access are met in the social environment. *People have a propensity for getting in each other's way.* Social institutions, traditions, and customs may conspire to block or inhibit our motivated behavior. When hungry, it is not enough to walk into a store and start eating the first food that comes to hand. Our society has prescribed a certain approach to the acquisition, preparation, and consumption of food. Failure to comply with the social limitations would create further difficulties, and the man who secured bread by throwing

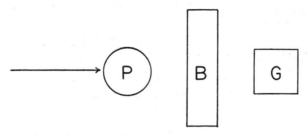

FIGURE 3. *The basic frustration situation.*

a rock through a grocery store window might find himself delayed in the eating of bread until he had properly (from a social viewpoint) been placed in a jail cell—a circumstance that would be a further social hindrance to the attainment of many other goals.

Still other hindrances come from the limitations of the particular human being himself. If the goal is graduation from college, a certain degree of intelligence is required; to be a dentist requires manual dexterity; to be a concert pianist requires musical aptitude. Our abilities, aptitudes, skills, and interests combine to set limits on the range of our behavior and often act to prevent gratification of motives.

Our label for all these interferences with smooth and immediate adjustment is *frustration,* which has been defined as "a serious or threatening nongratification of needs and desires because of environmental or intrapsychic obstacles." [1] Frustration is another of the basic concepts of psychopathology. Generally speaking, disordered behavior emerges

[1] A. H. Maslow and B. Mittelman (1951), *Principles of Abnormal Psychology,* p. 578. New York: Harper and Brothers.

when organisms undergo frustration. In its most elementary form it may be represented as in Figure 3, in which the strength and direction of the motive are indicated by the arrow, the individual by the circle, and the frustrating circumstance by the rectangle. This latter is usually referred to as a *barrier*, standing between the person and his goal. The barrier may be any one or a combination of the hindering circumstances just mentioned. The diagram emphasizes the essential nature of frustration: *it is a delay of goal-directed activity*. From our definition of frustration and from considering the diagram, it is apparent that frustration constitutes a threat to the organism in proportion to (1) the strength of the motive and (2) the psychological difficulty entailed in surmounting the barrier.

FRUSTRATION A NECESSARY PART OF ALL LIFE PROCESSES

The behavior of animals in a frustrating situation is another of those matters of general psychological interest, where the psychopathological aspects are only a part of a universally present phenomenon. Just as we have said that adaptation is essential for the very existence of an animal, frustration also appears to be a part of the general pattern of behavior. Since more or less frustration is always present, one can only speculate concerning the type of organic life that would develop in a perpetually regulated environment, where no effort was needed for adaptation. Ordinarily, when an organism encounters an obstacle, it varies its behavior until the problem is solved and the obstacle is surmounted. Such behavior is somewhat loosely called "trial-and-error." Although there is controversy as to precisely what the mechanisms may be and how uniformly they operate, in general we observe that successful attempts to solve problems are retained by the organism, whereas faulty solutions are abandoned. Thus, learning and habit formation would appear to be intimately related to frustration, since *learning probably only occurs when motives are frustrated*.

CONFLICT OF MOTIVES AND FRUSTRATION

The most frequent source of frustration we will meet with in psychopathology is that which arises when there is a conflict between motives operating in the individual at any given time. The organism may be driven by a number of needs, the satisfaction of which requires that behavior take different and contradictory directions.

Conflict of motives = frustration

One such conflict situation is created when an individual has strong approach and avoidance tendencies toward the same goal. As an example, note the college student who faces a final examination. He probably has strong motivation to avoid the examination based on the fear of failure. On the other hand, he must take the examination in order to continue his college career or, perhaps, to obtain the approval of his teachers, fellow students, and parents. The result of this particular conflict is often anxiety and inability to concentrate. As a frequent conflict situation, other examples are easy to find. The child who realizes the inevitability of punishment if he goes to the circus without parental permission, or the person who wishes to engage in sexual activity but is threatened by the fear of pregnancy, discovery, or venereal disease is meeting this dilemma.

FIGURE 4. *One type of conflict situation.*

Another conflict situation occurs when the individual is faced with a choice between goals all of which he wants to avoid. This time our hypothetical student is faced with two courses, one of which he must take to satisfy the requirements of his curriculum. He has heard that they are both especially difficult, and he would like to avoid both. Our student will probably show considerable uncertainty before he finally chooses one. Of course, other alternatives are open to the student; he might change curricula or even possibly he might leave school.

A third conflict situation is perhaps not a type of conflict at all; it is illustrated in Figure 4. Here the person must choose one of two equally attractive goals. The classical example is the fable about the hungry donkey who sat between two identical piles of hay, and, according to the story, starved to death. Unfortunately, this ending is most likely incorrect. Individuals faced with this conflict usually reach a rapid solution with little uncertainty. A more correct but less satisfying finish to the fable would relate that the donkey ran readily to one pile of hay. For another example, let us return to the student. Now he wants to go to the movies, but he must choose between two equally desirable pictures. After some slight hesitation, he will probably readily select one, unless another type of conflict situation is generated.

Suppose further that the two particular movies are being shown only once and at identical times. If he chooses one, he must necessarily give up the other. We now have the conditions for the fourth type of conflict. And the necessity of giving up one will probably diminish the desire for the original choice. In general, this type of conflict is probably much more common than the one shown in Figure 4.

All these situations constitute sources of frustration. But why? Is it not possible for the individual to gratify the motives successively? In probably the majority of life situations this solution is followed; it is the normal or optimal resolution of the conflict. The factor that creeps in to make resolution difficult is usually *time*. Many coexisting needs are of such a strength and their gratification demands actions of such a nature that the organism is presented with the baffling problem of trying to move in opposite directions simultaneously. In the simple dynamics of physics, an object acted upon by equal forces in opposed directions would remain stationary, or if there were the slightest departure from the equality of strength or the direct opposition of direction, it would move in a path that was a mathematical resolution of the forces acting upon it. The ability of living organisms to inhibit action or to deal successively with simultaneous needs is, of course, a great asset, and places the individual in a position considerably more advantageous than the inanimate object of the physicist. But in the situations stated above, where the organism is unable to inhibit action because of the pressing nature of the needs, the conflict of motives becomes a direct source of frustration, as real as the simple barrier situation and usually more serious in its implications.

The conflict between motives may be of all degrees of intensity, depending upon the strength of the motives involved. Conflict between weak motives has little significance for the general economy of the organism; one or both motives are inhibited, and expression becomes serial or absent. The stronger the motives involved, the more serious is the frustration. Conflict acts as a means of delaying gratification. If gratification of a need is essential for some phase of a person's adaptation, at any level, frustration is dangerous. This is doubly true if the need that is frustrated is of the type that increases in strength as the period of nongratification lengths, as with the cellular-level requirements of air, food, and water.

Another source of conflict, having the same dynamic characteristics as a conflict between differing needs, is the conflict between various techniques of satisfying a single need. For example, an individual's need may be for social recognition, and he may be in such a life situation that this could be gratified by demonstrations of athletic ability or by scholastic achievement. Since both techniques would be time consuming and demand effort that would exclude the possibility of successfully pursuing both alternatives, a real conflict situation could exist.

Levels of Awareness

DO PEOPLE RECOGNIZE THEIR ADJUSTMENTAL STRESSES?

The student might well ask, at this juncture, whether people are always aware of their adaptive struggles and of the frustrations and conflicts that they so often meet. Or, are these processes as little accessible to awareness as the movements of the electrons and protons that make up our bodies? This question has turned out to be significant in psychopathology, and upon its answer depends a great deal of our understanding of disordered behavior. If a patient in a mental hospital is asked the direct question: "Why are you behaving as you do?" or "What reasons do you have for thinking in such a way?" he may have great difficulty in giving an answer. The answer he does return may or may not have value in any attempt to understand his condition. A patient, who believed he was in prison for the crime of treason, was asked the question: "Why do you think the President of the United States is persecuting you?" The answer was, "Because the Lord has revealed that fact to me, and that is why I am here." As he amplified his account, it was apparent that he had a very well-organized group of beliefs concerning the circumstances of his situation, and that they were almost completely erroneous. Into his case history report went the comment of the examiner: "The patient shows a lack of insight for his condition."

INSIGHT

By *insight* the examiner meant a reasonably correct understanding of the psychological factors involved in the patient's own past history and present situation, that is to say, of the patient's motives, habits, and the environmental forces that influenced his behavior. At one time in the history of our science it was believed that the "normal" rational human being possessed this knowledge, and that one of the most emphatic ways of telling the "insane" from the "sane" was the absence of insight in the former. We now know that this is not strictly true, and that the concept of insight must include the idea that it is possessed to varying degrees by all people. No individual is completely insightful for the determiners of his own behavior, and no individual is completely without awareness of the forces that shape his life. In general, the mentally ill person does have *less* insight, but the reasons for this are not simple. The degree of insight is dependent upon the type of problems faced and upon the amount of stress these problems engender.

THE UNCONSCIOUS

In order to discuss the matter of insight it is necessary to introduce another basic concept of psychopathology, the *unconscious*. This term is used in a broad sense to mean any and all of the behavioral processes of which the subject is not aware. It is unfortunate that such a definition of "unconscious" is so general as to be a source of confusion. Miller (1942) has identified sixteen distinct ways that the word has been employed in writings on abnormal behavior. These usages are summarized in Table 2. It will be seen that many quite different aspects of behavior are included. For our present purposes we will use the term to mean "lack of awareness" and "lack of knowledge."

DEGREES OF DIFFICULTY IN RECALL

It is useful to analyze the concept still more closely and to differentiate various degrees of awareness. When a student registers for work in college, he is usually asked to fill out numerous forms, which require him to report his age, his home address, names of relatives, church affiliation, academic classification, phone number, and so forth. All these instructions are carried out with such ease, as far as memory is concerned, that the student usually attends only to the tedium involved in so much registrational red tape. Yet, ten minutes before starting to fill in the forms, probably none of the information that he has reproduced with such ease was consciously present to the student's awareness. This is true of a vast number of remembered experiences. We are aware of them only when the situation demands. Such memories are said to be easily recalled.

TABLE 2

DEFINITIONS OF UNCONSCIOUSNESS*

Type of Meaning	Definition
1. *Inanimate* or *subhuman*	Anything incapable of discriminating or behaving under any conditions whatsoever
2. *Unresponsive to stimulation*	Absent-minded, day-dreaming, anesthetized. A state in which stimuli from external environment are not affecting behavior
3. *Not mental*	Absence of sensation, emotion, thought, or any psychical attribute; absence of distinction from the physical
4. *Undiscriminating*, applied either to an individual or his actions	Absence of ability to discriminate between two or more stimuli
5. *Conditioned*, acting on the basis of conditioning; conditioned responses	Assumption that conditioning, a physiological process, is unconscious because it occurs at that level
6. *Unsensing* (applied to an individual); *unsensed* (as applied to his actions, emotions, needs, etc.)	
a. *Stimuli not reaching the organism*	Not knowing because not stimulated
b. *Inadequate stimuli affecting organism*	Stimuli inappropriate to sense-organ stimulated—light to the ear
c. *Sensory tract incapable of carrying stimuli*	Action of drugs, injury, etc., on sensory tracts
d. *Sub-liminal stimuli affecting organism*	Unconscious because below threshold
e. *Stimuli not reaching cortex*	Similar to Definition 2 above
7. *Unnoticing* or *unattending*	We are unconscious of those aspects of our environment to which we are not attending at any given time
8. *Insightless, not involving insight*	Not being aware of the task, or of the pattern of actions necessary to complete task (Gestalt meaning)
9. *Unremembering*, or *unremembered*	Includes all material that has been forgotten
10. *Acting instinctively, unlearned or inherited*	Instincts, reflex behavior, etc.

* Adapted by permission from *Unconsciousness* by J. G. Miller, published by John Wiley & Sons, Inc. 1942.

TABLE 2 (Continued)

Type of Meaning	Definition
11. *Unrecognizing* or *unrecognized*	Implies either that the existence of the process is not known, or that the existence is recognized, but the character of the process is not understood
12. *Acting involuntarily*	Without volition, without will. Rarely used in deterministic psychology
13. *Unable to communicate* (as applied to an individual); *incommunicable* (applied to actions, ideas, motives)	Anything incapable of verbalization or any other sort of communication
14. *Ignoring*, or *ignored*	Individual acts as if not recognizing facts of which he is really aware
15. *Psychoanalytic* meaning	(*a*) Processes repressed from consciousness; (*b*) they can only be made available to consciousness by special techniques; and (*c*) they are not under voluntary control
16. *Unaware of discrimination, unavailable to awareness*	Unconscious if the individual fails to react discriminatingly to his discrimination

But, as every student knows, there are some memories that no amount of searching and no effort after recall seem to revive. Incidents from our past lives, names, dates, and circumstances often elude us more or less permanently. We are, to one degree or another, unconscious of them; we cannot use them consciously because they seem not to be available. Ordinarily we excuse such lapses by saying we have "forgotten," that the passage of time or a wealth of intervening experiences has erased such memory of them as we once might have had. Research in psychology has shown in a fairly conclusive manner that such a concept of forgetting is oversimplified. Very little memory loss comes through sheer disuse and the passage of time. As Bartlett (1932) demonstrated so well, forgetting is usually an active process in which many factors contribute to alteration of failure of memory. Since Bartlett's work, extensive evidence has shown that interference between experiences is a far more critical factor in forgetting than simple disuse (see Osgood, 1953).

FREUDIAN EVIDENCE FOR UNCONSCIOUS MOTIVES

The most significant contribution to an understanding of that portion of our psychological life of which we are unaware came from the studies of Sigmund Freud. It was Freud who first capitalized on the idea, which had been suggested by several philosophers before him, that many of the vital determinative influences over our whole lives take place without our being at all aware that they are going on. It had been assumed, as a rather common-sense position, that if a person could not remember or recognize some aspect of his own life or situation, that such an aspect must have little or no significance for him. In the more formal circles of psychological science, it was postulated that memory depended in part on the *vividness* of the experience, and experiences not recalled were probably so lacking in significance as to furnish no good grounds for their being retained. From clinical studies of mentally ill patients and from close observation of the everyday lives of quite normal people around him, Freud gradually came to the conclusion that a great many of the thoughts and ideas that helped to determine a person's behavior were seldom or never present in the awareness of that person. His evidence indicated also that even more important determiners of behavior, the needs and desires of the person, were represented in consciousness imperfectly or not at all. He noted, for example, that the seemingly accidental mistakes in writing or conversation, the "slips of tongue or pen," did not seem to be merely chance errors, but could be fitted easily into the personality picture of a person if enough facts were known. The seemingly inexplicable forgetting of the name of an acquaintance, often under embarrassing circumstances, could be meaningfully explained if the incident were related to the total life of the individual doing the forgetting.

This idea of unconscious memories, unconscious wishes, and unconscious needs has such tremendous implications for psychology that some of the evidence for it should be reviewed. In 1914 Freud published his first extensive report of studies on these unconscious factors in behavior in a book, *The Psychopathology of Everyday Life*. He maintained that all our actions, no matter how trivial or insignificant they may be, are motivated and serve as delicate indications of our needs, wishes, and desires. Since the person is seldom aware of the reasons for his actions, many aspects of behavior are shrugged off as due simply to "chance."

Among the incidents cited by Freud was the forgetting of names. In each instance he showed that the name forgotten was connected in some way with circumstances of pain or annoyance. A man forgets the name of a business associate and must ask his office staff the name every time he wishes to write a letter to that individual. Search for a reason shows that the associate recently married a young woman in whom our subject was also interested. A man with violent political prejudices finds difficulty in correctly pronouncing the name of a rival political leader and many times must stop and correct himself. A professor, in a lecture, finds himself unable to remember the name of a rival in the same field of investigation. A patient receiving psychiatric treatment shows a complete inability to remember the name of the street on which he lived during a painful period of his life. As Freud says, the motive behind this "forgetting" is "an avoidance of awakening of pain through memory."

EXPERIMENTAL EVIDENCE

The evidence evaluating the extent to which the person is shielded from traumatic memories does not come solely from anecdotes and clinical histories. In typical experiments the subjects have been asked to list all the pleasant and unpleasant experiences they have had over a given period of time (as, for example, the Christmas vacation period). Usually, recall tests for the same experiences are also given at later dates. Table 3 summarizes the results of three such studies by Meltzer (1930), Stagner (1931), and O'Kelly and Steckle (1940). Such results

TABLE 3

PERCENTAGES OF PLEASANT AND UNPLEASANT EXPERIENCES
RECALLED AFTER VARIOUS PERIODS OF TIME*

Type of Experience	Original (O'Kelly-Steckle)	Immediate Recall (Meltzer)	15 Days (Stagner)	6 Weeks (Meltzer)	10 Weeks (O'Kelly-Steckle)
Pleasant..........	62	62.4	54.4	53.0	48
Unpleasant.......	37	37.4	43.4	39.8	40

* *Source:* L. I. O'Kelley and L. C. Steckle (1940), "The forgetting of pleasant and unpleasant experiences." *Amer. J. Psychol.*, *53*, 433.

would seem to indicate roughly that a preponderance of pleasant experiences are recalled, even after rather long intervals of time. A criticism of studies of this type is the possibility that people tend to have more pleasant than unpleasant experiences, particularly college students during a vacation period.

Far more serious criticisms of these studies have been advanced by Turner and Barlow (1951).[2] They were concerned with two major sources of error. First, they felt that the order in which the experiences were recalled might influence the percentage recalled. With one group where the pleasant experiences were recalled first, higher percentages of pleasant experiences were recalled. In a second group recalling unpleasant experiences first, higher frequencies of unpleasant experiences were obtained. When a proper counterbalanced recall order was used in a third group, there were no differences in recall for pleasant and unpleasant experiences. Second, they felt that the studies cited above had failed to equate the intensity of the original experiences. Their evidence shows that when intensity is equated recall is less difficult for the more intense experiences but without any differences between pleasant and unpleasant experiences. The results of Turner and Barlow place these studies in doubt. Until further evidence supports or rejects their findings, the main support for the existence of unconscious protection against traumatic experiences must come from the available anecdotal reports and clinical experiments.

One of the best of these is a series of studies of hypnotically induced conflicts run by Erickson who was able to demonstrate experimentally the operation of motives completely unrecognized by his subjects (Erickson, 1938a, 1938b, 1939a, 1939b, 1939c). An amusing example is the following.

During hypnosis the subject was instructed that after he awakened Dr. D. would begin talking to him about some abstruse subject in which he was not at all interested, and that although he would actually be profoundly bored he would try to appear interested. He was told that he would want very much to close the conversation, that he would wish for some way of shutting off this interminable flow of words, that he would look around him in the hope of finding some distraction, and that he would feel that Dr. D. was terribly tiresome. He was then awakened, whereupon Dr. D. began the conversation. Although the subject appeared to be politely attentive, Dr. D. would occasionally say, "Perhaps you're not interested?" The subject would reply with excessive emphasis, "Oh, yes, certainly, I'm very much interested." Now and then he would interrupt Dr. D., trying to pin him down to some definite point for discussion, but each time this effort was evaded.

[2] R. H. Turner and J. A. Barlow (1951), "Memory for pleasant and unpleasant experiences: some methodological considerations." *J. exp. Psychol.*, 42, 189-196.

At length the subject began glancing about the room and was noted casually to observe an open door. Finally he interrupted Dr. D. saying, "Excuse me, I feel an awful draft," and got up to close the door. As he did so he was asked what he was doing. He replied, "The air seems to be awful hot ('hot air!'); I thought I would shut off the draft." When the hypnotist pretended not to understand and asked him what he was doing the subject replied, "Why, I just shut the bore." His remark was repeated by the hypnotist for the benefit of those in the audience who had not heard it. When the subject heard his statement given as "shutting the bore" he started visibly, seemed tremendously embarrassed, and with much urgency turned to Dr. D. saying, "Did I say that? I didn't mean that. I just meant I closed the door." He was very apologetic in his whole manner and bearing.[3]

It should be pointed out that the subject had no recall, after hypnosis, of the instructions that had been given him during the hypnotic session.

REPRESSION

To this process of selective "forgetting," the term *repression* has been applied. It is assumed that the individual unconsciously rejects from his awareness those aspects of his past experience that have either immediate or remote potentialities for causing him pain. *Repression becomes an active protective device, which attempts to shield the organism from disruptive stimulation.* As such, repression becomes a name for a part of the same general motivational process that we have discerned as operating at all life levels, directing the organism toward the establishment of equilibrium.

Returning now to the matter of insight, it can readily be appreciated that no one can achieve complete insight for all aspects of his behavior. In the life of any ordinary mortal too much has been repressed; we are protected against insights that would harm us or give us pain. Since the material that has been repressed is, for all conscious purposes, forgotten and unavailable to our memory, it follows that we cannot be aware of many of the motivating circumstances that prompted the repression.

If we are unaware of a memory, or of a wish, or of a motive, does that mean that it is no longer a factor in our behavior? The evidence is abundant, both from clinic and laboratory, that such is not the case. The fact that we seem to forget selectively in a manner that protects

[3] M. H. Erickson (1939), "Experimental demonstrations of the psychopathology of everyday life." *Psychoanal. Quart., 8,* 340-341.

our self-esteem is only one contribution to the hypothesis that motives shape our behavior equally well whether or not we can name them or talk about them. In view of the universality with which unconscious motivation has been recognized naively in the everyday experience of people, it is somewhat surprising that the concept has not been readily accepted by scientific psychologists. The disobedient child or the person who has committed an "impulsive" crime both may be making quite honest statements when they say, "I don't know why I did it." One of the major aims of psychotherapy is to provide a patient with correct evaluations of formerly unconscious motives, and it has been found that many emotionally ill patients show a recovery that is proportionate to the degree of insight they can be aided to attain. Among the most potent sources of emotional stress is the feeling that one's actions are being caused by unknown factors over which there can be no control. Frequently the daily papers carry stories of people who have committed suicide because "they felt they could no longer control their actions."

Learning and Forgetting

Another property of living things, which is of crucial importance to psychopathology, is learning. Most modern views of the causation of mental disorders depend heavily on the recognized ability of the human being to be molded by his experiences. As has been mentioned, both good and bad techniques of adjustment are *acquired,* and the personality of any individual is very much the result of the habits he has learned in the course of his past life. The degree of flexibility a person will show in adjusting to new situations is a function of the old habit potentialities he brings to that situation. Also, the rapidity with which he learns and the length of time he will retain all depend upon the operation of many circumstances having favorable or unfavorable effects on the learning process.

Learning has been one of the most active fields of psychological research in the past fifty years. A great deal is known about the variables that influence learning. There has been an increasing effort to state the implications of this knowledge for psychopathology. The importance of these implications is far-reaching, not only in our attempt to explain why deviant behavior occurs, but also because the treatment of any condition that, at its roots, is a structure of *ineffective habits* must be re-education, the acquisition of new and more effective habits. Psychotherapy of any kind is effective in proportion to the amount and kind of learning it produces.

It is fortunate that we do not have to wait for a generally accepted theory of the learning process before applying the basic concept of learning to problems of psychopathology. Knowing the extent to which the behavior of the human being may be influenced by what it learns is itself a contribution. As far as we can see at present, all social behavior techniques are acquired, and the very personality of an individual is more a matter of learning than of inheritance. Learning is thus a double-edged sword since both the assets and liabilities for adaptation are incorporated through learning.

THE CONCEPT OF ASSOCIATION

A number of frequently used concepts in psychopathology come from studies of the learning process. One of these is the general principle of *association.* Even in the pre-scientific psychologies there was an attempt to explain the composition and derivation of the flow of ideas that appear in consciousness, and there was a somewhat general agreement that those ideas appear together which had in the past been associated by their appearance at the same time (the principle of contiguity) or which had elements in common (principle of similarity). As applied to learning and retention, the statement could be made that new experiences that occurred contiguously or that were similar to older and already learned behavior would be retained better than experiences that did not have this advantage.

Added to these basic associative principles were statements about such secondary determiners as the *vividness* or intensity of the experience, the *recency* of occurrence of the experience, and the *effect* (degree of satisfaction) of the experience. Other things being equal, it was supposed that ideas were retained with a firmness dependent upon the strength of these secondary factors.

Using these concepts as a background, the three most influential theories of psychopathology were constructed. We have already seen how Freud called upon association of ideas in his study of the motivation behind the "errors" of everyday life. Association was basic to the "psychobiology" theory of Adolf Meyer and of the theories of Pierre Janet and the "French" school of psychiatry.

THE CONDITIONED RESPONSE

In the meantime research workers in the field of learning were extending the associative principles and, by experimental work, were giving these principles more adequate definition. A Russian physiologist, Ivan Pavlov, succeeded in showing that a wide variety of new stimuli could be associated with basic biological response patterns in such a way that the new stimuli would elicit the old responses in a manner equivalent to the original biologically adequate stimulus. Thus, as every student of elementary psychology has learned, a dog may be trained to salivate to the sound of a buzzer as well as to the more biologically adequate stimulus of the sight or taste of food. This process of training Pavlov termed *conditioning* and referred to the newly learned stimulus-response connection as a *conditioned response*. In principle, this experiment of Pavlov did not add much that was new to the old associationism, aside from giving it a physiological basis. As a practical demonstration, however, of a laboratory technique for studying association, the conditioning experiment proved a stimulus for a vast amount of new research on learning. Also, in at least three major instances, the phenomenon of conditioning served as a point of departure for the erection of theoretical systems for the explanation of all behavior.

REDINTEGRATION

Growing out of the interest in conditioning, and with direct application to the field of psychopathology, came an explanatory principle originated by H. L. Hollingworth (1920) and termed by him *redintegration*. The word was borrowed from the Scottish philosopher Hamilton, who used it in a somewhat similar manner. Hollingworth defined redintegration as, *"that type of process in which a part of a complex stimulus provokes the complete reaction that was previously made to the complex stimulus as a whole"* (Hollingworth, 1920). This principle, Hollingworth felt, was true of all behavior. In a very general way his contention is too much in conformity with experience to be contested, and it has become a recognized part of almost all theories of psychopathology.

MEMORY

Earlier, in our discussion of levels of awareness, we used one aspect of learning, namely memory, as a test of the extent to which repression operated on any particular learned behavior. The memory functions are important in other ways. The longer and more completely the effects of experience are retained, the greater a part do they play in behavior at any given instant. Many factors other than repression serve to reduce completeness of recall. Injuries to the nervous system, maturational changes of old age, emotional disturbance at the time of learning or recall, all are effective in limiting performance.

Finally, since remembering, like learning, is an active process, the material that is retained may undergo transformations that result in the memory being quite different from the original impression. Since the person's behavior is influenced by the memory and not by the stimulus that originally implanted the memory, a recognition of this distorting effect is of importance in understanding a person's behavior. If I go to a filling station to get road directions and am told that "Highway 130" will take me to my destination, the information does me little good if I "remember" that "Highway 30" is the road to take. In many of the behavior diseases these distortions of memory are prominent symptoms.

RETENTION OF DISORDERED BEHAVIOR— THE "NEUROTIC PARADOX"

Although we think of disordered behavior as essentially *maladaptive,* the organism's retention of such behavior is not explained by the label. To do so we would have to assume that some creatures had a basic motivational bias opposed to adaptation, a sense of biological values, as it were, inverted from the normal. Such a supposition would bring us back to an old type of theory that the causes of mental disorders resided in the organism exclusively. Since the psychopathologist frequently notes that faulty modes of adjustment *are* retained in mentally ill people, there may seem to be a paradox involved in the statement that frustration results in the selection or retention of successful ways of adapting.

There are at least two explanations of this seeming dilemma. To begin with, there are many ways of reducing frustration, and in any given situation the barrier may be solved by use of any one of several techniques. Some of these methods are actually less effective than others, particularly if we take a long-time point of view. They may afford temporary or seeming relief, and in the end be no solution at all. Consider the case of an individual who was satisfied with the action of aspirin in reducing the pain of chronic headaches but never consulted a physician. If the headaches were due to the pressure of a brain tumor or were the result of inadequate lenses in his spectacles, his solution-attempt via the aspirin route would constitute an actual maladaptive act. During World War II an emergency treatment of emotionally disturbed soldiers was employed in which the patient was given strong doses of narcotics and kept in a stuporous condition for many hours or days. Such a treatment removed, at least temporarily, many symptoms, but could not be expected to constitute a cure since the essential causes of the breakdown had not been treated. From the individual's point of view in these situations, the technique of taking aspirin or of sleeping for long periods may seem to be a successful solution of his problem if the pain or discomfort were relieved. The goal toward which the individual consciously strives may be only a small part of the total need situation that created the goal. Retention of maladaptive techniques, then, may in many instances be due to the limited outlook or foresight of the patient. *The organism often responds to the immediate and narrow view of the situation,* not to its remote and complex implications. As we shall see, many people learn methods of evaluating this environment that preclude the possibility of response to the more inclusive aspects of life.

The other possibility of explaining the retention of maladaptive practices is the assumption that some frustrating situations are so narrowly constraining and so chronic that no other possible courses of action remain open. Dickens created such a situation in *Oliver Twist,* where the young Oliver, under Fagin's tutelage, acquired socially maladaptive techniques primarily because no alternatives were presented. This is a special case of adaptation, where actions necessary to preserve an equilibrium at the cellular and personal levels result in serious disequilibrium at the social level. It is noteworthy that complete adequacy of adjustment requires more and more comprehensive understanding of situations by the organism as we go from the cellular to the social levels of adjustment.

RELATION OF LEARNING TO OTHER BASIC CONCEPTS

The integrated nature of behavior is well illustrated in the interdependency of learning with all other aspects of the organism. What is learned, the rate at which learning takes place, and the length and amount of retention are all influenced by variables of motivation, heredity, environmental stress, physical health, and many others. We will limit our consideration in this section to motivational factors in learning.

As we remarked before, learning probably takes place only when some circumstance arises to frustrate a motive, or, in other words, when a problem is presented to the subject. Completely unimpeded progression toward a goal would call for nothing that was not already in the repertoire of the subject's responses. When frustration occurs, behavior must be varied if it is to be successful, and this variability, called forth by barriers, is essential to learning.

Problems are defined by the motives that are blocked. If the motive is hunger, the problem is "acquiring something to eat," and the techniques developed in solving this problem are oriented toward eating. Likewise, if the motive is escape from pain or fear, the behavior of the subject is oriented to those motives, and circumstances that prolong pain or fear are the problems. In general, we may logically say that a motivational situation of any kind will call forth variability that has as its purpose the reduction of the motive and restoration of the equilibrium whose disturbance gave rise to the motive. This is true of learning in general and is of specific importance to psychopathology. The processes that underlie disordered behavior are no different from the processes that underlie well-adjusted behavior. Both are adaptive, as we have seen, and their points of difference reside in the type of motive that produces directions of this behavior we call disordered or in the nature of the barrier confronting the person. Since living organisms are capable of retaining the effects of experience, and since those retained effects modify later behavior, by means of learning, any technique of adaptation may be preserved and may play a determining role in subsequent adaptive efforts of the subject.

The person in a conflict situation will vary his behavior until a successful issue of the frustration is discovered. If the conflict recurs, the probability is great that he will use the technique that was effective on the previous occasion. *The subject learns techniques that successfully resolve conflicts.* This is one way of stating a principle of learning whose general designation in learning literature is "the law of effect." This "law" has been subject to criticism on experimental grounds, but the net effect of the evidence seems to be that learning is influenced by factors *in addition* to the law of effect. In pathological behavior operation of this principle is seen abundantly. A casual look at some pathological behavior might lead to the conclusion that the subject was learning techniques that brought pain and trouble rather than the reverse. The patient who slashes his skin with a dull knife, the individual who disrupts his whole social adjustment by chronic overindulgence in alcohol, the person who commits suicide—all these behaviors may seem so obviously distressing to the subject and so lacking in adjustmental value as to be a complete denial of the principle expressed above. Yet, in the most maladaptive behavior (as viewed by the outside observer), detailed study of the case will show that the patient is using techniques oriented to *his* problems, and that, when his problems are known, the behavior becomes an understandable attempt to solve these problems.

A further circumstance of the relation between learning and motivation should be considered. If we say that the problem is defined by the motive, what then happens in a conflict where two or more motives of approximately equal strength are involved? In the past each motive has been associated with appropriate reduction techniques. When the motives operate simultaneously, each will continue to stimulate behavior appropriate to itself. In this lies some of the apparent confusion in behavior attendant upon conflict. In consequence of this stalemate of techniques adapted to the individual motives, often a new motive arises from the conflict, a motive to "escape conflict," and behavior takes a new direction, which is not appropriate to the motives arousing the conflict, but to the conflict itself. This is a further factor in the seeming unreasonableness of disordered behavior.

DISCUSSION QUESTIONS

1. What are the basic physiological needs of animals?
2. How important to the everyday behavior of man are these physiological needs?
3. How many basic social motives of man can you list?
4. Why would you expect conflicts between ego needs and superego needs?
5. What are some of the social frustrations in modern civilization?
6. How well can you recognize the motivation for your own behavior?
7. Are there any differences in your insight into your behavior for differing kinds of situations?
8. Why does conflict seem inevitably to produce frustration?
9. What are some of the criteria for acceptable and unacceptable resolutions of conflict?

10. Can you think of examples of faulty memory in your personal life that might be explained by the motivational schemes we have discussed?

SUGGESTED READINGS

J. Deese (1952), *The Psychology of Learning.* New York: McGraw-Hill Book Company, Inc.

S. Freud (1938), "Psychopathology of everyday life," in A. A. Brill (trans.), *The Basic Writings of Sigmund Freud.* New York: Random House, Inc.

J. G. Miller (1942), *Unconsciousness.* New York: John Wiley & Sons, Inc.

P. M. Symonds (1951), *The Ego and the Self.* New York: Appleton-Century-Crofts, Inc.

P. T. Young (1936), *Motivation of Behavior.* New York: John Wiley & Sons, Inc.

BIBLIOGRAPHIC SOURCES

The psychology of motivation has produced a stupendous literature. The general literature is discussed in Young's two books on motivation and emotion (Young, 1936, 1943). We have distinguished in the text between physiological needs and social motives. The more customary terminology is the analogous dichotomy of "primary" drives and "secondary" drives. The primary drives—or physiological needs such as thirst, hunger, and so on—are discussed in Young (1936, 1951). In addition, the excellent article by Stellar (1954) discusses the recent work of the physiology of motivation with special reference to the role of the hypothalamus. The secondary drives—or social motives—are examined in Miller (1951) as based on primary drives. An excellent general source on current topics in motivational study over several areas is the Nebraska symposium (1953), entitled *Current Theory and Research in Motivation.* Papers included are by J. S. Brown, H. F. Harlow, L. J. Postman, V. Nowlis, T. M. Newcomb, and O. H. Mowrer. Other important sources are Roethlisberger and Dickson (1941), Allport (1937), Miller and Dollard (1941), and Thorndike (1935, 1940). For a provocative paper on the problem of the measurement of social motives, Allport (1953) is suggested. Finally, no student of motivation should miss the splendid and very critical article by Koch (1951) from which a quote is applicable: "We are a science still groping for the identification of our basic variables" (p. 148).

"Ego" and "superego" have been established as basic words in psychopathology, and you were probably using them long before you began to read this book. The importance of these words in modern psychopathology may be traced, like so many other concepts, to Freud (1927). He postulated that the structure of personality or mental life is composed of three basic categories: the id, the ego, and the superego. The id consists of the basic drives. The other two we have discussed in the text. The interplay between these dimensions of personality fills a large portion of the psychoanalytic literature. Some of the most completely developed parts of Freud's theories are concerned with this interaction. One methodological point should be made clear. From the writings of Freud and many other analytic authors one gets the impression that these three categories denote some existing thing such as denoted by the word "chair." As you might expect no physiological investigation has discovered such entities. It is for the reason that reification is so easy with this terminology that we have used the terms "ego functions" and "superego functions." As processes, functions, or habits, these terms have meaning; as entities, the concepts mean little. The best introduction to ego functions is Symond's (1951) *The Ego and the Self,* which is a short, scholarly, and clear summary of the many viewpoints in this area. The annotated bibliography of 211 publications should be particularly helpful. Ausubel's (1952) *Ego Development and the Personality Disorders* is also suggested.

Good introductions to the topic of frustration are somewhat hard to obtain but Maier (1949), Maslow and Mittleman (1951), Rosenzweig (1944), and Symonds (1946, 1949) represent many points of view and should be helpful. Perhaps it is best to start with Symond's texts (1946, 1949) which review the various types of frustrating situations and methods of reacting to them.

Perhaps the best general sources on conflict are those by Singer (1949, 1950) which discuss the views of Freud, Pavlov, Guthrie, Luria, and others. Since these publications are not too easily available and since they will probably require some knowledge about the area to be understandable, other sources are suggested for initial study. Guthrie's (1944) associationistic analysis of conflict is readily available. One of the earliest experimental programs on conflict in humans was that of Luria (1932). Conflict situations are classed by Lewin (1935) in a book presenting the Gestalt approach to a theory of personality. In the text we have drawn heavily from N. E. Miller's (1944) penetrating account of a series of experiments done by Miller and his associates. There is perhaps no better illustration in the present psychological literature of a complementary program involving theory and experimentation (see Miller, 1952). The view that behavior always involves conflict is advanced by Mowrer and Kluckhohn (1944).

Another primary psychoanalytic distinction has been the division of the structure of personality into the categories of "conscious," "pre- or foreconscious," and "unconscious." "Pre-conscious" refers to that material which is not immediately conscious but which may easily and readily be brought into consciousness. As with the notion of id, ego, and superego, these terms pertaining to conscious experience or the lack of it are readily reified. To avoid this and following the lead of others, we have used the words "levels of awareness" or "conscious processes." We have drawn very heavily from the best single source in the area, Miller's (1942) *Unconsciousness*. Miller's (1950) short chapter in Reymert (1950) may be a useful introduction. As supplementary material, Margett's (1953) article gives a fascinating historical account of the concept of the unconscious.

Quantitatively, the study of learning is by far the most extensive area of investigation in modern psychology. Accordingly, the literature is immense. As a general introduction on the undergraduate level, Deese (1952) is suggested.

The best introductions to the present status of learning theory are the book by Hilgard (1948) and the papers by Spence (1951a, 1951b). For the major works of the leading learning theorists, Guthrie (1952), Hull (1943, 1951, 1952), Tolman (1949), and Skinner (1938) are paramount. Also, an article by Guthrie (1944) presents a theory of personality in terms of associative learning.

Many of the topics such as redintegration, forgetting, and memory are discussed with reference to the literature of human learning in the chapters by Hilgard (1951) and Hovland (1951) and the much more comprehensive treatment by McGeoch and Irion (1952). Brogden (1951) reviews much of the animal literature. For work done on the rat, Munn (1950) is standard.

The classic treatment of conditioning is the survey by Hilgard and Marquis (1940), *Conditioning and Learning*, with which every student of learning should be familiar.

The application of learning theory to the problems of psychopathology has been outlined in detail by several authors. Dollard and Miller (1950), Guthrie (1938), and Mowrer (1950a, 1952a, 1952b) should be consulted.

No single author has discussed the neurotic paradox more completely than Mowrer (1948). This paper has been reprinted with additional notes in Mowrer's (1950) *Learning Theory and Personality Dynamics*. Further information may be found in Mowrer (1952c).

The relationship between motivation and learning is discussed by Leeper (1935). Adams (1931) has an article presenting the Gestalt point of view. For a more recent and broad treatment of the problem, see Chapter 22 in Woodworth and Schlosberg (1954).

Finally, Stolurow (1953) has collected a number of major theoretical and experimental papers into one volume. All these papers are familar reading to the scholar in learning.

IV

Personality Development and Maladjustment

Every life is many days, day after day. We walk through ourselves, meeting robbers, ghosts, giants, old men, young men, wives, widows, brothers-in-love. But always meeting ourselves.

—JOYCE, *Ulysses*

Personality: the Central Topic in Psychopathology

If some industrious candidate for an advanced degree could make a word count of the frequency with which various words are used in textbooks and monographs in abnormal psychology, he would undoubtedly find that "personality" achieved a top frequency. Almost all psychopathologists are in agreement that personality is involved in the behavior disorders, whatever else they may believe in addition. The worst difficulty in using the word is the wide variety of meanings that have given it so broad an inclusiveness as to lead to occasional confusion.

DEFINITION

For our purposes we may view personality as *an expression of the organism's unique potentialities in any given situation.* The term implies a relatively persisting unity that behaves in varied ways as the conditions of life change. Personality *is the person* and, as such, is a unique organization of protoplasm that changes from moment to moment, is modified by its experiences, and yet always maintains an ele-

61

ment of constancy and predictability that identifies it. The individual, with his name, his family, his social group memberships, and his geographical location is a unit of relative constancy in a changing world. It is to this unity that we must turn when we seek to understand behavior. To the clinician particularly, the person is of supreme importance, since, in almost every instance, he never deals with lesser organizations. The physician, the social worker, the teacher are all working with personalities. They do not work with genetics, with brains, with incomes, or with learning processes, but with the combination of all these factors in the given specific individuals who make up their clientele.

Since the person is the repository and the target of so many genetic and environmental factors, it is surprising that we find in him some element of predictability. Each individual tends to behave consistently from day to day, and in differing situations. The mother or father of a large family, the policeman who knows his neighborhood, the physician who knows his patients are usually able to make a high percentage of correct predictions concerning the behavior of those people with whom they have intimate contact. The fact that references or recommendations are usually required in establishing credit or in securing a job is a recognition of the predictability of behavior. To the psychologist the personality is a unit that moves through life situations with characteristic degrees of adjustment or maladjustment. From a knowledge of factors that make up the personality he aspires to predict what the individual will do when confronted with any new situation.

Of significance to the psychopathologist is the fact that personality may be said to delimit and, in a way, select environmental impacts, thus creating behavior. Those aspects of the environment that will be responded to will depend upon the person who is responding. Everyone is familiar with the operation of this factor in discriminatory behavior. The woodsman reads worlds of meaning from visual, auditory, and olfactory inspection of his familiar environment; the city dweller needs the roar of traffic and the human social surroundings to make similarly detailed discriminations. In the same way a person with deep-seated insecurity detects the most delicate nuances of snub or ridicule; he interprets the slightest environmental changes as threatening forces directed against him. All these discriminatory reactions are functions of the personality. We can predict the reactions of the woodsman in the forest, of the city-dweller in the subway, and so on. The person may be compared to a filter that passes certain stimulations, rejects others, and is completely unaffected by still others. Evidently, each person lives in a world of his own, a world whose dimensions are shaped and determined by his own properties as a reacting organism. The meanings of objects or situations, and thus the behavior of people toward them, can be defined or predicted only by knowing the personality who creates the meanings. Conversely, the personality of an individual may be determined by a study of the meanings or discriminations we observe him making. R. D. Williams (1938) used the phrase "probe body" to indicate that the person measures, interprets, and responds to the universe around him, pointing out that the person plays something of the same role in the energy field of which he is a part as a meter in an electrical circuit. As Koffka (1935) has said, to understand a person's actions we must know the psychological environment in which those actions are taking place.

THE PSYCHOLOGICAL ENVIRONMENT

The concept of *psychological environment,* as defined by the Gestaltists, has certain useful applications to psychopathology. There is a useful distinction between the *psychological* and *physical* surroundings in which behavior occurs. Ordinarily, when we think of "environment" we think of a physical world, of a space that is measured in the physicist's units of length, weight, and time, of a space that possesses uniformities in experience to all people exposed to equal "quantities" of it. This constancy we assume implies that the units in which this environment is described are also constant, so that one yard is always of the same length as any other yard, one pound of the same weight as any other pound, and one minute of the same duration as any other minute. However, psychologists have always had difficulty in fitting their measures of behavior to these physical units. One of the earliest discoveries in experimental psychology was of the fact that the sense organs do not react equally to equal changes in physical stimuli. A subject who has no difficulty in discriminating between one ounce and two ounces may be unable to tell a difference between 16 and 17 ounces, although in each case the two weights are increased by the same additional amount. The same lack of correspondence may be detected in other situations. Anyone who has waited for a train knows that an hour may be an endless time, or that the hour may be very short indeed, if it is filled by visiting with a friend, reading an interesting novel, or watching a good baseball game. Evidence could be multiplied that physical dimensions are extremely elastic when we actually experience them. Le Comte Du Nouy (1937) has shown that biological time, using physiological processes such as healing time of wounds as the clock, is radically different from physical time, and Hoagland (1933) and François (1927) demonstrated experimentally that time estimation is a function of body temperature and not of astronomical constants alone. Who would be bold enough to say that the first mile of a fifteen-mile hike is as long as the last mile? Certainly not the weary pedestrian. It is apparent that we are missing some of the essence of behavior if we neglect these psychological ways of measuring and experiencing the environment. As soon as the environment is described through the eyes of a person who is behaving in it, physical units become changed in their actual effects on behavior. Much of the physicist's preoccupation with sources of "error" in his measuring instruments is directed at the human element. (See Boring's [1950] description of the astronomer's discovery of the "personal equation.") Consequently it has been proposed that we boldly *assume* the existence of another environment—the environment that is generated by the personality. As Du Nouy says, "From whatever angle we look at it . . . we are led to the conclusion that it would be interesting to borrow solely from a living organism the units which are used to define it" (1937, p. 144). *These units and dimensions of the psychological environment are determined by the personality.*[1]

If we assume, then, that every person has his own psychological environment, it is obvious that we must define our basic explanatory concepts in terms of that environment. Motives, for example, may be viewed as directions in which the personality moves toward goals. The physical direction of movement is not in itself psychologically significant; what *is* important is the degree to which this movement results in goal attainment. Motives and goals are highly individual, and are thus characteristic of the personality creating them. The strength of a motive is also dependent upon these same individual factors. Hunger is a strong motive, and food a desirable goal, but only to a person who has undergone a certain minimal period of food deprivation; to anyone who

[1] The reader is urged to consult the very important critical analysis of objective and subjective approaches to behavior theory made by Hull (1943) and to compare it with Koffka's (1935) discussion of the same points. Our position in this chapter attempts to use Koffka's concepts and to avoid Hull's objections—a risky business.

has just finished a hearty meal, hunger does not give direction, and food does not constitute a goal. Too often in the past psychopathologists have made the error of assuming that motives or the lure of goals were factors independent of the individual organism and that they could be measured in objective terms that were equally independent of the organism that was motivated. The same error is often made by moralists and others who would regulate the conduct of people through appeal to hypothetical universal conditions or requirements that they assumed to exist uniformly for all. To the suspicious or apprehensive person all other people in his psychological environment assume an appearance of aggressive threatening attack. He assumes, that is, uniform motivation in everyone, not realizing that people have those characteristics only in *his* psychological environment.

Another aspect of the personality-oriented environment is the fact that the individual tends to preserve those aspects of the environment that are associated with successful reduction of motives and to eliminate those aspects that interfere with such reduction. The constancy of the behavioral environment is maintained by the personality. This is of great significance to the psychopathologist, since *many of the strivings of organisms tend to preserve an environment that has elicited and continues to elicit maladjustive behavior.* This is a phenomenon lying at the heart of psychopathology. Since the individual is very often restricted in his appraisal of a situation by the limitations of his own personality, what seems gratifying and successful to him may, from a more inclusive point of view, actually be frustrating and maladjustive. Or, as is often the case in the personality disorders, the patient may be motivated in directions that are tension-reducing *for him* and be successfully meeting his problems, but at the cost of frustrating, annoying, or harming others in his social environment. A rather frequent example of perpetuating an environment harmful to the person is seen in those individuals who start their criminal careers by forging checks to meet some momentary financial need. If the first forged checks are accepted as genuine, and the immediate problem is solved, forgery becomes an advantageous technique and will be preserved in the personality. The long-term frustrating effects of such anti-social behavior do not operate as strongly in the criminal's psychological environment as do the immediate rewards. It should be explicitly recognized that the assumption of a personality-created environment does not also imply a belief in an omnipotence or omniscience of personality. People do not always know what is good for them to know. The pedestrian whose psychological environment includes a "street free of moving vehicles" may still be hit by the car he didn't see.

Frustration and the Development of Personality

INFANCY AND CHILDHOOD

There are many factors in the development of personality that are fundamental to psychopathology. Foremost is the helplessness of the human infant and his long period of dependence on others. One consequence of this slowly evolving maturity is the fact that emotional development of the child is based on his interpersonal relationships. Love and hate, fear and anger are associated with the human figures surrounding the infant. Early emotional patterns are built up in relationships with the parents, and in this critical period of dependency, basic attitudes, appetites, and aversions are initiated. Dependency forces on the infant a long period of constant intimate association with parents and creates the opportunity for emotional attachments far deeper than in the young of any other species.

In the normal course of development there is a gradual weakening of the strong affectional ties with parents. New interests, new objects of affection, and new independence of parental protection appear. In many instances, however, the early emotional relationship with the parents persists, with small change, long after it has served its maximal usefulness. This constitutes an obstacle to normal personality growth, and the child remains emotionally immature.

Examples of this pathological retardation in emotional growth are not hard to find. Long a favorite theme for the dramatist and novelist, it frequently is seen by college vocational counsellors and psychiatrists. It is easily recognizable in an obvious form in the "mamma's boy," the person "tied to his mother's apron-strings," the individual who has never been allowed or encouraged to make decisions for himself, who is overprotected and shielded from normal social contacts, and whose future is decided *for* him by parents. Neglecting for the moment the reasons for such actions on the part of parents, it is obvious that the effects on the personality of the child can be extremely serious. One example is the following:

Case 4. Miss G., a student in elementary psychology, came to the department "to talk over her future." She said that she had been in one of the branches of military service during the war and consequently was somewhat older than the average college sophomore. Yet, in spite of being twenty-five, she still did not know what sort of life work she should prepare for. An appointment was made to give her a vocational interest test and to discuss her plans. As she was leaving she handed the interviewer a letter, saying as she went out the door, "That's what I really came to see you about." The letter contained a list of things about herself that troubled her, starting with "I always feel self-conscious," and enumerating about twenty other complaints, some of which sounded rather serious. Among these were several statements to the effect that she "felt her personality was changing," that she would have periods when she felt outside herself, and nothing seemed real, that something seemed to be wrong with her mind, and that she felt no emotion toward people.

A series of interviews disclosed something of the background for these complaints. Miss G. and her brother, two years older, were the only children of a woman whose husband had deserted her while the children were very young, the patient being only two years old at the time. The family lived in a wealthy suburb of a large midwestern industrial city and had, until the father left, a better-than-average income, together with high social standing in the community. The circumstances of the desertion and the behavior of the father for a year or so before gave good grounds for suspecting his "mental competency"; although he disappeared completely, there appeared to be enough evidence to convince the mother that he was suffering from a mental disease. She reacted courageously to the new circumstances and, being a talented musician, managed to maintain the family residence and send the children through high school. The struggle was terrific, however, since, as Miss G. said, her mother's income was rarely enough to supply both adequate food and clothes; some months they would have food but no clothes, and every addition to their wardrobe could be paid for only by slimmer rations at the table. Miss G. was a bright student in the lower grades and took seriously her mother's frequent remarks that she would have to be brighter than other children because she could never depend on having anything else. In high school her grades started out well and then suffered a slump that was paralleled by an increasing state of emotional tension in the girl. This arose from the obvious discrepancies between her financial status and that of her friends; they had more clothes, they talked about and, a little later, drove their father's new cars, they were able to invite Miss G. to their homes for week-ends; Miss G. did not have clothes or a car, and she was ashamed to have her friends see the bare rooms and shabby furniture of her home, losing sight, in a typically adolescent manner, of the fact that as children her friends had been almost as familiar with her house as she was herself. The poor scholastic record alarmed her mother, and she became even more urgent in her emphasis on succeeding. She said that Miss G. was old enough to know facts, and that she should recognize that the reason they were so poor was because of the way the patient's father had treated them. If Miss G. were wise, her mother said, she would have nothing to do with men and should make up her mind that she could "make her own way in life," just as her mother had.

As a result of the pressure at home, Miss G. worked harder, but did not give up envying her friends. By the time she was through high school she was sure that the only way to be happy was to have money and *not be poor*. But she was also more dependent on her mother than ever, since the mother had continued to develop the theme of how hard she had worked to keep the family together and how all that she had done had been out of love for her children. A dynamic, forceful, and domineering woman, she completely overshadowed Miss G., who seemed to herself to be weak, helpless, and incapable. In only one respect did she fail to mirror her mother's ideas, and that was in the matter of money and the signs of success. The mother estimated success on something of an artistic and social level; Miss G. estimated success by the amount of money people had and the degree of ostentation they were capable of achieving with that money. Her mother, noting those trends, reproached her, saying that she was immature and superficial. After high school, Miss G. secured employment as a typist in a large office and performed so poorly that she was "demoted" to the lesser-paying job of receptionist in the office lobby. It was here that Miss G. found her first real interest in a vocational line. She made an excellent receptionist because, as she said, she "liked to be looked at," and as a receptionist, she felt she seemed "more important." Soon she secured a job as a dress model and, aside from her discontent at not being able to buy the clothes she displayed, she was reasonably happy. However, her mother felt that the employment was unsuitable for her daughter and started a campaign to remedy the situation. It was as a result of one of these discussions that Miss G. quit her job and enlisted in the armed forces, her first real rebellion against her mother. The mother, however, changed the rebellion into something else by pointing out how much more socially useful the patient was by doing this work than by modelling dresses. She warned again, however, that Miss G. should be extremely careful not to get mixed up with men and should work hard so she could "get to the very top." The patient did well in the service, although she had two or three episodes of extreme anxiety over slight affairs with men, which she dutifully related to her mother.

When she left the service after the war, she immediately returned to her home and wanted to resume her work modelling. Her mother vetoed this and said that, since she was now eligible for the G.I. Bill assistance in getting a college education, she would be "as crazy as her father" (a favorite saying) if she didn't go to college. Although Miss G. still wanted to become a model, she finally went to college, supervised by her mother, but with no real interest and a great deal of repressed hostility toward her collegiate work. Her complaints of unreality feelings and of "personality change" seemed to be a type of day-dream or fantasy escape from the growing dissatisfaction with domination, which she was able to overcome in no other way. Although she told herself many times a day that she loved her mother and that her mother knew better than she did herself what was good for her, she would dream at night that her mother was dead or that her mother was a disreputable person; during the day she would spend her time in imagining the delights of being rich and having everything she wanted. She was asked to join a sorority but refused because she felt that people would know she was poor. She could have had friends among the other students with little money, but she hated any suggestion of poverty in others. Consequently she led a very lonely life in which the distinction between reality and dreams was sometimes hard to make. At twenty-five she was hardly as mature emotionally as many children of fourteen.

In this case the influence of a dominant and overwhelmingly affectionate mother, acting year after year with a blind disregard of the actual psychological environment in which the girl was living, came close to producing a break with reality. It is probable that the mother herself had little insight for the biased and conflictual outlook she was creating in her daughter. Being deserted by her own husband, having the years of struggle for her children, possessing ambitions for her daughter with no corresponding insight for her daughter's personality, all these facets of the mother's background were being perpetuated in the daughter (see Burlingame, 1947).

Among the first to recognize the importance of events of infancy and early childhood in molding personality, Freud and his students have continued to emphasize the primary character of the emotional habits and attitudes formed during this period. They have, for example, pointed out the frustration inherent in personality expansion. The infant, at first completely dependent upon the mother, must go through a frustrating process of weaning and must relinquish its complete domination of the mother's time and attention. Still further frustration grows out of the constantly increasing emphasis on the inhibition of other spontaneous drive-expressions. Socialization of the child involves the acquisition of acceptable excretory habits, and the Freudians have attributed much deep emotional significance to the process of toilet training. Blocking and thwarting these primitive forms of behavior results in the usual consequences of frustration, and child psychologists report an increase in aggressive behavior during this period. The aggression may be directed toward any aspect of the child's environment, but the parents and those things that symbolize the parents are initially the chief recipients. Since much of the child's aggression is primitive in nature, parents and society in general react to the aggression by even stronger attempts at inhibitory training. This may be followed by extension of the child's aggression, creating a vicious circle that ends in maladjustment and the emergence of catastrophic behavior. On a small scale this may be seen in the little domestic pictures that emerge when Junior is being induced to eat his spinach or drink his milk. The social pressure from his parents starts with attempts at blandishments and demonstrations of spinach-eating, accompanied with attempts at verbal arguments of, "See, Junior, Daddy *likes* his spinach, and he's a great big man like you'll be if *you* eat your spinach." When this fails to produce the desired result, the next gambit is usually an attempt to make the spinach the means to an end: "If you eat the nice spinach you can have your dessert." Unfortunately this attempt at psychological subtlety results in the spinach becoming, not a technique for acquiring something sweet, but a barrier and a frustration separating Junior from his dessert. This produces the predictable aggressive response, and Junior begins to show a primitive emotionality. He may squirm, pout, cry, make an elaborately mascerated mess of the spinach, or even go so far as to question his parents' judgment about spinach or about diet in general. Since the parents are by now rapidly becoming frustrated themselves, aggression is met with aggression. Father says, "You'll *eat* that *spinach* before you leave the table if I have to force it down your throat," and mother at the same time says, "If you don't eat your spinach, you'll have to leave the table this instant and go to bed." Junior manifests still more disordered behavior, as do his parents. The scene ends by Junior receiving a spanking, which increases his distaste for spinach, or being allowed to forego the spinach, thus giving birth to a suggestion in his fertile young mind that could best be classified as "technique for conquering parents and doing what I want to do."

More serious as a consequence of the emotional struggle between parents and children is the finding that alcoholics often show in their background such factors as "domineering mother," "stern father," "state of insecurity in childhood" (Wittman, 1939). If the result of child-hood frustration is to deprive the individual of opportunities for developing maturity in his handling of the frustrations and emotional tensions of adult life, the result may be such faulty ways of compromise with adjustment as alcoholism. (For the background of childhood frustration in the etiology of alcoholism see also Schilder, 1941; Strecker, 1941; and Jellinek, 1942.)

An important aspect of childhood is the acquisition of techniques and tools for adjustment to the social environment in which the person must spend his life. It is perhaps unfortunate that the period of greatest learning is also the time when the child is least able to evaluate critically what is being learned. At the time when these basic techniques and attitudes are developing, the person is least able to discriminate the true from the false, the adequate from the inadequate, the successful from the unsuccessful, and so forth. Thus, every child learns much that may later lead to inefficiency, faulty adjustment, prejudice, and social ineptitude. During this period of life the child accepts standards and values, methods and tools from the environment that surrounds it. Much of what sociologists have called "cultural lag," the slowness of social evolution, depends upon the circumstances of early education. The emancipation difficulties of adolescence stem from the growing discrepancy between the demands of the individual's contemporary surroundings and those aspects of early training that did not prepare him for adequate behavior in those surroundings. The emotional aspects of this period are increased by the continued efforts of parents to maintain their own point of view and their own dominance.

Frustration, then, is frequent in the life of the child. However, tolerance of poor ways of meeting frustration is maximal. Legally and otherwise the child is recognized as being incompetent to meet the standards of adult society. Even such serious crimes as murder meet with only minimal punishment if they are performed by young children. Pathological situations may arise when the child is driven to conform to standards of behavior that are beyond his capabilities, or when strong and insistent desires cannot be gratified.

It should be recognized that frustration is inevitable if the child is to become a participating member of his social group. To what extent the effects of frustration are harmful must be determined experimentally. There have been many attempts to investigate the part early frustration plays in the later life of the individual. The usual difficulties of human experimentation are magnified in the efforts to answer this problem. It is almost impossible to submit human children to situations in which the kind and amount of frustration are controlled and then to follow the lives of the subjects for a long enough period of time to observe possible changes in personality. In clinical studies of individuals we must depend upon the uncertain evidence of people's memories, which may be distorted by the effects of the very factors we seek to study. In any case, it is seldom we can be certain that we are reliably informed of the nature of frustrating situations that happened many years ago (see Rappaport, 1942).

EXPERIMENTAL EVIDENCE

As comparative psychologists have become better acquainted with the details of motivation in lower animals, the psychopathologist has been able to devise experimental techniques that escape some of the difficulties of the human clinical study. Using animals with a relatively small life span, it is practicable to rigidly control the early life experiences of the animal and test it specifically for behavior alterations at any later period of its life. The social and humanitarian objections to possibly harmful human experimentation may also be avoided.

One group of investigations, using the rat, has been made on the effect of early food deprivation on later adult behavior with respect to food. If rats undergo periods of food deprivation, it has been observed that later, when food pellets are plentiful, they will carry large numbers of them to the corner of their cage. This behavior has been termed "hoarding." It evidently does not appear to any marked extent in animals who have always had plentiful food supplies (Wolfe, 1939; F. McCord, 1941; Morgan, Stellar, and Johnson, 1943). When young rats met frustration of their hunger drive for a fifteen-day period following weaning and were then tested for hoarding after a five-month period with unlimited food, they hoarded approximately 38 pellets to every 14 hoarded by a control group whose first food frustration occurred during the critical tests (Hunt, 1941). In a second experiment, animals whose initial frustration started a week after weaning did not show significantly more hoarding than did control animals during the test period five months later (Hunt, Schlosberg, Soloman, and Stellar, 1947). It would appear that frustration has a greater effect on later behavior when it occurs at the earlier ages, although more experimental evidence on this point is badly needed (see Beach and Jaynes, 1954).

The effect of early frustration on later behavior was studied in another way by Steckle and O'Kelly (1940). Immediately after weaning, a group of rats were placed in a specially constructed cage whose floor was covered with an electric grid at all points of approach to the animals' water supply. Thus the animals could only drink while standing on the grid and receiving an electrical shock. The animals were left in this cage for 32 days. They were weighed daily, and if an animal showed a continuous weight loss for three successive days, it was placed in a conventional cage with ample food and water until its weight had returned to its first-day level. Two control groups were also used. One group was deprived of water for 72-hour periods and then allowed free water intake until its weight level was restored. The second control group lived a normal cage life with water and food always present. At the end of the training period, the groups were given a two-week interval of free access to water. All groups were then placed on a 24-hour water deprivation and trained to secure their daily water-intake at the end of a straightaway. After the animals had learned to run rapidly through the apparatus, the floor of the alley, formed of an electric grid, was activated. The number of times, on successive days, that

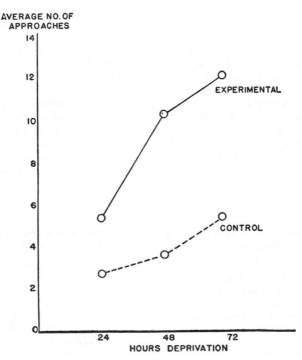

FIGURE 5. *Effect of early experience with shock on later persistence of response* (from data of Steckle and O'Kelly, 1941).

animals crossed or approached the grid were observed. Figure 5 illustrates the differences that existed between the groups with respect to approaches at three different levels of thirst motivation. The earlier experience of the experimental group with shock seems to have given them a greater persistence in their attempts to overcome the frustration of the charged grid.

Seashore and Bavelas (1942) subjected a group of children to a frustrating situation and noted the resulting behavior. The subjects were repeatedly asked to "draw a man," and after the subject was through, the experimenter would ask the child to draw a "better man," implying that the production was not good. This was continued until the child either refused to go on or until fifteen men had been drawn. Ten of the eighteen cases showed a steadily poorer performance as the critical attitude continued. It is evident from this that frustration of even a simple sort may actively interfere with optimal behavior in some children. Findings somewhat similar in their implications are reported by Scott (1946) in a study of fighting behavior in mice. If untrained fighters are placed with those more skilled at combat, and adequate adjustment is prevented, they adopt lower-level adjustments of less effectiveness.

In an attempt to relate dominative and cooperative behavior among nursery-school children to parental influences, Meyer (1947) correlated ratings of the children's behavior with ratings of parental variables. Table 4 shows those correlations that were significant. The dominance-cooperation ratio was secured by dividing the ratings for dominative behavior by those for cooperative behavior. High values of this ratio would indicate a preponderance of dominative behavior. The pattern of correlations found by Meyer is a decided verification of the relation we have referred to between aggressive behavior and frustration. Notice, for example, that the better the rapport between parents and child, the less assertiveness the child will show, and likewise, that the more disciplinary friction in the home, the higher will be the proportion of aggressive behavior shown by the child in the school situation.

TABLE 4

CORRELATION BETWEEN PARENTAL BEHAVIOR TOWARD CHILDREN
AND THE CHILDREN'S DOMINANCE-COOPERATION RATIO[*]

Parental Behavior Rated	*Correlation with Dominance-Cooperation Ratio*
Effectiveness of policy	−.65
Rapport with child	−.61
Understanding child's problems	−.59
Disciplinary friction	.57
Readiness of criticism	−.56
Democracy of policy	−.52
Readiness of explanation	−.49
Intensity of contacts	−.49

[*] *Source:* Compiled from data in Charlene T. Meyer (1947), "The assertive behavior of children as related to parent behavior." *J. Home Econ., 39,* 77-80.

These studies show that frustrations are capable of modifying the later behavior of the organism. In none of the studies given above, with the possible exception of the man-drawing experiment of Seashore and Bavelas, are the consequences of frustration necessarily harmful. In fact, it is easy to see the adaptive nature of the subjects' responses to frustration. It makes biological sense for an animal who has experienced hunger to store food beyond its immediate needs. The importance of such a mechanism for foraging animals, such as squirrels, is obvious. Early experience with electric shock seemed to impart a resistance to its effects and enabled the animal to secure more adequate gratification of its motives in the second situation. The children with unsatisfactory home lives showed a compensatory type of dominance behavior that presented as many potentialities for adequate adjustment as for poor adjustment. Two significant points, therefore, should be emphasized: (1) *the reaction to frustration is an effort to adjust;* and (2) *frustration often provides stimulation for learning of adjustmental techniques.* It should be realized that these principles are of general applicability to all frustrating situations, even when the results are extremely detrimental to the individual's long-term mental or physical health.

An animal experiment by Levy (1934) illustrates the more immediately harmful effects that frustration can produce. In a litter of six puppies, two were allowed to nurse with the mother, two were fed from a bottle with a nipple that required about five minutes' sucking to secure the milk, and the last two were fed from a bottle with an extremely large hole in the nipple, requiring only two minutes for complete intake. The results of this arrangement were noticeable in a very few days. The breast-fed puppies showed normal activity, the other four showed restlessness. The five-minute bottle-fed animals showed some sucking activity between feedings, and the two-minute bottle-fed puppies showed almost continuous sucking behavior, directed toward a variety of environmental objects and toward each other, going so far as to cause bleeding of their skins. These two dogs became extremely irritable and lost weight, although they were receiving the same amount of food as their more fortunate litter mates. The conclusion seems evident that the puppies' need for food was a complex motive and included a "sucking" component. When this component was not satisfied in a normal manner, a frustration situation was created. Studies of infants have shown differences in the behavior of bottle-fed and breast-fed babies that may stem from similar early frustration (Levy, 1928, 1937; Ribble, 1938, 1939).

Halliday (1943) has advanced, as reasons for the greater incidence of psychosomatic disorders in our contemporary culture, the increase in frustrations typical of present-day civilization. Among the changes that he believes have taken place in the last seventy years and that mean added frustration for the people of today are: decline in breast-feeding and delay of bowel training, restrictions in play area due to automobile traffic, loss of the patriarchal structure of the family, and a lack of economic or social security due to rapid changes in the structure of society. Mead (1947) reaffirms Halliday's argument and calls attention to the need for an approach to the problems of children that takes account of the nature of present social and cultural conditions.

FRUSTRATION TOLERANCE

Obviously, if children are to adapt successfully to the stresses of their environment it is necessary that they be exposed to those stresses in such a way that they may develop techniques of adjustment. Primarily, it is important that children develop *frustration tolerance,* which has been defined by Rosenzweig as "the individual's capacity to withstand frustration without failure of psychobiological adjustment, that is, without resorting to inadequate modes of response" (1944, page 385). In other words, the individual must be able to meet frustration in such a way that the learning of successful reduction techniques ensues. The problem of individual differences in frustration tolerance has been mentioned before, and it should be apparent to the student that "frustration tolerance" and "stress threshold" are terms referable to the same concept. Our next chapter is concerned with the ways that faulty techniques of handling frustration develop and with some of their consequences in personality structure.

General Summary

We have defined personality as the expression of the organism's unique potentialities in any situation, and have stressed the fact that personality has a persistent unity, a continuity that enables the observer to make predictions about the subject in a variety of situations. The personality may be said to define and select the environment. To this concept of the relation between the individual and the universe about him, we have given the name "psychological environment" and have said that it is the person's own interrelationships with that environment that determine his behavior, normal or pathological. Although people are motivated in their own unique psychological setting, there is a tendency on everyone's part to assume that his psychological environment is the one true and typical environment of all other people, thus leading to gross errors in his attempts to understand and anticipate what other people will do relative to other objects and to the subject.

Because the psychological environment is a creation of personality, and because personality has continuity, the environment will assume certain constancies that may be of pathological significance, since undesirable and maladaptive ways of behaving may be retained. The incomplete view that any person has of reality may serve as a factor in the retention of ways of behaving that are of momentary satisfaction but that possess long-range possibilities of maladjustment.

Frustration is seen as a necessity in the learning and development of the individual and also as the initial factor producing poor adaptation. The effects of frustration may be apparent in many later stages of development. The concept of frustration-tolerance was introduced as an important factor in determining what the effects of frustration will be for personality development.

DISCUSSION QUESTIONS

1. What does the term "personality" mean to you?
2. Can you distinguish between "personality," "character," and "temperament"?
3. What do people mean, if anything, when they remark: "He's got a lot of personality"?
4. Is the distinction between the psychological and physical environments necessary?
5. How is it possible for any organism to maintain maladjustive behavior?
6. What aspects of adult behavior would you guess to be determined by childhood training?
7. What is the adaptive as opposed to maladaptive significance of frustration in childhood?
8. Can you see differences in frustration tolerance among people you know?
9. Allport has said that all personalities are unique, meaning that no two people are alike. If this is true, how can we ever hope to have a *science* of personality?
10. What are the contributions of *habit* and *motive* to personality?

SUGGESTED READINGS

G. W. Allport (1937), *Personality, A Psychological Interpretation.* New York: Henry Holt & Company, Inc.

G. Murphy (1947), *Personality, A Biosocial Approach to Origins and Structures.* New York: Harper and Brothers.

R. Stagner (1948), *Psychology of Personality* (2nd Ed.). New York: McGraw-Hill Book Company, Inc.

BIBLIOGRAPHIC SOURCES

On personality in general, two of the most thoughtful books in contemporary psychological literature should be read by anyone who wishes to go further than the scanty introduction made in this chapter. These books are Allport's (1937) *Personality, A Psychological Interpretation,* and Murphy's (1947) *Personality, A Biosocial Approach to Origins and Structure.* The former contains the argument that, in the last analysis, personality is *unique* and that no two individuals should be expected to present exclusive similarities. The latter weaves the constitutional, motivational, and social factors into personality with the learning process as a central unifying concept. Other texts of equal scientific validity are McClelland (1951), Thorpe (1938), and Young (1952). Stagner's (1948) *Psychology of Personality* gives a survey of the various systematic approaches to the subject. Finally, every student should be familar with Hunt's (1944) two-volume work on *Personality and the Behavior Disorders.*

One highly developed method used in personality study is factor analysis which—in brief oversimplification—involves the administration of large numbers of tests and the mathematical resolution of factors from the responses to these tests. The technique and its results are described in detail in Cattell (1950a, 1950b) and Eysenck (1947, 1952). Do not confuse this method with psychoanalysis.

An important symposium on personality and theoretical models was edited by Krech and Klein and published in the *Journal of Personality* in 1951. The paper by Klein and Krech (1951) elaborates the thesis that ". . . all theories of behavior must be personality theories" (p. 5). In the other papers a variety of approaches are explored. For example, von Bertalanffy (1951) and Halstead (1951) on biological models, Hebb on neurological models, and so forth. Miller (1951) discusses theory in terms of the work on conflict. The entire collection of papers has been published separately as a book (Krech and Klein, 1952). The student will find every paper stimulating, well written, and certainly worth reading carefully. A necessary and excellent supplement to these authors is MacKinnon (1953), who takes a somewhat less optimistic view on present theoretical models and model building in the area of personality. An amusing simile comes from Blum (1953, p. vii), "Theories of personality are multiplying like the plague."

On developmental factors in personality there are several good sources, many of them psychoanalytically oriented, as would be expected from the emphasis psychoanalysis places on the events of infancy and early childhood. Buhler's (1930) *The First Year of Life,* Anna Freud's (1937) *The Ego and Mechanisms of Defense,* and Rank's (1929) *The Trauma of Birth* are classic. The best single source for this literature, however, is Blum's (1953) *Psychoanalytic Theories of Personality* which examines in detail the various psychoanalytic conceptions of personality development.

Perhaps the most scholarly presentation of the literature is Carmichael's (1954) *Manual of Child Psychology* with 19 chapters devoted to physical, psychological, and social development of the child, from pre-natal life to adolescence.

The texts on personality development by Harsh and Shrickel (1950), Martin and Stendler (1953), Senn (1953), or Slotkin (1952) may be useful. For literature surveys, Blair (1950), Eichorn and Jones (1952), and Stagner (1952) may be consulted. On the troublesome period of adolescence Zachary (1940) is suggested.

For different aspects of the influence of familial social factors on personality see Strecker (1946), Levy and Monroe (1948), Benedek (1946), and the papers by Baldwin, Sanford, Kuhn, and Winch in Hulett and Stagner (1951). The bibliographic score compiled by Heinicke and Whiting (1953) cites over 1,300 titles. On a somewhat broader context, Kardiner (1939) and Dollard, Doob, Miller, Mowrer, and Sears (1939) are both concerned with the relation of social forces to the growth and development of personality.

The literature on the effect of childhood experience on personality is extremely controversial. The best single source is Orlansky's (1949) exhaustive review which provides little support for the view maintaining that adult personality is determined by childhood training—one of the most widely held tenents of psychoanalytic theory.

Not quite so controversial but still in some doubt are the studies on hoarding as affected by infantile experience. For a review of the studies cited in the text and others, see Beach and Jaynes (1954). Negative results have been obtained by several investigators (see McKelvey and Marx, 1951) and, on the basis of a careful investigation, Porter, Webster, and Licklider (1951) concluded that, ". . . deprivation is a facilitating but not necessary condition for hoarding" (p. 305). For two theoretical analyses of hoarding, see Morgan (1947) and Marx (1950).

In addition to the literature on early experience and hoarding, there are a great many studies on the effect of varied infant and childhood experiences on later behavior. Beach and Jaynes (1954) have published an excellent survey of the literature on lower animals. In addition to hoarding, the topics of sensory discrimination, feeding, reproduction, social behavior, emotion, and learning are discussed. The student of personality and behavior development should be aware of this literature, and Beach and Jaynes is a splendid place to begin.

V

Behavior Mechanisms

*The desire which arises from joy and sorrow, which is re-
lated to one or to some, but not to all, the parts of the body,
has no regard to the profit of the whole man.*

—SPINOZA

We have discussed the general characteristics of frustration in Chapter III. There we concluded that some element of frustration was evident in all goal-oriented behavior, and that it served as an instigator of learning. The person's efforts to reduce the motivational forces acting upon him result in the development of new techniques of surmounting environmental obstacles. This is an effective factor in adaptation, and survival is dependent upon its existence. There are, however, many blind alleys in nature, and along with the development of successful ways of coping with frustration, there occur many instances of poor and failing solutions to difficulty. The very name, "trial and *error*," which has been given to many learning situations, indicates the unhappy fact that there are usually more wrong than right solutions. That this is true in a purely statistical sense, almost anyone who has placed bets in a horse-race or put chips on a number in roulette can testify. But even the mathematical confusion of probabilities in gambling has less complication than the possibilities of faulty adjustment of life problems. Because the living organism can retain the trace of past experiences, and because its awareness of the ramifications of any situation is at best incomplete, poor methods of dealing with problems tend to become incorporated in the personality. Some of these "errors" in adjustment occur with such regularity that the psychopathologist has developed a system of names to identify them. Before describing each mechanism in detail a few of the general principles of their development will be considered.

The Behavior Mechanisms

DEFINITION

A "behavior mechanism" can be defined as *sequences of learned responses to frustration or stress that occur without consideration of rational or realistic evaluation of the problem they are intended to solve.*
So defined, the term includes much of the behavior of all people, regardless of their psychopathological status. As Symonds (1946, page 169) has said, rational behavior is the end-stage of a long developmental history. The mechanisms originate in infancy and early childhood; they survive in adult behavior as a legacy of our formative years. They are used as unthinkingly as we say our name, speak our language, tie our shoes, or carry out any old familiar habit. Because they are such a fundamental part of our personality, they have the camouflage of the obvious and are recognized only with difficulty by the person employing them. They are learned and retained because at some time in our lives they performed a useful function. Some of them continue to be of functional advantage, but most of them are of the same degree of usefulness as our appendix and, on occasion, can be more troublesome. The mechanisms started as techniques of relieving simple frustrations, and they were satisfactory in the relatively uncritical environment of childhood. But the environment of the adult is not so tolerant, and the frustrations of the adult are complex.

As an illustration, suppose we follow the career of an infant who was frequently fed only *after* it had cried. The crying began as a sufficient motor response to the pangs of hunger. The appearance of food, the abatement of the hunger, and the return to comfort all revolved around the crying response. At age three this same child managed to climb to the lower branches of a tree and was unable to get down. Crying promptly summoned the parents, and the situation was relieved. At age seven the child asked permission to attend a motion picture and was refused. No psychologist is needed to predict the response to this frustration. The seven-year-old child used the techniques it started to learn in infancy, and for the quite adequate reason that they brought results. Suppose the parents prove unyielding in spite of the crying? A desirable and rational adjustment might include elimination of crying from the child's repertoire of problem-solving devices. When this happens, as it often does, the child has taken a very real step toward what we adults call "maturity." If the child continues to cry, by a circular process it may discover that parents will yield to a greater violence of emotional display. If the parents relent, they may discover that they have been instrumental in the development of a new mechanism, the "temper tantrum." As the child grows older, tantrums can come to be common automatic reactions to difficulties. Many unfortunate adults have discovered that the tantrum does not meet with the ready and unmixed success it once did, but because of the difficulty of insight mentioned previously they find it hard to connect their poor adjustment with the tantrum mechanism.

SOCIAL UTILITY OF BEHAVIOR MECHANISMS

Another reason for the long life and hardihood of behavior mechanisms lies in the social implications of many frustrating situations. As the child develops into a social being, he is guided more and more by the evaluative standards of the society in which he lives. Many of his impulses, drives, wishes, or desires not only cannot be carried out directly without violence to social dictates, but many of them cannot be recognized and acknowledged by the individual himself. To admit, for example, an aggressive desire for the harm or death of a near relative who is frustrating us would be so contrary to our own moral ideas of proper conduct as to cause us distress. To avoid such anxiety-producing thoughts or actions, and still to carry out our motives as best we may, many other mechanisms are either originated or perpetuated. In a way, what we are saying is that *mechanisms are not only used as means of solving problems, but as ways of disguising or avoiding the implications of some problem-solving techniques.* The small child may react to frustration by directly attacking its source. Anyone who has observed children has seen more than once instances of open and unconcealed aggression. The child may fly at the thwarting adult, little fists hammering, screaming "I hate you, I hate you! I wish you were dead, dead, DEAD!" It is probably fortunate for the health of parents that the child's strength and size are slight, otherwise parricide might be more common. When the child expresses death wishes, he does so without social inhibitions. In later life he has generally become socialized to the extent of inhibiting not only the overt behavior back of the aggressive death wish, but also the verbal expression of it and even, many times, the very thought of it. In its place, fulfilling the same function, but with a greater degree of social comfort and acceptance, are substituted various mechanisms. The mechanism reduces the possibility of anxiety and gives a feeling of escape from the problem. This is, in the long run, only a slight advantage, since nothing the behavior mechanisms can do will constitute either an adequate or a permanent solution, for the motive will remain in operation until attainment of an appropriate goal object reduces it.

Since all people employ mechanisms in their daily round of adjustments, it is natural to wonder why they have a special application to psychopathology. The answer is far from simple and can be only partially dealt with in this chapter. From the viewpoint of personality development, our particular interest is in those factors that sway the organism's adjustment from the ideal (if academic) state of perfect equilibrium with its environment. Thus, when a type of behavior is noted that satisfies the subject that he has solved a problem, but that is clearly seen by the objective observer to be a poor or faulty effort, it is evident that complication of some sort is to be expected.

BEHAVIOR MECHANISMS AND PERSONALITY

The role of behavior mechanisms in personality was first studied by Freud, who assigned them a place of major importance in the etiological processes of behavior disorders. It may be helpful here to imagine all people ranked in a continuum according to the proportion of their total behavior, which is comprised of mechanisms as distinguished from behavior oriented to reality. We would find the psychopathological problems at the far end of the scale, with a large behavior component of mechanisms. Occasionally this illustration may be contradicted by the discovery of a patient whose illness seems determined by the exclusive use of one mechanism in one frustration situation, but such cases would be rare. The general experience of clinicians reveals that maladjusted individuals in the course of their illness place ever heavier dependence on these ways of dealing with their problems, and mechanisms seldom work in complete isolation, nor do patients' problems occur singly.

The importance of mechanisms to personality cannot be comprehended by a quantitative approach alone, however. Their effect on efficient adjustment is ably illustrated by a consideration of chronic alcoholism, which is one of the more obvious end-results of the "mechanism-solution" of problems. As the old temperance leaflets used to say, the patient's first drink is the beginning of danger. Alcoholic stimulation operates on some personalities as an answer to their most earnest prayers. Because of its physiological action, shyness and social unease seem to vanish with the cortical inhibitions that supported them. The torture of insecurity and the misery of anxiety are replaced by confidence and the warm glow of a new world in which all problems come to appear simple and immediately soluble. More easily than the child with his temper tantrums, the tippling adult has achieved what seem to be some of his major life goals. One of the great dangers of alcoholism and other forms of chemical escapes from reality is the fact that they operate in a dual manner. They remove the awareness of fear and insecurity, and they substitute a blurred view of reality possessing many rewards of sensory excitation and pleasant fantasy. Best of all, from the subject's point of view, this miraculous cure may be purchased cheaply, administered when needed, and never requires a direct (and possibly painful or full of threats of failure) approach to the problems it seems to solve so well. It is in the latter "advantage," of course, that all mechanisms prove themselves to be false techniques. If the human being were as short-lived as many insects and his whole existence were centered around one supreme adjustmental effort, as in the reproductive behavior of the male honey bee, it is barely possible that a once-used mechanism would be effective. But since man's life consists of many days, one following another, postponement of problems does not mean their disposal, and as every student discovered when he started handing in arithmetic problems, a false solution is no solution at all. The alcoholic eventually finds that the simply structured universe of the night before never survives to the morning after. Faced with this situation he usually operates on the simple principle of fending off the disillusionment, of delaying the hangover. So, as the temperance tracts warn, the single drink grows into the "lost weekend." This quality of self-perpetuation is characteristic of most mechanisms. Since their exercise prepares the individual only for their *further use,* no positive gains of effective skills are attained. Instead of growing, the personality actually shrinks; in place of variability, the personality acquires stereotypy. In the alcoholic and the drug addict, this persistent use of the same adjustmental technique may grow to pathological proportions and spread into all aspects of their lives. The same trend is apparent in the other mechanisms we will study. To use the vocabulary of the conditioned response experiment, there is a "generalization" of the mechanism-response, and it is elicited by an ever wider variety of stimulation. The drinking that started as a solution to problems of social timidity may be resorted to in problems of work, finances, or love. The temper tantrum that appeared when a need for candy was frustrated may again appear when the subject is frustrated in defeat in a sporting event (ask any umpire, referee, or coach).

INDIVIDUAL DIFFERENCES IN THE USE OF BEHAVIOR MECHANISMS

The question of individual differences appears in connection with mechanisms. Why do so many people seem able either to abstain from alcohol or to use it as a mild form of stimulation or relaxation, and so many others develop into chronic alcoholics? Why does one person utilize infantile means of adjustment in a situation where another person behaves in a constructive adult manner? To a large extent, the answer must be sought in the individual circumstances of the life history of the person. A person, as Brown has remarked (1940), does not become a problem because he drinks, but drinks because he has a problem. Two sets of antecedent circumstances to the pathological employment of mechanisms must be considered. First, there are the simple facts of habit formation. As we have seen, animals and human beings have a strong tendency to repeat those acts that bring satisfaction, and by repetition the acts become firmly established as habitual modes of adjustment. Second, the circumstances that first elicit the mechanisms must be investigated. Obviously there would be no learning at all if there were no frustration. Particular kinds of frustration seem to produce learning of mechanisms; other kinds of frustrations produce learning of healthy and adequate techniques. Some methods of rewarding people's efforts in problem situations are more effective than other ways. The details vary from person to person, but certain general factors emerge.

Ideally, only competent solutions of problems should be rewarded, but even the wisdom of Solomon would not be sufficient to invariably insure such a state of affairs. When a grown person blames his failures on other people, it is relatively easy for the observer to detect the fault in his solution, but in the childhood of that person clarity of vision is harder to achieve. For example, the crying of a child was mentioned as one of its first responses to difficulty. When an infant cries, it is fed, and it would be difficult to say that the crying was not an adequate solution. At that early age adequacy can only be measured in terms of immediate results. Crying is reinforced by feeding, or soothing, or changing diapers. When the child, a year later, feels frustration or discomfort, crying has lost some of its adequacy, particularly for those needs that can be made known by verbalization. If the crying is still rewarded in situations that could be met more effectively by other means, then a beginning has been made in the formation of a behavior mechanism.

CLASSIFICATION OF BEHAVIOR MECHANISMS

Our classification of behavior mechanisms as given in Table 5 is taken from Thorpe and Katz (1948). Although they are grouped according to relative degrees of social acceptance, the student will recognize that there is a large range of variability in the actual social toleration accorded to any of the mechanisms, depending upon a host of

TABLE 5

CLASSIFICATION OF BEHAVIOR MECHANISMS*

Socially approved adjustment mechanisms:
    Compensation
    Rationalization
    Substituted activities

Socially tolerated adjustment mechanisms:
    Identification
    Projection
    Egocentrism

Socially criticized adjustment mechanisms:
    Sympathism
    Regression
    Dissociation

Socially disapproved adjustmental mechanisms:
    Repression
    Negativism
    Fantasy (daydreaming)

* *Source:* L. P. Thorpe and B. Katz, *The Psychology of Abnormal Behavior*, p. 69. Copyright 1948, The Ronald Press Company.

factors of individual, situation, particular cultural milieu, and so on. More important at the moment than deciding the exact degree of social approval of the mechanisms is the fact that the mechanisms do have social implications that act, in a reciprocal fashion, back onto the patient, exerting a secondary influence on his employment of the mechanism and the emotional reactions that can be expected when the mechanism-inspired behavior occurs in a social setting.

Although the mechanisms are listed and will be discussed separately, they seldom occur in isolation, either in normal or pathological instances. Some individuals more habitually use particular mechanisms, but since they are techniques for meeting problems, the average person has acquired at least the rudiments of several mechanisms by the time he reaches adulthood.

Compensation

The absence or deficiency of any aspect of personality may be met by a variety of vigorous efforts to remedy the lack. The defect, of course, may be real or imagined, since the criterion of its importance is its existence in the person's psychological environment. *Compensation* is an active attack on frustration and, as such, is one of the healthier of the mechanisms. As long as the person is able to achieve his goals and to maintain a sense of security, compensatory behavior is highly adaptive. If, however, the compensation is incomplete, or is overdone, or takes a form that leads to further problem-production, its adaptive characteristics may be overshadowed. Symonds (1946) has pointed out the fact that compensation is basic to most behavior mechanisms and that many of the other techniques are really ways of compensating. In proportion to their lack of success in tension reduction and their production of further problems, the other mechanisms may create still further need for compensatory action.

ILLUSTRATIONS OF COMPENSATIONS

Examples of compensation may frequently be seen in the behavior of all people, and dramatic instances of its operation are part of the familiar lore of our culture. Abe Lincoln, studying by the light of the fireplace and walking miles for books, Theodore Roosevelt developing from a puny and timid boy to an almost too vigorous and muscular man of direct and incisive action, Helen Keller making a life work of achieving mastery over sensory defects, one-eyed Wiley Post becoming a skillful aviator, hunch-backed Steinmetz achieving a dominant role in electrical engineering, deaf Thomas Edison inventing a phonograph, even Demosthenes mumbling through the pebbles in his mouth—the list could be extended almost without limit. Alfred Adler (1917a, 1917b, 1927, 1931) was so struck by the universal appearance of compensatory behavior in his patients that he formulated a whole theory of personality development around the phenomenon. He believed that all people, and particularly those who develop neurotic problems, are possessed of an inferiority of some aspect of their anatomical, physiological, or psychological makeup, and that the striving to compensate for that defect is of crucial importance in the development of their personalities. For Adler, the motive for behavior could be generalized as "striving for mastery," or as an avoidance of an "inferiority complex." The most important point of Adler's theoretical writings for our present purpose is his emphasis on the necessity of a feeling of *adequacy* to be maintained in the person and his demonstration of the many ways in which the person will strive toward this goal. Holloman (1943), writing from this point of view, attributes much of the motivation of outstanding Negro athletes to their "efforts to compensate for . . . feelings of inferiority." Symonds (1946) reports a similar instance, where an older brother achieved something of a reputation in his family for outstanding intelligence. The younger brother, although of average intelligence, gained the impression that he was stupid, and, in compensation, became an outstanding athlete. The reverse may also be true, of course, and many good students owe a part, at least, of their motivation to their feeling of inferiority in athletics.

COMPENSATION AND OVERCOMPENSATION

Compensation basically plays a conservative role in the behavior environment. When the restorative behavior is exaggerated, in *overcompensation,* the mechanism loses its conservative nature and becomes a behavioral defect. Like a pendulum swinging about a central resting point, the person may show evidence in his behavior that he has overdone his compensation. The observation of personality growth in a college class as it swings through the four years of its campus residence usually reveals many examples of overcompensation.

Case 5. One shy, retiring young man reported with other freshmen for pre-registration advice and counselling. His whole personality seemed to be painfully trying to crawl inside itself, and when he was asked to give his name, he blushed, stammered, and seemed to be on the verge of saying "I don't know, sir." He had made good grades in high school and said that he was interested in majoring in English Literature. After the registration he was not seen again by our office until shortly before the end of his freshman year. He had continued his good scholastic standing and said that he wanted to go out for dramatics. We encouraged him, but with silent reservations as to his chances of success. The following winter a young man strode into our office and demanded permission to drop several subjects and substitute courses in speech and dramatics. Although the name sounded familiar, the sun-lamp tan and the matinee-idol mustache covered and disguised the timid freshman of the previous year. A little conversation about the requirements of the university persuaded him to plod on in the paths of academic virtue. As he was leaving, he asked us to come to the next student production, in which he was playing the leading role. We went, and his performance showed no trace of fear, lack of confidence, or hesitancy. He seemed to be enjoying himself tremendously. The next year, although he no longer had to have papers signed by us, he came into the office and said that he needed help; at midterm he was failing in almost all his studies and had been before his Dean for warning. It developed that he had become so interested in dramatics that he had joined a group of Community Players and was attempting to carry on his school and town activities at the same time. He paid little attention to studies that were not offered by the dramatics staff and had conceived, in general, such a good opinion of himself that he was seriously thinking of giving up school and going to Hollywood to get a "good break for once." His success at dramatics had produced an irradiation of self-confidence and assurance that was so overpowering that one wished for just a little of the shy freshman to reassert himself. He did drop out of school, and after a fruitless year of "starving for his chosen art" and meeting with little success, he returned to the university, somewhat chastened, but on the whole a much more healthy personality. He had behaved very much like a pendulum in his compensations.

Sometimes the overcompensation is not so much a quantitative excess as it is a shift of activities into unsuitable areas. Legally reprehensible behavior is often of this type. Bill Carlisle, a train robber who acquired first notoriety and then a measure of fame in the West, was the son of a very poor man who turned to crime as an almost wholesale compensation. He robbed trains after notifying the authorities that the robbery would take place; he refused to take money or jewelry from women; he escaped from prison by working his way first into a job where he checked out boxes of prison-made shirts and then into one of the boxes; and finally, after being caught and serving for twenty years, he is now making an outstanding social adjustment as a businessman in a small town near the scene of his youthful depredations. The juvenile delinquent who steals cars is compensating for lack of privilege, and if he comes from a poor family, the fact is obvious to everyone. If, however,

he comes from a family of high economic status, even the juvenile
judge is sometimes inclined to fall back on a concept of "native incor-
rigibility." Study of such cases, more often than not, brings out an
overcompensation for lack of love and attention, for feelings of inferiority over manliness, and so on.

Sexual aggressiveness is often prompted by the same imbalance calling for compensation.

Case 6. One junior high school girl seen at our juvenile court is typical
of such cases. This girl had been involved in sexual difficulties with several
gangs of boys. Investigation showed that she came from a poor family, was
not asked to join the girls' secret societies or clubs, and was not able to wear
new outfits of clothing with each minor change in school-girl styles. She was
a pleasant, attractive person who was of above-average intelligence, and her
home background, apart from the financial aspects, was good. Her father
was a truck-driver who had been in an accident that prevented him from
following his occupation of long-distance trucking. However, he was able
to earn enough to own his own home and to provide the "necessities" of
life. The mother was a quiet, hard-working housewife, whose eight children
left her little time for activities outside the home. The girl, aside from her
present trouble, had always been a "good" girl and had an excellent reputation in the neighborhood. Only one thing was lacking in the patient's situation at home, and that was a personal feeling of love and security. The
feelings of rejection she met at school were matched by a similar lack at
home. Neither of her parents was particularly demonstrative and with so
many children probably could not give any one of them the affection that
this girl needed. The parents' attitude was that they "gave her a good
home." Consequently, when she found that she could secure attention and
recognition by sexual misconduct, it proved a ready source of compensation.

Overcompensation may be manifested in other ways that lead the
casual observer to form entirely erroneous opinions of the person. The
person who is basically shy may be loud and aggressive in his actions;
many bullies are "starving for affection," and many of the behavior
problems in a school are children who want to be noticed and want to
so much that even unpleasant and punishing attention is better than
being ignored.

What psychological mechanism is back of overcompensation? Very
probably it is the all-pervasive effect of success on the retention of performances. The overcompensated person has found a technique that
reduces tensions, that keeps off anxiety, and since the tensions are
constantly rising and the anxiety is always a threat in the background,

the situation is always appropriate for employing the technique. These factors tend to operate in all cases of compensation, so there must be additional elements to overcompensation. These elements are probably associated with the deeper needs underlying the particular lack that is the surface cause of the compensatory behavior. A small man does not develop a completely objectionable pugnacity solely because of his small stature, but because he has been frustrated in any number of ways, because he has not been able to find security, because he has not been loved, because he has felt a lack of power. If all these motives are frustrated in his childhood, he has many motivational tensions that are drained off in a common channel of compensating for lack of stature. Overcompensation is extremely reminiscent of the hoarding behavior of rats that have been starved in infancy; in fact, overcompensation may be thought of as a variety of psychological "hoarding," in which the individual stores up more of the compensatory achievement than he "really needs," or better, than he appears to need. As Wittels (1941) has said, "no human being can live without the phantom of omnipotence"; few are ever completely satisfied with moderate achievement, at least in our culture. The combination of frustrational training in childhood with the emphasis on success and achievement that forms the *leitmotif* of adult life makes it difficult for the individual to inhibit overcompensation and stop when he is in a precise state of balance (a hypothetical affair at best). The maladjusted individual is one whose background contains more than the usual number of these childhood frustrations and less than the average amount of (subjectively defined) success, and it is in such a soil that overcompensation seems to grow best.

SOCIAL ASPECTS OF COMPENSATION

Social psychologists have been interested in the manner in which compensation may work with entire groups of people in such a way as to influence that group's typical behavior. Vaughan (1928) has discerned compensatory behavior in many types of social groups. Labor strikes, for example, may be channels for compensation, for turning aggression that would otherwise be frustrated against the management and giving the general public an idea of the importance of the particular worker to society. Racial or religious groups may manifest striking behavior characteristics that are compensatory, such as the supposed predilection of Negroes for athletic competition, mentioned previously.

The marked aggressiveness characteristic of minority groups that have had to struggle in the midst of fierce competition has given us much folklore about the "typical" Italian, Irishman, or Swede, or the "typical" Catholic, Jew, Quaker, Episcopalian, and so on. According to Kimball Young (1946), many students of social behavior maintain that women's interest in fashions is a compensation for their sense of inferiority in a world dominated by men. In the days before women had started to attain an equal social position with men their clothes emphasized their femininity; since they have achieved equality in most aspects of social life, their clothes have tended more and more to resemble those of men, particularly in dress that is suitable for the situations in which they wish to establish their equality, as in business and recreation.

An interesting social aspect of compensation is the attempt people may make to overcome a lack in themselves by association with someone having the lacked characteristic. This phenomenon has been analyzed by Tramer and his associates (1939), who have termed it "completion."

COMPENSATION AND BEHAVIOR DISORDERS

Compensation as a factor in psychopathology may be seen to exist in a variety of disorders. Some people respond to their deep lack of security and their fear of insecurity by developing a compensatory rigidity; others attempt to compensate for guilt feelings. Some individuals may, exceeding the rat, hoard every imaginable article. The newspapers once were full of the discovery of a mansion in New York in which two brothers lived surrounded by tons of collected junk, ranging from empty dog-food cans to old mail-order catalogues. That a pile of hoarded articles fell and killed one of the brothers and that the other, who was blind and helpless, then starved to death, emphasizes the maladaptive nature of the mechanism. In severe behavior disorders, with their appearance of behavior mechanisms run wild, we are reminded of the malignant tumors, those cellular growths that start as physical compensations and end by becoming completely dominant in the organismic scheme of things and so maladaptive that they kill the organism that started them.

SUMMARY

In summary, compensation is a universal device for restoring equilibrium or for supplying a real or fancied deficiency in the individual's life. Many of the other common behavior mechanisms are secondary techniques of compensation. Compensation may be an effective adaptive device, or, in the form of poorly directed or too intense effort, may be maladaptive and a source of further stress. Compensation is apparent in social groups and forms a part of the basis for extreme maladjustment.

Rationalization

DEFINITION

Rationalization may be defined as the process of consciously explaining or justifying a thought, feeling, attitude, or action on what are meant to appear as logical and rational grounds, irrespective of the actual underlying motivation, which may be unconscious and unknown to the individual. "Alibiing," "giving excuses," "kidding one's self," are colloquial expressions for the same activity. It is a characteristic of human behavior as old as language itself; an old proverb says, "The poor workman blames his tools," and the fable of the fox and the grapes is standard fare for the second-grade readers. The fact that it is classed among the socially accepted mechanisms is an indication of what standard currency the rationalization has among men, that we allow it validity, and exchange excuse for excuse.

RATIONALIZATION AND AWARENESS OF MOTIVES

Although people have recognized rationalization in one form or another for a long time, it was not until psychology began to learn about the nature of unconscious motives that any estimate of its prevalence could be made. Again, it is to Sigmund Freud that we owe the beginning of this insight. Before Freud it was known and accepted that people often offered alibis for their sins of omission or commission, and that the reasons advanced corresponded with reality in varying degrees. However, it was assumed that the excuse-maker simply chose from among the possibly consciously known reasons one that sounded the most acceptable. Freud, as we have seen, was able to show that many times the rationalization is offered in lieu of a reason that is in accord with reality but that is unknown to the subject.

Mrs. Smith says, "Did you mail that letter to my mother?" Mr. Smith, feeling in his breast pocket, replies, "Oh fiddlesticks! I clean forgot it. You know, I was thinking about that Jones contract, and it completely slipped my mind." Mrs. Smith, who is the soul of kindness, says, "Well, be sure to mail it in the morning. Or, maybe you'd better give it to me, and then I'll be *sure* it gets mailed." Conversations of that type are so usual, so homely that it is a tribute to Freud's observational genius that he could discern a sinister motive back of Mr. Smith's husbandly veniality. Freud would say, of course, that Mr. Smith didn't really like his mother-in-law very well, and that inhibition of the instructional set to mail a letter was simply the working of the repressed antipathy to the old lady. Here we begin to see the inevitability of rationalization in any world that values harmonious interpersonal relationships. Suppose Mr. Smith had been that mythical creature of the 18th century philosophers, the rational man. Then, when he was asked about the letter he would have had to reply, "Why no, dear, I didn't mail it because I very much dislike your mother, and to connive in a relationship of which I so heartily disapprove is completely impossible to me. I won you away from your mother, I'm jealous of her, and if I have anything to say in the matter, you are not going to write her." Since we could not depend upon Mrs. Smith also being rational, Mr. Smith's remarks would probably have been the beginning of strained relations. But, to extend the example just a little further, if Mr. Smith had been completely incapable of rationalization, he probably would never have married Mrs. Smith, even assuming that he might have been very much motivated to do so. Romance would have dimmed the first time the future Mrs. Smith had asked Mr. Smith, after a period of silence, "What are you thinking about, darling?" and Mr. Smith would have been forced by his rational nature to forego the diplomatic "Of how beautiful you are, sweet," and answer, "I was thinking about how much you reminded me of that girl in the burlesque show I saw last time I was in Chicago, and that reminded me of how, in spite of my affection for you, I still have it in the back of my mind that it might be pleasanter to stay a bachelor."

Human social relations, as we know them, must be filled with these conscious and unconscious deviations from a true and realistic accounting for the operations of our personalities. Since a great part of rationalization comes because we must return an answer to the great social question, either spoken or implied, of "Why did you do that?" and since most of the time we literally don't know the answer, we respond by offering verbal formulae that meet with social approval. The effect on interpersonal relations of eliminating rationalization would be staggering. An approximate idea of what would happen can be gained from that favorite of the high school stage, *Nothing But the Truth,* where the hero becomes involved in a wager that he cannot go for twenty-four hours without uttering a single untruth. If you try to do this, even within the limits of conscious matters, you will hurt people's feelings, lose friends, and in general be regarded, if not with hate, at least with sorrow and regret.

LOGIC, LANGUAGE, AND RATIONALIZATION

Rationalization as a mechanism is almost completely dependent upon language and is hence an essentially human mechanism.[1] Rationalizations have two components: (*a*) an appearance of rationality and (*b*) communication. The appearance of rationality means that the rationalization must assume a logical form, as has well been analyzed by Symonds:

Rationalization is fundamentally fallacious thinking. In terms of the syllogism, rationalization is a selection of facts that can be used as minor premises in order to justify certain conclusions already reached. One notes three things in this analysis of the process of rationalization: first, that the conclusion is given. Usually this is an act performed, since rationalizations are very frequently explanations justifying behavior which has already taken place. Second, in a rationalization the major premise is also given, and with this no particular fault is found, except that it may not always be a sound generalization. The essential feature of rationalization is the search for a particular circumstance to be used for the minor premise which, taken with the major premise, will lead decisively to the conclusion. Rationalization, therefore, represents a selection of possible circumstances or reasons which will justify the course of action already pursued.[2]

This is made easy by the fact that our language has a structure that is at least superficially logical, and the form of almost any statement has an air of rationality if a subject, a verb, and a predicate are present. Actually, in most rationalizations, that is as far as logic enters into the matter.

Communication is the second necessary aspect of rationalization. Behavior must be justified *to* either one's self, or *to* others, hence again the need of language. Rationalization, more than any other mechanism,

---

[1] Casual observation of dogs shows that they seem to have acquired some of this human failing also. One aging "part-dachshund" can charge a strange dog with murderous growls and the precipitous rush of a jet-assisted take-off, but if the stranger holds his ground, our protector can reverse her course and trot away expressing casual indifference as well as any Thespian, even down to the detail of a protracted yawn and a pretended interest in an imaginary flea.

[2] Percival M. Symonds (1946), *The Dynamics of Human Adjustment*, pp. 454-455. New York: Appleton-Century-Crofts, Inc.

shows how much we depend on the opinions of others for the maintenance of our own self-esteem. Why else, on the face of the matter, should anyone feel that he must justify his behavior? Yet we find that people are constantly attempting this type of communication. Since a person may rationalize his behavior *to himself*, it is evident that the individual finds it painful to entertain knowledge of his own motives, even when the knowledge would remain private. Thus does the social environment become an internalized part of the personality.

It is obvious by now that rationalization is intimately connected with the concept of the superego that was discussed in Chapter III, Many actions are of doubtful social propriety, and the superego is the personal arbiter of those social standards. The person rationalizes in order to account for actions in a manner harmonious with the mores of the culture. He attempts to shield himself from the threat of social disapproval, whether from without or from within. Tension is built up by the threat of social rejection, and it can be reduced if the person can show himself or others that the action was logical.

This raises some interesting issues. Why should the external trappings of logic apparently have the effect of reducing anxiety? We know with fair certainty that man is not primarily a creature of logic, and that his behavior is constantly influenced by emotional forces that are independent of rationality. However, as L. C. Steckle (1949) has emphasized, man has come to have such a hearty respect for reason that it forms a major element of his entire system of values. Humans are constantly appealing to one another to "be reasonable," and debate has long been assumed to be one of the highest forms of human action. So much do we value reason that we are guilty of wishful thinking about it and pretend to see rationality where none exists. We have learned to expect that a reasonable account of our behavior exonerates us from guilt or blame, although even our legal codes do not take this view. We are again forced to see the wisdom in Socrates' remark that no man does that which to him is wrong. There is perhaps, in this pathetic quest for rationality, a lurking fear of the unknown or dimly sensed motives that steer us, and there is a rebellion against the thought that we are not the masters of our own destinies, but may be pulled this way and that by forces that are beyond our control.

Another point is the question of how the individual arrived at this state of dependence on the appearance of rationality. There are two phases to the problem. The first is the historical and is beyond the scope of this volume.[3] The second is concerned with the past development of the person and the factors in his life that gave rise to rationalization. Some of these latter are fairly obvious. Parents place great importance on instructing their children to "account" for their actions. Out of everyone's childhood must arise the echoes of that question, "But *why* did you do that?" and the often guilty bewilderment as to how the question should be answered. In most instances the question is either unanswerable, or there is no answer that would satisfy the parent. When Junior is caught dipping into his piggy bank and spending the funds setting up sodas for the gang, Mother and Father conduct the inquisition, asking "Why?" Junior, if he is young enough, will probably answer, "Because I wanted the money," but he is then asked, "But why did you want to steal it?" If he answered, "Because there wasn't any other way I could get money for the purpose of establishing a reputation as one of the boys," he would be showing preternatural insight, but he would not satisfy the anxious parents. What they are doing is addressing a question to God or to Nature in general, and what they are really asking is, "How could a son of such honest, respectable people as we, stoop to such a low, dishonest thing as stealing?"; they are motivated by a complex of fears that have as major elements such items as, "What if Junior grows up to be a criminal?" and "Have I been a poor parent, and is the guilt really mine?" and "What would the neighbors think?" The impression left on the child by years of this attention to the social aspects of his actions is seen in the readiness with which he is able to erect the fiction of sweet reasonableness about all his actions by the time he has become an adult. A student who was being gently reprimanded for an obvious and flagrant case of copying from another student's paper during an examination, said, "It's really your fault for seating us so close together and not watching us," and was disappointed when we were not put to rout by his logic. We may find ourselves automatically falling into a similar formula when stopped for speeding. One almost says to the policeman, "I wasn't going any faster than those other cars." It is to the credit of

---

[3] As far as we know, there has never been an attempt to systematically write this chapter in our intellectual history. Historical accounts of the development of thought in our civilization have mostly confined themselves to the realities and have let the appearances go, with the possible exception of Robinson (1921).

psychology when we do not quite make the remark audible to the officer, but the thought is there with surprising emotional force behind it.

One suspects that the educational system and the immense part played by science in our culture have their effects also. In school we are primarily concerned with a real world, and the child is trained to believe in the fiction of the "rational man" and is expected to act as one. Grades are assigned on the basis of memory for factual material, and the study material is designed to give knowledge of the world in which multiplication tables are the basis for reality. The smattering of science picked up by the average individual is a collection of facts about the world and very little about the way those facts are secured or about the application of this scientific method to that individual's own personality. These facts are stated in the language of reason, in declarative statements that "make sense." They represent a power that may be transferred to the person's own problematic situations, and the superficial aspects *are* transferred. Advertisers have recognized this, and appeals to "reason" and to "science" are persuasive lures to the prospective buyer.

ADAPTIVE SIGNIFICANCE OF RATIONALIZATION

But underneath all these superficial aspects of the development of rationalization is the basic dynamic reason for its use. *Rationalization is a protection against anxiety.* It keeps the person from knowing those of his motives and wishes that are at variance with his ideal or expectation concerning himself. Rationalization is a sophisticated, language-borne version of the primitive avoidance response. A person rationalizes so that he may remain comfortable in his relations with himself or with his associates. Like compensation, it is a conservative mechanism and, like compensation, it is subject to abuse. Indeed, even more than compensation, rationalization is a deleterious influence on adaptation, since it acts as a mask to reality. By means of a rationalized approach to life, a person may keep from himself facts that are vital to his adjustment. A minor example or two should suffice. If a person develops a state of abnormal fatigue, notices a constant cough, and sweats copiously at night, and still continues to say to himself that he's just a little run down, and he's tired because of working too hard, and he sweats because of the poor ventilation in his room, he may develop a rather extensive tubercular lesion before he is forced to do something rational about it. It is surprising to note how many doctors have played this intellectual game of rationalization on their own complaints. One doctor, who should have known better, minimized certain early signs of heart disease and insisted on leading a vigorous routine, until he had his first unmistakable anginal attack. A student who can find elaborate reasons for not writing term papers usually finds out this elementary fact of psychopathology sometime in the long midnight hours the day before the paper is due.

SUMMARY

To summarize, rationalization is a mechanism that protects the person against anxiety and rejection by others through the device of giving a seemingly logical appearance to behavior. It is dangerous because it gives a false picture of reality, and because it acts to decrease the person's realistic evaluation of himself and of the situations to which he is responding.

Substituted Activities

Strictly speaking, this mechanism is a variety of the compensation technique. The individual attempts to achieve tension reduction by changing from a frustrated activity to one that promises the same rewards or goal attainments but that can be carried out more easily. Its operation is very apparent in instances where the direct attack on a problem meets with strong personal or social disapproval, but where an indirect approach allows the person to remain within a region of acceptable behavior. For example, most unmarried people find many difficulties of a personal and social character in the way of direct sexual gratifications, and many substitutes or compromises are available, such as dancing, reading love stories, physical exercise, masturbation, sexual perversions of many kinds, and so forth. Freud (1938), in his *Three Contributions to the Theory of Sex,* attempted to show that many symptoms were attempts made by the patient to protect himself against strong sexual motives, that the symptoms were, in other words, *substitutions* of less anxiety-producing behavior.

SUBLIMATION

It is also Freud who differentiated between these substitutive activities that were of indifferent or negative social value and those that contributed to the social acceptability of the person. The latter he termed *sublimations*, arguing that the motivational forces were deflected into channels of socially meritorious behavior. Thus, when the sexually frustrated person finds an outlet for his thwarted impulses in creative writing, in social philanthropy, in teaching, and so forth, he has sublimated the motive, deriving from it the energy to engage in the acceptable activities. Although we cannot accept Freud's concept of energy as related to a single drive in all its details, we can recognize that he has distinguished a particular type of substitutive activity, a kind of compensation actually, which is of benefit to society. That sublimation, any more than other substitutive activities, is an effective adaptive device in and of itself, we cannot be so certain. Contributions to the social good are often made at the cost of extreme personal pain and even personality disintegration. Edgar Allan Poe made substantial contributions to literature and should have been a good test-case of the tension-reduction potentialities of sublimation. His life history shows him to have been throughout a most unhappy, anxious, and disorganized personality. There is little doubt that his personal frustrations drove him to the remarkable literary output he evidenced, but that his literary activities reduced his tensions is extremely doubtful. As we shall see in the chapter on treatment, something more is needed for successful adaptation than the uncontrolled and relatively blind action of any of the behavior mechanisms.

Substituted activities as adjustmental devices are a good illustration of the immense variability inherent in the human animal. Man has so many activity resources that a catalogue of the different substitutions would be a tremendous volume in itself. A man may collect stamps as a substitution, gaining prestige or a feeling of power, or simply satisfying the hoarding motive created by earlier deprivations. But what a variety of nuances may be found within this simple activity. The collector may specialize in the stamps issued by one country or group of countries, he may collect only stamps of given years or periods of years, he may collect only stamps that have pictures of airplanes or birds, he may become interested only in the postmarks of stamps, or in only the varieties of a single stamp. Collectors have written monographs, and thick ones too, on a single type of United States stamp. All these and many more are variations in a single type of substitutive activity. The same type of substitutive purpose may be achieved by developing an interest in other types of collection; people collect everything from ashtrays to zebras. A contemplation of the varieties of hoarding leads one to see that it is possible to create a psychology based on relatively few underlying motive states; the complexity of behavior comes from the unlimited number of activities through which these motives may be reduced.

SEXUAL ABERRATION AS SUBSTITUTION

The pathological implications of substitution are many, but we will confine ourselves to an examination of the *sexual perversions*. The term "perversion" is unfortunate for scientific usage, since it implies a moral condemnation of the activity so labeled, but the evaluative tone of the word emphasizes the extremely emotional nature of people's reactions to sex. Since the biological aim of sexual activity is reproduction of off-spring, any activity of a sexual nature that does not have this reproductive aspect as a main or incidental aspect could be termed perversive. With the widespread use of contraceptive devices and with the growth of at least a little tolerance with respect to sexual activity, it has been recognized that the sexual motive is not to be completely identified with reproduction, but is an urge for gratification with important bearing on the integrity of the individual as well as on the perpetuation of his race. With this being true, we find that psychopathologists have become increasingly reluctant to make any of the evaluations that are inherent in dividing sexual behavior into "normal" and "perverted" types. There is a field of study, however, that may be delimited by saying that the basic biological sex act consists of the genital union of male and female, and that all other types of sexual gratification and activity must be looked upon as falling into some such classification as: (*a*) preliminaries to sexual intercourse, (*b*) sequaliae of sexual intercourse, or (*c*) substitutions for sexual intercourse. Many actions in each of these categories have been considered at one time or another as perversions, and as Kinsey's (1947, 1953) surveys have shown, among a large number of our population at present any type of sexual activity that is not direct heterosexual intercourse is thought of as perverted. In this section we will deal only with those activities that are substitutes. This includes members of the other classes of sexual activity when they are not connected with intercourse, but are practiced in isolation from the sexual act.

Any classification of perversions, within the limits we have set above, is bound to be incomplete. At one time or another, almost every type of human activity has shown itself capable of being connected with sexual gratification. As an example, let us take *fetishism*. In this activity, any nonsexual object may attain the potency of a sexual object in stimulating and gratifying the sexual impulses. The fetishistic person may be stimulated by shoes, a lock of hair, underclothes, gloves, stockings, jewelry, perfume, or by nonsexual body-parts, such as hands, legs, feet, ears, eyes, and so forth. The inanimate object becomes a substitute for the sexual object, and contact with the object constitutes a sexual act for the subject, even leading to orgasm and ejaculation. That this is but an exaggeration of a normal state of affairs is apparent. Adornment, particularly in the female, has always had some element of emphasizing secondary sexual characteristics, such as legs, thighs, hips, breasts, lips, eyes, or hair, and masculine judgment of such appeals indicates their sexual stimulus value. The fetishist, however, for reasons as yet not completely understood, is content with the secondary symbols of sex and finds in them the adequate situation for sexual stimulation.

Sadism and *masochism,* the sexual satisfaction gained from inflicting and experiencing pain respectively, again show how a small part of the entire sexual process is singled out and elaborated as a substitute activity. There is an element of attack and submission in heterosexual intercourse, but in the substitute activity, the pain element becomes an end in itself. We can only speculate as to the motives for those activities. The aggressiveness in sadism suggests that it arises from some early sexual frustration, and that it symbolizes an attack on a threatening object, possibly on parent symbols. Masochism seems to portray a feeling of dependency, a need for being dominated.

In *homosexuality* a person of like sex is substituted for one of the opposite sex. The etiology of homosexuality is largely uncertain, although many factors have been assumed to be operative. Although some of these factors may be hereditary and constitutional, the largest role in this type of substitutive behavior is played by environmental training. The homosexual technique of sexual gratification seems to arise most often from such relatively nonsexual circumstances as antagonism toward parent of opposite sex or identification and sympathy with parent of opposite sex and rejection of like-sexed parent. The

Kinsey findings support the environmental hypothesis, showing (*a*) that 50 per cent of his male sample have had homosexual responses at one time or another in their lives with about 4 per cent exclusively homosexual, and (*b*) that 28 per cent of his female sample have had homosexual responses with from 1 to 3 per cent of the sample showing exclusive homosexuality. Terman and Miles (1936) have shown that no simple cleavage can be made between homo- and heterosexual personalities, but that all gradations exist.

Masturbation is such a common substitutive sexual activity that it can be considered typical of sexual adjustment in adolescence. Kinsey (1947) found that about 92 per cent of his male sample had masturbated, and the frequency of masturbation was highest in the adolescent group. On the other hand, Kinsey (1953) found with his female sample that about 62 per cent had masturbated with the highest frequency in the older age groups. Incidentally, Rosanoff had predicted in 1938 that about 65 per cent of females indulge in this practice, a figure quite close to the Kinsey findings. Masturbation becomes of pathological significance only under two conditions, (*a*) when the individual becomes alarmed or anxious about the practice due to erroneous information or impressions about its harmful effects, and (*b*) if, as an adult, he uses masturbation as an exclusive substitute for heterosexuality. With respect to the first consideration, the belief is still widespread that masturbation can result in physical or mental harm. In many of the older books for parents and in the manuals of sex information for adolescents, the opinion is advanced that masturbation can lead to such varied things as insanity, weak will, pimples, diseases of the kidneys, poor eye-sight, and "depravity." As a source of anxiety masturbation is still of great importance among adolescents, and if the alarming opinions about its harm are reinforced by the people they turn to for advice, serious emotional disturbances may result. The exclusive practice of masturbation by adults may be considered pathological, but there are social factors that modify even this opinion. Strictly speaking, heterosexual intercourse is prohibited by law and by moral and religious edicts, except between husband and wife. The unmarried person faces a real problem here, in that a normal biological adjustment may be in sharp conflict with a person's ideas of right and wrong. The exclusive use of masturbation, in such instances, can only be regarded as a compromise and as, for many persons, the lesser of several undesirable forms of sexual adjustment. Considered as a substitute activity, mastur bation may be the best adjustment a person can make in a given psycho-social situation. There are other motives, however, for this particular substitution. Many people resort to masturbation because of insecurity, lack of knowledge, or because of fear of venereal disease; the substitution is then a symbol of a more basic emotional disturbance.

There are many other sexual aberrations that have the character of substitutions, although the ones we have discussed are the most common. All these "perversions" have the common element of avoidance of the mature social situation of heterosexual intercourse, and in most of the patients who practice these forms of sexual expression there will be found factors of frustration and conflict over sexual motives. From a biological viewpoint such behavior is of doubtful adaptational value, although in the particular social environment that a person must adapt to, the avoidance of direct sexual expression may have conservative values for both the individual and the society.

SUMMARY

As long as substitutive behavior is a manifestation of the flexibility of the organism in its approach to problems, then it may be looked upon as possessing desirable features. If, however, the substitution is actually inadequate for tension reduction and is used persistently, irrespective of this, the mechanism is pathological.

Identification

DEFINITION

Following Masserman (1946), we may define *identification* as "wishful adoption, mainly unconscious, of the personality characteristics or identity of another individual, generally one possessing advantages which the subject envies and desires." As the proverb says, "Imitation is the most sincere form of flattery." Identification is another of those pervasive human behavior characteristics that are seen in all ages and in all cultures. There is even a type of structural biological adaptation that exemplifies the same trends and achieves something of the same results in other species. Among snakes, for example, some nonpoisonous species are extremely like more dangerous types, and there are flies that resembles bees and wasps (Romanes, 1892, vol. I); since these similarly appearing species always inhabit the same area, the evolutionists were quick to point out the adaptive and survival value of such resemblances. Parallels in human behavior are not unknown. Many primitive peoples identify with various animals, hoping that the animal's outstanding characteristic will be transferred to themselves. Clan and totem names aided in the identification. Among the American Indians animal identification was carried into the naming of children.

VARIETIES OF IDENTIFICATION

We may distinguish at least two types of identification. In the first, an individual imitates, copies, or emulates another person in some of his characteristics. Aspects of the other person are taken into the personality. The child may act in ways that copy mannerisms of his parents, the slightly older person may change his personality to resemble the hero or heroine of a recently seen movie, the timid person may attempt the swagger of a bully. One of the reasons for stressing biographical information about great men in school is to secure some measure of favorable identificatory reaction from the students.

In the second type of identification, the individual attempts to live his life through other people. The father who wanted to be a doctor attempts to influence his son to take pre-medical work in college, the mother who has felt deprived of a social life as a girl may attempt to experience vicariously, through her daughter, the good times she herself never had. This type of identification with others frequently leads to disappointment because the other person's wishes and motives are seldom sufficiently close to those of the person doing the identifying to lead to any sort of satisfactory tension reduction. Even in the rare case where the dutiful son does become a physician, the father's satisfaction is not on a very solid basis, since he usually finds that his enjoyment is still tempered by regrets that it is the son and not himself who has achieved the goal.

IDENTIFICATION AND THE INTERNALIZATION OF CULTURE

Identification is a strong force in the socialization of the child. He assumes the characteristics of his parents, and then, as his environment broadens, of the other people with whom he comes in contact. The whole development of the *self*, the basic element of personality, depends upon this mechanism. As James (1890) and Mead (1934) have emphasized, the personality of a child grows by virtue of the roles it assumes. As Mead puts it, the "I" is the actor, and by identification, various roles are played by the "I," each of the roles being a "me." Mead pointed out that identification with various roles is at the heart of our attitudes and our manner or style of behavior. When the small boy is being a gangster, he may snarl at his mother from the side of his mouth; if he has recently attended a movie showing West Point cadets, he may astonish his father by saying "sir" at the end of his sentences. If he finds out that a much admired baseball or football player eats a certain brand of breakfast food, he may urge his mother to include that brand in her purchases. Advertisers have taken abundant advantage of this mechanism in many ways. One cigarette manufacturer has for several years run a series of advertisements that show successful and glamorous people performing in their specialty and then relaxing with the manufacturer's cigarette. A partial list of the people who have appeared in this series includes a successful businesswoman, a society debutante, a motor-boat racer, a test-pilot, a champion swimmer, a trapeze artist, a champion midget racer, a polo player, a truck driver, a cowboy, a military pilot. Within such a list there are the potentialities of conforming to most smokers' favorite identifications. But our identifications are not all on such a superficial level. The growth of group membership implies the ability of the person to identify with the group, a tendency that we see around universities every home-coming day. Here the "old grads" return to "my school," their strangely proprietary interest in the school's football teams alternately a matter of gratification and discomfiture to college administrators. From his childhood, identificatory mechanisms may give the person his attitudes about religion, politics, his town, and his country. A person's ideals and his vocational interests owe much to this process.

Identification may also penetrate our lives in the realm of recreation and enjoyment. Croce's empathy theory of aesthetics states that enjoyment of the beautiful is based upon ability to feel with or into the artistic production. A statue of an athlete running is effective to the degree that it stimulates in the viewer some small part of the kinesthetic pattern that the sculptor attempted to portray. In literature the most powerful root of enjoyment is the identifications we are able to make with the characters. The aesthetic experience from Hamlet arises in the sense of conflict and desire for revenge that Shakespeare stirs in the reader. *Terry and the Pirates* is a successful comic because of the realistic ease with which the artist is able to produce characters with whom the audience can identify. The measure of great literature is the universality of the motives and problems with which it deals and the degree to which the reader can see himself mirrored in the characters of the production. In sports we see the emergence of hero figures, and our enjoyment in witnessing sporting events comes from our identification with these heroes or with the group in which they, and, vicariously, we, have membership.

In religion and in the formation of philosophies of life, identification is again a mechanism of primary importance. Into our concept of God we put our own wishes, and desires, and fears; God becomes a personal agent, an extension of our need for security, affection, or power. The ideals and moral codes whereby we orient our lives have a genetic history that includes a long series of identifications with the conduct and example of other people. Herein lies the power of parents and teachers as ethical forces, since the frequent contacts of children with them result in the major share of the identificatory incorporation of morals that the child receives.

PATHOLOGICAL ASPECTS OF IDENTIFICATION

With identification being the universal force that it is, we may ask, In what ways is identification undesirable or pathological? The most undesirable aspect of identification comes from the indiscriminate nature of the process, particularly in children. Without a background of critical experience, positive identification may be made with people or with character traits that are maladjustive. The child can as easily assume the bad as the good traits of a parent or companion. If father swears, so, probably, will sonny. If mother manifests a virulent hatred of some other racial or religious group, so will daughter. If the biggest heroes of the neighborhood are the gang who successfully robbed a grocery store, many who did not participate in the robbery may find that they wish they had. Immaturity in the parent will not lead to mature identifications in the child; parental conflict will be reflected in a conflictual personality in the child.

A further harmful possibility in identification is in the loss of flexibility that may occur. Normally personality should show changes with age, and this should also be true of our identifications. To identify with Buffalo Bill or the cowboys is appropriate and beneficial at age ten, but by age twenty such identification should be so integrated into the personality that it survives only as a liking for western shows or as an interest in the history of pioneer days. One should derive a great deal of vicarious pleasure from one's children, but should also be able to relinquish this identification when it is no longer appropriate. The child should retain sufficient flexibility to accept identifications that differ from those stimulated by the parents. Failure to do so may be a factor in preventing the child from growing into a mature adult who can establish new and independent interpersonal relationships.

In this latter type of pathological identification, the attempt to cling to old roles is symptomatic of the person's conflicts and fears. Identification, it should not be forgotten, is a technique for avoiding anxiety, and as long as the anxiety is focused on the same set of life circumstances, changes in identificatory aspects of personality cannot be expected. Thus identification, too, shows the conservative tendency of preferring present safety to possible future dangers.

SUMMARY

Identification is a process of social learning, in which we assimilate those characteristics of other people that contribute in some way to satisfying our needs or reducing our anxieties. To the extent that these borrowed characteristics strengthen our effectiveness in manipulating reality or lead us to further maturity of personality, the mechanism is adaptive. It is a poor way of adjusting when the assimilated habits interfere with more aspects of our adjustment than they support.

Projection

DEFINITION

Projection is a mechanism bearing some relationship to the second meaning of identification as discussed above. *In projection the individual ascribes to others wishes, motives, and fears that are his own but of which he is usually unaware.* Projection is akin to several errors of thinking that are familiar to psychologists in other connections. *Anthropomorphism,* the tendency to interpret the behavior of lower animals or other nonhuman things as if they were members of our species, is an example. Comparative psychologists have traced some of the early misconceptions about animal behavior to this variant of projection. The poet who "finds tongues in trees, books in the running brooks, sermons in stones, and good in every thing" illustrates the dependence of literary imagery on this mechanism. As a means of adjustment, projection serves the purpose of freeing the person from self-knowledge of undesirable attributes while still giving free expression to them, or the similar purpose of assuring him that he is not isolated and unique in his own motivational pattern.

Although occasionally a person will project good and socially acceptable wishes and motives into his acquaintances, it is more frequent, particularly in psychopathology, to find that projection is utilized to rid oneself of those thoughts, wishes, and motives that seem undesirable or dangerous to us. This attempt to escape the implication that we have anything bad in our personalities runs through all the mechanisms, but is brought to the sharpest focus in rationalization and projection. Biblical literature gives us the unforgettable picture of the Hebrew tribal rite of periodically casting the sins of the people into a goat and then chasing the goat into the wilderness. The tendency to make our associates the scapegoats for our own faults is so widespread as to need little additional comment. The remarkable thing about projection is the lack of insight shown by the projector.

Case 7. While the senior writer was recorder on an army board of inquiry concerned with separating soldiers from the army because of "habits and traits of character undesirable in the military service" (the percentage of readers with a military background will recognize this as a "Section Eight" board), he had the opportunity to make close observations of the behavioral reactions of his fellow board members. One man, a rather effeminate person in his mannerisms, would become extremely disturbed whenever we passed on a case of homosexuality. He would ply the soldier with questions, sneer at the answers, and give every evidence of hostility. During deliberations of the board, he would loudly announce his opinion of homosexuality in general and of the fate that homosexuals deserved in the military service. The phrase, "Hanging's too good for them" would occur frequently, together with references to sterilization and castration. He'd often assert that it was too bad that some of them couldn't be tortured so they would confess who the other obscene homosexuals on the post were. When a soldier appeared who was not a homosexual, whether he were an habitual alcoholic or an established case of mental deficiency, this board member would attempt to find a homosexual element. At the club his jokes all seemed to run along the same line, and so persistently anti-homosexual was he that his fellow officers sometimes allowed themselves speculation about his forty-five years of escape from matrimony and his own feminine appearance. It was no surprise to the psychiatrist and psychologist on the board when the officer was admitted to the hospital with an acute anxiety state concerning a homosexual advance he had made on another officer while under the influence of liquor the preceding evening. His hostile attitude toward homosexuality had been a protective device against self-recognition of these urges in himself.

DEVELOPMENT OF PROJECTION

Projection, like identification, starts as a part of the normal process of personality development. To see your motives externalized in the environment is a sign of a type of ego-expansion and indicates the dimensions of your psychological environment. Projection is one aspect of ego function. As Koffka has said:

. . . the skin need by no means be the boundary surface of the Ego. . . . The confines may be still wider. Mrs. P. will think Miss Q. an odious person and a bad teacher because Miss Q. finds Mrs. P.'s little boy a lazy and stupid brat. Her Ego has been touched through her child, just because her child belongs to her Ego. This is a grim truth, a truth which lies at the bottom of many a struggle that often enough has a tragic quality, the struggle of the young to free themselves from the parents.[4]

But projection represents a fairly primitive stage of ego-development, since it shows the person's inability to separate the self from other objects. We all recognize the infantile level of behavior involved in showering recriminations on a chair that we have stumbled over in the darkness or in cursing the hammer with which we have pounded our thumb. The same primitive lack of differentiation is shown in all forms of projection, and it is likely that the mechanism is, in the last analysis, a somewhat elaborated form of the primitive avoidance response.

Evidence for this view may be derived from observations of hunted animals. A rabbit, chased by dogs, will "freeze" under a clump of sagebrush, staying motionless, but with every sensory threshold lowered, prepared to spring into a run. Often some chance sound, unconnected with a threat to the animal, will set off further flight reactions. Under the influence of strong fear, the person is strongly set toward avoidance. When in such a state of apprehension, the threatening aspects of the environment loom large. It is clear that the ominous features of the environment are not due to the physical objects themselves, but to the part those objects play in the subject's psychological environment. He *projects* his emotional state into the environment; if the emotional state

---

[4] K. Koffka (1935), *Principles of Gestalt Psychology*, pp. 320-321. New York: Harcourt, Brace and Company, Inc.

is one of fear, the environment will appear fearful, and the person will make avoidance responses to the apparent sources of the fear. Projection, then, returns the source of the fear to the external surroundings, where we have learned to expect danger. To identify the danger with internal processes, to recognize that the source and the result are both within the personality, is a type of sophistication that few emotionally disturbed individuals are capable of making. This is particularly true with respect to those fears that furnish the basis of anxiety. As we will see, the anxious person has difficulty identifying the origin of his fear, and his search for an object often leads to an identification of the source in the behavior of his associates. The officer with repressed homosexuality was frustrated and afraid, but failing to perceive correctly the internal origin of his difficulties, he found his environment peopled with homosexual threats toward which he reacted by a variety of aggressive and avoidance responses.

The type of projective content shown by a person gives a great deal of insight for that person's own motivation, as we have seen in the homosexual officer described previously. The comment "Methinks he doth protest too much" is a genuine indicator of projected guilt. The person who takes an overharsh attitude toward sex, or lying, or theft, or laziness, or any other "bad" personality trait, may be suspected of harboring conflicts and frustrations of a similar kind himself.

EXPERIMENTAL EVIDENCE

An interesting example of what appears to be a projective mechanism created in rats is contained in an experiment of O'Kelly and Steckle (1939). A group of six male litter-mates approximately 100 days old at the start of the experiment were given daily exposures, as a group, to intermittent electrical shock in a small cage. The animals had all been housed in common living quarters since birth and were rated by the experimenters as being unusually tame and docile. No instances of fighting had been observed among any of the animals prior to the experiment. The shock apparatus that was used was so arranged that highly irregular sequences of shock would be given, ranging in duration from approximately half a second to about five seconds, with inter-shock intervals of from three to twenty or thirty seconds. The given sequence of shock was repeated every 105 seconds, and in any given sequence a total of 17 seconds of shock was administered. The phenomena that were observed as a result of this situation are best given in selections from the day-to-day protocol kept by the experimenters.

2-5-39
All six animals were placed in the shock cage together and given one hour of shock through the timing device. Animals make attack on cagemates coincidental with accidental bodily contact. When shock is turned off animals remain crouched.

2-7-39
Given one hour shock through timing device. Animals apparently becoming adapted to shock. Remain crouched, starting at initial appearance of shock. No change in position or behavior when shock is turned off. In an effort to break up this adaptation a short interval (1"-2") of strong shock was given. The reaction to this shock was immediate. Further, it sensitized the animals to the weaker shock. Reactions now at pre-adaptation intensity. Animals appear to be pairing off, into mutually antagonistic duos.

2-9-39
Essentially a repetition of 2-7-39. Animals adapted readily to normal shock (at end of five minutes), with behavior as previously described. Five-second interval of sensitizing shock (as above) returned the reaction to normal shock to pre-adaptation intensity. Animals again pair off into duos, mutually antagonistic. When shock and timer were disconnected and cage lifted from floor, groups immediately broke up and rats return to normal, nonantagonistic exploratory activity.

2-10-39
Animals placed in cage and given normal shock. Time of shock reduced to one-half hour. Immediate pairing of animals. Attacks more vicious, with biting. At the end of period shock disconnected, and animals left in cage with timer motor running. Fighting continued, *without shock,* four hours. Five hours after the shock had been disconnected the animals were huddled, asleep.

2-11-39
Animals observed prior to shock with only timer motor running. Were tense and stationary. No pairing or fighting. Shock connected, and animals gave practically no response to normal shock. Sensitized by full voltage for five seconds. Response to normal shock was now vigorous and vicious. Immediate pairing, blood drawn immediately. Shock continued for one hour. Animals observed continuously after shock turned off. Gradual diminution in aggressiveness. After an hour and a half without shock they were huddled and asleep.

2-13-39
Again tested by turning on motor before application of shock. Tense and stationary. 1.25 minutes of normal shock given through timer. Immediate pairing and fighting. Shock disconnected. Rather vigorous opposition continued. After *six hours* no apparent relaxation. Opposition and fighting still

intense. When cage picked up from floor, all fighting and tenseness immediately ceased. Rats returned to normal exploratory activity. Returned to home cage. No carry-over into cage activity. Animals eat, crawl over each other, in normal peaceable fashion.

2-14-39
Placed in shock cage and given thirty-five seconds of normal shock through timer. Immediate pairing and fighting which failed to change after cessation of shock. No apparent change in *nine hours* of observation. Again, however, immediate disruption of aggression when cage lifted from floor. No carry-over into home cage.

2-15-39
Placed in shock cage and timer motor, without clock, started. No fighting response. Tense and stationary. No shock given. In three hours all animals asleep, huddled. They were then given three seconds of shock. Response, immediate pairing and fighting, which broke up within an hour giving way to huddling and sleeping.

2-16-39
Given thirty-five seconds of shock. Intense fighting. *Eight hours* later some relaxation evident. Each contact, however, brought immediate attack.

2-18-39
Given fifty-one seconds of shock. Immediate pairing and fighting. Frequent observations maintained by experimenters yielded no evidence of relaxation in animals at end of *twelve-hour* period. Thirteen hours after administration of shock some relaxation in evidence. This would be in some one animal, and was by no means frequent or characteristic. Fifteen hours after start, squealing had almost ceased and attacks were slower and less vigorous. This seemed to be due to exhaustion or fatigue, rather than to loss of aggressive tendency *per se*. At *seventeen and one-half hours* after the start no pairings were observed. All animals either washing or asleep. This continued until for five minutes no aggressive behavior was manifested, and adjustment seemed relatively permanent. When timer motor turned off, definite response to cessation of noise. Rats awakened and looked about them, resuming tense position. Motor again started, with immediate pairing and attack as a result. This persisted for the three-minute period motor was allowed to run. Rats then returned to home cage. All attack ceased when cage was lifted from floor. Home cage behavior normal.[5]

At the time this experiment was reported we advanced the possibility that the animals' remarkable aggression was a variety of projection. If a rat is shocked in the same sort of apparatus, but in isolation, the animal will attack the sides of the cage, bite the grid and claw indiscriminately at any object in his surroundings. This ready externalization

[5] L. I. O'Kelly and L. C. Steckle (1939), "A note on long-enduring emotional responses in the rat." *J. Psychol.*, 8, 126-128.

of discomfiture may be tested by pinching the tail of a rat that is in a cage, with the tail hanging out. The animal will immediately attack a cage-mate. In the shock situation we have described, where more than one rat is being shocked at the same time, the attack behavior is directed toward other rats, with no further attempt at random attack of other portions of the environment. Since the rat attacked is similarly motivated, the situation is optimal for aggression. It does not require too great an imaginative jump to see the parallels with the behavior of people who project their own hostility and fear into other people, and then use the other person's responses to their own aggression as evidence of the validity of their delusions. Projection, in a social situation, presents the ideal conditions for a circular increase and perpetuation of maladaptive behavior.

Egocentrism

DEFINITION

It would not be hard to defend the proposition that all people are egocentric. Any individual can function only as himself; his perceptual world has the self as a point of origin, and the directions in his psychological environment are primarily above, below, in front of, in back of, to the left, to the right, inside, and outside, with the person in the center. Further, all parts of the psychological environment are interconnected by virtue of the integration and continuity of the personality. To this extent egocentrism is a necessary fact of personality. As an adjustment mechanism, *egocentrism* is an exaggerated attempt to increase the importance of the self in ways that are trivial, harmful, or simply unpleasant enough to have a bad result in the person's social adaptation.

DEVELOPMENT OF EGOCENTRISM

The infant starts out with elemental and direct egocentric behavior. As parents come to realize when they walk the floor with a crying baby in the small hours of the morning, there is no concept of social give-and-take in the infant. Increasing socialization involves learning to inhibit and defer many wishes and motives in the interests of social harmony. The concept of "enlightened self-interest" begins to take effect, and the mature individual finds that his ego interests are best secured by means of group action and cooperation. The person who has never received an adequate amount of attention, whose prestige value in his own eyes has never reached an optimal point, may find that he is consistently directing his behavior into patterns of self-interest that have as their immediate goal the attraction of attention and recognition rather than the long-term goals of group integration. The child who can receive recognition from his parents only by excessive action and dramatic extremes will grow into the adult with the same motives and the same techniques of achieving them.

Egocentricity is not solely brought about by the past experience of the individual. Some social situations seem to generate cooperation, and others to bring out the "every man for himself" type of motivation. The experiments of Lewin and his students have shown this with great clarity. Lippitt (1940) demonstrated that artificially created group situations among children, in which democratic principles prevailed, brought out more use of "we" in referring to activities than did the autocratic atmosphere, which produced a host of "I" reactions. Bavelas (1942) found that cooperation between children at a camp increased when the leaders adopted more democratic ways of dealing with the group.

Egocentricity may be produced by isolation, either geographical or cultural. Long periods away from contacts with others may result in a narrowing of interests and a preoccupation with that which is purely personal. The height of egocentrism is probably achieved in those individuals who are able to completely gratify their needs for recognition and attention independently of any social factors. This is the type of operation of the mechanism that may be seen in the completely withdrawn; a similar state would seem to have been attained by many mystics whose meditations and internal contemplations do away with the need for exterior recognition. A more socially advantageous type of egocentrism is found in those people who have become so identified with a cause that they manifest egocentric behavior for the cause, treating any fancied slight or handicap that the cause meets as a personal trauma.

FORMS OF EGOCENTRISM

The forms of egocentric behavior range from flag-pole sitting to temper tantrums, and from sexual exhibitionism to the "See!!! No hands" of the juvenile bicycle rider. Common selfishness is only a minor example. "Taking care of Number One first" is at the heart of much of our competitive struggle, some of the aspects of which we will try to analyze in the next chapter. There is no biological objection to competition as such; animals have been, and will be in competition as long as ecological balances and pressures are a part of life on this planet. What is pathological about egocentricity is its fatal short-sightedness, a myopia that sometimes amounts to a blindness. The lack of insight that is shown by after-dinner speakers who seem unable to relinquish their commanding position, by committee members who must make comments with no relevancy to the matter under discussion, by small children who whoop, yell, stand on their heads, climb over the visitors when attention is on a serious conversation rather than on the children, by the hot-rod driver who careens through a residential zone scattering children and dogs to the right and left of him (and is rather hurt when you remark that such driving should be confined to the race track) is phenomenal. One otherwise amiable person was given to perfectly astounding examples of marathon speaking; after one of his stints he would sit down and say in not too soft a whisper, "Boy, I really showed 'em *that* time." Although in faculty meetings people would groan when he arose to speak, he seemed to interpret it as good-natured joking. The only time his comment approached the objective truth was one time when he said, "I knocked 'em dead with that one"; since many of them were asleep we could not but agree. While the chairman would fidget, clear his throat, leaf through his papers, and look at his watch and the room clock, this gentleman, serenely oblivious, would continue at his happiest position, the "center" of attention.

The tragedy of egocentric behavior is that it is so patently designed to achieve the very goals it trends away from. The egocentric person is pathetically eager to be liked, and admired, and respected, and the maladjustment lies in his technique, which gives him but the crumbs of that which he is seeking. It is remarkable testimony to the strength of this motive that the crumbs are hoarded so avidly. The meek little man who has just committed a particularly revolting murder waits as eagerly for his press clippings as the politician who has just launched the first explanation to his constituency of his behavior back in Washington.

Egocentricity is pathological, not only because the technique often has the opposite result from what is sought, but also because it serves as a means of limiting variability of behavior. The egocentric person becomes so single-minded in his quest for personal satisfaction that he misses opportunities to achieve that goal by other techniques. As in identification, too much emotional involvement in any one aspect of life results in a fruitless stereotypy of response and precludes the possibility of personality change that is essential to successful and mature adaptation.

SYMPATHISM

It is difficult to draw very much of a distinction between egocentrism and *sympathism*. In the latter the person contrives to put himself in a position where others will notice him and express their concern over his difficulties.

The senior writer's dog went through a phase in the development of her personality where this mechanism was overworked to the point where diminishing returns resulted in experimental extinction. While still a pup, she was hit a glancing blow by a passing car, with no injury other than a bruise on one front paw. She was, however, smothered with sympathy, allowed to break regulations, fed at irregular hours and with substances having more taste than canine food value, and was in general accorded a position in the domestic economy far beyond her usual lot. For two or three years after the incident she would resort to a pronounced limp, holding her forepaw in the air every time that disciplinary stress impinged on her. The technique that had brought sympathy on one memorable occasion had become a part of her personality.

Sympathy from other people is, in our culture, almost a part of the infant's birthright. The very young infant has almost immediate attention paid to its every pain and discomfiture. As the individual develops through childhood much of this sympathetic attention becomes harder to secure, and, in those people who win through to emotional maturity, only a small part of the need for sympathy survives. Some children, however, are unlucky enough to have parents who continue the lavish display of sympathy each time the child is hurt or frustrated, and as a result the grown person still expects and works actively for the pity of others.

As a mechanism, sympathism supplies the person with assurance that he is loved and with material for confirming his rationalizations about his inadequacies. Sympathy is not, on the face of it, extended to one who is willfully guilty, and an expression of sympathy over failure is testimony that the subject is, as they sang in the gay nineties, "more to be pitied than censured." Sympathy gives social status to weakness and acts as a tacit permission for the person to continue his weakness

The mechanism is akin to egocentricity because it involves an attempt to attract attention to the self, and in such a way that the self gains in importance.

HYPOCHONDRIASIS AND SYMPATHISM

Although we shall soon see that hypochondriacal complaints are usually initial attempts to give a meaningful self-explanation for physiological symptoms of anxiety, the social effect of physical symptoms is to attract attention to the possessor. With this attention usually goes a rather genuine sympathetic attitude. The sympathy that is garnered from a hypochondriacal complaint may then serve to fixate the complaint as a technique for gaining further sympathy as well as for its original purpose of accounting for an otherwise inexplicable symptom.

Sometimes, in spite of the general principle that sympathism is an outgrowth of very early patterns of infancy, we find that a person stumbles on this mechanism rather late in his life. At one of the Army tuberculosis centers it was rather common to receive patients who had never been ill "a day in their lives" before a suspicious shadow was discovered on a routine chest X-ray. Many apparently healthy soldiers with such X-ray findings were sent to this hospital for more definitive diagnostic work and for therapy of their minimal tubercular lesion. A problem that would develop repeatedly would be that of a rapidly progressing invalidism on the part of these patients. When first received, they would complain and snort at the idea of absolute twenty-four-hour bed-rest and would thump their chests to show how healthy they were. After a few weeks of being waited on constantly and of tasting the satisfactions involved in complete freedom from other cares, many of these patients would give up all resistance to the hospital routine and would start a systematic hypochondria, complaining of first one symptom and then another. One patient, who had been a promising young scientist before the army and tuberculosis, halted any intellectual conversations with visitors because they were too "tiring" and worked himself into a depressed state that could only be relieved by sympathy and by the recital of hard luck that a sympathetic ear stimulated in him. The psychological nature of this man's troubles was fully revealed when the medical board announced, after the patient's third month of hospitalization, that the supposed tubercular lesion was an X-ray artifact and represented no serious lung pathology. After a short period of psychotherapy, the patient achieved insight for some of the factors in his illness and was able to return to productive work.

Regression

DEFINITION

Thus far we have spoken primarily of mechanisms representing immature and sometimes infantile methods of achieving tension reduction. In adults they appear as fixations of early levels of adjustment. *Regression,* on the other hand, implies that a person has achieved a more mature state of adjustment, but under the influence of stress, relinquishes the later-learned techniques and returns to the immature and infantile. Thus, one could overcome or "grow out of" an egocentric orientation, only to slide back to it in times of emotional crisis. When the new ocean liner, the *Titanic,* was wrecked on an iceberg, crewmembers with revolvers were necessary to keep the men back while women and children were placed in the lifeboats. The panics that sweep through crowds trapped in burning buildings show how stress can produce regression in almost anyone.

FRUSTRATION AND REGRESSION

Regression is a reaction to frustration, an attempt to restore optimal conditions by utilizing techniques that have had past success at tension reduction. As such, it is only a small part of the larger matter of "habit selection." When a person confronts a problem he must select, from among the large repertoire of habits that constitute his behavior potentialities, that way of acting that is most appropriate to the problem at hand. That such selection is not automatic and perfectly tuned to the requirements of the problem is a common observation.

Hans Zinsser (1940) tells of a professorial friend of his who came home from his laboratory one evening to be reminded by his wife that they were to dine with the president, and that he should hurry and change into his formal attire. He went to his bedroom, thinking about some of the problems of the day; his wife waited for an hour, then went upstairs and found that her husband, absorbed in his meditations, had completely undressed, put on his pajamas, and was sound asleep in bed.

In working mathematical problems, as in proving identities in trigonometry, the student must select a method of approach, and, if that doesn't work, must try something else. In driving a car a person is frequently confronted with a situation where several types of behavior are possible; in driving on a two-lane highway one is faced with the choice of passing in the face of oncoming traffic. In social groups one selects a subject for conversation, or selects an answer to a given comment.

Rational adaptive behavior depends for maximum effectiveness on a wise selection of habits in the sense we have indicated. Only rarely can the behavior mechanisms be included in such a category; they are usually shortsighted selections, and the factors determining their selection are usually only distantly and indirectly related to the needs of the present situation. The role of regression in this state of affairs seems to be primarily that of making mechanism-selections more available than rational selections. We may assume that most of the mechanisms are learned as a part of normal social development, but that only exceptionally are they employed, unless the internal need-state so changes the objectively apparent situation as to make the mechanism dominant over the more immediately suitable behavior potentialities. When a man is being reprimanded by his employer, the most suitable conduct may be a relatively silent assent with the employer's statements. The tensions arising from other provocations, however, may produce regression to a more elementary or primitive rage reaction. The conflicts and frustrations that produce emotion also bring about behavioral regression. This has been recognized from a very early period in the study of behavior. Aristotle (Klemm, 1914), no doubt under the influence of the Platonic view of an ideal life of reason, mentioned the childishness of the fearful and angry person, and he referred to the "passions" as being of animal origin. Seneca (Estrange [trans.], 1865), with a characteristic Stoic detachment, condemns the passions because they cause a return of the individual to "rash and beast-like behavior." The ease with which emotion could distort judgment was emphasized by the scholastics, and as early as St. Augustine we find a very clear definition of the regressive nature of emotional behavior. In his *Confessions* (Pilkington [trans.], 1876) there is a vivid world-picture of Augustine's own behavior at the two extremes of emotional·influence.

The modern period with respect to regression started with Freud. In place of the general observations concerning the simplification or "lowering" of behavior under the influence of emotion, Freud proposes a concrete series of developmental steps in personality down which the regressing person could tumble. Freud discovered, in the analysis of a patient, an intense but repressed homosexual motivation (*Collected*

Papers, 1924). The factors surrounding this case, together with much other clinical material, led him to think of regression as a major dynamic factor in mental disorder. He had formulated a theory of sexual development to which the concept of regression was directly applicable. According to Freud, the sexual functions of the normal individual develop in an orderly manner through several stages, from infancy to adulthood. In the first stage sexual gratification (the sex drive being assumed active throughout the person's life) is accomplished through stimulation of the oral regions, as in drinking or sucking, and later through the anal region as in excretory acts or fecal retention. In this stage the individual is sexually self-centered or auto-erotic. He manifests this egocentricity, as we have seen, in all aspects of his behavior. During childhood the early ego-sexuality is gradually replaced by a latency period in which the training regimen imposed by society causes a diminution of overt sexuality, and any sexual expression is gained through association with members of the same sex, what is essentially a period of homosexuality. It is during this period that boys play with boys, girls with girls, and that rather strong group pressure is brought against the child who does not conform to this pattern. The third stage in normal sexuality is the heterosexual, where the ego-oriented and the homosexual trends give way to an interest in persons of the opposite sex. Homosexuality would then be thought of as a fixation of the sexual development at an intermediate stage or as a regression back to that stage. Dynamically, the regression to earlier or more primitive levels is brought about by frustration of normal heterosexually motivated behavior. The regression may be of any degree, so that, as is often seen clinically, the regression is back to the auto-erotic stage, that is, to a stage of personality development that is typically egocentric. Freud was able to show that these regressions brought about profound alterations in the general behavior of the patient, his whole habit repertoire, as it were, shifting with the change in the sexual adjustment.

The English psychologist and anthropologist Rivers (1920) advanced a somewhat similar idea, saying that disordered behavior comes about because of a dominance of primitive forms of motivation, activated by conditions of unusual stress. He cited, as an example of this, the war neuroses he had seen. These were caused, he said, because of the conflict between the primitive desire to preserve one's life and the demands of social duty.

Before reviewing the experimental work that has been done on regression, it would be well to point out that at least two types of regression have been distinguished: (1) a selection of earlier-used behavior techniques, the motivation remaining constant; and (2) a shift to more primitive forms of motivation, with the behavior changing appropriately with the change in motive. We have seen examples of both types in our earlier discussion of other mechanisms. In sympathism, for example, the individual may often vary his habit selection until he finds a type of behavior that is appropriate to his motivation.

EXPERIMENTAL EVIDENCE

Regression, considered in either of the above ways, is a behavior mechanism most suitable to animal experimentation since it can be objectively defined in terms of overt behavior and since it does not depend, at any stage of its operation, on the verbal report of the subjects.

Typical of the experiments producing regression in rats are those reported by Hamilton and Krechevsky (1933), Sanders (1937), and O'Kelly (1940a). If rats are trained to find a reward by running first in one direction and then by running in another direction, and are then given an electrical shock before they reach the point at which they must choose the first or second direction, the shock causes a large percentage of a group of animals to choose the earlier-learned direction of running. This choice of an earlier-learned habit that is no longer effective in gaining the reward is rather clearly an instance of regression. Further animal experimentation by Martin (1940), Mowrer (1940), O'Kelly (1940b), and Klee (1944) has indicated that the regressive response is an adaptive reaction to punishment that is associated with the habit that is being performed, and that regression is always in a direction that is behaviorally an avoidance of punishment. As Klee has pointed out, however, this response, which may be adaptive in purpose, may be actually so maladaptive that the animal starves to death because of its inability to regain the flexibility needed to form new habits that lead to reward. A pertinent subsidiary finding is that regression is not produced if the shock is not immediately a part of the behavior of the animal before it makes a choice (Martin, 1936; Sanders, 1937), and that regression is not influenced in any marked manner by brain lesions (Biel and O'Kelly, 1940a, 1940b) or by early experience with electrical shock (Steckle and O'Kelly, 1940, 1941).

Using human subjects, Lewin and his co-workers have been able to set up experimental situations approximating real-life conditions and have observed regressive components of the reaction to frustration. Barker, Dembo, and Lewin (1941), working with children in a play situation, frustrated their play with toys. Before their study of regression, they worked out the type of play activity characteristic of children at different chronological age levels, finding a steady progression in the complexity of play, chiefly in terms of the type of fantasy and the organization of play units. When the play activity was frustrated, the behavior of the children became more primitive than their former level; they showed what appeared to be a regression to the same type of play activities characteristic of younger children. The writers were careful to point out, however, that this regression is not an actual resumption of earlier-learned activities in an unmodified form, but that it closely simulates it.

REGRESSION, EMOTION, AND ORGANIC INJURY

As we will see later, emotion and organic injury may tend to produce regressive behavior. Under emotional influences, the behavior of the individual shows a loss of deliberation and inhibition. Emotion, like alcohol, acts to decrease normal inhibitory influences and to make easier the type of regressive behavior described by Rivers (see Miller and Miles, 1936). When brain injury results in the loss of higher cortical control, release symptoms, which are a form of regression, are elicited. Emotion and brain injury are at least similar in their effects in that loss of cortical dominance gives forth with regressive behavior.

It is probable that *all* disordered behavior shows a high degree of primitive or childish components, and that a substantial portion of these early-level behaviors are the type of simplification and habit selection that we have called regression. The term, as such, is purely descriptive, and as we have indicated, probably represents a multiplicity of factors in the situation that are capable of activating or re-activating other behavior mechanisms.

Dissociation

Dissociation may be defined as any gross disparity between the various psychological components of personality, whether it be between emotion and thought, or between thought and action, or between emotion and action. At the level of everyone's experience, dissociation may be made clear by the example of "logic-tight compartments." In the church that the senior writer attended as a boy, it was a matter of some comment among the communicants that one of their fellow members could be notorious for cruelty to his wife and for grasping financial practices, and yet be able to secure a certain amount of local fame as an ardent backer of the church and one of the best impromptu deliverers of prayers at the Wednesday night prayer-meeting. He had successfully dissociated his personal and business life from his religious activities, with no evidence that either system interfered appreciably with the other. A colleague is an outstanding liberal, of courageous and unalterable principles. He has on many occasions given abundant evidence of the sincerity and extent of his attitudes. He is an inflexible disciplinarian in his official position, a man whose conservative interpretation of rules is as much of a matter of dependable prediction as his liberal actions in other respects. Again we have an example of the inconsistencies that may appear in the behavior of a single individual.

The adaptive purpose of dissociation seems to serve as a device for allowing the person to carry out motives that are fundamentally contradictory and that would lead to conflict if permitted to operate in conjunction. The religious businessman with hostility toward his wife to whom we were introduced in the last paragraph could not conform to both the business and the Christian ethics *and* the personal necessity to treat his wife cruelly if these diverse motives were ever permitted to interact. The dissociation in this case acts adaptively by allowing the personality to maintain some sort of social adjustment.

Training in dissociation, as we have mentioned before and will discuss again, begins when the child learns that different standards of conduct are appropriate to different situations. The average child is brought up to believe in some version of cooperative, golden-rule, live-and-let-live, turn-the-other-cheek modes of behavior regulation. At about the time that such inhibitory training is beginning to take effect he is introduced to the my-country-right-or-wrong, you-must-succeed, get-ahead-in-the-world, survival-of-the-fittest, devil-take-the-hindmost type of competitive emphasis in behavior. Both of these regulatory frameworks demand some recognition and conformity if the person is to adapt effectively in our culture. Since the motives are so opposed, as Horney (1937) has seen, our times demand a certain amount of dissociation as the price of survival. The problem is frequently seen in counseling college students. The large number of contradictions between early religious training and the tenor of materialistic science give rise to conflict situations that are unavoidable, but many persons work through them by using the technique of dissociation. The lack of logical consistency in a culture that has grown through centuries, with accretions from this period and that, makes a certain amount of dissociation necessary. The inconsistencies of social customs and mores would be an unending source of amazement to a completely rational person. That a person may be fully and appropriately dressed in less than a square foot of clothing on the beach in the afternoon, and yet feel naked and ashamed if an appearance is made at dinner in a dress that is too short or a white tie instead of black goes far beyond logic and demands a flexibility of logical approach whose nimble dance must become at times sheerly dissociative. To strain for logic where none exists is productive of anxiety and of disordered behavior. The neurotic dogs who were required to both lift a leg and plant it more firmly in a stationary position were in no more illogical an environment than the human beings of the depression who went hungry while economic forces produced actual destruction of food, or the men caught in war who found twenty years' training in peace and brotherly love capped by an introduction to effective means of slaughter. All societies have probably exhibited the same inconsistencies, although many facts suggest that our present culture possesses them in a more acute form. As long as vital motives may operate without a person being aware of their nature, and as long as emotional aspects of motivation may be rationalized, we will have need for some type of dissociative mechanism.

Repression

We have discussed repression in Chapter III, where this mechanism was defined as a selective "forgetting," or loss from awareness, of thoughts, memories, or wishes whose nature would be such as to give pain or discomfort to the individual. Repression, like regression, would seem to be a basic defense process that creates the opportunity for use of other adjustment mechanisms. A little earlier we showed how "forgetting" to mail a letter created a situation where rationalization was used to explain an otherwise inexplicable lapse of memory.

We have also discussed much of the experimental evidence on repression. Although a great deal more needs to be done in the laboratory before we will be able to describe precisely the factors that produce repression, there would appear to be little doubt that such a mechanism exists and is of basic importance in adjustment.

The pathological aspects of repression come from the effect it has on insight and from the way in which life data are selected for repression. Since unpleasant and dangerous content is most readily repressed, the person is many times deprived of knowledge and insight that would be valuable for intelligent solution of problems. In all disordered behavior there is a confusion and bewilderment about processes, which are made apparent only by their manifestations. The material selected for repression conforms to no law of logic or of common experience. We may forget a name and yet be aware of no adequate reason why that particular name should be forgotten; selective forgetting operates on the basis of relatively unconscious motivational factors, and our conscious awareness is only a spectator in a play that remains confusing because we never know the plot that is being acted out. This breeds a sense of uncertainty in the best-adjusted person, and, of course, a more intense bewilderment in the individual with more unresolved tensions and conflicts.

Negativism

It is difficult to fit this mechanism into the same frame of reference with most of the adjustment techniques, although it has, in common with them, the conservative tendency of preserving the organism from situations that threaten it. *Negativism* is defined as a persistent oppositional effort to attempts made to guide or direct the person's conduct. As a component in the temper tantrum it may be seen frequently in children.

Ribble (1944) has described negativism in very young babies who have not had adequate "mothering."[6] It is manifested by a refusal to suck, an apparent loss of appetite, and a failure to assimilate food. The accompanying postural reactions are of extreme interest, in that they exemplify the avoidance reaction at its most direct and primitive level. As Ribble describes it:

[6] *Mothering* is used by Ribble to denote those activities of rocking, singing, soothing, and other maternal behavior that is not experienced by infants who are maintained in the hygienic isolation of many modern nurseries.

. . . close examination will reveal more or less hypertension or rigidity of all the body muscles. Arms and legs resist extension. The torso is arched slightly backward. The muscles of the back and the back of the neck are particularly tense. This extensor reaction, or hypertonic reaction as it is sometimes called, is also at times accompanied by vomiting and by frequent periods of violent screaming during which it is extremely difficult to quiet the child. Still other common accompaniments are breath-holding, shallow breathing, and constipation. Apparently the tension is present in both the striped muscles and in the smooth visceral muscles.[7]

Although negativism, in its primitive form of avoidance of potentially harmful situations, may be seen in lower animals and young children, as a pathological mechanism it becomes of serious importance as it gains a fuller association with the developing system of personal and social needs. In normal development negativism reaches a peak about the third year and then gradually decreases (Murphy, 1944). If a child is opposed to a course of action that has been suggested to it, and further force is exerted to compel compliance, it will often be found that the struggle for obedience has entered a phase different from the initial negativism. The oriental phrase, "loss of face," describes the ego-involvement in negativism. Integrity of the personality seems to demand that conduct not be forced by coercion. Governments have had to recognize this component of negativism, and many modern states have constitutional guarantees against the direct use of force to gain obedience in social behavior. In Dale Carnegie's (1938) *How to Win Friends and Influence People,* the supposed efficacy of his techniques depends upon a studious attention to means of avoiding a negativistic response to appeals. Negativism becomes a serious hindrance to adjustment when it helps to put the person in a position from which he cannot retreat without loss of prestige. Personal integrity is so tied up with the "illusion of free-will" that situations that threaten the illusion are traumatic. The proverb, "A man convinced against his will, is of the same opinion still," expresses negativism and its ego-roots very well.

Negativism is a force to be reckoned with in psychotherapy, as we shall see later. When a person senses that a situation is going to lead to a loss of protection or to pain, his *resistance,* as it is technically termed, increases. One of the tasks of the psychotherapist is to over-

[7] M. A. Ribble, "Infantile experience in relation to personality development," in J. McV. Hunt, ed., *Personality and the Behavior Disorders* (2 vols.), p. 633. Copyright 1944, The Ronald Press Company.

come this resistance in order that insight may be achieved. In this respect, negativism is complementary to repression, protecting and maintaining its effectiveness.

Fantasy

Kurt Lewin (1936) called attention to the fact that the personality is organized in many dimensions and at many levels. Among those levels is the world of fantasy. In imagination one may behave in many ways, respond to motivational forces, perform locomotions, work out problems and experience deep emotion. As you sit at your desk, with this book open in front of you, you may be turning physical time back and be living in the approximate environment of the last dance or party you attended, or you may be jumping ahead in time and shivering over the examination that isn't due for another week. Or, because such imaginations may bring painful emotions, you may be thinking of how nice it would be to spend a winter in Florida, or to have been born with more money, or better looks, or more brains. You may, in your imagination, be a football player; you may be a chorus girl, a debutante, an airline pilot, a bank president, a criminal, a movie star, or anything else at all, so versatile and flexible is the imagination. *All these activities that have existence only for you and within you we may term* fantasy. Lewin speaks of personality as varying along a dimension of reality-irreality. Fantasy is in the zone of irreality, since the fantasy is relatively independent of other than the psychological limitations of the personality.

Daydreaming is a part of the normal imaginal processes and is linked to dreams on the one hand and to logical and creative thought on the other. Along the continuum of reality-irreality, logical thought is at the reality end, dreams at the irreality extreme. All this imaginal activity is subject to the same determining principles as any other type of behavior; that is to say, it is motivated, it is influenced by the capacities and the past experiences of the individual, and it has the same characteristics of accomplishment and fatigue we see in any type of performance. Further, fantasy is a part of the adaptive efforts of the person.

DEVELOPMENT OF FANTASY

The distinction between fact and fantasy or between different levels of reality comes about by a developmental process in the child. Young children separate what we adults call reality from their own imaginative productions very indistinctly (Murphy, 1944), and, as study of the validity of testimony given by eye-witnesses of an event shows, even adults have not completely succeeded in making the distinction. Gradually, as with the other adjustive techniques, fantasy is modified by the socialization process, and the levels of reality become more clearly heterogeneous. Lewin (1935) has shown that the feeble-minded children make this differentiation more slowly and never achieve the same degree of heterogeneity achieved by the normal child.

As an adaptive reaction, fantasy may serve in young children as a way of modifying painful or frightening experiences (Bender and Vogel, 1941) and help the child deal more effectively with his emotional problems. As the child grows older, not only does he begin to separate the degree of irreality, but the fantasies themselves are more closely integrated with reality. The imaginative content of the four-year-old shows an abundance of fairies, brownies, gnomes, and other fabulous creatures. The adolescent's imaginal content has fewer fairies and pumpkin coaches and more of the directly autistic images of himself as hero and situations filled with possibilities of security, prestige, wealth, power, and so forth. Although the motivational sources of fantasy do not change in kind through the developmental period, the difference in content reflects differences in the type of problems faced at the different age levels. That the high school junior dreams of dates and football, while the businessman dreams of new contracts and expansion, is a function of the differences in social role that come with increasing age. The content of fantasy is always an indicator, directly or indirectly, of the problems facing the person.

FANTASY AND ADJUSTMENT

The pathological importance of fantasy should not be underrated. Because of its widespread distribution among all persons there may be a tendency to minimize the role it plays in maladaptive behavior. Fantasy is stimulated by frustration, and as a solution attempt, it operates at a level of irreality that gives it little power to actually modify many of the factors critical to the original frustration. If an assignment is due and the person merely daydreams about the task, no direct attack is made on the problem. Fantasy may have its place in problem solution if it serves as a period of planning and if the plans so formulated can be carried into action. In such a case fantasy approaches what we usually think of as creative thought. The novelist may actually use fantasy in this manner as a working tool, as C. S. Forester told an interviewer:

The idea for his new novel, *The Sky and the Forest,* was conceived by Mr. Forester some ten years ago. . . . "I let it soak into my subconscious. I have an analogy for that process. If you drop a piece of timber—with a rope around it—into the sea and pull it up every now and then, each time you look at it you will find that it has acquired more barnacles. This same thing happens with an idea for a novel." He said that he usually pulls the ideas up and looks at them when he is lying around in bed in the morning, smoking cigarettes and thinking that he really ought to get up. "That's the time of day when it is good to be a writer. You pull up the things that you haven't done and admire the shapes and patterns of the barnacles—what astonishing creations they are! Their possibilities are endless. Here, at last, is the matter for a really good book." [8]

Fantasy, however, in most of the emotional problems of life, does not produce constructive solutions at a level of reality. As in the other mechanisms, fantasy relieves anxiety sufficiently to bring a satisfaction with the technique as it stands. Then, the availability of fantasy as a technique assures its use in an ever-wider variety of problems, until there is real difficulty in finding one's way back to reality in any important issue.

Another pathological feature of fantasy is the part it plays in procrastination. Daydream solutions of problems are postponements of real solutions. In some cases this may have an advantage of a sort, in that it permits an implicit trial-and-error process to go on, and gives better assurance that action, when it finally is executed, will be correct and appropriate. However, most fantasy formation is not concerned with probable solutions, nor, generally, even with remotely possible solutions of problems. Escape from reality is the primary goal and the chief result of fantasy. Since reality provides the final criterion of ad-

---

[8] From interview with C. S. Forester by Robert van Gelder, reported in *Book-of-the-Month Club News,* Harry Scherman, ed., July 1948, pp. 11-12.

justment, the escape itself is a fantasy, because there is, of course, no way that any animal can run away from the world in which it is immersed.

Summary

This chapter has been primarily concerned with some of the ways in which reaction to frustration can be of pathological significance. These rather stereotyped reactions to stress are termed "behavior mechanisms," and we have seen that they are ways of solving problems that have both good and bad points, but that, in general, are inferior substitutions for direct attacks at a level of reality. Without exception, as we have seen, the mechanisms have their origin in the attempts all people make to reduce tensions and effectively achieve their goals. The mechanisms become harmful when they prevent the person's resolution of difficulties in ways that are genuinely effective. In the use of mechanisms the person has shifted his emphasis from the demands of the problem to the demands of the emotional accompaniments of the problem, and has adopted as his criteria of solution a diminution of these painful emotional experiences without respect to actual reduction of the problem itself. The final criterion of effectiveness of any mechanism must be based on both biological and social components of adaptation. The mechanisms in themselves are neither good nor bad techniques of adjustment, but are the one or the other, dependent upon the extent to which they promote or interfere with adaptation at all life levels.

DISCUSSION QUESTIONS

1. Can you recognize the operation of the behavior mechanisms in your own personality? Is it easier to identify the use of mechanisms in yourself or in others?
2. Why are the behavior mechanisms so effective in adaptation even when they are faulty techniques?
3. Can you suggest some other classification schemes of the behavior mechanisms?
4. How important is social interaction in the development and use of the behavior mechanisms?

5. Can you cite other examples of compensation and overcompensation?
6. Is a mechanism like rationalization necessary in our culture?
7. Can you explain in detail how the operation of a behavior mechanism reduces anxiety?
8. What attitude should society take toward sexual aberrations?
9. What is the significance of the large-scale surveys of sexual behavior such as those of Kinsey and his associates?
10. Can you think of any customs of our culture that might tend to encourage the maladaptive use of the behavior mechanisms?

SUGGESTED READINGS

C. S. Ford and F. A. Beach (1951), *Patterns of Sexual Behavior*. New York: Harper and Brothers.

R. R. Sears (1944), "Experimental analysis of psychoanalytic phenomena," in J. McV. Hunt, ed. (1944), pp. 306-332. *Personality and the Behavior Disorders*. New York: The Ronald Press Company.

P. M. Symonds (1949), *Dynamic Psychology*. New York: Appleton-Century-Crofts, Inc.

BIBLIOGRAPHIC SOURCES

On the behavior mechanisms in general, see Symond's (1946) *The Dynamics of Human Adjustment,* Brown's (1940) *Psychodynamics of Abnormal Behavior,* Shaffer's (1936) *Psychology of Adjustment,* and Hilgard (1949). A particularly useful source is Symond's abridgment of the 1946 book into *Dynamic Psychology* (1949). Each successive chapter is a detailed and clear exposition of a particular defense mechanism.

The best source for compensation is probably the work of Adler, cited in the text. Cameron (1951) is also suggested. On rationalization, James Harvey Robinson's (1921) *Mind in the Making* is still good reading.

As might be expected the literature of sexual psychopathology is immense. Historically, the standard clinical and anecdotal approach was represented by Krafft-Ebing (1904) in his *Psychopathia Sexualis,* whose Victorian concern with Latinizing the most significant statements provides the only argument the writers have had for being compelled to take Latin in high school. Also important and extremely influential is the more urbane *Studies in the Psychology of Sex* by Havelock Ellis (1942). For complete bibliographies of the literature on studies of the normal and pathological aspects of sexual adjustment, there are no better sources than Kinsey, Pomeroy, and Martin (1947) and Kinsey, Pomeroy, Martin, and Gebhard (1953). And, of course, these two books contain an immense amount of information about the sexual adjustments of rather large groups of individuals in our culture. Another splendid source is Ford and Beach's (1951) *Patterns of Sexual Behavior,* representing both a cross-cultural and a phylogenetic approach. For two extended and interesting case histories on fetishism, see Bergman (1947) and Greenberg (1951). The word "sadism" comes from the name of the eighteenth century monster the Marquis de Sade whose practices and writing sometimes pass beyond belief. The term "masochism" comes from the name of the Austrian Chevalier von Sacher-Masoch (1836-1905) justified in part by his novels. The fascinating biography by Cleugh (1952), *The Marquis and the Chevalier,* is recommended. The literature on the homosexual is surprisingly large; Henry's (1948) *Sex Variants* is suggested. We recommend, in addition, the autobiographical article by Jane Mac-Kinnon (1947) on the homosexual woman.

The role of identification in personality is discussed by Helene Deutsch (1944) in the *Psychology of Women* and by Balint (1943). Wells' (1935) article on regression contains an inclusive bibliography and is delightfully written, but should be supplemented by the more recent papers of Antonitis and Sher (1952), Gill (1948), and Sarbin (1950). For additional information on repression, Cannicott and Umberger (1950), Glixman (1948) and especially Zeller (1950a, 1950b) should be read. On fantasy, Ames and Learned (1949), Davidson and Fay (1953), Symonds (1949b), and Thetford (1952) are pertinent references; Freud's (1938) *The Interpretation of Dreams* is classic. The relation of negativism and ego development is discussed by Ausubel (1950).

As we have said, many of the concepts in this chapter are directly related to the psychoanalytic movement. We strongly suggest that you supplement this text with the papers by Sears (1943, 1944) systematically evaluating the scientific status of these concepts.

VI

The Physiology and Psychology of Emotion

Of points where physiology and psychology touch, the place of one lies at "emotion."

—SHERRINGTON

One of the oldest beliefs about human behavior concerns the intimate linkage between emotion and the general physical condition of the body in health and disease. Long before we had any understanding of the exact nature of the mechanisms involved, it was recognized by physicians that the "mental attitude" of the patient was often the crucial factor in determining recovery from illness. Novelists of other days made much of this phenomenon, and there is a modern psychological flavor to the old ballad of Barbara Allan:

'O it's sick, and very, very sick,
    And 't is a' for Barbara Allan:
O the better for me ye's never be,
    Tho your heart's blood were a spilling,'

He turned his face unto the wall,
    And death was with him dealing:
'Adieu, adieu, my dear friends all,
    And be kind to Barbara Allan.

'O mother, mother, make my bed¹
    O make it saft and narrow!
Since my love died for me today,
    I'll die for him to-morrow.'

134

In the light of so much folk-knowledge and such an abundance of clinical evidence it is surprising that a systematic exploration of the relationships between emotional behavior and physical illness has been so recent. The principal reason appears to be that our knowledge of the physiological aspects of emotion has only in recent years become organized around central unifying concepts. Since a grasp of modern psychopathology depends upon correctly understanding the psychology and physiology of emotion, we will spend some time on the topic.

THE DIFFUSE NATURE OF EMOTION

One of the difficulties encountered by a scientific study of emotion is the fact that the typical phenomena may be viewed from more than one level of description. As Woodworth and Schlosberg (1954) point out:

. . . one can find three different aspects of emotion. In the first place, an angry man *behaves* in a particular way: his actions are gross and powerful, often without regard to the finer requirements of the situation; he may "have the strength of a demon" but be "blind with rage." In the second place, he manifests clear symptoms of internal *physiological changes* in his rapid breathing and flushed face. Finally, he has characteristic *introspective experiences* that he can report.[1]

But concentration on one aspect of emotion cannot give us an adequate account of emotion. Since so much of the distinctive character of emotional experience depends upon its internal aspects, both physiological and psychological, observations of overt behavior can never succeed in yielding a full account of the phenomenon. Further, we meet with very little success if we ask a person to describe his own emotions. This is not due to any lack of awareness of the experience, since most people can quite accurately recognize when they are "emotional"; nor is it due to any subtlety or lack of intensity of the emotional experiences, since they are among the most dramatic and attention-compelling aspects of the organism's activity.

The most serious obstacle to a scientific treatment of emotionality is the massive and diffuse character of the process. In spite of our recognition that behavior is always influenced and determined by a multiplicity of variables, and that ultimately the whole organism takes part

[1] R. S. Woodworth and H. Schlosberg (1954), *Experimental Psychology* (2nd Ed.), p. 107. New York: Henry Holt and Company, Inc.

in any response, much of our behavior seems to concern one organ or organ system so predominantly that we find it possible to talk almost as if that particular part of the organism were alone concerned in a given act. Sensory phenomena, such as seeing, hearing, touching, tasting, and so forth can be discussed fairly well and can be defined with a fair amount of accuracy in terms of the specific sense organs most involved. The various motor skills, associated as they are with definite parts of the skeletal muscular system, lend themselves to easy description. Running, walking, swimming, driving, and fighting give us little difficulty. Even such highly internalized activities as thinking or reasoning seem to be understandably described as minimal or implicit trial-and-error manipulations of the environment by means of symbols.

Emotions, however, are such inclusive psychological phenomena, concerning so many parts of the organism and coloring so much of the organism's relations with its environment, that no single organ system and no single aspect of the environment seems to tell enough of the story of the emotion to make it meaningful in reconstruction. It is probably for this reason that description of emotionality was so much more complete and realistic when done by the creative artist than when attempted by the scientist. Indeed, almost all the general types of emotional behavior were described by poets and novelists long before they were verified and accorded status by science. This state of affairs is of significance for our study of emotion and psychopathology. Emotional behavior is *dramatic;* people are somehow lifted out of their routine existence by emotion. Such things catch the attention of the artist. The emotional experiences of a human being are, in a sense, his stock in trade. Art is partially a re-creation of emotional situations, in stone or on canvas, in the words of poetry or story, or by the collaboration of dramatist and actors on the stage.

EMOTION AS A CONSEQUENCE OF FRUSTRATION

What is it then that the artist has been describing so well for so many years and that the scientist is just beginning to understand? The reader could probably answer this question for himself by simply remembering the last movies he has seen or the last novels he has read. In common with all these more or less artistic attempts to depict life are the elements of motivation and frustration, of strivings toward personal goals, and of failure and success in these endeavors. What the artist discovered was that emotion is connected intimately with motivation and is aroused by the failure and/or success of the person in achieving the goals he has created. Emotional behavior is a consequence of frustration, of "the interruption of tendencies."

If we were concerned with the general theoretical topic of emotion-ality, we would have to qualify this statement in such a way as to adequately include *all* types of emotional experience since some types of pleasant and less intense emotions are not so obviously related to frustration. Since, however, our interest is primarily in the pathological behavior of organisms, we will be chiefly occupied with following the consequences to the organism of those frustrations that produce the more intense (and usually unpleasant) emotional states of anger and fear.

Emotion, then, is a type of behavior that appears when the motivated organism is blocked or thwarted while carrying out those activities that are necessary for the achievement of its goals. We can picture emotion as originating in blind random struggling of the primitive organism against the restraining and inhibiting forces of its environment. In the course of organic evolution many organismic structures have become specialized for more effectively dealing with these environmental ob-stacles. Anatomically and physiologically most mammals are well equipped for the violent behavior that is the most primal expression of what we have called "emotion."

The Anatomy and Physiology of Emotion

PHYSIOLOGICAL MECHANISMS IN EMOTION

Physiologically, as Cannon (1936) was one of the first to suggest, the emotional animal is in a state of increased readiness for fighting or for running away. The entire bodily economy is organized for the expenditure of great amounts of energy in overt muscular activity. Cannon concluded that the actual bodily changes, which resulted in preparation for emergencies, were not distinguishably different for those psychological emotional experiences that we regard as almost diametrically opposed, namely rage and fear. He felt that whether the behavioral situation called for aggressive attack or for hasty retreat, the physiological mechanism functioned in precisely the same way; since its primary role seemed to be as a liberator of energy it is apparent that nothing is lost in the way of adjustmental efficiency at the psychological level. Although this point of view has been widely accepted, there is a growing amount of strong evidence indicating differences between the physiological expression of anger and fear. Wolf and Wolff (1943) were able to make direct observations of changes in the activity of the stomach of a human subject during many types of emotional experiences. Since the patient worked in the laboratory of the experimenters, he was observed daily, and changes in the appearance of his stomach were correlated with the emotional situations that occurred in the course of his daily experience. Among other results, they noted that the changes in stomach appearance and function accompanying rage and other aggressive emotions were just opposite to those occurring during fear. Further experimental investigations of Grace, Wolf, and Wolff (1951) of four patients with exposed colons have strongly supported these findings. Hypofunctioning of the colon was experienced in relation to feelings of fear, depression, and dejection. Anger, resentment, and anxiety were associated with hyperfunctioning of the colon. In addition to other differential changes in the colon, they note:

The circumstances under which each of these patterns of reaction occurred were distinguishable with respect to the stimulus, the nature of the individual, his past experiences, his current state, and the conditions during exposure to the stimulus situation.[2]

Although there is still a great deal we do not understand about the exact relationships involved, future research like this will most certainly introduce changes in our present conceptions.

THE AUTONOMIC NERVOUS SYSTEM

The bodily equipment for dealing with emergencies consists primarily of the autonomic nervous system and the motor units that it supplies. As the reader may remember from other physiological and psychological studies, the autonomic nervous system supplies innervation to smooth muscles and glands. This means that the walls of hollow viscera and of blood vessels, other smooth muscles in the heart and in the iris of the eye, and the glandular tissues of the body, both duct and ductless, act in ways that are strongly influenced and determined by the nervous impulses that pass along fibers of the autonomic nervous

[2] W. J. Grace, S. Wolf, and H. G. Wolff (1951), *The Human Colon*, p. 226. New York: Paul B. Hoeber, Inc.

system. Figure 6 shows schematically a few of the ramifications of this part of our nervous system.

Autonomic is derived from "autonomy," which means independence or self-government. There are several features of the autonomic system that are contributory to this appearance of independent function. In

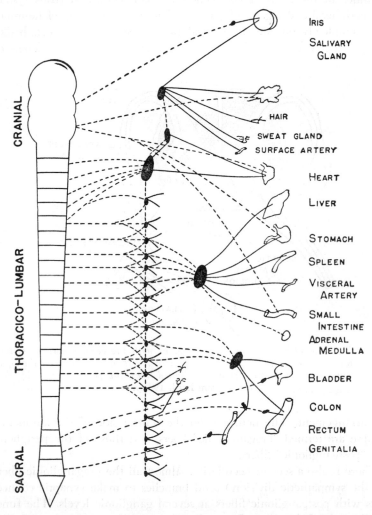

FIGURE 6. *Schematic representation of the autonomic nervous system* (modified from Bard, 1934; after Cannon, 1915).

the first place, this part of the peripheral nervous system is completely motor in function. Unlike the motor nerve fibers in the skeletal portion of the peripheral nervous system, which have only a single neuronal process between central nervous system and peripheral destination, the autonomic nervous system is distinguished by the occurrence of *two* neurones in the simplest connection between central nervous system and peripheral end organ. This means that an entire group of neurones exist completely outside the central nervous system, their cell bodies grouped together in ganglionic clumps. Figure 7 shows the details of

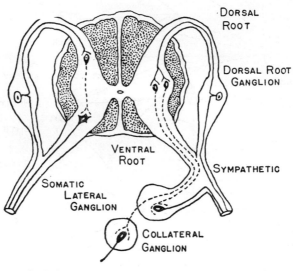

FIGURE 7. *Detail of the autonomic connections with the central nervous system. On the left, is a simple sensorimotor reflex arc of the somatic system; on the right, the preganglionic neurones are shown by dotted lines, the postganglionic by solid lines* (from Bard, 1935).

this arrangement. The neurones on the central side of the autonomic synapse are termed "preganglionic" fibers, and those of the peripheral side "postganglionic" fibers.

There is also a second peculiarity. Almost all the preganglionic fibers (in the sympathetic division) send branches to make synaptic connections with postganglionic fibers at several ganglionic levels. The functional result of this type of neural organization is an extreme diffusion of action, since nervous excitation can spread to widely separated parts of the body. The autonomic nervous system almost literally creates a distribution system outside of the spinal nervous system.

The preganglionic fibers leave the spinal cord at three rather distinct levels, as shown in Figure 6. The central thoracicolumbar level is termed the *sympathetic,* the upper (cranial) and lower (sacral) levels are called the *parasympathetic* divisions of the autonomic nervous system. The functions of the sympathetic and parasympathetic are both directly and indirectly antagonistic. As can be seen in Figure 6, many of the organs are supplied with fibers from both divisions. In the heart, for example, the parasympathetic exerts an inhibitory effect, the sympathetic an excitatory effect, on its actions. In the digestive tract, the sympathetic is inhibitory, the parasympathetic excitatory. This antagonism should be borne in mind; we will make use of it soon.

There is still another remarkable fact about the autonomic nervous system. Notice in Figure 6 that several of the viscera receive preganglionic fibers directly from the spinal cord without the usual synapse. Of major significance for us is the fact that the medulla of the adrenal gland is thus innervated. The adrenal medulla, when stimulated, secretes *adrenalin.* The researches of Gaskell (1921) and Langley (1921) have shown that the secretory cells of the adrenal medulla correspond to the postganglionic fibers both embryologically and morphologically, and that the action of adrenalin on any tissue is similar to the action of nerve impulses in the sympathetic postganglionic fibers on such tissues.

We spoke a moment ago of the diffuse nature of autonomic activity. It should be recognized that the sympathetic plays the major role in this unitary action. Parasympathetic fibers do not spread as widely. In general they supply only organs rather close to the ganglion from which the postganglionic fiber originates. Bard (1934) states that this restricted distribution of parasympathetic fibers constitutes an arrangement whereby the central nervous system can exert effect on single organs more readily than is the case with the sympathetic, where a nerve impulse in one part of the system spreads throughout the whole range of organs supplied by sympathetic fibers.

CENTRAL NERVOUS SYSTEM CONNECTIONS OF
THE AUTONOMIC NERVOUS SYSTEM

Turning to the central connections of the autonomic, we find again the same remarkable polarities and antagonistic controls that characterize the more peripheral segments. It is possible to secure evidence of autonomic activity in animals whose spinal cords have been severed, indicating the presence of purely spinal autonomic reflexes. Sahs and Fulton (1940) transected the spinal cord in monkeys and showed that vasoconstriction and vasodilatation in response to temperature changes on the skin could still take place. Dusser de Barenne and Koskoff (1932) and Sherrington (1900) demonstrated that evacuatory and sexual responses can also be mediated at spinal levels. The responses are sluggish and lack the coordination that is present in the intact organism. If the brain stem is severed above the medulla oblongata, autonomic responses are better integrated and show a wider range. Blood pressure is under more control and does not fluctuate as widely as in the spinal preparation. Swallowing, sneezing, coughing, vomiting, and salivation are manifested. If the brain lesion is above the level of the pons, pupillary reactions to change in light intensity are added to the animal's autonomic repertoire. These findings for the lower levels of the central nervous system demonstrate the primitive and vegetative nature of the autonomic apparatus. In basic outline this role of the spinal cord and midbrain remains the same for all vertebrates, and is little less complex in the primitive fishes than it is in the highest primates.

Above the pons we come to that level of the central nervous system which is the crucial central focus for the integration of visceral function. This integration results from the interplay between posterior and anterior sections of the hypothalamus and from regulation of hypothalamic function by the cerebral cortex. The forepart of the hypothalamus has parasympathetic, the posterior sympathetic representation. Since the hypothalamus receives afferent nerve fibers from the cerebral cortex, thalamus, and corpus striatum, it plays a part in relaying impulses from sensory areas into autonomic motor channels.

At this level are controlled the heat-regulating mechanisms of the body, water metabolism, some sexual and digestive functions, and, most important for our present purpose, both the skeletal and visceral components of emotional expression. It has been known for many years that animals whose cerebral hemispheres have been removed show violent emotional responses to almost any type of stimulation. In addition to the overt behavior of snarling, growling, biting, and struggling, a wide variety of visceral changes also occurred. Bard (1934) and Ranson, Kabot, and Magoun (1934) found that direct electrical stimulation of the hypothalamus gave responses similar to those observed in the decerebrate preparations. Fulton (in Howell, 1947) cites an unpublished experience of Dusser de Barenne who:

. . . inadvertently injected a small amount of strychnine into a cat's hypothalamus (intending it for the thalamus). The cat recovered from its ether anesthesia and within a few seconds a frightening seizure of unleashed fury developed in which the cat dashed madly from one end of the room to the other, from the floor to the ceiling, savagely attacking anything in its path.[3]

Bard and Mountcastle (1948) showed, by ablation studies in the cat, that the cerebral cortex and the hypothalamus are intimately associated in the production of emotional behavior. They further demonstrated that specific brain areas are concerned with the inhibition of emotional response.

Equally good evidence of the sub-cortical control of emotion comes from clinical neurological observations with humans. Injuries that interrupt the motor pathways from the cerebral cortex may result in a facial paralysis, in which voluntary movement of the facial muscles is impossible. If the patient is placed in a situation that stimulates emotion, such as sorrow or mirth, the facial muscles move to form the appropriate expression (Wilson, 1924, 1929). The reverse situation, in which lesions occur in the thalamic and hypothalamic region, may result in preserved voluntary expressive movement and destroyed or diminished emotional expression. This suggests two conclusions: (1) that emotional behavior is mediated at the sub-cortical level of the hypothalamus, and (2) that emotional expression is controlled or inhibited in the normal animal by higher centers in the central nervous system. It is also evident that emotional expression is as intimately a matter of autonomic activity as of overt skeletal muscular movement.

SUMMARY

Let us summarize briefly the physiological material we have just covered. Emotional expression is both overt and internal. It is mediated primarily by the sympathetic division of the autonomic nervous system and by several areas of the central nervous system, particularly the posterior portion of the hypothalamus. The whole mechanism of emo-

[3] J. F. Fulton, ed. (1947), *Howell's Textbook of Physiology* (15th Ed.), p. 250. Philadelphia and London: W. B. Saunders Company.

tional expression is inhibited, controlled, or regulated by the higher centers of the cerebral cortex. The motor destinations of the sympathetic nerve fibers in the smooth muscles and glands are widespread, and the mode of excitation is diffuse, due to the multitudinous branching of the preganglionic neurones. Finally, the sympathetic division of the autonomic is *usually* functionally antagonistic to the parasympathetic division. This allows us to say, *as a rough approximation,* that the normal flow of nonemotional vegetative life depends upon the parasympathetic, and that the sympathetic becomes dominant during times of emotional upset.

Psychosomatics

THE SYMPTOMS OF EMOTION

What is the significance of these facts for comprehending the psychology and pathology of emotion? Let us examine in more detail what might be called the "symptomatology" of emotion. Table 6 summarizes reports and interviews gathered from combat soldiers in the United States Army concerning their bodily state either just before or during periods of intense danger. All these symptoms are the result of sympathetic dominance; in times of stress the peaceful vegetative balance of our circulatory, digestive, and excretory systems is destroyed. Notice how many different organ systems are involved, and how painful or uncomfortable most of the symptoms seem to be. Superficially it may be difficult to see how these symptoms justify Cannon's statement that emotion is physiologically an organization of the body for emergencies. Such, however, is really true if we understand what type of emergency the body is being prepared to meet. It is obvious that a person who felt as bad as Table 6 indicates would be very poorly prepared to carry out any complex intellectual task, such as taking an examination, teaching a class, or participating in a dramatic production. If the emergency is one that requires physical effort, however, Cannon's assertion is amply confirmed. The increased activity of the heart stimulates more rapid blood circulation, assuring a more abundant supply of energy to muscles and facilitating removal of the waste products of muscular activity. The whole complex of digestive symptoms is due to the shift from parasympathetic facilitation of digestion to sympathetic inhibition of digestive processes. The relative volume of blood supplied

TABLE 6

EMOTIONAL SYMPTOMS OF SOLDIERS IN COMBAT*

Symptom	Percentage of Soldiers
Violent pounding of the heart............	86
Sinking feeling in the stomach...........	75
Feeling sick in the stomach..............	59
Trembling and shaking..................	56
Cold sweat............................	55
Tense feeling in the stomach.............	53
Feeling of weakness and faintness........	51
Vomiting........................	24
Involuntary defecation..................	10
Involuntary urination...................	10

* Source: E. G. Boring, ed., *Psychology for the Armed Forces*, 1945, p. 384. Reprinted by permission of the National Research Council and the Infantry Journal Press, Washington, D.C.

to the digestive organs decreases, and that to the skeletal muscles increases. Partly as a result of increased activity of the sympathetically stimulated adrenal cortex, and partly by direct stimulation from postganglionic sympathetic fibers, the superficial arterioles of the skin dilate or constrict, imparting the change in skin coloration so characteristic of emotion. Increase in the amount of adrenalin in the blood results, through action on the spleen, in an increase in number of circulating red blood corpuscles. Blood sugar is increased by the effect of adrenalin on the glycogen stored in the liver. Since blood sugar is the most readily available form of energy for muscular action, this phenomenon may be readily fitted into the "emergency" concept of emotionality. The vital role of sympathetic activity in times of stress has been demonstrated by an experiment of Campos, Cannon, Lundin, and Walker (1929) in which animals were forced to run until exhausted and then were given injections of adrenalin. The effect of this hormone was to increase materially their muscular effort and to extend the duration of their activity.

The role of sympathetic activity in aiding the animal to cope with stress is also illustrated by those experiments in which the sympathetic nervous system has been systematically severed in such a way as to render it either totally or partially useless. Cannon, Newton, Bright, Menkin, and Moore (1929) found that cats could remain healthy after complete removal of the sympathetic if they were not subjected to unusual stress. Acute changes in temperature, partial anoxia, fatigue, and hemorrhage were poorly tolerated. In recent years our knowledge of sympathetic functions has been increased as a consequence of the discovery that partial sympathectomy may afford relief to patients suffering from various consequences of abnormal vasospasm.

As the evidence accumulates it becomes more and more apparent that the influence of the autonomic nervous system is felt in almost every type of adjustive reaction that the human organism performs. Because of the direct participation of the sympathetic system in emotional reactions, every psychological situation involving stress, excitement, frustration, or conflict is also a physiological situation. Here we can see the justification for the statement that the sciences of psychopathology and tissue pathology have an increasing amount of overlapping concern and interest. To tell the complete story of a degeneration of cells in the liver and kidney of a patient, we must know not only the number and kinds of tissue changes that may take place under a variety of immediate physiological conditions but also the laws of emotion, and we must be able to understand the assortment of events that determine frustration in that patient's life history.

THE SCOPE OF PSYCHOSOMATICS

To this fairly recent trend in psychopathology the term *psychosomatics* has been applied. Psychosomatics *traces the interrelationships between emotional expression and adjustment on the psychological level and the effect of its physiological accompaniments on bodily health and disease*. It is probably not an exaggeration to say that the psychosomatic emphasis has been one of the truly great events in the history of psychopathology. As the true relationship of the autonomic nervous system to adjustment became apparent, the psychopathologist was able to utilize research methods and data from every field of medical physiology and pathology, and in return has been able to contribute much to the understanding of many puzzling aspects of somatic diseases.

Functional symptoms involve the revolution of a vicious somatopsychic circle—emotional reaction, conflict, functional derangements of organs expressive of the emotional conflict, more emotional reaction, more functional incapacity, and so on, until the human machine runs down, or perhaps gives out, and there remains the scar of structural pathology.[4]

[4] E. A. Strecker (1943), "The leaven of psychosomatic medicine." *Annals of Internal Medicine, 18,* 737.

Let us examine some of the important contributions psychosomatics has made to systematic psychopathology. There are several, but all of them probably grow out of one, *namely the establishment of the concept of adjustment or adaptation as universally applicable to all biological events, from the most minute change in cellular chemistry to the most complex psycho-social happenings.* As we have seen, organic life itself depends upon the maintenance of many equilibrial relationships; energy exchange factors are critical for living. Within the body many complex mechanisms exist for maintaining steady states of temperature, acidity-alkalinity, salt and mineral content of the tissues, and for protecting the body from overly strong energy impacts, and so forth. Animal psychologists and ecologists have long realized that equilibrium is not achieved by internal means alone, since the animal is immersed in an environment that makes continual demands upon it. Cannon (1932) has quoted the French physiologist, Charles Richet, as saying:

> The living being is stable. It must be so in order not to be destroyed, dissolved or disintegrated by the colossal forces, often adverse, which surround it. By an apparent contradiction it maintains its stability only if it is excitable and capable of modifying itself according to external stimuli and adjusting its response to the stimulation. In a sense it is stable because it is modifiable—the slight instability is the necessary condition for the true stability of the organism.[5]

The "adjustments of external stimuli" cover a great deal of the animal's behavior and may be said to be the whole problem of the psychologist. The social scientists, working from entirely different points of view, have reached the same conclusions. Hendrick (1947), in explaining Freud's formulation of a psychological theory of motivation from intensive study of clinical material, says:

> This induction of a fundamental property of life, derived from psychoanalytic observation, coincides with the ultimate conclusions of scientists in other fields. For example, the physiologist Cannon, after a life of investigation of organic function, maintains that all bodily processes are devised to maintain a definite physio-chemical equilibrium which he terms "homeostasis." The essence of Cannon's conclusions about "homeostasis" coincides remarkably with the significant statements of Freud's own most speculative

[5] Reprinted from *The Wisdom of the Body* by Walter B. Cannon, by permission of W. W. Norton & Company, Inc. Copyright 1932 by the publishers. Page 20.

work, *Beyond the Pleasure Principle* (1920). Their investigations have been in separate realms, yet their final conclusions in regard to the fundamental processes of life are the same: the psychoanalyst, that psychological processes are initiated by the need to restore an emotional equilibrium which is experienced as pleasure; the physiologist, that all organic processes are initiated by the need to restore a physico-chemical equilibrium which is experienced as health.[6]

The psychopathologist, like other biological scientists, frequently speaks of "the organism as a whole," or talks about the "unity" of the organism. By these phrases he means that all aspects of the life cycle of any living creature are interdependent, that the organism does not have parts that function in isolation. What happens to change one aspect of the organism results in changes in other aspects. Justification for this point of view comes from an abundance of observational data. Ritter (1919) collected enough evidence to fill two volumes; they make exciting reading even today. The psychopathologist, as noted above, also had arrived at the same conviction from his studies. The missing link in the whole problem was knowledge of the integrating mechanisms that knit the organism together. There is still a great deal that we do not know, but our present state of insight for the operation of the autonomic nervous system goes a long way toward perfecting our understanding of "the organism as a whole." We can see now something of the relationship between internal regulative processes and overt motivated behavior. When motivated behavior is frustrated or when there is a conflict of motives, the implied threat to adjustment results in internal, as well as external, compensatory changes. The external changes are manifest as emotion and trial-and-error behavior. The internal changes are the physical symptoms of emotion and, under certain circumstances, of anxiety.

EMOTIONAL INFLUENCES ON DISORDERED BEHAVIOR

It would be unfortunate if the reader, at this juncture, assumed that the unifying effect of autonomic organization was a totally favorable state of affairs for human adjustment. The variety of bodily changes involved in even the simplest emotional reaction have a general connotation of regression to the simple and primitive. Behavior in contemporary human society is most efficient when the organism is capable

---

[6] Ives Hendrick (1947), *Facts and Theories of Psychoanalysis* (2nd Ed.), p. 93. New York: Alfred A. Knopf, Inc.

of responding to complex and heterogenous stimulus situations and when the various aspects of the situation can be evaluated in a way that leads most adequately to goal-directed activity. To perform in such a manner requires a high degree of rationality, or physiologically speaking, maximal control of action by the cerebral cortex. When the person is frustrated in a complex *social* setting, cortical control becomes of even greater importance. Unfortunately, it is in just such situations that emotional response is the most likely to occur, and adjustmental efficiency to suffer.

An experiment by Patrick (1934) demonstrates the disruptive effect of emotional stimulation on human subjects in a problem-solving situation. The subjects were trained in an experimental room having several exit doors, only one of which would be unlocked on any given trial. The task was to discover which door would permit escape from the room. The essence of solution was the discovery that the door unlocked in an immediately previous trial would never be unlocked in the following trial. Under normal conditions the subjects rapidly became acquainted with this fact and followed various orderly ways of discovering the unlocked door. Emotional stimulation (electrical shock, shower of cold water, etc.) was introduced without warning and continuously during the trials in which they were operative. The effect on the subjects' methods of solution was profound. In place of the orderly, rational trial-and-error solution attempts, the subjects would typically show perseverative reactions of tugging repeatedly at a given door, trying to get out of the door successfully used in the previous trial, or running at random around the experimental room.

An even more extreme example of the possible disorganizing effect of emotion is found in studying the role of emotion in precipitating convulsions. Fremont-Smith (1934) observed 42 unselected epileptic patients. In 31 of the group emotion was indicated as a precipitating factor. In eight of the patients seizures were precipitated by emotions occurring while the patient was under direct observation. Fremont-Smith concluded that stimulation of the sympathetic nervous system was a link in the etiology of the seizures.

In simple emergencies where the frustrations are directly presented and can be dealt with by strenuous physical action the autonomic functions directly support adjustment. Dockeray (1946) relates an incident in which a student, out for an evening ride in his car, saw the automobile directly ahead of him overturn. The student exerted a great physical effort in righting the car and in extricating a girl who had been pinned under it. He took the victim to a hospital, took his own date to her home, and then, on arriving at his own doorstep, collapsed. His emotional state both aided and interfered with adequate adjustment, depending on the level of complexity of the environmental demands.

A survey of the type of behavior that results when the emotional organism is placed in problem situations indicates many ineffective pathological response patterns. As Patrick found with his college students, emotion frequently produces *perseverative reactions,* in which the same unsuccessful futile act is tried again and again. The subject appears unable to vary his attack on the problem; his behavior becomes stereotyped and inflexible. Examples are numerous. In depressed states patients persistently run through the same crying, sobbing formula of "I am no good. I have committed the unpardonable sin." Their self-accusations cannot be modified by rational arguments, nor can their behavior be easily changed by ordinary environmental manipulations. This same phenomenon may be seen in the intense grief reactions of otherwise healthy people. The irrational escape behavior of a crowd caught in a burning building has this character of perseveration.

As long as emotion is aroused only by transitory situations of superficial or temporary importance to the person, the social disorganization need not have serious consequences. Emotion rises with the situation, and when the situation changes the emotion dies down. The fear engendered by an airplane trip through rough air ends when the plane has reached its destination; the anger or annoyance over a flat tire dies down when the tire is repaired. Even the grief of bereavement and the intense love of courtship undergo changes with time. Both psychologically and physiologically, then, we are dealing with essentially reversible reactions with no aftereffects of permanent importance, particularly if the behavioral disorganization does not result in some further adjustmental difficulty.

PATHOLOGICAL ASPECTS OF EMOTION

To assume pathological importance emotion must not only be intense, it must be *chronic.* Most physical consequences of emotionality can be tolerated for only a short time. Emotion as an emergency mechanism may be compared to the low gear on an automobile or the rich emergency adjustment of the airplane engine. Useful for short periods of time when intense effort is required of the mechanism, long-continued use results in general strain and harm to the whole machine. Emotional states make such demands upon the organism. When they recur frequently or over an extended length of time, harmful consequences, both physical and psychological, may ensue. Disruption of the adequate function of many body organ-systems is brought about by the sympathetic mechanisms. This results in a variety of somatic symptoms, whose totality may represent every region of the body. Patients may complain of headaches, palpitation of the heart, shortness of breath, stomach pains, skin eruptions, aching bones and joints, cold extremities and excretory difficulties, making a pattern of symptoms that are characteristic of only one type of etiologic agent, chronic emotionality. The alarm and concern that such symptoms cause the patient result in still further emotionality, thus establishing one of the vicious circles of cause and effect so often seen in psychopathology.

What are the causes of chronic emotionality? Most simply stated, the causes are emotion-provoking situations that persist. In more psychological language, chronic emotionality arises in situations where frustration and conflict block gratification of the organism's motives steadily over long periods of time. Such conditions may be (a) *largely external to the organism,* and consist of environmental features that are themselves barriers to adequate adjustment. Or the conflict may have only superficial relationships to the external world of the patient and be (b) *primarily a product of his own motivational conflicts.* Both circumstances are important, although the psychosomatic results are about the same for each. In a broader sense we shall see that the psychodynamics of both are also similar. Because, from an immediate, practical point of view, environmentally engendered emotionality can be more easily controlled and because it presents a less complex picture, we will consider it first.

PSYCHOSOMATIC REACTIONS TO
ENVIRONMENTAL THREATS

The most common external source of chronic emotionality is physical danger. Explorers, men at war, victims of disasters, all may be exposed to intense environmental threats. If these are prolonged, psychosomatic symptoms appear. This is particularly true when the element of frustration is great, when it appears that the efforts made to surmount the threat are fruitless. Even here, of course, individual susceptibility varies, some being able to withstand more stress than others

Slade (1933) gives an interesting account of the reactions of people in an isolated community in Australia to an earthquake of severe intensity, which extended over a period of several weeks. He noted many symptoms consistent with our understanding of pathological emotionality. A large number of the populace developed physical symptoms of emotional origin, and physicians were kept busy attempting to treat weakness, fatigue, and the like. Many symptoms of cortical release developed, as an "increase in laughing and jesting," and complaints of memory loss. Many developed an apparent indifference to the danger of their situation, acting like "veterans after prolonged trench warfare" and "a don't-care attitude characterized many." He also noted that, until publication of the newspaper could be re-established, people were very susceptible to rumor and panic.

Kubie (1943) has summarized the various symptomatic forms that reaction to environmental stress may take. His list is reproduced below. Notice the surprisingly wide range of behavioral abnormalities that may appear:

1. Simple exhaustion, from which the patient recovers promptly with sleep and food.

2. State of more severe exhaustion, with inability to sleep or rest.

3. Overwhelming exhaustion, complicated by varying degrees of starvation, avitaminosis, dehydration and acidosis, with or without wounds, infection, fever, burns, concussion or blast injuries.

4. Confusional states, varying from mild low-grade disorientation, with rapidly alternating levels of clarity and confusion, to profound delirious reactions, with total disorientation, severe emotional disturbances, hallucinations and stupor.

5. Diffuse dissociated states: amnesias, fugues, somnambulistic wanderings, trance-like "twilight states," pseudoconvulsive states and states of immobility which may for a period resemble cataleptic and catatonic reactions.

6. Localized dissociations: hysterical paralyses, hysterical spasticities, tics, tremors, ataxias, vertigo and hysterical sensory disturbances involving distance receptors, skin receptors or internal sensory function.

7. Acute anxiety states of widely varying severity. These may be (a) diffuse and continuous, (b) episodic or (c) "phobic," in that they are precipitated only in certain special situations.

8. Acute emotional eruptions which swing swiftly through the whole gamut of fear, rage, tears and elation. These may occur in a setting of confusion and delirium (category 4) or of transitory diffuse dissociations (category 5).

9. Visceral disturbances. These may involve, for instance, (a) the heart, i.e., "soldier's heart," effort syndrome of neurocirculatory asthenia; (b) the respiratory system, with typical air-hunger and dyspnea; (c) the gastrointestinal system, with hysterical vomiting, any degree of dyspepsia,

one of the ulcer syndromes or severe and debilitating diarrhea; (d) the genitourinary system.

10. Acute psychotic and psychopathic disturbances: (a) profoundly retarded depressions; (b) hypomanic or manic excitements; (c) paranoid states, with or without megalomania, more or less systematized suspiciousness, explosive rages, and insubordination and rejection of all military regulation and commands; (d) schizoid trends, with seclusiveness, ideas of reference, typical delusions and acute hallucinatory experiences.[7]

Reinartz (1943) has given a very good description of the psychosomatic results of stress in flight personnel. After pointing out that the usual psychoneurosis among fliers has a long background of maladjustment before overt symptoms appear, he discusses the type of disorder appearing in previously well-adjusted persons:

. . . flying stress or operational fatigue is used to describe a condition that may be observed as an *abnormal* flying strain being placed on a *normal* individual. It is particularly found in those members engaged in battle flying. These well-coordinated individuals, presumably because of the care used in their selection for specific assignments, free from psychogenic disorders, can break only on exposure to overwhelming stresses. The assumption is that, at some level of pressure, the most firmly integrated individual will succumb.

The condition is characterized by symptoms which begin slowly, but once having begun, develop rapidly with deterioration and disintegration of the mental and physical constitution of the victim. They "crack up" so to speak. It is the sum total of symptoms raising themselves above the diagnostic threshold which brings the individual to the attention of medical personnel.[8]

Reinartz lists the following symptoms: lack of enthusiasm, listlessness, loss of physical energy, loss of power of concentration, restlessness, sense of guilt, loss of appetite, disturbances of sleep, increased concern about the heart, digestive disturbances, loss of ability to fly at high altitudes, and feelings of faintness.

The war reporting of Ernie Pyle and the drawings of Bill Mauldin indicated almost as well as scientific study the effects of fear and exhaustion on men.

[7] Lawrence S. Kubie (1943), "Manual of emergency treatment for acute war neuroses." *War Medicine, 4,* 587. By permission of the American Medical Association.

[8] Eugen G. Reinartz, "Psychiatry in aviation," in Frank J. Sladen, ed. (1943), *Psychiatry and the War,* pp. 271-272. Courtesy of Charles C. Thomas, publisher, Springfield, Illinois.

A soldier who has been a long time in the line does have a "look" in his eyes that anyone who knows about it can discern. It's a look of dullness, eyes that look without seeing, eyes that see without conveying any image to the mind. It's a look that is the display room for what lies behind it— exhaustion, lack of sleep, tension for too long, weariness that is too great, fear beyond fear, misery to the point of numbness, a look of surpassing indifference to anything anybody can do. It's a look I dread to see on men.[9]

Treatment of these conditions is usually quite simple. When the patient is removed from the threatening situation, given adequate rest and an opportunity to understand the source of his symptoms, recovery is the rule. This fact emphasizes the essentially external nature of the causes for this particular type of breakdown. There can be complications, of course. Autonomic disturbances can cause irreversible changes, and too long an exposure to emotional tension may result in a variety of somatic conditions whose treatment must be directed at the specific defect. Stomach ulcer, for example, once started, must be treated by medical procedure; it cannot be expected to disappear even when the sources of stress are removed.

In addition to the physical changes themselves, the patient is exposed to the danger of developing secondary emotional reactions to the physical symptoms. It is possible for a person to become convinced of inferiority or personal inadequacy in the stress situation. This is particularly true during war, when men feel a deep sense of guilt when removed from their organizations. The conviction that they have "let their buddies down" or that they "can't take it" interferes with recovery and substitutes another source of emotional stimulation for the original dangers. The period of actual stress may cause personality changes that become self-perpetuating.

Let us summarize the stimulus conditions necessary for emotional response. When motives are frustrated, when tendencies to action are interrupted, we experience emotion. Taking this as a guiding dynamic principle, we can then say that such stimuli as arouse fear or anger must have the psychological meaning of barriers to us. Those things that produce fear are simply the aspects of our environment that threaten our security or our lives. Advantage is taken of this principle in one of the standard lie-detection techniques much used by our police forces.

[9] Ernie Pyle (1944), *Brave Men,* p. 270. New York: Henry Holt and Company, Inc.

Because almost every person suspected of a serious crime is in an emotional state when exhaustively questioned by the authorities, it is something of a problem to determine a guilty person by means of techniques that register the physiological changes of emotion. To overcome this difficulty, each suspect is presented with a standard group of stimuli, among which are many having nothing to do with the crime in question and some having direct bearing on the crime. Suppose, for example, that a murder has been committed with a revolver. The suspects are presented successively with five or six guns, one of which is the weapon used in the crime. The innocent suspect will usually show approximately the same emotional reaction to all the revolvers; the guilty person will have a heightened reaction to the pertinent weapon. It is the one that most threatens his security. He is, we could say, *sensitive* to that particular stimulus.

All persons are sensitive to immediate threat of physical danger, and that threat can become excessive in proportion to the degree to which the person is helpless in the face of it. This is the common dynamic basis of all psychosomatic disorders: *that the person is constantly exposed to emotion-provoking stimuli in situations where the possibility of escaping or minimizing the stimuli is impossible.* It is this that at least partially sets off the psychosomatic disturbances from many other types of pathological behavior.

PSYCHOSOMATIC REACTIONS TO INTERNAL CONFLICTS

We now turn to those psychosomatic disturbances that are primarily a product of the patient's personality and that may have little relationship to momentary changes in his present environment. To introduce these conditions are three very short case reports, describing what might be any three patients in an average day's practice of any physician. The first part of the report in each case gives the situation as it appeared before inquiry into the behavioral background of the difficulty. The last part of each study gives the information secured by short psychiatric interviews. Note how the latter information contributes to understanding the patient's physical problems.

Case 8. A man 49 years old, with a wife 35 and two healthy children, described himself as desperate because he was sexually impotent. Pathetically he told of treatments to regain potency and happiness; genitourinary instrumentation, general and prostatic massage, hydrotherapy, electrotherapy, heliotherapy, a sheaf of prescriptions for endocrine products, faithfully taken. His impotence was no better. Indeed to it had been added annoying sensations and sharp pains in the perineum, burning on urination, nocturnal emissions, headaches, insomnia, loss of energy and concentration, etc.

The man with the impotence had been dominated far into manhood by a positive aggressive mother. He was 14 years older than his wife whose sex needs were strong. His symptoms appeared after an unsuccessful attempt at sexual intercourse. He thought his wife was irritated and impatient at his failure.

Case 9. A married woman, aged 42, complained of severe nausea, "sick stomach," vomiting, anorexia, headache, backache, vertigo, etc. She had had two rest cures, numerous gastrointestinal roentgenograms, special corsets for gastroptosis, and now she was having weekly gall-bladder drainages.

The woman with the gastrointestinal symptoms had lost sexual desire. Sexual relations had become unpleasant and painful. By various subterfuges she had decreased the frequency of the sex act, but was filled with anxiety, lest her husband should tire of her and leave her.

Case 10. A 22-year-old student wanted to leave college since he felt he was too sick to go on and as he said: "I would rather quit than flunk. It's no use trying. I can't concentrate." Tuberculosis had been suspected. He had had many dietary and rest treatments, efforts to increase his weight.

The young student was enormously relieved at being given the opportunity of relieving his mind, deeply troubled and remorseful because of masturbation. During much of his life he had been tied too tightly to the apron strings of an emotionally possessive mother. She had warned him excessively about "girls." The masturbation had not been continuous from childhood but had been resumed soon after entering college, upon the heels of three hetero-sexual experiences, occurring in a setting conducive to embarrassment, feelings of inferiority, and fear of discovery.[10]

In each of these cases the physical symptoms seem to have grown out of the life circumstances of the patient. The patient is seen as expressing, by means of bodily ailments, various aspects of life problems and conflicts with which he is faced. The problems themselves are different from those faced by the soldiers in our last section. The influence of a dominating mother coming out as physical fatigue, chronic sexual maladjustment manifested as nausea and vomiting—the symptoms are similar but the problems are not the same. The meaning of stress is not as obvious in these cases. An exploding airplane, a sinking ship at sea, an earthquake-torn city are obvious and immediate sources of stress on the person who experiences them and, as was emphasized, are capable of producing disordered behavior in the majority of persons.

[10] E. A. Strecker (1943), "The leaven of psychosomatic medicine." *Annals of Internal Medicine, 18,* 738.

The stresses that originate within the personality, however, are more particularly individual in nature.

In the last section, we spoke of the sensitivity of an individual to a particular stimulus. *Each of us, likewise due to the particular circumstances of our individual life experiences, develops sensitivities, or lowered thresholds, to those aspects of life that symbolize threats to our own integrity or adjustment.* The badly maladjusted person is simply one whose thresholds are very low for a great many potential threatening situations. Such a person will spend a large proportion of his time being emotional.

To illustrate this phenomenon, consider the person whose experiences have built up in him a deep suspicion and distrust of other adults in his social environment. Anyone with whom he has social transactions is a potential threat, a source of frustration to his desires for security or well-being. People, then, are for him stimuli for fear responses, and if he continues to associate with people, it must be at the expense of constant emotional turmoil. If, to extend the example, the only possible way he can earn his living is in an occupation that involves association with people, he is placed in a conflict situation. Since all this, for the most part, is unconscious, our patient is in the position of being afraid but without recognizing the source of the fear, that is, he is anxious.

In Chapter IV we discussed the origin of such maladjustment and conflict in the early life of a person and its chronic influence on the developing personality. We saw that much of the frustration and conflict are well established by adulthood and that most of it functions at an unconscious level. When the person's persistent attempts to adjust are ineffective, at either a biological or social level, there is the development of anxiety and the further elaborations of attempts to remove the fear. All these circumstances within the organism often result in the disordered behavior termed *psychoneurosis* or *psychosis*. In addition, another type of reaction may be seen, one connected closely to bodily disorder, and termed *psychosomatic disorders*. Some of these psychosomatic disease conditions will be discussed in the following section.

Psychosomatic Disorders

Although it is beyond the scope of our treatment to review every type of psychosomatic illness, the outline presented in Table 7 indicates how many diseases, from almost every chapter of the medical textbook, have a definite emotional element in their causation. We will summarize the essential psychological findings in a few of these syndromes.

TABLE 7

DISEASE CONDITIONS OF PSYCHOSOMATIC ORIGIN*

1. *Gastrointestinal system*
   duodenal ulcer; mucous colitis (disease of mucous membrane of the colon, with colic, diarrhea, and passage of membranous threads in the stools); visceroptosis; "stress dyspepsia"; some cases of constipation
2. *Cardiovascular system*
   essential hypertension; effort syndrome; neurocirculatory asthenia
3. *Respiratory system*
   asthma
4. *Genitourinary system*
   nocturnal enuresis; vaginismus (painful spasms of the vagina due to local hypersensitivity); some types of menstrual disturbance
5. *Locomotor system*
   many cases of "fibrositis," "neuritis," "sciatica," and "lumbago"; also some postural defects
6. *Endocrine system*
   exopthalmic goitre, hyperthyroidism
7. *Nervous system*
   migraine, cholera, some cases of epilepsy
8. *Skin*
   some types of prurigo, exzema, pruritis, psoriasis, uticaria, rosacea complex

* Source: Adapted from James L. Halliday (1943), "Concept of psychosomatic affection." *The Lancet,* 265, 692.

DISORDERS OF CIRCULATORY SYSTEMS

Changes in the function of the circulatory system are among the most dependable of the physiological aspects of emotion. It was suspected relatively early in the history of psychosomatics that various circulatory disorders might be related to chronic emotionality. Hypertension (high blood pressure) has been connected for a long time in the popular mind with the emotional display of anger. We are all familiar with the fiery red skin of the enraged person. It is a possibility that chronic high blood pressure could be, in part at least, a reflection of some underlying emotional state. Saul (1939) made a detailed psychoanalytic study of seven patients whose hypertension was of the "essential" type, that is, where the increase in blood pressure could not be identified as a direct concomitant of other physical pathology. During the long series of analytic interviews the patients' blood pressure was taken before and after each session. Common to all these patients was a basic conflict between a desire for freedom and independence and attraction to a dominating parent. Characteristic of the patients' reactions to the conflict was an intense hostility and rage that was always sternly repressed. When, during therapy, they had opportunity to give vent to their hostility, blood pressures were decidedly reduced. The following is typical of the cases in this series:

He was mild-mannered and submissive. He was strongly attached to his mother in an oral form as was seen by his indulgence in periodic candy jags. His rage from rebellion against his own submissiveness, and oral dependence, and from thwarting of these wishes, was expressed early in life by temper tantrums, which lasted until after adolescence. Threatened with loss of love because of them, he succeeded in controlling them and became milder in personality. Within a year after suppressing them his blood pressure rose from normal on repeated examinations to 160 over 100 and went slightly higher during the next decade. Physical examination was negative.[11]

Saul concludes that the hostility in patients suffering from hypertension was intense and chronic. "However gentle the exterior, the analyses made it clear that these individuals were chronically boiling with rage." [12] The hostilities were, in addition, always very inhibited, and with no adequate outlet, either through socially constructive activity or through organized psychoneuroses. "The hostility was never adequately expressed but never relinquished."

Saul's findings have been confirmed by other studies, and a tentative description of a "hypertensive personality" can now be made. According to Dunbar (1943) high blood pressure tends to occur in individuals with a lengthy past history of illnesses, who are usually married, with large families, who have had overprotective and dominating mothers and who have a relatively low educational level. They give histories of lifelong conflict over authority accompanied by a fear of the possibility of personal failure. They show a chronically repressed hostility, with a surface appearance of calm self-control. They have a strong desire to be dominant, but are usually unable to accept responsibility if the opportunity arises.

Similar to the hypertensive in many aspects of his background is the person who develops coronary heart disease. The coronary arteries, which supply blood to the heart, are richly supplied with nerve fibers

[11] Leon J. Saul (1939), "Hostility in cases of essential hypertension." *Psychosom. Med., 1,* 153-216.
[12] *Ibid.*

from both the parasympathetic and the sympathetic, the latter acting as constrictors of these arteries. Chronic emotionality thus has a direct effect on the nutritive supply of the heart and can combine effectively with many physical factors to produce cardiac disease. As summarized by Dunbar (1943) the personality of the patient with coronary disease is quite similar to that of the hypertensive patient. There is the same background of conflict with authority, rebellion against parents, and desire for dominance. An odd difference between the two types occurs in their education and vocational background, more of the coronary victims having completed college and belonging to professional groups. A possible explanation of this comes from Dunbar's finding that the coronary disease group apparently have few of the overt neurotic traits of the hypertensive group, but do show a pronounced compulsive drive for work. This work compulsion, arising as a technique for reducing anxiety, may well be strong enough to carry them through the long preparational period of the professions.

Much more research is needed, however, before we can feel much security in these supposed relationships between patterns of personality and types of disorders. As with most clinical investigations, controls are difficult to apply. We do not have enough studies of cardiac patients who have *not* sought psychiatric care, nor of people with the "cardiac" personality who do not manifest somatic symptoms.

RESPIRATORY DISORDERS

A frequently occurring physical complaint of the psychoneurotic is "shortness of breath," or "difficulty in breathing"; and respiratory changes are a prominent feature in any intense emotional state. It is not surprising, then, to find that bronchial asthma is another of the psychosomatic syndromes. Bronchial asthma is essentially a spasm of the bronchial muscles, which interferes with both inspiration and expiration of air. Like hypertension it may have a variety of causes, all of which ultimately involve the autonomic nervous system. One of the leading factors in asthma is, of course, general or specific allergies; other factors may be tuberculosis, endocrine abnormalities, heart and kidney disease, and so forth. Whatever part these factors play in the production of asthma in any given patient, one influence is common to all— emotionality. In a monographic study of bronchial asthma French and Alexander (1941) found the asthmatic personality to be characterized by anxiety, a low degree of self-confidence, and overdependence on parental or parent substitutes. In their family background appeared rather consistently a rejection of the patient by one or both parents. The parents compensated for this emotional attitude by overt overprotection and an equally compensatory solicitousness. This combination of hostility and suffocating protectiveness engendered feelings of insecurity in the child, accompanied by more or less constant fear of isolation or failure of support. The asthmatic attacks themselves tended to be precipitated by situations that seemed to threaten separation of the patient from the parents. In older patients the initial parental attachment was often transferred to the sexual partner, and asthmatic attacks were often precipitated by insecure or illicit sexual relationships.

GASTROINTESTINAL DISEASES

Although psychosomatic medicine has been looked upon as a recent development, physicians have recognized the role of emotion in diseases of the digestive organs for many years. Dunbar (1947a) cites references to medical writings of 1884 in which cases of gastric disturbances are traced to financial losses and confirmed by the disappearance of symptoms when the financial conditions were bettered. Since that time research has abundantly confirmed the clinical observations. We have already mentioned the study of Wolf and Wolff. They found that prolonged resentment increased the blood supply to the stomach membranes, increased the acidity of the stomach contents, and increased the motility of the stomach musculature. As a result of these changes small ulcerated areas appeared, suggesting that ulceration of the stomach could be a secondary consequence of emotional experience. Similar findings were reported with respect to the colon and ulcerative colitis in the experimental work of Grace, Wolf, and Wolff. Mittelmann and Wolff (1942) investigated the past history of patients with gastritis and peptic ulcer. The appearance of symptoms was correlated with periods of emotional conflict and anxiety. During interviews in which these disturbing situations were discussed with the patients there was a measurable increase in the acidity and motor activity of the stomach. The experimenters were able to secure similar reactions in normal control subjects when emotional reactions of hostility and resentment were aroused by artificial laboratory situations.

As with all psychosomatic conditions, there appears to be a predilection for association between peptic ulcer and a particular personality type. As gathered from various sources, this syndrome would appear to occur predominantly in ambitious, conscientious young men who show a strong drive toward success. These individuals have underlying inferiority feelings that are strongly overcompensated. They have need for affection and dependency, which is in conflict with their need for recognition of superiority.

Psychoanalytic studies by Alexander (1934, 1948) of a number of patients suffering from several types of gastric disturbance led him to classify three dominant types of condition on the basis of associated personality structure. These were (1) the gastric type, with ulcers or dyspepsia; (2) the diarrhea type; and (3) the constipation type. He summarized his findings as follows:

The most conspicuous feature of the gastric cases . . . is intense receptive and acquisitive wishes (intaking or incorporating tendencies) against which the patient fights internally because they are connected with extreme conflict in the form of guilt and sense of inferiority which usually lead to their denial. "I do not want to take or receive. I am active and efficient and have no such wishes." Our assumption is that the stomach symptoms are conditioned by the repressed and pent-up receptive and aggressive taking tendencies which serve as chronic psychic stimuli of the stomach function. In some cases the receptive and acquisitive wishes are not *internally* inhibited by conflicts but *externally* by circumstances.

The dynamic formula of the colitis (diarrhea) cases is: "I have the right to take and demand, for I always give sufficiently. I do not need to feel inferior or guilty for my desire to receive and take, because I am giving something in exchange for it." Our assumption is that the diarrhea, apart from expression aggressions, serves as a substitute for the giving of real values.

Finally in the constipation cases the dynamic background of the symptom may be verbalized as follows: "I do not take or receive and therefore I do not need to give." Our assumption is that the constipation is a reaction against the obligation to give.[13, 14]

However, evidence somewhat in opposition to these studies is provided by Krasner (1953). He investigated three groups: one consisting of patients suffering from ulcerative colitis, a second with duodenal ulcer, and a third of normal controls hospitalized without apparent

[13] F. Alexander, C. Bacon, *et al.* (1934), "The influence of psychologic factors upon gastro-intestinal disturbances: a symposium." *Psychoanalyt. Quart.*, 3, 501-588.
[14] The student should not take the language of Alexander's conclusions too literally. As expressed, these are Alexander's *inferences*, and not the verbal behavior of the patient.

psychosomatic ailments. All these individuals were given an extensive battery of tests including an intelligence test, a personality inventory, an interest test, and a supplementary questionnaire. Although the colitis group had a reliably higher mean intelligence quotient than the other groups, there were, in general, no consistently reliable differences between the ulcer group and the colitis group. There was evidence that the two psychosomatic groups differed greatly from the nonpsychosomatic group, and, on the basis of this fact, Krasner suggests the possibility of a *general psychosomatic personality* as opposed to a specific personality type for every illness. Clearly, much more evidence of this type is necessary.

HOW ARE PERSONALITY AND DISEASE ASSOCIATED? A SUMMARY

The evidence we have reviewed suggests one of two or three possible conclusions. Since there appears to be some type of association between personality and disease, we should consider the nature of the relationship between them. Do personality types act partially as causes of particular disease syndromes? Or, on the other hand, is the personality type itself caused by the disease, in the sense of being a factor that a person must adjust to? The evidence is not clear-cut on this important point. Bauer (1945) found what appeared to be a family line of congenital predisposition to gastrointestinal illness; families of peptic ulcer patients showing a significantly higher incidence of all sorts of stomach trouble than families of control groups. Unfortunately it has not been possible, thus far, to make complete personality studies on successive generations of families apparently susceptible to a given type of illness. Even granting the possibility of making such investigations, it would be difficult then to identify the relative importance of the constitutional factors and the influences stemming from the environment. We again have the difficulty of arriving at a positive conclusion, and, after reviewing the effect of emotion on the organism, we should be reluctant to attribute to ·constitution a completely causal role of psychosomatic illness.

If we take a somewhat broader point of view toward "personality type" and consider the phrase to include the habit patterns of the individual as well as his constitutional endowment, explanation becomes a little clearer. If chronic emotionality leads to disease, then it is obviously necessary to ask why a given person behaves in an emotional manner in a particular life situation. The psychoanalytic studies we have quoted show that some people gradually build up certain habitual ways of reacting to other people and create continuing situations in which it becomes excessively difficult for them to gratify their motives without conflict and frustration. Then, after they have been in such a self-created situation for some time, they develop the somatic symptoms we have been studying. From this point of view we can say with more assurance that personality is a critical factor in psychosomatic disorders.

Having arrived at such a stage of our analysis, we can then fruitfully employ the concept of constitution. The organic weaknesses, the predisposition of a given person for a particular type of illness, and the fact that some people develop ulcers and some asthma may be partially constitutional factors. The stress of emotion is itself not sufficiently selective to account for the facts. Under emotion, strain is placed on many organ systems; the system that becomes disordered is presumably weaker or less resistant to the stress. Whether this weakness is completely a constitutional matter is impossible to answer at present. The concept of multiple causation is more likely. The past history of the organism plays a part. Early rheumatic fever may leave a cardiovascular system so weakened that it fails under chronic emotion. To say that constitution may have been the determining factor in the damage from rheumatic fever simply emphasizes the interpenetrating nature of all causal factors in organic life.

Our second possible conclusion, that the disease shapes the personality, is also true and has been abundantly confirmed. Disordered function becomes a barrier to adjustment and calls for further struggle on the part of the patient. Psychosomatic disorders in particular may represent the vicious circle of emotionality as a cause of disease, the disease as a further source of emotionality, and so on to an intensification of the original symptomatology.

DISCUSSION QUESTIONS

1. Can you argue for a fundamental division between mind and body?
2. Can you devise alternative definitions for emotion?
3. Can you recognize any possible psychosomatic components in your past illnesses?

4. Can you recall the physiological and psychological symptoms in some examples of your past emotional behavior?

5. How can emotion act as a causative factor in disease?

6. How can emotion *help* the organism adapt?

7. Do the personality traits of the psychosomatic patient represent the cause or the result of the disease?

8. In light of the material we have covered in this chapter, do you feel there is any basis for the old belief that recovery from physical illness is at least partially a function of the patient's desire to get well?

9. Do you feel, from what you now know, that it would be desirable to modify social customs and mores in such a way that more direct physical expression of aggression would be possible?

10. How is it possible to maintain that diseases have *multiple causation* when we know that bacteria and viruses have been identified as *the* cause of many diseases?

SUGGESTED READINGS

H. Flanders Dunbar (1954), *Emotions and Bodily Changes: A Survey of Literature on Psychosomatic Interrelationships, 1910-1953* (4th Ed.). New York: Columbia University Press.

R. R. Grinker (1953), *Psychosomatic Research.* New York: W. W. Norton and Company, Inc.

M. L. Reymert, ed. (1950), *Feelings and Emotions: The Mooseheart Symposium.* New York: McGraw-Hill Book Company, Inc.

BIBLIOGRAPHIC SOURCES

The literature on the psychology and physiology of emotion and on psychosomatics is incredibly extensive and the student is referred here for the most part to secondary sources that contain full bibliographies.

On emotion we have a number of good reviews of the psychological literature. Young (1943), Ruckmick (1936), Beebe-Center (1932), and Prescott (1938) all have representative discussions of the psychological problems of emotion. Chapters 5, 6, and 7 of Woodworth and Schlosberg (1954) are especially valuable. For provocative theoretical approaches to emotion, see Brown and Farber (1951) and Schlosberg (1954). The physiological background of emotional experience is presented exceptionally well by Bard (1934), Gellhorn (1950, 1953), Lindsley (1951), and Morgan and Stellar (1950). For supplementary information on the physiology of the nervous system, Fulton (1949) is the standard text.

However, the best single source at present for emotion is probably *Feelings and Emotions,* edited by M. L. Reymert (1950). This volume is the publication of 47 papers that were given at the Mooseheart Symposium in 1948. The approach is catholic: psychologists, physiologists, psychiatrists, neurologists, anthropologists, and sociologists were present. For a broad overview of the scope of investigation in emotion, we strongly suggest this book.

For a specific discussion of the relationship of emotion to disease, the paper by Menninger (1949) is excellent. According to Menninger, there are four possible roles that emotion may play in disease. First, emotion may be a causative factor by blocking physiological function which in time would of course lead to disease. Second, emotion may appear as a symptom, that is, concomitant to disease development. Third, emotion may act as a complicating factor in disease. The disordered individual may develop organic illness; with organic disease, stressful events may occur; or emotion may be precipitated as fear of a present organic disease. Fourth, many physical handicaps are life-long and emotion may be involved in the acceptance of these.

Parenthetically, as a footnote to the section on emotional influences on disordered behavior, perseverative reactions have also been demonstrated experimentally with lower animals. If rats are trained to find food at one arm of a T-shaped alleyway, and are then given a severe electric shock while running to the food, it becomes very difficult to eliminate the habit of turning in the first-learned direction when the food has later been shifted to the other arm of the T (J. A. Hamilton and Krechevsky, 1933). Similar perseverative reactions occur in rats that have large areas of their cerebral cortex removed and in human subjects under the influence of alcohol and other toxins. It would probably be too much to say that emotion results in "functional decortication," but the general trend is apparent.

On the mind-body relationship, which is at the heart of any theoretical inquiry into psychosomatics, the best historical sources are Boring (1950) and the same author's essay on physiological psychology, *The Physical Dimensions of Consciousness* (1933). A sensible and penetrating attempt to pierce the semantic fog that so often surrounds this problem is found in the appendix to Muenzinger's (1942) textbook. A long and difficult essay on the same topic with many stimulating, if debatable, points is Kantor (1947). Finally, there is the urbane and erudite treatment by Griffiths (1943).

There are so many texts on psychosomatics that choice is difficult. The following are suggested, any one of which is more than adequate: Alexander (1950), Alexander, French, *et al.* (1948), Altschule (1953), Cobb (1950), Dunbar (1947, 1949), and Weiss and English (1949). Miles, Cobb, and Shands (1952) have published a book of case histories. A fascinating historical account is given by Raginsky (1948). Finally, Hoch (1952) has written a scholarly and lively paper summarizing the concepts and methods of this discipline.

Further, the standard bibliographic reference work on psychosomatic medicine is Flanders Dunbar's *Emotions and Bodily Change* which, in the third edition of 1947, listed 2,400 titles. More recent work is given in the fourth edition of 1954. Since 1938, a scientific journal, *Psychosomatic Medicine,* has been published which contains experimental and clinical studies.

In a broader context, two sources are suggested. The first is Selye's (1950) *Stress* which is a review of the literature on physiological adaptation to almost every conceivable external and internal stress stimulus. Over 5,000 references are cited. The second source is the Proceedings of the Association for Research on Nervous and Mental Diseases published as *Life Stress and Bodily Disease* (Wolff, Wolf, and Hare, 1950). Held in New York in 1949, the conference heard 49 papers on the relationship between stress and physiological response. Many of the papers supplement the sections of this text which are concerned with circulatory, respiratory, and gastrointestinal disorders.

Parenthetically, an unusual personal account of stressful experience is Byrd's (1938) account of his difficulties while manning an advanced Antarctic weather station alone during the winter season. His description of his psychological reactions as he was slowly being overcome by carbon monoxide is a masterpiece of introspective report. Supplement this with Grinker and Speigel (1945).

In addition to all these sources, some shorter and more specifically supplemental to the text are available. Hambling (1951, 1952) presents ten case studies on hypertension in some detail. A critical survey of the literature on hypertension is given by Manus (1949). For a history of hay fever and asthma from Hippocrates to the twentieth century, see Abramson (1948). Finally, Barnacle (1949) and especially Grace, Wolf, and Wolff (1951) should be consulted as background material for gastrointestinal disorders.

—————————————————————————————————— PART TWO

The Problems of Disordered Behavior

We shall now begin, not with postulates, but with an investigation.

—S. FREUD

Introduction

We have completed our survey of basic psychological principles of most importance for understanding the subject matter of psychopathology. In this section we will examine the varieties of disordered behavior, the various "mental diseases" that furnish the problems of psychopathology. All science starts with observations of phenomena occurring in the universe about us and, in the preliminary stages of its work, attempts to classify them in ways that will demonstrate their interrelationships. Although classification alone does not result in a completely satisfactory description, further progress is difficult without adequate classification. In both chemistry and biology the initial phases of the science were devoted to an attempt to arrange the pertinent phenomena in some sort of orderly sequence of interrelationships. In chemistry this led to the basic distinction between elements and compounds, and to the periodic table; in biology the Linnaean taxonomy led to a glimpse of the fundamental continuity of development from simple to complex animals and ultimately to theories of evolution.

During the major portion of its history, psychopathology has been occupied with the effort of classifying the great number of types of behavioral disorder that have been observed and described. As a result, the literature of the science is burdened with an imposing nomenclature of "disease types" and "symptom complexes" and "syndromes." In the course of our discussion we will meet with "psychoses" and "psychoneuroses" and "constitutional reaction types," with "schizophrenia" and "manic-depressive psychosis" and "involutional melancholia," with "neurotic character disturbances" and "mental deficiency," and a hundred more terms referring in one way or another to the multitudinous aspects of disordered or pathological behavior. *All these words refer to ways in which people have been observed to behave.* Some of the words are meant as shorthand descriptions or references to

171

rather constantly occurring groups of symptoms, such that when one symptom of the group is observed in a given individual, the other symptoms of that group may be expected to occur in the same person. Some of the words refer primarily to the possible causes of the disorder. "Manic-depressive psychosis" receives its name purely on the basis of observable symptoms of mania and depression; "neurasthenia," on the other hand, is a term that denotes a specific cause, being used to describe a condition in which a weakness or lack of vitality in the nervous system was postulated as a cause of the behavior in question.

Whatever the origin of the terms or the basis of classification of disordered behavior that they imply, it is clear that the behavior they label constitutes our problem. Before a discussion of causative factors can be meaningful to the student he must have some idea of the nature of this problem. Thus this section is devoted to a descriptive summary of the types of disordered behavior, following a more or less conventional classificatory scheme. In this section, through case studies and description of symptoms, the points of divergence and the areas of resemblance between ordered and disordered behavior should become apparent. *At the outset it should be quite definitely understood that no possible classification of behavior can result in mutually exclusive categories.* The same is true, of course, of all biological facts. There are common elements that cut across the arbitrarily erected dividing lines. A classification of infectious diseases, for example, can only separate the possible infections in a partial manner. Certain symptoms, such as fever, dehydration, increased white-cell count, and cardiovascular changes may be common to all or a great number of the possible infectious diseases. The same is true of behavior disorders. Certain aspects of mental disease are protean in their manifestations; indeed, the naive observer may be more impressed by the *similarities* than by the *differences* on his first introduction. Only continued and detailed consideration of the behavior will show that differences do exist, and that they are sufficiently reliable to warrant certain distinctions that the classifications make between various sorts of disturbed behavior.

To approach classification as merely an exercise in terminology, however, is not our aim. We wish to determine the continuities and interrelationships that exist between all mental disorders. In order to do this we must adopt a consistent point of view, an hypothesis, concerning the basic ways in which these disorders are related. The hypothesis we use is only one of several possible ways of accounting for the phenomena, and the student should keep this in mind in his study of the material to be presented.

Stated briefly, our hypothesis is as follows: *All behavior disturbances are attempts of the organism to restore a disturbed equilibrium at any or all of the levels of adaptation to life.* Symptoms are the overt manifestations of this struggle, and the whole gamut of "diseases" are basically and inherently attempts to avoid pain and injury. We view the organism as being placed in problem situations, of having strong motivation to solve the problems and attain the goals appropriate to the motives involved. We assume that the organism brings certain potentialities in the way of abilities and skills to bear on the problems, and that its success is dependent upon the appropriateness of such assets to the particular problem involved. We further assume that, for a given organism, some problems are not immediately soluble with its particular equipment, and that repeated attempts at solution meet with continued frustration and failure. Behavior is, however, subject to variation in kind and direction until some sort of resolution of the disequilibrium is achieved. The type of behavior that results in problem solution, we further assume, will be retained and repeated in similar situations. If the solution of the problem is only partial, or if it involves further disequilibrium in other aspects of the individual's life, the solution techniques so learned are sometimes pathological. *The classification of mental diseases is then looked upon as an approximate catalogue of techniques for adjustment that have proven inadequate in one way or another, but which have had sufficient rewarding results to insure their retention by the organism.*

If we look at the variety of mental disease in this way, we should expect to find some sort of internal relationship between them. To a certain extent we might anticipate that a hierarchy of maladjustment could be found, and that there would be a development of disordered behavior from simple and elementary to complex and all-inclusive. This follows from the assumption of trial-and-error behavior in problem solution. If faulty solution attempts fail to remove the barrier, other techniques must be used. If the result is an adequate solution of the problem, the behavior is not of immediate concern to the psychopathologist. If, on the other hand, these additional solution attempts also fail, we have the picture of an organism being driven to ever more drastic and deviating ways of dealing with its difficulties.

Our classification scheme, then, will start with what appears to be the most elementary example of a life-problem situation and the first evidence of disordered reaction to it. These are, respectively, *avoidance of pain or injury,* and *anxiety.* We shall attempt to show that anxiety is itself painful and intolerable, and that it thus becomes the source of an avoidance motive in its own right. In its attempts to avoid anxiety, the organism then shows one or many of the possible problem-solution techniques. Because anxiety poses peculiar requirements of its own with respect to avoidance techniques, we shall try to demonstrate that it plays a significant role in the development of all other types of disordered behavior, and that *all types are basically techniques of reducing or avoiding anxiety.*

VII

Anxiety

Life is a dream in the night, a fear among fears,
A naked runner lost in a storm of spears.

—SYMONS

Fear of danger is ten thousand times more terrifying than
danger itself, when apparent to the eyes; and we find the
burden of anxiety greater, by much, than the evil which we
are anxious about.

—DEFOE, *Robinson Crusoe*

Anxiety and Fear

THE PSYCHOLOGICAL EXPERIENCE OF FEAR

We have seen that living is a constant struggle to maintain an equilibrium that is always being disturbed by our own demands and by the environment that surrounds us. When motives are impeded, when conflict seems to reduce the possibility of attaining the ends demanded by our needs, when internal weakness or environmental circumstances appear as obstacles to our adjustment, we often experience the emotions of *fear* or *apprehension.* So universally are these emotional experiences found in the maladjusted person that it is not overemphasis to say that *fear is the passageway to disordered behavior of all kinds.* This chapter will be devoted to a discussion of the many ways that fear acts as a factor in psychopathology.

To define "fear" is difficult. The dictionary tells us that fear is "an emotion characterized by dread or expectation of harm." The Greeks spoke of fear as "an irrational recoil from an object." Although we commonly think of fear in terms of those things we are afraid of, the fear itself is primarily an internal state of readiness to avoid or retreat from that which appears threatening to us. Such situations are common in the lives of all animals, and man's development of complex social structures has not eliminated the sources of harm or danger. Rather, if our impressions are at all reliable, mankind faces a greater variety of threatening circumstances than any other animal.

A true picture of fear as a psychological experience can only be achieved by examining the general adjustmental setting in which it occurs. Physiologically, fear is an emergency reaction, a provision for ensuring effective avoidance of harm. When we are afraid, our hearts beat faster, sending the blood more rapidly through the skeletal muscles of the body; an increase in the rate of breathing delivers a larger amount of oxygen to the bloodstream. Many other physiological changes occur, all of which tend to prepare us for more vigorous action. In a primitive way, and under certain specific conditions, fear is an optimal adjustive response to stress. Even in the conditions where fear is pathological and maladjustive, its properties spring from the original adaptive purpose that it served.

OBJECT-FEAR AND ANXIETY

All fears have the element of avoidance or "readiness to run" in common, and to some extent there is no clear dividing line between "normal" and pathological fear. A secondary classification can be made, however, which is of critical importance to our subject. For the moment, let us differentiate between (1) *object-fear* and (2) *anxiety*. In object-fear, the avoidance reactions are made with respect to real circumstances that imply physical or social harm. A child running from an angry dog, a man leaping out of the path of an oncoming car, the attempt to raise money to avoid foreclosure of a mortgage—in such instances the threat is actual and present. Secondly, in object-fear, there is a recognition by the person of the particular aspects of his situation that are causing the avoidance response. He knows and can verbalize the real source of his danger. He has, in the sense we have used the word, *insight* for the factors causing the fear. His avoidance responses, therefore, are most likely adaptive and remove him from the threatening circumstances. Such fear reactions are most usual and common to all of us; without them it is doubtful if we could survive for long in a world that does present very real dangers to our adjustment at all points of the life continuum.

At the other extreme of the psychological scale of fears is the pathological condition that is commonly called *anxiety*. In anxiety the person goes through the same sort of fearful experience but lacks insight for the causative factors. He is unable to tell what he is afraid of. In its most extreme form, anxiety appears as "objectless fear" or fear without apparent cause. Fear of the mysterious or the unknown is an appropriate example of anxiety. The old Cornish prayer,

> From ghoulies and ghosties
> And Long-Leggety beasties
> And Things That go "bump" in the night;
> Oh Lord, deliver us

originated as a formula for protecting the suppliant from unknown dangers. Primitive peoples the world over have endowed the universe around them with such threatening qualities. As knowledge increased, anxiety concerning the unknown decreased. Among individuals in our own culture there is a certain degree of recapitulation of this sequence. As children we entertain more anxiety about the dark and all it may contain than we do as adults. With experience and education we find most such fears-without-object becoming of minimal importance.

Because of this lack of insight in anxiety there is frequently a failure on the part of the anxious person to identify his disturbed condition for what it is. The physiological symptoms may receive his major attention, and such fear as he experiences may be an alarm reaction to his bodily disturbance. Thus, it is rather frequent for a physician to meet a patient who has come for medical advice because of a "heart attack," and to find that the patient has been attending to the rapid heart beat and increased respiration which often accompany anxiety. This is well described by Stekel:

The "nervous heart" is the most common form of anxiety feelings. This is easily understandable. In ordinary fear the heart beats faster. The patients experience either a violent commotion in the heart which manifests itself in palpitation, or they complain of their heart "standing still." The changing of the rhythmical beats of the heart from rhythmical to arhythmical is also a common source of complaint. The heart is said to "flutter." Others say: "I feel a vibration as if I had no heart, a sense of void, as if there were a stone in its place; there is a weight inside me, as if my heart were some foreign substance." Another lady says: "A vague feeling as if everything were too tight, as if my heart were trying to escape from my body. I feel a sense of oppression, of pulling, as if it was made of indiarubber." Some complain that the heart is not in order. It beats very fast, then intermits, and then begins to go slowly again. Something must be wrong.[1]

Finally, we come to a most important distinction between object-fear and anxiety. In the former we are reacting to threats that are a part of our known present situation. In anxiety the reaction is to some danger or conflict or frustration that is vaguely or poorly localized in both time and space. The type of experience that we ordinarily speak of as "worry" may have a large component of anxiety. Worry is an unpleasant reaction to vague future threats in which the elements of the situation are only approximately identified. Thus, a parent "worries" about his children, a businessman "worries" about the future state of the market, a child "worries" about the darkness outside his bedroom. In each case some part of the situation is recognized as threatening or frustrating. In addition, however, all these anxiety situations deal with a type of "future" that is vague and indefinite, and in which no definite avoidance reaction is possible. Further, in each case, as clinical studies tell us, the individual is not aware of all, or even the major, motives involved in his emotional experience. Trouble is anticipated in some particular zone of life experience, but the person is unable to answer in any specific way *why* he expects the grief to occur in just such a situation. The motives that give rise to the anticipated frustration are buried below his level of awareness and, as in all anxiety experiences, the emotion is dominant and the reaction is vague and not well directed toward removing the causes of the fear.

In summary, then, anxiety is a form of fear experience that is differentiated from normal object-fear in several ways. First, there is a lesser degree of insight for the causes of anxiety. Secondly, anxiety is sometimes experienced most directly in terms of its physical manifestations and is not correctly identified by the person. Thirdly, anxiety is fear prompted by anticipation of future threat and thus provides no immediate effective avoidance response.

[1] Wilhelm Stekel (1923), *Conditions of Nervous Anxiety and Their Treatment*, p. 35. (Translated by Rosalie Gabler.) London: Routledge and Kegan Paul, Ltd.

Symptomatology of Anxiety

PSYCHOLOGICAL SYMPTOMS

The principal psychological symptom of anxiety is a feeling of fear and apprehension, which may be diffuse and vague with respect to any specific aspect of the environment or the patient's life as he knows it. In anxiety there is often reported a feeling of "impending doom," or a conviction that "something terrible is going to happen," although the patient is unable to state in what area of his life this will happen and cannot give any good grounds for the feeling. These emotional experiences form a constant background to the patient's activities, effectively hindering him in the performance of any task. They may extend even into his sleep, causing insomnia or waking him after a short period of drowsing (see Wexberg, 1949, and Riesenman, 1950). Quite commonly the patient reports various sorts of terrifying dreams in which he is threatened by death or disgrace. In less extreme cases the apprehension is milder and is manifested primarily by boredom or a "what's the use of it all" emotional coloring to everyday happenings. In such cases the dominant subjective feeling is one of fatigue and exhaustion. The patient finds that even the contemplation of performing a task in the future is painful.

PHYSIOLOGICAL SYMPTOMS

Attending these psychological symptoms, and many times overwhelming them, are the physiological manifestations. Identical with the bodily changes in any strong emotion of fear or anger, they are clearly an expression of the mobilization of the body for physical effort. The role of the autonomic nervous system and the glands and vegetative organs that it controls are of paramount significance. We have already mentioned the changes in heart-rate, blood pressure, respiration, digestive and excretory functions. In addition, there is often a state of increased tension in the striped or skeletal musculature, due to increased metabolic activity. The person may experience these symptoms as an "inability to relax," a state of "jumpiness." They are often a part of the explanation of the restless sleep and the excessive fatigue of the anxious person. They may constitute a vicious spiral to the anxiety that originally caused them, since the patient often reverses cause and effect and attributes the cause of his symptoms to one or another of the organs that are responding to the general emotional situation.

ACUTE ANXIETY

When these symptoms occur with sudden great severity, the condition is referred to as *acute anxiety,* or *anxiety state.* Here the symptoms may become so intense as to amount to a panic. The following instance is typical:

Case 11. The patient, A. Z., had his first acute anxiety attack following a pre-Lenten drinking party. At the party he had succeeded in gaining a rather advanced state of intoxication and had been put to bed by friends. The following morning he slept until after noon, thus missing all opportunity to attend Mass. Being a strict and ardently religious Catholic, this caused him considerable emotional disturbance. His immediate reaction was to blame his wife and friends for not waking him in time to go to church. After some argument and soothing, he seemed to be calmed and to forget the incident.

A few hours later, while seated at the table eating, he complained of a feeling of faintness, jumped up, and rushed outdoors. His wife followed and found him seated on the back steps, breathing heavily. He said that he was deathly ill and needed more fresh air. When she urged him to go back into the house and lie down, he refused and instead asked to be taken for a ride in the "fresh air." Since he appeared so urgent and desperate, Mrs. Z. consented to drive him around. They had gone only a few blocks when he began to cry and said that he felt he was dying. His wife, very much alarmed, returned to their home and called their physician. Mr. Z. continued to talk in an agitated manner, requesting that his relatives be summoned, that the priest be called to administer the last rites, that he was afraid to die, and other similar remarks. His appearance was of extreme fright, with dilated pupils, contorted facial expression, rapid irregular breathing, excessive perspiration, and a coarse shuddering tremor, which periodically engulfed his whole body. By the time the doctor came he had convinced both himself and his wife that he was suffering from a heart attack. A sedative was administered and the panic slowly subsided.

The patient's description of his attack as seen in retrospect, is interesting. "If you haven't experienced it, there aren't words that can make you realize what a dreadful feeling came over me. I felt that I was going to die in some terrible manner in the next few minutes, and that I was completely helpless to do anything about it. In some dim way I seemed to feel that I was being punished for something, but whether it was for something I had done or something I was going to do I couldn't decide. My only impulse was to move around, to run away from the horrible empty feeling inside me. Although the doctor told me it was something in my mind, it still

seems too vivid and real to be completely mental. It must have had something to do with all the drinking I did the night before."

In this case it is apparent that a connection existed between the
drinking and the anxiety. The patient, however, showed only a partial
insight for its nature, ascribing the panic to a fancied physiological
effect of the alcohol. Nearer the truth is the possibility that he unconsciously pictured the drinking as a voluntarily sinful act, which had
the effect of producing another departure from his moral code, namely
missing attendance at church. The fear of impending doom was almost
a literal interpretation of the Biblical statements as to the consequence
of sin. Therapeutic interviews later disclosed a long background of
conflict between the patient's desires to conform to the teachings of his
religion and his desires for conformity with the social group to which
he belonged. This group was fond of parties and rather heavy indulgence in drinking. In the patient's past history was found a rather
constant pattern of alternation between party-going and "swearing-off."
In this he demonstrated the basic pattern of the incipient neurotic. On
either horn of his dilemma he was uncomfortable, since gratifying one
set of urges meant stifling the other. The end result was inevitably
an emotional disturbance, which, in the appropriate circumstances,
emerged as a panic state that dominated his entire personality.

CHRONIC ANXIETY

In some personalities anxiety becomes chronic. It is seldom manifested in dramatic "panics" or "attacks," and it does not lead to active
formation of other types of symptoms. Instead, the person seems to
have a constant undercurrent of apprehension and fear of the future,
which does not quite reach the surface of his personality, and yet
which is reflected in any detailed study of the everyday stream of his
life. Such individuals are the "worriers," whose anticipation of the
worst possible outcome of any adventure effectively prevents them
from ever having any.

An old gentleman of our acquaintance showed such a pattern. For
twenty years he never started out on an automobile trip without dire
predictions of disaster. He would never venture into the mountains
during the winter, spring, or fall because of the "danger of being
lost in a blizzard." He disliked and avoided business or vacation proj-

ects that would take him into strange populated areas "because of all the dangerous city traffic" and had equally firm fears about the desert, the plains (tornadoes), and the seashore. When social circumstances and a very influential wife would combine to expose him to a new environment and he found it to be safe, he would then become enthusiastic. On the whole, however, he contrived to lead a life sufficiently narrow to protect himself from even a very active apprehension. Negation of change was a firmly established pattern.

It is possible to show experimentally how chronic anxiety may affect human activity. An example of this type of study is Taylor's (1951) experiment showing the relationship between conditioning and chronic anxiety. Using a test of anxiety (Taylor, 1953), she selected from a large group of college students two experimental groups consisting of students who were presumably (a) highly anxious and (b) non-anxious, respectively. The individual subject was seated facing a small, circular, opaque window. The window was lighted and suddenly became brighter. About one-half second later, a brief puff of air was applied to the subject's right eye, causing a reflex eyeblink. However, after a number of repetitions of pairing of the light change and the air puff, the eyeblink began to occur with the change in brightness preceding the air puff. Thus, the eyeblink became a conditioned response. In comparing the two groups, Taylor found (as shown in Figure 8) that the anxious group conditioned much more rapidly than the non-anxious, and, in addition, reached a much higher level of conditioning at the end of eighty trials.

FREE AND BOUND ANXIETY

A useful distinction in classification is sometimes made between "free-floating" and "channeled" or "bound" anxiety. In the former there is only the pervasive uneasiness of the anxiety, without a definite cause being identified. Persky, Grinker, and Mirsky (1950) have published an excellent example.

Case 12. Illustrative . . . is S. S., a 37 year old male barber who complained of fear of death, suffocating sensations, numbness of hands and lips and panic attacks. His symptoms began about one year prior to his first visit after a saphenous vein ligation. At first he had a great deal of preoccupation with the possibility of embolism about which he had read, but gradually his anxiety became generalized. There developed a generalized foreboding and apprehension which was present constantly, becoming irregularly worse in attacks of panic during which he would show all the somatic manifestations of acute anxiety such as dilated pupils, tremor of the facial muscles and hands, pallor of the face, tachycardia and hypernoea

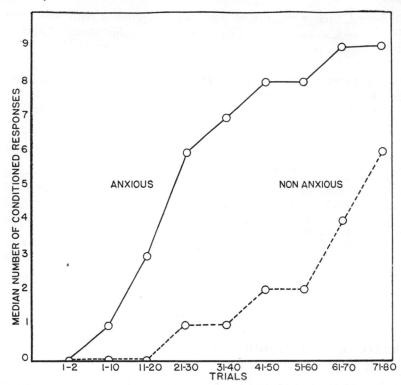

FIGURE 8. *Rates of conditioning for groups of anxious and nonanxious individuals* (from Janet A. Taylor [1951], "The relationship of anxiety to the conditioned eyelid response." *J. Exper. Psychol., 41,* 81-92. Reprinted by permission of the American Psychological Association).

and he would be impelled to run from his shop into a doctor's office. Physical examination was essentially negative. Psycho-dynamic studies revealed that the patient's nuclear anxiety was related to a strict and forceful father who compelled the patient to leave school and become a barber, which he detested, in the father's shop. Strong unconscious hostility to the father, protected by passive homosexual and submissive attitudes toward him, was accentuated by the operation which symbolized punishment (castration) and his ego was constantly deluged by signals of danger (anxiety) indicating that the disturbing hostility was approaching consciousness. No defensive maneuvers against the anxiety were possible.[2]

[2] H. Persky, R. R. Grinker, and I. A. Mirsky (1950), "The excretion of hippuric acid in subjects with free anxiety." *J. clin. Invest., 29,* 110-111.

In bound anxiety the patient associates the anxiety with something specific as is shown in the following example from Persky, Grinker, and Mirsky (1950).

Case 13. "Illustrative . . . is B. C., a 19 year old female who had, two months prior to hospital admission, developed spasmodic twitchings of the entire body. These began after being awakened suddenly by children of her employer who frightened her. Neurological examination revealed no evidence of disease of the nervous system. The past life was full of evidence of rejection by mother and grandmother. In adolescence she had been sent to a reform school on the false charge of having sexual relations. After discharge she really became promiscuous and was sentenced to a house of correction. Later she fell in love with her employer and with his wife lived out a triangular sexual arrangement. The patient's twitching represented a conversion symptom reminiscent of jerkings of her body while being whipped at reform school. Under pentothal the patient admitted a fear that her present life would evoke punishment from her mother and a return to reform school. This fear was expressed only in her symptoms although the symptoms themselves evoked secondary apprehension and crying.[3]

Causes of Anxiety

ANXIETY AS A PRODUCT OF CONFLICT AND FRUSTRATION

Anxiety arises from conflict and frustration. It would never appear if all a person's motives were smoothly and immediately satisfied. Since anxiety is allied to fear, the motives whose frustration cause anxiety are usually motives of escape or avoidance. So, in looking for the causes of anxiety, it is evident that we must investigate more carefully the nature of the avoidance response and the situations that prompt it.

DEVELOPMENT OF ANXIETY FROM PRIMITIVE AVOIDANCE BEHAVIOR

Drives or motives originally arise as consequences of tissue-needs. At a vegetative level, activity in the organism is in response to these needs. How does such response come about? Let us begin with a very simple example. If a baby brings its hand near a hot object, say a candle flame, and is overstimulated in a painful manner, a general

---

[3] *Ibid.,* p. 111.

avoidance reaction will ensue. The tissue-need in this case was evidently *to get less of the stimulation,* to reduce the strength or amount of stimulation. Most tissue-need states, such as hunger and thirst, also are accompanied by uncomfortable or painful stimulation of various sorts. If a baby becomes hungry it will go through much the same type of frantic random action, and if motion pictures were taken of the candle incident (with the camera outside the child's field) and of the pre-feeding behavior, it would be difficult to say whether the baby's movements were prompted by hunger or pain. In both pain and hunger, the common element is avoidance of overstimulation. Because of a certain teleological orientation of our everyday speech and thought, we often make the mistake of saying that the baby "avoids" the candle and "seeks" the food. At a later stage of development and learning this may be true in part (see Hebb, 1949), but it is not the case with a naive organism. The situation is probably similar for all vegetative needs. Restoration of equilibrium is originally an avoidance reaction, *a protection against overstimulation.* Failure to respond in this manner would mean death for the organism (see Holt, 1931).

There is, however, one very important difference between the candle incident and the hunger situation. In the former, restless random avoidance reactions are all that is needed to reduce the level of harmful stimulation. In the latter, and in most appetitive situations, random avoidance movements of themselves are not enough. The baby, if not fed, could move around in its crib until exhausted by starvation, without bringing it closer to an adequate satisfaction of its needs. Because the goal is so specific, and because in later life avoidance and seeking activity become so well blended, it is easy to lose sight of the fact that the behavior originally grew out of avoidance responses.

If these avoidance drives are frustrated, the situation may become rapidly intolerable for the organism. The situation assumes the proportion of an emergency, and soon all the reserves of bodily energy are called upon in an attempt to break through the barriers that restrain the organism in its attempt at avoidance. This mobilization of bodily resources is the biological basis of emotion. It is from such a state of affairs that we see those familiar symptoms of emotionality, the rapid heart-beat, the increased respiratory rate, the cessation of digestive action, the blushing or pallor, and all the rest. These symptoms will be about the same in the baby or young child when almost any type of drive is frustrated. As the infant develops and behavior becomes more differentiated, it becomes able to cope with many of its frustrations. It develops smooth and rapid avoidance of candle flames and many other forms of immediately painful stimulation. It learns techniques of satisfying hunger and thirst. In proportion to the adequacy of these techniques frustration is diminished and so is the corresponding emotionality.

Consider, however, those situations in which the individual cannot identify some of the essential elements of the frustration. Usually the unidentified element is either the motivational complex or the type of goal that will reduce the tension. The possibilities of making direct avoidance responses are then materially lessened, and the behavior will assume more or less the characteristics observed in the baby who has no adequate technique for avoiding hunger pangs. That is to say, the person's behavior will be relatively random and poorly oriented with respect to the precise needs of the situation. In this state of affairs *the person will then follow any pattern of action that has any appearance of successfully removing the discomfort of the frustration.* The emotional symptoms of the frustration become motivational in character, and impart a generalized direction of *avoidance* to the individual's activities. The organization of responses to anxiety follows the same general course as the development of any other complex behavior, and our analysis of the learning process is as applicable here as in any other learning situation.[4]

TYPES OF CONFLICT LEADING TO ANXIETY

What sort of conflicts result in anxiety? We have already seen that they must be imperfectly identified by the patient, that they must, to use the current terminology, be largely unconscious. In addition, to produce more than a passing twinge of dimly felt fear, they must

---

[4] Apparently, however, a learning theory analysis of the development of responses to anxiety requires a rather complicated extension of present theories to account for the facts. One such difficulty is the lack of extinction of these responses under experimental conditions that should produce extinction. A possible interpretation is that permanent or partially permanent conditioning occurs with avoidance responses to strong fear stimuli. See R. L. Solomon and L. C. Wynne (1954), "Traumatic avoidance learning: the principles of anxiety conservation and partial irreversibility." *Psychol. Rev., 61,* 353-385.

have an element of persistence. For the most part, this means that the conflict must be between vital and enduring motives. The slight and momentary frictions of daily living, the delay at the bus stop, the poorly cooked meal, or the passing discomfort of a head cold are not enough to produce anxiety. The situation lasts for too short a time, the motives involved are superficial, and the gratification is not too long delayed. Anxiety, it should be remembered, is an emergency response to important exigencies. It is an old, indeed a primitively archaic response, but it arises only when the person *is* in the sort of situation which, for him, is threatening to his integrity. As Mowrer (1939) has pointed out, anxiety may be a reflection of the discrepancy between this emergency mobilization and the lack of adequate action which follows. Such situations are reflections of disequilibrium at basic life levels, and the results of such disequilibria are the important drives and motives of our lives. This means that anxiety is connected with conflicts among basic cellular, individual, and social motives.

In looking at the gamut of vegetative needs of the organism it is evident that our culture generally makes fairly adequate provision for their supply. Air is free, and people who refrain from climbing very high mountains or stratospheric flying or submarine adventures are seldom frustrated in their need for oxygen. The possible exceptions to this are usually acute consequences of various physical diseases, such as pneumonia, or of certain chronic conditions, such as asthma, where often the "air-hunger" is secondary, psychologically speaking, to other types of conflict.

Food is something more of a problem, particularly when it is linked to our general economic condition. Consistent frustration of hunger may produce explosively aggressive behavior and may also produce a threatening apprehension and anxiety. But, if the presence of food be granted, there is very little inhibition to the manner of ingestion, or to the particular food selection, imposed by society. Aside from certain localized social taboos, as against cannibalism, and certain religious prohibitions, the average individual who is lucky enough to get sufficient food does not find himself involved in much conflict over the realization of his goal. Conflicts centering around the hunger drive are usually secondary to other problems on either a physiological or a social level, as in the allergies and the semi-voluntary restrictions of diet of the person who feels a social need to lose weight.

The problem of shelter, like that of food, is so closely connected with various socio-economic factors that probably most of the potential for anxiety arises from these aspects of the situation.

Thirst is likewise only rarely a primary factor in the development of anxiety. For the great majority of the earth's inhabitants, water is not a scarce item, and few restrictions have been developed in connection with securing or consuming it.

Common to all of the basic needs thus far mentioned is one circumstance that rather effectively limits their role in the causation of anxiety. Consistent and chronic frustration of any of these needs leads within a very short time to the death of the organism. Almost all human societies are so organized that the person deprived of the minimum essentials of life is cared for by the collective action of the society. This care may be a crude and direct abandonment of the sufferer or an equally direct execution of him, or it may take the form of charitable support, as is the case with most of the peoples we call "civilized." In either case, the problem does not continue as a chronic state of severe need, a requisite condition, as we have seen, for anxiety.

One biological-need factor that directly meets our criterion, namely the sexual drive, remains. Tensions on this level can persist for long periods of time without directly causing the death of the frustrated organism, although a general frustration of sexual expression would, obviously, serve to eliminate a species. It is also true that no other biological motive is so completely regulated; in our culture such regulations and taboos penetrate almost all aspects of sexual relations. It was this fact that probably led Freud to erect a psychological system based entirely upon the consequences of sexual frustration. We know now, of course, that frustration and conflict at various levels of social motivation are just as effective causes of anxiety, but, as far as the basic drives are concerned, Freud was correct in placing the strongest emphasis on sexual needs, since they are, of all the biological urges, the most consistently subject to frustration.

It should be clear that our behavior is never the result of needs operating in isolation. This is true to some extent of all living organisms, and it is especially and completely true of the socialized human being. We behave in a social environment, and our needs are worked out in terms of that environment. So when we talk of the sexual need and its frustrations we should recognize that both the need and the barriers to its expression are as much a social as a physiological characteristic. Indeed, as Cameron (1948) has said, all the problems of psychopathology are, in reality, "biosocial" problems. This is particularly true of the whole of sexual activity. Adequate, normal heterosexual behavior is perforce a social act, involving more than one person. It is possible that some of the force and pervasiveness of its social regulation proceeds from a recognition of this fact. Certainly, it is the manifest difficulty of integrating adequate sexual behavior into the over-all demands of the social environment that makes sex a large factor in anxiety and other forms of disordered behavior.

Neither sexual abstinence nor sexual expression as such is an adequate cause of anxiety. Rather, it is the conflict between the desire for sexual activity and the opposing forces of the person's social and moral training that leads to anxiety in this important sphere of adjustment. When so much of our early training is directed toward inhibition of sex behavior, it is not unusual to find that sexual acts or thoughts can reactivate a fear of censure or punishment. As one young woman told her physician, "after having been married for two years I still feel uncomfortable and embarrassed when my husband makes love to me. I seem always to see an image of the disapproving face of my mother." This patient had received a thoroughly repressive training in sexual matters as a child. She was the only daughter of a woman who had divorced her husband shortly after the birth of the child and who had taught the child that sex was a "nasty business." As a result of such training a real conflict was established with an incapacitating anxiety as the product.

An examination of the role of sexual behavior and mores in other cultural groups tends to support the supposition that anxiety with sexual causation is the result of conflict. Margaret Mead (1928, 1935) has shown that no adolescent anxiety reactions occur concerning sexual matters in those groups whose mores do not include so strong an emphasis on sexual suppression. Similar studies indicate the great amount of anxiety that may be occasioned in a person over any aspect of behavior that is subject to strong social inhibitions within his group. Again we may cite the complex way in which sexual motivation is allied to ego-satisfaction and to community standards. When we speak of mature sexual adjustment as involving a monogamous marriage between two people whose sexual relations are only a part of a more extensive social contract, we have indicated the immense amount of integration of a large number of motives needed to make this adjustment possible.

The sources of anxiety may be traced, perhaps even more frequently, to conflicts between more purely individual and social motives. In our culture the emphasis on success and achievement through competition, the needs for security and recognition by our fellows, the motivation to comply with the standards of our group, all are fruitful sources of anxiety. In many instances these motives are given greater urgency by their connection with the underlying biological urges. When "reaching the top" is made one of the most important life goals, and when the society in addition evolves all sorts of stipulations as to the manner of accomplishing this goal, there is great possibility of conflict. Urgency is given to our strivings, and poignancy to our conflicts, by the underlying necessity to provide ourselves with food and shelter. Many an aggressive impulse toward a person in authority looms in direct opposition to the necessity of holding a job.

A rather frequently occurring example of these lower-level motivational conflicts, which may only appear in awareness as feelings of anxiety, is found in the repressed hostility that is engendered by many of our interpersonal relationships. Parents with extremely overprotective attitudes toward their children often express anxiety of various kinds. Superficially they appear to "worry" about the possible threats and disasters that the children may encounter. Deeper clinical study reveals, however, that they have deep-seated hostility toward the children, that the hostility gives rise to all sorts of wishes and fantasy, which picture harmful situations in relationship to their children. These wishes, so contrary to their own training and their own higher ideals, produce conflicts, and thus anxiety. The following case illustrates this principle in another type of social relationship:

Case 14. J. C. was a recent graduate of an Officer's Candidate School. He had done so well as to receive a special commendation from the commanding officer of the school. He was, therefore, treated somewhat leniently when he disappeared for three days shortly after reporting to his first duty assignment as an officer. Instead of facing charges of AWOL or being brought before a board of inquiry, he was reprimanded and sent back to duty. When, the next week, he again disappeared and did not show up for ten days, a different approach was made. J. C. was placed in the hospital for observation. When interviewed, he said that he had felt a great sense of restlessness and uneasiness ever since becoming an officer and had started drinking as a means of relief. His drinking bouts had confused him still further and he had spent his time while absent from the post in alternating between drinking and worrying about what would happen to him if he came back to duty.

His past history showed that he had done well in college and had a position of some responsibility in a bank prior to entering the army. Shortly before going to Officer Candidate School, he had met a waitress and had married her after knowing her less than a week. He received enough leave to take her to his home town and introduce her to his family. The marriage and the personality of the girl were twin causes of a great deal of family concern. His leave was spent in family quarrels in which J. C. hotly defended his bride and came close to breaking relations with his mother and sister, toward both of whom he had always been unusually close. When notified that he had been accepted as an officer candidate, he sent his wife to his mother's home, an arrangement that had little to recommend it save a compelling economic necessity. The wife and mother quarreled bitterly and both wrote J. C. frequently while he was in OCS presenting him with an ever-increasing problem of choosing between them.

Shortly after his graduation, J. C. wrote his mother an angry letter, telling her that he was in love with his wife, and that he never wanted to see his mother again. He then asked his wife to join him at his new assignment. It was the afternoon of the day that he made this decision that he went on the first spree. During intensive interview the patient denied that his problem presented any conflict to him, although he could give no other adequate reason for his state of tension and uneasiness. He said that he had made a decision and that he was happy in anticipation of soon being reunited with his wife. He attributed his "nervousness" to overwork and concentration while in the OCS.

It was then decided to probe the matter more deeply, and the patient was given an intravenous dose of sodium amytal sufficient to make him more relaxed and somewhat drowsy. He then told of a persistent, recurring dream he had been having, in which his wife and mother were walking down the street of his home town, apparently on a shopping tour. Suddenly a truck or a streetcar would run down his wife, missing his mother. With his wife lying on the ground, horribly injured and bleeding, J. C. would run to his mother, paying no attention to his wife, and take her away from the scene of the accident. It was this dream that terrified the patient, but upon awakening he could only recall that he felt worried about his wife and felt that something terrible had happened to her. As the time approached for her journey to his new station, the anxiety increased. This material was interpreted to the patient as a natural expression of hostility toward his wife, who had been the agent in the breaking of emotional relationships with his family. The dreams were easily seen as a direct expression of primitive emotional wishes that his wife be eliminated; since these wishes were so contrary to the love he had for her, he was placed in a violent conflict situation, which he had attempted to escape by literally running away.

Are people always aware of these conflicts? In the main they are not. The socially inhibiting factors rarely are external to the person. Rather, they are as much a part of his personality as are the desires that they oppose or regulate. The moral, social, and ethical lessons learned in childhood are not remembered individually; they operate below the level of awareness. We become aware of them only indirectly through the emotions we feel in situations where they motivate us to avoidance. One is aware of his inhibitions toward theft only in situations where he is tempted to steal. If he is constantly placed in such situations, and if the motives toward theft are strong, the conflict may achieve that chronicity which is essential for the development of anxiety. If early training has produced a strong enough avoidance to theft, the person may quite possibly refuse to recognize that he has a desire to steal. This refusal we call repression, and it fulfills a condition for the arousal of anxiety.

REPRESSION AND ANXIETY

Anxiety always involves conflict between more or less completely repressed motives. This appears to be true even in those instances where a person appears to have a clear sense of the alternative ways of behaving that are before him. Hidden in the background are many of the motivational factors that have created his indecision. A man may be considering the offer of a new job, perhaps one which possesses many advantages over his present position. His reluctance at leaving the old job may appear to him as equally based on rational considerations. Only a thorough study of his personality may reveal that the reluctance was largely a deep-seated fear of failure, and that the new undertaking contained as many threats as rewards. If we are taught to be contemptuous of such fears of failure, and if they are incompatible with what we believe to be our personalities, they may easily be repressed. If so, they may be manifested only by that fear that does not recognize its object, that is, by anxiety.

The materials repressed are such wishes, needs, and memories as meet with strong personal and social disapproval. Since we are brought up to think of ourselves in ways that meet with the approbation of our parents and their culture, and since many aspects of an individual's life can never fully conform to these ideals, it is obvious that all of us have much to repress. If repression were synonymous with elimination of undesirable material, we would have to look elsewhere for a dynamics of anxiety. Unfortunately the repression is more apparent than real. We noted many ways in which repressed memories and motives influenced everyday behavior, in such matters as "slips of the tongue," seemingly chance forgetting of names or errands, and so forth. We concluded that repression was an attempt to protect the person from painful or uncomfortable feelings. This protection can be successful only if the environment does not provide forms of stimulation that activate the repressed material. Seldom, however, is a person fortunate enough to encounter such an environment. Such phenomena as language and constantly recurring internal drive conditions make environmental escape from critical stimulation difficult. The person who has suffered bereavement finds that, no matter how resolutely he attempts to completely repress memories of the loved one, chance words, snatches of a song, intonations of a voice heard on the street, can revive the painful emotions connected with his loss. In the same way the anxious person finds his fearful emotions stimulated in countless ways. When the conflicting motives are persistent, even his dreams betray him, and sleep brings new terrors. Among many combat veterans, sleep was regarded with dread because of battle dreams in which the repressed memories of fighting and of its fears were relived.

The repressed material, then, acts as a threat to good adjustment. It is as if the person were saying to himself, "If only I could keep myself from even thinking about acting in this way or that, I could remain happy." But since the individual rarely is cognizant of the tempting or the inhibiting motives, he feels only the vagueness of the threat, and this is manifested as anxiety. He is actually aware primarily of a disturbed bodily state, and as we have already said, his avoidance behavior is an attempt to reduce this uncomfortable bodily state.

INDIVIDUAL DIFFERENCES IN ANXIETY

From this analysis we can see that some anxiety is the lot of all of us. Unanswered is the important question of why some people are more anxious than others, so anxious as to be termed as being in "anxiety states" and regarded as sick patients. The conflicts normal to life in our culture can be accentuated by the type of training an individual has received, by the habitual ways in which he attempts to reduce his difficulties. The girl we mentioned a few paragraphs above was taught certain techniques for dealing with sexual problems. In a normal marriage relationship these techniques proved ineffective and thus reinforced the conflict. These poor ways of meeting problems are at the heart of all pathological anxiety, since they intensify the difficulties of normal adjustment to our complex social structure instead of making the task easier.

The efficiency with which a person meets his conflict situations is dependent upon his past training. If the past training is poor, the chances of successfully adjusting to the conflicts inherent in our social life are reduced. If the training is good, a much higher level of conflict will be tolerated before the onset of anxiety symptoms.

What, in general, is the type of past training that is favorable for the development of anxiety? Answered most broadly, we can say that a background of habits, beliefs, and convictions that are mutually contradictory and that have internal inconsistency leads to the creation of conflicting motives, and, because the training has been inconsistent, does not provide the possibility of resolving conflict by any type of unitary action.

Although the person may be unaware of the basic conflicts from which his anxiety has sprung, he is usually only too aware of its manifestations. Several investigators have shown that both children and adults quite generally harbor many unreasoning fears of various kinds. As we saw, these fears, whether they be of the dark, of examinations, or of high places, are usually the person's attempt to focus the anxiety that arises internally on some plausible external circumstance. Sometimes the object of the fear is directly connected with experiences related to the conflict. Anxiety evidenced during school examinations is very often based upon conflict over a desire to please parents or teachers, on the one hand, and a real or fancied intellectual inadequacy on the other. In such instances the student's explanation of the reasons for his anxiety may appear genuine and final. A deep clinical study, however, is usually able to show that the apparent conflict is superficial and is only a repercussion of more persistent disharmonies in the personality.

Summary

Earlier in this chapter we developed the point that most motives seem to be, in their most primitive stage of development, characterized by an *avoidance* of uncomfortable or painful stimulation. Although a large number of our most important motives later acquire adequate goal objects of such a nature that the direction of behavior is toward such goals, a substratum of the primal avoidance behavior remains and, as such, represents one of the basic defenses of most animals. By means of avoidance dangerous intensities of stimulation are evaded, and impairment or destruction of the organism is prevented. This avoidance mechanism seems to be a generalized property of all motile organisms throughout the phylogenetic scale, with man being no exception. Indeed, observation of human beings seems to indicate that avoidance is not limited to those situations in which actual physical injury is imminent, but that it also forms a large component of motivation in any situation where pain or unpleasantness occurs. We not only draw our hands back from the hot stove; we also attempt to find ways of escaping early from a boring party or we try to keep from thinking about unpleasant things that have happened to us in the past. The avoidance motives, then, help determine the direction of our behavior at ego and social levels of adjustment as well as at cellular levels.[5]

It is true, of course, that all adult human life cannot be explained on a simple (hedonistic) basis. There are too many instances of people accepting and even actively seeking uncomfortable or painful situations; there are too many examples of the contrary capacity of maintaining socially integrated behavior even at the sacrifice of ease and comfort. Nevertheless, the avoidance motives are a part of the pattern, and in psychopathology they are often of critical importance in determining the direction of behavior. The techniques of avoidance that we acquire as a consequence of our experiences with harm and threat are primarily suited to the type of situation where the danger is immediate and obvious. When the danger is vague or poorly identified, our previous techniques of avoidance are likely to prove ineffective, and the anxiety continues undiminished. As we have seen, "running away" is of no avail when that from which we are retreating is carried along with us as a part of our personalities. Direct aggression is equally ineffective. The person is forced to deal with a pain whose source cannot be localized in the environment around him. The same statement could be made about many of the common vegetative drives at early stages of their development. Here too, the discomfort is internal, and the attempts to avoid it are just as unsuccessful. But hunger and thirst can be allayed if food and water are found. The restless, relatively random

---

[5] That fear is a motive that produces selective learning has been clearly verified experimentally by Miller (1941, 1950).

attempts to escape the pangs of deprivation eventually result in a large variety of adequate environmentally oriented techniques of drive reduction. *In anxiety we see the same process, but still at a primitive level of restless avoidance.* Because the environment contains few easy sources of drive reduction for the pain of anxiety, the organism is confronted with a persistent, unreduced motivational imbalance. Therefore we conceive of anxiety as a problematic situation in its own right.

The goal of an individual suffering from anxiety is reduction of pain, and this goal acquires psychological value of such magnitude as to dwarf almost any other normal human concern. The pain of anxiety is more compelling, to judge by the variety and persistence of the attempts to escape it, than almost any other type of pain. Any technique that gives the slightest promise of success is assiduously pursued, even when the resulting behavior exposes the person to the risk of further maladjustment. Most of the examples of disordered behavior that we are to study can be interpreted as attempts to solve the problem of anxiety reduction.

If anxiety is viewed as a motivating condition, and its reduction as a problem, then we should be able to analyze the behavior of the anxious person in much the same way we approach the behavior of any organism in a learning situation. We would expect that failure of any solution attempt would be followed by variability of behavior with modified techniques. We would further expect that successful techniques would be retained and used whenever the problem was again presented. This is precisely what we do find in a study of the anxious patient. He attempts to resolve his anxiety by one means or another, and, if the anxiety still remains, he tends to vary his behavior until a solution is found that gives him surcease from discomfort. Sometimes this final solution is personally and socially adequate. Animals have survived through the ages because at least a number of individuals have been able to make successful adaptations. Our present interest, however, is in those instances where the problem solutions are inadequate in one way or another. We will find, in looking at certain clinical conditions, that the patient has discovered personally satisfying techniques of anxiety reduction to which he clings because they have removed pain. However, the technique, from an over-all point of view of social adjustment, actually creates even greater problems for both the individual and society. In the condition termed "conversion hysteria," for example, a person may develop a complete blindness or a partial paralysis. This solution may be precisely the state of affairs that will remove him from the anxiety-producing situation. A pianist dreading his first recital may find himself unable to move his arms and thus be protected from the risk of playing before a critical public. Evaluated from the standpoint of the individual's musical career, this type of adaptation is clearly faulty. Since he persists in such behavior, however, we must conclude that he is more strongly motivated to avoid playing in public. But, since he evidently has had some motivation for accomplishment as a musician, the physical symptoms that effect his withdrawal cannot solve all his problems. Thus, he actually remains in a conflict situation, and the avoidance of one discomfort is done at the cost of creating another.

The maladjusted person whose attempts to reduce anxiety are faulty typically finds himself in situations where the adjustment attempt itself brings about new conflicts and reinforces the old ones. Thus anxiety persists, and the attempt to escape becomes more and more a dominant life motive. It is possible that, since all of us dwell in an unstable environment, this attempt to escape the discomfort of anxiety is one of the major social motives. In most instances, however, our personal training and the social situation in which we exist provide useful and adequate techniques of avoidance; only when factors in either the person or the environment lead to faulty techniques does this dominant motivation force the individual into disordered behavior.

DISCUSSION QUESTIONS

1. Are we well advised in making a distinction between anxiety and fear?
2. Can you think of anything to add to our description of anxiety symptoms?
3. Are there any biological advantages to anxiety?
4. How strong a motive is anxiety in our own culture?
5. What are some useful and adequate techniques of handling anxiety?
6. What are some of your own experiences with anxiety? Try to identify those aspects of the situation that might have stimulated it.
7. What is the role of anxiety in the psychosomatic disorders?
8. Do subhuman animals experience anxiety?
9. Some philosophers claim that greater anxiety will occur when people have greater freedom to work out their own destiny. Can you evaluate this opinion?
10. Is anxiety more crippling when it is "free-floating" or when the person has "attached" it to some aspect of his environment?

SUGGESTED READINGS

P. H. Hoch and J. Zubin, eds. (1950), *Anxiety*. New York: Grune & Stratton, Inc.

R. May (1950), *The Meaning of Anxiety*. New York: The Ronald Press Company.

O. H. Mowrer (1950), *Learning Theory and Personality Dynamics*, Chapter 19. New York: The Ronald Press Company.

BIBLIOGRAPHIC SOURCES

The student may wonder why we have started our discussion of the behavior disorders with the problem of anxiety. The answer was given by Freud (1936) when he stated that anxiety is ". . . the fundamental phenomenon and main problem of neurosis."

The distinction made in the text between anxiety and object-fear is psychoanalytic in origin (Freud, 1936). Other scholars have not made this separation (White, 1948; Dollard and Miller, 1950), and Rado (1950, 1952) has argued specifically against it. An excellent discussion of the issue may be found in May (1950).

There are many good papers on the psychological symptoms of anxiety. One extensive and readily available source is N. Cameron (1947). One of the most vivid descriptions was written by the philosopher Kierkegaard (1946) in *The Concept of Dread,* originally published in 1844. For an extensive study of anxiety dreams, the student should see Harris (1948, 1951). The relationship between fatigue and anxiety is discussed in Shands and Finesinger (1952). The student interested in the measurement of fatigue should consult Schwab and DeLorme (1953).

A definitive paper on the physiological symptoms of anxiety is by D. E. Cameron (1944). May's (1950, pp. 57-67) discussion is quite stimulating. For an example of a detailed clinical and experimental investigation of one patient, see Crede, Chivers, and Shapiro (1951). The use of the electromyographic technique in the study of muscular tension under stress is developed in detail by Malmo, Shagass, and Davis (1951). Further information on physiological indices may be found in O'Kelly (1953). One issue not discussed at this point in the text is the use of physical and chemical treatment to reduce anxiety in psychiatric patients. These methods include the use of electroshock, neurosurgery, and a variety of chemicals such as insulin or metrazol. For two excellent reviews of this literature the student may read Freed, Spiegel, and Wycis (1949) and Lowenbach and Suitt (1950). Our own discussion is in Chapter XVII.

The study by Taylor (1951) cited in the text is only one of a rapidly growing literature on the effects of anxiety on human activity. In general, two experimental techniques are involved. Experimenters either select subjects suffering from a chronic anxiety state (as did Taylor) or they attempt to experimentally induce anxiety by placing subjects under stress.

With conditioning, anxious subjects are found to condition faster and extinguish the conditioned response slower than the non-anxious subjects. Welch and Kubis (1947a, 1947b) and Bitterman and Holtzman (1952) have reported these results with the conditioned psychogalvanic skin response. Taylor (1951), with the conditioned eyeblink, did not find reliable differences in extinction for her groups. Incidentally, Taylor's study was not confirmed by Hilgard, Jones, and Kaplan (1951); however, further investigation (Spence and Taylor, 1951, Spence and Farber, 1953) did support Taylor's work.

In other areas of learning, anxiety has been found to be detrimental. For example, in verbal learning, the anxious subject generally makes more errors and takes longer to learn (Malmo and Amsel, 1948; Lucas, 1952; Taylor and Spence, 1952; Montague, 1953). In the learning of motor skills, the anxious subject is slower in learning on the stylus maze (Diethelm and Jones, 1947; Farber and Spence, 1953) and in mirror drawing (Ammons, 1950). Beier (1951a) showed decrements in mirror tracking.

One of the most important areas in this literature is the effect of anxiety on intellectual functioning. A number of experimenters have reported detrimental effects of anxiety on reasoning and thinking ability (Diethelm and Jones, 1947; Welch and Diethelm, 1950; Beier, 1951a). However, in a study involving the formation and shifting of concepts, Wesley (1953) found no consistent relationship between anxiety and response tendencies.

For general reviews of the experimental literature, consult Holtzman and Bitterman (1952) and Welch (1953).

One large area of investigation not mentioned in the text is the experimental analogue of anxiety (or fear) in the learning of infra-human animals. One line of investigation stems from the conditioning experiments beginning with Pavlov, Bechterev, and particularly Liddell (Hilgard and Marquis, 1939; Liddell, 1950, 1952). A second and related series starts with the work of Mowrer (1939) and Miller (1950). These latter experiments are concerned primarily with modern learning theory and have investigated two hypotheses: first, that fear is a learned drive, and, second, that the reduction of fear is reinforcing to learning. There are several excellent summaries of this work, Mowrer (1950), Schoenfeld (1950), Dollard and Miller (1950), and Miller (1951).

The literature on children's fears is extensive (Beverly, 1942; Jersild, 1940, 1948; Liss, 1944; Ross, 1951). For a discussion of the theoretical importance of this material, see May (1950). For the use of projective techniques in the study of children's fears, see England (1946) and Darkey and Amen (1947).

The text perhaps does not emphasize enough the intimate relationship between anxiety and repression. Freud (1936) was the first to recognize that anxiety can only be understood when repression is recognized. Freud had two theories about the connection between anxiety and repression which can be expressed in one quotation (1936, p. 53), "It was anxiety which produced repression and not, as I formerly believed, repression which produced anxiety." For an excellent discussion of Freud's two theories, see Mowrer (1950).

Another area not mentioned in the text is the measurement of the existence and amount of anxiety. On the basis of some of the studies mentioned above, it has been suggested that conditioning might be used. Schiff, Dugan, and Welch (1949) reported a correlation of .52 between psychogalvanic skin response and clinical diagnosis. However, Hilgard, Jones, and Kaplan (1951) and Bitterman and Holtzman (1952) report very low correlations of this type. Spence and Taylor (1951) offer cogent reasons against the use of conditioning techniques.

A very large number of tests have been used for diagnosis. Clinical evidence has suggested that the Rorschach test might be valuable. There are a number of experimental papers but the issue is quite confused (Elizur, 1949; Kates, 1950; Eichler, 1951; Garlow, Zimet, and Fine, 1952) with some studies reporting positive results while others are generally negative. Kates (1950) found six reliable Rorschach indices which differentiated between anxious and obsessive-compulsive patients. Eichler (1951), with normal subjects and experimentally induced stress, obtained four reliable Rorschach signs out of fifteen test indices. Even more conflicting is the use of the Wechsler Bellevue Intelligence Scale. The evidence is divided between positive results (Rashkis and Welch, 1946; Purcell, *et al.*, 1952; Moldawsky and Moldawsky, 1952) and negative results (Heyer, 1949; Shoben, 1950; Warner, 1950). The Taylor Scale (Taylor, 1951, 1953), developed from the Minnesota Multiphasic Personality Inventory, has been widely used. The MMPI itself was used in a number of studies, and Welch (1952) has developed an anxiety index for it. Other tests include the Saslow Screening Test (Saslow, Counts, and DuBois, 1951; Gleser and Ulett, 1952), a questionnaire developed by Sarason and Mandler (1952), and Freeman (1953). An additional technique involves the electroencephalogram (Malmo and Shagass, 1949; Schiff, Dugan, and Welch, 1949; Ulett, *et al.*, 1952, 1953). A particularly interesting method is that of Malmo and his associates (1947, 1949, 1951) who present a standard series of pain stimuli and record many behavioral indices.

If, after wading through the preceding paragraphs, the student is still interested in further readings in anxiety, we suggest two sources for a beginning. May's (1950) book, *The Meaning of Anxiety*, is a scholarly, readable, and detailed study of the field. The second source is a symposium edited by P. H. Hoch and J. Zubin (1950) published with the title *Anxiety*. There are thirteen papers covering the historical, social, psychological, clinical, and physiological approaches to anxiety This small book contains a remarkable amount of information.

VIII

The Psychoneuroses

All things are taken from us, and become
Portions and parcels of the dreadful past.
—TENNYSON

CLASSIFICATION AND TERMINOLOGY

The classification of the psychoneuroses, as of all mental disorders, has shown progressive changes with the years. Because there is still no complete uniformity in the terms used to designate the various types of psychoneurosis, we begin our study of these conditions by a few remarks on nomenclature.

The classifications that have been made of these conditions have all been based on differentiation between groups of related symptoms. None of the accepted systems of nomenclature are based on modern notions of causation. This may be one reason for the changes we have noted. Another reason is the historical circumstance that the different symptom-complexes were first described and studied in widely separated eras. Thus, *hysteria* is a term first used by Greek physicians of the time of Hippocrates; it has survived with only minor changes to the present. Other terms are of recent origin, and many of them are short-lived, giving way to more suitable, more definitive, or more comprehensive names. *Shell-shock* and *combat fatigue* refer to syndromes that were described in World Wars I and II respectively, and both terms refer to conditions that go by other names in less troubled times. The general trend, as can be seen from an inspection of Table 8, is to expand the nomenclature in the direction of greater specificity of designation. This is the expected accompaniment of our increase in knowledge concerning these conditions.

TABLE 8

COMPARISON OF DIAGNOSTIC TERMS

Type of Symptom	*Older Term*	*More Modern Terms*
Functional paralysis, sensory disorders, amnesias, etc.	Hysteria	Conversion reaction Conversion hysteria Dissociative reaction
Phobias, compulsions, obsessions, doubts, timidity, depressions, etc.	Psychasthenia	Reactive depression Obsessive-compulsive neurosis
Hypochondriasis, functional disorders of various organ systems, fatigue, exhaustion	Neuresthenia	Anxiety state or reaction Psychosomatic condition Combat fatigue or stress reaction

The term *psychoneurosis* is used interchangeably at present with the shorter term *neurosis*. At one time a distinction was made between the two, based on a belief that some disordered behavior was mental or psychological and other conditions were due to actual pathological changes in the nerves. Now either term may be used, since they are now taken to mean the same thing. The patient whose behavior fits into this category is referred to as *psychoneurotic,* or often just *neurotic*.

Psychoneuroses as a group are to be distinguished from psychoses. These two types of condition furnish the chief problem of the psychopathologist. Differentiation between them is easier to make etymologically than in actual fact. Since the distinction is one of the first questions that occurs to the student, we shall discuss these differences in a somewhat formal and arbitrary way here and allow the likenesses and differences to assume their proper perspective as we describe the many types of each condition in turn.

The term *psychoneurosis* has come to refer to those types of symptomcomplexes or syndromes in which the disturbances of behavior do not affect a person with enough severity to terminate completely his chances of making some kind of social adjustment. They are reactions to conflict or frustration that are made within the accepted limits of social living. The anxiety states that we discussed in the last chapter, although painful and disruptive of effective and happy living, were not, for the most part, so intense or inclusive as to take away completely adjustive capacity as ordinarily defined by the society in which these patients live.

The *psychoses,* on the other hand, are usually disordered reactions of such intensity or such inclusiveness with respect to all parts of the personality that any sort of compromise with normal social requirements is impossible. It is among the psychotics that we find the majority of individuals who must be committed to hospitals for the protection of themselves and of other people in their environment. The legal term, *insanity,* applies to some (but not all) psychotics.

At least three principal points of difference between the neuroses and the psychoses may be stated. (1) The psychotic reactions are more intense or severe; (2) the psychotic reactions involve more areas of personality adjustment; and (3) the psychotic reactions usually involve more social and personal danger. These statements should be understood as referring to the clear-cut majority of patients showing these reactions. There also exists, however, a large area of overlapping conditions in which it is difficult to make a clear distinction. Indeed, one of the most prevalent problems of the clinical psychologist and of the psychiatrist is that of making a differential diagnosis between psychosis and neurosis. Examples can be found of persons who, on the basis of other considerations, are clearly neurotic, who show symptoms more intensely than many psychotics, whose total personality seems clearly involved, and who are distinctly in need of hospitalization for their own protection. As we shall see later, when we discuss the possible causes of these conditions, it should be expected that many individuals will behave in ways that combine features of both neurosis and psychosis.

There are many ways a person may seek to defend himself against anxiety. Probably no two psychoneurotic patients could be found who had exactly the same problems or reacted in exactly the same way in their attempts to solve their problems. However, there is enough similarity in both problems and techniques to justify attempts at classification. Table 9 gives a short description of neurotic reaction types. In the following pages we will study the characteristics of each type in turn.

The anxiety reactions have been described in the last chapter. This material and the information from Chapter VI on the psychosomatic disorders should be recalled since some degree of anxiety and some somatic complaints are found in almost all psychoneurotic reactions.

TABLE 9

Type of Psychoneurosis	*Definition*
1. Anxiety reaction.............	The anxiety is diffuse and not restricted to definite situations or objects . . . neither is it "bound" nor controlled by any psychological defense mechanism . . . in such reactions, both the psychological and physiological aspects of the anxiety are felt by the patient
2. Obsessive-compulsive reactions..	The anxiety may be observable in connection with obsessional fears of uncontrollable impulses . . . or may manifest itself in a displaced form through useless or excessive, and often repetitive activity
3. Phobic reaction...............	The anxiety in these cases becomes detached from some specific idea or situation in the daily life behavior and is displaced to some symbolic object or situation in the form of a specific neurotic fear
4. Neurotic-depressive reaction.....	The anxiety in this reaction is allayed . . . by self-depreciation . . . the reaction is often associated with the feeling of guilt for past failures or deeds
5. Conversion reactions..........	Synonymous with "conversion hysteria" . . . instead of being experienced consciously, the impulse causing the anxiety in conversion reactions is "converted" into functional symptoms in organs or parts of the body
6. Dissociative reaction..........	The personality (ego) disorganization appears to permit the anxiety to overwhelm and momentarily govern the total individual, resulting in aimless running or "freezing" . . . the anxiety may be either discharged or deflected into various symptomatic expressions such as fugue, amnesia, etc.
7. Psychoneurotic, other.........	All other psychoneurotic reactions. Does not include "mixed" types which are classified under major component.

* Based on (1) *Nomenclature and Method of Recording Diagnoses,* War Dept. T.B. Med. 203, Washington, D.C., 1945; and (2) Committee on Nomenclature and Statistics of the American Psychiatric Association (1952), *Diagnostic and Statistical Manual, Mental Disorders.* Washington, D.C.: American Psychiatric Association, Mental Hospital Service.

Obsessive-Compulsive Reaction Types

SYMPTOMS

We have seen that anxiety is a form of fear, and that fear is a part of the generalized avoidance-reaction to threat or danger. Since the threat or danger is poorly localized or recognized in anxiety, the whole environment may assume menacing properties, and the patient may seek to shun as much contact with his environment as he possibly can. Such an individual *constricts* himself, both with respect to his relationship with other people and in his inner world of thinking, speculation, and fantasy. His style of life is structured in such a way as to avoid any possibility of anxiety-producing situations occurring.

This type of reaction to anxiety and the type of personality that it produces is often termed the *obsessive-compulsive reaction,* principally for the reason that extreme forms of such a technique of adjustment result in obsessive and compulsive symptoms. *Obsession* has been well defined by Masserman (1946):

> A persistent, conscious desire or idea, recognized as being more or less irrational by the subject, which usually impels *compulsive acts* on pain of *anxiety*.[1]

Compulsions are acts that the subject must carry out, in spite of recognition on his part of their unreasonableness. Again, the motive force is avoidance of anxiety that would result if the act were not performed. Minor examples of both obsessions and compulsions may be found in the everyday life of most persons. The old childhood games of touching every other picket on a fence or avoiding the cracks in a sidewalk have a compulsive flavor, as does the almost irresistible urge to place one's tongue against an aching tooth or the cavity where a tooth has been extracted. The maddening persistence of a chance bit of melody or of a rhythmic phrase that obtrudes itself seemingly against our most violent protest illustrates the obsession. Many otherwise rational individuals cannot free themselves of various forms of prejudice, and

[1] J. H. Masserman (1946), *Principles of Dynamic Psychiatry*, p. 287. Philadelphia: W. B. Saunders Company.

they confess their helplessness in the same breath with their acknowl-
edgment of the unreasonableness of the fixed belief.

Obsessions and compulsions, as was noted above, are techniques of
avoidance. "Step on a crack and break your mother's back" shows the
avoidance motive as clearly as pages of examples from the clinic. The
greatest difficulty for both subject and observer, however, is to discover
what is being avoided. The obsessive-compulsive has, in this regard, the
same problem as the person who is simply anxious. In both instances
the individual is aware of discomfort or fear but is poorly aware of the
reasons for it. Obsessive and compulsive behavior is adopted as one
technique of reducing and then preventing anxiety. Since the anxiety is
generally diffuse, the reactions to it tend also to extend over wide areas
of a person's life. If all the environment appears dangerous, then defenses must be built to cope with any aspect of the environment that
impinges on the subject. Thus the safeguards gradually come to play a
greater and greater part in the personality and eventually may become
completely dominant.

THE OBSESSIVE-COMPULSIVE PERSONALITY
AND ITS SOCIAL ORIGINS

The obsessive-compulsive type of personality is quite common, and
it is likely that most of us possess some elements of such behavior. Lesser
intensities of the reaction are almost necessary for successful living in
our culture. Neatness, compliance with relatively rigid routines, refusal
to expose oneself to obvious risks and dangers, fulfillment of obligations
and promises are the normal behavioral techniques out of which the
neurosis grows. These techniques are, for the most part, quite evidently
habit patterns that we have acquired. The motivation for carrying them
out comes partly from the circumstance that they aid us in gaining
essential satisfactions and partly because the well-imbedded habit itself
comes to act as a motive in its own right. There is no essential break
then between the motivation of the normal person and that of the
obsessive-compulsive neurotic, and there is continuity in the behavior
itself. In both instances the individual is attempting to deal with his
problems by learned techniques. The difference lies in the degree of
rigidity and the intensity with which these techniques are carried out.

An example may be found in considering the normal habits of
cleanliness. Hygienists tell us that the hands should be washed with
soap and water before we handle food, and social dicta demand clean

hands as an item in interpersonal relationship. We have learned a number of elementary facts (and some misconceptions) about the relationships between hand cleanliness and freedom from bacterial contamination. Thus, hand-washing becomes a technique for achieving cleanliness, which may even be raised to the level of symbolic analogy. "To come with clean hands" symbolizes freedom from corruption, and ceremonial washing of the hands is practiced in various religious rites. In Matthew's account of the trial of Christ before Pilate, the following occurs:

When Pilate saw that he could prevail nothing, but that rather a tumult was made, he took water, and washed his hands before the multitude, saying, I am innocent of the blood of this just person: see ye to it. (Matthew, 27:24.)

A not uncommon symptom of the obsessive-compulsive state is a compulsive hand-washing. A patient may scrub his hands literally hundreds of times during a day, carrying the practice to a point of actual tissue damage to the skin. Extensive clinical investigations have shown that such behavior is a symbolic attempt to free the patient of guilt. He is behaving, in short, like Pilate in the Biblical example just cited.

Case 15. A landlady in a small college town complained to the university authorities that one of the students rooming at her house spent so much time in the bathroom that other roomers were suffering considerable inconvenience. An interview with the student disclosed a compulsive type of hand-washing, which he felt must be completed before he could go out of the house, or before he could study, or before he could retire in the evening. He had first to soak his hands for ten minutes, alternately in hot and cold water, then vigorously brush them with a stiff brush and strong soap, soak them for another ten minutes, and repeat the washing procedure. He could give no adequate reason for his behavior, but he knew from painful experience that if he did not carry out the sequence he would be restless, uncomfortable, and anxious.

The symptoms had started only within the past year, although he said he had always been afraid of "germs" and, even as a small boy, had never been comfortable on camping trips or doing any kind of work that involved dirt. During the war he had been an enlisted man in the Quartermaster Corps and had been assigned to the Graves Registration service. His group had performed their somewhat grisly duties in an area where battle losses were high and where many badly dismembered and mutilated bodies had to be searched for identification and then buried. While the patient had reacted strongly against such work, he had managed to perform his duties without incident. It was after his return to the United States and at about the time of his discharge from the Army that the compulsive hand-washing began. Further interviews revealed that the patient had suffered intense feelings of guilt during his army experiences because he was in such "safe" work, and each time he assisted in the recovery of a body and in a burial he became more impressed with "the unworthiness of people who were not engaged in the actual fighting."

Consciously he tried to reassure himself by noting that the disagreeable nature of his own work was in some way an atonement for his "avoidance of duty." In spite of this rather obvious fact he came out of the army with a strong feeling of guilt. Out of this background the hand-washing appeared as an apparent attempt to dissipate anxiety, to "cleanse himself of guilt." He had little conscious awareness of this motivation, although after talking over his past history several times the connection became apparent to him.

SYMBOLISM IN PSYCHONEUROSIS

Such a naive and strained symbolism may strike the reader as illogical and, when carried to such extremes, as irrational. Since we will meet again with this type of symbolic connection between actions, let us look more closely at symbolism in general. A *symbol* is something that is used to stand for something else. Often the connection is quite arbitrary, and justification reduces to a mere matter of convenience. Many symbols used in mathematics and the sciences are of this type. They have meaning because they are accepted by general agreement as equivalent to the object or process that they stand for. Such symbols may be very useful in certain limited ways; they may be manipulated logically to arrive at new revelations about the objects for which they stand. Algebraic equations furnish a good example. "Let x stand for the (unknown) number of apples that may be raised in an orchard when certain other variables are in operation." Mathematical operations will then yield a value for x, and something new is known about the object for which x was a symbol. As we shall see later, in the chapter on social factors in psychopathology, most language behavior involves this property of symbols. But what of the symbols that are used by the obsessive-compulsive person? Here, the symptom is a symbolic way of escaping from a problem situation. Up to a certain stage in the process, this type of symbolic behavior is no different from that of the person using algebra to calculate his yield of apples. However, the apple-grower does not try to carry the use of the symbol x quite as far as does the neurotic. He emphatically does not try to market xs, whereas the neurotic does try to use the symbol as if it *were* the thing it stood for. Such behavior is so clearly unsophisticated from a rational point of view that we should immediately think of looking for some elementary and primitive type of causation for it. The use of the symbol as if it directly and completely stood for the object is found among primitive people (as in the black-magic technique of piercing the heart of an image of an enemy for the purpose of causing that person's death); certain remnants of this primitive approach to symbols are found in our own culture in our attitudes toward certain religious and nationalistic symbols. For example, the flag of our country becomes invested with properties that carry symbolism to a fairly extreme degree, as in the regulations that forbid the flag to touch the ground or to be flown after sunset except under quite definitely specified conditions. A young man in love may be rendered euphoric by being granted the most trivial of favors if he feels that the gift is a symbol of the affection of his loved one. Obviously the difference between this type of symbolic behavior and that which is used in mankind's more logical moments lies in the nature of the reaction to the symbol. In the more primitive type, the person reacts emotionally to the symbol, with the same type of emotional reaction he would show to the real object. It is the emotional reaction that is the common link between symbol and object.

Returning to the obsessive-compulsive, we can say that in his ritualistic behavior he is reacting emotionally to that which the ceremony had come to signify in his past experience. Save that the symbolism is more distinctively personal, the process itself does not differ in any essential way from much of the symbolic ceremony in which members of the culture in general engage. Even the rigid manner of clinging to its expression and the distress which follows a failure to observe its demands may be found in many forms of culturally accepted behavior (for example, the case of A. Z. in Chapter VII). What, then, is the difference between the obsessive-compulsive neurotic and the rest of humanity? Primarily the compulsive neurotic reaction is differentiated as an illness because of the high degree of individuality of the symbolism. Demanding expression, as we have seen, the needs of the neurotic find outlet in behavior at variance with the general mode of behavior in the social group. Obsessions and compulsions, if they dominate the life of the individual *and if they are not shared by the society in general,* lower the patient's efficiency and preclude the possibility of effective behavior in spheres removed from the content of his neurosis. Thus, in the case just reported, the student lost a great deal of much-needed study-time and experienced difficulty in his social relationships with others because of his compelling need to carry out the hand-cleansing ritual. The obsessive drive toward neatness and order may result in a drastic lowering of accomplishment in all other aspects of life. Familiar to everyone is the housewife whose pride in a "well-kept house" keeps her family in a state of continuous turmoil; one such woman would not allow her husband to smoke his pipe in the house, her children to have playmates or pets in the house, or herself to neglect a daily ritual of mopping and dusting even when she was ill. In such cases clinical inquiry will disclose that the compulsive behavior is necessary to satisfy some deeply-lying need or is an elaborate way of avoiding a threat of catastrophic stress. As the psychoanalysts have shown us, only a person who is desperately afraid of "dirtiness" would elevate cleanliness into a passion. Freud, in some of his earliest writings, stressed the fact that many neurotic symptoms are behavioral expressions of a person's need for avoiding even less desirable types of behavior. The fact that the patient himself only poorly understands what he is trying to avoid intensifies the emotional aspects of his behavior.

ANALYSIS OF OBSESSIONS

While our interpretation of compulsions may appear quite reasonable and easily understood, there may be some question about the application of such reasoning to the obsessions. The most obvious difference between the two is probably that the compulsion is usually manifested in overt behavior, whereas the obsession is intrinsically implicit and only indirectly detected in the patient's actions. Also, in the compulsion, anxiety is generated if the act is not carried out; in the obsession, anxiety arises from the content of the persistent ideas or thoughts entertained by the patient. But these differences are, at best, superficial. Basically, obsessions and compulsions serve the same purpose of defense against anxiety and do it in pretty much the same way. The real psychological difference between the two types of symptom seems to reduce to a question of proximity of the anxiety to the personality. *Compulsive behavior appears to be a device for protecting the person against the conscious experience of anxiety, whereas obsessions confine or contain the anxiety in a small area.* Figure 9 may make this distinction clearer. In the compulsion the person is represented as utilizing his symptom as a shield against anxiety. The obsession, on the other hand, does arouse anxiety, but prevents its engulfing the whole personality. The patient is, as it were, kept so busy thinking about the obsessional material that he has no time to think of other problems.

The obsession, then, is a protective device that works in the same way as the compulsion, but at closer quarters. Both techniques are found frequently enough in the same person to justify the term *obsessive-compulsive* neurosis. The two symptoms, moreover, have a dynamic interrelationship. Obsessions are the thoughts from which compulsive actions spring. Excellent examples of this relationship may be found in

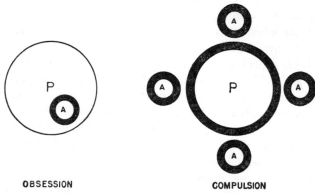

OBSESSION   COMPULSION

FIGURE 9. *Schematic representation of obsessions and compulsions. In the obsession, anxiety is internalized; in the compulsion, anxiety is externalized and avoided.*

the experiences reported by many of the early Christian holy men. When one of these individuals retired from the world, depriving himself of the normal bodily satisfactions of food, sex, and comfort, he would frequently become obsessed with vivid fantasies and dreams of that which he had relinquished. Visions of mouth-watering banquets and of beautiful dancing girls appeared to distract him from his holy meditations. Since these experiences were interpreted as satanic temptations, vigorous attempts were made to combat them. The techniques used usually were various types of compulsive actions, repeating the phrases of a prayer over and over again, carrying out spiritual exercises, or reducing life to a series of rigidly determined routines.

PHOBIAS

A rather special type of obsession that further illustrates the connection with compulsion is the *phobia*. Phobias are strong, unreasoning fears, usually directed at some specific environmental object. A common phobic fear, shared in some degree by most people, is that directed toward snakes. Many people show the same type of reaction toward small rodents, spiders, dogs, and so forth. Many of these phobias fortunately do not interfere to any great extent with normal social adjustment, since the object feared is not a constantly present part of the social environment. However, other phobias occur that are seriously detrimental to a happy life. Prominent among these are fear of high places, of closed places, of open space, of crowds, of noise, of light, of darkness, of moving vehicles, of water, or indeed of any aspect of our usual human surroundings. The intense fear engendered by exposure to the phobic stimulation leads the patient to expend great effort in his attempt to avoid the traumatic situation. The best first-hand description of phobic experience is to be found in W. E. Leonard's *The Locomotive God* (1927), the autobiography of a life-long psychoneurotic sufferer. Leonard's fears of open spaces became so acute that he was unable to leave his house. The analysis he makes of his fears is of interest to us. He noted that they started in an "objectless terror," and in many instances the phobia developed as an intellectual effort to find an adequate environmental causation for the emotional experience. This is a confirmation of the point we developed earlier, that the psychoneurotic symptom develops out of anxiety and is best conceived as a means of reducing or avoiding the anxiety.

The phobia is essentially an avoidance reaction, in which the pain of an internal conflict has become identified with some aspect of the environment. The relation between the internal conflict and the specific content of the phobia is often complex and obscure and is discovered only after prolonged clinical study. In some instances, however, the etiology is more readily apparent.

Case 16. A young man, being treated by a psychiatrist for a psychoneurotic illness whose chief symptoms were fears of high places and of crowds, became interested in aviation. In spite of urgent warnings by the psychiatrist, he decided to take flying lessons, arguing that the best way to overcome the fear of heights was a direct attack. In his study of the patient, the psychiatrist had found that the fear of high places was based upon a strong, but repressed, urge to commit suicide.

The suicidal motive was of long standing and was based on the rather infantile belief that self-destruction was a sure way to gain the parental love and affection that the patient felt was denied him. The fear of high places was thus an avoidance reaction against being placed in a situation where the conflicting motives could be aroused. The patient persisted in his flying lessons and reported triumphantly to his psychiatrist that he no longer felt fear and was thus discontinuing his treatment. The psychiatrist was not greatly surprised to read in the papers a few months later that the young man had died in a seemingly inexplicable airplane crash. The patient had been flying alone in a light plane and had dived the ship from a thousand-foot altitude directly onto the landing field below. Witnesses reported no apparent effort on the part of the pilot to prevent the crash. Evidently the patient's conflict had been resolved in the direction of suicide when the protecting phobia reaction was taken away.

Another case, which illustrates something of the type of circumstances that precipitate phobias and also reveals how little insight a patient may have for their causation, is the following account reported by Bagby (1928):

Case 17. A girl of good heredity displayed from her seventh to her twentieth year a severe phobia of running water; the sound of splashing water especially excited intense fear. She had no recollection of the following incident, until it was recalled in her twentieth year in the way to be described. When seven years old, she had spent a day in the woods with her mother and aunt. The mother returned home early; but the child insisted on remaining longer with her aunt. When the mother was gone, the child disobediently ran away alone. The aunt, on searching for her, found her wedged among the rocks at the foot of a small waterfall, with the water splashing down upon her head; the child was screaming in fear. The child, after being rescued, desired that her mother should not know of her disobedience and its consequences. The aunt promised, "I will never tell," and departed the next morning without having revealed the facts. The phobia was first manifested shortly after this incident, and continued until, thirteen years later, the aunt returned to visit the family. Having been informed of the nature of the phobia, she greeted the girl with the words "I have never told." This greeting provoked the recollection by the patient of the forgotten incident after which the phobia rapidly disappeared.[2]

It will be noted that the unusual fear of water was initiated by a frightening experience that occurred in childhood, and most phobias probably derive their content from such early sources. It should be emphasized, however, that identification of the source of content of a phobia is not enough information to enable us to understand the reasons

[2] E. Bagby (1928), *The Psychology of Personality*, pp. 44-47. New York Henry Holt and Company, Inc.

for its appearance. Many people have had terrifying experiences of even greater intensity and have escaped without phobic consequences. *Only when the frightening experience can be utilized as a technique for avoiding still more painful experience does a phobia develop.*

SUMMARY

The obsessive-compulsive neurosis occurs in rigid, constricted person-alities who protect themselves against disturbing stimulation by an active process of eliminating the possibility of unknown or unan-ticipated occurrences. When motivational conflicts or environmental pressures become too strong for their habitual type of personality organ-ization to handle, they respond with exaggerations of the same tech-niques, thus developing the symptoms we have called obsessions, compulsions, and phobias. Although these symptoms are attempts at adjustment, they result in an actual crippling of the individual as far as normal and mature social adjustment is concerned. As in most psychoneuroses, the secondary anxieties that are created and maintained by the symptomatic behavior present further problems of adjustment to the patient.

Neurotic-Depressive Reaction

SYMPTOMS

This condition, often termed *reactive depression*, is characterized by overwhelming feelings of sadness, sorrow, grief, and self-depreciation. It is differentiated from a very similar psychotic condition, not so much in terms of intensity of reaction, but rather by the conditions of onset. In the psychoneurotic depression the patient usually develops his sad-dened emotional tone as a more or less appropriate reaction to a life situation. It starts from the type of experience that produces sorrow or grief in most people—death of a loved one, loss of prized possessions, unfulfilled expectations, and so forth. The behavior becomes unusual only because of its abnormally long duration and great intensity. The psychotic depression, which we will discuss in the next chapter, does not usually start in such obviously appropriate situations and is not as clearly oriented to events in the patient's external environment.

The following case illustrates the main features of this type of be-havior, occurring as it does in a very simple and directly obvious situa-tion.

Case 18. N. D. entered the psychiatric section of an army hospital in the seventh month of his military service. He was admitted following an attempt at suicide; he had been forcibly restrained from cutting his throat with a razor and at the time had told his companions that he wanted to "kill myself to help my mother." His depressive symptoms started about two months before, when he had received a letter from his mother telling of the great need the family felt for the patient's services. The mother was attempting to work a small share-crop farm with only the help of the patient's younger sister. After receiving this letter, the patient appeared apathetic and depressed and expressed guilt feelings over having left his mother. He applied for an extended furlough and, when his request was refused, went on two drinking bouts that resulted in minor disciplinary action by his immediate superiors. He failed to stand formations and stayed in the barracks, frequently crying or lying face-down and incommunicative on his bunk. Two days before admission to the hospital he received another letter from the mother, and this was shortly followed by the suicide attempt.

The neurotic-depressive reaction is in many ways similar to the obsessive reactions discussed earlier. There appears to be the same type of fixed mental content of which the patient cannot rid himself, and much of the depressed patient's behavior seems compulsive in nature. However, in this condition the reaction is primarily at an affective level, the obsessive thinking and compulsive actions coming as a secondary consequence of the dysphoric emotionality.

DYNAMICS OF THE REACTIVE DEPRESSION

The feature of neurotic depression that is most frequently revealed by clinical study is the relationship between the depressed effect and feelings of guilt or unworthiness. The patient's grief, it would appear, is only partly directed toward the environmental situation that precipitated it and is primarily a reaction to internal inadequacies of his own. These failures need not be directly connected with the precipitating situation, although more frequently than not they are. A common and easily understood example of this reaction is seen in the response some people make to bereavement. Usually the relatives who show the most profound outward signs of grief at a funeral are the ones who have some reason for feeling guilty over their relations with the deceased in past years. In our culture, as in many others, a prominent and public display of sorrow is taken as a type of atonement for past unkindness. It is possible that the ornate funerals provided for underworld characters by the very people who hastened their departure is illustrative of this mechanism. As Thomas Mann said in *The Magic Mountain,*

"What we call mourning for our dead is perhaps not so much grief at not being able to call them back as it is grief at not being able to want to do so."

Case 19. J. L. was admitted to the hospital on the recommendation of his battalion surgeon. The patient was a master sergeant in an infantry organization. At the time of his admission he had been on active duty for three years, coming into service as a part of a National Guard contingent from one of the southern states. He had been an excellent soldier and had risen rapidly in rank and responsibility. His outfit had just completed extensive field training and had been alerted for overseas shipment at the time J. L. was sent to the hospital. Following the last stage of training, J. L. had been given a fifteen-day furlough, which he had requested for the purpose of visiting his home and marrying a girl he had been engaged to since before entering the army. He had returned from the leave unmarried and had been uncommunicative when his friends had asked questions.

Two days before entering the hospital he had gone to the battalion medical officer for some medicine to "get him to sleep"; inquiry revealed that he not only had difficulty in sleeping, but felt excessively fatigued, irritable with the men in his outfit, and unaccountably depressed and saddened at the thought of assuming combat responsibility for others. On the day of admission he had gone to his commanding officer and requested that he be reduced in grade to private, giving the above reasons. The commanding officer sent him to the chaplain, and the chaplain sent him to the medical officer who sent him to the hospital. A series of interviews soon showed something of the background for the depression. When J. L. had returned to his home, he had found plans actively under way for his marriage, and the small town in which he lived planning to make it something of a community occasion. He had been glad to see his fiancée, and for the first two days at home had felt very happy at his prospects. On the evening of the second day, while making love to her, he found himself making frankly overt sexual advances, which his girl resisted. The next day he awoke feeling ashamed and guilty over his conduct of the evening before. That afternoon he again saw his fiancée and stated that such feelings of unworthiness swept over him that he was firmly convinced that he could never marry her. He had broken the engagement, fled town, and spent the rest of his leave in a nearby city, alone in a hotel room, crying and drinking.

Further probing over the sexual episode, which seemed to be the precipitating factor, revealed that he had, several months previous to his furlough, visited a prostitute while drunk one evening; it was his first sexual experience of this type and left him with feelings of disgust. When he was making love to his girl, memories of this experience returned, seizing him with such force that, as he said, "I knew right then that I was completely unworthy of her and could never ask her to marry such a low person as myself."

As in the obsessive-compulsive reaction, the symptoms appear to be ways of preventing intolerable anxiety. The free emotional expression of grief has long been known by most people as a technique of living through or recovering from the effects of bereavement. The reactive depression owes some if its effectiveness as a tension-releasing device to this "have a good cry, and you'll feel better, dearie" principle. The depressed person is not tense with repressed sadness, but is expressing it freely in his behavior.

SOCIAL FACTORS IN REACTIVE DEPRESSION

More important, however, to the understanding of the reactive depression is insight for the social role that the patient is playing. The symptoms are interpersonal communications. The patient is telling the people around him how sorry he is that things are the way they are. Although superficially the communication deals with the precipitating event, actually the intent of the patient is to confess and atone for the sins and errors that have gone before. The wayward son who is prostrated at his mother's funeral goes through such a violent reaction because his past life has produced guilt as much as because his mother's death itself is an emotional trauma. As in the obsessions and compulsions, we can discern social influences at work. Public grief and public confession are mandatory in some cultural groups; in some societies the whole process has been so well formalized that professional mourners exist—individuals who can be hired to publicly wail and grieve. In our culture, with the Christian emphasis upon the doctrine of forgiveness of sins through confession and repentance, most people as children are supplied with the basic seeds of the anxiety-dispelling technique of the neurotic-depressive reaction.

Finally, as Becker (1933) has pointed out, the sorrow in bereavement has a large element of appeal to others for help and assistance; that this appeal is usually quite irrational is, of course, beside the point. What should be emphasized is that the neurotic-depressive person is turning to other people and to established social customs as a refuge against anxiety. That the need for aid from others is a part of the depressed reaction is borne out by Becker's observation that bereaved people manifest a general tendency to anger and aggression, directed toward those who do not suffer or mourn as deeply as the patient. This aggression is patent evidence of the strong nature of the drive that is being frustrated and that the drive is socially oriented.

It should be emphasized that the depressed patient does not have insight for the total significance of his mood disturbance. He knows that he is sad or unhappy, he is often vaguely aware of a sense of guilt, and he frequently expresses a need for help from others. Only with well-managed psychotherapy, however, does he gain an integrated understanding of the factors contributing to his depression. J. L. could not see the connection between his early sexual and ethical training and his reaction in breaking his engagement until a rather large number of psychotherapeutic interviews had taken place.

SUMMARY

The neurotic-depressive reaction is an overly intense but initially appropriate grief response to conditions of bereavement or frustration, the reaction often persisting long after what is regarded as a normal recovery period. Causative factors in this condition appear to be feelings of guilt and inadequacy. The symptoms attempt to prevent anxiety through a process of confession and atonement whose efficacy appears to be socially determined.

Conversion and Dissociative Reactions
(Conversion Hysteria)

These reactions are in many ways the most interesting conditions studied by the psychopathologist. Historically, they were among the first set of disorders to be described and were classed under the general name *hysteria*. The name "hysteria" itself goes back to Greek medicine and is derived from the Greek word for uterus, reflecting a belief that hysteria was exclusively a disease of women and was due to disturbances of the female generative organs. We now know that the disorder may be found in both men and women. It should be further pointed out that the commonly used term "hysteria" refers to agitated emotional behavior and *not* to the conditions we are considering here.

THE ADAPTIVE ASPECTS OF THE HYSTERICAL
    REACTION

The symptomatology of hysteria is complex and varied to a degree that makes adequate synoptic definition of the term almost impossible.

It is manifested by a variety of physical symptoms that more or less crudely mimic most known bodily disorders. In addition it presents behavioral symptoms in great number. Diagnostically, hysteria always poses a problem to the physician or clinical psychologist. The physical symptoms, as we shall see, are often such faithful copies of organic conditions as to mislead or puzzle fairly expert diagnosticians. The behavioral symptoms often are of such dramatic nature as to furnish news reporters with abundant good story material. In addition, the symptoms are often such poor imitations of organic conditions and occur in such circumstances as to call undeserved accusations of malingering down upon the head of the hysteric.

Our definition of hysteria will be most meaningful if we attempt to phrase it in terms of the part it plays in the struggle against anxiety. An adjective frequently used as part of the diagnostic term indicates the way in which the hysterical person copes with anxiety. The adjective is *conversion,* and most commonly the disorder is referred to as *conversion hysteria.* This is a reference to the process, which seems to take place in these patients, of converting their anxiety into symptoms that then become relatively independent of the rest of the hysteric's personality. A very simple example of the conversion mechanism will make this clearer:

Case 20. A student was referred to the counseling service of our university by his academic advisor because of failing marks in a foreign language, grades which were at variance with *A* and *B* grades in his other studies. The student stated that he was not particularly worried about the poor grades, since "there's nothing I can do about it." He elaborated by explaining that the language class came at a late afternoon hour, and that since the first week of the school year he had been developing blinding headaches at about that time and had been unable to attend most of the class meetings.

Further interviews disclosed little concern for the headaches; he had not complained about them to the student health center nor to his own physician. He seemed to regard the whole situation as somewhat unfortunate, but he did not exhibit normal concern about either the language grades or the headaches. Study of his case showed a long history of difficulty with grammar and languages, dating back to junior high school. Since he had never learned the essentials of English syntax, he found the foreign language extremely difficult. When the connection between headaches and the feelings of frustration and insecurity with respect to the language was pointed out to him, he merely laughed and said it sounded as if that might be the case, but "it would take more than that to convince him."

A little thought about this case will show that the headaches served a very utilitarian purpose. They enabled him to escape the frustration of a school situation that evidently, in some way that the counselor could not identify, aroused a great deal of anxiety. (The past history of persistent failure in language subjects, with consistently good grades in other courses, many of which required just as extensive verbal ability as the language, points to an emotional variable of some kind at work.) The attitude of indifference that the student assumed, both toward his precipitating problem and toward the escape symptom, is very characteristic of the hysteric; in fact, it has become almost a signpost pointing to the diagnosis and goes by the descriptive appellation of *la belle indifference*. In military hospitals it was a common experience to see a litter deposited carefully on the floor of the admission office, containing a young man with the superficial appearance of good health, lying complacently and relaxed, with a sweet smile on his face. The following type of dialogue would ensue:

EXAMINER: Well, son, what seems to be the matter?
PATIENT: I'm paralyzed from the hips down, and can't move my legs.
EXAMINER: When did this happen?
PATIENT: We were just starting out on a fifteen-mile hike when all of a sudden I fell down and just couldn't move from then on.
EXAMINER: That's pretty serious. I suppose you're worried about it?
PATIENT (smiling reassuringly): Oh, no, sir. I never worry much. It'll come out all right.

If we follow the dynamics of the condition, this apparently paradoxical happiness in the face of defect is understandable. The patient apparently has solved his problem—he has rid himself of anxiety by developing symptoms that honorably take him out of the anxiety-producing situation. His technique has something of the end results achieved by the obsessive-compulsive, but the goal is accomplished with much less effort and in a much more uncritically direct manner. Whereas the obsessive-compulsive person is constantly patching up his defenses and cannot relax for a moment in his ritualistic battle against anxiety, the hysteric achieves a sudden and complete solution, one that is dramatic and socially acceptable.

Hysteria, then, may be defined as a solution to the problem of anxiety in which the patient develops physical and behavioral symptoms that enable him to avoid the anxiety-producing situation and also *effectively reduce his anxiety to a level of comfortable tolerance.* This way of handling conflict situations is well described in the song that advises the listener to collect his troubles, "wrap them in a box, tie it with a ribbon, and throw it in the deep blue sea."

If the hysteric is so successful at coping with the perturbations of anxiety, we might well ask why the hysteric is considered to be a neurotic. Why, if he surmounts his problems with such success, do we not recommend that all other neurotics go and do likewise? The question is more serious than it possibly sounds, and its answer is related to very important considerations of psychopathology. Hysteria is a pathological condition because the patient achieves relief from anxiety at a biological and social price that is too dear. He incapacitates himself for other aspects of biological adaptation, and he can only survive socially in certain limited cultural settings. His symptoms, as we shall see, can only exist in a tolerant environment, for they almost uniformly preclude an effective social participation. In other words, only with respect to anxiety reduction is the hysteric successful and then only in a setting that will tolerate his symptoms. If the environment proves hostile to the symptoms, if it takes them away from the hysteric, he is again faced by anxiety and is driven to still other stratagems.

SYMPTOMATOLOGY OF HYSTERIA

Although the task of describing hysterical symptoms is almost like the labor of cataloguing the whole field of bodily and psychological ailment, we will attempt to review some of the more frequent and some of the rarer, but dynamically illuminating, manifestations of the condition.

The symptoms of hysteria may be divided for descriptive purposes into (1) sensory, (2) motor, (3) internal organic, and (4) behavioral. In every patient there will be found some combination of these four classes; rarely, if ever, do they exist in isolation. Moreover, they seldom present exactly the same appearance in the actual patient as the artificial isolation of textbook description might suggest. One further caution is necessary: *there is a very real possibility that many of the symptoms of the hysteric are suggested to him by the examiner,* and that the exact form that they assume will depend to some extent on the examiner's concept of hysteria or of other organic diseases.

SENSORY DISTURBANCES

The sensory disturbances in hysteria may affect any sensory system. In order of frequency, as they occurred over a three-year period in a large army hospital, the skin senses came first, interoceptors second, the eyes third, ears fourth, and chemoreceptors fifth.

Sensory disorders, irrespective of their origin, may be divided into types on the basis of the nature of the disturbance. Sensory function is (1) diminished or absent, (2) exaggerated, or (3) distorted. Diminished auditory acuity and blindness are examples of the first class, excessively sensitive hearing (hyperacusis) or inability to use the eyes under normal daylight illumination illustrate the second class, and astigmatism or cutaneous sensations of crawling objects are typical of the third class. Any of these disorders may be caused by injury to the sense organ, by structural defects of the sense organ, or by injury or disease of the neural mechanisms that serve the sense organs. Thus, blindness may be due to defects in any part of the structure of the eye itself, as in cataract, or by disease or injury of the optic nerve or its central projections. In hysteria any or all of these sensory disturbances may occur, but *invariably without the structural defect appropriate to the impaired function.* Hysterics may become blind or show loss of visual acuity, they may become deaf or complain of continuous ringing in the ears, they may develop a loss of skin sensitivity or aching painful muscles and joints, all in the absence of any adequate organic cause. Fortunately the hysterical symptom usually shows some points of difference from the similar symptom arising from organic factors, thus making the diagnostic problem somewhat easier than would otherwise be the case. In spite of the differences, however, many hysterics have been treated over long periods of time for organic conditions that they did not have.

Sensory disturbances of cutaneous functioning are seen in almost every hysteric. The patient frequently is unaware of the symptom until it is found by the examiner, a fact that led Babinski, a noted French neurologist, to remark that the examiner himself probably suggested the symptom by his procedure in looking for it. As part of a complete neurological examination, the patient's skin is stimulated lightly with a pin or with a wisp of cotton, the stimulus object being applied at frequent intervals along the extremities and over the torso. The patient is requested to tell the examiner if the sensations are similar or different at the various points of stimulation. This examination may disclose areas that "feel different" or where sensation is completely lacking. Closer exploration of these areas usually shows a peculiar distribution of the anesthesia or parenthesia, one that corresponds to external anatomical topography rather than to cutaneous nerve distribution. Favored locations for anesthesias are the extremities, and the distribution of impaired function may correspond to the hand or arm, or to the foot

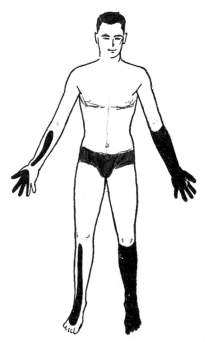

FIGURE 10. *Distribution of cutaneous anesthesia in organic lesions and as an hysterical symptom. Organic anesthesias are indicated by the black areas on the left, hysterical anesthesias by the black areas on the right.*

or leg. This distribution has given rise to the phrase "stocking and glove" anesthesias, as seen in the hysteric. Figure 10 illustrates typical distributions of anesthesia in hysteria and in cases of organic lesions to sensory nerves. Girdle or belt areas are also quite frequent, again with little correspondence between the locus of the disturbance and the cutaneous nerve distribution.

The anesthesias are good illustrations of the broadly uncritical nature of all hysterical symptoms and suggest something of the basis on which many physicians and others have accused the hysteric of malingering. The hysterical symptom conforms so closely to what an uninformed "common sense" guess would be about the anatomical and physiological properties of the body that suspicion of conscious fakery is hard to shake. A wider survey of the evidence, however, is against the "malingering" interpretation. In those past centuries when people took seriously the concept of witchcraft and strenuously searched out the supposed witches, the victims were subjected to painful torture and almost inevitable execution afterwards. One of the most damning proofs that a prosecutor could advance against a person suspected of witchcraft was the existence of "devil's marks," which were areas of cutaneous anesthesia. In spite of the horrible consequences of finding these stigmata, thousands of hysterics continued to manifest the symptoms and were duly tortured and burned. The patient is usually unaware of the existence of his cutaneous disturbance until it is discovered by an examiner. Another feature of hysterical symptoms that differentiates them from the efforts of the malingerer is their persistence in inappropriate situations. The person who is consciously trying to deceive others will attempt to maintain a symptom picture that is consonant with his deception. The hysteric, on the other hand, is not disturbed at inconsistencies and usually shows several of them in his behavior. In conducting an examination of the skin senses on an hysteric, instructions can be given the patient to answer "yes" if he feels the pin point, and "no" if he does not. With his eyes blindfolded an hysteric will often respond with a series of Yes's and No's, failing to realize the incongruity of reporting an absent sensation. The malingerer is constantly on his guard to prevent any action that will betray his pretense; in this respect the hysteric differs greatly. It is not unusual to find an hysteric with a paralyzed leg, who while undressing for a physical examination, quite unconcernedly stands on the supposedly paralyzed leg while removing the other shoe. A patient with complaints of such excruciating pain in the back that he cannot perform the lightest type of work may be seen at the patient's recreation hall helping move a piano, carrying chairs, and standing on ladders to string crêpe paper in preparation for a dance. Very rarely does a malingerer have the genius to be as inconsistent as the hysteric.

Returning to the cutaneous symptoms, it should be noted that, in spite of the frequence of their occurrence, they do not, in general, serve the hysteric in any directly useful way. They are secondary symptoms, and the absence of evidence of their purposiveness is another point in favor of the idea that they are suggested by the examiner. Just as the necessity of hiking fifteen miles "suggests" a paralysis, the neurological examination procedure suggests the anesthesia. We will discuss the suggestibility of the hysteric a little later.

Next in frequency to cutaneous symptoms are those that are referred to the various kinesthetic and organic receptors in muscles, joints, and viscera. During World War II so many patients came into our hospital with complaints of pain in the back that the condition seemed almost endemic. Included in this group are also the symptoms of abdominal pain, headache, stiff joints, muscular cramp, and so forth, all, of course, without a corresponding organic lesion as a cause. These symptoms have one feature in common—all of them are disabling to the patient and prevent him from carrying out a normal social adjustment.

Hysterical disorders of vision do not occur as frequently as the complaints just discussed, but they have usually a sudden onset and are sufficiently dramatic to attract much attention. A complete hysterical blindness is relatively rare; in an army series of a thousand cases only two such instances developed.

Case 21. One was in a former Hollywood cameraman who had been drafted into the army much against his will and with a very great loss of income and status. He was assigned to an Air Force training center as an instructor to aerial photographers. One afternoon, while demonstrating the proper placement of arc-lights for the best effects in taking motion pictures, he complained that the brightness of the lights hurt his eyes. Within half an hour he reported that he was unable to see and was led to the station hospital. Examination showed his pupils to have normal reflex reaction to changes in light intensity. When a moving object suddenly approached his eyes, he would blink, yet claim that he had seen nothing. He spent a month in a general hospital without improvement. On the day he came before the medical board and was informed that he would receive a medical discharge from the service he first reported that he could dimly perceive the outline of objects; by the time he was ready to leave the hospital for Hollywood his vision was practically normal again. The personal gain from symptoms was obvious in this case to the point of casting grave doubts on the validity of his symptoms. A series of interviews under hypnosis, however, showed that many of the determinants of his symptoms were quite independent of his army experience, and that the army had served merely as a precipitating factor to an illness that would possibly have occurred under other conditions equally frustrating.

Case 22. The second case fell into a pattern that is familiar to all psychologists and psychiatrists who work with industrial and civil compensation claims. A young second lieutenant of infantry was on maneuvers in Louisiana. While on a simulated night attack, a signal rocket exploded directly in front of him. He was startled and momentarily dazed by the occurrence, but managed to carry on his duties for the rest of the night. The next morning he complained of headache and of black spots before his eyes. The spots spread rapidly during the day and his eyes became bloodshot. The medical officer who examined him suspected that the flash of the rocket had possibly done some ocular damage; the patient's eyes were bandaged and he was confined to bed for a period of several days. When the bandages were taken off, the eyes had resumed their normal appearance but the patient complained of complete blindness. Light narcosis with sodium pentothal, accompanied by strong suggestion that his vision was restored, enabled him to see normally for a few hours, after which "things would shut down" on him and he would be as blind as before. The patient was retired from the service, and when last seen was being led by his wife, but was lifting his feet properly to avoid obstacles and giving other automatic and reflex evidence of intact vision.

A more common visual defect in hysteria is *tubular vision.* This is a concentric constriction of the visual field, usually occurring bilaterally and confining the patient's vision, as the name suggests, to such an area as he would see if looking through a pair of narrow tubes. This symptom bears some resemblance to the anesthesias, in that the patient is quite often not aware of the defect until he has received a perimetric examination. Figure 11 shows a normal visual field contrasted with

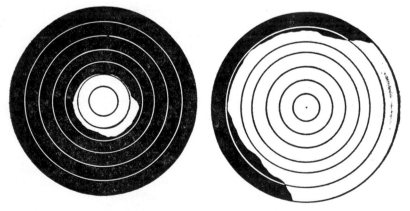

FIGURE 11. *Visual field of hysteria as compared with the normal visual field. The hysterical field is on the left.*

that from a hysteric. As with most hysterical symptoms, the disorder does not interfere with normal automatic visual coordinations. Here again there is a possibility that the symptom is suggested to the patient by the examiner.

The auditory disturbances of hysteria parallel the visual. Complete deafness is rare, although it occurs at times as a residual of accidents or other experiences that suggest auditory impairment. A pilot developed a complete loss of hearing following a harrowing flight through a thunderstorm in which the static in his radio ear phones had been severe. Partial disturbances of hearing are more frequent. The following two cases illustrate typical instances.

Case 23. Miss M. was referred to the university psychology department for a determination of auditory thresholds by a local otologist. She had complained of a persistent buzzing and ringing in her ears for the past five months. The symptoms had progressed to the point where they interfered with her work as a stenographer, since often she could not accurately hear dictation. Tests of pitch and loudness thresholds, however, showed no real loss of acuity. A Rorschach test showed a personality structure consistent with hysteria. A series of interviews, aimed at tracing the psychological situation in which the symptoms developed, disclosed the following pertinent information. Approximately six months previous she had gone to a party at a friend's mountain cabin, and while more or less under the influence of alcohol and a moonlit night had engaged in a rather abortive attempt at sexual intercourse. The next day she experienced a panicky fear that she was pregnant and, after hurried consultation with some of her intimate girl friends, began to take large doses of quinine sulphate.

She continued this medication for two weeks, remaining in a state of fearful agitation. The quinine produced unpleasant symptoms of nausea and ringing in her ears. Her regular menstrual period then occurred, and she gradually recovered her normal spirits. Unfortunately the man who was a party to the original incident was an office associate and a frequent escort to dances, shows, and other parties. A mild "petting" experience with this man about a month after the original incident was followed by feelings of nausea and a return of her auditory symptoms, which became chronic and persistently annoying enough to prompt her to seek medical advice. A diagnosis of hysterical akoasm was made and she was referred to a psychiatrist for treatment.

The next case illustrates quite well the difficulties attendant at times upon making a diagnosis and the role of the psychiatrist or clinical psychologist in protecting the patient from the consequences of his symptoms.

Case 24. A. N. was sent to the army general hospital from a field command for observation and treatment of a suspected brain tumor. He had complained of blinding headaches, dizziness, and a buzzing sound in his left ear. A neurological examination was essentially negative, although differences in the strength of reflex movements was noted, those on the right being weaker. Opthalmoscopic inspection by the first physician who examined him seemed to indicate signs of increased intercranial pressure. A tentative diagnosis of a tumor on the auditory nerve was formulated, and the patient was scheduled for examination and operation by the neurosurgery department.

As a more or less routine procedure the patient was also seen by the psychiatrist and the psychologist. The psychiatrist noted that the patient was an immature-appearing "happy-go-lucky" boy of nineteen, who described his symptoms dramatically but with little apparent emotional involvement. The psychological examination included an intelligence test and the Rorschach. The intellectual level was "average adult," and no scatter was apparent on the subtests. (By "scatter" the clinical psychologist was referring to the variation in test performance from one part of the intelligence test to another; scatter is often observed in individuals with some organic or psychotic impairment of thinking.) The Rorschach showed no organic signs, but did indicate the presence of some anxiety in a person with an hysterical personality structure. Psychiatrist and psychologist agreed in presenting a diagnosis of hysteria. A recheck of the neurological examination and an examination of the patient by the eye clinic gave normal findings. The past history of the patient showed that a sister had died of a brain tumor, and that it had been located on the auditory nerve, giving much the same symptomatic picture as was presented by our patient.

In this case the family background of the patient contributed enough to his symptoms to give them a striking resemblance to an organic condition and almost precipitated a craniotomy. It has often been remarked by physicians that hysterics receive more maldirected medical and surgical treatment than does any other diagnostic classification.

Complaints that center around the interoceptors are widespread in all psychoneurotics but they have a distinctive flavor in the hysteric. Here, as in his other symptoms, the hysteric reveals a flair for dramatic description, which is quite unmatched in other neuroses or in most of the organic syndromes. When asked to describe his headache, most people are able to achieve such phrases as "a sick headache," "a sharp pain," "a dull ache," and the like. The hysteric often produces such descriptions as these: "it feels like a red-hot nail is being driven into my temples," "it feels as if iron claws were tearing my head apart from the inside," the "pains are stabbing, shooting bursts from left to right." When observed while these assaults are occurring, the hysteric seems calm out of all proportion to the intensities of symptom he has described.

Pain may be experienced in any region of the body, but the head, abdomen, and muscles of legs, arms, and back constitute the main sources. The sensory disturbance of this type is usually associated with a corresponding motor disorder, the patient experiencing difficulty in moving the affected parts, or as in the case of the headache, associating the sensory disturbance with memory defects.

MOTOR SYMPTOMS

The most common motor defects in hysteria are the paralyses, convulsive episodes, and gait or posture disturbances. In all these symptoms the escape from anxiety and frustration is usually easy to recognize, for, irrespective of the lack of organic basis for the complaint, the hysteric is disabled for the ordinary tasks of life. The boy who became paralyzed in his legs escaped the frustration of life in the infantry; Menninger (1937) reports the case of a woman who took to her bed shortly after her marriage and stayed there twenty years, unable to move hands or feet, thus escaping the tasks and worries of a farm wife.

Hysterical paralyses show the same inconsistencies with anatomical nerve supply that are seen in the anesthesias. The paralysis may affect only an isolated segment of an extremity in a way that would be impossible on the basis of injury to motor nerve and may be accompanied by an equally impossible anesthesia. The paralysis often shows an interesting point of evidence for its purposiveness when attempts are made to remove it in therapy. In military practice it was often necessary to attempt a temporary removal of such symptoms in order to make the patient ambulatory and get him to his home with a minimal amount of trouble. In such instances a direct attack was made on the symptom by means of strong suggestions from the medical officer that the patient was recovering function. These suggestions were usually most effective if given while the patient was under a light dosage of some narcotizing substance such as sodium pentothal or sodium amytal. The physician would tell the patient that the medicine was removing his symptoms and at the same time attempt to passively manipulate the paralyzed extremity. Often the patient would manifest resistance to the removal of the symptom and would counteract the physician's manipulations with oppositional contraction of antagonistic muscles. The "paralyzed" muscles would reveal themselves to be extraordinarily capable of contraction in the direction opposite to that being suggested by the therapist, often to such a vigorous extent that the patient and his bed would be moved around the room by the therapist's efforts to move the "paralyzed" member. This manifestation of resistance is seen in more indirect ways in any attempt to treat the symptoms of psychoneurosis. Often the symptom may be removed, but the chances are very much in favor of the patient developing another symptom serving the same anxiety-escaping purpose. This is an essential point in understanding neurotic disorders. The symptoms are the patient's adaptive techniques, and removal of the technique without doing something about removal of the problems that prompted the technique simply forces the patient to other expedients.

These principles have been demonstrated in a series of experiments by Seitz (1953). Using posthypnotic suggestion, Seitz showed that the removal of symptoms was followed by the spontaneous substitution of other related symptoms. One patient, a 41-year-old single white man, suffered from an hysterical tremor of the hands and forearms. In the first hypnotic session, the patient was told that the tremor would disappear. In the posthypnotic period, the tremor was replaced—without suggestion—by a twisting of the neck to the left. During the second hypnotic session, the suggestion was made that both the tremor and the twisted neck would be gone. This time the patient substituted nausea, gagging, and sweating. The third session resulted in the substitution of a "bursting headache." In the final session all the previous symptoms were told to disappear. The result is best told in Seitz's own words:

This time the patient exhibited a dazed facial expression posthypnotically. He shook his head a few times as if to clear it, then arose from his chair and advanced toward the investigator. His hands were outstretched in a grasping position toward the investigator's throat.[3]

The patient was quickly hypnotized and the tremor reinstated. This series of experiments show clearly that the symptoms are the patient's method of solving his problems, that the symptoms are symbolically related, and that removal of the symptom does not solve the basic problem facing the disturbed individual. As nonsensical or bizarre as the hysteric's behavior may appear, it is his method of dealing with

[3] P. F. D. Seitz (1953), "Experiments in the substitution of symptoms by hypnosis: II." *Psychosom. Med.*, 15, 408.

serious problems, and the only effective way of bringing about permanent changes in the behavior is to attack the basic problems.

Many hysterics who do not have actual paralyses develop bizarre disturbances of posture or gait that may have the same crippling effect.

Case 25. One patient seen recently, a student, had been forcibly evicted from a tavern after creating a minor disturbance. He had fallen in such a way as to bruise his right arm. The next day he went to the Student Health Service, complaining that motion of the arm was limited to about 10 degrees around the elbow, and when he appeared he was carrying it at an odd angle, from which he claimed it could not be moved. Detailed examination of the arm, including X-rays, showed no damage to the joint or bones. A month later the arm was being carried at the same angle, and the physician reported some danger of permanent damage due to calcification of the immobilized joint. Vigorous psychotherapy aided the student, but when last seen the arm was genuinely limited in motion due to the long period in which it had been maintained without exercise.

In addition to hysterical pains in the back or legs the patient may develop a gait so characteristic as to receive a distinctive name, *astasia-abasia.* In this condition the patient is quite able to move his limbs in a coordinated fashion as long as he is lying down, but if he attempts to move about, the coordination breaks down and he is either unable to walk or staggers in a drunken manner. One army patient was continually being arrested by military police for intoxication because of his astasic walk. Extreme instances are easily confused with vestibular disorders and cerebellar tumors.

A motor disorder that does not occur with great frequency, but which is a dramatic symbolization of the dynamic purpose of hysterical symptoms, is the *convulsive attack.* This may simulate a typical grand mal epileptic fit, or it may consist only of a fainting attack. In either instance it occurs in situations that are similar to those that provoke temper tantrums in children, namely as a response to frustration. A point that usually differentiates the hysterical seizure from its organic counterpart is the low frequency of injury in the former. When the hysteric faints or convulses, he does it in such a manner that the possibility of harm or injury is minimized. The attacks seldom come when the patient is alone, he falls in such a way that he does not strike or bruise himself, and he does not suffer a loss of consciousness. One psychiatrist with a wide experience in handling such cases said that he could tell an hysterical attack by simply saying to the patient, "you can wake up now."

An organic convulsion or a real fainting spell seldom would respond to the test phrase, the hysteric almost invariably would. In clinical experience with the electroencephalograph it sometimes happened that a person suspected of epilepsy would experience a seizure while having his brain waves recorded. Those who turned out to be hysterical would show no evidence of disrupted cortical function on the EEG tracing, a finding quite at variance with the tracings from epileptics having attacks.

SUGGESTIBILITY IN HYSTERIA

Earlier in our discussion the dependence of the hysterical symptomatology on the culture was mentioned. Society aids in determining the form of the hysterical symptoms, although often in roundabout and seemingly negative ways. During the time in our history when most people believed in witchcraft and in divine possession, hysterical symptoms assumed what appeared to be an almost infectious character, and outbreaks of these symptoms would occur in large numbers of the population, spreading over wide areas. These instances emphasize what the reader has probably already noted, that the hysteric is an extremely suggestible person. He reacts to his environment with a great deal of sensitivity, and his symptoms take on a coloring of the setting in which he has been immersed. This is shown in the type of symptom selection in hysteria. If, in interviewing such a patient, you ask if other members of the family have shown this symptom (say a lame back, or a headache), the chances are very good that the patient will answer affirmatively and tell you about his mother's headaches or his father's backaches, which were "just like mine." The hysteric who shows convulsions usually will be found to have witnessed convulsive seizures in others. The sensitivity of the hysteric to suggestion should always be taken into account when evaluating the reports from examinations of them.

The suggestibility of the hysteric shows itself in other ways. As we have said, it is often possible to remove particular symptoms by strong and authoritative suggestions. Many paralyses have been removed by administration of sugar pills accompanied by emphatic assurance that the medicine "always works in cases like these." The symptoms may be removed by strong suggestion from other than professional sources. The miracle-healing at religious shrines, the frequent benefits from chiropractic manipulation, and the success of many cult movements in restoring the "lame, the halt, and the blind" owe their results to the suggestibility of people with hysterical defects. It is unfortunate that none of these therapeutic agencies makes any sort of consistent follow-up of the people who have thrown away their crutches and their Seeing-Eye dogs as the result of suggestive treatment. They would find that, until the problem that caused the symptoms is dealt with, the hysteric will be forced to return to his old symptom or to develop a new one.

"COMPENSATION" NEUROSIS

Brief mention should be made of "compensation" neurosis, since it is essentially hysterical in character and has been illustrated in many of the cases presented in this section. By compensation neurosis we mean the disabling symptoms that occur as the aftermath of accidents or other unusual happenings. In our civil law many such situations present the possibility of determining blame and responsibility and give the injured person the right to receive redress in the form of damages, compensation, pensions, and so forth. Department stores are frequently involved. If a customer slips and breaks her leg while in a store, it is often possible for her to bring suit against the store and recover damages. Workmen are entitled to compensation for time lost due to injuries or illness in which the working conditions have been at fault. This social situation thus furnishes ample motivation for the development of hysterical symptoms or the hysterical prolongation of symptoms initially due to an organic lesion that has recovered. As long as compensation is forthcoming the symptoms remain; in many instances the worst handicap to psychotherapy of hysteria is the existence of such remunerative secondary gain. In the treatment of head injuries the physician should be constantly on the alert to detect and forestall the transition from headache directly due to the injury to the neurotic residual that can easily develop to a point of maintaining the patient as an invalid long after he has completely recovered from his original injury.

THE GANSER SYNDROME

In our review of the symptoms of hysteria we have not exhausted the variety of manifestations that may appear. We have said nothing about hysterical *aphonia*, for example, although this inability to use the voice often occurs. Neither have we mentioned *narcolepsy*, an irresistible tendency to fall asleep while the patient is going about his daily routine, nor *somnambulism*, in which the patient walks in his sleep. In fact, the hysterical person may mimic any type of disturbance, including the more severe psychotic states. This latter is rather unusual, but since it occurs with some frequency in connection with medico-legal affairs, it is worthy of mention. In most legal codes it is possible for an accused person to receive more lenient treatment at the hands of the law if it can be established that he is irresponsible or insane. Thus, many individuals who have been indicated for serious offenses are placed in psychopathic hospitals for periods of observation in order to determine the status of their sanity. Under these circumstances some people show a peculiar type of behavior that has been termed the *Ganser syndrome*. Here, the patient, without a great deal of conscious awareness, begins to behave in a childishly simple burlesque of psychosis. He acts in the way he believes a "crazy" person should act. He reports fantastic delusory and hallucinatory experiences of a type never seen in actual psychotics. One patient maintained that he saw a family of big green alligators following him around and that they had ice cream cones in their jaws. They lose knowledge of the most elementary kind. If given a key and asked its function, they say it must be something to light cigarettes with, and if shown a door, they attempt to use the key in a reverse position, with the usually inserted part of the key toward them. If asked to look out the window and tell the season of the year, they respond with the opposite of the actual season. In simple arithmetic they make ludicrous errors, saying that two plus two are eighteen, and so on. The attempt to escape punishment is so obvious that these people, in common with most other hysterics, have often been accused of malingering. The simplicity of the performance, and the fact that it only occurs in individuals who may be diagnosed as hysterics on other grounds is evidence against malingering. The hysterical simulation of psychosis is only another example of the by-now-familiar conversion technique.

DISSOCIATIVE REACTIONS

Related to, but sometimes distinguished from, the conversion reactions are those "behavioral" symptoms that make such good newspaper copy: the dissociative reactions. We will consider the amnesias and multiple personality. In these conditions distortions of personality structure are paramount rather than functional somatic complaints. The hysterical amnesias represent behaviorally, as White (1948) has pointed out, a loss of personal identity. Multiple personality is the state of two or more independent personalities within one individual. Our discussion assumes that the basic developmental mechanism of the dissociative reactions is identical to conversion hysteria and thus is a variant of the latter.

HYSTERICAL AMNESIA

Amnesia, or loss of memory, is not an uncommon accompaniment of many organic injuries to the cerebral cortex. In concussion, for example, there is often an amnesia for events immediately before the accident and for varying periods of time following it. As a general rule these memories are completely and irrevocably lost; they cannot be recovered by any therapeutic process.

The amnesias of hysteria do not follow this plan. They occur suddenly, without physical trauma, and are usually recoverable, sometimes in psychotherapy and equally as often spontaneously. They usually involve a flight from threat, and in such instances are referred to as *fugue states*. The following case is typical.

Case 26. B. R. had been a student at a western university. During his senior year he had married a girl from his home town, and after graduation had started work as a chemist for a large industrial concern in a nearby city. He was drafted early in the war and spent a year as an enlisted man stationed at a plant producing war gases. Because of his ability and college background, he was sent to an Officer Candidate School in Chemical Warfare in Maryland. He successfully completed the training and was commissioned. On the evening of the commissioning ceremonies he went to Baltimore with some of his fellow students to spend the evening in celebration. That same evening he was missed by his companions shortly after they had entered a night club. Assuming that he had returned to the hotel at which they were staying, they were not alarmed, but when they got back to the hotel he was not there. Six days later he walked into his wife's parents' home, saying that he didn't know how he had arrived there and that he remembered nothing from the time he had entered the night club in Baltimore to the time he opened the front gate of his in-laws' home.

He voluntarily reported to the military police and was sent to an army hospital. Extensive interviews failed to revive any trace of memory for the time he was traveling or any motivation for the flight. However, his past history showed that he was following a familiar pattern. He had taken an extra year to graduate from college because he suddenly quit in the last quarter of his last year and spent four months in aimless wandering. Just prior to his marriage he had disappeared for two weeks. He had been promoted in the chemistry department of the company at which he had been employed and had suddenly requested a vacation. Obviously the prospect of assuming new responsibilities as an officer had called forth the same flight-technique. Under hypnosis the memories were recovered and this hypothesis was confirmed. Just before running away he and his companions had been discussing their future officer careers, and the patient had thought, "I might fail to be a good officer and be disgraced." The trip then followed, with no object in mind other than getting away from the threatened responsibility.

Such amnesic flights may be extremely elaborate. A case is reported in which a minister disappeared from his New England home and spent several months in Philadelphia as the operator of a newsstand. During this time he had no memory of his identity as a minister, he had assumed a new name, and he had shown a good adjustment in his adopted role. Inquiry into his past life showed that conflicts had piled up in his old life to the point of forcing his escape. This method of solving problems by putting oneself in a position where they no longer operate is characteristic of the hysteric. Whether the method be by way of sensory or motor disturbances, aches and pains, or running away, the anxiety situation is *converted* into a nonthreatening circumstance. The hysteric solves his problems by escaping them.

MULTIPLE PERSONALITY

Multiple personality received its literary recognition most ably in the story of Dr. Jekyll and Mr. Hyde. Whether Stevenson recognized the psychiatric implications or not, be portrayed the essential elements in this particular hysterical technique. Dr. Jekyll, it will be remembered, was a kindly, conventional physician, and Mr. Hyde was a devilish fiend fit for inclusion in the gallery of Dick Tracy characters. Dr. Jekyll did good by day, Mr. Hyde did evil by night. Mr. Hyde carried out, we might say, the repressed motivations of Dr. Jekyll. This most dramatic of hysterical manifestations was reported extensively by Morton Prince (1906), whose patient has assumed a permanent place in the hall of psychopathological fame. The case he reported was a Miss Beauchamp, a sober, good, and dutiful girl in the best Victorian tradition. Her difficulty lay in the fact that suddenly and undependably she would change into an irresponsible mischievous hoyden whom Prince named "Sally." Sally would smoke, tell suggestive stories, play practical jokes, and in general behave in a way that would shock the staid Miss Beauchamp. Since these personality changes occurred during the course of psychotherapeutic interviews, we are again confronted with the possibility that Dr. Prince played an unwitting role in the transformation by suggesting some of the basic outline of the shift.

The number of reported cases in the literature is quite large,[4] and they have been contributed by an impressive list of authors. One of the most recent to be reported at some length is by C. H. Thigpen and H. Cleckley (1954).

Case 27. Eve White was (at time of examination) a twenty-five-year-old married woman faced with serious marital and personality problems. A demure, retiring individual, Eve White was quiet, industrious, and, as the authors put it, "in some respects almost saintly." During the course of therapy the authors were led to suspect the existence of another personality. White could not remember a previous therapy session. Later she wrote a letter to one of the authors expressing concern over this lapse of memory. In the middle of the letter the handwriting suddenly changed and a new line of discourse was established. On the succeeding therapy day, the suspicions of the authors were startlingly confirmed when a second personality became dominant for the first time.

This new personality, Eve Black, had been co-existing with Eve White since childhood. Like "Sally" in the case of Morton Prince, Eve Black's behavior was the opposite of White. Black was shrewd, rowdy, and provocative; she enjoyed joking and pranks. Uninhibited and frank, Black lived for the moment. Furthermore, Black was aware of the existence of White while Eve White knew nothing of her other personality. Black delighted in placing Eve White in embarrassing positions: "When I go out and get drunk," Eve Black with an easy wink once said to both of us, "She wakes up with the hangover. She wonders what in the hell's made her so sick." [5]

Psychological testing of both personalities revealed some differences.[6] White had the higher intelligence quotient. Rorschach test records led to different diagnoses for the two personalities. The electroencephalographic examination showed divergent brain rhythm patterns. The handwriting expert noted consistent and surprising disparities but maintained that expert analysis showed that both samples were by the same person.

As therapy progressed, a third personality appeared. "Jane" (as she was named) was by far the most mature of the three. Jane was aware of both White and Black, and she sympathized with the problems of White. On some occasions, Jane would intercede to solve some of White's difficulties. As therapy continued, Black was less and less able to control White. At the time of publication, Eve Black was being superseded by both White and Jane, and no further information was available on the outcome of the case.

[4] For an extensive review of some 76 selected cases and a discussion of the factors involved in multiple personality, see: W. S. Taylor and Mabel F. Martin (1944), "Multiple personality." *J. abnorm. soc. Psychol.,* 39, 281-300.

[5] C. H. Thigpen and H. Cleckley (1954), "A case of multiple personality." *Idem,* 49, 141.

[6] An analysis of these personalities was made with a new testing technique that produced many interesting insights. See: C. E. Osgood and Zella Luria (1954), "A blind analysis of a case of multiple personality using the semantic differential." *Idem,* 49, 4(1), 579-591.

This case is consistent with others in the literature and shows the lengths to which the individuals will go (or perhaps must go) to escape the situation facing them. We see that the person is again carrying out an escape from anxiety, and the multiple personalities are really variants of the amnesias and serve the same purpose.

SUMMARY

The reaction of conversion hysteria is manifested by a large number of somatic and behavioral symptoms that have the dynamic function of providing escape from frustration and anxiety. The efficacy of the symptoms in accomplishing this purpose depends upon social factors, and if the symptom is removed without altering the conflicts that caused it, new symptoms will appear.

Traumatic Neurosis

REACTION TO DEATH AND THREAT OF DEATH

Man is born and, for the most part, remains the weakest of mammals. No other creature is as helpless at birth, and if man is judged solely on the basis of sensory acuity or muscular strength he must be placed far down the list of living things in any rating of adaptive capabilities. That man has mastered his environment more than any other creature is due to the many evolutionary circumstances that gave him a better brain, an upright posture, opposable thumb and forefinger, and so on. But, with all of his triumphs, man is peculiarly vulnerable to all sorts of physical injury. Because of his weight he cannot endure falls with the same indifference as the lighter mammals or the insects; he cannot endure the same ranges of cold or heat as can many another creature; his ability to move swiftly from one place to another is dependent upon artificial devices that are capable of escaping from his control and turning from servants to enemies; his operations in water or in the air are dependent upon these same artificial devices, and the same risks are involved. Finally, he has turned to cooperative effort as a means of controlling his environment; the social aggregations that result contain many potentialities for harm that do not exist for the more solitary animals (unless they come within man's sphere of influence). In addition to these facts that make man's life a more dangerous adventure, there is the general fragility of living protoplasm to consider. The combination of chemicals that manifests life is delicate and is under constant threat of dissolution. A bolt of lightning, the muddy rush of a flash-flood, the burning heat of a forest-fire, the destructive chemical action of poisons, the disintegrative attack of other living creatures from bacteria to members of our own species—all these things and many more must be avoided or conquered if life is to be maintained.

With life such a tenuous and risky undertaking, it is almost astonishing to find that most humans grow up with a firm conviction of their own immortality. Intellectually most people know, by the time they have reached adulthood, that everyone dies and that there are no exceptions to that rule. Emotionally, however, this biological fact means very little to most people. As long as your own demise is indefinitely far in the future it is not a cause for alarm. If you were sentenced to die exactly two weeks from today, at ten in the morning, the emotional reaction would be severe. *Fear* of death would then be actual and ever-present; you would be face to face with a realization that a time would come when you would not be living. Your conviction of personal immunity from harm would have disappeared.

These considerations may seem an unnecessary elaboration of the macabre, but they are fundamental human realities that play a large part in the symptomatology of the type of neurosis we are now considering. A *traumatic neurosis* is an emotional disturbance following either bodily harm or strong threat of injury. In Chapter VI we described the reactions of soldiers who had been exposed to the dangers and fatigue of long-continued combat. Many of their reactions could be called traumatic neuroses. The same problem emerged in merchant seamen cast adrift on life rafts after their ships had been torpedoed; it was severe enough in this group to warrant special investigation and research. In civilian life the incidence of traumatic neurosis is very large, although no reliable figures exist as to exact numbers. Our civilization carries so many threats of sudden death that many of the population become exposed to violent accident every year. The psychological injury may be as real and even longer lasting than any physical harm incurred.

SYMPTOMATOLOGY

The symptoms found in traumatic neurosis duplicate to an appreciable extent those found in the other neuroses we have discussed. The immediate reaction to the traumatic event, particularly if the person escapes physical injury, may be an unnatural calm or possibly even a mild euphoria. In some cases reported there has been an amnesia for the events directly after the accident. In an automobile racing accident, two cars collided and then rolled end over end. The driver of one of the cars loosened his safety belt, climbed out of his car, and ran over to the other car, which was upside down on top of its driver. The first driver seized the hot exhaust pipe of the other racer and pulled the car off the driver. He received serious burns on the hands, yet when questioned about the incident by the ambulance doctor he remembered nothing after the two cars had collided. Concussion of the brain was suspected, but the most searching physical examination failed to reveal that the driver had received any blow to his head. In the cases reported by Blain (1943) of merchant seamen studied after escaping from torpedoed ships, many similar incidents of amnesia were seen.

Following the first reaction to trauma is a gradually increasing anxiety and depression. The anxiety is manifested by the same symptoms we described previously; there is the persistent uneasiness and sense of foreboding, the restlessness and irritability, and the later development of elaborate avoidance symptoms. The depression seems centered around a sense of guilt (Blain, 1943) in most of the military cases, and in all cases has some more or less conscious element of a fearful knowledge that death is inevitable.

Lastly comes the most chronic aspect of the neurosis. The patient develops techniques for avoiding anxiety, but in the typical case they meet with only partial success. Phobias, ritualistic behavior and compulsive thoughts, physical symptoms similar to those of conversion hysteria, and symptoms of autonomic instability may all be manifested. That they are unsuccessful is shown by the frequency with which sufferers from this neurosis complain of nightmares, of persistent ruminations about their accident, and of a complete inability to maintain a stable emotional equilibrium. Such symptoms may continue for years and reduce the patient to the status of permanent invalidism. The extent of the personality changes that may follow an accident are briefly depicted in this case reported by Miller (1940) from his experience in the British Army during World War I:

Case 28. Captain A. J. S., age 37, had served through the Boer War with distinction and was in France by October 1914. After a period of trench-feet he became very anxious and tired. By April 1915 he noticed that he had lost his mental alertness, he forgot things, and his mind had blank intervals. He never exhibited hysterical symptoms, but perspired a great deal and had palpitations. He remembers being taken prisoner in May 1915, and remaining in a bad prison camp until the Armistice. In 1919 he was depressed, apathetic and cynical. He had a paranoid attitude towards anything which remotely reminded him of captivity. There were screaming fits at night. His pre-war character his wife described as reserved but gentle, a good officer, conscientious, but a poor mixer. After the war he was a "changed character." [7]

The next case is of a merchant seaman seen during World War II by Blain:

Case 29. A 27-year-old English boy presented three kinds of symptoms. He was mildly depressed; he had attacks of increasing tension when he felt he must cry out and yell when in a social group, at which he would leave and go to the men's room, weep for a few minutes, and come back feeling all right; and attacks similar to nightmares before going to sleep at night. In these attacks he would be ready to go to sleep when he would start thinking of various incidents—torpedoing in the Channel, a week of bombing in Harley Pool without sleep for a solid week, ships sinking around him in convoys, his 2nd mate who had gone crazy, planes diving, bombs dropping, home, his wife and the child he hadn't seen, etc.—the events of the last voyage with shortage of food, no refrigeration, bad feeling among the ship's company. Then memories followed each other faster and faster, racing around his head until he thought it would split. He would look around and objects appeared far away, his hand ten feet off, the house across the street ten blocks away. He would get up, walk about, smoke a cigarette and it would all pass off. Then he would go to sleep without further trouble. During this time he had palpitations, sweating, trembling, waves of hot and cold over his body . . . (before the war) he had been doing well in business and had married a short time before the war opened.

He was trained for the sea. He joined up and had had two years and three months of a tough life—no real vacation, any number of bad actions, seen ships and men lost time after time, and didn't crack up through it all. Then a series of events occurred which appeared significant. The last trip began with delays—going aground in the harbor, removal of stores, more delays. Then long tropical experience with no refrigeration and shortage of food, grumbling among crew and officers. Ulcer-like symptoms developed with increasing severity for three months, culminating with a collapse with terrific abdominal pain on deck the second night in New York. He was taken by ambulance to a hospital. There were no X-ray findings, no blood, and the diagnosis was spasm. Discharged in two weeks as physically sound and told to rest up for a few weeks for his nerves, he was never aware of being nervous or emotionally upset until just before leaving the hospital.

[7] From Emanuel Miller, *The Neuroses in War,* p. 66. Copyright, 1940, by The Macmillan Company and used with their permission.

Then he got despondent and unhappy and went to a hotel where his agents paid his room and board.

He soon spent the few dollars he had borrowed and could get no cash advance on his pay due in England. His consul could do nothing for him. He felt ill but could get no help. Although entertained at canteens and given free theatre tickets, he hadn't a nickel for subway rides or cigarettes. He came to me [Dr. Blain] after three weeks, after telling the consul if nothing could be done for him, he wanted to go back to sea and bloody well get knocked off. After a few minutes of talking, he suddenly came out with a terrific blast against his last skipper and for ten minutes poured out a mass of hostility that gave me the surprise of my life. Instead of all his other troubles, before and since his collapse, this one feeling that the skipper had grafted on the stores, was incompetent and had not properly kept his vessel fit, suggested itself to me as either the cause of his break or the last straw in a series of similar disappointments or causes of being let down. Then followed being sent out and told he was all right when he knew he was not fit to look after himself—government and old legal barriers prevented his having any money. A jeweler in New York took his watch for repairs and sold it, saying he thought the owner had gone back to sea. The boy was treated at my office and lost all symptoms, got back his zest for living and sailed away on a ship not bound for home.[8]

This case shows very well the fact that the neurosis may delay its appearance until some time after the happenings that are its basic causation. It should also be noted that the patient's symptoms included many variants of the reactions we have already studied.

PERSONALITY VARIABLES IN TRAUMATIC NEUROSIS

The neuroses we have considered thus far for the most part seem to be outgrowths or manifestations of particular sorts of personalities. The neurosis appears to be an exaggeration of the ways that the person habitually behaved. In the obsessive-compulsive neurosis and particularly in conversion hysteria, the pre-neurotic personality presented most of the features later noted in the actual illness. The situation is slightly different in the traumatic neurosis. Almost every personality seems susceptible, and there are few criteria in the pre-traumatic personality for the prediction of its onset or of the type of symptoms it will present. Kardiner (in Blain, 1943) mentions three personality factors that may be of value in predicting this type of breakdown: a history of

[8] Daniel Blain, *et al.* (1943), *Proceedings of a Conference on Traumatic War Neuroses in Merchant Seamen,* pp. 17-19. New York: New York Academy of Medicine.

stammering, a history of chronic autonomic disturbances, and a disposition to epileptiform reaction. Kardiner feels very strongly that the traumatic neurosis is not derived from disturbances in social relationships, but is a very primitive reaction of poorly organized defense against those aspects of the environment that appear threatening. He calls attention to the fact that the person in the traumatic neurosis reacts by withdrawing from the source of danger and then generalizes the danger potentiality to everything else in his surroundings and continues to withdraw from all these. He hazards the guess that people who have not developed adequate techniques as children for mastering their environment will be more susceptible to traumatic neurosis.

INTELLECTUAL AND EMOTIONAL APPRECIATION OF LIFE PHENOMENA

We said earlier that the traumatic neurosis can be thought of as an emotional reaction to the possibility of death. It would be interesting to spend a little time in consideration of the meanings that death may have for people. Human beings are in a unique situation in this respect. Because of their ability to verbalize and to generalize from their observations of nature they do have knowledge that enables them to predict future aspects of their life cycle. This power of prediction is reflected by the over-all accuracy of the actuarial tables stating life expectancy for individuals of any given age. In this general way, our knowledge causes us concern only in proportion to the dwindling of our life expectancy as we get older. Even the more specific knowledge that we each must die and will inevitably arrive, in due course of time, at our own death-scene is not a source of chronic anxiety to most people. An observant friend, a physician who spent four years in a Japanese prison camp, told of one engrossing discussion that served to distract a group of the prisoners, all of whom had recently undergone experiences in which death appeared a certainty and whose everyday life was marked by the sickness and death of their comrades. The question they debated was why the human being could experience such a painful emotional reaction to the prospect of imminent death, of death that might occur that day, or the next hour, or the next minute, but could maintain such an appearance of indifference over the general devastating fact that no living thing was immortal. Their conclusion was important, because it is consistent with the phenomena we have been considering. They felt that the reason most people do not fear death when life is not immediately threatened is because most people, down deep, really believe themselves to be immortal. This emotional conviction was proof against rational argument and could only be shaken or destroyed by another emotional experience that brought a person actually face to face with the prospect of death. In this respect, as the physician remarked, the average person behaves very much like the patient with conversion hysteria; his calm in the face of his own ultimate dissolution is similar to *la belle indifférence* of the hysteric. Also, like the hysteric, the calm and the complacency are superficial. Abundant observational evidence shows that in primitive and highly sophisticated cultures alike reactions to the concept of death occupy a distinctive position in their activities. There are spells and incantations to ward off death, there are the "supreme sacrifices" for propitiation of the gods, requiring that a member of the group die in the ceremony, there are ceremonial suicides. In our culture we see the many careful euphemisms for death, "passing away," "gone to his rest," and so on, and we whistle more loudly when we pass cemeteries. Much of the emotional attitude that places the physician in a peculiar institutional niche stems from his powers to intercede with death. The power of our emotional shrinking from death was shown in some of the cases of reactive depression we cited above. In the traumatic neuroses we catch a glimpse of another aspect of the meaning of death to humans. The fear and avoidance reactions we see in the traumatic neurosis indicate that to us death means a loss of mastery, a loss of our self-dominance over the environment. In acute fear of death, as manifest in the traumatic neurosis, all objects in the environment assume this threatening quality and are possible sources of new destructive disruption of the personality. Death is the final frustration against which no technique avails.

SUMMARY

In the traumatic neurosis disruptive behavior develops as a consequence of exposure to situations that acutely threaten the continued existence of the person. The emotional conviction of immortality is replaced by a generalized fear of the surrounding world, which requires the threatening significance originally attached to the traumatic situation. The symptoms of this neurosis represent a cross section of the ways already mentioned as defense against anxiety.

General Summary

We have now described some (but not all, by any means) of the ways a person may try to avoid or reduce the painful drive of anxiety. Although this chapter has been primarily devoted to a presentation of symptoms, we have tried to show how these symptoms are related to the motivational conditions that produce them. It now remains to see what final general statements we can make about the psychoneurotic behavior patterns. Probably the single most important thing for the student to understand is that *these ways of behaving are habits that the anxious person has acquired.* So far as we know, no person is born psychoneurotic, and all psychoneurotics may learn other, less distressing ways of dealing with their frustrations and conflicts. Given the adequate conditions of assistance, ineffective ways of dealing with anxiety may be replaced by habits more conducive to good adjustment.

As a second generalization, we may say that *no psychoneurotic type of adaptation is of long-run utility to the patient,* even in those conditions where the behavior offers a temporary shield. Avoidance or reduction of anxiety that does not eliminate the fundamental conflict or frustration in which it is rooted commits the patient to a continuous servitude to this strong avoidance drive.

A third general statement to be remembered is that the *neurotic mechanisms,* completely aside from their long-term impotence, *are also crippling to adjustment by virtue of the activities which they preclude or distort.* It is no more possible for the psychoneurotic to lead an efficient and happy social and interpersonal existence than it is for a person with tuberculosis. In both instances the pathological situation forces a displacement of normal activities by those connected with the disease problem.

DISCUSSION QUESTIONS

1. Should a distinction be made between conversion reactions and dissociative reactions?
2. Is a neurotic reaction to chronic stress inevitable?
3. What is the importance of anxiety in the neurotic disorders?

4. What explanation can you give for the high incidence of traumatic neuroses in our services during war?
5. What are some socially approved phobias?
6. How prevalent is psychoneurosis in our culture?
7. What sort of case could be made for and against conceiving of conversion hysteria as malingering?
8. What is your own attitude toward your death? Do you find any relationship between this aspect of your personal philosophy and other aspects of your behavior?
9. Are there any aspects of contemporary public life that suggest causation similar to that of the traumatic neurosis?
10. If you were a judge, would you let the knowledge that award of compensation might be an encouragement to neurosis color your decision-making in cases of this kind?

SUGGESTED READINGS

N. Cameron and Ann Magaret (1951), *Behavior Pathology.* New York: Houghton Mifflin Company.

A. Kardiner (1941), *The Traumatic Neuroses of War.* New York: Paul B. Hoeber, Inc.

L. P. Thorpe and B. Katz (1948), *The Psychology of Abnormal Behavior,* Part V. New York: The Ronald Press Company.

BIBLIOGRAPHIC SOURCES

By almost unanimous contemporary agreement, the use of the word "hysteria" as a technical term for those psychoneurotic symptoms described as such is distasteful. Unfortunately, as someone has pointed out, the word has been in the terminology so long that efforts to displace it may never be successful. Most classifications of the psychoneuroses (such as in Table 9) do not use the word, substituting instead the terms "conversion reaction" and "dissociative reactions." Nevertheless, hysteria as a technical term continues to predominate in the literature and in texts such as the present one. Perhaps textbook writers should take the initiative and relegate the word to a passing footnote.

On the psychoneuroses in general a rather complete presentation of symptomatology may be found in Thorpe and Katz (1948) or in Wechsler (1929). Historical development of our knowledge concerning these disorders is discussed briefly but well in Hollingworth (1930) and at more length in Zilboorg (1941). For an historical account of the terms "psychosis," "psychoneurosis," and "neurosis," as well as a strong critique of them, see Bowman and Rose (1952).

There has been little specific experimental interest in the language of the neurotic. One interesting study was done by Lorenz and Cobb (1953) who analyzed the formal linguistic categories of grammar and syntax such as substantives, adjectives, verbs, and so forth, for large samples of the language of neurotics. Their data definitely suggest a different pattern of speech for the neurotic. Another fascinating technique is the method developed by Dollard and Mowrer (1947, reprinted in Mowrer, 1953) called the DRQ or "Discomfort-Relief Quotient." The quotient is simply the number of "discomfort" words expressed during therapy divided by the number of discomfort plus relief words. The DRQ is designed to measure tension through the course of therapy and appears to be quite successful (see Mowrer, Hunt, and Kogan, 1953). Mowrer (1953) has written an excellent chapter (17) on the role and measurement of language in psychopathology.

The anxiety reactions were discussed in detail in Chapter VII. An additional source on the disorder termed "anxiety neurosis," "neurasthenia," or "effort syndrome" is Cohen and White's (1951) survey of the literature. Particularly of interest is the clinical description and discussion of the various terms that have been used to denote the disorder. A great deal of literature is discussed on differential physiological measures between this group and normal controls.

The obsessive-compulsive reaction type has been discussed by Frink (1921) with an analytical point of view, and by Ross (1937) from a more eclectic position. For the associational process in this neurosis see Guthrie (1938).

A clinical study of 100 cases of reactive depression has been made by Myers and Von Koch (1945), and D. E. Cameron discusses the relationship between anxiety and depression. An idea of the symbolism of the reactive depressive may be gained from Fenichel (1945). For a reasonable critique of the concept of neurotic depression supported by 12 brief case studies, see Ascher (1952).

The classic writing on hysteria is Janet's (1920) *The Major Symptoms of Hysteria.* The basic presentation of the psychoanalytic position on hysteria may be found in Freud's (1943) *A General Introduction to Psychoanalysis;* the case material in Abse (1950) is also suggested. An interesting book with an odd title is Sadger's (1920) *Sleep Walking and Moon Walking.* A description of sensory symptoms and some of the ways they may be treated by suggestion is contained in MacCurdy (1918). Perhaps the best source for symptomatology is the study by Purtell, Robins, and Cohen (1951). These authors compared 50 women diagnosed as hysterics with 50 normal controls. Symptoms were recorded in detail, and it was noted that no hysteric patient had less than 11 symptoms (with a mean number of 23 for the group) whereas the average number of the control group was about four. For a case of hysterical fugue and treatment by hypnosis see Collier (1953). Hysteria as a learning phenomenon is examined in detail by McGill and Welch (1947). The Ganser syndrome is described by Bleuler (1924). For historical sidelights on hysteria, see Zilboorg's (1935) *The Medical Man and the Witch During the Renaissance,* and White's (1896) *A History of the Warfare of Science with Theology.*

The chief monographic source on the traumatic neuroses is Kardiner's (1941) *The Traumatic Neuroses of War.* Grinker and Spiegel's (1945) *Men Under Stress* is also pertinent here. Stein's (1952) review is suggested. The relationships of traumatic neuroses to the compensation neuroses of hysteria is well discussed in Huddleson's (1932) *Accidents, Neuroses, and Compensation.* The analytic point of view concerning behavior oriented around death may be found in Menninger's (1938) *Man Against Himself.* According to Kalinowsky (1950), the incidence of traumatic neuroses in the German Army in World War II was negligible. Incidentally, for material, he had to visit individual German psychiatrists since, unfortunately, "After the war the Occupation Authorities discouraged publications on military psychiatry" (p. 340). An interesting experiment (with an odd title) is Sharp (1950). A combat division psychiatrist, Sharp reports on the combat records of 395 mild neuropsychiatric cases which were allowed to accompany the division into combat despite their diagnosis and the doubts of command. Only nine were lost for neuropsychiatric disorders. Only 44 of the total were lost for all reasons, less than would be expected by chance based on division statistics. A detailed analysis of 20 traumatic war neurotics, five years after separation, is the article by Futterman and Pumpian-Mindin (1951). They state, "The patients still present the same symptomatology as was seen immediately after the war. In many of our cases symptoms have persisted unchanged since they first began. In others there have been periods of lesser or greater remission with recurrences precipitated by external anxiety" (p. 401). Nine case studies are presented in detail. A somewhat more encouraging report is Brill and Beebe's (1951) follow-up study of 995 neurotic enlisted men. Since separation, 54 per cent have shown improvement, 13 per cent are worse, 30 per cent show no change, and 3 per cent are unclassified. Although, as they note, combat was the most frequent source of breakdown, it is interesting that 35 per cent of the sample developed the disorder before any overseas duty.

In the preceding chapter we examined some of the studies of the relationship between learning and anxiety. A somewhat broader experiment is that of Hall and Crookes (1952). Five groups were used, four psychoneurotic (anxiety, depression, hysteria, and obsessional) and one normal control. All the subjects did two tasks: first, a verbal learning series, and, second, a psychomotor task. With a variety of measures, the anxiety group was somewhat close to the normal group while the depression group was worse than the control or anxious group. Smaller samples for the hysteria and obsessional groups make comparisons difficult, as they note, but the data indicate that the hysterics were the best of the neurotics on verbal learning but were very poor on motor performance. The obsessional group was the reverse, being the worst of the neurotics on verbal learning but closest to the normal controls on the performance task.

As a supplement to the implicit views expressed in this chapter on the relationship between learning and neurosis, Dollard and Miller (1951), Guthrie (1938), and Mowrer (1952) are again suggested. In addition, the problem of the neurotic paradox, as mentioned in Chapter III, should be recalled (Mowrer, 1948, 1950).

In perhaps no other area of psychopathology is the problem of terminology more difficult or obscure than in the psychoneuroses. There is little common agreement on classification, and the official medical classifications are constantly undergoing change. The solution to this problem is certainly not immediately apparent, but one possibility might be considered. A major source of names is the behavior, and, in recent years, there have been attempts to get more adequate and reliable descriptions of disturbed behavior by the use of rating scales and check lists. The varieties of scales and lists being used is discussed in an article by Lorr (1954). From these scales a number of attempts have been made to construct new classification schemes. As an example, one of these is Wittman and Sheldon (1948) for psychotic behavior. The most extensive investigations have been made by Wittenborn and his associates (see Wittenborn and Holzberg, 1951; Wittenborn and Mettler, 1951; Holzberg and Wittenborn, 1953) who combine this technique with factor analytic methods. Whether such techniques, dependent solely on overt symptoms, will be completely successful remains, of course, to be seen. It is encouraging, however, to see the problem attacked directly and in a systematic manner.

Parenthetically, an interesting dialogue concerning attitudes toward death appears in Morton Thompson's (1949) novel about Ignaz Philipp Semmelweis, the discoverer of the cause of puerperal fever. Semmelweis, as a medical student, is talking to one of his professors, and remarks that his attitude toward people and toward life has changed, that since he has started to study medicine people "are no longer people. They are organs and diseases and symptoms, chemicals. . . ." The professor answers: "I will tell you a secret, Mr. Semmelweis. No layman ever feels that he will die. Deep within him he knows that someday, before it is too late, the secret of eternal life will be discovered. Others may die. But not he. And the doctor, Mr. Semmelweis, knows that from the day he begins the study of medicine that someday he will die. He knows that nothing can save him. No layman ever really feels that he will become ill. He may fear it, but he does not actually believe it because he cannot imagine pain and make it real. All doctors know that illness is as inevitable as deterioration and they know this in terms of themselves. This is the difference, Mr. Semmelweis. To the layman, the layman is immortal. To the doctor he is very mortal indeed." [9]

[9] From *The Cry and the Covenant*, by Morton Thompson. Copyright 1949 by Morton Thompson, reprinted by permission of Doubleday & Company, Inc.

The Psychoses

So weary with disasters, tugg'd with fortune,
That I would set my life on any chance,
To mend it or be rid on't.
                    —SHAKESPEARE, *Macbeth*

TERMINOLOGY

We have already indicated some of the points of difference commonly used to distinguish between *psychosis* and *psychoneurosis;* some of these differences were matters of degree or intensity of symptom, and some were qualitative variations in the kind of behavior manifested. In general the psychoses always present the sharpest points of contrast with what we popularly refer to as normal behavior. The psychotic patient seems to be receding from his cultural surroundings to such an extent that we say his "whole personality" is involved,[1] although, as the reader will no doubt recognize, we have tried to show that this same "whole personality" is affected in the behavior we term *psycho-neurotic* or *normal* as well. We will spend a little time trying to arrive at some working definitions of "psychosis" as soon as we present a few more of the terms we will meet in this chapter.

PSYCHOPATHOLOGY AND THE LAW

The definition quoted in footnote 1 and the features of psychotic behavior listed in the preceding chapter will probably suggest that we are now writing about "insanity," and that the *psychotic* patient is the

---

[1] This definition from a textbook is representative: "A major mental disorder, usually involving the total personality; the individual's mental functions are so profoundly disturbed that he is incapacitated from participating in everyday activities" (Thorpe and Katz [1948], p. 898).

actually *insane* person who fits the lay conception of what abnormal psychology concerns itself with. Because of the widespread confusion of these terms, it is important to clarify their contemporary usage. *Insanity* is, strictly speaking, a legal concept and is defined in legal statutes in a number of ways that have certain points in common. Historically, until the early part of this century the medical and legal usages were almost synonymous and derived from the same beliefs about this form of disordered behavior. More recently, reflecting our increased scientific understanding, medical terminology has changed. To establish the insanity of a person in a court of law, it must be demonstrated either that the person does not know the difference between "right" and "wrong," or that he is unable to exercise that control of his actions generally expected and observed in the average individual. The establishment of this point is important and necessary in at least three types of legal action: (1) In determining criminal responsibility, an accused person has, as a possible permissible plea, the allegation that he is not guilty of a crime because of insanity, or, as it is sometimes phrased, "being of an unsound mind." Almost universally insanity is an exonerating circumstance in this connection. (2) In attempting to establish the competence of an individual to execute any legal action, insanity is a disqualifying condition. Contracts, wills, sworn testimony, commitments to sell or purchase, and so forth are not acceptable or valid if the person involved is insane. (3) The responsibility of society for the individual, as formulated in law, involves the concept of sanity in several respects. First, if a person is adjudged insane, a guardian is usually appointed by the court to handle his financial and legal affairs. Second, in most states, hospitalization of a mandatory sort for the mentally ill person must be preceded by a court hearing to establish his insanity. In some states special combined panels of lawyers, physicians, and laymen are appointed to hear evidence and decide the question of sanity; in many places these are called, with medieval flavor, "lunacy commissions." That hospitalization of any kind should be a legal and not a medical responsibility is something of a paradox, yet the historical and circumstantial reasons are comprehensible enough. The type of patient legally termed insane is not only sick; he is also a potential threat to society or to himself. Since such people do kill or harm others, commit suicide, behave rashly and recklessly in business and social transactions, and since their hospitalization of necessity may involve an involuntary confinement for a long period of time, the legal processes incident to medical treatment of these patients are patently not motivated solely by the professional ambitions of the bar.

However justifiable the motives for legal definition of mental disease and however necessary the admixture of law with medicine may be, the fact remains that for some time there has been a steadily growing divergence between the legal and medico-psychological concepts of disordered behavior. The psychological sciences give little basis for any procedure of validly determining universal "right" from "wrong," acknowledging this to be a socio-ethical project, and still less are they able to furnish a test that will establish any person's ability to make this differentiation. Further, science has a deterministic bias that casts doubt on the reality of the "free will," which is so obviously the underlying assumption of the condition that a person "exercise control of his actions." The psychological sciences are unable to locate or describe the agent that the law infers as a controlling force in the individual. Thus, when a psychiatrist is called upon to examine a person and to make a statement about his sanity, the statement is not a scientific conclusion but is literally what many psychiatrists frankly call it, an "opinion." This situation is not met in psychiatric professional procedures; divergence of opinion about diagnosis exists, but agreement among competent examiners may be obtained on the basis of explicit criteria, whereas agreement between "expert" witnesses about sanity or insanity is exceptional. Most court hearings in which the person accused of a serious crime is examined by psychiatrists retained by defense and prosecution result in contradictory testimony. This gives the average layman the understandable but erroneous impression that very little must be known about such conditions if the experts disagree. The truth of the matter is that they have been asked to answer a question that is scientifically unanswerable in the form on which the law states it. If, as often happens, the opposed psychiatrists are asked what the medical diagnosis of the accused might be, their answers are surprisingly in agreement. The latter is a matter of scientific description and classification; the former is not.

Thus, as can be seen, *insanity* and *psychosis* are not synonymous. Most psychotic patients would be called insane, but not all. Some insane persons, within what we believe to be the intent of the law, are not psychotic, but may be psychoneurotic or mentally defective or simply visitors from another culture so different that it fails to prepare them for conformity to our own. *Insanity* is not, at present, a scientific term and will not be used in this text.

ORGANIC AND FUNCTIONAL

These two words are often used to qualify the description of many mental disease syndromes. A psychosis may be "organic" or "functional." By *organic* it is meant that the disordered behavior seems to grow out of, follow, or be caused by a specific injury or deformation of a part or system of the body. The deviant behavior following an injury to the brain or the confusional state following an overdose of some drug would be called *organic*. The *functional* disorders are those for which no injurious agent or defect has been identified and for which there appears to be evidence that the disease has been acquired as a set of faulty habits. If no evidence exists for functional causation, and if no specific organic agent has yet been found, the condition is termed *idiopathic*. For example, epilepsy that cannot be traced to definite sources of toxin or injury is called "idiopathic epilepsy." We will later explore the merits of this distinction between "organic" and "functional," as well as some of the controversies it has caused. It is enough to say here that the distinction is probably not crucial to understanding the behavior of the psychotic patients, however essential it may be in their treatment.

CLASSIFICATION OF PSYCHOSES

There have been many attempts to classify the psychoses. The earliest classification to meet with any general agreement was made by Kraepelin, the German psychiatrist, and was based on the hypothesis that all psychoses were clear-cut, sharply defined conditions with definite specific causes, differentiated symptoms, uniform clinical course, and definite prognosis. In this idea he was influenced by the example of the bacterial and traumatic diseases that had been fitted into such a scheme. Further study showed that Kraepelin's types were sometimes too broad and sometimes too restrictively narrow; to compensate for this, modifications in the classification have been made periodically, in the light of clinical experience.

The classification we will follow in our discussion of these psychotic disorders is presented in Table 10. It will be noted that this classification reduces the number of disorders to five major types and a small number of subdivisions within these. This has been done in the conviction that most psychotic behavior has a common dynamic basis, and that the amount of duplicative behavior among the types as previously distinguished was so great as to disprove their practical utility. In the psychoses with organic etiological factors, for example, there would be almost no end of distinct psychoses if each drug, toxin, and type of structural or physiological injury and defect that can produce psychotic behavior were to be considered separately. The symptoms in most of the organic disturbances may be comprehended on the basis of a few principles, and the symptoms themselves are closely similar irrespective of the causative agent. We will consider these problems further in the next chapter.

TABLE 10

A CLASSIFICATION OF PSYCHOSES*

Type of Psychosis	*Description*
1. General	These disorders are characterized by varying degrees of personality disintegration and failure to test and evaluate correctly external reality in various spheres. In addition individuals with such disorders fail in their ability to relate themselves effectively or happily to other people or to their own work.
2. Schizophrenic disorders (*a*) General	This term represents a group of psychotic disorders characterized by fundamental disturbances in reality-relationships and concept formations, with consequent affective and intellectual disturbances in varying degrees and mixtures. The disorders are marked by strong tendencies to retreat from reality, by emotional disharmony, unpredictable disturbances in stream of thought, and by a tendency to "flatten-out" the emotional and libidinal struggle which gives the appearance of "deterioration"—not necessarily fulfilled—that may progress to "dementia."
(*b*) Schizophrenic reaction, latent	Certain individuals are found on examination to present definite schizophrenic ideation and behavior . . . beyond that of the schizoid personality, but not of an advanced stage as in acute or chronic schizophrenic reactions. These individuals may be incipient schizophrenics, and they may maintain their borderline adjustment over long periods. Among their friends, these individuals are regarded merely as queer or eccentric; under close examination, however, they show evidence of psychotic symptoms. They represent essentially borderline psychoses. . . . Hospitalization of such cases is rarely necessary.

TABLE 10 (Continued)

Type of Psychosis	*Description*
(c) Schizophrenic reaction, simple type	This type of reaction is characterized chiefly by reduction in external attachments and interests and impoverishment of human relationships. It often involves adjustment on a lower psychobiologic level of functioning, usually accompanied by apathy and indifference but rarely by conspicuous delusions or hallucinations. In contrast to the long history—without any, or slight, change in symptomatology—of the schizoid personality, there is characteristically a change in the simple type of schizophrenic reaction.
(d) Schizophrenic reaction, hebephrenic type	Such reactions are characterized by shallow, inappropriate affect, unpredictable giggling, silly behavior and mannerisms, delusions often of a somatic nature, and hallucinations.
(e) Schizophrenic reaction, catatonic type	The reaction is characterized chiefly by conspicuous motor behavior, exhibiting either stupor, mutism, negativism, and waxy flexibility, or excessive motor activity and excitement. The individual may regress to a state of vegetation.
(f) Schizophrenic reaction, paranoid type	This type of reaction is characterized by schizophrenic (dereistic and autistic) thinking and unpredictable behavior, with mental content composed chiefly of delusions of persecution, occasionally of grandeur, hallucinations, a fairly constant attitude of hostility and aggression, and ideas of reference. Excessive religiosity may be present and, rarely, there may be no delusions of persecution, but instead an expansive and productive delusional system of omnipotence, genius, or special ability. The systematized paranoid hypochondriacal states are included in this group. It will be borne in mind that some patients manifest their paranoid ideas only when depressed, and others only when they are manic.
(g) Schizophrenic reaction, acute undifferentiated type.	The acute group of this reaction includes a wide variety of schizophrenic symptomatology, such as confusion of thinking and turmoil of emotion, accompanied by secondary elaboration manifested by perplexity, ideas of reference, fear, and dream states, and dissociative phenomena. These symptoms appear precipitously, often without apparent precipitating stress, but exhibiting historical evidence of prodromal symptoms. Very often it is accompanied by a pronounced affective coloring of either excitement or depression. The symptoms often clear in a matter of weeks, although there is a tendency for them to recur.

TABLE 10 (Continued)

Type of Psychosis	*Description*
(*h*) Schizophrenic reaction, schizo-affective type.	This group shows mixed schizophrenic and affective reactions. The disorder, however, is basically schizophrenic.
(*i*) Schizophrenic reaction, childhood type.	This group denotes those individuals who show schizophrenic symptoms in the period of life preceding puberty.
3. Paranoid disorders (*a*) Paranoia	This type of psychotic disorder is extremely rare. It is characterized by an intricate, complex, and slowly developing paranoid system with the individual usually regarding himself as particularly singled out. The patient often endows himself with superior or unique ability, and even considers himself appointed for a Messianic mission. The paranoid system is particularly isolated from much of the normal stream of consciousness, without hallucinations and with relative intactness and preservation of the remainder of the personality.
(*b*) Paranoid state	This type of paranoid disorder is characterized by transient paranoid delusions. It lacks the logical nature of systematization seen in paranoia; yet it does not manifest the bizarre fragmentation and deterioration of the schizophrenic. It occurs most frequently in individuals between 35 and 55 years of age, and it is ordinarily of a relatively short duration, though it may be persistent and chronic.
4. Affective disorders (*a*) Manic-depressive reaction	This group shows marked swings in mood of either mania or depression. In general, the patient (1) may be restricted to one phase or the other, that is, showing only mania or depression, or (2) may alternate between manic and depressive phases.
(*b*) Psychotic depressive reaction	This differs from the neurotic depressive reaction chiefly in degree. If the patient manifests evidence of gross misinterpretation of external reality (*e.g.*, in matters of guilt and unworthiness), it technically becomes a psychosis.
5. Involutional melancholia	This reaction is characterized most commonly by depression, with or without agitation, without previous history of either manic or depressive illnesses. It occurs in the individual's middle life and in his later years. It tends to have a prolonged course and may be manifested by worry, guilt, anxiety, agitation, paranoid and other delusional ideas, and somatic concerns.

* Based primarily on War Department Technical Bulletin, T.B. Med. 203, *Nomenclature and Methods of Recording Diagnoses*, pp. 16-19, October, 1945; and secondarily on Committee on Nomenclature and Statistics of the American Psychiatric Association (1952), *Diagnostic and Statistical Manual, Mental Disorders*, pp. 5-6; 24-28. Washington, D.C.: American Psychiatric Association, Mental Hospital Service

Even at the risk of appearing to labor a point, we will repeat our earlier caution concerning the arbitrary nature of diagnostic classifications in psychopathology. To the same extent as in the psychoneuroses, the behavior we are describing is as noteworthy for its variability from patient to patient as for its elements of constancy. Dividing lines between the types of psychosis are not sharp, clear or definite; only when we draw back from consideration of the individual case and survey the accumulated mass of recorded behavior of large groups of these patients do we see constellations of symptoms that tend, on the whole, to indicate that some groups of patients behave more in one fashion than another. Again, as with the psychoneurotics, the "textbook" cases we present are usually selected to illustrate particular points in our presentation. Even when we do this, the student will note that some aspects of the behavior we describe could as well be classified in some adjacent category. Although this is certainly not a comfortable situation to those who, quite rightly, would like to see a cleanly compartmentalized classification system, it is an honest and a realistic reflection of the present state of affairs in this corner of science.

General Description of Psychotic Behavior

PSYCHOTIC BEHAVIOR

What is psychotic behavior? How can we view it against the background of adjustmental striving with which we have been concerned? What distinctions, if any, can be made between psychotic behavior and the psychoneurotic behavior we have recently discussed? To answer these questions we must go back again to our starting point, the concept of adaptation to stress. We have seen that, when the stress is sufficiently intense, compensatory or adjusive behavior becomes more and more exclusively devoted to reducing the disproportionate threat to equilibrium. If these efforts are unavailing, the behavior undergoes further transformation to an end phase that is termed a "catastrophic response." The catastrophic response reflects the inability of the individual to maintain equilibrium, and the proper balance and integration between all the need-demands upon the person break down. A simple illustration should suffice. Automobile accidents have been caused by bees stinging drivers. A bee sting represents a sudden and, to some people, an almost catastrophic stress. The driver whose attention is so completely usurped by his efforts (usually disorganized and catastrophic) to reduce the pain of the sting finds that he is unable to maintain the balanced behavior that other needs in his situation demand. He releases the steering wheel, he looks away from the road, he puts on the brakes, he swears or cries, he searches for the bee—and he has an accident. Or, on a more complex level, let us take the businessman whose occupation demands ever more effort to ensure success or even to maintain financial solvency. He devotes more hours to business, he stays home less, he is instantly on guard against anything threatening to disrupt his schedule. He thus has friction with his wife who wants to have friends in for bridge or wants to spend a large sum of money on the house, with his children who want to use the car, want to go on vacation, or want him to play with them, with his friends who want him to play bridge or poker or who have more successful businesses of their own. When he finally is forced to see his physician, he is told that he must "lead a more balanced life," that he is "heading for a nervous breakdown," or that he must "go away for a while." The patient finds that, in his efforts to solve problems in one area of his life, he has accumulated tensions in other areas. In spite of his doctor's advice, he may have placed himself in such a position that he cannot go away, cannot lead a more balanced life, and cannot avoid heading for a nervous breakdown. He may, in fact, be so preoccupied with his business problems that he hardly hears the doctor, hardly notices his wife's resentments and the growing estrangement with his children and friends. He would be, then, approaching the type of condition we call psychotic.

Psychosis may have many causes, since the word is essentially a shorthand description for a state of preoccupation with some pressing adjustmental problem that is so intense as to preclude any sort of balanced adjustment for the person's life as a whole. Thus, we will see that a person with a brain tumor may act in a completely psychotic manner because the derangement of his nervous system is so severe that all his efforts are required to maintain simple vegetative life and possibly some small semblance of ego integrity. The childhood background of another patient may have so handicapped him with a sense of inferiority, insecurity, and lack of love as to warp his whole adult behavior into a constant preoccupation with these problems and a total disregard of the other conditions of adult life in our culture. Still a third person may have suffered such a hereditary or developmental handicap as to necessitate his whole activity being directed to overcoming the deficiency, again with the danger of sacrificing compliance with other needs.

In this sense, our definition of psychosis is formulated against both a biological and a social background. The living creature adapts or perishes, and the human creature must adapt to social as well as physical realities. That which makes the psychotic often "dangerous to himself or others" is the same disharmony in meeting adjustmental demands that was at the heart of neurosis. As in the neuroses, we believe that the primary problem of the psychotic, whatever it may be, is transformed into an attempt to escape anxiety. Psychotic behavior grows out of this elemental problem of anxiety-reduction and is separated from neurotic behavior more in degree than in kind. The psychotic patient may be said to be a person who either *has not used the usual neurotic techniques for dealing with anxiety,* or who *has been forced to abandon them by the continuing severity of his problems.* Accordingly, most psychotics should show anxiety symptoms sometime in the course of the development of their illness. One study, at least, specifically indicates this (Billings, Ebaugh, *et al.,* 1943), and in personal clinical experience it has almost invariably been true that histories on psychotic patients show that they have had symptoms of anxiety before the more psychotic manifestations developed. Table 11 illustrates a comparison between anxiety-related factors in the backgrounds of psychoneurotic and psychotic soldiers examined in the Billings and Ebaugh study. The hypothesis that people will vary their attempts to solve anxiety problems until they find a solution or until they are overwhelmed by the consequences of their behavior seems substantiated by these data. Psychotic behavior may be thought of then as extreme, last-ditch attempts to reduce anxiety or to maintain integrity.

According to our hypothesis, some of the psychotic types we will review should show similarities to milder psychoneurotic reactions. We should be able to trace the development of disordered behavior in some persons through a neurotic stage into ever more severe and extreme deviations until we finally arrive at an established psychosis. This should be most true of the so-called functional disturbances and probably less true of the organically caused conditions. In the latter, the stress that forces disordered behavior may have occurred suddenly and in the life of a person whose pre-traumatic adaptation was excellent. Many well-adjusted people are hit by automobiles, shot, fall down stairs, develop tumors, catch poliomyelitis, or otherwise succumb to environmental threats of unpredictable occurrence. Even in the organic conditions, however, we shall see that the pre-traumatic personality plays a large and important role in determining the precise nature of the symptoms shown by any individual.

TABLE 11

COMPARISON OF ANXIETY-RELATED SYMPTOMS IN THE HISTORIES OF
PSYCHOTICS, PSYCHONEUROTICS, AND NORMAL SOLDIERS*

Symptom	Per Cent Occurrence in Psychotics N 37	Per Cent Occurrence in Psychoneurotics N 36	Per Cent Occurrence in Normals N 100
Bedwetting after age 10	34	39	7
Nail-biting after age 10	43	41	16
Restlessness	43	33	7
Uneasiness	51	33	5
Sleepwalking	12	11	5
Nightmares	51	44	12
Playing alone	59	42	3
Moodiness	76	44	9
Religious conflicts	13	5	1
Disturbed psycho-sexual development	54	50	6
Excessive smoking	11	14	5
Hypochondriasis	57	75	11

* Source: Abstracted from tabular material in the study by Billings, Ebaugh, *et al.* (1943).

In our discussion of the legal aspects of psychotic behavior we saw to what an extent the psychotic patient stands out against his social background. One of the key factors in defining psychotic behavior is an evaluation of the cultural setting of the patient. Historically, the first type of psychiatric patient to be hospitalized was the psychotic. His preoccupation with his own problems makes him a poor participant in community life. His hallucinatory and delusional experiences often lead him to misinterpret so grossly the behavior of people around him that his subsequent actions may prove inconvenient or dangerous. Just as a drowning man will clutch at his rescuer and actually impede the efforts to save him, so will the psychotic cut himself off from and even attack the community upon which he basically depends for his well-being.

The psychotic deviates markedly from his social group in his ways of thinking, and in this, as in other aspects of his behavior, he becomes a matter of community concern. Rightly or wrongly, all social groups evolve particular sets of convictions, distinctive conventional ways of thinking and acting, and standards of acceptable and non-acceptable behavior and thought. Deviations from these mores, particularly if they are openly and overtly expressed, call forth reactions of aggression, resentment, and hostility from the group. How small the deviation may be to go beyond the group's tolerance is shown in the sad fate of many a school teacher who was fired for such sins as smoking, adopting an unconventional hair arrangement, or teaching material unacceptable to the group's standards. The psychotic, wittingly or not, manages to deviate in most of the group-determined properties to an extreme that is not tolerable. In this respect his illness is different from influenza or appendicitis, and this has been one of the factors making mental disease a disgrace bordering on the criminal in the attitude of the majority of the group. Psychotic behavior as such is not the source of this group reaction of repugnance. Within any social group may be found generally accepted beliefs as bizarre and as lacking in agreement with reality as anything the psychotic ever produced. It is when the psychotic's thinking diverges from the group's thinking that he is regarded as dangerously ill.

Because the psychotic is forced to such extreme efforts, he creates secondary social problems at an alarming rate. The psychoneurotic seldom becomes so completely out of touch with his group (as long as he remains neurotic) that they regard him in a hostile manner. In response to these secondary sources of frustration the psychotic may develop more aggression and do so directly against the impeding social group. This may lead to still more pronounced withdrawal from society or to attack that the psychotic looks upon as provoked and richly warranted. The psychotic person becomes not only asocial but antisocial.

More than in the psychoneuroses we notice how completely the loss of adaptive capacity penetrates all levels of the patient's life. Not only at the social level, but at the cellular and ego levels as well, the psychotic manifests defeat in his struggle to adjust. Even in the functional disorders, which do not have a primary organic causation, we find the life span of the psychotic is shorter than that of the population as a whole. In addition we find that many of the psychotics manifest physiological disturbances almost as deviant as their psychological symptoms (Hoskins, 1946). A manner of living that is out of harmony with the culture leads to biological difficulties in satisfying the most elementary drives. It is not uncommon for the receiving room of a psychiatric hospital to see patients coming in half-starved, cold, and dirty beyond the most lax notions of sanitation. Here again one gains the impression of a person so busy with other more important matters that eating, sleeping, and bathing are inconsequental and irrelevant.

In summary, *psychotic behavior is characterized by a disruption of the integrated adaptation to stress at all life levels.* The psychotic is preoccupied with some problems to the exclusion of others. He is attempting to reduce anxiety by extreme means and is often driven into psychosis by the failure of more moderate attempts at adjustment. These strivings bring him into conflict with society and thus produce secondary difficulties. His maladjustment finally involves his whole life and becomes the dominant aspect of his personality.

HALLUCINATIONS

Hallucinations are sensory experiences for which no adequate sensory stimulation can be discovered. If, on a dark night, a person reports seeing a figure dressed in shining white walking toward him and if no changes in light intensity falling on the eye can be discovered, the experience is called hallucinatory. If a person says that he hears a voice and no sound stimulus can be discovered, his experience is likewise hallucinatory. The mysterious and "unnatural" aspects of this type of phenomenon are responsible for much of the superstitious attitude that has, at one time or another, characterized psychotic persons as being possessed of spirits. Even some fairly recent medical definitions of hallucination have retained a little of the conviction that such experiences arise from some unknown and unknowable stratum of life. Hallucinations have been defined as "sensory experiences without stimulation," which is akin to saying that they have no cause; such a definition is an unwarranted admission of failure, since we have a fairly respectable amount of knowledge about hallucinations.

From a psychological point of view hallucinations fit into something of the same category as what may be called "thoughts" or "images." The implicit verbal and imaginal manipulations that the human can make are almost unlimited. The artist may see his glorious canvas in "his mind's eye" long before he has plied his brush; the truant schoolboy may verbally and visually construct his rendezvous with a whipping while he is still enjoying the swimming or movie trip for which he left school. Almost everyone has had hallucinatory experiences at night while asleep—dreams are as hallucinatory an experience as could ever be had by the sickest psychotic. In short, the hallucination is of the same natural order of events as fills the majority of our waking life and a great deal of our sleep.

Realizing how coextensive hallucinations are with normal experience, some have tried to differentiate the hallucination from normal imagery on the basis of "insight," saying that the psychotic person does not realize that his hallucinations are caused by internal stimuli and do not have an objective reality. This comes near to being true, but is not dependable as a completely sweeping generalization. Many psychotics are troubled by their hallucinations because they realize that the experience is not "real," and many instances are on record where daydreams or other sorts of usual imagery have been mistakenly identified as having objective reality. Further, by special experimental techniques, hallucinations may be induced in otherwise non-psychotic persons, and their actions reveal a lack of insight for the internal nature of the hallucinatory stimulation. Under hypnosis, it is possible to tell the subject that when he is freed from the hypnotic session he will have any sort of sensory experience; in the vast majority of instances the subject will act precisely as if the suggested experience were taking place and will give a verbal report that betrays no knowledge of the artificial nature of the experience. For example, a girl is told, under hypnosis, that when she awakens she will have a small puppy dog in her lap. Upon termination of the hypnosis, the subject will pet the "dog," talk to it, and act in every way as if a dog were actually there. Auditory and cutaneous hallucinations are suggested with equal ease.

What then differentiates hallucinations from these other imaginal experiences? The best answer is simply that they are not basically differentiated. Hallucinations are only extremely vivid types of imagery which, under special circumstances, are accepted as genuine sensory stimulation in both psychotic and non-psychotic persons. The conditions under which this may occur are those that diminish the person's discriminatory ability. Sleep, toxic delirium, intense preoccupation with one field of stimulation, fatigue, shock—all these are conditions in which the hallucinatory experience has been reported. All these conditions have a state of lowered discriminatory ability in common. That hallucinations occur so frequently in the psychotic we can take as evidence that these patients are much more deeply immersed in their problems than are the psychoneurotics; the psychotic is so preoccupied with his serious difficulties that he makes less effort to differentiate between "thought" and "reality."

The content of hallucinations and the sensory department in which they occur have been studied intensively. The material of hallucinations, like that of dreams, is formed from the experience background of the subject. In hallucinations we see reflected the preoccupations, the interests, and the motives of the patient. Often great insight for the nature of a patient's difficulties may be gained by careful study of his reported hallucinatory experiences. From a statistical point of view we can say that the great majority of hallucinatory experiences are devoted to unpleasant or threatening material. The patient typically sees someone threatening him, hears voices calling him foul names, smells unpleasant odors, and tastes putrid substances. Since a psychosis, like all disordered behavior, is a reaction to great stress, the disagreeable nature of most hallucinations should be expected. The patient, after all, is dealing with circumstances threatening to his equilibrium, and the hallucinations tend to reflect those threats.

Hallucinations occur most frequently in the auditory sphere and are usually experienced as voices uttering relatively complete sentences, usually of an accusatory or revelatory nature. One patient, a physician, heard a voice telling him that he would be the most able diagnostician in the world if he could "tune in the radio in his stomach"; another patient could not sleep because voices coming from the walls told him he was "the worst of all homosexuals"; another patient committed suicide because voices told him he was to "be tortured in the morning." Visual hallucinations occur less frequently but have the same types of content. A patient woke from a sound sleep to see his mother, who had been dead for years, standing by his bed; another patient was troubled by seeing blood stains on his clothes and hands; a soldier, recovering from a prolonged drinking bout, saw a squad of marines standing by his bed, ready to lead him out for an early morning execution. Olfactory hallucinations occur in many patients. One patient was convinced that he exuded an odor of decay and gave that as a reason for his efforts to avoid people; an old widow who had lived alone for many years claimed that she was able to tell whether a person's soul was "black or white" by the distinctive odor they presented. Tactual hallucinations are most commonly seen in persons who have received injury to the nervous system through poisons, drugs, alcohol, and so forth. Many chronic alcoholics and cocaine addicts complain of the uncomfortable and painful feeling they have that they are being bitten or crawled upon by countless numbers of "bugs." The tactual hallucination may be, although rarely, quite well differentiated. One patient reported that the devil was writing messages in fire upon the skin of her abdomen and would trace with her finger the exact distribution of the painful sensation; another female patient felt that the skin of her face was turning into rose petals and complained of the sharp pains that this transformation occasioned.

ILLUSIONS

Hallucinations are usually differentiated from *illusions,* the latter being defined as "faulty or mistaken interpretations of sensory stimulation." Common examples of illusory experience are the familiar appearance of water on a highway as a person drives along it on a bright day or the mistakes in judgment of length when confronted with particular arrangements of linear visual stimulation as shown in Figure 12. Of

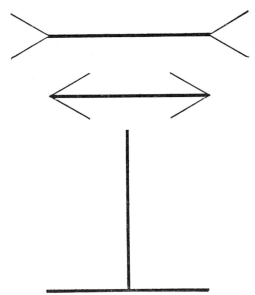

FIGURE 12. *Illusions of length. The two feathered lines are the same length; the vertical and horizontal lines in the lower drawing are the same length.*

more significance to psychopathology are the illusory interpretations individuals make of imperfectly received stimulation or of stimulation received against a background of motivational set or attitude that warps the perception. The sensitive person who dimly hears a conversation and believes the participants are talking about him and the emotionally involved witness to a situation whose testimony shows that he has perceived only what he was motivated to perceive are frequently encountered in our study of disordered behavior. Here again, however, we must stress the continuity between "illusory perception" and all other perceptual experience. All perception is influenced by factors of motivation and attitude, of past experience and expectation. All stimulation is selectively transformed into perception, and only a mechanical recording apparatus approaches true fidelity in reception or reproduction of experience. To the extent that the psychotic is more involved in his problems, has stronger motives or more vivid anticipation of what a situation will turn out to be, to that extent he may be more subject to illusion as he is more subject to hallucinations. In addition, there is no sharp distinction that can be drawn between an illusion and an hallucination. Some illusions work on such a minimal amount of direct sensory stimulation and such a large amount of internal patterning that they approach the hallucination. The "mirage" experiences of persons dying of thirst are of this type; a minimal amount of sensory stimulation may so strongly suggest water as to dominate completely their experience.

DELUSIONS

Appearing as commonly in the psychoses as hallucinations are the *delusions*. A delusion is a belief or conviction that is firmly held irrespective of and with immunity to objective evidence as to its truth or falsity. The *obsessions* we discussed in the last chapter fall into a continuum with delusions on one side and the usual strong emotional convictions of everyone on the other. Most patients with delusions are as unable to analyze their beliefs critically as is the neurotic or the "normal" person. Delusions deserve a separate name only because they generally depart farther from objective reality than either the obsessions or the prejudices. Dynamically, however, they appear to have the same causative basis in the needs and wishes of the organism and are clung to because they meet needs more than because of any *intellectual* incapacity of the person to evaluate reality.

Delusions are, with respect to content, separable into two types, the expansive and the derogatory or persecutory. In the expansive delusions the individual directly compensates for inadequacy by believing that he is more capable or better equipped than is in reality the case. A patient may believe that he has the strongest body, the biggest heart, the most potent sexual organs of anyone in the world. He may believe that he has the power of God, of Satan, or, as one atomic-age patient said, of the "Manhattan Project." He may believe that he is the richest man in the world, or the smartest, the most musical, the most scientific, or the most religious. In the derogatory type the patient may feel that he is unworthy to associate with human beings, that he is lower than the "beasts of the field," that he is afflicted with loathsome diseases, that his body is maimed or distorted, that his internal organs are rotted away, or that various mechanisms or foreign bodies have been implanted in him. In the persecutory type of delusion the patient may believe that conspiracies exist to deprive him of his possessions, his loved ones, or his life, that designs are being made on his reputation, that other humans or supernatural powers have taken possession of his faculties and are compelling him to actions that will disgrace or destroy him.

Because the delusions are established on emotional grounds, rational argument does not change them. Just as we have seen in the hysteric, the delusional patient is capable of blandly ignoring the lack of correspondence between his beliefs and the reality surrounding him. The "richest man in the world" may be hospitalized in an institution that requires him, as a part of his activity program, to perform such ignoble tasks as weeding the garden, cleaning the stable, and so on, but he is not bothered by the incongruity. The patient with "omnipotent powers of the universe" may plead with an attendant for a small extra privilege or may stare wistfully at the bars and locks that separate him from the world without for a moment giving up his conviction that all things are possible to him. The physician mentioned earlier, who received diagnostic information via the radio in his stomach, firmly believed in the existence and location of the radio despite his expert anatomical knowledge that should have rendered the belief absurd. In the same way we have seen the obsessional patient cling to his beliefs in the face of a rational knowledge that they were untenable; and who has not argued religion or politics with opponents who were capable of a sublime disregard of evidence? Propaganda, cleverly used, may convince great numbers of people of the truth of palpably false statements. The delusions of the psychotic are probably distinctive mostly in their individuality rather than on any more qualitative grounds.

The Schizophrenic Disorders

GENERAL CONDITIONS

Viewed either as a problem in psychological research or as a matter of public health, schizophrenia occupies a dominant place in the field of psychopathology. About 45 per cent of the hospital psychiatric cases are schizophrenics. There were approximately 22,000 first admissions of schizophrenics to state mental hospitals in 1949 (Federal Security Agency, 1952). Considering only the lost earning and productive power of these patients who are removed from society, the economic loss from schizophrenia is tremendous.

As a research problem schizophrenia has received more attention than any other psychosis. Investigations have been carried out on almost every aspect of the schizophrenic's life and body. Anatomists, chemists, physiologists, pathologists, endocrinologists, physicists, semanticists, psychologists, psychiatrists, sociologists, and anthropologists have all contributed. At the present time we may say that our understanding of the syndrome is still far from complete. We know less about schizophrenia now than medicine knew about malaria in 1800. In the pages that follow we can do little more than describe the various clinical pictures that are included under the term; in the third part of this book some of the factors that play a part in this psychosis will be discussed. Schizophrenia is still a challenge to the psychopathologist—probably it is his most important problem.

Schizophrenia has a long past but a relatively short history. In very early accounts of behavior we see described actions and experiences closely resembling the symptoms of this disease. The first formal description, however, was given by the Belgian physician, B. A. Morel (1860), who noted that many young people developed a state of emotional apathy and intellectual dulling that was progressive and led to deterioration. To this condition he gave the name *demense precoce, or dementia praecox,* an early or premature dementia. The disease was thought to be confined to adolescence. Kraepelin, in his famous classification, grouped together a number of somewhat dissimilar symptom patterns that appeared to have emotional and intellectual slowing in common, under the heading of dementia praecox. These "forms" of the disease were (1) simple dementia praecox, (2) hebephrenic, (3) catatonic, and (4) paranoid. His descriptions of symptoms were clear and masterful; more than any other student, Kraepelin defined the area of behavior we now still consider under schizophrenia.

For the word *schizophrenia* we are indebted to E. Bleuler (1924). Objecting that many dementia praecox patients actually do not show symptoms of their disease until they are 30 or even older and that thus the implication that this disorder was a disease of youth was erroneous, Bleuler suggested "schizophrenia," a word of Greek coinage meaning a "splitting of the mind." Bleuler's term was based on his observations that the schizophrenic patient manifests an extreme dissociation both in emotion and intellect, between reality and his actual content of behavior. Contemporary usage favors "schizophrenia," although "dementia praecox" is still used as an exactly equivalent synonym.

SYMPTOMS COMMON TO ALL FORMS
OF SCHIZOPHRENIA

The "types" of schizophrenia are named on the basis of particular distinguishing features that emerge against a background of symptoms that all schizophrenics have in common. The most prominent of these are *emotional and intellectual dissociation*. Schizophrenics rather uniformly show changes in their emotional expressions and in their ways of thinking.

Emotionally the schizophrenic gives the appearance of either apathy or indifference to the usual emotional stimuli or he over-reacts to such situations. He may maintain a phlegmatic calm in such distressing situations as the death of intimates, threat of imprisonment or torture, pleading of friends and relatives, and so forth, and yet may fly into a violent outburst of rage if some minor aspect of his daily routine displeases him. He may show a stoic indifference to damaging financial losses and break into fits of uncontrolled sobbing over a trivial remark. This lack of appropriateness in emotional expression is responsible for the descriptive term, "dissociation." It is one of the features of schizophrenia that makes for difficulty in the management or treatment of the condition. Examiners commonly report an inability to "get next to" the patient, to establish rapport with him. The schizophrenic's habitual emotional reactions are so foreign to what would be expected in most people that they engender a feeling of strangeness, as if the patient were having experiences beyond the ken of the observer. Some experienced clinicians regularly use this feeling of a lack of empathy as an aid in diagnosis. On closer inspection, however, the seeming inappropriateness of affect is a function of the incomplete understanding of the observer. If the examiner could know the preoccupations of the patient and could understand the relative values the patient places on his own internal thoughts, conflicts, and frustrations, as opposed to the demands of the superficial external situation, he would see that the schizophrenic is displaying an emotional reaction appropriate to the former. One such patient, in an Army hospital when the initial landings were made on the Normandy beachheads, burst into tears when he heard the news. This reaction was in decided contrast to the air of optimistic speculation that affected the rest of the ward. After a rather long talk, it was possible to gain a little understanding of the patient's atypical reaction. This patient had a strong conviction that he was under sentence of death, which would be carried out when the tank-destroyer organization to which he had been attached would return to the United States. The patient had been sent to the hospital from a port of embarkation and had heard or fancied that he had heard his company commander remark that "they'd be back to get him some day." The news of American army success was full of implications of doom for this patient.

Blunting of affect or apathy is often made more understandable and appears less a deviation in kind from the ordinary laws of emotional expression if an attempt is made to understand the situation from the patient's point of view. This emotional flatness, if seen in ordinary life situations, would be taken as an indication that the person showing it was "uninterested." The wooden faces that sometimes confront the professor as he addresses his early morning class might be straight from a psychopathic hospital. A study of 12 persons who survived long periods in a Nazi concentration camp showed that the defense mechanisms developed by these prisoners all included a sense of detachment and emotional frigidity (Bluhm, 1948). In the schizophrenic this lack of interest has simply spread to most of the matters that ordinarily concern people. He is, to repeat, too concerned with his own affairs, and he has devoted his emotional life to them. It should not be forgotten that many of the schizophrenics are actively hallucinating and reacting with some emotional force to these imaginal products. They may also be caught in the web of strange delusional systems that color their environment with different and unreal values, as did the soldier described previously. Evidence of the great emotional strain in the schizophrenic are the automatic nervous system signs of affective tension. The patients have cold, mottled, sweaty extremities, tremor, vasomotor instability, and many other signs of sympathetic nervous system upset.

Dissociation of intellectual process in schizophrenia is perhaps even stranger at first glance than the emotional changes. Emotional behavior in any person may be irrational, but almost by definition we expect thought to be rational. Thinking is one of man's most direct behavioral relations with the realities that surround him. The schizophrenic shows many apparent deviations from this relationship. His thinking seems to proceed by rules of a logic of its own and grinds out conclusions that the rational person cannot foresee in his premises. Schizophrenic thinking "doesn't make sense." Delusions are not the only examples. In his speech the schizophrenic often reflects the peculiar nature of his intellectual processes. Many authorities have discerned, in these intellectual symptoms, a *regressive* return to childish ways of behavior and others have felt that the schizophrenic, like a senile person, *deteriorates* in his abilities. These two hypotheses have been advanced with such persistence as to be accepted uncritically by many writers on the subject. Because our analysis of the schizophrenic as a person bound up in his own problems does not lead to either of these points of view of the intellectual symptoms of the disease, we will spend some time in reviewing the evidence for regression and deterioration.

We have mentioned *regression* as a technique for reducing anxiety or escaping problems by having recourse to ways of behaving that were effective or appropriate at some earlier time in the patient's history. The application of this concept to schizophrenia was made by Freud (1924) and was supported by an authority on child psychology, Piaget (1923). Piaget, in studies of children, emphasized the autistic nature of their thinking, meaning that the thinking was oriented around the individual to the more or less complete exclusion of environmental realities. Superficially it might appear that the schizophrenic, with his great attention to his own problems, conformed to the same pattern. Experimental studies of the thought of children as compared with the thinking of schizophrenics, however, do not show the identity that Piaget predicted (McDonald, 1915; Cameron, 1938). The evidence is entirely too slim to warrant a statement that the schizophrenic attempts to solve his problems regressively.

Another variant of the regression hypothesis stems from a comparison of the schizophrenic's thinking with that of primitive man. It was assumed by some anthropologists from field studies that primitive man thought in a "primitive" manner, and that the schizophrenic had regressed to a pre-historic cultural level. This hypothesis has been sharply criticized by Cameron (1944), who doubts, on the basis of the experimental evidence, whether the intellectual and emotional symptoms of schizophrenia have any regressive aspects:

The fact that schizophrenic disorders do appear among adults in "primitive" (*i.e.*, nontechnological) civilizations and among young children of our own contemporary technological civilizations, as well as the results of comparisons that have been made between the logic of normal children and adults and that of schizophrenics, contradicts the regression hypothesis. Moreover, the contention is supported by the same evidence that schizophrenic disorganization represents neither a retracing of the ontogenetic-phylogenetic path of development, nor a removal of outer layers of thought to expose any "primitive nucleus." Instead, it presents us with a development, new and unique for a given individual's life history, that can be made quite intelligible in behavioral terms.[2]

The question of *deterioration* is even more confusing than that of regression. Any casual visitor to a state hospital for the mentally ill will remember seeing patients who give every overt appearance of personality disintegration. Many of them must be fed and closely supervised in their excretory functions, many of them sit silently for hours, unkempt in appearance, saliva drooling from their lips. Any sort of conversational attempt elicits only a blank stare or at best a mumbling rejoinder without relevance or meaning. Even in an examination situation, with skilled professional study, the patient may appear in no more favorable an intellectual light.

Case 30. A young schizophrenic who was being given an intelligence test responded to every problem situation with a monotonously intoned "Red, white, and blue, you and me too." After a few minutes even this much effort was abandoned, and he lapsed into a silence broken only by infrequent giggles and odd facial distortions. When this boy's parents first came to visit him they were shocked at the changes that had taken place in the few months since he had left home. He had been near the top of his class in high school and had completed a trade school training with high recommendations. When he had been drafted into the Army, his Army intelligence test had shown him to be in the top 30 per cent of all recruits.

[2] Norman Cameron, "The functional psychoses," in J. McV. Hunt, ed., *Personality and the Behavior Disorders,* p. 904. Coypright, 1944, The Ronald Press Company.

Now his intellectual output was lower than that of many hospitalized mental defectives. Viewed from the objective evidence, it would seem an obvious conclusion that his intellectual powers had deteriorated.

Such observations as these convinced many students of schizophrenia that the disease was characterized by a steadily increasing dementia, by a steady loss of intellectual ability, until the end result would be a vegetative state of mental decrepitude. The course of the disease in many patients seemed to bear this out. Almost all custodial hospitals have many patients who are little better than vegetables. Too, another class of patient furnishes what seemed to be a parallel to the schizophrenic "deterioration." In a certain number of aged people the hardening of arteries attendant upon old age produces alterations in circulation of blood in the brain and an attendant destruction of brain tissue. These patients do show a steady downhill course with respect to their mental powers. Each year of their hospital stay finds them closer to a vegetative state. Many psychiatrists consider the schizophrenic to be manifesting a similar loss of abilities.

This belief in deterioration is supported by evidence. Babcock (1930) attempted to measure intelligence loss in the schizophrenic by means of objective tests. She assumed that the score on a vocabulary type of question would give a reasonable estimate of the pre-morbid intelligence level, and that the disparity between vocabulary score and the score made on other types of problems would yield an index of the degree to which the patient had deteriorated. She defined deterioration as follows: "By mental deterioration is meant impairment of mental functioning with no implications as to possible causes, whether physiogenic or psychogenic, and whether the condition is permanent or temporary" (Babcock, 1930, p. 5). Her results indicated that schizophrenics do show deterioration; they were confirmed in subsequent studies by Schwarz (1933), Vigotsky (1934), Davidson (1937), and Trapp and James (1937). However, studies by Wittman (1933) and by Kendig and Richmond (1940) showed little actual loss of capacity. We have already referred to the study by N. Cameron (1938), which led to similar conclusions. As the matter seems to stand at the moment, schizophrenics will show "deterioration," if the term is defined as a numerical decline in test score, under some conditions of testing. Lack of rapport, the momentary condition of the subject, the skill of the examiner all play a part, as they do in any determination of intelligence. Qualitative studies, which attempt to scrutinize the *methods* by which schizophrenics approach problems, may show no evidence of a deterioration of intellectual abilities.

Another approach to the question of thinking in schizophrenia has been made by workers who apply the same techniques to the schizophrenic as have been found to differentiate normals from brain-injured patients. Goldstein (1924) noted that patients with severe brain injury have difficulty in dealing with abstractions and try to reduce every problem to an extremely concrete status. This defect cripples them in their attempts to classify objects, to comprehend relationships, or to perceive the principles governing a class of actions. This was thought to be due to an inability of the patient to take a "categorical attitude." Bolles (1937) found that schizophrenics appear to have the same type of difficulty in test situations. This was later confirmed by Bolles and Goldstein (1938), and using a different type of testing situation, by Kasanin and Hanfmann (1938). Goldstein and Scheerer (1941) have created a formal test for exploration of the abstracting-categorizing capacity and have published results indicating that schizophrenics have great difficulty in achieving success on the problems in this test. Cameron (1938) has criticized this general way of determining deterioration; he found that a careful approach to the patient, with adequate time taken to secure cooperation, would show the schizophrenic capable of a rather high-level performance. He feels "that the abstract capacity level can be found in most schizophrenics provided the painfully patient technique necessary for effective rapport with this group is developed" (Cameron, 1944, p. 903).

We may conclude from our examination of the evidence that *the schizophrenic does show a considerable decline in his intellectual efficiency under the average conditions of testing or in the usual social situations where he is most frequently observed, but that the defect does not represent a loss of basic capacity.* If he can be motivated to increase his efficiency, he is still capable of something approaching a normal performance. Confirmation of this conclusion comes from certain clinical observations that have been made on sudden remissions of the psychosis. Occasionally, following a severe infection, a sudden emotional shock, or even without identifiable reason, a patient will change from severe withdrawal to a comparatively normal status. The same result has been seen after inhalation of mixtures of oxygen and carbon dioxide (Loevenhart, Lorenz, and Waters, 1929), and sometimes after other more modern forms of shock therapy (see Chapter XVII). The patient, seemingly deteriorated, can then converse in a normal fashion and show every evidence of normal mentation. If he were deteriorated in the same sense as the senile dementia patient, this would, of course, be impossible.

SCHIZOPHRENIA, SIMPLE TYPE

Simple schizophrenics are characterized most prominently by a relatively mild withdrawal from social and interpersonal relations. Since they are seldom aggressive and have few delusions or hallucinations, they are hospitalized less frequently than the other types. Their lack of interest in other people and their indifference to social standards are reflected in the types of vocational and avocational choices they make. Many become vagabonds, hobos, prostitutes, or minor delinquents. They are often able to make a satisfactory marginal adjustment for years in solitary occupations that do not demand close association with others.

The onset of this form is usually slow, beginning as far back as pre-adolescence. The patient loses interest in his work and friends, adopts more solitary ways of amusing himself, and may become moody and irritable. He is usually indifferent to attempts by others to stir him from his apathy. He may wander around the country, stealing and doing odd jobs, enduring pain, discomfort, hunger, filth, danger, and social disgrace with the same lack of emotional reaction.

Intellectual efficiency is not as greatly interfered with in the simple form as in some of the others. Formal testing usually reveals little defect, although the patient will be discovered to hold highly original and usually illogical ideas on most subjects.

Case 31. One of the writers spent a rainy afternoon with a sheepherder he had met while on a fishing trip in the high country in Wyoming. The herder had charge of 2700 sheep, a considerable part of the fortune of his employer, and was solely responsible for their welfare for weeks at a time. This man had quit school after completing the tenth grade and had drifted into bootlegging. When prohibition was repealed, he had "bummed" for a year around the country and then had taken the job as sheepherder "because people got on my nerves." During his lonely weeks with the sheep he had occupied his time in thought about politics and religion. He believed that unless the nations of the world adopted Christianity in their dealings with each other Christ would make a second appearance on earth and assume a ruling role over all nations. When asked how he knew this to be true he answered that he felt it in his heart and head and if it weren't true he wouldn't feel it both places. A little later the talk drifted to the financial condition of his employer. The herder was able to calculate the value of his herd, work problems in percentage and interest that came up, and showed a good grasp of financial abstractions. A little later he told of having sexual relations with his animals with the same lack of emotional concern he had shown in talking about the weather. Here was a simple schizophrenic making an adequate adjustment because he had found a situation that made no demands with which he could not comply.

The following case presents many of the characteristics of the simple schizophrenic, particularly the atypical ideas that these patients develop:

Case 32. J. E. was a 25-year-old white male who was admitted to an Army psychiatric service after ten months in the Army. He had volunteered because he felt that he "was no use to his wife and family anyway." Early in his training his officers noted that he frequently went on sick call, that he was awkward in drill, that he resented discipline, could not take or transmit orders, and that he was a chronic complainer. His fellow soldiers rated him as "stupid, lazy, undependable, careless, irritable, and sulky." Immediately prior to entering the hospital he had been AWOL for a period of 23 days. When he was apprehended, he told the military police that the 23 days had been like a dream and that his head ached and felt like a balloon.

His past history showed that as a child he had many neuropathic traits, such as bed-wetting, nail-biting, terrifying nightmares, finicky appetite, and temper tantrums. When he was about ten, his parents noted that he was developing an undecisiveness about his actions and his teachers reported that he started to have difficulties in his school work. He failed the second, sixth, ninth, and tenth grades. During high school he became increasingly restless and asocial. He left school at age 17 without graduating. Shortly after this he had his first sexual intercourse with a girl he had been going with in high school. The girl had an operation for an ovarian tumor shortly after this and the patient became very disturbed, saying that he was responsible and that he had ruined the girl. He attempted suicide, jumping out of a second story window, but escaped with minor injuries. Since that time he had indulged in ten further suicide attempts, most of which had been so poorly planned as to be completely abortive. At the same time as the first suicide attempt he developed a compulsion to stick his hand through closed windows and doors; he has had minor surgery on several occasions, and both his hands carry many scars. Dating from age 17, also, is a conviction that his body is changing because "urination gives me a thrill." At age 21 he began to develop a conviction that he was gradually changing to a female, and that his penis was accordingly becoming smaller. He had other ideas of bodily change. His head sometimes felt "ten times its normal size, and hollow as a log." Since early childhood, and becoming more intense with the years, were morbid fears of water, fire, lightning, and becoming insane. Since entering the Army he had developed a fear of being bombed and cowered in his bunk unable to sleep, "because he could see the bombs coming down through the canvas." Three years before entering the Army, he married but only lived with his wife a short time, claiming that she "drained my energy."

His family history is not remarkable. The father is a first-generation immigrant from Roumania, financially comfortable. The mother is a precise and demanding person who quarrels with the father because of his heavy drinking. The patient is an only child who was humored and spoiled by both parents.

In appearance the patient is somewhat obese and gives an appearance of oddity and awkwardness. Throughout the interview he cried and laughed with no apparent relation to the conversation. He occasionally remained silent for two or three minutes with a withdrawn look on his face. His thinking and ambitions are both bizarre; samples of his ideas have been given above. He has an ambition to be a famous violinist and talks confidently of his ability, but he has never bought a violin. The patient showed some insight for his condition, saying "my nerves are all shot."

This case illustrates the slow onset, the changes in interests, the loss of efficiency, and the odd emotionality. It should be noticed that this patient also showed many features of compulsivity and at least a suggestion of anxiety during childhood.

The simple schizophrenic is thought generally to show a steadily progressing loss of integration. The induction experiences of the Army showed, however, that a systematic search through the population would turn up a large number of individuals who conformed quite well to the description of this syndrome, but whose condition had, like our sheepherder's, remained stationary for years. Cameron (1944) has expressed the opinion that very few patients should be included in this group, since he has found that the more painstaking and thorough the examination, the more of the so-called "simple" schizophrenic patients show delusions or hallucinations or other symptoms that would classify them as belonging in some other sub-group.

SCHIZOPHRENIA, HEBEPHRENIC TYPE

This form of schizophrenia contains most of the symptoms that are popularly associated with "craziness," or "insanity." The word *hebephrenic* is of Greek derivation and means literally "youthful mind." Like the simple form, the hebephrenic develops slowly and insidiously from early youth, usually reaching a state of social disorganization in late adolescence or early adulthood.

The chief identifying symptoms are silliness, fragmentation of affective and intellectual processes, and the formation of extremely bizarre delusional and hallucinatory content. The hebephrenic manifests many seemingly meaningless facial grimaces, ritualistic movements of the extremities, and odd mannerisms of voice and action. When not subjected to treatment, the apparent deterioration of intellectual efficiency is rapid and the patient's hospitalization is usually a prolonged, if not permanent, matter.

If we attempt a summary of the hebephrenic in one descriptive sentence, we could say that his whole behavior is characterized by a complete break with the usual human concepts of reality. In all phases of his personality he appears to have evolved a psychological world of his own, a world in which he gains the emotional satisfactions he has been unable to secure in the reality from which he has fled. In his behavior he expresses, not only the satisfactions of his fantasy world, but also many of the hostilities and aggressive impulses generated out of his frustrations in the real world.

The "silliness" of the hebephrenic is, of course, an evaluation by the examiner and arises from the circumstance that much of the patient's behavior is so highly individualized as to make little sense to anyone not privy to the circumstances in which it occurs. Silliness is expressed by the giggling and laughing with no apparent adequate social stimulus, by the odd manner of speech, and by varied patterns of ritualistic motor activity. The giggling is usually an expression of the patient's preoccupation with delusional or hallucinatory material, or it may be due to the individual way in which he sees the external world. At times, in interview situations, the inappropriate laughter seems no more than the discharge of tension in an emotionally difficult situation, more intense, but of the same kind, as is seen in a group of soldiers before a battle, in a group of students before an examination, and which has been aptly called "gallows-humor." One patient's delusional content pictured people as animals, and the patient's reactions to his warped perceptions often occasioned mirth on his part. He could describe the sort of animals various people appeared to be, and sometimes his descriptions were sufficiently apt to stimulate amusement in his "normal" examiners.

The language of the hebephrenic presents extremely bizarre features and deserves even more research attention than has been given to it. Basically at least two trends may be discerned: (1) a substitution of sound-association for meaning-association, and (2) an elaborate and private symbolic association between words. The first tendency leads the hebephrenic to utterances that have been graphically described as "word-hash" or "word-salad," in the course of which many new words (neologisms) are coined. Samples of hebephrenic speech are better appreciated if heard from the patient or from a recording, but imperfectly rendered though they may be by written symbols, the following gives some idea of the sound-association principle at work:

UT
by H. R. H.

1

Ago and Geodd when fane was
acted, lode and sod the Miries does,
Code to God and then the facted ane
Kabyles and train the tacted brain.

2

Fesoured and pealed than Game can,
lame! Odd and breath the pulse is ran
Syllus and Death, the challonees iraes
fetter Man tode the chancre deliries.

3

The Prose accounting Mense the gulling
tense, deleaned the faitaned, a Probity annulling
Those, as traited, tonsures traminoed
The fasted fires of Pedantry is dominoed.[3]

In this poem there is some fragmentary hint that meanings are being expressed, although the main impression is of word selection for the sake of sound alone. Even more devoid of meaning is this sample, which was delivered over and over again, both spontaneously and when the patient was questioned: "Jondary, jondag, jikkle jikkle jikkle, mat-mitty, mat-mitty, mat-mitty, jongwhing jat-jitty, johnwhing, etc., etc." A hint of one possible role these otherwise meaningless productions may have comes from a patient whose curious verbal mannerisms are cited in another chapter. This man would be unable to speak a word

[3] W. Muncie (1939), *Psychobiology and Psychiatry*, p. 155. St. Louis: The C. V. Mosby Company.

unless it was preceded by "what," somewhat as follows: "What-when what-are what-we what-going what-to what-eat." Since this patient had preserved a fairly high degree of contact with other individuals, it was possible to discuss his verbal mechanism at some length. He felt very seriously that words had great power, but that as long as he said "what" before he said any other word, the power of the following word would be eliminated. "What," in effect, was a talisman, a *magic word* that shielded him from harm. That is to say, his language habit arose from a highly individual symbolism, a meaning attached to "what" that was peculiarly his own. Another patient said that he talked as he did "so no one would understand him," since, as he said, "if people understand you they more frequently don't get what you're driving at," and he felt that *he* understood what he was saying. He had the typically schizophrenic indifference to the people around him and did not feel that communicating with others was an important function of speech.

The ritualistic movements and mannerisms of the hebephrenic may stem from the same group of motives and partake equally of the characteristics of hebephrenic speech. The familiar religious gesture of crossing one's self is a normal example of manneristic symbolism, as is raising one's hat or using one's hands in gestures expressing bewilderment or enthusiasm. One hebephrenic, who was laboring under a severe sexual preoccupation, continually made movements with his hands that clearly symbolized sexual intercourse. The gesture was so stylized and practiced that it went on constantly, irrespective of other activities the patient might be carrying on. Many of the motor mechanisms have a symbolism as obscure (or possibly lacking) as do some of the speech mechanisms. A patient in our university hospital would many times a day carry out an elaborate routine of spitting on his hands, wiping the back of his neck, and attempting to masturbate, all as a rigidly connected series of movements as inflexibly unvarying as an involuntary reflex. Other patients indulge in grotesque burlesques of winks, lip-smacking, pouting, speech-like movements of the jaws, and so on. The faint resemblance these movements bear to our usual ritualistic gestures in society at large encourages the speculation that they serve some hidden symbolic purpose of the patient. It is as if the hebephrenic had created his own world, laid down his own rules of communication, and represented it by his own set of symbols.

The following history of a hebephrenic illustrates not only much of the silliness and intellectual loss of contact with reality, but also, since it is given largely in words of an exasperated medical officer who wrote it, shows some of the social impact the hebephrenic's indifference to society may have:

Case 33. This befuddled tramp gives a fantastic tale of volunteering for service during one of his episodes of "bumming" about the country, volunteering largely because he didn't have anything else to do and had not been able to hold a job in civilian life and also because he thought that his many inventions would be of value to the Army. After six months of being observed as odd, inefficient, lacking in common sense, dirty, careless, unable to transmit orders, lacking in personal pride, tough, loud, mean, lacking endurance, bragging and talking to himself, he went AWOL for six months. It was also noted that he wet the bed, occasionally told fantastic stories, and drank excessively. During these drinking episodes he would become mean and dangerous and other soldiers were afraid of him at these times. He suddenly returned from AWOL, bumming his way back to his home station after war was declared, stating that he wanted to help his country. After two months in the guardhouse, during which time the above-noted behavior traits became more than the guards could stand, he was referred for psychiatric examination.

His past history reveals that he was raised by a grandmother who was showing signs of senile decay during the patient's childhood. The patient had been rejected by a mother and father who were criminals and drunkards. The whole family, including collaterals, have been relief and community problems for years. The patient was an only child. He was a weakly baby and was considered bashful and overly dependent upon his grandmother. He showed many morbid fears of people, being injured while playing, animals, and so on. He took an immediate dislike to school and was a continual truant. The children would call him "that queer guy, Johnny."

When he was 15, he was placed in an industrial school. He remained there for a year and a half, and completed, under duress, a sixth-grade education. The social service report from this school states that the authorities there considered him "crazy." When he was released from the school, he started his life of vagabond independence, wandering around the country getting into many kinds of trouble. He started taking dope and drinking excessively. According to his story, at each turn of his road there have been Negroes ready to kill him and people who have tortured and persecuted him. In 1936 he spent 15 days in jail for stealing his grandmother's clothes and her supplies from the relief agency. He worked one day for WPA but was fired. His sexual history is told with much enthusiasm and is extremely chaotic, with a history of much overt homosexuality and innumerable graphically described perversions. He married in 1938, but soon separated, shortly before the birth of a child. He has made no attempt to help his wife and shows no interest in seeing his child. Since 1934 he has had frequent attacks of gonorrhea, without treatment.

Direct examination reveals a bizarre and wooly-haired creature who is untidy, silly, and illogical. He rattles on at great length about being able to invent practically anything and particularly new types of bombs and shells. The psychomotor activity is scattered, illogical, and vague. He is a bundle of morbid fears of spiders, high places, lightning, people, injuries, and so forth. He has had delusions of strange powers for the last 13 to 20 years. He also believes that he can read anyone's mind. He blocked frequently during interview and appeared to be having vivid hallucinatory experiences.

We have said that the delusional content of the hebephrenic is scattered and bizarre. This is in contradistinction to the delusions of the paranoid, to be considered a little later, where the delusional content is highly elaborated and systematic, with at least a superficial regard for consistency and the appearance of reality. Among the frequently seen delusions of hebephrenia are the wide variety of bizarre beliefs they entertain about their bodily structure and function. Often the initial clue to the person's illness will come from his narration of somatic difficulties. In the medical service of a large Army medical technician's school one day a student reported to complain of illness. His chief difficulty was headaches, a not uncommon complaint among the students, who worked long hours at their studies and laboratory tasks. This student's complaints, however, differed in one important respect: his freely volunteered hypothesis of the cause for the headaches. According to the patient, his head pains were based on an escape of blood from their vessels into his skull cavity. He was sure of this because he could shake his head and "hear and feel the blood sloshing around in there." He felt that all his arteries and veins were rotted away and that the heart was "pumping away his life's blood." Another patient had the belief that his bowels had become infested with radium and had become so deteriorated that "my insides are an aching emptiness." The widespread uniformity with which these patients form somatic delusions that express decay and emptiness gives some hint of the disintegration that affects their personality. The somatic delusions show an interesting sidelight on the schizophrenic thinking defects.

A rather ready way to distinguish between the hypochondriacal complaints of the less seriously ill psychoneurotic patient and the more serious somatic delusions of the psychotic is to note the manner in which the complaint is presented. The psychoneurotic talks chiefly about the symptom itself, often elaborating dramatically, as we have seen, the details of how he feels. The schizophrenic, on the other hand, commonly presents the complaint itself with little elaboration, but then spends a good deal of time in telling the examiner his hypotheses of its causation. If the neurotic speculates about the cause of his disturbance, he usually finds a rather conventional medical reason, whereas the reasons of the schizophrenic are quite generally bizarre and improbable. It is possible that the patient is trying to express, in a curiously warped symbolic way, his general state of personality disintegration. We see this way of talking used to convey such a meaning in our common parlance. A person who has been going through a period of suffering or grief might say, "I feel all gone inside," or "I've had the heart completely taken out of me." If the observations of Goldstein concerning the loss of abstract thinking can be applied here, *it is possible that the schizophrenic is merely taking in a very concrete manner the abstract habits of expression prevalent in his culture.*

Delusions of control and influence may occur. The patient may believe either that he is influenced by an outside force or that he has powers of thus controlling others. A hebephrenic college student first came to the attention of the student health service because he had told his roommates that he had worked out a way to make love to girls any place in the world by means of a system of thought control. He said that he could prove this very easily, by listening to the voices of feminine radio stars, then make love to them, and he would notice by changes in their voices whether or not he was successful. He added that, to that time, he had not had a single failure. Delusions of control and influence resemble the productions of the paranoid, but are not as well organized; the forces at work are more poorly conceived, and the delusions themselves are unstable. Through these delusions we get another glimpse of how the world appears to the patient. To the hebephrenic the world is filled with uncontrolled or unfathomable forces that operate in chaos without organization or system.

The hallucinations in hebephrenia have no particular distinguishing characteristics. The patient may hear voices or have visual experiences that are congruent with his delusions. As with psychotics in general, it is sometimes hard to determine where a delusion ends and an hallucination begins. The patient may report that he "feels as if he were dead inside." This is a delusional belief but may also be an hallucinatory sensory experience. The delusions of bodily change are usually accompanied by strange, hallucinatory verifications of the belief.

In summary, the hebephrenic presents a complete break with reality, both intellectually and emotionally. His behavior is completely oriented around his preoccupations, and his communication with others is fragmentary and bizarre. From a social point of view the hebephrenic's behavior is meaningless and absurd, although a knowledge of his background and the type of problem he faces may sometimes make his actions appear more meaningful.

SCHIZOPHRENIA, CATATONIC FORM

The simple schizophrenic manifested indifference toward society, the hebephrenic appeared completely oblivious of society, and the *catatonic* carries out an actual aggression toward society. The catatonic form is differentiated from other types of schizophrenia chiefly on the basis of motor symptoms so distinctive as to be unmistakable. The catatonic patient shows two opposed extremes of energetic muscular activity: (1) the generalized inhibition of movement, and (2) an excessive and excited muscular aggression.

As contrasted with the simple and hebephrenic forms, catatonia may have a sudden onset in persons who have shown only minimal signs of a schizoid personality. Also, more than in the other forms, the catatonic shows spontaneous remissions; in many instances a patient has recovered after a single catatonic episode and made an acceptable social adjustment for years without further symptoms. The general prognosis for catatonia is better than for the other types, although some patients show a characteristic downward and chronic course, becoming permanent custodial problems.

Considering first the inhibitory symptoms, it is important to realize at the start that we are not dealing with a passive lack of action, but with an extremely active and forcibly inhibitory effort. The patient may assume a posture and hold it for hours, apparently inaccessible and stuporous. Attempts to converse with him are fruitless; he shows no sign of having heard. A hand moved rapidly toward his eyes does not elicit a blink, nor does his face show a change of expression. In this "stuporous" state the patient may go for hours without eating or drinking, he may retain his excreta or carelessly fail to exercise control over his defecation or urination. His nearest relatives may visit him after an absence of years and be unable to elicit the slightest sign of recognition. Some patients, while in this state, manifest a curious "pseudo-passivity," in which they will allow the examiner to place their limbs in any position and will then maintain that position until again changed, a phenomenon termed *cerea flexibilitas* or "waxy flexibility."

At the heart of this inhibitory state is the general catatonic characteristic of *negativism*. The catatonic seems highly motivated to do just the opposite of what seems customarily to be indicated. Other people move around, actively adapting to the momentary shifts of emphasis in their environment, but the catatonic does the opposite. He resists the attempts of ward attendants and nurses to minister to his needs, he fights all compulsion from without by actively inhibiting the movements that would make that compulsion effective. This is admirably illustrated by some patients who can be made to carry out orders if the verbal form of the order is the opposite of what the nurse or attendant wants the patient to do. If you want the patient to lie down, you tell him not to lie down or to stand up. If you want him to brush his teeth, forbid him to do so. The fact that his behavior may sometimes be controlled by this negative approach shows the simple and direct attack that the catatonic is making on his problems of adjustment. He acts as if convinced that his chances for equilibrium lie in the direction opposite to that of the society around him.

That the catatonic "stupor" is more apparent than real is shown by the completeness with which the patient can describe events that have taken place around him during his inactive and withdrawn period. While he has been rigidly inactive and inaccessible, he has been a keen observer of his environment. His inactivity is comparable to that of the small hunted animals who crouch in frozen immobility while the hunter searches for them. If anything, their perceptual sensitivity is heightened and not depressed.

An amusing incident on the closed ward of one hospital illustrates this. A class of student nurses were gaining experience on the psychiatric section as a part of their regular training course. One girl, possibly from reasons of insecurity, was given to making rather free and frank comments out loud about the patients as she moved around the ward. One patient, a catatonic, had for several days sat immobile on the side of his bed. The nurse, as she was making the adjacent bed, remarked to a fellow worker concerning the "stupidity" of the catatonic. Her back was to the patient and she was bent over adjusting a sheet. Suddenly, in the midst of her comments about the patient, he let out a loud cry and planted a well-aimed foot on the nurse's posterior. When she recovered, straightened up, and looked around the catatonic had resumed his "wooden Indian" expression and his former posture.

The incident taught a lesson that had been imperfectly learned in the classroom, that the catatonic is actively opposing an environment toward which he is maintaining an attitude of watchful alertness.

The other phase of catatonia is the catatonic excitement. This may follow or precede the immobile stage in a cyclical manner, or it may be the given patient's only type of catatonic manifestation. In terms of sheer energy release the catatonic excitement has no parallel in schizophrenia. Activity runs the gamut from purposeful and savage attack to a sheerly random and ever-changing pattern of purposelessness and restlessness. When started, this behavior may continue as perseveratively as did the "passive" phase. Patients frequently become exhausted, emaciated, and dehydrated through their incessant activity and their refusal to take nourishment.

The catatonic excitement is frequently the first sign of psychosis noted in the patient. He may suddenly, with no apparent provocation, attack someone close to him. Some of the seemingly senseless wholesale murders that create newspaper stories are performed by persons in catatonic excitements. A recent example was of a young farmer who came in from the field at noon, ate his lunch, picked up the kindling axe, and killed his wife and two children. In a college dormitory, while waiting in line at the cafeteria, a student suddenly threw his tray and its contents over the cashier and ran screaming out of the hall. Although these attacks seem spontaneous, closer inquiry shows, more often than in other forms of schizophrenia, immediate environmental and emotional precipitants for the behavior. The catatonic excitement sometimes resembles a runaway, grossly exaggerated temper tantrum, in which the individual reacts to frustration by a primitive disorganized aggression against everything even remotely connected with the frustrating circumstances. The following case illustrates many of the catatonic features:

Case 34. L. B. M. was 22 years old when he was first seen in the army psychiatric hospital. He had been in the army three months at the time. In spite of the fact that he had entered the facts of his mental illness on his Selective Service questionnaire and had tried to tell the examiners at the induction board about his illness, he had been drafted. During his three months of service his officers had noted that he was unable to transmit orders and that he was inefficient in his work. Just before being hopitalized he had walked the floor all night long, acting suspicious and aloof, and had stood out in the rain a whole day without apparent reason.

The patient was a Negro boy, the fifth of seven children, from a highly intelligent and race-conscious family. The father was an extremely domineering, strict, and rigid person whose professional and business success had placed the family on a high economic and educational level. The patient's mother was a tense, emotional, aggressive person who set high standards for her children. One sister was hospitalized for schizophrenia, and a brother was considered "odd" by his family and by others in the community.

The patient's past history indicated that he had wet the bed until age 8, bit his nails, and had terrifying nightmares from early childhood to the present, had violent temper tantrums and was frequently moody and sulky. His intelligence was of superior adult level; he graduated from high school at age 14 and from college with honors in a pre-medical curriculum at age 18. During high school and college he actively participated in social activities, although his associates reported him to be moody and subject to depression if he could not be the leader. In college he seems to have been a very serious, intense, and somewhat haughty person who continually checked the mistakes of his teachers. In spite of this, one of his professors wrote that he had never had a more brilliant student. After graduation from college his work record was very erratic, consisting mainly of common labor jobs, with frequent changes. He was fired on two occasions for inefficiency. He was considered by his employers to be undependable, temperamental, careless, and erratic. During this time he had no hobbies, and his recreational outlets seem to have disappeared, being replaced by an increasing seclusiveness and passivity. His sexual development was irregular. He had intense conflict over masturbation and over an incident at age 11, when he was seduced by an older man, a factor that was expressed in the content of some of his delusions. He did not smoke or drink and appeared as an extremely rigid, shy, and withdrawn person.

The development of his illness seemed to date from his college graduation, when he noted an increasing inability to concentrate, numerous accidents while working, loss of initiative, and a feeling of being dazed. About a year after he was graduated, he became acutely disturbed and combative and was admitted to a private psychiatric hospital, where he was given a course of insulin shock therapy. He became calmer and was discharged as "in remission." He went back to his irregular career of menial labor until he was drafted.

His appearance on examination was of a typical catatonic, untidy, rigid, tense, slow-moving, manneristic, and distant. He sat slouched in his chair with an averted gaze and a bowed head, speaking in a barely audible voice. The speech was sparse, frequently blocked, often irrelevant to the topic at hand, rambling and scattered, often breaking over into a word-hash, with many automatic phrases being inserted throughout. He showed flattening of his emotional expression. He voiced feelings of uselessness and hopelessness, claiming to be a hindrance to the world. He told of feeling that he was controlled by others and that he was "as good as dead." He felt that voices were accusing him of being a homosexual and calling him foul names.

Because catatonics recover more frequently than other types of schizophrenic patients, we have been able to get more firsthand accounts of the illness as it appears to the patient. These reports show that the patient is responding in very understandable ways to the world as he sees it during his illness.

Case 35. Milici (1942) has reported an intensive study of such a case. A 17-year-old girl, who went through both a stuporous and excited phase of catatonia without being able to convey the horrible secret to anyone, became convinced that her father and other people were trying to kill her. She felt extreme terror and showed it by such disturbed behavior that her father called an ambulance and she was taken to the hospital. The patient felt she was being taken to her death. When she arrived at the hospital "she was exhausted yet wildly excited and resistive, her mind raced furiously. She was put in a small room which had only a mattress on the floor. She screamed, pounded on the door, tried to climb out of the window. She thought she saw fumes entering through small openings in the wall, was certain she was being gassed. She thought she was in Hell. She feared the mattress and kept walking in circles around it until she was so faint she could not stand. She slept not at all, stared out of the window, was certain a scandal had been made of her doings and that this was widely published. She thought her mother was in an adjoining room, since she heard her voice calling to her. . . . At dawn, Eleanour entered a day hall with other disturbed patients. This, she felt, was surely purgatory. She was dazed. She was afraid to talk, believing she would be heard elsewhere through the radio. She searched for members of her family, certain they must be present, since she continued to hear them calling to her. She screamed repeatedly when she could not locate them, made tremendous efforts to get out through every door." [4]

The catatonic is frequently preoccupied with thoughts of death. His delusions, as in the case cited here, often center around his own death and that of his loved ones. Here we see the same emotionally threatening attitude toward death that characterized the victim of the traumatic neurosis. In the catatonic these preoccupations are even more serious and invade even more of the personality. As Milici says in introducing the case history we have just read:

Both in the incubation period and in the stupor proper, there is a considerable preoccupation with the death theme, expressed as a delusion of dying or being dead, as a plain desire to die, with active suicidal attempts,

[4] Pompea Milici (1942), "The catatonic death reaction." *Psychiat. Quart., 16,* 53-54.

or as a fear of being killed. The patient may say that he has been drugged, that he is in his grave, in Heaven, burning up in Hell, changing into a skeleton. Frequently others, particularly close relatives, are "dead" or "dying" also. Often, there is absorption with thoughts of a relative already deceased and with whom the patient insists he is in visual and verbal contact. Or a person expresses the fear that he or others, usually members of the family, are to die, to be killed. They are to commit suicide, are to be cut into pieces, shot, drowned, boiled alive, electrocuted, poisoned; they are being changed by spirits. There may be ideas of a more general nature, talk of shooting and war, of dynamiting the environment and destruction of the world.[5]

What is the source of this train of gloomy thought in the catatonic? In the traumatic neurosis we saw the patient shocked into an emotional realization of the threat of death by some sudden and intense psychological experience. In some catatonics a similar episode appears in the history, usually the death of some close associate, but this is not true in a sufficiently large number of cases to constitute a general explanation, or to justify a direct comparison of the catatonic and the neurotic. By conceiving of the catatonic reaction as an attack on the environment the place of death becomes understandable. As Freud showed, death fantasies are means of expressing aggression; in our dreams we may kill our enemies or our friends-turned-enemies. Or we may be so aghast at the thoughts that spring unbidden into our minds that we turn the death fantasy against ourselves, and the aggression is turned inward. The delusional and hallucinatory content of the catatonic, as was noted by Milici, abounds in such bloodthirsty fantasy, and usually against people with whom the patient has had intimate associations. The hostility theme that was revealed in the patient's negativism is carried on at a symbolic level as well.

It is sometimes said that the catatonic exemplifies a *regressive* solution to life's problems, that he is returning to primitive and early-learned forms of behavior, possibly even returning to a purely reflex and instinctive level of defense as old as the existence of mammals themselves. This hypothesis is based primarily upon observations of the catatonic stupor. Here the patient often assumes a posture reminiscent of that taken by the fetus in the womb, head down between the drawn-up legs. The inactivity of the stupor, as we have remarked before, gives the impression of the immobility of a hunted animal, ready to spring into action if necessary but prepared to stay frozen as long as

[5] *Ibid.*, 39-40.

danger demands. This also is looked upon as a primitive mammalian defense, almost reflex in nature, and completely irrational. The "fetal curl" can be disregarded as evidence since it is by no means the only typical catatonic posture, and since the same position may be taken by many non-catatonic, non-psychotic persons as one of the many possibilities for comfortable limb arrangement (see Landis, Forbes, *et al.,* 1934). The primitive nature of much emotional behavior, however, whether it occurs in the catatonic or in anyone else, is easily recognized, as has been shown by Landis and Hunt (1939) in their studies of the movements and expressive patterns of people who have been subjected to sudden emotional stimuli sufficient to produce a startle reaction. Since we have recognized that the catatonic is in a highly emotional situation, the regression hypothesis is, to that extent, probably true.

To summarize, the catatonic form of schizophrenia manifests stuporous and excited phases that may alternate with any degree of rapidity or may be found singly in a given patient. The catatonic is negativistic and appears to be carrying out an active, if emotional and inefficient, aggression against his environment.

SCHIZOPHRENIA, PARANOID FORM

Paranoid schizophrenia is characterized by the presence of fairly well-organized delusional systems, usually of a persecutory or grandiose nature. This condition should not be confused with *paranoia,* another psychotic disorder that will be discussed. The *paranoid* schizophrenic shows much the same disorders of emotion and thinking as other schizophrenics, although they seldom appear as completely ineffective as the other types. The paranoid form seems to appear at a somewhat later period of life, the majority of such patients presenting their active symptoms in the late twenties and early thirties (Noyes, 1934). Although there is less deterioration of intellectual efficiency in this group, the prognosis is usually doubtful, since their delusional systems seem very resistant to therapy.

The paranoids manifest an extreme degree of *intellectual dissociation,* in that they are able to maintain elaborate systems of delusional beliefs side by side with a fairly well-oriented acceptance of reality in other phases of their lives. Like the simple schizophrenic, the paranoid may be able to make a marginal social adjustment for years, staying out of hospitals and out of serious trouble. The paranoid most often becomes involved with social authority when his delusional content motivates him to defensive action.

Case 36. A university student had made a good record for three years in college, not only in his studies but in his social relations. He was arrested for provoking a fight with an employee of a local store. He told the police that this man had been spreading false accusations about him for at least two or three years. When the university psychiatrist examined the student, he found evidence that the young man had been actively delusional since his freshman year and had kept a diary that set forth the details of the patient's growing preoccupation with persecutory forces in his environment. Further inquiry into the past life of the patient showed that his parents had noted personality changes dating from his junior year in high school; he had become more apathetic, indulged in strange arguments, gave vent to suspicions and accusations against neighbors, his teachers and even against his parents. During all of this period of developing psychosis he had been able to do above average work in his studies and to conceal from casual acquaintances all hints of illness.

The delusions of the paranoid schizophrenic are predominantly of a persecutory nature. The patient believes that others are talking about him, planning to injure or kill him, trying to influence him for evil, seduce him sexually, and so forth. The following case presents some of the typically schizophrenic delusional content:

Case 37. R. W. S. volunteered for the army to "cure myself." After 16½ months of service he entered the psychiatric hospital after having failed in an attempt to obtain a cadaver for "experiments in restoring life." The patient's story of his past life, when checked by social service investigation, turned out to have been a complete fabrication. He stated that he was an orphan who had "been on my own" since age 3. He told a long story of many beatings and hardships of life on the road. He said that he had finally become associated with the Ringling Brothers circus, first as a trapeze artist and then as a female impersonator. He stated that he had written many "true" stories about homosexuality and had published them in leading magazines. According to his story he had been on the point of signing a Hollywood contract when his "nervousness" became so bad that he joined the army, because "that's where the best doctors in the world practice."

From the social history it was established that he had been a well-behaved youngster, who had given no trouble until he was a junior in high school, when he was arrested for impersonating a female and sent to the reformatory for two years. When he was released from the reformatory, he apparently lived a vagabond life until his entry into the army.

In appearance the patient was a short, thin person who talked constantly during the interview and expressed considerable irritability if he was interrupted. He frequently wrinkled his face up in odd grimaces, and laughed in an incongruous manner. He stated that people had been trying to kill him for at least eight years. For the past five years, according to his statement, he had been gradually changing into a woman, and he will soon be able to have children. His whole appearance and manner of behavior are so feminine as almost to be a burlesque. On mental test problems his answers showed poor attention and an inability to maintain a direction of action long enough to complete the simplest sort of task.

It is worth noting that this patient, in spite of his rather bizarre delusional content and his apparently obvious psychotic condition, was able to perform military duty for almost seventeen months before he was brought into the hospital. The ability of the paranoid to preserve some remnant of socially acceptable behavior is unique among the schizophrenics.

Also worthy of notice in this case is the preoccupation with homosexuality. Many authorities, particularly the psychoanalysts (but also see Rosanoff, 1938) trace the origin of the paranoid state to repressed homosexuality, claiming that circumstances, either internal or external, which threaten this repression, serve to stimulate the persecutory preoccupation. Rosanoff, for example, has substituted the term "chaotic sexuality" for the more conventional terminology we have adopted, believing that the disturbance in normal sexual development is a primary etiological characteristic of this condition. There is some plausibility in this contention. Clinical experience with paranoids shows a rather frequent homosexual content in their delusions, and it is possible that the intense social taboos against homosexual activity serve to create conflicts, fear, and apprehension in the person whose sexual motivation is of this kind.

Although paranoid delusions are primarily persecutory, there is usually a hint of the expansive and grandiose, even in these. In addition, some paranoids show a rather full development of the expansive type of delusion, as the following case illustrates:

Case 38. S. E. was admitted to the hospital from the city jail, where he had been serving a sentence for "peddling without a license." The jail physician had recommended psychiatric observation after the patient had told him a story of being the Swedish ambassador to the United States who was travelling around the country in disguise to study "conditions." In appearance, S. E. was untidy and disheveled, a small man who appeared to be about forty-five years of age. He stated his age to be "six thousand and twelve," and said that he was the owner of the whole "continent of Sweden under God." He claimed that the medicine he was selling from door to door was made "from the innermost private essences of time without end, amen." For over a thousand years, according to the patient, evil men had been trying to get his secret of perpetual life and even now were "operating on him." He said that he had discovered a super-radio with which he could tell where his enemies were, and that at the proper time he would "order the armies into action" and give his whole fortune of several billion dollars to the support of "genuine Swedish Christianity." He maintained that he was not bothered by being placed in jail or being taken to the hospital, because his "super-ordered powers" would enable him to walk out through the thickest walls at any time he chose.

In seeking for some rationale to the paranoid schizophrenic's behavior we might ask what the patient is trying to express through the medium of his symptoms. We see the picture of a person who feels that he is being hunted, pursued, threatened, but who at the same time is frequently convinced that he possesses miraculous powers or that he is singularly favored in wealth, longevity, health, or other attributes. It is plausible to think that the persecutory trend may be a way of saying, "See how very important I am. People hate me and persecute me because I am so important." The expansive delusions are direct expressions of the same thing. By these devices, which are essentially verbal in character, the paranoid is able to make an adaptation to a world in which he actually feels insecure and inferior. Just as we have seen certain parallels between the catatonic and the traumatic neuroses, and between the hebephrenic and the obsessive-compulsive, in the paranoid we can discern some similarities with another psychoneurosis, conversion hysteria. In both conditions we observe the startling ability to dissociate a symptom complex from any sort of reality evaluation; in both conditions we see a further dissociation of emotional or affective expression from its appropriate application. The hysteric, for the most part, disposes of his conflicts by physical symptoms, the paranoid by his elaborate delusional system, but in both instances the solution appears, for the patient to be successful. The reduction of anxiety that is seen in many people who develop either hysteria or paranoid schizophrenia may be a factor in making these conditions difficult therapy problems. A person who is reducing anxiety by any type of behavior will be loath to relinquish it.

SCHIZOPHRENIC REACTION, ACUTE,
UNDIFFERENTIATED TYPE

Although statistically this heading is provided for that rather large number of schizophrenics who show mixed symptoms of the other forms, there is one rather distinctive reaction included here, which we will call a *schizophrenic panic reaction*. These patients have a sudden and severely acute psychotic illness that runs a short but stormy course and subsides in a relatively short time. Common to these cases is an extremely agitated fright reaction that has many of the characteristics of an exaggerated psychoneurotic anxiety state, but accompanied by delusions and hallucinations. The following case is typical:

Case 39. J. N. was carried bodily into the psychiatric ward by six attendants who maintained control of the patient only by dint of great exertion. The patient was crying and screaming, giving an appearance of being in mortal terror. Strong sedation was administered and he gradually relaxed and fell asleep.

His illness had started quite suddenly two days previously. He had been lying on his cot in the barracks reading, when he imagined he heard two fellow-soldiers discussing him. One of them referred to him by name as a "queer," and the other said that they'd better get rid of him "tonight." The patient felt frightened, but continued a pretense of reading. When the lights were put out, the patient slipped into his bed without removing his clothes, and as soon as the room appeared quiet, he left the barracks and the post and walked into town. All this time he felt he was being watched and followed, and when he went into an all-night restaurant he thought he saw one of the soldiers who had been plotting against him talking to the waitress. He ordered a cup of coffee, but when he tried to drink it he noted a bitter taste and was certain he had been poisoned. He ran out of the restaurant and spent the night in a wild and aimless flight into the desert. He was found late the next day stumbling along, with no clothes on and mumbling incoherently that "they were getting him."

The patient's past history was uneventful. He was raised in a small town in Kentucky and had graduated from high school with average grades. His family was poor, but had a good reputation in the town as sober and responsible people. The patient had secured employment at a hotel as combination night clerk and bell-boy and had held the job successfully until he was drafted. He went through basic training uneventfully and had been doing satisfactory duty as a member of a tank-destroyer team. His sexual adjustment seemed within normal limits; he had no overt homosexual experiences, and as far as could be determined, had not impressed any of the men in his outfit as being peculiar in any way. No substantiation of his story about being called a "queer" could be elicited from any of the men in his barracks. They had noticed nothing out of the ordinary about the patient's conduct on the evening he had left or at any other time.

When the patient was interviewed the day following his admission, he was somewhat calmer but still presented an agitated appearance. He spoke in vague terms of the plots existing against his life, he felt that the examiners and hospital attendants were involved, and he could not be reassured of his safety. He cried and begged the examiner to have mercy on him, but if they were going to kill him to do it quickly, without torture. He was disoriented as to time and place, having no concept of where he was or how many days it had been since his illness started. His intellectual efficiency was low and he gave every appearance of being a deteriorated schizophrenic of long standing.

A week of sedatives, hydrotherapy, and small dosages of insulin worked a complete change in the patient. He gradually lost his fears, stated that the whole thing seemed like a bad dream, and became anxious to return to duty.

Similar cases occurred with some frequency as a result of the stresses of combat. Conditions of this type were described in the chapter on emotion. Grinker (1943) described the condition in his medical report of the North African campaign. The patients are disoriented, dazed, emotionally disturbed, and either agitated or apathetic with respect to environmental stimulation. They have hallucinatory experiences and various amounts of delusional content. When the stress is removed and suitable therapeutic measures are instituted, the patients recover rapidly.

As yet there are no reliable hypotheses to account for this acute schizophrenic reaction. It seems obvious that the person is involved in a catastrophic type of response to stress, but unanswered are the important questions of identifying the variables that operate to produce such severe reactions in some individuals and that spare others with seemingly the same exposure to stress and equally good or bad past histories.

A word should be said concerning the so-called "mixed" types of schizophrenia. Actually, few patients present a textbook picture of a single form of the disorder, but rather have features of all types. We have seen in the case studies that catatonics may have persecutory delusions and that paranoids may present some of the aspects of silliness and intellectual fragmentation described as hebephrenic. Since we are relatively sure that schizophrenia is not caused by the action of a definite infectious or traumatic organic factor, this is what we would expect. The schizophrenias, as we have described them, are simply ways of behaving that some people have learned in their attempts to meet life's difficulties, and variations in such techniques from person to person are to be expected. The roots of causation of schizophrenia go deep into *every* variable of which life is a function. In chapters to come we will scrutinize in turn factors of heredity, maturation, constitution, organic neurological conditions, and social or cultural factors, and will find, at the end of that survey, that the story of schizophrenia is still only fragmentary. It remains one of the frontiers of science.

The Paranoid Disorders

PARANOIA

Paranoia is of such rare occurrence that it is of interest to us more as a further illustration of how far from reality this fusion of verbal and emotional processes may lead than because it constitutes a serious problem in public health. The victim of paranoia is distinguished from the paranoid schizophrenic primarily by the high degree of isolation from other aspects of reality orientation that is achieved by the paranoiac. The paranoid schizophrenic, as we have seen, suffers some impairment in almost all spheres of reality testing, although even there not to the same extent as other schizophrenics. The paranoiac may be completely capable of adequate social adjustment in aspects of his life that are not involved in his delusional system. He suffers no general loss of intellectual efficiency, and he does not show the hallucinatory behavior that so interferes with the schizophrenic's perceptual processes.

Paranoia usually develops slowly and with few outward signs of social disorganization in the patient. Typically, the patient comes to the attention of society only in later phases of his disorder when he has begun to prosecute vigorous action on the basis of his delusional system. He may be looked upon as eccentric or a "crank" in his community, but because he preserves a goodly amount of social inhibition he may avoid all the outward appearance of psychosis.

The delusions of the paranoiac resemble, and possibly grow out of, the rationalization techniques used by everyone. The symptoms are methods of freeing the patient from responsibility or for compensating him for frustrating inadequacies. Because the delusions are built up slowly from what appear to be rationalizations, they often possess a compelling internal logical structure. If the suppositions on which the delusional system is erected could be granted, then the patient's beliefs have every hallmark of reasonableness. This feature of the delusions has often led people associated with paranoiacs to accept their productions as fact, sometimes with startling consequences, as the following case testifies:

Case 40. Captain B. Y. was a reserve officer who had come on active duty a few months before December 7, 1941. He was stationed on one of our islands in the Pacific at the opening of hostilities with the Japanese and was in command of a company of Coast Artillery. The captain had been a civil engineer in private life and had had a successful private practice. After the attack at Pearl Harbor, he was made security officer, responsible for intelligence work in the small district where his company was stationed. He discharged his duties with efficiency and initiative and soon had completed the routine screening of the civilian inhabitants of his district. In his report he noted that he had uncovered information of such highly confidential nature that he could not write it; he requested permission to report in person and lay his findings before higher headquarters. Permission was granted, and his report so impressed the staff intelligence section that Captain Y. was relieved of his local command and attached to headquarters for further investigative work.

For a month the captain kept large groups of soldiers searching the countryside and continued to submit sensational reports to the staff. These reports, in meticulous detail, complete with maps, geological data, names, dates, and figures, advanced the hypothesis that the Japanese enemy was being shielded by rich plantation owners and by members of the ex-nobility of the islands. The captain claimed to have found that the plantations had constructed secret air fields and that the old island nobility had given the Japanese secrets of the sea-caves that honeycombed the shore-line of the island. According to the captain, and supported by his geological studies, these sea-caves extended back for miles underground and were big enough and contained a depth of water sufficient to float the Japanese miniature submarines. The captain felt that this was all part of a detailed plan for a careful concentration of Japanese ground troops and a surprise attack on the defenses of the islands from within. So ably had the captain marshaled his arguments and so well did his hypothesis link together scraps of information gained by intelligence from other sources, that responsible officers gave serious attention to his reports. Suspicion of Captain Y.'s integrity arose slowly, as his searching operations turned up consistent blanks and as independent investigation of many of the persons he had named in the alleged plot showed them to be completely loyal and innocent of his charges.

The final eye-opener came when the captain reported that an attempt had been made on his life. According to his story, he had been seated in his quarters shortly before retiring when a man dressed in army uniform opened the door and fired at him with a heavy service revolver. The military police who investigated the charge were unable to find evidence of a gun having been fired, and the enlisted man who had been stationed at a guard post less than fifteen feet from the door of the captain's quarters had noticed nothing unusual. When the total situation was discussed with the captain, however, and when the intelligence officers told him flatly that they believed him to be mistaken, the captain, without anger, simply reiterated his convictions. He was placed in the hospital for observation and a diagnosis of paranoiac agreed upon. He was then shipped back to the States and given further examinations preparatory to sending him before a medical retiring board. These examinations showed no intellectual defect and, with the single exception of his system of beliefs about the Japanese infiltration, showed him to be a man of mature judgment. His wife had met him when his ship came in from the islands and accompanied him to the inland hospital from which he was to be retired. She accepted his story as literally true and made great efforts to prove that he was being made the victim of a plot. For all practical purposes she became as deluded, as paranoid, as was the patient.[6] Captain Y. was retired, still vigorously believing himself to be right. He returned to civilian life and made an acceptable adjustment to his old profession of engineering, resolved to sometime write a "now-it-can-be-told" book about his discoveries.

Paranoia illustrates, in more severe form, another of the general human modes of behavior. The paranoiac bends all his resources of reason and intelligence to the support of an hypothesis that is factually untenable but emotionally satisfying. He refuses or is unable to take a point of view sufficiently objective to examine the validity of his premises in the same way he evaluates the internal coherency of his argument. This tendency may be observed in almost equally severe form in connection with people in general when their basic beliefs about religion or politics or any other deeply basic issue are concerned. Political speeches contain many examples of refusal to see enough of the facts of a situation to pass an unbiased judgment or to form a rational opinion. The great religious controversies of history have shown how incapable of compromise an individual becomes when he uses the technique of rationality to support an emotional conviction. The old proverb says, "A person convinced against his will holds the same opinion still," and the emotional energy that attaches to rationalization gives added proof to the truth of the saying.

It is purely a matter of speculation, but rather provocative, to think of the role that paranoiacs may have played in history. One of the outgrowths of their delusional systems is the conviction of superiority, the

---

[6] This phenomenon, called *folie à deux*, is not unique. Many times the relatives or close associates of a patient identify so strongly with him as to become as ill as the patient himself.

Messianic complex. They may feel that, due to their abilities or their special knowledge, or due to direct command from on high, they are destined to become great leaders. Several public figures in history have had careers that suggest this element in their personalities. There was, for example, much publicly printed psychiatric speculation concerning Adolf Hitler and other dictatorial figures during contemporary times, and earlier European history gives us Ivan the Terrible, the first czar of Russia, and Tomás de Torquemada, the inflexible inquisitor general of Spain. That a paranoiac could achieve a position of leadership is completely within the realm of possibility, and if he has the means for making his delusions determiners of a future reality, he could be very dangerous indeed.

PARANOID STATE

The paranoid state deserves a separate place in our classification primarily because of a need to categorize the rather common temporary semi-delusional behavior that appears in many individuals, most commonly in the period of middle maturity. In this condition the patient develops short-lived delusional beliefs, usually of a persecutory nature, arising from situational inadequacies or frustrations. From a long-time point of view the condition is not serious, but unfortunate behavioral and social consequences may grow out of the actively delusional period of illness. Many incidents are reported in the daily press where a husband or wife, suspicious of his mate's fidelity, institutes divorce proceedings, inflicts bodily harm, or even commits murder.

The paranoid state may be a part of other types of maladaptation. In chronic alcoholism a frequent symptom is the development of paranoid ideas of infidelity, discrimination, and so on. The same sort of thing may be seen in individuals laboring under handicaps of physical illness or disability. Some tubercular patients, separated from their families by long periods of hospitalization, become paranoid. Deaf people frequently develop suspicious convictions about the behavior of others. In disorders affecting the cerebral cortex the same persistent beliefs may occur.

The psychological mechanism in the paranoid state does not seem to differ materially from that discussed in paranoia above. The individual projects his own inadequacies onto the environment and defends the projection by various forms of rationalization. That paranoid ideas of infidelity and discrimination by superiors are so prevalent and that the disorder occurs primarily from age 35 on suggests the validity of ascribing the paranoid delusions to this mechanism. It is at middle age that the individual first starts to experience competition, sexually and in his work, with younger people. To face the fact that age brings with it a reduction in some types of adjustmental potential is too bitter a fact for many individuals to face; the easier way is to seek for the causes of inadequacy in circumstances exterior to himself. The preservation of ego adjustment, consequently, results in a loss of perspective and reality orientation at the other adaptational levels.

Case 41. Illustrative of the paranoid state is a shocking murder that took place in a town near our university. A young man had just finished serving a one-year prison sentence for theft. He returned home and accused his wife, who had supported their children and maintained the family integrity, of being unfaithful to him while he was in prison. He was unable to give reasons for such a belief and the wife protested her innocence. Nevertheless, goaded by his beliefs, he continued to quarrel, and, as a climax, strangled his wife. When seen later, after his arrest, he admitted the possibility that he could have imagined the whole thing.

Another instance is told in the letter of a woman who wrote to a nationally syndicated newspaper advice column, complaining that her husband locked her in their home every day when he went to work and would never let her associate with other people unless he was present. A former colleague resigned a job through a completely unsubstantiated belief that his supervisors were discriminating against him because of his religious beliefs; the facts were that this person had been so involved in personal financial problems and so emotionally disturbed about his personal security that he was unable to perform with any degree of effectiveness. In spite of his lowered efficiency he had received what was actually extremely tolerant treatment.

The paranoid states, with their vaguely formed beliefs concerning threat from people around them, shade imperceptibly into the sort of emotional response we generally refer to as "jealousy." As everyone knows, jealousy is a painful type of emotional experience, extremely disturbing to all parties concerned in it. Jealousy grows from the same soil as the paranoid states, a lack of personal security in interpersonal relations. The jealous person is actively afraid of being deprived of sources of emotional satisfaction, and his fear reflects a belief that he does not have the capacity to retain the source of satisfaction by his own efforts. The jealousy reaction, like all fearful emotions, stimulates such strong and primitive avoidance behavior that rational considerations go by the board. A jealous man literally "makes a fool of himself." As Cameron (1947) pointed out, the insecure individual has such a lowered perceptive threshold toward anything that is even remotely connected with his insecurity that he is constantly susceptible to misinterpretations of social situations. The jealous person perceives deep significance of a threatening sort in the slightest action of his loved one. He tortures himself for hours with fanciful reconstruction of possible circumstances that reflect on her faithfulness or devotion. The revelation of some of these fantasies occurring in supposedly "normal" people convinces the unbiased observer that the paranoid states are continuous, with emotional behavior supposedly within the range of tolerable adjustment.

Affective Disorders

THE GENERAL NATURE OF THE AFFECTIVE REACTIONS

The *affective* disorders, considered together, constitute the second largest group of hospitalized mental illnesses. Approximately 10 per cent of new admissions to mental hospitals in 1949 were either manic-depressive or involutional melancholia cases (Federal Security Agency, 1952). These disorders occur with somewhat less frequency than the schizophrenias, and they present a brighter picture with respect to remission and recovery. Few of the affectively disturbed patients spend more than five years in any single hospitalization, although they may return with recurrences of their illness.

The affective psychoses are so called because of the fact that their major symptoms are derangements of emotional expression. The patient is either too happy, too sad, too irritable, too optimistic, or too pessimistic. His exaggeration of emotional expression is accompanied by signs of intellectual disturbance but not to the same extent as in the schizophrenic. There is less delusion-formation, and hallucinations are rare. Thinking in formal test situations, if his emotional state permits him, is much freer and less influenced by bizarre personal preoccupations than is the schizophrenic's.

Although these points serve to differentiate the affective disorders from schizophrenia, many patients in practive display features of both conditions. There is nothing mutually exclusive about the diagnosis, although for many years following Kraepelin's original description of the two conditions an attempt was made to separate them precisely. Even today many patients present difficult problems in differential diagnosis between schizophrenia and manic-depressive psychoses or involutional melancholia. An old criterion that has been much criticized in more recent years was that of recovery. It was thought that schizophrenics rarely made spontaneous recoveries, and that the affective reactions did so quite commonly. More careful study, however, has disabused us of the idea that any of these disorders run an inevitable course, comparable to some infectious diseases, for example. Remissions, either spontaneous or as a result of therapy, are seen in both schizophrenia and the affective states.

The classification of sub-types of affective disorders presents some problems. Basically all emotional distortions seen in these conditions range between the two poles of manic elation and deep depression, and any individual patient at any particular time could be placed somewhere on a continuum between these two extremes, as could, it might be parenthetically added, all other persons. The affective disorders tend to occupy the extremes, but even at these extremes there are gradations that are sufficiently distinctive to be named. We will follow Cameron's (1944) suggestion, at least in part, and differentiate the manic extreme into *subacute mania, acute mania,* and *hyperacute mania.* The depressions we will describe under the headings, *retarded depression* and *agitated depression. Involutional melancholia* will be described separately, although there are probably as good grounds for including it in the general classification of depressions as there are for distinguishing it.

Characteristic of all affective disturbances, particularly in comparison with schizophrenia, is the rapidity with which the symptoms change. Schizophrenia tends to become relatively static, with little day to day or month to month change in the patient's condition, whereas the affective disorders manifest almost continually changing aspects. Observation of this feature led one of the early workers in the field, Kahlbaum (Zilboorg, 1941) to use the name *cyclothymia* to designate the disorders in which mania alternated with depression, and Kraepelin to use the name *manic-depressive* psychosis. The pattern of emotional variation between excitement and depression can occur in several varieties. The patient may alternate between mania and depression, passing directly from the one to the other, or he may show a progressive but slow change that goes through all the stages of mania into a period of normal emotional response and thence to stages of depression. Frequently patients are found who alternate between normal and either depression or excitement, but not in both directions. Other patients remain with fair consistency in the various stages of mania or depression without achieving either the opposite extreme or the normal median position. One patient seen at the University of Colorado Psychopathic Hospital had maintained a regular 24-hour cycle between elation and depression for the several years that he had been under institutional supervision. Most patients, however, do not show anything approaching regularity in their emotional shifts, and the type of alternation can be established only by study of the patient over a long period of time.

SUBACUTE MANIA

This term includes all those emotional deviations in the direction of mania that range from a mild euphoria to a relatively uninhibited excitement in which contact with reality is still predominantly retained. The person's mood and behavior show changes in the direction of greater spontaneity and increased general activity. The person laughs more, takes a more dominant part in conversations, has a feeling of increased fluidity of thinking, shows greater wit and sparkle in his speech, finds it easier to originate and carry out projects. He cuts down on his hours of sleep, plunges into more activities than he may have time for, and quite commonly loses weight. As the mania progresses he may act like a person who is mildly intoxicated, losing some of his usual inhibitions over speech and action. His reactions to frustration may also become less inhibited, and he shows an irritability that is out of proportion to the situation.

Some individuals are what have been called "hypomanic personalities" and are able to maintain a low degree of subacute mania for years as an habitual performance level. These people often are able to initiate and keep going a vast variety of constructive projects as long as they are able to have adequate assistance from less euphoric helpers who supply the attention to detail and the persistence that the hypomaniac lacks.

The increase in general activity of the subacute mania carries over into all phases of the individual's interests. Along with his elated mood there is often an increased sensitivity to the opinion of his associates, and an attempt to dominate situations. Criticism is accepted poorly, and the patient will show a compensatory burst of activity aimed at demonstrating the errors in the criticism. His social and erotic interests show a corresponding increase also. He tries to participate in more and more organizations, attend more and more parties, and engages in more and more flirtations and amatory conquests.

In all this activity, although there is no sharp break with reality, the person runs a grave risk of damaging his reputation, efficiency, and financial and business interests. Since society has a rather great superficial tolerance for the "life of the party" type of personality traits being expressed by the patient, it often happens that he experiences nothing but encouragement in his activities until they expand to the point of disaster.

Case 42. A college student, known as a "big wheel" on the campus, became involved in several extra-curricular activities that demanded so much time that he received failing grades on his midterm report. His reaction to the poor grades was to try out for a school play, thus adding another distracting factor. He came to the attention of the authorities after several of the town merchants complained that he had run up bills that they could not collect. It appeared that he had, as a part of his growing euphoria, decided to be the best-dressed man on the campus, and had purchased seven new suits with accessories, bought his dates roses by the dozen, rented cars for long periods of time, had run up restaurant bills by inviting the whole play cast to after-rehearsal "steak-snacks," charged gasoline for all his friends' cars, and supplied his fraternity with all the latest classical and popular phonograph recordings. Only the timely intervention of a father whose financial position was solid enough to meet his son's obligations saved a disagreeable situation. With prompt psychiatric treatment the boy was able to return to school the following year.

The course of subacute mania is unpredictable. In some instances it lasts but a short time and is followed by a return to a normal level of behavior. In other cases it is simply a phase in a progression toward an even more intense reaction. Even less is known about the basic causation of this condition than of the schizophrenic reactions. The psychodynamics are, in many cases, obscure, a situation that has led some writers on the subject to class the affective reactions as consequences of endocrine or metabolic disturbances. Since there is even less evidence for that point of view, it is probably nearer the truth to regard the condition as psychogenic and functional.

Regarding the condition from a psychological point of view and searching for the origins of this type of behavior in everyday life of all people, we might sum up the manic as a person exemplifying the trite old adage that "nothing succeeds like success." The manic has progressively utilized a technique of casting off inhibitions and has experienced a new feeling of release with each newly fallen inhibition. Unlike the schizophrenic, who removes obstacles in the real world by forming a fantasy world of his own, the manic finds that the obstacles of the real world can be overcome by simply disregarding them. If he talks fast enough, keeps busy enough with momentary tasks, invents ever new projects, he is relieved of the necessity of facing the persistent and unsolved inner conflicts. With each new sign of success at this technique, he receives an added boost to his activity, until, like an engine without a governor, he runs so fast that he exhausts himself.

ACUTE MANIA

The acute manic attack bears a superficial resemblance to the catatonic excitement. In both states the patient is hyperactive, irritable when any attempt is made to control him, and is careless of bodily needs for food, water, or excretion. Here, however, the resemblance ends. The catatonic is intellectually bizarre and out of contact, being motivated primarily by his inner preoccupations. The manic represents an exaggeration of normal elation and has, if anything, a heightened awareness of his surroundings, noticing aspects of the situation that escape others. He is particularly observant of other people and sometimes shows an embarrassing awareness of small details. One manic patient, in the height of his excitement, was being visited by the ward medical officer, a man who was a little self-conscious about a very slight deformity in his lower left arm, which was twisted from an old elbow fracture. The patient, on first seeing the physician, immediately said, "Hi, Twisty, the old meat hook ain't what it used to be, is it?"

In his excitement, the manic presents the same symptoms we have noted in the subacute mania in an exaggerated and accelerated form. He is constantly moving around, singing, laughing, joking, making puns, slapping people on the back, moving furniture, trying to stand on his hands, interested and actively interfering with any sort of activity that others may be trying to carry out. If any attempt is made to check this activity, the patient may become assaultive and pugnacious; the sensitivity of the subacute mania is also increased. This behavior, with its lightning-like quality, may go on for as short a time as a day or as long a time as several months. If the patient can be placed in a relatively quiet, non-stimulating environment, his behavior tends to become calmer. If, however, attempts are made at forcible restraint, the reaction is usually in the direction of even greater energy output.

In all of this excited manic behavior there is no evidence of the intellectual aberrations seen in the catatonic excitement. The stream of talk shows no clear break with rational associations, the written productions of the patient are within the realm of the understandable. The quality of thought does suffer; the patient is not able to pursue any topic long enough to permit of sound judgment. Interference with intellectual functions arises primarily from the pressure of general activity and emotional elation. Although there may be some delusional formation, the beliefs are usually as quickly aroused and dispelled as any other activity. Hallucinations are rare, and when they occur have more the character of illusions, in that the patient spends so little time in any activity that he often misinterprets environmental stimulation. One manic was sure that the senior writer was the governor of his home state, since we both were of about the same stature and complexion and parted our hair on the same side. As long as he was in the hospital, he insisted on talking about state affairs and wanted a commission in the state highway police.

The following case is illustrative of many points in the acute manic excitement, particularly the rapidity of the onset and the extremes to which pressure of activity may lead:

Case 43. Mrs. L. T. was a young married woman, 27 years of age, who lived in a small midwestern town. Her husband was comfortably employed as a bank teller and, although childless, they led a close, home-centered life. Mrs. L. T. was president of her garden club, worked in the P.T.A., taught a Sunday school class, and played golf every Thursday afternoon. Her health had always been excellent, and she had never shown signs of emotional instability, although she had mood fluctuations that were mild and at most went from a mild sort of sadness to a pressure of activity sufficient to accomplish the tasks expected of her in her personal and community life.

Her illness began suddenly. One morning she found it necessary to drive to a neighboring town to do a small errand in connection with her church work. After completing the errand, she started back home, feeling unusually happy and light-hearted. The thought flashed through her mind, "What a nice day to go on a trip," and then, "I've enough money in my pocketbook (she had been collecting funds for her church) to take me anyplace at all." At the next crossroad she turned her car, and without knowing or caring where the road led, started driving at a high rate of speed, her feeling of joy and release mounting. She drove all the rest of that day and all through the night, stopping only for gasoline, not feeling fatigued and not worrying about home or her husband. Mr. L. T. had notified the police when she failed to appear at home, and pick-up orders were sent out. However, Mrs. L. T. in some way managed to reach Chicago without meeting the police and with something over a hundred dollars in her pocketbook. She stopped her car in the middle of a busy Loop street, and with the ignition keys in her hand, walked to the curb and stopped a man, saying, "Hey, sexy, want a good car? Here." She then handed him the keys. She disappeared in the crowd, made her way to a department store, and created a scene in the women's clothing section by wildly insisting on being served ahead of other customers and then stepping out of a dressing room clad only in her undergarments. When the clerks attempted to detain her and call the police, Mrs. L. T. attacked, pulling hair and screaming. By the time the police arrived she had disappeared, with one of the store's coats on.

Her next port of call was a cocktail lounge in a small hotel, where she ordered several elaborate drinks, made amorous advances to the bartender, and interpreted his air of cool neutrality as an unflattering rebuff. She hurled a glass at the bar mirror, shouting obscene remarks. The bouncer at this establishment, being made of sterner stuff than the department store personnel, managed to hold her until police aid could arrive. She was taken to the station, and booked on a charge of drunkenness. Luckily a police surgeon was in the building, and at his insistence a blood alcohol determination was made. This showed such a low level that the surgeon suggested she be taken to a hospital for observation. While in the police station, Mrs. L. T. attempted to tear off her remaining garments, tried to make love to the police, wanted to be made a policewoman, insisted that she was the "spirit of youth," howled obscene comments about the police surgeon's ancestry, laughed hysterically, bit a policeman's thumb, talked wildly of suicide, and attempted to reveal the intimate details of her marital love life. At the hospital she continued to behave in somewhat the same fashion; when her husband arrived she overwhelmed the bewildered man with kisses and in the next instant slapped his face and said that he had never appreciated her. She gradually became calmer, and within a week was discharged, again the perfect garden club member, P.T.A. and Sunday school sponsor, and golf-playing young matron. Her retrospective account of the illness was limited to "I don't know what came over me, but it seemed such a wonderful idea to go on a trip that I couldn't resist it, and the farther I got the happier I felt. Through it all, as far as I can remember, I never felt better in my life. I can't understand what made me do it, though."

We see here rather clearly the emotional release that comes from shedding inhibitions. In this case we unfortunately have no information concerning the factors that made this well-disciplined young woman cast off her shackles. We can only surmise that beneath the placid surface of her small-town respectability there had been an accumulating aggressive tension that was finally enough to overpower the discipline and send her off on her manic episode.

HYPERACUTE MANIA

This term refers to the terminal state of an increasing manic excitement. The patient in hyperacute mania has become so active and uncontrollable that he constitutes a real danger to himself. His activity frequently leads to utter exhaustion and collapse, with a severe strain on his heart and vascular system. All the behavioral characteristics of the manic are present in an even more exaggerated form. Delusional material is more freely expressed, and the patient seems to have lost most of his contact with the environment. In this extreme form of excitement the points of distinction from a violent catatonic excitement or an extreme febrile delirium almost vanish. Any obvious relationship between the causes of the mania and the subsequent behavior has disappeared, and the patient presents simply a picture of an organism in extremely wild disorganization. These patients present difficult problems of treatment and nursing care. Aside from heavy sedation with drugs, there is no way of controlling their behavior. Forcible restraint is largely ineffective since the patient merely struggles the harder because of his bound position, and exhaustion is not prevented. The slightest attempt to interfere with his activity meets with the unreasoning resistance and aggression of a wild beast. Fortunately such extremes of manic excitement are not common, and their duration is limited because of the physical limitations of the patient.

RETARDED DEPRESSION

One of the most remarkable experiences in clinical psychopathology is to witness the transformation of a manic excitement into a retarded depression. Day does not differ from night more than an excited manic differs from a retarded depression. The fact that these two conditions may exist in the same patient within a time interval of twenty-four hours or less contributes to the effect. The type symptoms of depression are lowered general activity, a sad dysphoric mood, a loss of spontaneity, and heightened susceptibility to fatigue. The depressive phases of affective disorders show the same distribution on an intensity scale as we have seen in the manias. The depression may range from a mild "subacute" depression, through an acute phase, to a hyperacute, almost stuporous state.

The *subacute retarded depression* may be difficult to distinguish from a reactive depression on the one hand and from slight feelings of fatigue, boredom, malaise, or sadness on the other. The main distinction between the psychotic depression and the psychoneurotic depression lies in the nature of the precipitating factors. As we have seen, the reactive depression usually has its inception in grief- or guilt-provoking situations and is distinguished from the normal reaction only in its greater intensity or longer duration. The psychotic type of depression usually grows out of more endogenous causes and is more closely allied to the normal mood fluctuations experienced by everyone. Most people notice changes in mood level from day to day or week to week without being able to identify particular reasons to account for them. The subacute depression differs from these normal fluctuations only in the intensity and duration of the depressed period. The patient shows a slowing in his activity and notices that routine tasks take greater effort. He loses his capacity to enjoy the lighter aspects of living; jokes and wit may become irritating or painful. The duties of social intercourse appear as burdens. He loses his feeling of self-confidence and increasingly seeks to withdraw from environmental contacts. He finds himself unable to sleep, typically waking at a very early hour and brooding over his problems. His preoccupations with disaster may spread throughout his personality, so that all perceptions are colored by his pessimism. He becomes gloomy about his personal health, about his business prospects, about his abilities, and about the injustice and unhappiness that may come to his dependents.

The efforts of well-meaning friends and relatives to deal with the depressed person are fraught with danger. The commonest approach is an attempt to "cheer him up." This usually takes the form of offering the patient more social distractions, parties, trips, visits from friends, opportunities for new amusements, and so on. All these tactics, of course, only serve to deepen the patient's depression and to irritate him the more. If his verbal statements of gloom and futility are ignored or "laughed off," the patient may be allowed to become dangerously depressed without receiving competent professional treatment. The danger of suicide is always present in the depressions, and the patient's statements of his mood are among the earliest danger signals. The old belief that people who talk about suicide never essay the act is erroneous, and in the light of such consistent evidence to the contrary, it is amazing that people still cling to the belief. Very few suicides trouble completely to conceal their motives. It is true that depressed patients, when thwarted in their suicidal aims, are able to exercise extremely clever deceptions, but this is a secondary reaction. *Any person whose behavior has shown the type of symptom we have been discussing and who mentions suicide should be taken to a psychiatrist as soon as possible.* The newspapers seldom miss a day in reporting suicide or suicidal attempts, and their frequency is high enough to warrant attempts to educate the public on the prodromal signs of suicide. Most suicides could be prevented by adequate attention to the complaints of the patient himself. The following case is typical:

Case 44. G. D. was a well-to-do farmer who had raised a family and had seen them all successfully established in homes of their own. He and his wife were looking forward to retirement; they planned to sell their farm, "move into town," and enjoy their leisure by traveling. Mrs. G. D. had been troubled by shortness of breath and a "stitch in her side" for some time, and they paid a routine visit to their family physician. He told them that she had a minor heart ailment that was not immediately dangerous, but would require rest and dietary management. G. D. reacted to this with more perturbation than did his wife. He felt that it would involve a change in their plans and that the doctor was concealing the truth about the gravity of his wife's ailment. He gradually became more worried and preoccupied, lost sleep, and found that the effort of doing chores was, for the first time in his life, almost too fatiguing for him to get through. He told his relatives that retirement was impossible because he was sure he would not be able to sell the farm, that he was getting too old to make such a drastic shift, and that he would be letting his children down if he spent his last dollars on himself. He said, on several occasions, that he "might just as well go down behind the barn and blow my brains out" because of "the way things were going." His change of mood so alarmed his wife that on their next visit to the doctor she told him about her husband's behavior. The physician talked to Mr. G. D. and told them both frankly that his condition was much more serious than his wife's; he then recommended a visit to a psychiatrist. On that same day, after they had returned home, Mr. G. D. came into the kitchen and found his wife lying on the floor, unconscious. He tried briefly to revive her, but she had apparently had an acute heart attack and was already dead. He called his relatives, who lived less than a mile away, told them that terrible things were happening, and asked them to come as soon as they could. He then took his shotgun, went behind the barn, and killed himself.

In this case it should be noted that, at no time, did Mr. G. D. approach the state of disorganization of behavior that is commonly thought of as psychotic or insane, and yet he gave multiple evidence of depression sufficiently severe to alarm the physician. If relatives had been able to recognize the symptoms, tragedy could possibly have been prevented.

Just as in mania, it is difficult to formulate the psychodynamics of the depression. In mania we recognized that the person was escaping his troubles by a "flight into reality," by keeping so busy with other aspects of the environment that the troublesome aspects of life were temporarily avoided. The depression, which is so closely associated with the mania, must have something in common with it, despite the gross differences in symptomatology. The depression is, let us say, still a flight into reality, but for the escape is substituted an overly intense preoccupation with the problematic aspects of the patient's life. It is as if the patient had run from his problems as long as he was able, and finally, all escape routes blocked or exhausted, he is forced to consider the frustrations and conflicts from which he has futilely tried to escape. Just as the escape gave a cumulative sense of freedom and elation, so the inhibitions and blocking of actually considering the problems give a cumulative sense of impotence and failure. It is possible that the psychotic depression also has the features of atonement for guilt, which were noticed in the psychoneurotic depression. In the case of G. D., just presented, relatives reported that he had reproached himself on many occasions for allowing his wife to work so hard that her heart was damaged. The content of many depressives' remarks refers to an overwhelming sense of guilt for either real or imagined lapses from their ideals of correct behavior.

The *acute retarded depression* moves the patient to a more extreme position on the continuum of affective slowing. Activity becomes almost completely suspended; gloomy thoughts are the patient's constant companions. Almost any intellectual problem becomes too difficult to carry out. Preoccupations with failure and impotence are manifested by hypochondriacal complaints and delusional systems in which punishment for guilt plays a major role. The patient eats or excretes only with great urging and assistance. His whole attitude toward the environment is one of dull hopelessness. The danger of suicide is very great, and even under institutional care many acutely depressed patients belie their seeming intellectual dullness by outwitting supervisory personnel in suicide attempts.

Attempts to converse with the acutely retarded patient or to give him psychological examinations are extremely difficult. He may start a

sentence and never finish it; he speaks in a low tone of voice and reduces his answers to monosyllables. Any problem situation demanding
a choice of response may result in blocking through the patient's inability to make a decision. Even in this picture of lowered intellectual
efficiency, however, certain differences from the schizophrenias still
stand out. The depressed patient is usually correctly oriented both for
space and time. He has some insight for the circumstances of his hospitalization and rarely misinterprets it to the same extent as the schizophrenic. The following is illustrative:

Case 45. E. D., aged sixty, was admitted to the hospital because he was
depressed, ate insufficiently, and believed that his stomach was "rotting
away." The patient is described as a friendly, sociable individual, not
quarrelsome, jealous, or critical, and possessing a sense of humor. He was
considered even-tempered, slow to anger, tender-hearted and emotional.

At fifty-five the patient suffered from a depression when he was obliged
to resign his position. This depression continued for about nine months,
after which he apparently fully recovered. He resumed his work but after
two years suffered from a second depression. Again he recovered after
several months and returned to a similar position which he held until two
months before his admission. At this time he began to worry for fear he was
not doing his work well, talked much of his lack of fitness for his work, and
finally resigned. He spent Thanksgiving Day at his son's in a neighboring
city, but while he was there he was sure that the water pipes in his own
house would freeze during his absence, and that he and his family would
be "turned out into the street." A few days later he was found standing by
a pond, evidently contemplating suicide.

He soon began to remain in bed and would sometimes wrap his head in
the bed clothing to shut out the external world. He declared he was
"rotting away inside" and that if he ate, the food would kill him. He urged
the family not to touch the glasses or towels he used lest they become
contaminated. On arrival at the hospital he appeared older than his years.
He was pale, poorly nourished, dehydrated, with his lips dry, cracked and
covered with sores. His facial expression and general bearing suggested a
feeling of utter hopelessness. He was self-absorbed and manifested no
interest in his environment. When urged to answer questions, there would
be a long delay before attempting to answer but he would finally speak
briefly, hesitatingly, and in a low tone. He occasionally became agitated
and would repeatedly say, "Oh, doctor, why did I ever get into anything
like this? Doctor, I am all filled up! I can't get anything through me—
what am I going to do? Oh, dear! Oh, dear!" In explaining his presence in
the hospital he said he realized he had been sent by his family because
they believed he would be benefited by the treatment, but added, "I don't
know how they can send me here when they have not the means. My

wife cannot pay for me and by this time she must have been put out of the house."

After several months the patient began to improve although hypochondriacal ideas persisted for a considerable period. Finally when the matter of his ground parole was considered he seemed in a normal mood and indicated that he was beginning to think somewhat differently concerning his gastro-intestinal tract. At that time he commented, "There's a good deal of life in the old horse yet." A month later he passed into a mild hypomanic state. He became alert, animated, talkative, exuberant in spirits, and confident in manner. This mildly excited state continued for about two months when he settled down into what seemed to be his normal mood and state of activity. After a few weeks he was discharged but several months later he again showed signs of depression and hanged himself before arrangements for recommitment had been made.[7]

The suicidal termination of this patient's history should especially be noted. The danger of suicide is never completely absent in the affective disorders.

The *hyperacute retarded depression,* like the hyperacute mania, is almost indistinguishable from any other stuporous condition as far as behavioral appearance is concerned. The patient is mute and inaccessible to communication. He usually must be forcibly fed by tube and similarly aided in excretion. His activity is reduced to the point that he does not move even under conditions of deadly threat, and his responsiveness to environmental stimulation of any kind is minimal. The condition can be differentiated from other types of stuporous disorders only on the basis of past history and, possibly, in terms of the manner in which the patient responds to treatment.

AGITATED DEPRESSION

Some depressed patients show the gloomy and dysphoric mood shift without a correlated reduction in activity. This type of behavior is referred to as *agitated depression.* Here the patient shows the same type of depressive development as is seen in the retarded depression, but with an increase in general activity accompanying the deepening mood change. Restless movement, inability to sleep or eat, and other features of mania may be present. The stream of conversation is under pressure, but differs from the manic chiefly in the perseverative nature of the speech content. The agitated depression may sit all day, rocking back

[7] Arthur P. Noyes (1934), *Modern Clinical Psychiatry,* pp. 147-148. Philadelphia: W. B. Saunders Company.

and forth vigorously and crying in a loud tone, "Oh, my God; Oh, my God; I'm a sinner, a sinner, a sinner." He wrings his hands, tears flow from his eyes, and he presents an exaggerated picture of disconsolate grief. His speech reveals numerous delusional beliefs that center around feelings of unworthiness, sinfulness, and bodily change. Because of increased activity, his frequent suicidal impulses are difficult to control. The patient may make efforts to maim or disfigure himself. One patient succeeded in amputating his penis and testicles with a piece of spring he had somehow been able to tear from his hospital bed. Another patient killed himself by running headlong across his isolation room and butting his head on the concrete wall. A young woman who was operated on for acute abdominal pain was found to have swallowed over half a pound of wire nails.

The agitated depression is differentiated from the catatonic excitement or the delusional hebephrenic primarily on the basis of history, as in the acute retarded depression. The agitated depression, in addition, usually maintains a better orientation and somewhat more intellectual integrity than do the schizophrenics, although the problem of differential diagnosis may sometimes be difficult.

INVOLUTIONAL MELANCHOLIA

Insofar as symptoms are concerned, involutional melancholia shows few points of difference from the other depressions we have just described. Some writers, as a matter of fact, doubt whether the condition exists as an independent entity (Jameison and Wall, 1932). However, in certain people who have had no previous occurrence of a mental disease, late middle age brings an episode of depression so deep as to be considered psychotic. The fact that it occurs around the time of menopause in women and in males at an age when they are experiencing some decline in their virility has suggested the possibility of a distinctive reaction type, caused possibly by endocrine dysfunction or associated with other beginning organic changes of old age. The clinical evidence seems to be against this supposition, although it has been defended by Werner, Hoctor, and Ault (1941). Studies in which depressed patients diagnosed as involutional melancholic were given large dosage of the hormones whose absence was thought to be responsible for the condition have, on the whole, failed to show improvement in the patients as a result of the medication (Palmer, Hastings, and Sherman, 1941; Ripley, Shorr, and Papanicolaou, 1940).

More plausible is the possibility that the climacteric period of entrance into old age presents psychological problems of such difficulty to some people that they are unable to cope with them by their usual mechanisms. After a person passes the most productive and energetic period of his life, he begins to realize that many of his ambitions, ideals, and ego-goals will never be attained. He may reflect upon the disparity between what he wanted to do or be in his youth and what he actually became. He may feel that his chances are now irrevocably gone. In this affective reaction there is much to remind us of the attitude of the traumatic neurotic toward death. For the first time the individual realizes that "the moving finger writes and having writ moves on," and that life once lived cannot be retraced. Both sexes, to somewhat different degrees, lose their sexual attractiveness, and the female may realize that she can no longer bear children. Old conflicts, long submerged during maturity, may make themselves felt again, and the person may no longer have the techniques of escaping them. In such a frame of mind it is not to be wondered at that some people are not able to face the death of a loved one, the triumph of a younger competitor, a divorce, or financial difficulties. These factors serve as precipitants for the psychosis, but the groundwork has been laid throughout the person's life. Involutional melancholia, according to Noyes (1934), occurs most commonly in persons of an inhibited, serious, narrowly rigid type of personality whose life habits have led him in a straightforward path of devotion to detail. These people commonly have had few recreations or diversions and have developed few skills, interests, or hobbies outside their immediate working life. Consequently, when their older years bring shifts in plans, and ways of living, they have no resources to meet the new demands. As William James has said, "We believe ourselves immortal because we believe ourselves *fit* for immortality" (James, 1890, p. 349). The melancholic no longer possesses this belief.

The content of behavior in involutional melancholia reflects these psychological background factors. The patient shows, in addition to his depressed mood, great anxiety and apprehension, preoccupation with thoughts of death, and delusions of bodily change. As one watches the patient, the impression is unmistakable that he is expressing misery and anguish. Regret is freely expressed for the way his past life has been wasted, and he cries out with fear for what the future is sure to bring. The general picture is quite similar to the agitated depression. Here also, the danger of suicide is very great, and the more so since the basic content of the disorder is a burning dissatisfaction with life.

The following case exemplifies many of the psychologically causative factors and most of the representative symptoms:

Case 46. Miss A. N. was one of two sisters and was the leading citizen of a small town in Ohio. Their father and mother had died in an accident when the girls were in their late teens, leaving them extremely secure financially and in possession of one of the biggest houses in town. Our patient never married, although she had many suitors. She preferred, in her own words, "to stay in daddy's house and keep the old home together." Her sister was not so constant and soon married and moved away. Miss A. N. devoted her time to charity and community affairs. In the course of time she found that age had crept upon her and that she had reached the age of fifty-five without ever having gone farther away than to Cleveland or Chicago. When she chanced to mention this to her friends, they urged her to plan a trip for herself. "Who," they told her, "deserves to enjoy herself more than you who have given so much of yourself to others?" The only difficulty appeared to be one of finances. The town banker tried to explain to her that she had, from time to time, and against his advice, dipped into the principal of her inheritance for some charitable purpose or another, and what was left, though sufficient to support her for many years, was not enough to take an extended vacation. Nevertheless, she decided to spend some more of her principal and laid out a tour that would take her around the world. She would see the great cathedrals of Europe, see the missions in Africa that she had worked so hard to support, see the Holy Land, and India, and the Orient. With her friends helping, she put together clothes, bought luggage, and studied travel folders.

Then something happened. Her sister came for a visit and confided that her husband was in desperate trouble. He had used his firm's assets to invest in a new enterprise, and it had failed suddenly and with no possibility of regaining the funds. His business needed capital to meet current expenses. Could Miss A. N. help them? She immediately canceled her plans for the trip and turned over the money she would have spent and more to the sister, minimizing the extent of her sacrifice and saying that "it was the only thing a sister and a Christian could do." It was shortly after this incident that friends began to notice that Miss A. N. was "getting old." She herself noticed that her memory was poorer and that she could not marshal the same enthusiasm for church suppers and Sunday school picnics. She also, for the first time, began to worry about expenses. She would send cuts of meat back to the market, saying they cost too much and were more than she needed; she argued with the handy man who had looked after her house and grounds. She asked her lawyer if he could sell her property and find her a smaller cottage "in which to die." When the time came to make her yearly pledge to the Church, she went to call on the minister and, to his surprise, burst into bitter weeping, saying that she had sinfully expended "dear daddy's money" and could no longer do her

Christian duty. The minister was sufficiently alarmed by her behavior to say something to her physician, who called on her and received an even more shocking surprise. Miss A. N. confided in him that she was "paying for her vicious sins" and that her body was wasting away so rapidly that she would no longer require his professional services. He noted that she had closed up all the rooms in her house and was living in the kitchen, apparently sleeping on a few blankets placed on the floor. He persuaded her to go to the hospital, where she received psychiatric and psychological examinations. On admission she was emaciated and tremulous, appearing to be at least seventy years old. Her appearance, however, remained neat and proper in the fashions of an older generation. She wore an old-fashioned bonnet and smiled sweetly but sadly at her examiners. Sitting primly in her chair and frequently pausing to wipe the tears from her eyes, she whispered her story in a barely audible voice. She had, so she said, committed the unpardonable sin, not once but many times. When asked what the unpardonable sin might be, she looked incredulous and replied that *everyone* knew that she had done so, but that she couldn't bear to have them feel sorry for her. She said that her body had dried up and that since she had no soul she would soon be gone, rotted away. Although all her life she had tried to do good, she had never succeeded in pleasing "chick or child" and now that she was old "they were all turned against her." From putting together many such interviews it became apparent that her illness had started soon after she had given her sister the money she had intended for her trip. The very night that she had finally decided to give this money she had dreamed that in some way she had poisoned her sister and that she had refused to listen to the sister's pleas for help. The dream had been so vivid that it had awakened her, and she remembered thinking what a fool her sister was to have trusted the man she married. The next Sunday, while reading her Bible, she had chanced across a statement to the effect that "he who calls his brother a fool has committed an unpardonable sin and shall be condemned to eternal hell." She at once remembered her recent meditation about her sister and said to herself, "I have committed the unpardonable sin." From then on she carried the load of guilt with her; her Church work seemed a mockery, and when she heard people making plans for the future her certain knowledge that her own was hopeless caused her pain. While in the hospital she became steadily worse until one night she was discovered weaving her crocheting thread into a cord strong enough to hang herself. Suicidal precautions were intensified but she managed to work a stick piece of wood from a piece of hospital furniture and lacerate her arm. The bleeding was easily stopped but the cut became infected, and she developed a generalized septicemia. Her recovery from this illness was accompanied by a lifting of her depression and she was later discharged from the hospital.

In this case we see the rigid personality whose interests were centered in maintaining the symbol of her father's place in the community throughout her early adult life. When the sense of what she had missed convinced her that she should vary her behavior, the incident of the sister acted as a notice that she would never escape the pattern she had erected. The disappointment and the fact that giving her sister the money actually crippled the patient in her main technique for gaining security, namely her charity work, were too much for her to absorb with her limited psychological resources. The dream, which had an obvious motivation in her frustration and disappointment, crystallized her feelings of anxiety and apprehension, the Biblical statement about damnation only confirming the opinion. The hostility she could not turn against the sister or against the circumstances of being old and living all her life in the same place she turned against herself; in effect she consigned herself to damnation.

DISCUSSION QUESTIONS

1. Is psychotic behavior *qualitatively* or *quantitatively* different from other behavior?
2. Can you give specific examples of difficulty in differential diagnosis between psychosis and psychoneurosis?
3. What is the role of anxiety in the functional psychoses?
4. Do you think that organic correlates of the "functional" psychoses will ever be discovered? Reasons?
5. What is the economic importance to society of these disorders? Try to find estimates of how much time and money are lost to the patient by his hospitalization as well as mental hospital costs.
6. Why would you expect therapy of psychotic patients to be more difficult than that of the psychoneurotics?
7. What might there be in common between Rodin's statue of "The Thinker" and some of the symptoms shown by catatonics?
8. How adequately do you think motion pictures have portrayed psychotic behavior? Can you discuss the differences between "good" and "bad" portrayals?
9. Suppose you were hitchhiking and were picked up by a person whose subsequent behavior convinced you that he was a paranoid psychotic. How would you act?
10. Should the legal interpretation of psychosis be liberalized so that *all* psychotics could be hospitalized instead of penalized, or should the law be made more strict so that "insanity pleas" could not be a possible recourse to the criminal?

SUGGESTED READINGS

C. Beers (1908), *The Mind That Found Itself*. New York: Longmans, Green & Company.

N. Cameron (1944), "The functional psychoses," in J. McV. Hunt, ed. (1944), *Personality and the Behavior Disorders*. New York: The Ronald Press Company.

B. Hart (1931), *The Psychology of Insanity*. New York: The Macmillan Company.

BIBLIOGRAPHIC SOURCES

In the first edition of this book, the Army Medical Department classification of the psychoses was used exclusively. In 1952, the American Psychiatric Association published a new classificatory scheme for the various types of mental disorders. Actually, the latter was based heavily on the former, particularly with respect to the functional psychoses. Rather than use the new schema, we have changed the old classification only to include some new types differentiated by the *Diagnostic and Statistical Manual, Mental Disorders,* prepared by the Committee on Nomenclature and Statistics of the American Psychiatric Association (1952). If possible, it is suggested that you obtain a copy of the 1952 manual and examine the method of classifying the mental disorders, not only for the functional pyschoses but also for all the behavior that is the subject matter of this book.

One particular problem in classification, among many, is the question of the independence of the involutional psychosis as a separate category. Although it is treated as a separate entity in Table 10, our discussion in the text raises the possibility that the involutional psychosis should be treated as a variety of the affective disorders. Although this is not a critical problem, it illustrates the difficulty in constructing a consistent and satisfactory classification scheme.

In the discussion of the general characteristics of psychotic behavior, our general position led us to the hypothesis that at least some psychotic patients possibly passed through a neurotic stage initially. The evidence presented seemed to indicate that anxiety symptoms were present in the histories of psychotic patients prior to the psychotic episode. Nevertheless, the student should be aware that many psychopathologists are opposed to these hypotheses, believing apparently that the functional psychoses and the psychoneuroses are independent. They feel further that no neurotic ever becomes psychotic except perhaps in very rare cases. It is very difficult to resolve these points of view without much more evidence than is presently available.

For the historical background of our present-day attitude toward the psychoses the best source is Zilboorg (1941), whose *History of Medical Psychology* is to the psychiatric field what Boring (1950) is to systematic psychology. Zilboorg traces the development of the concepts of schizophrenia and the affective disorders and has an excellent discussion of the problems earlier writers faced in their attempts to bring order to the field.

On the important question of psychopathology and the law, there is no single secondary source that presents both the scientific and the legal side of the question. An old book that had a great deal of influence was Maudsley's (1875) *Responsibility in Mental Disease;* Chapter IV summarizes the forensic situation up to that time. Surprising is the modern sound of much that Maudsley says, since it is apparently true that the law changes much more slowly than science. More recently there is the report issued by the Commissioners in Lunacy for New York State (1938), which discusses the concept of legal responsibility in some detail. Weihofen's (1933) *Insanity as a Defense in Criminal Law* and Green's (1944) article critically reviewing the "tests" of mental incompetency are examples of legal writing. In the psychological literature, Higginson's (1950) chapter in Mikesell's (1950) text is recommended.

On the psychoses in general, the little book by Hart (1931), *The Psychology of Insanity,* will always remain a classic for its clear descriptions and its warm human interest. It is still one of the best interpretations of mental disease. An equally interesting book that constantly emphasizes the relationships with the everyday world around us of psychotic people and behavior is Menninger's (1937) classic *The Human Mind.* Of standard psychiatric texts, the following may be consulted for varying points of view and for case material: Alexander and Ross (1952), Bleuler (1924), Billings (1939), Cobb (1952), Henderson and Gillespie (1940), Muncie (1939, 1948), Noyes (1934 or 1940), Strecker (1952), and Strecker, Ebaugh, and Ewalt (1951). On mental disease as a social problem, Landis and Page (1938) present much of the basic statistics, and Deutsch (1938) provides the historical setting. For an idea of the variety of scientific disciplines that research on mental disease affects, the symposium edited by Bentley and Cowdry (1934), *The Problem of Mental Disorder,* or the Milbank Memorial Fund Conference (1952), *The Biology of Mental Health and Disease,* should be read. In these are reports by investigators in everything from anatomy to zoology on their contributions to the problem.

For a provocative account of verbal hallucinations, Arnow (1952) is suggested. An interesting experiment is reported by Altschule (1951) who found that he was able to control hallucinatory phenomena by carbon dioxide inhalation. Albee (1951) has found some indications that the content of schizophrenic delusions may be a prediction of possible recovery. He found that, among those schizophrenics who improved and had delusions, their delusions tended to be more self-condemnatory in nature. Among schizophrenics who did not improve, their delusions tended to be persecutory in nature. However, as Albee points out, these are not absolute categories and more research seems desirable. For the literature on hallucinations and delusions in children, Despert (1948) is an excellent source. Delusions of pregnancy are well known, and Wallenberg-Chermak (1952) presents several cases including two cases of males with delusions of pregnancy. Sometimes it is difficult to separate delusion from fact; Atkin (1953) and Money (1948) discuss the problem in detail.

On schizophrenia, bibliographies of pertinent journal literature are listed in most of the texts referred to. More complete as a review of the literature is Cameron's (1944) treatment that we have used several times in this chapter. For much more extensive reviews of the literature, the work of Lewis (1936) and Bellak (Bellak, 1948, 1949; Bellak and Willson, 1949) should be seen. Bellak, after reviewing more than 3,500 papers, reports on more than 40 separate causal categories that may be involved in this disorder. On anxiety in schizophrenia, Shulman (1950) and Standish, Mann, and Menzer (1950) are suggested. Every major psychopathologist has had some point of view about the schizophrenic disorders. Simon (1949) presents short statements about the beliefs of eight: Kraepelin, Bleuler, Meyer, Freud, Jung, Kasanin, Kallmann, and Myerson.

On the language of the schizophrenic, Goodstein (1951) is an excellent introduction. Cameron (1947), Cameron and Magaret (1951), and Kasanin (1944) should also be seen.

One of the major problems in schizophrenia is the diagnostic fact that there is often much confusion between schizophrenic and psychoneurotic phenomena, especially in the earlier stages of schizophrenia or in mild cases. Several authors have commented on this problem (Bigelow, 1953; Mace, Koff, Chelnek, and Garfield, 1949) and Lewis (1949) has suggested criteria for differential diagnosis. An aid here should be the established psychological tests, but recent evidence on, for example, the Wechsler-Bellevue (Brecher, 1946; Garfield, 1949; Harper, 1950; Klein, 1948) and the Minnesota Multiphasic (Hunt, Carp, Cass, and Winder, 1948) has not been too favorable. Certainly the most obvious problem is the ill-fit between the names and the behavior of the disorder.

On the organic etiology of schizophrenia, Hoskins (1946) has an important and readable essay in which he presents the evidence for a more organic interpretation than we have given in this text. The organic approach is always implicit and constantly explicit in the Milbank Memorial Fund Conference (1952) and in the investigation headed by Heath (1954) on *Studies in Schizophrenia*. All three of these volumes are major contributions, and it is hoped that they can be examined in detail. In particular, the chapter by Wolf and Cohen (1950) in the Milbank Conference on the histopathology of schizophrenia is suggested. The organic approach may be illustrated by the experiment of Rupp and Wilson (1949). These investigators report the pathological findings on 37 individuals diagnosed as functional psychotics (20 of them schizophrenics). After death, it was found that 36 of the 37 had serious organic heart disease, several had central nervous system damage, and many had extensive visceral disease. Just what connection the organic damage has to the behavior disorder, if any, is, of course, the central unsolved problem. Even more confusing is the fact that other pathological studies of schizophrenics have been negative.

An interesting personal account of how it feels to be a catatonic has been written by a patient with some psychological training who went through a schizophrenic episode (Boisen, 1936). A fictional account of a schizophrenic episode that is based on the author's personal experience is *The Snake Pit* by Mary Jane Ward (1946).

On the paranoid disorders and particularly on the determinants of paranoid thinking are the articles by N. Cameron (1943, 1951). For details of at least one historical figure who was a paranoid, see Dakin's (1930) *Mrs. Eddy, The Biography of a Virginal Mind*. Bonner (1951) discusses the problem of the differential diagnosis between paranoia and paranoid schizophrenia.

The affective disorders have a less extensive bibliography than does schizophrenia. The student is again referred to the standard texts and to Cameron's (1944) review. On the manic-depressive psychosis, depressive type, Campbell (1950) offers detailed symptomatology on 200 mild cases and discusses the problem of differential diagnosis with psychoneurosis. For a survey of the literature on the involutional psychosis, see Tait and Burns (1951). With the increase of the aged in the general population, it is not surprising that the incidence of involutional psychoses is also increasing (Malzberg, 1948). Finally, the book that started the mental hygiene movement in the United States, Beers' (1908) personal account of his experiences while going through an affective disorder, *The Mind That Found Itself*, should be required reading.

X

Behavioral Reactions to Tissue Defect, Disease, and Trauma

An attempt to relate phylogenetic and individual differences in behavior to brain structure is . . . rather like an adventure in correlating the mysterious with the unknown.

—K. S. LASHLEY

CLASSIFICATION OF THE ORGANIC DISORDERS

Many forms of organic defect, disease, and trauma may bring about alterations of behavior that are sufficiently severe to be termed *psychotic*. Drugs, poisons, disease, and injury may so alter behavior that it appears irrational and incomprehensible to the social group and prevents effective adjustment, thus meeting our criterion of psychosis. By this definition a person who is very drunk is suffering from an "acute alcoholic psychosis," and the confusion following a severe blow on the head is also a temporary psychotic episode.

Classification of the organic psychoses is usually made in terms of the precipitating agent, such as alcohol, drugs, syphilis, and so forth. A somewhat more general classification is shown in Table 12 based on classes of precipitating agents.

The chief value of classification in this way lies in the indication given for treatment and prophylaxis. An additional distinction is made in the *Diagnostic and Statistical Manual* (1952) between "acute" and "chronic" disorders. The former refers to conditions where brain dysfunction is reversible or temporary, whereas the latter denotes permanent damage. It is obvious that such a differentiation is critical to treatment.

However, etiological classification results in a great many names and

TABLE 12

Psychoses due to constitutional factors:
  (1) Congenital cranial anomalies
  (2) Mongolism

Psychoses due to infection:
  (1) Epidemic encephalitis
  (2) Meningitis
  (3) Brain abscess
  (4) CNS syphilis (general paresis)

Psychoses due to intoxication:
  (1) Alcoholic intoxication
  (2) Drug and poison psychoses

Psychoses due to trauma:
  (1) Head injury
  (2) Birth injury

Psychoses due to circulatory disturbances:
  (1) Cerebral arteriosclerosis
  (2) Senile sclerosis

Psychoses due to convulsive disorder:
  (1) Epilepsy

Psychoses due to metabolic, nutritional, or growth changes:
  (1) Senile brain disease
  (2) Alzheimer's disease
  (3) Endocrine disorders
  (4) Familial amaurosis

Psychoses due to new growths (tumors or cancers)

Psychoses due to unknown, uncertain, or hereditary causes:
  (1) Multiple sclerosis
  (2) Huntington's chorea
  (3) Pick's disease

* Condensed and adapted from: Committee on Nomenclature and Statistics of the American Psychiatric Association (1952), *Diagnostic and Statistical Manual, Mental Disorders.* Washington, D.C.: American Psychiatric Association, Mental Health Service.

implies distinctions in symptomatology that do not exist in reality. There are actually only a few major varieties of symptoms, all having in common some interference with effective functioning of the central nervous system. We will first review some of these general characteristics of the organic behavior defects. This chapter will then conclude with a discussion of a few of the diagnostic types listed in Table 12.

Additional treatment of many of these types will be found in Part Three of the text.

Behavioral Consequences of Organic Brain Dysfunction

A classification of the symptoms shown by all patients with organic brain disturbances results in three rough categories of behavior: (1) release symptoms; (2) interference or decrement symptoms; (3) substitution or compensation symptoms. Physiological and psychological factors enter into each group to differing degrees. The release phenomena and the substitution symptoms are made possible by a disruption of physiological equilibria, but their course and content are largely determined psychologically. The decrement symptoms are best understood as signs of physiological deficit, and since many of them are symptoms of omission, the psychological element does not loom as large.

RELEASE SYMPTOMS

The many different parts of the central nervous system exhibit a hierarchical organization of function. In the course of evolutionary development, the central nervous system has become more and more complex, changing always in the direction of greater development of the cerebral structures. The vertebrate nervous system in its simplest form consists of a spinal cord and a cephalic ganglion (clump of nerve cells). The cephalic ganglion has undergone a series of modifications in phylogenetic development, resulting in the overgrown cerebrum of man. The lower brain centers and the spinal cord are relatively similar in most mammalian forms, but the cerebrum, and particularly the cerebral cortex, has been an index to the general state of development of any species. Figure 13 indicates these phylogenetic changes in central nervous system structure.

What behavioral assets go along with this bigger brain? The comparative psychologist tells us that there are several: a better memory, capacity to make delayed reactions to stimuli, keener and more comprehensive perception, ability to abstract or generalize from sensory data, a richer repertoire of associative possibilities for varying behavior, quicker and more effective learning, and so forth. All these things are made possible through the increase in number of nerve cells in the central nervous system and through increase in the complexity of their organization. Herrick (1924) has estimated that there are nine billion neurons in the human cerebral cortex alone. Since there is the possibility of functional connection between any or all of them, the combinations of possible neural pathways reaches astronomical proportions,

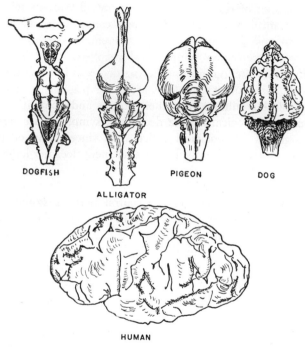

FIGURE 13. *Comparison of brains of various vertebrates.*

and the possibilities for variation in human behavior are tremendous. Added to this quantitative complexity is a growing amount of specialization of various parts of the brain for various types of organismic function. Thus, in the human brain, there are specialized areas for vision, motor function, hearing, and probably many other functions. There is also a topographical specialization, which gives primary integrative control of one side of the body to the cerebral hemisphere on the opposite side. Our knowledge of the neurophysiology and physiological psychology of the brain is still in its exploratory stages. It is only a little more than a hundred years since men first came to suspect the ways that the brain was involved in behavior. However, in this short time, certain reliable correlates between brain function and behavior have been established.

One of the first discoveries concerning the brain and behavior was the fact that the cerebrum, and particularly the cerebral cortex, exercises a limiting or inhibiting control over muscular action. Sherrington (1947) showed in 1906 that, when the functional connection between the cerebrum and the lower parts of the central nervous system was interrupted by surgical operation, a peculiar type of paralysis was obtained. The animal's musculature increased its tonus, and the animal's limbs would be extended stiffly. This state of affairs is termed "decerebrate rigidity." Sherrington deduced that the cerebrum in some way controlled or inhibited the excessive tonus of muscles. Clinically, the type of paralysis characterized by increased tonus and spasticity of musculature is called an *upper motor neuron paralysis,* implying that the neurological defect is to be found at some higher level of the central nervous system. In contradistinction, if the nerve fibers are cut between a muscle and the spinal cord, the resulting paralysis is characterized by a flabby, "flaccid," collapsed state of the muscle, and is called a *lower motor neuron paralysis.* Decerebrate rigidity is seldom seen in its ultimate form except in animals that have undergone experimental surgery. In humans, the best examples are to be found in infants who have grave developmental defects of the cerebral structures.

Another feature of the behavior of decerebrate animals is the ease with which emotional reactions may be elicited. In recognition of the manner in which the operated animal would show signs of anger to completely indifferent stimuli, Sherrington called the emotional display *sham rage.* The emotional behavior of the decerebrate animal shows a lack of control and an uninhibited vigor corresponding to the increase in muscle tone, which was also noted. With the cerebral cortex no longer functional, these primitive forms of response appear to be *released.*

Release phenomena occur not only in decerebrate animals, but also to a lesser extent in those that have sustained injury to a *part* of the brain. The inhibitory role of the cerebrum is decreased, and the behavior reflects the difference. A familiar example in any hospital is the emotional behavior seen in people who are regaining consciousness after a general anesthesia. Patients who are usually well controlled often swear and shout obscenities or cry and laugh seemingly without adequate stimulation. Much the same phenomena take place in the delirium of fever or drug poisoning. The actions of a person who is going through the various stages of drunkenness furnish a very good demonstration of the consequences of progressive release of cerebral control. Among the first inhibitions to be released are the 'fine social discriminations; the subject loses the more subtle (or more superficial), polite manner; he makes statements and tells stories with no acute discrimination of the sensibilities of his audience. He is more easily stimulated to tears or laughter. As the intoxication progresses he loses more and more motor coordination and more and more social control. His staggering gait and unsteady fumbling show over- and under-energization of muscles. The latter stages show what amounts to a *functional decortication,* and the drunk loses consciousness. His symptoms on an evening's party parallel the symptoms of the organic psychoses. In all organic lesions of the brain more or less "release" symptomatology is present. It may be detected by clinical observation and by psychological tests.

INTERFERENCE OR DECREMENT SYMPTOMS

Along with the positive release of control in organic conditions there is always more or less loss of pre-traumatic behavioral potentialities. An intact central nervous system is necessary for many of the more highly integrated types of activity. Injury to the brain is reflected in many types of decrement in function. Severe trauma results in loss of consciousness, preceded or followed by disorientation, loss of muscular power, loss of abstracting or generalizing ability, loss of higher speech functions, and so forth. We will also see that organic damage and its resultant sensory or motor incapacities may lead to personality and social maladaptation.

There is no definition of consciousness that would satisfy every student of human behavior, but all are in agreement on one point, that consciousness involves an awareness of the environment and a capacity to deal with it in a discriminatory manner. It is evident from observation that loss of consciousness accompanies many of the severe forms of stress on the brain. The most immediate cause is a relative cerebral anoxia. When the cerebral cortex fails to receive an adequate supply of oxygen, the complex integration upon which consciousness depends is impaired. Cerebral anoxia can result from mechanical decrease in blood supply, as in strangulation and blows on the head; from constriction of cerebral blood vessels, as in intense emotion; from chemical changes in the blood constituents, as in carbon monoxide poisoning; or from any factors that interfere with proper oxygenation of the blood in the lungs or with its circulation.

The adaptive significance of loss of consciousness is hard to determine. It has been said that unconsciousness has a primitive adaptive value and is closely related to the death feint seen in some insects and vertebrates when closely threatened. It is true that complete cessation of motion has a protective value to the pursued animal, but whether it is equivalent to unconsciousness is doubtful. The small mammals who adopt this ruse are able to leap into further running activity if danger approaches too closely, and this bespeaks awareness during the feint. There is a type of Andalusian goat that shows a cataleptic reaction (feinting) to any sudden intense stimulation. These animals will fall if shouted at in a loud tone of voice or if disturbed in any other way. Since they would then be easy prey for any carnivore that fancies goat flesh, this behavior appears more pathological than adaptive.

For the human being, in any of the ordinary conditions of living, unconsciousness is a disordered, catastrophic form of behavior. The unconscious person is defenseless, unable to discriminate or make adjustive movements, and cannot meet either internal or external demands. There are many degrees of unconsciousness, of course, and many degrees of maladjustment rising from them.

From a physiological point of view, unconsciousness is not always as unfavorable a symptom. The loss of consciousness accompanying intense pain probably serves to protect the organism from even more severe catastrophic responses. However, what is physiologically desirable is not always to the best interests of the organism as a whole. For example, a flier caught in the flaming wreckage of an airplane crash may lose his life if the pain from his burns causes loss of consciousness and a cessation of his struggles to escape. Such instances, which could be multiplied endlessly, illustrate a basic fact concerning psychopathology, namely that there is often a severe conflict between the momentary physiological adjustments of the organism and its long-term over-all needs. This conflict becomes particularly acute with human beings who are attempting to adjust to a complex society.

Loss of consciousness is not the only severe decrement symptom in organic conditions. There are many others, among the most serious of which are the *aphasias*. Aphasia is a loss of some language function, ordinarily due to impaired cortical functioning. There are many disturbances of speech based upon pathology of the larynx and other vocal speech mechanisms, resulting in aphonia, hoarseness, monotony of speech, and so forth, but none of these is classed as aphasia. Aphasia is a loss of the symbolic aspects of communication. The precipitating cause is an injury to the cerebral cortex, usually in the "dominant" hemisphere.

Cerebral dominance requires a word of explanation. As is well known, most people show a preference for the use of one hand or the other in motor manipulations. The majority of persons seem to be right-handed. Along with the right-handedness go many other indications that the right side of the body takes the lead in motor and sensory adjustments, and it is as true to the facts to refer to a person as right-eyed or right-legged as to say that he is right-handed. Due to the fact that nerve tracts to and from the cerebral cortex cross in the lower brain regions, the left hemisphere of the cerebrum is connected with the right side of the body, and the right hemisphere with the left side of the body. Thus, injuries to the left hemisphere produce paralysis of muscles on the right side.

Aphasia results when the dominant hemisphere is injured. During World War II there were many head injuries. Analysis of the known cases of aphasia from the war showed that in only two cases of a total series of almost a thousand was the brain injury known to be in the non-dominant hemisphere. The precise location of injury necessary to produce aphasia is unknown. For many years it was thought that aphasia resulted from injury to the second and third convolutions of the frontal lobe of the dominant hemisphere, a locus known as *Broca's area*, after the French neurologist who described the correlation. More recent research has shown that various aspects of the disturbance can be produced by lesions in almost any portion of the dominant hemisphere; with still comparatively little known about the precise relationship between the location of injury and the symptom, we must be content for the moment with this generalization.

Although the chief symptom of aphasia is the reduced ability to deal with symbols, this defect is only a part of the larger clinical picture of a brain-injured patient. The types of personality alteration found in aphasic patients include:

1. A reduced capacity for abstract thinking
2. Disturbances of attention and concentration
3. Memory defects
4. General impairment of intellectual efficiency
5. Increased irritability, fatigability, increased anxiety and tension, euphoria, and various psychosomatic disturbances
6. Reduced ability to make an adjustment to new situations
7. A strong tendency towards perseveration
8. Social withdrawal; development of shyness and seclusiveness
9. An inhibition of the use of much of that speech potentially available because of repeated experiences of failure
10. Neurological muscular and sensory handicaps due to destructive nature of lesion[1]

Aphasias are classified under two main divisions, the *expressive* and the *receptive,* although most cases actually have symptoms referable to both. The expressive aphasia shows as an inability to express ideas through spoken and written language. This includes difficulties in speaking, naming, oral reading, writing, and spelling. The receptive aphasia is an inability to comprehend either written or spoken language.

The diagnosis of aphasia depends upon careful neurological and psychological examinations, since symptoms superficially similar to those of aphasia are sometimes seen in hysteria and the psychoses, whereas neurological defects of the superficial speech apparatus or of hearing may produce aphasia-like symptoms. Tests for aphasia include estimates of the patient's ability for oral reading and conversational expression, naming, repeating test phrases, spelling, both oral and written, arithmetical calculations, auditory comprehension, and comprehension of silent reading.

In most cases of aphasia, although the patient is unable to indulge in ordinary communication, his ability to utter emotional expletives is relatively unimpaired. Patients may be able to swear or speak habitual expressions of joy, and speech therapists have found that many of them are able to use language in singing the words of songs. This is further

[1] This list is quoted from the *Report of the Conference on Aphasia of Clinical Psychology and Neurology Branches, 22-26,* September 1945, p. 1. Neuropsychiatric Consultants Division, Surgeon General's Office, United States Army.

evidence that the cause of aphasia lies in the destruction of parts of the brain that integrate complex functions of abstraction and thinking and not in those parts that integrate the primitive sensory-motor connections of speech or writing as such.

By a slow process of re-education the aphasic is able to gain back some part of his lost language ability. In some instances the patient may be able to function at as high a level as before his injury, although most cases retain some trace of their defect. The fact that these patients can be taught to use symbols after having lost the ability is taken to mean that some other portion of the brain takes over the functions of the part that has been injured. This is a matter of some neurological interest, since the human brain shows little of such flexibility with respect to most sensory and motor defects caused by brain injury. No one has yet established the exact manner in which substitutive functions work nor the areas that assume the function, although the best guess is probably that the comparable area on the hemisphere opposite the lesion is the locus.

Specific organic defects may be in sensory or motor functions. These symptoms are of great value in the neurological examination because they aid in localization of the source of neural pathology. We have briefly mentioned the paralyses in connection with the localization of upper and lower motor neuron lesions. Some of the specific paralytic syndromes are of psychological interest. Infantile paralysis, for example, often imposes a psychological defect that may be as crippling as the motor disturbance itself. The dramatic nature of the illness, the many degrees of obvious incapacity it may cause, and the fact that a great many of its victims are children are all factors in producing inadequate personality reactions during the long convalescence the patient must usually go through. One case, typical of many others, was told by one of the leading students of the psychological aspects of this disease:

Case 47. The patient, a boy of fifteen, had weathered the acute period of his illness and had been left with atrophy and weakness of one leg. Before his illness the boy had been a moderately active person with no obvious signs of maladjustment. Because he was one of a family of seven children he had not received a great deal of attention or spoiling before contracting polio. When he returned from the hospital, however, he became the center of attention for the whole family. The father bought him a complex motor-driven wheel-chair, his mother spent long hours massaging his leg, his brothers and sisters gave up their allowances to buy him presents.

It is not surprising that the patient relished this new experience. Unfortunately his physician became dissatisfied with his progress; although the leg was pronounced strong enough to walk on and braces were fitted, the boy complained of great pain, of the discomfort of the braces, and indicated clearly that he preferred to get around in his wheel-chair. Attempts were made to get him to go to a sanitarium; he consented reluctantly, but was back in a week, saying that the exercises caused him such discomfort that he had insisted on coming home. The boy's physician then took matters into his own hands and issued stern instructions to the family. The patient was not to be babied, he was to practice his exercises before being fed, the wheel-chair was to be traded-in for a strong pair of crutches, and the patient was to resume his schooling. This regimen, along with judiciously supplied encouragement and privileges, resulted in a much more rapid rate of recovery, and the patient was saved from what might well have become a life of invalidism.

Sensory defects are often as serious, particularly when they interfere with communication, as do blindness and deafness. Studies of these groups show a host of psychological consequences of their disabilities, some of which may be etiological factors in personality disorders. Although many individuals with sensory handicaps solve their problems by compensatory development of substitute skills, to others the defect becomes an insoluble problem, or the solutions achieved are more personally than socially satisfying. During World War II psychologists and psychiatrists played an important role in helping soldiers who were newly blinded or deafened to find ways of maintaining their sense of personal integrity and their social usefulness. The emotional trauma connected with the period of initial adaptation to their new status was the most difficult period in their adjustment.

This same type of reaction was noted in the paraplegics and in the amputees. Most of these patients went through a longer or shorter period of almost complete hopelessness; behaviorally this was indicated by a quiet but determined withdrawal from social contacts. They would show lack of interest or irritability toward anyone who attempted to distract them by offering occupational therapy, diagnostic testing, or even suggestions about hospital routine. Typically these patients showed ambivalence about their wives and families, fearing that their handicap would produce changes in their interpersonal relationships. In the patients making healthy adjustments this period of withdrawal would gradually change, the patient would begin to take an interest in his surroundings, engage in diversional activities, and start some type of constructive planning for the future. A few individuals would show changes in the opposite direction, their behavior becoming more and more catastrophic and less and less adaptive. The withdrawal would deepen, the patient turning his face to the wall and lying for hours without moving or speaking, the general picture resembling that of a severe depressive reaction. Others would regain a social orientation of their behavior but would become childishly dependent upon the hospital personnel, not only with respect to their defects but for all other phases of living. It was this latter group that responded best to psychotherapy and to a type of general hospital and ward management that provided the sort of incentives and rewards that would motivate the patient toward adaptive effort.

All decrement symptoms are not of the massive and easily recognizable kind we have been discussing. With many types of brain damage the interference with normal behavior may be so slight as to pass unnoticed in ordinary social intercourse. However, if these patients are given careful tests of intellectual functioning and emotional reaction, the defects become evident. Such psychological examinations are extremely important since they can be an aid in the early diagnosis of slowly developing pathological brain states, such as tumors, abscesses, hemorrhages, and so forth, and also because they provide a way of determining whether or not a patient is sufficiently recovered to resume his pre-traumatic occupation. Some of the behavioral changes found in the aged are deficit symptoms due to local changes in the circulatory supply to the cortex. Minimal in themselves, many times the cumulative defect is such that the senescent individual finds his adjustment difficult.

In summary, decrement symptoms are due to a destruction of structures necessary for adaptive behavior. The loss may be general, as in unconsciousness, or may be confined to specific symbolic, motor, or sensory functions. In many instances the defect is so slight as to escape casual notice and can be detected only by special examination devices.

SUBSTITUTION OR COMPENSATION SYMPTOMS

Since injury interferes with the organism's attempts to maintain an adequate adjustment, the injury can be considered as a problematic situation. Many of the reactions of the traumatized person become understandable when viewed in this way.

The reduction of sensory, motor, associative, and abstracting abilities in these patients must always be taken into account. A critical evaluation of their milieu is lacking, and although their basic motivation is not greatly altered, their ability to employ varied techniques of adjustment suffers. When to this is added the increased problems brought about by the decrement and release factors characteristic of their injury, it is not surprising that their behavior appears pathological.

Compensation symptoms can be divided conveniently into three types, corresponding to the various contributions they make to the individual's maintenance of equilibrium. These mechanisms we shall label (1) *protective;* (2) *replacement;* and (3) *perseverative* reactions. They should not be thought of as distinct and segregated forms of response but as components of the organic patient's everyday efforts in dealing with his own peculiar problems.

The *protective* mechanisms involve avoidance of situations that expose the individual to danger of failure. Either consciously or without insight, the patient may go to as great pains to maintain a simplicity of situation within his powers of adjustment as does the back-injured patient to avoid working conditions that place a strain on his back. As Goldstein (1939) has said: "a defective organism achieves ordered behavior only by a shrinkage of its environment in proportion to the defect" (page 46). As in other instances, it is easy to point out similarities between the behavior of these patients and the symptoms we have already encountered in the psychoneurotics and the psychotics. We again see the primacy of the primitive avoidance response in circumstances that direct a threat against the organism.

It is possible that some of the extreme conservatism of elderly people may be motivated by a desire not to place themselves in situations that are beyond their capabilities. Clinical psychologists have also noted difficulty in persuading patients to participate in psychological tests in situations where the individual has some reason to doubt his own capabilities. Once in the test situation, such patients often attempt to finish as rapidly as possible, as if escape were their dominant motive.

The *replacement* mechanisms substitute, for the lost or diminished abilities, other activities that appear to the patient to fulfill the same purpose. Defects that leave a void in the patient's life cannot be tolerated. They are replaced as rapidly as possible with activities that satisfy him. Amputees showed the intensity of this frustration by the avidity with which they sought prosthetic devices and by the detailed criticisms and emotional protests they made about faulty appliances. Gaps or losses in memory are filled by false memories, by circumstantial accounts that appear plausible, giving the patient a sense of continuity, which is objectively lacking. Difficulty in carrying out varied or numerous tasks because of lost flexibility in memory and attention is compensated for by the development of *circumstantiality.* In this device the patient strives for a photographic reproduction of past events. In order to reproduce the simplest memory he must tell all the temporally and spatially associated elements of the situation he is narrating. Since much of the reproduced material is highly irrelevant to the patient's original memory, and since the irrelevant associations can give rise to further irrelevancies, the organic patient often appears rambling and inconsequential in his speech.

The behavior of the organic patient also shows *perseveration.* Proportional to the shrinkage of his behavior repertoires, there is an increase in the repetition of those habitual forms of response that remain. This is apparent in both verbal and non-verbal behavior. The mechanism seems to be an attempt to preserve some adequacy of behavior in spite of lost skills. It is also possible that perseveration is the motor accompaniment of decreased discriminatory ability. If the patient perceives complex situations incompletely, it is likely that his reactions will be simpler and less differentiated.

Perseveration is well illustrated in performance on the Rorschach test. A typical patient will give the same simple response to several successive ink blots, such as "piece of wood" or "ink" or "a bone of the body," or will name the colors on the chromatic cards. The patient appears satisfied with his answers and considers them an adequate performance. He will also give many of what Piotrowski (1937) has called "automatic phrases," monotonously making the same remark when each card is presented to him, such as "Gosh, what d'ya know!" or "I'll do my best, sir." These expressions fulfill the superficial requirements of social communication and are also considered satisfactory by the patient.

Experimental demonstration of the differences between perseveration and the normal quality of *persistence* has been accomplished by Hamilton and Ellis (1933). Two groups of rats were trained to secure food by pulling various lengths of string, at the end of which food was attached, into their cages. One group, after this preliminary training, was subjected to extensive brain lesions. Following this both groups were satiated with respect to hunger and then given further opportunity to pull in string. The normal group pulled in very little string under satiation conditions, whereas the operated group continued the activity extensively, in spite of the less appropriate nature of the activity. A detailed description of the behavior of one of their brain-injured animals well portrays the rigidity and stereotypy of the disordered organism:

"Rat No. 7 . . . was the wildest of the original colony. At the slightest opportunity he would escape from his cage and was on all occasions almost impossible to handle. After operation this was reversed. No signs of wildness remained and no effort was made to escape. Indeed, he had become so phlegmatic that the experimenter, wondering if motor coordination was intact, lifted the animal from his box (shoe-box size) and placed him on the floor at ½ meter distance. This was 10 days after operation. The animal had retained vision and apparently sense of smell as well, for he at once moved, sniffing along the floor, toward the box, crawled up over its edge and in. Several days later this experiment was repeated with the same results.

"Twenty days after operation the following systematic series (of observations) was undertaken:

"*a.* It was found that the rat could find his way back to the box from any point within a radius of 1 meter when the box was placed in the center of the room (*i.e.,* no guide such as running along a wall was possible).

"*b.* A normal rat was placed for 72 hours in a similar box, then both normal and operated animals removed, placed 1 meter from their boxes, and the respective behaviors observed. The normal rat began a hasty investigation of the room, moving for the most part away from the box, and in general, seemingly unaware of, or indifferent to, its presence. No. 7 went directly to his box and climbed in. Four seconds after the experiment began No. 7 was already in his box; 25 seconds later the normal animal had reached the far wall of the room and showed no signs of behavior that would lead back to the box.

"*c.* The next experiment with No. 7 consisted in allowing him to reach his box by returning with the wall as a guide. Using different walls and different rooms the animal was placed beside the baseboard, the box next to this wall, and record kept of the distance from which he was able to return. From any distance within 3 meters the return was prompt and smooth.

"*d.* A wide (indoor) staircase was used for the next experiment. The animal was placed 3 meters from his box, right shoulder to the stair rise, and permitted to return five times along the same path (a new stair step was used at each return). Upon the sixth opportunity the rat was carried not 3 but 4 meters away. Instantly, upon being set down, he ran in the direction of the box precisely 3 meters and stopped. There ensued a most obvious seeking behavior. He snuffed about, left the wall but quickly returned, reared up and tried to climb over the step as if it were the box, failed, sniffed again, and then moved slowly along with the right shoulder against the stair rise and thus finally to his box which he entered immediately after a few preliminary sniffs along its side. The hesitation at the 3 meter distance lasted 8 seconds. This experiment was repeated on different days with the *same* results each time.

"At no time was the animal given a food reward upon return to his box. The experiments above reported were carried out under varying conditions of hunger—from very hungry to satiation—and showed no quantitative or qualitative differences whatever. Further investigations of hunger in the case of this rat were made as follows:

"It was discovered that he would not eat at any place but in his own box. Once his familiar food dish was placed on a low table 25 cm from his box and the animal allowed to go for 48 hours without food, yet he did not leave his box to reach the dish. On several occasions at his customary feeding time (evening) he was placed (after 24-hour hunger) in another box with food, but he refused to eat. When taken from his box and allowed to return, the rat was often forced to run across sunflower seeds, but at no time did he stop, even when very hungry, to eat these but seemed oblivious to them in his desire to reach the box." [2]

SUMMARY

In this section we have distinguished three general categories of the behavior characteristic of organic brain disturbances: release symptoms, interference or decrement symptoms, and substitution symptoms. For present purposes, these behavior classes may serve as a guide through the following section, which offers an examination of some diagnostic types traditionally termed the "organic psychoses." In Chapter XIV we will reconsider this behavior and its organic correlates in a broader biological and psychological context.

The Organic Psychoses

SENILE PSYCHOSES

In 1949, 10 per cent of hospital admissions were from among the ranks of the senile. If we add to this group those individuals who have cerebral arteriosclerosis, which is usually a circulatory senility, we find that in 1949 about 25 per cent of psychiatric admissions were attributable to causes associated with the approach of senescence. As other types of public health work and medical science in general progress, the

[2] J. A. Hamilton and W. D. Ellis (1933), "Behavior constancy in rats." *J. genet. Psychol.*, 42, 135-137.

problem of the senile will become greater, since more people will live long enough to develop the anatomical and physiological changes of age.

For purposes of classification, because of real differences in the neuro-pathological findings, a distinction is usually made between *senile psychosis* and psychosis with *cerebral arteriosclerosis*. The changes in neural tissue of the brain in senility show an actual atrophy and disappearance of nerve cells, with a proliferation of connective tissue in replacement. The gross weight of the brain is reduced by as much as 10 per cent (Weil, 1945). In cerebral arteriosclerosis, which can, but rarely does, occur in young individuals, the blood supply to the brain or to some part of the brain is diminished; in this lowered state of nutrition atrophic changes may take place, although the simple lowered blood exchange is itself sufficient to produce alterations of cerebral function. As Weil (1945) has said, in practice it may be difficult to separate tissue changes due to sclerotic blood vessels from those due to primary senile changes. In either case, the behavioral symptomatology is much the same.

In the early stages of senile psychosis there may be a gradual loss of the effects of social learning and inhibition. The person becomes careless in his dress and manner, forgetting social niceties. His emotional relationships with those around him change from love and affection to hate and hostility. He shows himself to be irritable at slight inconveniences, and concern for others turns into a selfish and egotistically oriented attitude. His attention to the environment lessens and is replaced by preoccupations about himself. With the lessened interest in events around him goes an impairment of recent memory, accompanied by a greater interest in the past and by forgetful, repetitive accounts of the same incidents. Emotional reactions become freer and less inhibited. His feelings are more easily hurt, and many senile individuals develop paranoid preoccupations. As the condition progresses, the memory defects become more severe, the patient's vitality becomes less, and the incidence of delusions and hallucinations increases. Senile psychoses present a genuine deterioration that may progress to the point where the patient has lost all contact with the environment and lives out his remaining life on a vegetative level.

Within this general framework of symptoms we find various subgroups. Some patients are predominantly agitated or excited, and their behavior approaches that of the agitated depression or the catatonic schizophrenic. Other patients show a paranoid trend that resembles that seen in paranoid or hebephrenic schizophrenia. Others show retarded depressions. In all cases of senile dementia we may note that the content of the psychosis represents an exaggeration of the personality traits of a lifetime and that the person brings to this last great adjustmental problem as many of the techniques of the past as survive the brain destruction that he is undergoing. Occasionally these senile changes will start prematurely between the ages of forty and sixty, and two types of neuropathological conditions have been described to account for some of these cases. In *Alzheimer's disease* there is a rapidly progressive deterioration, thought to be associated with the abnormal proliferation of thread-like cellular growths around the cortical neurons. In *Pick's disease,* the symptoms are essentially the same, perhaps with more neurological disturbance, such as aphasia, paralysis, sensory defects, and so forth. The apparent cause of this premature senile psychosis is a rapid cortical atrophy, occurring diffusely over the entire brain, but presenting bilaterally symmetrical areas of very intense degeneration. Since other than cortical structures are also involved, the neurological complications of this condition are readily accounted for. As with Alzheimer's disease, there is no satisfactory knowledge of etiology.

The psychotic condition associated with *cerebral arteriosclerosis* can be differentiated from senile psychoses only when the age of onset is sufficiently early to make general senile changes unlikely. Arteriosclerosis is a hardening and thickening of the walls of the arteries and arterioles, due primarily to calcification of the innermost coat of the blood-vessel. It occurs inevitably as a part of the changes of old age, but may occur somewhat earlier in life as a distinctive pathological process. When this is the case, the sclerosis is usually not generalized, as in senility, but tends to attack one or another localized part of the vascular system. Why, in some people, the cerebral arteries are singled out, is not known, but possibly we have here another instance of constitutional predisposition. The age of onset of cerebral arteriosclerosis as a presenile condition is usually between the ages of fifty and sixty-five. More commonly than in the senile psychoses, the behavioral disturbance is accompanied by localized neurological defects, as in Pick's disease.

The psychological content of this psychosis is dependent upon the previous personality structure of the patient. Paranoid preoccupations are common, and most of the patient's increasing intellectual deterioration is ascribed to causes in the environment. During the early stages it is possible to notice the person's lack of self-confidence and his rather bewildered attempt to find explanations for defective functioning, which is, at this stage, obvious to the patient. As the condition progresses the insight seems to disappear in proportion to the increase in delusory content and the growth of intellectual deterioration. Many of the features of psychosis with cerebral arteriosclerosis are illustrated in the following abbreviated case history:

Case 48. Colonel C. had been a brilliant, successful, and wealthy lawyer whose practice had ranged through all phases of his subject. In addition he had achieved something of a reputation as an author, lecturer, and socialite. When the United States entered World War II, he was called on active duty and assigned to a responsible position in the legal department of the Army. He acquitted himself well and was soon known for the amount of legal work he could assimilate. At the time of his illness he was forty-nine years of age; his last physical examination had found him feeling well except for occasional headaches and dizziness, which he attributed to the confining nature of his work reading legal documents. The examining medical officers noted nothing unusual save for a slightly higher than average blood pressure, and he was cautioned to watch his diet and exercise and cut down a little on his smoking.

About a month after this examination the first symptoms of his illness appeared. He had been acting as a reviewing authority on courts-martial decisions and confirmed a sentence of death, feeling that the verdict of the court had been fair and consistent with military law. Later the same day he received a telephone call from an officer who had been interested in the case and who protested to Colonel C. that the verdict of the court should not be upheld. The colonel vigorously defended his decision, but found, to his annoyance, that he was becoming angry and could not remember details of the case nor could he remember the legal points that were applicable to the case. After this conversation he departed for his quarters, taking the papers on the debated case with him. That night, unable to sleep, he read the case over and was suddenly struck by the thought that the facts were possibly different than he had thought them. Several statements in the report of the trial seemed completely new to him, although he was reasonably sure that he had studied each sentence of the brief that afternoon. Without stopping to try to reason why this should be, he decided that he ought to visit the military post at which the trial had taken place. This post was several hundred miles distant from his own station, but he was so agitated lest he had done the condemned soldier an injustice that he hastily packed a bag, and without permission, started to drive to the other post. On his arrival, early in the forenoon he went to the officers' club and asked for breakfast. As he was eating a pancake he found a small chip of glass embedded in it. He suddenly had a feeling that "the scales had dropped from his eyes," and he saw that the reason he could not remember in the evening what he had read in the afternoon was because someone had substituted new pages in the brief, probably some friend of the man who was sentenced to death. Now they were trying to poison him. He immediately left the club and, finding the post provost-marshal, demanded that the entire kitchen staff of the club be placed under arrest. This request started a chain of events that resulted in the colonel, alternately white and purple with anger, being deposited in the closed ward of the psychiatric section of the hospital.

On admission he was extremely upset because no one would believe his story, and he threatened the entire staff of the section with legal action. When he found that he was to be detained irrespective of his wishes, he demanded a pen and paper and spent the evening quietly writing a statement concerning his unfair treatment. In the morning he had a sheaf of papers that he requested be mailed to the President of the United States. Psychological examinations showed that he had considerable intellectual impairment, that his memory was poor, and that his emotional control was defective. Aside from his delusory content, however, he seemed to be fairly intact, although even a very short period of questioning brought out a strong expression of irritability and further threats. The neurological examination showed a right-sided weakness and changes in the fundus of both eyes, which suggested arteriosclerosis. This diagnosis was confirmed a few days later when the patient had a minor stroke, which increased the weakness of his right side and brought into prominence some aphasic difficulties that probably had existed before to an extent sufficient to aid in the original mixup about the brief. The officer was retired from the Army, and at his own request was sent to a private institution.

GENERAL PARESIS

This disorder, sometimes called "general paralysis of the insane" or "dementia paralytica" is almost as important in the history of psychopathology as conversion hysteria, since it was around this disease that Kraepelin organized his classification of mental disorders. *General paresis* is a combined behavioral and neurological condition produced by a syphilitic infection of the meninges and the cerebral structures. In 1949 paretics constituted 4 per cent of new admissions to mental hospitals; there is some reason to believe that the frequency of this disorder is declining as venereal disease control and syphilitic treatment improve. An interesting biological problem is posed by the fact that only about 2 or 3 per cent of people who contract syphilis ever develop paresis. Why the spirochete invades some nervous systems and not others is still unknown, although the most likely hypothesis is that some nervous systems are less resistant than others, since there is evidence that from 50 per cent to 70 per cent of cases of general syphilis have a temporary central nervous system involvement during the secondary state of the disease (Noyes, 1934).

General paresis is one of the possible forms of tertiary syphilis and, as such, appears some time after the original infection, the lapse of time being from about two to thirty years. According to Noyes (1934), the incubation period is from ten to twenty years in approximately half of the cases; in one-fourth of the cases the period is under ten years, and in one-fourth the period is over twenty years. This latency period constitutes one of the more serious social aspects of the disease, since the peak of its incidence is in the period when the patient is from thirty-five to forty-five years of age and at the height of his social, family, and economic responsibilities. The onset of the disorder is usually gradual, and in the case of an official with public responsibility or a technician in the position of a railroad engineer, or aircraft pilot, the consequences could be extremely hazardous. Since the presence of neurosyphilis can be detected by seriological tests of the blood and spinal fluid, most of modern industry is to some extent protected. The physical examinations of bank presidents and state and national officials, unfortunately, are not as stringent as those required for airline pilots or railway employees.

General paresis is important to the psychopathologist for another reason. Like the senile disorders there is a definitely established correlation between brain defect and disordered behavior; however, unlike the senile disorders, there is the possibility of restoring the paretic to relatively normal functioning by means of therapy. By inducing high body temperatures, either through the use of malaria or other physical means, it is possible to secure improvement of what is otherwise a steadily progressive dementia in about 80 per cent of all cases. This furnishes a way of gaining insight for the role of brain pathology in the production of behavior pathology, since it is possible not only to see how a person with brain defect behaves, but also to see how his behavior is changed as a result of changes in the pathological agent.

Although the presence of neurosyphilis may be detected by examination of a person's spinal fluid many months or even years before he develops neurological or behavioral symptoms, it is the latter that usually are first noticed. The onset is so gradual, however, that persons in daily contact with the patient may have difficulty in saying when they first noted personality changes. The changes themselves will not, by now, be unfamiliar to the student, since they parallel those seen in most of the behavior disorders. There is an increasing indifference to the finer social and aesthetic discriminations in behavior; the patient becomes untidy, careless, forgetful, irritable, and indifferent to things that have before claimed his interests. He may show many release symptoms, drink more heavily, indulge in sexual irregularities, neglect his business, show a lack of his usual foresight and judgment, and become apathetic and unconcerned when reproached or disciplined. His mood may become euphoric, or he may show depression. Probably he will show hesitation or confusion if sudden decisions or judgments are required of him. If the patient does not secure treatment, and if he does not meet with a fatal accident in the course of his disorder, the dementia proceeds rapidly in severity, the end phase being the completely disordered vegetative state.

Accompanying the behavioral symptoms are many neurological signs of cerebral impairment. Useful for diagnostic purposes are various reflex changes, the progressive weakness and incoordination of muscles, and the frequent incidence of convulsive seizures. Among the reflexes, more than half the cases of paresis show the *Argyll Robertson* pupillary disturbance, in which the pupil does not react to changes in light intensity, but continues to react in accommodation. The weakness and incoordination may be shown by the difficult, tremulous writing, by tremor of the protruded tongue, and by speech defects that are evidenced when the patient is asked to repeat test phrases containing difficult consonant combinations, such as "Methodist Episcopal," "General Electric," or "rough riding artillery brigade." These neurological difficulties show a progression that parallels the behavioral and generally terminate in a state of such weakness and ataxia that the patient becomes bedfast.

Usually at least three main types of behavioral symptomatology are seen in various paretic patients. These are: (1) the simple dementing type, in which there is an uncomplicated loss of intellectual efficiency and emotional control with the production of few delusions or hallucinations; (2) the expansive or euphoric type, characterized by rich delusional formations, usually of the grandiose type we have seen in some manics and in some hebephrenics and paranoids; and (3) a depressed type, in which the patient shows the same sort of hypochondriacal and nihilistic delusions as seen in the functional affective reactions. It is probable, although there has been little research on the matter, that the paretic manifests symptoms that were in keeping with his former personality structure.

REACTIONS TO ALCOHOL

Alcohol as a substance of human consumption has been associated with man since before recorded history, and drunkenness has been a variant of human behavior as far back as we have records. In that time men have devoted some of their best verbal talents to the praise of alcohol and to its condemnation. For better or for worse, the various forms of alcoholic beverage form a part of the social environment in our culture and must be recognized as an important variable in psychopathology.

TABLE 13

BEHAVIORAL EFFECTS OF VARIOUS CONCENTRATIONS OF BLOOD-ALCOHOL

Alcohol in Blood (mg. per cc.)	*Behavior*
0.01-0.07	Growing sense of euphoria and energy release, with impulsivity and beginning of motor incoordination
0.1-0.2	Motor incoordination serious, with staggering gait and fumbling. Mental confusion, appears "drunk"
0.2-0.3	Emotional release, crying, groaning, etc. Loss of sphincter control
0.3-0.5	Stupor merging into coma. Collapse with slowing of pulse and respiration, which may end in death

Alcohol is one of a series of chemicals that have a selective depressant reaction on the nervous system; the action of alcohol illustrates the pharmacological *principle of dissolution,* that drugs in general act on higher and more complex structures before acting on lower or less complex ones. Alcohol depresses first the cerebrum and then works downward to the brain-stem level, fortunately producing unconsciousness before the toper can ingest enough to depress the vital breathing and heart action centers. Occasionally we read of an individual who, on a bet, drinks a large quantity of whiskey in a short time, with fatal results. Usually, the ingestion of alcohol is accompanied by oxidation and excretion, which dissipate some of the effect of the substance. If the rate of intake is too rapid, the toxic effects may keep so far ahead of these dissipative effects as to produce death. When intake rates remain lower, the physiological effects are primarily felt as a depressive action on the higher parts of the central nervous system and are, in general, reversible; if the person stops his intake, the depressant action ceases as the alcohol is oxidized, and recovery of normal central nervous system function is achieved.

Alcohol is absorbed into the bloodstream from the stomach and the small intestine. The behavioral effects of alcohol are correlated with the amount of its concentration in the bloodstream, as shown in Table 13. The rate of absorption from stomach and intestine is conditioned by many factors, including the dilution of the beverage, the state of fullness of the stomach (before or after meals), and the rate at which the beverage is consumed. It has also been shown that the "experienced" or habitual drinker shows a slower absorptive rate.

Although there is no question about the short-term effects of alcohol on physiological function, there is no agreement about the long-term effects of continued heavy drinking. Some authorities state that chronic overindulgence in alcohol results in permanent defects in neural structure as well as in degenerative conditions of the liver and kidneys; unquestionably these pathological findings are seen in the post-mortem examination of many chronic alcoholics and are manifested behaviorally in some of the disorders associated with chronic alcoholism. It is possible, however, that these effects are due to the vitamin B deficiency, which is associated with many cases of alcoholism.

Turning from the physiological to the psychological aspects of alcohol, we find that drinking is one of the most frequently used techniques for the reduction of anxiety. The fact that men have turned to alcohol throughout the course of history is indicative of the value that has been placed on this substance as a means of reducing tension. Since the technique is admittedly artificial and temporary, and since alcohol has no real potency in solving adaptive problems, it is obvious that the benefits to be gained from its use are also temporary. Further, the more difficulties an individual has, the more constantly must he use alcohol if he has adopted this mechanism in his attempts to adjust. For this reason most students are in agreement that alcohol is not a primary cause of behavior disorders, but is, rather, symptomatic of deeper personality disturbances that have been unsatisfactorily resolved by the use of alcohol.

Since alcohol acts upon the higher levels of the nervous system, the first behavioral effects of drinking are markedly similar to the effects of any other injury to the cerebral cortex. There is euphoria, a loss of the more subtle aspects of social discrimination and manners, defective judgment, and a loss of insight for inadequacies in the patient's own behavior. It is this stage of alcoholic intoxication that most maladjusted persons are seeking. Shyness is mitigated, worries and anxieties are temporarily forgotten or appear trivial, personal ethical or moral inhibitions that have caused conflict or frustration of motives disappear. The person gains a sense of freedom and happiness alien to his sober state.

If the effects of alcohol stopped at this point, or if the drinker stopped taking alcohol at this level of intoxication, some of the more serious problems of alcoholism would be avoided; however, even this mellowing effect has its dangerous side, since, as in all the adjustment mechanisms, the problems and the conflicts are not resolved and will return as soon as the drinking either stops or continues to deeper stages of intoxication. For most alcoholics, however, drinking does not stop at a level of mild intoxication, but continues to higher stages of blood-alcohol concentration. The reasons for this behavior are evident. First, the pleasurable effects from a little alcohol create a strong motive for continuing the drinking activity, and second, as intoxication progresses, the insight and inhibitory control become lessened to the point where an individual is no longer able to gauge the effects his drinking is producing. As we pointed out, the excretion and oxidation of alcohol is a slow process. Starling (1933) reports that the removal of alcohol proceeds at a constant rate of about 0.012 per cent per hour. This means that the blood concentration in mild intoxication of 0.15 per cent would not be eliminated for over ten hours. The intoxicated person, even if his intake is slow, is storing up alcohol faster than he is excreting it. For this reason alcoholic intoxication frequently progresses to extremes. The symptoms of advanced intoxication are characterized by an increasing confusion, helplessness, incoordination and stupor, ending in unconsciousness, coma, and sometimes in death.

With the continued use of alcohol as a method of adjustment come further psychological symptoms. The chronic alcoholic is completely dependent upon alcohol. He is an *addict* to whom the necessity for alcohol has overshadowed all other considerations. Because of this compelling motivation, he has less time for interest in other aspects of living. Because he gets drunk frequently, his participation in normal social pursuits suffers. This leads to an appearance of social disintegration of the personality. As his social adjustment fails, he has more emotionally painful reasons for drinking, and a vicious cycle is established. In every sense of the word, the chronic alcoholic conforms to our conception of the neurotic, whose false solutions of problems never remove them but constantly place him in more and more serious conflicts, calling for even more application of the reality-denying mechanisms. As an economic, social, or personal unit, the alcoholic is a failure.

Alcoholism must be considered, then, from two standpoints: first, as a type of behavior that grows out of maladjustment, and second, as a causative factor in further maladjustment. Only certain people become alcoholics; there are many people who drink heavily and constantly who are in no way psychological problems and are probably of only minor interest to the student of alcohol physiology.

Well remembered is an old steel-worker who had never missed a day's work in thirty years, who was sixty years of age, and had consumed a quart of whiskey daily as long as he could remember. In all his life he had never been arrested for drunkenness, had never been in financial difficulties, had never beaten his wife, and had achieved a reputation with his employers for dependability and ingenuity. He drank whiskey in the morning on arising, with his meals, and before he went to bed. He was a tremendous fellow in all his appetites, a hearty eater, a sports enthusiast who at sixty was still an avid bowler and a fisherman who would walk six miles to a good spot on a Sunday. He had raised four children and provided them with a college education.

He was, admittedly, an exception, but he illustrates the point that alcoholism is a product of a disturbed personality, and that the addiction to alcohol does not come from the chemical alone but from the individual who *needs* it to carry on in the world. The chronic alcoholic is an insecure person who has found that alcohol gives him a feeling of security, or, better stated, helps him *avoid the pain* of insecurity. The insecurity has causes that go back into the person's childhood, and to find the causes of alcoholism we have to investigate the factors that shape personality.

The *effects* of alcoholism are a part of the picture of organic reactions in general. *Acute intoxication,* as we have seen, is a temporary psychosis, the patient's reaction to a disturbance of brain function. As in other organic conditions, the content of the behavior, what the person actually does while he is intoxicated, depends on the background of his individual personality. Some drunks are happy, some are sad, some are boisterous, some quiet, some paranoid, some aggressive, some passive, all depending upon the multiplicity of habits and attitudes that they happen to have at the time they become intoxicated. There is an old folk-saying to the effect that you find out what a man really is by observing him when he has been drinking. Modern psychology would make only a small modification in this bit of wisdom by saying that in drunkenness the person reveals that aspect of his personality that is inhibited during his sober intervals. Many repressed homosexual or homicidal motives first appear as overt components of the person's behavior during a drinking bout, often resulting in extreme emotional disturbance when the individual recognizes these trends in himself. Indeed, the most striking effect of alcohol is the way it releases the façade of social appearances behind which most people have hidden or repressed many of their deeper motives. The lack of judgment and coordination of the intoxicated person makes him something of a hazard to himself and others; he is frequently involved in accidents, he may be injured or injure others in fights; he makes promises and contracts indebtedness with a freedom which may prove embarrassing or harmful; his sexual drives, functioning in a relative freedom from inhibition, cause social complications and may be an important factor in spreading venereal diseases. In every way but its duration the acute alcoholic intoxication does not differ materially, either from a social or individual point of view, from the other behavior disorders we have discussed.

Even more suggestive of the extreme disorders is the state known as *pathological intoxication.* Some people seem to have what amounts to an allergy to alcohol, in that even small amounts precipitate violently disturbed behavior, the intensity of which has no relation to the amount of alcohol imbibed. The disturbance usually lasts for only a few hours, and the patient usually has an imperfect memory for his behavior when he recovers. The following case is illustrative:

Case 49. One evening about eleven, while the senior author was Officer of the Day at his military station, he was called to the main gate of the post by the military policeman on duty, who said that he had a very drunk soldier who would not consent to being escorted to the guardhouse. On arriving at the gate we found a small, stocky, neatly dressed soldier sitting apathetically on a bench in the guard station. The guard said that four MPs had tried to drag him away, but that as soon as they touched him he would act "like a crazy man," screaming and resisting with all his strength. The torn clothes of the MPs confirmed the guard's statement. The soldier had escaped a blackjack only because he appeared so obviously strange in his actions that the guards were sure that he was not an ordinary drunk. When I approached him and asked him to take a ride with me in my car, he seemed to comply. His arm linked securely in mine, I started to lead him toward the car while the MPs followed to watch the magic of my methods.

As we almost immediately veered off the road onto the golf course I discovered that the little man was *leading me,* a silent fury lending strength to his vise-like grip on my arm. The MPs, watching me dig my heels into the seventh green as I tried to break our flight and let go of the soldier at the same time, finally came to the rescue, and we all joined in the silent, violent struggle against the man's uncanny strength. We finally transferred him to the receiving ward of the station hospital where he managed to tear the shirt from the physician administering a sedative injection. The next morning the patient awoke and was puzzled by being in the hospital, claiming no memory of the incident of the night before. He said that he last remembered having a beer with a companion at about nine in the evening. An investigation of his record showed that a similar incident had happened earlier in his life, while he was still in high school. Then he had seriously injured a friend of his after they had both drunk a small amount of wine.

Sinclair Lewis has a good description of pathological intoxication in *Arrowsmith,* where the hero prevents a schoolmate named Angus Duer from killing a man and finds that Duer has no memory of the incident the next day.

There is no satisfactory theory to account for this reaction, although it seems probable that such patients are making what is almost a hysterical dissociation. The state is also, in its low threshold for alcohol, reminiscent of brain-injured patients in general, whose tolerance for alcohol is much reduced by their injury. There is a possibility that this state is related to the epileptic equivalent reactions we have discussed previously, and that alcohol simply sets off the seizure mechanism.

A condition termed *acute alcoholic hallucinosis* illustrates the way in which the personality of the patient colors reactions to alcohol, and how alcohol may serve as a trigger mechanism and then play a minor role in the disorder. In alcoholic hallucinosis, the patient, usually after a heavy and prolonged drinking bout, begins to hear accusatory and threatening voices, to which he reacts with extreme fear and anxiety. The appearance of the patient is similar to that of the person in an acute panic state. The voices may be supplemented by visual hallucinations. Most interesting, and probably accounting for the extreme fear the patient experiences, is the fact that he is otherwise quite well oriented and alert, with none of the confusion that marks so many of the organic conditions. The hallucinosis usually subsides rapidly, rarely lasting longer than two weeks. Noyes (1934) reports that occasionally this condition marks the beginning of a typically schizophrenic psychosis, thus emphasizing the incidental role of alcohol in its production.

The alcoholic disorder that has stimulated more cartoonists and writers than any other is *delirium tremens*, the D.T.s of the joke book and popular lore. Contrary to the impression that might be gained from such sources, this condition is an extremely serious alcoholic psychosis. The symptoms usually appear following prolonged drinking bouts in chronic alcoholics who have many years of heavy drinking behind them. The patient has a suddenly appearing delirium in which he is confused, has vivid and terrifying hallucinations, is disoriented and so tremulous and physically fatigued that movement is difficult. The hallucinations may be in any sensory departments, although the tactual and visual are the most frequent. The patient may imagine that insects or snakes are crawling over him, and the tactual impression is supplemented by visual hallucinations of them. He has illusions concerning objects in his visual environment; the wallpaper design or the furniture turns into moving threatening objects. He mistakes the identity of people and fancies he is at places other than he actually is. He may have to be restrained to prevent self-injury. He is constantly restless and usually finds sleep impossible. On recovery the patient is found to have an almost total amnesia for the illness. Because of his physically exhausted condition, he must be nursed carefully, since the restlessness puts strain on a body already worn out. Many patients die of cardiac failure during the episodes.

Recent research has shown that delirium tremens has a combined etiology of general toxicity due to the effects of alcohol on the liver and other organs, and a vitamin deficiency occasioned by the lack of food intake so characteristic of long drinking sessions. This is aggravated by the loss of resistance secondary to physical exhaustion.

Psychologically, delirium tremens is again somewhat similar to panic states; the general form of the symptoms is found in almost all the toxic reactions; the threatening misinterpretation of the environment takes much the same form as that found in the catatonics.

Another manifestation of the combined effect of alcohol and vitamin deficiency is *Korsakoff's psychosis,* which is characterized by amnesia, disorientation in space and time, and by a marked tendency toward a confabulatory compensation for the memory defects. Definite pathological changes in the brain have been identified, and there is the possibility that this disorder can be produced as a consequence of infectious processes or other severe stresses on the brain as well as by alcohol. The disorder usually appears suddenly, and the patient finds himself unable to recall events that happened within the near past, often, indeed, being unable to remember enough of a conversation, as it is going on, to answer intelligently. Because the patient may appear unconfused and alert, and because he produces his confabulations so readily and with every appearance of reason, the casual observer is apt to feel confused himself, but not be able to quite identify the source of his uneasiness. The general impression in such instances is that caused by those vaudeville masters of "double-talk," who can return a nonsensical answer with such apt expression of voice and face as to lead the auditor to believe he has misunderstood. The Korsakoff patient has an accompanying polyneuritis that is manifested by pain and tenderness over the course of the nerve trunks of the extremities and by frequent paresis or paralysis of specific muscle groups.

REACTIONS TO DRUGS, TUMORS, ABSCESSES, AND OTHER DISEASES

Since, as we have already emphasized, the behavioral reactions to brain dysfunction are closely similar, irrespective of the specific source of the brain disorder, we will bring this survey to a close by a few remarks on a large number of miscellaneous sources of brain disturbance and their behavioral concomitants.

Factors that affect brain function may have either a local or general action. Tumors and abscesses usually occupy definitely circumscribed areas of the brain, and their interference with function is dependent in nature and degree upon their location. If the lesion is in the occipital visual areas, the main disturbances are visual; if in the motor areas, the disturbances will be in muscular functions, and so on. The types of disturbance that come with injuries to the frontal lobes are of particular interest because of the use of frontal lobotomies as therapeutic measures in the treatment of behavior disorders. All localized lesions interfere to some extent with the association functions of the brain and produce more or less difficulty in thinking and some degree of inhibitory loss with a consequent loosening of emotional expression. The localized lesions rarely produce sweepingly psychotic disturbances of behavior as do the more disseminated lesions we have discussed previously. The chief behavioral incapacity of a general type is probably confusion, disorientation and, in the terminal stages of the disease, stupor and coma. In brain abscesses there may be an associated febrile process with delirium.

Most exogenous toxins, such as drugs, most infectious diseases, and most systemic diseases have a generalized effect on the brain that is similar to that of alcohol. Because of differences in absorptive rate and because of other features, such as ease of access, taste, and so forth, no type of drug acting upon the nervous system has had as much usage as alcohol. Nevertheless, from the point of view of psychopathology, cocaine, morphine, belladonna, hyoscine, marihuana, peyote, or hashish are all used for just about the same set of motives, namely, that they act as a source of tension reduction. *There is no good evidence for any physiological factor, acting independently of a person's psychological need, in making these substances "habit-forming." They are craved for precisely the same reason that alcohol is craved, namely, because they appear as adequate ways of adjustment to the patient.*

The toxic effects of drugs, or of fevers, or of systemic diseases of kidneys, heart, liver, and so forth, on the brain are well known. The patient shows various degrees of delirium; he may show depression or excitement; he is disoriented, has fleeting illusions, hallucinations and delusions, and through all the symptoms expresses the repressed motivational aspects of his personality. If, as is usually the case, the patient recovers, and the disease has not produced permanent changes in brain structure, he again assumes the mask of social adjustment. If irreversible changes are incurred, the patient's subsequent psychotic behavior is little different from the various types we have already described in detail. Predominantly these behavior aberrations illustrate the reaction of a person to stresses that either force inadequate response or induce catastrophic behavior.

General Summary

Now that we have examined the characteristics of organic disorders, let us consider for a moment the significance of these disturbances for psychopathology. Firstly, there is the matter of the resemblance of the behavior to the "functional" psychoses we have already studied. In the functional disorders there was no clear organic "cause" for the symptoms; in the psychoses of organic origin the "cause" seems clearly evident. Studies by the hundred of the brains, the rest of the nervous system, the endocrines, the blood, and all the other vital systems of the schizophrenic have failed to reveal structural alterations that could not be found with equal frequency in the non-schizophrenic, or functional alterations that could not be explained more plausibly as a result of the schizophrenic's mode of life than as a cause of it. Yet the symptoms are essentially the same. Recognition of this fact may then lead to two alternative types of deduction. We could say that, given common symptoms and given a connection apparently established between these symptoms and definite alterations in the structure of the brain in the organic disorders, the schizophrenic symptoms must therefore be caused by still undiscovered structural alterations in the brain. This is the argument that has driven the tissue pathologist to ever more searching examinations of the brains of dead schizophrenics and that has been the inspiration for those theorists in psychopathology who are termed "organicists." Yet the quest for tissue pathology in the functional disorders has had the outcome that two writers on neuropathology have summed up in the following decisive words:

> . . . *all the neurohistological data described for schizophrenia are irrelevant, and have nothing to do with the schizophrenic process, whatever that may be.*[3]

What is wrong with that which appears to be inescapable logic? This is a real problem, and the fact that distinguished investigators still believe the logic correct (see Hoskins, 1946) should increase the care with which we examine it.

The second deductive path we might follow would proceed in this way: Since the symptoms of organic psychoses and schizophrenia are similar, and since the brain pathology of the organic is absent in the schizophrenic, the two types of disorder must have something else as a common etiological element. At first glance this would seem to be a somewhat anarchistic denial of the significance of the brain damage in the organic, and so it is in the sense that it denies the assumption un-

[3] Frederick Wertham and Florence Wertham (1934), *The Brain as an Organ, Its Postmortem Study and Interpretation,* p. 485. New York: The Macmillan Company.

derlying the whole organic position, namely that a structural defect is the *direct* and *single* cause of the disordered behavior that follows the defect. Our reasons for rejecting this assumption have already been stated in a previous paragraph. What role, then, does the brain damage play in the organic? Also, what are the common factors in organic psychoses and schizophrenia?

The answer to the first question would appear to be that the brain damage is important as a *source of stress* and as a factor crippling or hampering the organism in its adjustment to all stresses. Because the brain, more than any other organ of the body, can play this double psychopathological role of being both a source of stress and the chief agent for dealing with stress, injuries to the brain are the most rapidly reflected in behavior. Injury or defect to other organs emphasizes, of course, that they too have the same double importance, but not to the same extent. A weak heart, arthritis, an inflamed appendix, poor eyesight, malfunctioning kidneys, all may change the direction of behavior by creating new problems, but they do not interfere with the very structural basis of all organismic adjustment as does defect of the brain.

Our answer to the second question is that the common factors in the organic psychoses and the schizophrenic disorders are the adjustmental stresses, the *problems* that the organism faces. Psychologically considered, these problems become strikingly similar, as much so as the ways that are taken for their solution and as the final stages of disorganization and catastrophe when all solution attempts fail. What, in broad outline, are these problems? Basically, they are problems of survival in a given social environment whose properties are conferred by the ego development of the individual. That is to say, they are problems of behaving adequately with respect to self-sufficiency, to security, to achievement, to recognition, to the emotional interpersonal relationships. We have seen that the schizophrenic, the manic, and the depressive many times express these fundamental strivings in their symptoms, and that they also express their fears and anxieties over conflicts and frustrations of these universal motives. In the organic symptoms we see the individual engaged in the same *struggle for competence;* if real memories are gone, false memories are substituted; if real love and respect and power are slipping, delusional replacements are made; if once-sharp abilities are dulled, something in the environment is responsible; if the world is becoming too complex and bewildering, there is protection in withdrawal, and there is armor against revealing the defect by being irritable toward others; and with it all, the problems are demanding and baffling and they preoccupy the person so fully that he appears self-centered, moody, or depressed. The symptoms grow out of the problems, and the problems are the common element. We can extend the statement to say that these same problems are the common factor in all psychopathology, since we have them activating the "normal," the psychoneurotic, and the functional psychotic, and the patient with organic defects.

DISCUSSION QUESTIONS

1. Under what conditions can release, interference, and substitution symptoms be seen in the behavior of normal individuals?
2. What sort of relationship exists between specific etiological agents and behavior manifested in the organic psychoses?
3. Can you suggest a more adequate classificatory scheme of the organic psychoses?
4. Would you expect that treatment of the senile psychoses is extensively effective?
5. How effective do you feel that legal prohibition of alcoholic beverages would be as a solution to the problem of alcoholism?
6. What are some of the common factors in the organic and functional psychoses?
7. Can you show similarities between psychoneurosis, functional psychosis, and organic psychosis?
8. Can you use the behavioral alterations that might occur following a brain injury to illustrate the concept of "multiple causation" of psychotic disorders?
9. If a mild, retiring, and modest person and an excitable, sociable braggart both became victims of neurosyphilis, what might you speculate about the types of symptoms they might display?
10. Do nonliving machines ever show alterations of behavior which resemble those of the psychotic?

SUGGESTED READINGS

K. Goldstein (1948), *Language and Language Disturbances.* New York: Grune & Stratton, Inc.

L. P. Thorpe and B. Katz (1948), *The Psychology of Abnormal Behavior,* Chapters 20-26. New York: The Ronald Press Company.

BIBLIOGRAPHIC SOURCES

In reading about head injuries a good place to begin is with the article by Meyer (1904), which is of interest historically, and because Meyer's views in 1904 and his logical approach to the problem are still worth while today. Goldstein's (1942) *Aftereffects of Brain Injury in War,* and Head's (1920) *Studies in Neurology,* and (1926) *Aphasia and Kindred Disorders of Speech* are primarily concerned with symptoms of brain injury. Halstead's (1947) *Brain and Intelligence* shows the possibilities of a quantitative experimental approach to these problems. Halstead's book also contains an extensive bibliography.

The physiology of the central nervous system as it relates to organic defect can be approached through a reading of Sherrington's classic work (1906), which was reprinted in 1947. The famous doctrine of levels conceptualized by Hughlings Jackson is best read in Head's (1920) work, or it can be traced through Jackson's original papers in the *Selected Writings* edited by James Taylor (1931). A standard text in neurophysiology is Fulton (1949).

The history of research and thinking on aphasia can be obtained from the introductory chapters of Head (1926). As an extended summary of a life of significant research and thought in the area including a survey of types, tests, and several case histories, Goldstein's (1948) *Language and Language Disturbances* is indispensible. Weisenburg and McBride (1935) and Berry and Eisenson (1942) are good clinical discussions of symptoms and treatments. Leutenegger (1951) is suggested for bibliographic material. On recovery and retraining of aphasics, see E. D. Freud (1951), Gronich and Pangle (1949), and especially Wepman (1951).

Supplementary material on the various organic syndromes can be found in the standard neurological and psychiatric texts already cited in other connections.

The volume, *Mental Disorders in Later Life,* edited by O. S. Kaplan (1945) and a similar volume edited by Stieglitz (1943) give abundant material on most phases of senility. One important research issue is the measurement of intellectual decline in the aged. The specific paper by Botwinick and Birren (1951) and the more general article by Hunt and Cofer (1944) should be read. Cases of Alzheimer's disease may be seen in Neuman and Cohn (1953); this paper and Newton (1948) contain literature reviews. For cases of Pick's disease, Josephy (1953) and Polatin, Hoch, Horwitz, and Raizin (1948) may be consulted.

The literature on alcohol is, speaking conservatively, somewhat controversial in nature. Many books with the appearance of objectivity seem to be inspired more from emotion than from respect for facts. However, Strecker and Chambers' *Alcohol, One Man's Meat* (1945) is an understanding treatment of the neurotic alcoholic. Bowman and Jellinek (1941) discuss the general problem of mental disorders with an alcoholic factor in their etiology, and Jellinek (1942) has a monograph on alcohol addiction. The *Quarterly Journal of Studies on Alcohol* is an excellent source for much of the literature on alcoholism. A fine introduction to the area of alcohol and drug addiction is Wilkins' (1952) short but succulent discussion of the area, its problems, and sources of literature. For illustrative case histories of many of the alcoholic disorders in the text, Hampton (1947) is a good source. The same may be said for May and Ebaugh (1953). Statistical incidence figures for first admissions to mental hospitals for alcoholism reflect the magnitude of the problem. In 1949, first admissions for alcoholism with psychosis was 5 per cent of the total first admissions; on the other hand, for alcoholism without psychosis, first admissions were 6 per cent of the total (Federal Security Agency, 1952).

General sources on psychotic reactions to drugs and other exogenous poisons are somewhat difficult to find. One source that discusses several drugs is Hoch, Cattell, and Pennes (1952a). Many drugs induce transient psychotic-like phenomena and suggest the possibility of experimental investigation into drug intoxication without dangerous results. One of these is mescaline, made from a Mexican cactus and widely used at one time by Mexican Indians. There are several reviews of this literature: Hoch (1951, 1952a), and Hoch, Cattell, and Pennes (1952b). One of the great English prose writers, Aldous Huxley, took a small amount of mescaline and reported the results in a small but beautifully written book, *The Doors of Perception* (1954). Bromide intoxication is apparently an increasing problem; for further information see Levin (1948), Tweed (1948), and Tillim (1952). Even broader in scope may be barbiturate intoxication; Tichy (1953) presents a review of the literature. On opiate addiction there are several fine sources, one of which is Wixler's (1953) small book. There is some question as to the incidence of drug-induced psychosis. Malzberg (1949) reported that psychoses due to drugs and other exogenous poisons accounted for only 0.2 per cent of all first admissions to New York State Hospitals in 1948. Levin (1950) criticizes these statistics as being unduly low because of official diagnostic categories, and he reports data to the effect that bromide psychoses alone account for 3.3 per cent of first admissions. More current statistics on a national scale show that psychosis due to drugs and exogenous poisons accounted for 0.4 per cent of all first admissions to state hospitals in 1949 (Federal Security Agency, 1952). However, Levin's objection apparently applies to these data also.

Parenthetically, there has been some question as to the veracity of the case study about the steel-worker who consumed such a large quantity of alcohol (see p. 348). Inquiry of our informant, Dr. L. C. Steckle, brings the following reply:

"I know for a fact that during prohibition when I was working with the old gentleman there was never a working day went by when he did not smell of alcohol from the time he came in in the morning until he went home at night. That he had a bottle hidden about the shop somewhere was a well-known but equally well-ignored fact. I recognize that a quart bottle of whiskey a day adds up to a lot of money over a period of a few decades but keep in mind that it is but a small amount per diem. I recall that during prohibition one could buy a pint of grain alcohol for $2.50 and that makes a quart of hundred-proof whiskey in anybody's language. However, the point is that so far as memory serves me your account is reasonably accurate."

PART THREE

The Causes of Disordered Behavior

The chess-board is the world, the pieces are the phenomena of the universe, the rules of the game are what we call the laws of Nature. The player on the other side is hidden from us. We know that his play is always fair, just and patient. But also we know, to our cost, that he never overlooks a mistake, or makes the smallest allowance for ignorance.

*—*T. II. HUXLEY, *Lay Sermons*

Introduction

We have now had a glimpse of some of the problems of psychopathology. Our scientific task is next to seek for the causes of disordered behavior. That these causes are legion we already know. In our discussion of basic concepts in psychopathology we saw that the behavior of living organisms is a function of many variables, some of which are within the organism and some of which operate in the environment of the organism. It is the organism-environment matrix that we must now subject to scrutiny. In doing so, nothing will be more strikingly evident than the impression that psychopathology is a very young science and that it is dealing with problems of great complexity.

For purposes of presentation and discussion we will divide this section into separate chapters dealing with heredity and development, with the role of the various organ systems, and with the interactions between the person and his culture. The division is clearly artificial. All these factors exert mutual influence on each other, and all are affected in their practical outcome by the settings that the other factors provide for them. To take but a single example, the sure operations of genetic heredity are dependent upon many chance variations of the social milieu for their association and outcome. What person will be the mate of any other is determined more by the individual history of both persons and by the social forces acting upon them than by heredity, yet the result of these individual and social circumstances is to produce a definite genetic integration that is a factor in the life and behavior of the offspring and of its parents.

As we shall see, research in psychopathology has seldom been able to proceed along all these many fronts in any integrated manner. The advances have been made piecemeal, by specialists in this and that small sector of biosocial knowledge. The total field of influence is too great; it prevents any one person from grasping it all in detail. Human planning has thus far been unable to encompass unified research plans for an all-embracing attack on the question of why organisms sometimes behave in a disordered manner. The question is simple, but the answer is not. Man has discovered a paradox. The more he finds out about nature, the less he knows. The sheer diversity of facts has itself bred handicaps. So many things are being discovered and described that the task of extracting coherent theories that cover all behavior is less possible now than at any time in man's intellectual history. We find it so with psychopathology. The unifying principles are few, and the integration they achieve is so lacking in detail that disordered behavior is more often misunderstood than explained. In the first part of this text we discussed a few of the basic concepts. In this part we shall attempt, as best we can, to see how well our problems are illuminated by the application of a representative sample of the known facts.

XI

Genetic Factors in Psychopathology

All the books that deal with inheritance in man cannot fail to give the impression that nearly all of our definite information about human inheritance concerns malformations, diseases, mental defects, and trivial characters of several sorts.

—THOMAS HUNT MORGAN

INTRODUCTION

A misconception in the field of psychopathology that is most widespread and that often has a macabre significance is that of "hereditary taint" in mental disease. According to usual belief in this matter, if mental disease "runs in a family," it will strike those unfortunates with the inevitability of death or taxes. This conviction has been utilized with good effect by dramatists and novelists for centuries. Examples from the modern theatre include O'Neill's *Strange Interlude* and Ashton's *A Bill of Divorcement*. These plays give only a hint of the anxiety, fear, and unhappiness that such beliefs have caused in the lives of countless human beings. A frequent matter for which the psychiatrist or psychologist is expected to offer advice is whether persons whose family background contains mental illness should marry and have children.

Most of the theories of the causation of mental disease seem to stress the functional, learned, or environmental aspects of these conditions. Nevertheless, an understanding of the hereditary and constitutional variables in behavior is also necessary.

Since the vigorous rebellion against "instincts" staged by the early behaviorists, psychologists have been unduly neglectful of genetic variables. Recent research has also tended to show that the dichotomous attitude of "heredity *or* environment" is a false way of viewing the problem. From the moment of conception the organism is nurtured in an environment, and exterior forces act upon the developing organism, resulting, in each instance, in a unique individual, both in structure and behavior. In general it can be said that there is no ultimate distinction between heredity and environment; they are important as integrated factors in the production of the behaving person.

Another reason for desiring more information on the genetics of mental disease springs from the need to formulate the therapeutic and prophylactic measures necessary in the control of mental illness. It has often been said that the geneticist is a biological and medical pessimist and that he can only give a person the advice: "Choose your parents wisely, my son, and you will have all perfection for your own," whereas the environmentalist says: "Give me your child at an early enough age, and I will make him merchant, thief, beggarman, or chief." Optimism purchased at the price of neglecting evidence is usually paid for dearly; nevertheless, the course of therapy or mental hygiene can be radically altered by what is eventually known concerning the inheritance of mental disease or the organization of personality traits that make mental disease possible. If the major forms of pathological behavior were found to have an hereditary basis, then ultimately we probably would have to pay very serious attention to the eugenicists and devise a sweeping program of genetic selection in order to protect the culture as a whole.

Now, although it is not impossible, as we shall see, to modify genetic potentialities in this way and that by environmental hammering, nevertheless, to the average human being (including the psychiatrist, psychologist, and social worker) there appears to be a fatalism and an inevitability about inheritance, a feeling that not as much can be done for a patient if the genes are stacked against him. To anticipate a little, such an attitude is right to a certain extent. There *are* limits set on the alteration of any individual by an environment. No amount of stuffing with rich foods and vitamins will change the height or weight beyond certain limits; no amount of tuition, even under the highest head of pressure that can be generated by the educational psychologist, will push an imbecile or an idiot through college mathematics. So, for practical as well as theoretical reasons, the problems of heredity are important to the psychopathologist, since he badly needs to know these limits.

It is true that in some instances the contribution of the germ plasm to the end result is so constant as to be predictable over a wide range of environmental situations. To take an obvious example, the structural organization of tissues that differentiate one species from another seems to proceed in a way that makes the betting odds a certainty that no dog will ever sire or gestate a giraffe, and that each species will, on the whole, continue to produce offspring having species characteristics in common. Even the amazing experiments of Loeb (1913) and Pincus (1936), in which eggs are fertilized without the aid of the male germ cell, the sperm, the resulting organism closely resembles the species from whence came the egg. It is true that alterations of the fetal environment can produce monsters, but normal embryological growth is featured by a relative constancy and correctness of the environment. Hence we must examine the possible variations in human germ plasm to determine the extent to which differences in its properties contribute to pathological behavior.

Heredity and Psychopathology

TRAITS AND THEIR INHERITANCE

Very little is known about the genetics of behavioral traits. What evidence there is seems to point to the greater influence of life experiences in trait determination. Most behavior pathology seems dependent upon environmental vicissitudes. However, the facts must be examined before we draw a conclusion.

Many investigators (Goddard, Tredgold, Keeler, etc.) have studied the occurrence of feeble-mindedness in families and believe it to be an inherited defect. Most geneticists extend these findings to say that all levels of intelligence are determined by gene composition (Gates, 1946, 1952). There are at least three ways of testing this and other genetic hypotheses: (1) the examination of family records or pedigrees; (2) comparison of identical twins with fraternal twins, siblings, and random samples selected from pertinent populations; and (3) artificial selection or breeding experiments.

FAMILY PEDIGREES

One of the earliest and most direct ways of investigating the influence of heredity on a psychological trait was the study of that trait's occurrence in successive generations of a family line. A survey of the

"I see he has his father's eyes!"

FIGURE 14. *Popular conception of the inheritance of behavioral traits* (from *Laugh Parade,* Avon Comics, Inc., 1946. Reproduced by permission of King Features Syndicate, Inc.).

royal families of Europe, made by Woods (1906), included 671 persons. Outstanding ability and degeneracy seemed roughly to follow family lines. Galton (1914) concluded that eminent men in Great Britain had equally eminent relatives over a hundred times as often as chance expectancy. Goddard (1914) investigated the background of a feeble-minded girl, Deborah Kallikak, tracing her family back to the mating of a normal soldier and a defective barmaid during the Revolutionary War. There were 480 descendants identified; among these were 143 mental defectives, 33 prostitutes, 24 alcoholics, 3 epileptics, 3 criminals, and only 46 that were unquestionably within the normal range of intelligence. The soldier later married a normal girl. This family in the same number of generations had produced only two alcoholics, one mental defective, and one probable psychotic. Other defective and illustrious family lines have been traced with similar results.

The force of such data as an argument for the genetic determination of intelligence is minimized when we consider the type of environment created by and around defectives. There is also the large possibility of error in attempting to estimate intelligence of people who did not leave concrete records of accomplishment. The diagnosis of mental deficiency is a difficult matter for the present-day clinical psychologist with a battery of well-standardized tests; it is infinitely more liable to error when made on the basis of family lore or the reminiscences of untrained observers. Dependence upon unskilled or casual observers always leaves the suspicion that judgments of behavior may be based upon moral values, social prejudices, or hearsay evidence. Thus membership in an economic stratum below that of the observer could possibly (and very often does, as can be verified by casual observation) result in a judgment that the subject was "worthless," "shiftless," and so forth. Myerson has termed much of such evidence "statisticalized gossip." For this reason, if for no other, family-line evidence for the influence of genetic variables is most valuable when *all* the familial members have been investigated by trained observers. Unfortunately, in our generation such studies do not exist, since competent training in objective social work and other sociological techniques, to say nothing of objective psychological techniques, are matters of the very recent past.

Geneticists do not, of course, rest their case solely on the possibilities of the hereditary determination of intelligence. The occurrence of several types of structural abnormalities has been traced in families. *Syndactilism,* a condition in which the digits of hands and feet are fused together and otherwise deformed, is inherited as a dominant characteristic. Many types of eye defect (atrophy of optic nerve, malformed lens, glaucoma, color blindness, night blindness, cataract, and so forth) have been described as inherited. Glandular defects of the thyroid and pituitary are described by Penrose (1944) as genetically determined. All these physical abnormalities can have a very profound effect upon the behavior of the person who possesses them.

The influence of inherited defect on general behavior is best illustrated in the serious mental disease known as *Huntington's chorea.* This disease is characterized by massive atrophy of the convolutions of the cerebral cortex and the corpus striatum. There is a marked reduction in the number of nerve cells. The condition was first described by George Huntington, a physician who practiced medicine in the same part of Long Island as did his father and grandfather. All three of them had seen cases of the disease, occurring in the same families. No case of this disease is known to occur in persons whose parents have not also had the disease or who do not come from families in which some other member has been afflicted.

The onset of Huntington's chorea is gradual, the first symptoms appearing usually between thirty and forty-five years of age, although earlier ages are recorded. The patient becomes irritable, careless in dress, shows a progressive loss of memory and develops an increasing emotional and intellectual deterioration. Accompanying the psychological changes are neurological symptoms of increasing severity. Irregular, jerky movements of the muscles of the arms, neck, and face appear. As these grow worse, irregular flexions and extensions of random muscle groups may occur with a frequency as high as eighty times a minute. Since the muscles of the lips, tongue, and respiration are involved, speech becomes hesitating, explosive, and often unintelligible. As the choreiform movements spread to the muscles of the trunks and legs, gait and posture are involved, resulting in a weaving, shuffling manner of progression. The final stage of this disease is a profound dementia. There is no effective treatment. The average length of life after the first symptoms appear is between ten and twenty years.

Another disease, *idiopathic epilepsy,* is thought to have a genetic determination. Lennox and Gibbs (1939) have shown that electroencephalographic (EEG) recordings, brain waves, of epileptics are characteristically different from those of normal persons. They found that a large percentage of the families of epileptics have similar EEGs, irrespective of whether or not they have clinical symptoms of epilepsy. Recent surveys of the EEG patterns from the general population, however, show that approximately 20 per cent have similar EEG abnormalities with no history of epilepsy.

The evidence from family-line studies such as we have cited has not been conclusive. In most instances it has been impossible to answer the main question: Is the trait inherited, and does it appear without major environmental determination? In general it can be said that certain structural patterns have persisted through several generations without appreciable alteration from environmental factors. Such patterns may be important factors in determining behavior. Indeed, in Huntington's chorea, the structure pathology becomes of paramount importance. But for purely behavioral traits the evidence is not so clear. Intelligence of members of a family seems to be rather consistent from generation to generation; extremes tend to beget extremes. Here, though, we must recognize with Galton that there is a strong tendency for the extremes to approach the average with succeeding generations.

Also unanswered is the question of the effect of very good or very poor environmental opportunities for learning upon intelligence test scores. Studies have been reported on the change in test achievement of orphans who have been adopted into homes of various economic and cultural levels. Wellman (1934), Skeels (1940), and others believe that favorable environmental influences produce increases in the intelligence quotient. Other studies have shown that children reared in culturally isolated environments (southern rural areas, on canal boats in England, and so forth) constantly perform more poorly than children whose surroundings offer more adequate and varied opportunities to learn. All these facts would make it appear that intelligence is susceptible to training. Critics have pointed out the possibility that these conditions are artifacts of the tests and that increase in test score is not necessarily indicative of an increase in basic intelligence (see McNemar, 1940).

IDENTICAL TWIN STUDIES

Another approach to the question is to be found in comparing the personality characteristics of identical twins, fraternal twins, siblings, and the general population. Identical twins are believed by most embryologists and geneticists to have been formed from the union of a single sperm or ovum. Thus they have the same chromosonal and gene structure in their germ plasm and go through almost identical developmental stages until birth. Since they have such similar inheritance, differences that are observed between them at various stages of their lives could be attributed to environmental influences. Many such studies have been made on a wide variety of the possible similarities and differences in environment that may be achieved by rearing identical twins together or rearing them apart. If they develop in vastly different environments, any likenesses that persist might reasonably be genetic in nature. Fraternal twins, on the other hand, have no more genetic likeness than do any other brother or sister. Since fraternal twins are so similar in age, they are more likely to be exposed to similar environmental forces than are siblings of different ages. Siblings have a genetic background with more common determiners than do persons picked at random from the general population. This furnishes the investigator with a graded series of intensities of genetic similarity.

One of the best studies of this type is that of Newman, Freeman, and Holzinger (1937). They studied 50 pairs of identical twins, 52 pairs of fraternal twins of the same sex, and 52 pairs of siblings of the same sex. Table 14 shows typical findings with respect to differences in height,

TABLE 14

MEAN PAIR DIFFERENCES IN SELECTED TRAITS*

Trait	Identical twins	Fraternal twins	Siblings
Differences in standing height....	1.7 cm	4.4 cm	4.5 cm
Differences in weight............	4.1 lb	10.0 lb	10.4 lb
Differences in Binet I. Q........	5.9 points	9.9 points	9.8 points

* Source: H. H. Newman, F. N. Freeman, and K. J. Holzinger (1937), *Twins: A Study of Heredity and Environment*, p. 72. Chicago: University of Chicago Press.

weight, and intelligence quotients between identical twins, fraternal twins, and siblings. Fraternal twins show no more likeness than do other siblings, in spite of the probability that they received the usual similar treatment accorded twins in our culture. This seems to point to genetic factors operating to give constancy to traits. In order to test this assumption further it is necessary to study the effect of dissimilar environments on identical twins. Here the heredity would presumably be the same, and environmental forces would operate to produce divergence.

Newman, Freeman, and Holzinger were able to locate 19 pairs of identical twins who were reared apart for a major portion of their early years. Twelve of the cases were separated during the first year of life, five during the second year, one during the third year, and the last during the seventh year. The duration of separation was from eleven to fifty-three years. The extent of relationship between the pairs in height, weight, and I. Q. is compared with identical twins reared together and fraternal twins reared together. Correlation coefficients are shown in Table 15. These data demonstrate the greater resistance of structural features to environmental modification. Intelligence, as measured by the Stanford Binet Test, appears sensitive to environmental influence, as shown by the lowering of the correlation of identical twins reared apart. Whether this means that the intelligence-test items are susceptible to environmental change or that intelligence as a trait is modified by the environment is still an open question.

TABLE 15

CORRELATIONS FOR THREE GROUPS OF TWINS*

Trait	Identicals reared apart	Identicals reared together	Fraternals reared together
Standing height	.969	.932	.645
Weight	.886	.917	.631
Intelligence Quotient	.670	.881	.631

* Source: H. H. Newman, F. N. Freeman, and K. J. Holzinger (1937), *Twins: A Study of Heredity and Environment*, p. 53. Chicago: University of Chicago Press.

Studies of the personality of non-psychotic identical twins show more resemblance in traits than would be expected if genetic factors did not operate. Out of many such studies we will briefly review that of Burks (1942). A pair of twin girls were separated before they were two weeks old and reared in families widely different in their circumstances. The environmental differences are summarized by Burks as follows:

In Adelaide (twin A), wide travel up to teen age, irregular early schooling, strict discipline, birth of an "own" daughter to foster parents when subject was about 5; in Beatrice (twin B), few changes in residence or school, illness of 6 months in fifth year, mild discipline, constant companionship from both foster parents, effective guidance from one of her high school teachers, presence of a foster (nonadopted) sister a year younger, taken into family when subject was about 7. The socioeconomic status of the two families was not widely different and was moderately above average.[1]

In spite of the differences in family setting, there were many similarities in the development of the twins. Their intelligence test quotients were about the same. Twin B, who had the more schooling, made the higher score. They had similar interests in play, sports, and other activities. However, interest patterns, as indicated by the Strong Voca-

[1] By permission from *Studies in Personality*, p. 67. Edited by McNemar & Merril. Copyrighted 1942, by McGraw-Hill Book Co., Inc.

tional Interest Test, were not particularly alike. In some aspects of personality they were more alike than their environmental dissimilarities would suggest. Both showed a history of nail-biting, enuresis, and early puberty. Gait, handshake, and writing tempo were similar. Differences appeared in "social-emotional" traits, "B, whose home situation was more free from pressure having a more cheerful mood level, resulting in, or at least accompanied by, greater warmth and skill in the handling of social relationships" (page 67). In general, then, the differences appeared in those forms of behavior more directly dependent upon social relations, the likenesses in those behavior patterns that are more directly dependent upon structure (intelligence, sports, age of puberty, and so forth).

However, as we pointed out earlier in the chapter, *any* genetic potential is modified by the environment in which it is activated. It is possible that the two foregoing tables simply indicate that height and weight need more drastic environmental changes to alter them, whereas intelligence is sensitive to subtler changes. S. J. Holmes (1936) cites a case of identical twins who showed unequal development in height and weight:

Case 50. At birth they were attached to one placenta and had almost exactly the same weight and head circumference. Their finger prints and palm patterns are remarkably similar. Up to school age they could scarcely be distinguished. In their second school year they began to exhibit differences in growth. One twin *M* developed diabetes insipidus and grew less rapidly than the other who was free from this malady. X-rays showed that the pituitary fossa was larger in the larger twin. The cause of the unequal development of the twins is unknown.[2]

Other similar cases could be cited, and it is unquestionably true that systematic environmental alteration would change the manifestations of most genetic determiners.

If environmental stresses are allowed to operate differently upon individuals of similar genetic background, gross structural differences may be obtained. The question may then be asked: how would such differences affect behavior? A study by Biel (1938) shows some of the difficulties to be met in trying to give a definite answer. Biel severely limited the food intake of half the members of a number of litters of

[2] By permission from *Human Genetics and Its Social Import*, p. 122, by S. J. Holmes. Copyrighted 1936, by McGraw-Hill Book Co., Inc.

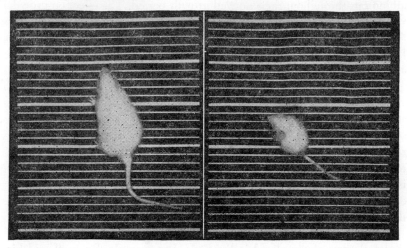

A

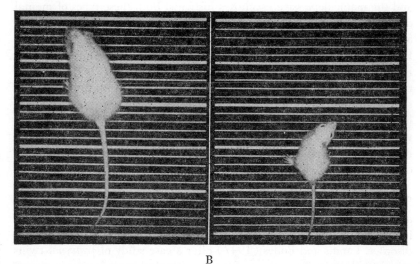

B

FIGURE 15. *The effect of early inanition upon body-size* (from W. C. Biel [1938], "The effect of early inanition upon maze learning in the albino rat." *Comp. Psych. Monog.,* 15, No. 74, 33. By permission of the Johns Hopkins Press, Baltimore).

albino rats throughout their normal growth period. The effect on growth was marked. At fifty-five days of age the rats on a full diet had a body length of approximately 10 cm, their starved littermates of only 5 cm. Figure 15 illustrates the degree of stunting. When both groups of animals were tested in maze-learning situations, the undernourished group did as well as the control group of normal animals. The structural changes did not detrimentally influence ability to learn a maze. In a subsequent experiment, Biel (1939, 1940) showed that even more severe conditions of malnutrition, carried out for longer periods of the rat's life, did have a detrimental effect on its maze performance. These results suggest that the influence of structural differences on behavior is not easily predictable, and that neither the genetic potential nor the environmental alteration of that potential can be generally related to the actual expression of a trait in behavior.

Some investigators have extended the identical-twin method directly to populations of disordered individuals. For example, Rosanoff and his co-workers (1931, 1935) have studied the occurrence of schizophrenia and the manic-depressive psychoses in twins. Both these types of mental disorders are generally considered to be of unknown origin, and both, as we have seen, are serious generalized maladaptive modes of behavior. Rosanoff finds that when one identical twin is schizophrenic, the other is affected in 68 per cent of his cases; the comparable figure for fraternal twins is 15 per cent. The findings for manic-depressive psychoses are similar, 70 per cent of identical twins and 16 per cent of fraternal twins being affected. In support of these data, Kallmann (1952) reports that with one identical twin schizophrenic the expectancy for the other to be schizophrenic is 86.2 per cent. With fraternal twins the expectancy drops to 14.5 per cent.

Such findings cannot be easily disregarded, since environmental factors for identical twins and fraternal twins usually show the same amount of variability. To such reports we can add case studies of identical twins reared apart, each of whom developed the same mental disorder. Landis and Bolles (1947) offer a case study of *fraternal* twins raised under similar, very unfavorable environmental circumstances. One twin developed schizophrenic behavior, the other remained normal. On the other hand, Kallmann (1938) reports cases of both schizophrenia and manic-depressive psychosis developing in identical twins of widely differing environmental experience. In his more recent work, however, Kallmann (1952) has found no consistent pattern between environmental background and the development of schizophrenia in his twins. One-fourth of his identical twin pairs developed schizophrenia despite dissimilar environments, whereas one-half of his fraternal twin pairs showed different behavior even with similar backgrounds.

If there is a strong genetic background to these disorders, then clearly we would expect the presence of a behavior disorder in the parents to affect the expected rate of the behavior in their children. In his original study of 1,087 schizophrenics, Kallmann (1938) found that when both parents were schizophrenic 86 per cent of the children were also schizophrenic, whereas the incidence of the disease in the general population is only 0.85 per cent. Further findings by Kallmann (1952) on 953 additional schizophrenics agree with these data: with two normal parents, the expected rate of schizophrenia in the children is 0.9 per cent; with one schizophrenic parent, 16.4 per cent; and with two schizophrenic parents, 68.1 per cent. In summarizing this literature, Kallmann states that

. . . no analysis of a statistically representative group of blood relatives of schizophrenic or manic-depressive patients has so far been completed in any country without showing a significant increase in the expectancy rate for either psychosis.[3]

Surveying the whole range of evidence from the study of the identical twins, the conclusion appears inescapable that genetic similarity forces a greater similarity in the behavior of twins than could be accounted for by any assumption of a completely environmental origin of their behavior. Further, this genetic factor seems to operate most importantly in those aspects of personality in which differences in structure are basic to differences in behavior. This is most clearly demonstrated with respect to intelligence, Huntington's chorea, and epilepsy. Since the findings from twin studies are similar for schizophrenia and manic-depressive psychosis, many authors have made the deduction that a structural defect lies at the root of the etiology of these diseases.

Only a partial agreement can be expressed at present with respect to this conclusion. The plasticity and learning capacity of the human organism must always be considered. Until we have worked our way through the evidence accumulated by those who have studied the en-

[3] F. J. Kallmann (1952), "Genetic aspects of psychoses," in *Milbank Memorial Fund Conference* (1952), *The Biology of Mental Health and Disease*, p. 284. New York: Paul B. Hoeber, Inc.

vironmental factors in mental disease, we must suspend our judgment. The possibility that appearance of abnormal behavior in a family is an indication of mutually shared experience arises as a legitimate doubt of the hereditarian position.

BREEDING EXPERIMENTS

In all the studies cited thus far, under both the family-line and identical-twin methods of investigation, the results may be interpreted as showing a genetic bias. All of them, however, have had to reckon with a relative lack of control of environmental factors. The random variations of environment in human society are so numerous and so inconstant from person to person that conclusions are always open to at least a slight suspicion that environmental factors might have operated in some way to prejudice the results. Fortunately, some aspects of the problem may be studied in lower animals by experimental methods.

As everyone knows, domestic animals have been bred for various structural and behavioral characteristics. Dogs, cats, sheep, cattle, and many other species have been capable of wide modification. In light of the long history of animal husbandry it is remarkable that few detailed studies of the relationship between genetic factors and behavior have been made. Valuable data on trait specificity, modes of inheritance, structural concomitants of behavioral traits, and many other such problems await the investigator.

A few studies that have been performed for the specific purpose of observing genetic factors in animal behavior are very suggestive of the power of this type of attack. Lashley (1932) has put it very well in his introduction to a genetic study by C. P. Stone of wildness and savageness in rats:

It is almost impossible to obtain conclusive evidence concerning heredity with human material because of the lack of adequate records of earlier generations, nor can we identify hereditable traits of behavior in man with any confidence. It is therefore necessary to turn to experimentation with animals for at least a tentative answer. The demonstration of different hereditable traits, clearly suggestive of temperamental differences in man, and the measurement of their modifiability in the individual by training marks an important step toward the solution of the problem of the origin and stability of temperamental differences.[4]

[4] Calvin P. Stone (1932), "Wildness and savageness in rats of different strains," in Karl S. Lashley, ed. (1932), *Studies in the Dynamics of Behavior,* p. ix. Chicago: University of Chicago Press.

The advantage of such studies lies not only in the control of conditions of inheritance and sources of data but also in the possibility of following experimentally the variations in such inheritance through several generations in a relatively short period of time. Experimental manipulation of environment is comparatively easy in lower animals, as we have seen in Biel's study of inanition.

One of the earliest studies of temperament was made by Yerkes (1913). After defining a series of standards of savageness, wildness, and timidity, he rated a number of wild rats and relatively docile laboratory stock. The tamer rats were crossed with the wilder, and the offspring rated by the same techniques. The half-breed offspring were less wild, timid, or savage than the first generation wild rats, but exceeded the tame parents in all ratings. A second generation of these hybrids approached the tamer parents in all ratings. These results were essentially confirmed by Coburn (1922), who inferred that temperamental differences were due to multiple genetic factors.

A study by Phillips (1912) is of interest in that an animal on a very different part of the phylogenetic scale was employed. He observed the docility and tameness of crosses between Mallard and Black ducks. The two species are closely related structurally, but the Black Ducks are extremely wild and are seldom tamed even in captivity, whereas the Mallards are easily tamed. If hybrids that are ¾ Black and ¼ Mallard are produced, the birds are wild and untamable, but a cross of ¾ Mallard and ¼ Black gives offspring that are wild in infancy but are susceptible to taming with increasing age and training.

TABLE 16

BEHAVIOR VARIABLES RATED IN STUDIES OF WILDNESS AND SAVAGENESS*

1. Resistance to catching in the home cage; running about the cage to avoid seizure by the experimenter's hand; clinging to the floor of the cage when caught; crawling behind or under other animals to avoid the experimenter's hand
2. Tense muscles of the body, particularly the sides and abdomen while in the experimenter's hand
3. Jumping, clawing, squirming, wriggling, etc., for the purpose of escaping from the experimenter's handclasp
4. Squealing when caught or while being held
5. Urination either in drops, jets, or a stream
6. Defecation
7. Biting the gloved hand when caught or as held in the hand
8. Opening the mouth, as if to bite or strike, but not actually biting
9. Laying back ears
10. Gnashing of teeth; chattering
11. Hissing noise (somewhat like the hissing of a goose)

* Source: Calvin P. Stone (1932), "Wildness and savageness in rats of different strains," in Karl S. Lashley, ed. (1932), *Studies in the Dynamics of Behavior*, p. 14. Chicago: University of Chicago Press.

The most definitive experimental attack on the problem of temperament was made by C. P. Stone (1932). He used a three-point rating scale for the intensity with which each of the behavior characteristics reproduced in Table 16 was present in various genetic combinations of albino and wild rats. The animals were rated on ten successive days. The ratings were made

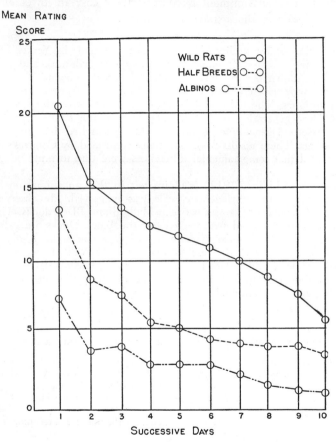

FIGURE 16. *Mean ratings of various strains of rat for temperamental character- istics on successive test days* (drawn from Stone's [1932] data).

in three situations: (1) while capturing and removing the rat from the home cage and then holding him in the experimenter's hand; (2) weighing the animal and observing his behavior then and while placed on a screen near the scales; and (3) after the animal had been allowed thirty minutes of relative freedom in a small enclosure and was then recaptured by the experimenter. The results of this experiment in terms of mean composite ratings for wild rats, half-breeds, and albinos for the ten successive days in the first situation (being held in the experimenter's hand) are shown in Figure 16. It will be observed that the three groups show differentiation in behavior that is clearly associated with their genetic composition. Of even greater significance to the mental hygienist, psychiatrist, and clinical psychologist is the reduction in mean score with successive days' handling. This illustrates that at least some genetic traits can be greatly modified in their expression through environmental manipulation. Notice that the mean wildness-savageness score for the wild rats at the end of the tenth day is comparable with that of the albinos on the first day, and that the differences between the three groups that existed on the first day have been much reduced by the tenth day.

In a sense this may be said to leave us back where we were at the conclusion of our review of human studies. That is, the evidence indicates that behavioral traits are at least partially determined genetically, but that later learning may modify them. One further item of information is needed however. Can behavioral traits be determined by selective breeding? Can the genetic constitution of animals be so manipulated that environment produces little effect? Huntington's chorea seemed to yield an affimative answer on the human level. Some animal experiments that are pertinent in this respect will next be reviewed.

A great deal of the search for evidence on the inheritance of psychological traits has centered around studies of human intelligence. We have seen that at least one of the reasons for this has been the comparatively early development of intelligence tests, which furnished a reliable trait measurement, and seemed to define a rather specific constellation of behavior characteristics. The same situation holds true for the experimental studies at lower animal levels. R. C. Tryon (1940) has rendered a significant contribution to this problem in his investigation of the inheritance of maze-learning ability of the albino rat.

Tryon pointed out that earlier attempts to study the inheritance of psychological traits were inconclusive for at least two reasons: (1) because accurate measuring devices were not available, and (2) because adequate methods of studying hereditary causation had not been developed by geneticists. According to Tryon, the following three steps are necessary:

(1) to choose as the original experimental population, *P*, a random sample of animals from the species,
(2) to measure accurately the behavior differences of these on a valid scale and under rigid conditions of environmental control, and then,

(3) by sundry systems of mating, to determine the nature of the hereditary factors at work.[5]

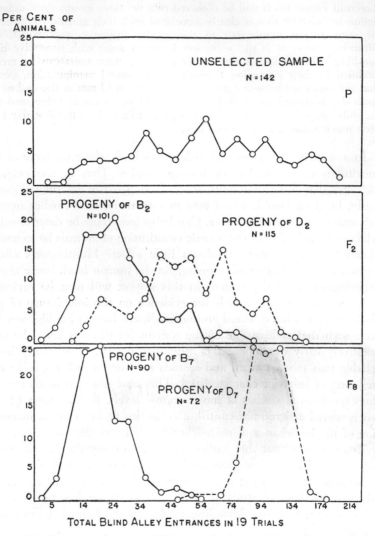

PER CENT OF ANIMALS

UNSELECTED SAMPLE
N = 142

P

PROGENY OF B₂
N = 101

PROGENY OF D₂
N = 115

F₂

PROGENY OF B₇
N = 90

PROGENY OF D₇
N = 72

F₈

TOTAL BLIND ALLEY ENTRANCES IN 19 TRIALS

FIGURE 17. *How maze learning ability may be improved by selective breeding* (modified from Robert C. Tryon [1942], "Individual differences," in F. Moss, ed. [1942], *Comparative Psychology* [Rev. Ed.]. New York: Prentice-Hall, Inc.).

[5] Robert C. Tryon (1942), "Individual differences," in F. Moss, ed. (1942), *Comparative Psychology* (Rev. Ed.), p. 344. New York: Prentice-Hall, Inc.

Accordingly, Tryon selected a random group of rats from the general colony maintained at the University of California (step 1); studied, modified, and improved a maze of high reliability (step 2); and then systematically mated the slowest learners on this maze (those making the most errors), and the animals that learned the most rapidly in each successive generation (step 3). Figure 17 shows the results from successive generations. Differences appeared noticeably in the third generation, and by the eighth generation there was almost no overlap between the "dull" and the "bright" animals. Ability to learn a maze would appear to be genetically determined.

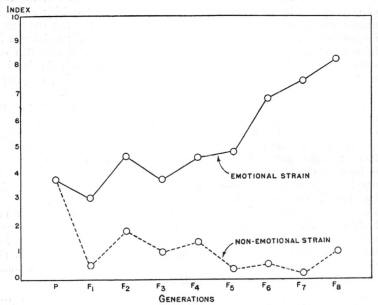

FIGURE 18. *Results of selective breeding for emotionality in eight generations of rats* (drawn from Hall's data, 1938).

Further experiments using these "bright" and "dull" animals showed that the maze-learning ability was general for many different types and patterns of mazes. In a particularly interesting study, Tryon showed that the ability differential was maintained under many drastically altered environmental conditions, which changed the types of cues (kinesthetic, visual, etc.) at various times during the course of learning. However, when the same animals were tested on discrimination apparatus, the advantage of the bright group and the constancy of the individual differences broke down, illustrating that for the rat, at least, there is no "general" intelligence, but rather there are many specific abilities. This fact is worth remembering in considering the studies on human intelligence and its inheritance. If an animal as low in the phylogenetic scale as the albino rat has so complex an organization of traits composing its intelligence, it could be surmised that the students of the genetics of human "intelligence" have been guilty of oversimplifying their definitions and possibly have been tempted to make hasty generalizations.

Another study that indicates the possibility of genetic determination of behavior traits is that of Calvin Hall (1938). Hall defined emotionality in the rat in terms of defecation and urination. If rats were placed in a strange situation, he observed that many of them showed various signs of autonomic disturbance. The number of repeated exposures to the situation in which defecation and urination persisted was taken as a measure of the degree of emotionality in the animal. Since some rats adapt quickly and others require more exposures to the frightening situation, the test constitutes a measure of individual differences in fearfulness. After determining a fearfulness index (number of days in which defecation and urination occur out of a total of 12 trials in the situation) for a number of animals selected at random, Hall selectively bred the most and least fearful, carrying the experiment on to eight generations at the time of his report.

Figure 18 illustrates his results. We find the same tendency at work that was noted with respect to intelligence. Within a relatively small number of generations the two strains of rats are significantly different in their reaction to a specific test situation. When tested in other situations, it was found that the emotional rats were less aggressive; out of 138 opportunities to fight over food, there were four fights in which emotional rats participated and 64 encounters between the nonemotional (fearless) rats (Billingslea, 1941). The emotional rats were less susceptible to epileptic seizures after air-blast stimulation than were the nonemotional animals (Martin and Hall, 1941). The relationship of learning ability to emotionality is uncertain (Anderson, 1938a, 1938b; A. W. Yerkes, 1916; Thorndike, 1935; Vaughn, 1937; O'Kelly, 1940). Probably future investigation will show that Hall's concept of fearfulness-timidity will resolve itself into a number of specific traits, as was the case with the concept of intelligence.

There are other animal studies dealing with temperamental differences and their inheritance. All show essentially the same type of conclusions, namely, that specific traits or abilities are genetically influenced, and that they are to some extent modified by environmental influences. As a field of research, the question is still open, and much essential work remains to be done. For example, animals selectively bred for intelligence, savageness, fearfulness, activity level, and so forth, should be mated to form generations with known genetic backgrounds in various combinations, such as "bright, timid, highly active animals," and "dull, savage, lethargic animals." With such known genetic constitution the determination of limits of environmental modification would more closely approach the real-life problems that face the psychopathologist.

THE QUESTION OF RACIAL DIFFERENCES

It is frequently said that certain diseases have *racial* characteristics in human beings. The evidence just discussed, in which differences between strains of lower animals have been found, might be construed as bearing out the contention that "race" among humans has similar determinative aspects for psychological abnormalities. For this reason it is worth while to devote a brief space to the discussion of race differences in behavioral traits and capacities.

In the first place, it can safely be said that the majority of psychologists are at present in agreement that most *psychological* differences that have been observed between races are socially determined. The "oriental impassivity," the volatility of the Mediterranean peoples, the silent reserve supposed to be typical of the Amerindian may all be attributed to social learning and adaptation to the mores of the cultural group. These factors will be discussed more fully in Chapter XV.

However, there are a few facts that should be taken into consideration at this time. We have cited Huntington's chorea as an example of an inherited nervous system defect that produces mental disease. There is another neurological disease that is apparently inherited and that caused grave mental deficiency, *familial amaurotic idiocy*. This disease has been considered to be more frequent in occurrence among Jewish people, thus indicating a possible racial basis; if such a statement turned out to be true, it would be most interesting, but also most puzzling, since by no stretch of the genetic imagination could the Jewish people be looked upon as a *racial* group, no matter how much they and their critics may maintain that they are. But research on the neuropathology of the disease showed that when diagnosis was adequately made, there appeared to be only about 57 Jewish cases to 43 Gentile cases (Weil, 1945, page 239), and the matter evens up on a relatively random basis.

For examples of what appears to be a genuine racial difference we must go far below the behavioral sphere into the field of cytology. If the red blood corpuscles of large numbers of Negroes are examined, it will be found that approximately 7 per cent of the Negro population will possess red corpuscles that become deformed under conditions that do not harm normal red cells. The chief circumstance producing the abnormal cells is a drastic decrease in the oxygen supplied to the blood.

The condition is termed *sicklemia* or sickle cell anemia, as the abnormal cells become so deformed in shape as to remain in the capillaries. This is often a serious factor that must be considered before administration of general anesthetics to Negroes. This condition has not been found as an hereditary defect in other races.

Although there are probably many more such "racial" differences, they are insignificant in comparison with individual inheritance and the great capacity for learned adjustment shared by members of all races.

THEORETICAL FORMULATIONS

We have reviewed the evidence, as gathered by various methods. Although only a few representative studies were described, they are typical of the general findings on this problem. We will now consider how these facts have been integrated into theory.

There are two extreme points of view. On the one hand it is claimed that heredity exercises a major influence on behavior, and on the other it is stated that behavior is environmentally determined. As in most controversies, such extremes are seldom generally held and a compromise position is often most clearly or reasonably indicated. The simplest form of such a compromise would be to say that both are important, that each makes its contributions to behavior, each in its own manner. Although such a rapprochement has a superficial appearance of being scientifically equitable, it unfortunately assumes an independent operation of the two not warranted by the facts. As we shall see when we discuss the development of individuals, any theory of genetic determinants must also explain how environment works on the genes (or how the genes work out their destiny in a specific environment, which amounts to the same thing). Equally, the most extreme environmentalist cannot escape his obligation to account for the structural organization of the protoplasm that his environment is molding. It is at this point that many of the extreme positions become weak and must be rejected.

As an instance of compromise between these extremes, let us look at the blastophoric theory of Myerson (1925). Whereas most geneticists postulated mental illness to be due to specific genetic combinations, Myerson maintained that the illness was the result of a weakened, defective, or abnormal total germ plasm, produced by environmental injury. According to this idea, the total germ plasm of the person is abnormal. The theory was based upon examination of family lines in which mental disease had occurred. The findings indicated that when mental disease first appeared in the family it occurred in the later decades of life, the mental diseases of old age. With succeeding generations diseases appeared at earlier and earlier age levels, and the diagnostic type changed from the senile disorders to schizophrenia and manic-depressive psychosis. The last stages showed the cumulative effect of generally poor germ plasm by a high incidence of feeble-mindedness. Such a weakening of the germ plasm he called *blastophoria*.

Notice that this theory does not go far enough. The environmentalist could ask: Why does the individual live such a large proportion of his life span before the incidence of the disease in the earlier generations? How could deterioration of somatic tissue affect germ plasm? (Experiments reported by Hanson and Cooper [1930], who subjected rats to daily doses of alcohol vapor for ten generations, failed to show any deterioration of health or learning ability of the offspring.) Myerson says "The environment . . . by its penetration, may even increase the mutation rate or injure the genotype for several generations . . ." (1934, page 36). But geneticists as a group reject the possibility of somatic changes in an individual having remote effects upon his progeny. Each individual receives a unique combination of genes and thus has a unique potentiality for future development. In breeding, the mating of closely related persons tends to emphasize common elements, since the probability of similar gene compositions is increased. But this is again a genetic influence. It is true that a limited number of mutations may be produced by the action of X-ray and other physical forces, but this is action directly upon the germ plasm and, from all we know now, is not essentially linked with a blastophoric degeneration of a family line.

In fairness to Myerson it should be noted that he has been much more concerned with emphasizing that recourse to heredity as an explanation of mental disease is usually a way of disguising our ignorance of its causative factors. As he says, an analysis of the writings on any disease syndrome show that the heredity hypothesis is usually abandoned coincidentally with the beginning of real progress in understanding of the specific factors responsible for the condition. "Our knowledge of a disease apparently runs in reverse ratio to the importance we lay on heredity" (1934, page 36).

Although the combination or arrangement of genes that any individual receives is unique, the possible expressions of this potentiality are infinitely great. As far as the evidence seems to indicate, the germ plasm is extremely sensitive to environmental influences in shaping the somatic structure of the individual. Let us take an hypothetical illustration. Suppose we have, by selective breeding, developed two types of corn; one of these strains yields a minimum of 100 bushels per acre under normal growth conditions, the other under the same conditions yields 10 bushels an acre. If we sow both types of seed in extremely barren soil and give them a minimum of attention, the yield of both types will be much less. Probably, the sparse-yielding corn would fail to produce at all. If we planted the high-yield corn in barren ground and the poor corn in the best possible soil, it is conceivable that the latter would give the better yield. To attempt a prediction of yield from the knowledge of the ancestry alone would be somewhat less than infallible; to predict on the basis of environmental factors alone would be equally liable to error, since there would be no good way of explaining why the two types of corn did not yield the same when raised in the same soil. Very often we are attempting to do the same things in our interpretations of behavior. Depending upon our bias toward genetics or toward the power of environment, we tend to assume constancy of the neglected factor (see Howells, 1945, 1947).

Summary

There is enough consistency in the results of studies from many points of view and using many different methods to warrant a conclusion that genetic factors in mental disorder cannot be completely ignored. Although there is relatively little that anyone can do about his heredity, so far as changing it is concerned, it should be evident that a knowledge of the family history of the individual who is mentally ill can aid in understanding his disability. The corrective influence of environmental manipulation, which *can* be controlled to a great extent, may compensate for many genetic handicaps. Much remains to be done in the way of research on heredity in mental disorder. We do not know enough yet to give practical advice on the important question of whether persons whose family history records behavior abnormalities should have children. Nor do we know precisely how to regulate the environment of the feeble-minded or other inheritor of defect so that his liability may be minimized.

DISCUSSION QUESTIONS

1. Can you list some of the difficulties encountered in scientific study of the genetic basis of behavior?
2. What are the advantages of studying genetic problems in lower animals?
3. What are the difficulties involved in generalizing from the results of subhuman animal experimentation to the problems of human psychopathology?
4. What are the relative contributions of heredity and environment to behavior?
5. Is the heredity-environment controversy a real problem?
6. On the basis of the studies cited in this chapter, what importance must we assign to the hereditary basis of psychopathology?
7. Can you suggest specific experimental work that might be done on genetic factors in psychopathology?
8. Supposing it was discovered that a particular behavioral disease syndrome was inherited, and you were contemplating marriage to a person with one parent who had died of this disease. What considerations would enter into your decisions in this matter?
9. Do you feel that sterilization is an acceptable public health measure in our present state of knowledge concerning psychopathology?
10. Could all of the Kallmann and Rosanoff statistics on inheritance of mental disease be interpreted from an environmentalist viewpoint?

SUGGESTED READINGS

C. S. Hall (1951), "The genetics of behavior," in S. S. Stevens, ed. (1951), *Handbook of Experimental Psychology,* pp. 305-329. New York: John Wiley & Sons, Inc.

A. Scheinfeld (1950), *The New You and Heredity.* Philadelphia: Lippincott.

BIBLIOGRAPHIC SOURCES

The literature on heredity is almost embarrassingly plentiful, although of very uneven quality. On the basic genetic facts the popular presentation of Scheinfeld (1950) forms a good introduction. A somewhat more technical introduction is the beautifully written text by one of this century's greatest geneticists, Richard B. Goldschmidt (1950). A summary of studies is given in Gates' (1946) two-volume review. Haldane (1948) discusses, in detail, some of the techniques of modern genetics. A popularly written and profusely illustrated book on genetic abnormalities is Whitney's (1946) *Family Skeletons*.

Probably the best introduction to the genetic approach in behavior is the extensive review by Hall (1951) in Stevens' (1951) handbook. Much of the experimental literature discussed here may be found reviewed in that article. Two papers which examine in detail the methodological aspects of genetic investigation are Hall (1947) and Scott (1949).

The amount of polemic on the heredity-environment controversy is immense. Pastore (1949) has collected, in a small but fascinating book, the views of various scientists on this issue in recent times. In 1947, six papers were published in the *Psychological Review* representing a symposium on heredity and environment. Hunter's (1947) summary is especially valuable for a discussion of the recent history of the controversy in psychology. All the papers are of unusually high quality. For one detailed solution of the issue, Anastasi and Foley (1948) is recommended.

The best single source summarizing the literature on the genetic basis of mental deficiency is Penrose's (1949) *The Biology of Mental Defect*. This text contains descriptions of many of the disorders we have mentioned, such as Huntington's chorea and juvenile amaurotic idiocy. For more detailed information on Huntington's chorea, see Schiele (1946) and Leese and Pond (1952). Cares (1951), Dunn (1947), and Jervis (1950) present detailed pathological, histochemical, and statistical information on familial amaurotic idiocy.

Some of the most extensive investigations of the role of heredity in epilepsy have been conducted by Lennox (1947, 1951). Lennox concludes that although epilepsy is not directly inherited a disposition toward the disorder is. The variable of birth trauma in idiopathic epilepsy has been suggested by the data of Neilsen and Courville (1951).

Further information on identical twins raised apart is given in Burks and Roe (1949). Oestlyngen (1949) has published a brilliant critical article on the use of the twin technique.

No single investigator has produced more evidence on the genetic basis of behavior disorders than Franz J. Kallmann. His original investigation of 1,087 schizophrenics was published under the title *The Genetics of Schizophrenia* (1938). A long and very critical review of this work was written by Pastore (1949). Hurst's rejoinder (1951) and Pastore's reply (1952) should also be read. In 1937, Kallmann became the head of the Department of Mental Genetics at the New York State Psychiatric Institute, and he has published further research based on twin investigations (Kallmann, 1946, 1950). Hurst (1952) has summarized this work in detail, and Kallmann's (1952) own summary should be consulted.

Searle (1949) has extended the work of Tryon to other types of behavior. This study, and other recent papers, are discussed in the chapter by C. S. Hall (1951) in the third edition of *Comparative Psychology*.

XII

Constitutional Factors in Psychopathology

Caesar: *Let me have men about me that are fat;*
Sleek-headed men and such as sleep o'nights:
Yon Cassius has a lean and hungry look;
He thinks too much: such men are dangerous.
Antonius: *Fear him not, Caesar; he's not dangerous;*
He is a noble Roman and well given.
Caesar: *Would he were fatter!* . . .
SHAKESPEARE, *Julius Caesar*

The Concept of Constitution

Regardless of whether one ultimately believes in the efficacy of the genes to limit behavioral potentialities, whether one believes that the environment will contain sufficient forces to shape protoplasm into any form, or whether one adopts the more reasonable point of view that both work together, still, in the end, all are forced to consider the individual organism. If we look at the individual human being as he presents himself for examination at any time, we are cognizant of a many-sided organization of properties. Superficially we may note height, weight, skin color, hair color and length, eye color, sex, gait and posture, hair distribution, fat distribution, size of appendages such as ear, nose, external genitalia, and so forth, and as many other features as time or interest would dictate. A more searching examination, with the aid of a variety of instruments to extend our unaided sensory capacities, would reveal countless other features: blood pressure, pulse rate, electrical discharge pattern of heart and other muscle organizations, vital capacity, chemical composition of the fluids of the body, temperature,

391

neurological integration, appearance and function of the internal organs, and so on. All these features, plus many more, are integrated into a vastly complex but deceptively unitary organism. The anatomist, the biochemist, the physiologists, and members of other biological specialties cooperate to give a meaningful picture of the person who presents himself for examination. This person is immersed in an environment that is partially of his own making, partially completely beyond his control. His behavior, in which we are interested, must be correlated on the one hand with this environment, on the other with the host of physical and chemical facts of his structure and physiological function. This latter problem has resulted in, among other things, the concept of *constitution*.

Constitution may be thought of as those features of the interrelationship between all its characteristics that give the organism consistency and continuity. Thus, body-build may be considered a constitutional aspect of the person, as may his blood type, his average speed of reaction, his ability to withstand stress, and so forth. The relationship between constitution and behavior is one of the oldest problems in psychology. It has implications of great interest to the psychopathologist.

Morphological Type and Personality

There have been many attempts to relate body-build and personality traits. Casual observation many times suggests that some such relationship exists. Although we usually learn by bitter experience that all fat people are not jolly and that some short individuals do not arrogantly compensate for their small stature, it is a great temptation to classify personality in this way.

DEGIOVANNI'S TYPES

According to Roback (1952), the scientific attempts to correlate temperament with bodily proportions originated with DeGiovanni, an Italian physician, and his students. DeGiovanni noted anatomical relationships from which he formulated the "law of deformation": "Individuals having a small trunk tend to assume a longilinear body which corresponds to the phthisic habitus; individuals having a large trunk tend to assume a short body which corresponds to the apoplectic habitus; individuals having a normal trunk tend to maintain normal proportions of the body." [1] Corresponding to these structural relationships Viola and Naccarati developed a classification system of body forms: (1) the *microsplanchnic,* thin, tall individuals; (2) the *macrosplanchnic,* or stout individuals; and (3) *normosplanchnic,* or persons with constant proportion between vertical and horizontal diameters of the body. These investigators found psychoneurotics generally among the microsplanchnics, and manic-depressives among the macrosplanchnics. Some confirmation was given by Naccarati and Garrett (1924) in an examination of 54 college students. They concluded that "temperamental disturbances of an emotional nature are found in those of low morphological index (relatively large trunk and short extremities) more often than in those of high morphological index (relatively small trunk and long extremities)." [2]

SIGAUD'S ENVIRONMENTAL BODY TYPES

Sigaud, a French pathologist, based a morphological typology on the relative prominence of those bodily systems influenced by various environmental factors. The atmospheric environment is in interaction with the respiratory system, the alimentary or food environment with the digestive system, the physical environment of gravitational forces with the muscular system, and the social environment with the cerebral or nervous system. Therefore, there are four types of individual: the respiratory, the digestive, the muscular, and the cerebral. Each type overemphasizes one system or another at the expense of the rest, and thus the individual's adjustment to the whole environment is shaped in a way correlated with his particular body type. A description of one of these types (taken from the writings of two of Sigaud's pupils, Chaillou and MacAuliffe, as cited by Roback) will suffice to indicate the approach:

The face of the muscular man is well formed, lending a somewhat square aspect to the countenance; the eyebrows are deep and not arched, the hair grows down on the forehead almost to a straight line, the organs are fairly proportioned, and the bodily musculature is highly developed. [3]

---

[1] S. Naccarati and H. E. Garret (1924), "The relation of morphology to temperament." *J. abnorm. soc. Psychol., 19,* 263. Reprinted by permission of the American Psychological Association.

[2] *Ibid.,* p. 263.

[3] A. A. Roback (1927), *The Psychology of Character,* p. 89. New York: Harcourt, Brace and Company, Inc.

Sigaud's approach was in some ways in agreement with contemporary modes of thought. He thought of organic form being the result of protoplasmic development in a specific milieu. "Varieties and variability of form are in the last analysis but morphological imprints engraved as a result of the efforts of the organism to adapt itself to the environment" (quoted by Roback, 1952, page 90). Of course, the critical point is not so much the origin of structural form, but its influence on behavior. MacAuliffe offers evidence on the former problem. He made elaborate series of measurements to demonstrate how the four constitutional types

"Fortunately, I'm an adopted child"

FIGURE 19. *Body-build has a large genetic element in its determination* (from *Collier's* magazine, March 9, 1946. By permission of the Crowell-Collier Publishing Company, New York).

developed under different environmental influences. He felt that different geographical locations favored different types. In fruitful agricultural districts the digestive type would be prominent, the respiratory type in mountainous regions, and the cerebral type developed best in city life. However, few data are offered to support the relationship of these types to individual personality differences in behavior.

KRETSCHMER'S TYPOLOGY

By far the most influential typology was that of the German psychiatrist, Kretschmer (1925). In his examination of large groups of patients with mental illnesses, he distinguished four general physical body-types: (1) the *asthenic,* composed of individuals who were slender, with long bones and slight muscular development; (2) the *pyknik,* made up of the stocky, plump, rounded persons; (3) the *athletic,* with wide shoulders, sturdy, well-developed musculature and good strength; and (4) the *dysplastic,* a group of people showing endocrine disturbances resulting in extremely disproportionate development, as in pituitary giantism, cretins, and so forth. The pyknik body-build he believed to be associated with affective mental disorders (manic-depressive psychosis) and also with *cyclothymic* personality. The asthenic habitus he associated with schizophrenia and with the *schizoid* personality type. In addition, the athletic and dysplastic types were more frequently found among the schizophrenias than among the affective psychoses.

For the purposes of the psychopathologist, Kretschmer felt the most important aspect of his system was the differentiation between the asthenics and the pykniks. These types he related to several differing manifestations of personality. The pyknik body-build he found in (1) the gay chatterbox, (2) the quiet humorist, (3) the silent good-tempered, (4) the happy enjoyers of life, and (5) the energetic practical man. The asthenic body-build is related to (1) the polite individual, (2) the sensitive man, (3) the world-hostile idealist, (4) the cold, masterful natures and egoists, and (5) the dried and emotionally lamed. On the basis of further studies he reported that 58 out of 60 pykniks suffered from manic-depressive psychosis and 81 out of 85 asthenics were schizophrenics.

After the publication of Kretschmer's book, *Physique and Character,* in 1925, a great many investigations were made to determine the validity of his classification. The results have been somewhat variable and contradictory. Most studies report low correlation between the types and personality characteristics as measured by other methods. According to Sheldon (1944), the American experiments may be summarized as follows:

(1) The descriptions of the physical types and the criteria for their recognition were found to be confusing and unsatisfactory. In fact, it was soon made evident that types as such do not exist.

(2) Yet in a number of instances where investigators side-stepped this stumbling block, accepting what may possibly be called the *spirit rather than the letter* of Kretschmer's claims, and proceeding to grade physiques according to their manifest general tendencies—in a considerable number of such instances significant positive correlations were found between physical tendency and psychotic tendency.

(3) However, no American students, using Kretschmer's technique as he presented it, have been able to demonstrate significant relationships between physical type and temperamental or normal psychological characteristics.[4]

JAENSCH'S "B" AND "T" TYPES

Our review of earlier attempts to define morphological types would not be complete without mention of E. R. Jaensch's typology based upon two clinical conditions, hyperthyroidism (Basedow's disease) and tetany. The latter or T-type is distinguished by hyperexcitability of the peripheral motor nerves, the temperament is subdued, and the person appears tense and anxious. The B-type of individual tends toward hyperthyroidism, the person sweats easily, reflexes are hyperactive, eyes are slightly protrusive, and pupillary reactions are rapid. Lest this seem a rather arbitrary way to parcel off mankind, let it be said that Jaensch discovered a very important psychological correlate of his two types. They differ in the type of imagery which they experience. Both types, as do probably all children, possess eidetic imagery; that is, they are able to recall vividly the details of former visual stimulation. The T-type experiences a persistent and vivid eidetic imagery that is poorly controlled and is connected with their inability to relax. The eidetic imagery of the B-type is less vivid and remains more under the child's control. Jaensch's clinical results show that both types of imagery exist but the attempt to relate this imagery to glandular secretion has not been successful.

[4] W. H. Sheldon (1944), "Constitutional factors in personality," in J. McV. Hunt, ed., *Personality and the Behavior Disorders*, p. 533. 2 vols. Copyright 1944, The Ronald Press Company.

SHELDON'S SOMATOTYPE CONTINUA

William H. Sheldon, a psychologist and psychiatrist, has, since 1924, been engaged in a brilliant attack on the problem of morphology and behavior. Realizing that the weakness of the earlier research lay in the assumption of dichotomous or trichotomous "types," Sheldon started to look for graded series of anthropometric measurements that would bridge the gaps between the polar extremes assumed by earlier investigators. Convinced that random measurements of the various aspects of human physique had not shown outstanding success, Sheldon photographed four thousand college students in standardized postures, from frontal, lateral, and dorsal positions. Inspection of these four thousand photographs revealed no "types" in the old sense of the word, but only what Sheldon termed "dimensions of variation."

In order to determine how many such dimensions existed, Sheldon employed two criteria in his examination: "(1) Could the entire collection of photographs be arranged in an ascending (or descending) progression of strength of the characteristics under consideration, with agreement between experimenters working independently? (2) In the case of a suspected new component of structural variation, is it, upon examination of the photographs, found to be impossible to define this apparently new component in terms of mixtures, regular or dysplastic, of the other already accepted components?" (Sheldon, 1944, page 538.) Application of these criteria showed three primary axes of structural variation. These Sheldon termed *endomorphy, mesomorphy,* and *ectomorphy.* The following descriptions indicate their meanings:

When *endomorphy* predominates, the digestive viscera are massive and highly developed, while the somatic structures are relatively weak and undeveloped. Endomorphs are of low specific gravity. They float high in the water. Nutrition may of course vary to some degree independently of the primary components. Endomorphs are usually fat but they are sometimes seen emaciated. In the latter event they do not change into mesomorphs or ectomorphs any more than a starved spaniel will change into a mastiff or a collie. They become simply emaciated endomorphs.

When *mesomorphy* predominates, the somatic structures (bone, muscle and connective tissue) are in the ascendancy. The mesomorphic physique is high in specific gravity and is hard, firm, upright, and relatively strong and tough. Blood vessels are large, especially the arteries. The skin is relatively thick with large pores, and it is heavily reinforced with underlying connective tissue. The hallmark of mesomorphy is uprightness and sturdiness of structure, as the hallmark of endomorphy is softness and sphericity.

Ectomorphy means fragility, linearity, flatness of chest and delicacy throughout the body. There is relatively slight development of both the visceral and somatic structures. The ectomorph has long, slender, poorly muscled extremities with delicate, pipestem bones, and he has, relative to his mass, the greatest surface area and hence the greatest sensory exposure to the outside world. He is thus in one sense overly exposed and naked to his world. His nervous system and sensory tissue have relatively poor protection. It might be said that the ectomorph is biologically "extraverted," as the endomorph is biologically usually reversed—the ectomorph is the introvert, the endomorph is *one* type of extravert. The hallmark of ectomorphy is the stooped posture and hesitant restraint of movement.[5]

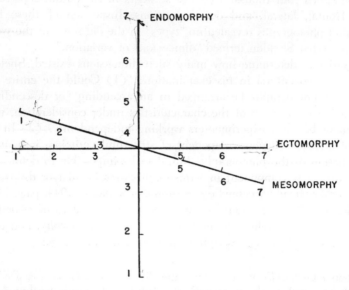

FIGURE 20. *Schematic representation of Sheldon's somatotype continua.*

If Sheldon had stopped here he would, on the whole, have merely been in basic agreement with the typologists before him, as the morphological divisions just quoted are very similar to those of Kretschmer and the rest. But, since these "types" are conceived as extreme or terminal positions on continuously varying dimensions of body-build, they furnish dimensions for the description of any person, no matter what

[5] W. H. Sheldon (1944), "Constitutional factors in personality," in J. McV. Hunt, ed., *Personality and the Behavior Disorders,* p. 540. 2 vols. Copyright 1944, The Ronald Press Company.

his particular physical habitus may be. This can be seen by examining Figure 20. The precision with which any individual may be located on these axes is limited only by the fineness of discrimination of the examiner. Sheldon scaled the axes in terms of a seven-point scale of equal-appearing intervals. The somatotype, or body-build designation of any individual, may be expressed in terms of his position on each of the three axes. Thus, a 7-1-1 somatotype would be an extreme endomorph, a 1-7-1 would be an extreme mesomorph, and so forth. An individual at the exact center of the system would be a somatotype of 4-4-4. Sheldon reports seventy-six different somatotypes that have been distinguished to date.

The next step in Sheldon's research is the critical one. Although it is a real contribution to anthropology to devise an effective classification system of body configuration, it is of little use to the psychopathologist unless it can be demonstrated to have some relationship to behavior variables. This problem was approached by the same general method that had proved so fruitful with the somatotypes. The first step was to discover significant and differentiating temperamental or personality variables. The literature on temperament and personality measurement was thoroughly searched for variables. The trait definitions so obtained were "modified and rewritten until they appeared to embrace or to imply all of the specific characteristics mentioned in the literature." After this process and with the addition of a few traits from his own clinical experience, he had a list of 50 traits.

Sheldon then studied 33 young men in a series of analytical interviews, once a week throughout a year. Each of these men was finally rated on each of the 50 traits, using a 7-point scale. The ratings on each item were then interrelated, in an attempt to discover the positive or negative relationships that might exist between the various traits. The traits were then classified into groups that showed high intragroup correlation and low intergroup correlation. Three such groups were found, containing 22 of the original 50 traits. By studying additional subjects, the list was increased to 60 traits, 20 in each group. Sheldon labeled the three groups of trait clusters *viscerotonia, somatotonia,* and *cerebrotonia,* respectively. The characteristics of these traits he describes as follows:

Viscerotonia, the first component, in its extreme manifestation is characterized by general relaxation, love of comfort, sociability, conviviality, gluttony for food, for people and for affection. The viscerotonic extremes are people who "suck hard at the breast of mother earth" and love physical proximity with others. The motivational organization is dominated by the gut and by the function of anabolism. The personality seems to center around the viscera. The digestive tract is king, and its welfare appears to define the primary purpose of life.

Somatotonia, the second component, is roughly a predominance of muscular activity and of vigorous bodily assertiveness. The motivational organization seems dominated by the soma. These people have vigor and push. The executive department of their internal economy is strongly vested in their somatic muscular systems. Actions and power define life's primary purpose.

Cerebrotonia, the third component, is roughly a predominance of the element of restraint, inhibition and the desire for concealment. These people shrink away from sociality as from too strong a light. They "repress" somatic and visceral expression, are hyperattentional, and sedulously avoid attracting attention to themselves. Their behavior seems dominated by the inhibitory and attentional functions of the cerebrum, and their motivational hierarchy appears to define an antithesis to both of the other extremes.[6]

Table 17 lists the traits that fall under these three headings.

Although Sheldon disclaims any major interest in the degree of relationship between physique and temperament as such, nevertheless the final test of the adequacy of his generalizations and his separate findings for somatotype and temperament is a determination of the degree of relationship between the two. Table 18 gives the correlations between the various somatotypes and temperament components. It will be seen that each somatotype shows a high degree of correlation with one of the three components of temperament, and a negative correlation with the other components. In other words, the viscerotonic personality is found more often in the endomorphic body type, the somatotonic in the mesomorphic somatotype, and the cerebrotonic in the ectomorphic body type.

Sheldon's work is extremely significant for several reasons. In the first place, he has demonstrated empirically that a relationship exists between the physical pattern of cells we term a body and the behavioral traits of the organism, thus giving substantial support to the general concept of integration. This clears up what seemed to be a difficulty with the organismic approach to behavior. It was apparent theoretically

[6] W. H. Sheldon (1944), "Constitutional factors in personality," in J. McV. Hunt, ed., *Personality and the Behavior Disorders,* pp. 543-544. 2 vols. Copyright 1944, The Ronald Press Company.

TABLE 17

SHELDON'S SCALE FOR TEMPERAMENT*

I VISCEROTONIA	II SOMATOTONIA	III CEREBROTONIA
1. Relaxation in posture and movement	1. Assertiveness of posture and movement	1. Restraint in posture and movement tightness
2. Love of physical comfort	2. Love of physical adventure	2. Physiological over-response
3. Slow reaction	3. The energetic characteristic	3. Overly fast reactions
4. Love of eating	4. Need and enjoyment of exercise	4. Love of privacy
5. Socialization of eating	5. Love of dominating, lust for power	5. Mental overintensity, hyperattentionality, apprehensiveness
6. Pleasure in digestion	6. Love of risk and chance	6. Secretiveness of feeling, emotional restraint
7. Love of public ceremony	7. Bold directness of manner	7. Self-conscious motility of the eyes and face
8. Sociophilia	8. Physical courage for combat	8. Sociophobia
9. Indiscriminate amiability	9. Competitive aggressiveness	9. Inhibited social address
10. Greed for affection and approval	10. Psychological callousness	10. Resistance to habit and poor routinizing
11. Orientation to people	11. Claustrophobia	11. Agoraphobia
12. Evenness of emotional flow	12. Ruthlessness, freedom from squeamishness	12. Unpredictability of attitude
13. Tolerance	13. The unrestrained voice	13. Vocal restraint, and general restraint of noise
14. Complacency	14. Spartan indifference to pain	14. Hypersensitivity to pain
15. Deep sleep	15. General noisiness	15. Poor sleep habits, chronic fatigue
16. The untempered characteristic	16. Overmaturity of appearance	16. Youthful intentness of manner and appearance
17. Smooth, easy communication of feeling, extraversion of viscerotonia	17. Horizontal mental cleavage, extraversion of somatotonia	17. Vertical mental cleavage, introversion
18. Relaxation and sociophilia under alcohol	18. Assertiveness and aggression under alcohol	18. Resistance to alcohol and to other depressant drugs
19. Need of people when troubled	19. Need of action when troubled	19. Need of solitude when troubled
20. Orientation toward childhood and family relationships	20. Orientation toward goals and activities of youth	20. Orientation toward later periods of life

* Source: Adapted from W. H. Sheldon (1944), "Constitutional factors in personality," in J. McV. Hunt, ed., *Personality and the Behavior Disorders*, p. 543. 2 vols. Copyright 1944, The Ronald Press Company.

and logically that body-pattern should be a significant variable in behavior, and yet the volume of negative results from attempts of Kretschmer and others to test typologies seemed to indicate a lack of such significance in fact. Although Sheldon's results do not give us a complete working statement of body-personality relationships, they serve to point the way toward the eventual truth of the matter.

TABLE 18

CORRELATIONS BETWEEN SHELDON'S SOMATOTYPIC AND TEMPERAMENTAL COMPONENTS*

	Viscero-tonia	Meso-morphy	Somato-tonia	Ecto-morphy	Cerebro-tonia
Endomorphy............	+.79	−.29	−.29	−.41	−.32
Viscerotonia............		−.23	.34	−.41	−.37
Mesomorphy............			+.82	−.63	−.58
Somatotonia............				−.53	−.62
Ectomorphy............					+.83

* Source: W. H. Sheldon (1944), "Constitutional factors in personality," in J. McV. Hunt, ed., *Personality and the Behavior Disorders*, p. 544. 2 vols. Copyright 1944, The Ronald Press Company.

A second point of significance lies in the possibility that the geneticist will now have a more precise trait-index for use in his studies. As Penrose (1944) has pointed out, geneticists have been most successful when they have had definite, well-defined traits to work upon; thus, they have had their most outstanding results in the area of specific aspects of somatic structure, such as eye color, conformation and number of digits, and so forth. The more closely behavioral traits can be related to obvious and measurable aspects of structure, the more confidently can the geneticist apply his methods of analysis.

A third advantage pointed out by Sheldon is that such a system as his provides a method of classifying patients by a schema that is oriented toward both the individual and his disease. Since the adoption of a schema with continual gradations, the old system of polar extremes, with its forcing of patients into limited categories, becomes obsolete. Although much work remains to be done before such a classification becomes a practical reality, it should be taken as a serious indication of what the future contains in the way of introducing a satisfactory terminology for personality description.

Against these positive gains which the work of Sheldon makes should be set a word or two of caution. The correlation coefficients displayed in Table 18 were derived from sets of somatotype and behavior ratings made by the same person. This means that there is an element of bias which, although unmeasured, almost certainly would operate to increase the apparent relationship between somatotype and personality variables. The definitive and critical experimental work on the Sheldon somatotypology remains undone. As we have noted previously, the general trend of experimental results in the body-type field has been disappointing. The intellectual climate of American psychology has not been particularly favorable toward the introduction of even as sophisticated a typology as Sheldon's, and therefore few research workers have cared to embark on the arduous and difficult labor that would be involved in a rigorous evaluation of Sheldon's proposals. We have taken so much of your time with them, however, because the Sheldon approach does, in its application of quantitative scaling methods, point the way toward eventual clarification of this relationship between body-build and personality that has intrigued thinkers through so much of man's intellectual history.

SUMMARY

All the typological approaches save Sheldon have proceeded under the assumption that people are sharply divided into differing physical categories, with clear lines of cleavage separating them. Such an assumption is simply untenable in the light of our knowledge of the distribution of biologcal traits in general. People are not "heavy" or "light," "tall" or "short," "thin" or "stout." For any structural attribute of the organism, careful measurement of a large number of people will show that weight, height, or girth is normally distributed. As we find more and more ways of measuring psychological traits we find that the same generalization holds for intelligence, emotionality, sensory acuity, or any other feature of behavior. These traits are distributed in accordance with the normal probability curve or some other mathematical relationship that provides a number of degrees of the trait, with relatively continuous variation from one extreme to another. Because of this fact, the typologists, who assume an abrupt transition in both physical and psychological qualities of organisms, can expect very few people actually to fit their "types."

However, if we are to be consistent with the principles of integration and field organization that we have already stated, it must be admitted that some relationship does exist between physical structure and behavior. Body-build *is* characteristic of the organism and is a relatively fixed and persistent characteristic. Our ignorance of the details of its significance and the sterility of the typological theories we have just viewed should not lead us to reject the relationship altogether.

The Prevalence of Type Concepts in Psychology

The human compulsion to think in terms of a few limited categories and to force facts into them is well illustrated when we examine the various analytical theories of behavior. Freud placed much emphasis on the stages in development of mature sexuality and their distortions in abnormal individuals. There were two possible ways in which a person could show such a developmental abnormality. He could either fail to mature beyond some infantile state of development, or, having once achieved a higher level, various conditions could produce a regression to some earlier stage. By designating these stages, such as "narcissistic," "pre-genital," "anal-erotic," and so forth, it is inevitable that patients will be artificially forced into such classifications. Thus a typology arises spontaneously, and the classification in practice becomes open to the criticisms that have been leveled against all type systems.

Jung created psychological types when he coined the terms "introvert" and "extravert." Later he extended the classification to include various composite characteristics, such as the "extraverted thinking type," the "introverted sensation type," and so on. His book, *Psychological Types, or the Psychology of Individuation* (1923), is a thorough discussion and analysis of the type concept as it has affected history, literature, aesthetics, philosophy, and psychiatry. His point of view is well expressed by the concluding paragraph of his book:

> To deny the existence of types is of little use in face of the fact of their existence. In view of their existence, therefore, every theory of the psychic process must submit to be valued in its turn as a psychic process, and, moreover, as the expression of an existing and recognized type of human psychology. Only from such typical presentations can the materials be gathered whose *cooperation* shall bring about the possibility of a higher synthesis.[7]

As this indicates, Jung argues not only that types exist, but that the thinking process of human beings itself is typological. To the extent

[7] C. G. Jung (1923), *Psychological Types, or the Psychology of Individuation*. p. 628. New York: Harcourt, Brace & Company, Inc.

that Jung is saying that all behavioral variables are polar, to the extent that extreme limiting values may be named, he is certainly correct. But it does not then follow that the numerous individuals of the world will correspond to these extremes. Rather, it would seem from most of what we know about the distribution of traits in nature that most individuals would tend to cluster around intermediate values. In fact, if polar continua are discovered in which individuals cluster around the extremes, it is likely that what has appeared to be a single continuum is really plural, two continua laid end to end perhaps. For a type is, in the last analysis, only a life circumstance in which the arrangement of causative agents has produced uniformities in behavior (or structure) sufficiently plain to be recognized by the observer. As such, a type is not a reliable concept since often those things that seem to be similar, as far as appearances are concerned, are produced by vastly different combinations of forces.

We see the difficulty in the practical clinical situation of trying to arrive at the diagnosis that best fits a given patient. After the psychiatrist, psychologist, and social worker have presented all their respective findings, it is only the rare or unusual case that fits the "textbook" description of a diagnostic category. This happens because textbooks perforce are more or less limited to describing diseases or syndromes and not individuals. The individual, as we have said, is unique, and only partially does his behavior accommodate itself to the schematic abstract from many people's behavior that is implied by any diagnostic term. Wherever, in the book, we talk about disease, as "schizophrenia," "reactive depression," "constitutional psychopathic state," and so forth, it should be remembered always that no one person ever exactly corresponds to the description, and that it is a summary of similarities that have been observed sufficiently often to justify their inclusion under a rough general label.

In rebuttal to such statements, it has often been said that one of the aims of science is classification and that classification unavoidably involves types. No one would argue against the proposition; what is not included in the objection, however, is the qualification that classification is only a subsidiary to the principal task of science, which is to describe the dynamic processes needing study. Classifications in science are not fixed and immutable. As effective description advances, classifications change. Whales were classed with fishes until adequate dissection showed them to have an anatomy and physiology similar to other mammals. Even such seemingly undisputable type-systems as "living-nonliving" have no real permanency. The discovery of the filterable virus, which may exist in an essentially crystalline state, but which reproduces and metabolizes, has shaken the boundary lines of the dichotomy.

There is, then, no essential evil in types, but also nothing sacred. When the type concept is utilized in the manner of Sheldon, with a recognition that nature is continuously variable, it can be productive and a stimulus to effective research. When it is used as a comprehensive system to fence the infinite variety of nature into a small, finite number of mutually exclusive categories, it can be a source of error and false thinking.

Sex Differences in Mental Disorders

One constitutional factor that has a firmly established genetic basis is that of sex. The structural differences characterizing the two sexes are a function of specific chromosomes, and sexual differentiation is completely developed during embryonic life.

Although frequent sex differences in behavior are matters of common observation, the question of their origin is far from clear. It was thought at one time that the sexes were as clearly differentiated in their behavior as in their structure, and most authorities were inclined to explain such differences as due to a fundamental genetic disparity between them. As psychological research on the topic accumulated there was a noticeable trend toward discounting sex differences and attributing the differences in their behavior to the different social environment that surrounds men and women. This is still a basic research problem, and in most areas of behavior the constitutional and social factors are interwoven in a way that makes assessment of the proportionate part played by each very difficult.

Men tend to excel women in skills that demand strength or a combination of strength and coordination. Height and weight differences favor men. Women, on the other hand, show reliably greater ability to resist disease and have a greater longevity than do men. For the United States, in 1950, the life expectancy for male infants was 67 years, as compared with 72 for female infants. At almost every age of life women show greater resistance to physiological stress than do men. Scheinfeld (1949), in a popular book on sex differences, has advanced a series of statistical findings that cast considerable doubt on the old sayings and beliefs about the "weaker sex" being the female.

With respect to the relative incidence of mental disease among the sexes, women again make a more favorable showing. Dayton (1940), in a comprehensive statistical study of the population of Massachusetts mental hospitals between 1917 and 1933, reported that there were 6

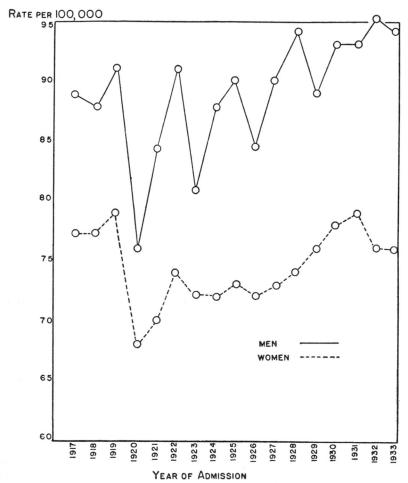

FIGURE 21. *First admissions "with mental disorder" to Massachusetts mental hospitals, 1917-1933 by year and sex* (from Neil A. Dayton [1940], *New Facts on Mental Disorder, Study of 89,190 Cases.* Courtesy, Charles C. Thomas, Publisher, Springfield, Illinois).

males with mental disorder to every 5 females, and furthermore, that the admission rate for females had shown a decline during this period, whereas the male admission rate had increased. Figures 21 and 22 illustrate the trends.

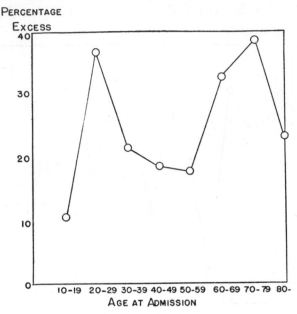

FIGURE 22. *Percentage excess of male admission rate over that of female, in each age group. First admissions "with mental disorder," 1917-1933* (from Neil A. Dayton [1940], *New Facts on Mental Disorder, Study of 89,190 Cases.* Courtesy, Charles C. Thomas, Publisher, Springfield, Illinois).

One of the largest statistical studies of the problem of mental disease was done by Landis and Page (1938). From a consideration of all available statistical evidence on admission rates, recovery rates, and mortality rates for mental diseases, they conclude:

At all ages the incidence of first-admissions is higher among the male than female population. This sex difference may be due in part to the greater home care extended to women patients and in part to the greater resistance which women show to all forms of disease.[8]

[8] C. Landis and J. D. Page (1938), *Modern Society and Mental Disease*, p. 42. New York: Rinehart and Company, Inc.

More recent data confirm these studies. Table 19 shows the number

TABLE 19

NUMBER OF ADMISSIONS PER 100,000 POPULATION BY ADMISSION GROUP AND SEX:
STATE HOSPITALS, UNITED STATES, 1949*

Admission Groups	Number per 100,000	
	Males	*Females*
All admissions.................................	107.27	89.34
First admissions..............................	76.97	61.71
Psychoses..................................	55.73	50.51
Psychoneuroses............................	2.21	3.25
"Without psychoses"......................	14.26	4.22
Other.......................................	4.89	3.73
Readmissions.	23.75	22.39

* Source: Based on data from Federal Security Agency (1952), *Patients in Mental Hospitals, 1949*. Washington, D. C.: United States Government Printing Office.

of admissions per 100,000 population to state hospitals in 1949. With the single exception of the psychoneuroses, the frequency of male admissions is greater than that for females. Also, male readmissions exceeded readmissions of women. In evaluating this latter comparison, however, it must be noted that slightly more men (25 per cent) than women (23 per cent) were discharged in 1949.

We will consider the social factors that might lead to sex differences in admission rates for mental disease in Chapter XV. These factors undoubtedly play a large part in a society such as ours, where such great differences in attitudes and standards exist for the two sexes. Of fundamental determinative importance, however, are the real constitutional differences that have been shown to exist and which play a part in determining further social distinctions.

Individuality as a Constitutional Factor in Personality

We have remarked several times that the human individual is unique. By this we have meant that each person has characteristics that make him different from any other person who ever existed. The common saying that "no two people are alike" is receiving more and more scientific confirmation. One of the implications of "field theory," for example, is that no two organizations will be precisely alike, and that the laws of science are laws of the dynamics of organization and not laws of the similarity of the organizations themselves. Statistical studies show that definite categories do not exist in nature, but that they are created by the limitations of our measuring instruments. This concept is expressed in the physicist's adoption of statistical techniques in his investigation of energy quanta and is equally obvious in the psychologist's measurements of intelligence. When many factors operate together to produce a result, as in the living organism, it is not surprising that individuality amounts to uniqueness.

CELLULAR BASIS OF INDIVIDUALITY

Of great potential significance for the psychopathologist are the studies of individuality at the lower biological levels of cellular functioning. Many of these investigations have been summarized by Leo Loeb (1945). In defining individuality, he makes a distinction between a *mosaic* and a *general* component. The individual is a mosaic of different tissues and organs, each of which has its own function, but exists interdependently with all other tissues and organs of which the body is composed. Current methods in genetics concentrate on studying the particular organs and their genetic determiners as an approach to the study of individuality. But there is another component, consisting of properties that are common to all parts of the organism and that differentiate not only between species but between individuals. "There is inherent in every higher individual organism something which differentiates him from every other individual, which can be discovered by observing the reactions of certain cells and tissues belonging to one individual toward the tissues and cells of another individual of the same species."[9] ". . . there is also a substance in the body fluids of one individual which responds toward all the cells and tissues of another individual in accordance with the degree of the genetic difference between these two individuals."[10] This characteristic Loeb names the *individuality differential*. There are also similar characteristics common to all members of species, genus, order, and class; all of these are termed *organismal differentials*. There are two principal ways of studying these differentials: by transplantation and by serological methods. The basic experiment is described by Loeb as follows:

[9] From Leo Loeb (1945), *The Biological Basis of Individuality*, p. 4. Courtesy, Charles C. Thomas, Publisher, Springfield, Illinois.
[10] *Ibid.*, p. 5.

Various organs or tissues are transplanted from one animal, *e.g.*, a guinea pig, into two other guinea pigs not directly related to the first guinea pig from which the tissues were taken. . . . It is seen that the reactions of the hosts of the multiple grafts toward the latter differ in accordance with the degree of genetic relationship between host and donor, but the host behaves in approximately the same way toward the various tissues from the same donor. In one animal the reactions are severe to all the tissues, in the other one they may be very light. These reactions consist in the activity of the lymphocyte, the connective tissue cells and blood vessels of the host towards the grafts; in addition, tissues, especially the more sensitive ones, are also influenced by the degree of their compatibility with certain constituents of the blood of the host, and the degree of this sensitiveness again depends upon the genetic relationship between host and transplant. In general, tissues are injured by the body fluids of a strange host. . . . However, in all the species which we have studied so far it is the *lymphocytes* which sense or recognize the finest degrees of similarity or difference in the constitution of the individuality differentials between host and transplant . . . the genetic relationship between host and transplant determines the intensity of the reaction of the host against the individuality differentials of the transplant.[11]

Much evidence for the above general statement has been collected. (There are 711 pages in Loeb's book, with references to 920 papers, and the author explains that the bibliography is incomplete!) By the reaction of host to transplant the uniqueness of the physiological and chemical substrata to behavior is securely established.

It is beyond the scope of this book to review completely the studies of individuality on the psychological level, but the general trend of such research confirms, in a coarse way, the discoveries made by Loeb. For example, Gesell, in his analysis of "growth careers" of infants, came to the conclusion that the strength of a behavior trait in the first year of life was quite closely predictive of its strength in the fifth year (Gesell, 1946, pages 324-325), and that individual differences in behavior traits at birth were marked. In a study of thirty infants, followed by repeated observation over a period of ten years and more, consistency of individual differences was noted in all but one case.

One large area of individual differences is of direct concern, namely, the capacity to withstand stress. As we saw in Chapter II, this characteristic of the organism is probably critical in determining the overt expression of maladaptive behavior. Gesell observed that the course of individual differences was least easily predicted when the organism

[11] *Ibid.*, p. 6.

was subjected to unfavorable conditions. This was true, he thought, because of the "internal developmental reserves." Whenever the normal processes of the organism are interfered with, the organism attempts to carry on by regeneration, compensation, or substitution.

These reserve factors . . . are not a single generalized capacity. They are specific biochemical and somatic structures almost infinite in number and variety, and of many degrees of availability. They are present in defective as well as normal individuals. They are probably most abundant in the most vital and best endowed. Vitality is an index of the plenitude and vigor of these very insurance factors. In spheres of behavior they operate not only during the period of growth, but also in old age, at least in the most "vital" individuals.[12]

Although it is probably true, as Gesell says, that the ability to resist stress is dependent to some degree upon constitutional factors, it should not be forgotten that in the course of life experiences many techniques are acquired for dealing with stressful situations.

INDIVIDUAL DIFFERENCES IN RESISTANCE TO STRESS

A convenient way of summarizing the relationship between stress and the constitutional factors in psychopathology is the formula cited by Bauer (1945, page 16):

$$D = I/R$$

in which D stands for disease (for us, particularly disturbance of psychological functions), I represents "injury" or environmental stress (actually, the psychological stress for that organism for that particular time and situation), and R represents the individual's resistance to stress. If this formula holds, it may be said that the greater the stress the less important the individual's ability to resist.

As an example, we may refer to the experience among British soldiers at the evacuation of Dunkirk; a remarkably high percentage of the troops finally taken off were in such a state of exhaustion and fatigue that they showed many of the symptoms of pathological behavior.

[12] Arnold Gesell (1946), "The ontogenesis of infant behavior," reprinted by permission from *Manual of Child Psychology*, p. 328, by L. Carmichael. Published by John Wiley & Sons, Inc.

Thinness of faces, pallor or sallowness of complexion and loss of weight are the commonest physical aspects. They had lacked not only sleep for a number of days, but food, which had been scanty in many cases for a week or more, and they had marched long distances. Mentally some were tense and others apathetic. Those who were tense were apt to talk very readily about their experiences. Sleeplessness and terrifying dreams of battle experiences were common; the former were usually easily countered by hypnotics, and normal habits of sleep were soon resumed in most cases. Sargent and Slater described cases of irregular tremor of the hands, and in one case a pill-rolling tremor, which, however, was not controllable by voluntary movements. They noted also occasional true nystagmus, and one case of hysterical twilight sleep with disorientation and subsequent amnesia.[13]

However as the stress becomes less, the constitutional factors of resistance to stress become more and more significant. In the actual occurrence of mental disease under the usual conditions of environment, the R-factor probably represents the basis of incidence. Bauer believes this principle to apply to all forms of disease:

This resistance is inversely proportional to what we call the individual predisposition. This predisposition is not a simple entity but the product of various structural and functional components of the individual, both constitutional and environmental in nature. They determine whether or not a disease may result from the action of an insignificant and slowly acting injurious agent, and they also account for the individual differences in the clinical picture and course of such a disease.[14]

A basic assumption behind the psychiatric program of the Army during World War II was that men differed in their capacity to withstand psychological stress, and accordingly that men whose tolerance was low should be kept out of service. Various types of examinations and tests were devised to eliminate those individuals who had already shown signs of instability and those whose thresholds were low. It is well known that in spite of all efforts in this direction, the rate of psychiatric disorder remained at a high level throughout the war. An immediate conclusion was that the tests were not completely effective

[13] Reprinted from *Psychological Effects of War on Citizen and Soldier,* p. 193, by R. D. Gillespie, by permission of W. W. Norton & Company, Inc. Copyright 1942 by the publishers.
[14] Julius Bauer (1945), *Constitution and Disease* (2nd Ed.), p. 16. New York: Grune and Stratton, Inc.

screening devices, and most of the evidence bore that out. However, studies by Fry (1951) and by Wells and Woods (1946) have indicated that resistance to stress is not a single capacity, but is, as Gesell has suggested, a manifold of factors.

Fry, as Chief Psychiatrist of the Student Health Service at Yale University, made a follow-up study of several hundred former Yale students who had entered the military services at some time during the war. Among these young men there were a considerable number who had been given psychiatric examinations and treatment for psychoneurotic conditions during their college careers. They had passed military medical screening by concealing the psychiatric aspects of their past history or had been inducted by accidental oversight on the part of their draft boards and ineffective psychiatric processing on the part of the Army. On the basis of the current ideas concerning the tolerance of men to stress, these individuals should have been among the first to break down. A careful check of their records in service showed Fry, however, that a large proportion of them not only did not break, but also achieved many forms of special recognition for excellence of their performance. The study by Wells and Woods showed confirmatory results. Such studies do not show, of course, that a previous psychoneurosis in itself is a good recommendation for military service. Army records showed far more cases of individuals with a past history of mental illness who *did* break down. What such studies do show is that there are many unknown variables in this particular capacity, and that its analysis is one of the major problems of psychopathology.

Spiegel (1944), after a tour of duty as a battalion medical officer in the North African campaigns, reported on psychiatric problems among combat troops. In discussing the factors that led soldiers to break he referred to the stresses of exhaustion, fatigue, and fear, and to the histories of previous breakdowns in civilian life, and then went on to say:

Another component, more interesting, yet not quite so clear, was something which for discussion purposes might be referred to as the X-factor. It was something that corresponds to whatever courage is; something which, when present, indicated good morale. . . . It seemed to explain why a tired, uninspired, disgusted soldier had the clinical appearance of an anxiety state. It seemed to explain why some units could outdo others; it seemed to aid in controlling the ever present fear; and it seemed to aid in resisting fatigue. . . . Here was a critical, vulnerable and, to be precise, an influenceable component which often decided whether or not a man would be overwhelmed by his fear, anxiety, or fatigue. Here was a factor which often decided whether or not a man became a psychiatric casualty.[15]

Spiegel infers that the X-factor was a function of the emotional interrelationships of the social group, and he emphasized its susceptibility to good or poor leadership, to bad news, to rumor, and so forth. Whatever the X-factor may be, the laboratory of war confirms the observations from other sources that individual differences in resistance to stress do exist, and that they possibly stem from biological sources as yet undescribed and unidentified.

Liddell (1936) and Maier (1939) have both shown that there are wide individual differences in the incidence of "experimental neurosis" in animals and thus presumably some difference in animals' ability to withstand the stresses produced in the experimental situation. Further experiments utilizing selective breeding are necessary to answer the question completely.

That the final outcome in stressful situations is determined by a multiplicity of factors should by now be clear. When a number of individuals are subjected to the same environmental stresses, the order in which they succumb may depend on the operation of variables which are not usually of major importance in themselves.

Case 51. An excellent illustration is found in the story of Captain Robert Scott's gallant trip to the South Pole. It will be remembered that Scott, with four companions, walked approximately a thousand miles through difficult terrain and in severe Antarctic weather. They reached the Pole but died of starvation and exhaustion when only a short distance from a relief depot on their return journey. All the party were exposed to a number of identical stressing agents. The intense cold, the vitamin deficiencies induced by their inadequate diet, the frequent emotional stresses induced by their misadventures in climbing the difficult Beardmore glacier, the daily fatigue from hauling their heavy sled—all these factors were impartially distributed. Yet there was an immense range in the capacity of these five men. Chief Petty Officer Evans, the largest and strongest man of the group, was the first to die and did so long before the others. The last to die was Captain Scott, who found strength enough to write several pages of letters and detailed directions for the future conduct of the expedition. The journal of this trip is excellent source material for the study of behavior under stress. There were many contributory reasons for the

[15] Herbert X. Spiegel (1944), "Psychiatric observations of the Tunisian Campaign." *Amer. J. Orthopsychiat., 14,* 383.

differences in vitality shown by the party, but the one that stands out was the difference in *motivation* among the men. Evans had no interest in the results or purpose of the expedition, other than a desire to do his duty acceptably. The expedition was a mission of the British Navy, and to Evans it was an assignment and nothing else. Much of the same was true of Captain Oates, an army officer who had been assigned as an expert in horses to supervise the care of ponies that were used in several phases of the exploration. Oates was the second person to collapse; he deliberately walked out of the tent into a raging blizzard, choosing that method of death in order not to delay his surviving companions. The next to die was Lt. Bowers, a navy officer, the youngest and most active man of the party. Bowers had become genuinely interested in the scientific aspects of the expedition and had shown himself a consistently valuable asset; however, basically he was not vitally concerned with the success or failure of the project. Dr. Wilson, the fourth person to die, was the scientific leader and second in command of the entire expedition. He was the oldest of the Polar party and had spent much of his past life as a semi-invalid. Yet his motivation was extremely strong. He was in the Antarctic by choice and felt a deep sense of responsibility for the successful conduct of the scientific work. Captain Scott, as we said, was the last to die; he survived the others long enough to write several entries in his journals and the reports and letters necessary for the welfare of the expedition as a whole. Scott's state of motivation was very high. He had the responsibility of being in command of the largest scientific expedition that the British had ever sent to the Antarctic; he felt attainment of the South Pole was necessary in order to stimulate the public sufficiently to guarantee future work; he had a personal ambition to reach the Pole due to a previous failure on his part a few years before. All these factors combined to impart to Scott a greater resistance to collapse.

One other aspect of resistance to stress should be mentioned. The various organs of the body, as Loeb showed, have individuality; this individuality extends to their particular degree of resistance to stress. An old concept in medicine was the idea of *loci minoris resistentiae,* or point of least resistance. It had been noted that individuals tend to have multiple difficulties centering around a particular organ system. Thus, a person with the lungs as his weak point might be subject to colds, bronchitis, and other respiratory disorders, and end with tuberculosis or cancer of the lung (or possibly both). Bauer and Aschner carried out an extensive study on the families of 255 cases of peptic ulcer and contrasted the presence of digestive disturbances in these families with those in the families of 400 patients suffering from a wide variety of conditions other than digestive. The results are presented in Table 20. All the differences are statistically significant. Bauer concludes:

TABLE 20

THE RELATIVE INCIDENCE OF DIGESTIVE TRACT DISEASE IN THE FAMILIES OF
PEPTIC ULCER PATIENTS AND PATIENTS HOSPITALIZED FOR OTHER AILMENTS*

	In the family are to be encountered			
	Peptic ulcer	*Carcinoma of the stomach*	*Carcinoma of the digestive tract*	*All chronic stomach disease*
	Percentages			
255 cases of peptic ulcer...	17.25 ± 6.69	13.73 ± 6.1	17.25 ± 6.69	53.33 ± 8.84
400 cases of various diseases other than affections of the digestive tract......	3.5 ± 2.6	3.5 ± 2.6	4.75 ± 3.01	15.25 ± 5.08

* Source: Julius Bauer (1945), *Constitution and Disease* (2nd Ed.), p. 49. New York: Grune and Stratton, Inc.

What is it then that is transmitted through the germ plasm and accounts for the evident predisposition to peptic ulcer, cancer, and various other disorders of the stomach? It can be nothing but a constitutional biologic inferiority of the stomach bearing upon its structure, quality, and reactivity.[16]

Data similarly could be presented for each of the other organ systems of the body. Many of these defects can be shown to have a definite genetic determination. Since the nervous system is no exception to this, we might expect that many of the constitutional factors we have discussed would have a bearing upon specific life situations in which the individual is attempting to adjust in the face of stress. Accordingly, in the evaluation of any patient of any abnormality of behavior it is of great importance to consider the constitutional makeup of the person in conjunction with the many environmental factors that are usually given a leading role in the production of mental disease.

The Psychopathic Personality

Before closing this chapter we turn to a consideration of one of the unanswered questions in the psychopathology of personality, a type of behavior disorder that has been variously termed "constitutional psycho-

[16] Julius Bauer (1945), *Constitution and Disease* (2nd Ed.), p. 49. New York: Grune and Stratton, Inc.

pathic inferiority," "constitutional psychopathic state," and preferably, *psychopathic personality* or merely *psychopath*. As the earlier "constitutional" labels imply, this condition may be apparent from such an early age in the life of the individual as to lead one to believe that he was "born that way," although other factors in the situation cast some doubt on that thesis.

We describe him here because of a compelling suggestion gathered from case histories of the psychopathic personality, a suggestion that the condition begins very early in life, is not basically hereditary, but is so much a part of the complete behavior of the person as to suggest a basis in constitution (as we have previously defined it).

The psychopath is a person who, showing none of the characteristics of the psychotic or psychoneurotic person, nevertheless appears incapable of making an adjustment to society. Legally regarded as sane and responsible for his actions, he shows, over a long period of time, that he is unable to avoid social failure. Furthermore, the psychopath is seldom of deficient intelligence and may be, as judged from intelligence tests, unusually well endowed. In spite of his intelligence he does not appear capable of profiting by experience or of altering his behavior when it meets with punishment and disgrace.

One of the best descriptions of the psychopath to be found in psychiatric literature is given by Cleckley (1941), who sketches twenty-one points of his clinical profile.

1. He is usually a very attractive person superficially, alert, clever, and with a psychometric test intelligence which does not show deterioration with the years.

2. He shows none of the symptoms of irrationality of the psychotic nor few of the symptoms of psychoneurosis.

3. He shows no sense of responsibility to other people. "No matter how binding the obligation, how urgent the circumstances, or how important the matter, this holds good. Furthermore, the question of whether or not he is to be confronted with his failure or his disloyalty and called to account for it appears to have no effect at all on his attitude" (page 239).

4. He has a disregard for the truth that covers his accounts of the past and his promises for the future. "One gets the impression that he is incapable of ever attaining the slightest comprehension of an attitude in other people which causes them to value truth and cherish truthfulness in themselves" (page 239). In spite of this, he uses the phrases related to truthfulness but regards them as techniques for gaining his own immediate goals.

5. He never accepts blame for his condition or for the troubles he

causes himself or others. He may use the forms of apology, but with the same insincerity as he employs phrases about truthfulness and honor.

6. He shows no sense of shame. The average psychopath in the course of his life has been involved in difficulties without number, yet without any evidence of regret.

7. He shows a propensity for cheating and committing crimes which is difficult to explain on any basis of the hope for gain that could be accepted as reasonable in a thief. "He will commit theft, fraud, and other deeds for astonishingly small takes and under much greater risks of being discovered than will the ordinary scoundrel. He will, in fact, commit such deeds in the absence of any apparent goal at all" (page 240).

8. He shows a poverty of judgment in the conduct of his affairs which is singularly at variance with his formal intelligence test score.

9. He is apparently unable to learn or profit by experience. "Few more impressive examples of this could be offered from the records of humanity than the familiar one of the psychopath, in full possession of his rational faculties, who has gone through the most indescribably distasteful confinement of many months with delusional and disturbed psychotic patients and after fretting and counting the days until the time of his release, proceeds at once to get drunk and create disorder which he thoroughly understands will cause him to be returned without delay to the detested wards" (page 240).

10. The psychopath is egocentric in a highly exaggerated way. In Cleckley's words, he shows little if any capacity for "object-love" as opposed to "self-love." "His absolute indifference to the hardships, financial, social, emotional, physical, and others, which he brings upon those for whom he professes love confirms one's intuitive appraisal of his true attitude during analytical studies" (page 242).

11. There is a general poverty of affect. Although he goes through the pantomime of emotion, the rapidity with which he changes and the evident shallowness of the expression militate against ascribing to him genuine affective experiences. "Vexation, spite, quick and labile flashes of quasi-affection, peevish resentment, shallow moods of self-pity, puerile attitudes of vanity, absurd and showy poses of indignation are all within his emotional scale and are freely sounded as the circumstances of life play upon him. But mature, wholehearted anger, true or consistent indignation, honest, solid grief, sustaining pride, deep joy, despair are never found within this scale" (page 243).

12. The psychopath lacks insight for the way his behavior affects others. "The patient seems to have little or no ability to feel the significance of his situation, to experience the real emotions of regret or shame, or determination to improve" (page 246). This lack of insight is the more puzzling since the psychopath has the intelligence, the freedom from emotional turmoil, the absence of delusions and hallucinations which are the usual criteria for the existence of insight.

13. The psychopath does not show the usual type of responsiveness to

kindness or consideration from others. His history will be full of examples of this type of reaction. The majority of "hitchhike murders," where a kindly motorist is rewarded by being killed, are probably the work of psychopaths. Although the psychopath seems to attract an unusual number of benefactors, their attentions are seldom recognized in any other manner than the exploitative.

14. The psychopath shows a peculiar pattern of dependence on alcohol. Cleckley has shown that the psychopath does not use alcohol in a way similar to that of the psychoneurotic alcoholic who drinks as a means of feeling more comfortable or adequate. Rather, the psychopath shows the double characteristic of being sensitive to alcohol and of seemingly drinking for no other purpose than becoming unconscious. Cleckley's case-reports consistently show their subjects going off on solitary drinking bouts in which they may lie in muddy fields or in a car parked on a country road for days, dousing each reviving flicker of consciousness with more whiskey. Further, they may show extremely bizarre behavior following minimal amounts of alcohol. One of our cases attempted to drive a stolen ambulance into his ward, and would have succeeded if the doors had been a little larger. Another case, after three drinks, made such violent advances to a barmaid that he was thrown from the establishment, only to go around to the back entrance and attempt to kindle a fire in the kitchen. One of Cleckley's cases broke into a library and urinated from the window on people walking in the street below.

15. The psychopath's drinking exploits seem to be motivated by a need for disgrace, if the motive may be judged by the results. "He often seems to be striving, beyond these fantastic preliminary activities, for a state of stupefaction or semi-stupefaction. This state, one sometimes feels, is dearer to him than wealth, fame or the love of woman" (page 252).

16. In spite of the drive towards unconsciousness hinted at above there is a surprising lack of motivation towards suicide, even in situations where the ordinary mortal might well consider this solution to his difficulties.

17. For a person who shows as promiscuous a sexual life as the psychopath there is an extremely casual attitude towards sex. "None of the psychopaths personally observed have impressed the writer as having particularly strong sex-cravings . . . indeed they have nearly all seemed definitely less moved to obtain genital pleasure than the ordinary run of people. One gets the impression that their amativeness is little more than a simple itch and that even the itch is seldom, if ever, intense" (page 253). Their promiscuity seems more a function of their general lack of the inhibitions most people find controlling their social behavior.

18. So many psychopaths come from normal and even superior families that heredity can probably be discounted as a factor in the etiology of this disorder.

19. Because the condition is capable of many intensities of manifestation, and because many psychopaths are able, by one means or another, to show some type of social accomplishment (Cleckley reports cases who have com-

pleted medical school, been "successful" businessmen, obtained the training and secured positions as college professors, etc.), the contention that the condition is completely active and present from birth is doubtful.

20. The psychopath is unable to establish and work towards long-term goals, either good or evil. His behavior appears motivated by short-term incentives, which may be contradictory from day to day or in conflict at any given time. His impulsiveness and immediate attempt to gratify his wishes at whatever the long-range cost is illustrative.

21. Finally, the psychopath "seems to go out of his way to make a failure of life. Almost consistently he cuts short, by some incomprehensible and untempting piece of folly or buffoonery, any activity in which he is succeeding, no matter whether it is crime or honest endeavor. Nor, in well-marked cases, is it possible for wealthy and influential and devoted relatives to place him in any position, however ingeniously it may be chosen, where he will not succeed in failing with spectacular and bizarre splendor. Considering a longitudinal section of his life, one gets such an impression of gratuitous folly and nonsensical activity in such massive accumulation that it is hard to avoid the conclusion that here is true madness—madness in a sense quite as vivid as that conveyed to the imaginative bystander by the terrible word *lunatic*. When one further considers that all this skein of apparent madness has been woven by a person of unimpaired and superior intellectual powers and universally regarded as sane, the surmise intrudes that some unconscious purpose to fail has been active, some unrecognized drive at social and spiritual self-destruction" (page 255).[17]

The following case study shows some of the points in this clinical profile:

Case 52. Pvt. Richard C. was transferred to psychiatry from a general medical ward where he had been under observation for "dermal ulcerations" over a period of two months. His transfer was prompted by a strong suspicion on the part of his medical ward officer that the ulcerative craters in his arms and legs were either produced or helped along by the patient's own efforts although all attempts to prove the suspicion had been unsuccessful. It was thought that the closer twenty-four-hour supervision afforded by the psychiatric ward would facilitate a test of the officer's hypothesis. On arrival at the closed ward Dick, in his wheelchair, presented a striking appearance. Built on somewhat the lines of Clark Gable, he had prematurely silvered hair, a gentle and serene expression, and had managed to contribute an exotic touch to his army-issue hospital attire by draping a white silk scarf around his neck. Although he knew that he was suspected of deliberate attempts at self-injury, he showed nothing of this knowledge in his manner. On initial interview he told his story in a frank and straight-

[17] Adapted from Hervey Cleckley, *The Mask of Sanity*. St. Louis: The C. V. Mosby Company, 1941.

forward manner, suitably demonstrating emotional expressions appropriate
to the various parts of his tale. His story, briefly, was as follows:

After a boyhood in a small town in Colorado, where he had attracted
attention as a singer in church choirs, he had been sent to an eastern musical conservatory by a wealthy benefactor and had been trained for operatic
work. He made his debut in Italy and for "three or four years" had sung
on the Continent and elsewhere. He had met a girl, also of the opera company, and they had married, leading on idyllic existence "as only two
artists very much in love could aspire to," until during a fateful week in
Vienna a sudden illness led to his wife's death. At this point, overcome by
emotion, he bowed his head and delicately touched his handkerchief to his
eyes. With every appearance of bravery, he mastered his emotions and
continued. He "had no heart for singing" after that and had returned to the
United States, where he decided to "throw himself into science." Accordingly, he matriculated at Iowa State University and specialized in electrical
engineering, graduating "in front of my class." He had planned on returning to Colorado to practice his profession when the draft caught him and
he had "oh, so gladly" entered the army to "do my little bit, and give my
all" for the war effort. After two months, which he claimed were the
"most enjoyable in my whole life," spent at a basic training camp, he had
been assigned to a mountain infantry regiment for further training. It was
then that he called the doctor's attention to the sores on his arms and legs,
and he was hospitalized. All efforts at treatment, with all the wonder drugs
at the army's disposal, had failed. It was at this point that the possibility
of the patient producing the lesions himself occurred to the ward officer.
Dick, when asked directly about this possibility, laughed gently and said
that we should be tolerant of the unfounded suspicions of the "young
man" who had been his physician. He felt that "the poor boy" was so
frustrated about Dick's case that he had become "hasty and emotional"
about it all, but Dick let us know that he bore the "poor boy" no hard
feelings.

Routine social service reports, the arrival of Dick's chart, and further
conversation with his former ward officer disclosed information considerably at variance with the story told by the patient. When he had first
arrived in the medical ward, he had created a very favorable impression. He
was cooperative, helped other patients, talked intelligently on a number of
topics to his doctor and nurses, and generally had become the "pet" of the
ward. He told essentially the same story that he told us, and the ward
officer, who was about to be married, managed to get the patient a leave
to accompany him to the town, several hundred miles away, where the
marriage was to take place, for the purpose of singing at the wedding. Dick
promptly sought out alcoholic refreshments and at the ceremony sang "Oh
Promise Me" in a manner more appropriate to "Sweet Adeline" at closing
time in a bar. The groom, an ardent amateur motion-picture fan, complained that, when the films of the wedding were developed, Dick seemed
to be the most prominent figure in every scene. This thespian hamminess
was the only characteristic of the entertainer that was ever objectively

verified. After the party's return to the hospital, relations between Dick and the ward officer stayed at a more suitable degree of professional distance, with the skin ulcers growing steadily worse. On ward rounds one evening, the Medical Emergency Officer was surprised to find Dick lying in bed roaring out, in a voice afterwards reported by the officer as exceptionally tuneless, various obscene camp ditties. Closer inspection showed that Dick's blood alcohol was elevated, and a search of his bed produced a small remnant of a fifth of whiskey. Since Dick had been in bed for a week, under constant observation of at least four other patients, the question of his liquor source was investigated, but with no tangible results until Dick manfully confessed that he had persuaded the night nurse to buy it for him, thus placing the nurse in a military-legal situation of some seriousness. She was tried by a court-martial, and Dick appeared, handsome and looking every inch a soldier, to testify against her. As he said to the court, no sense of gratitude or loyalty to the nurse would keep him from telling "the Truth," which he did with such good effect that the nurse was permitted to resign her commission for the good of the service.

It was at this point that Dick was transferred to the psychiatric section. Social service returns meanwhile had begun to filter in, and when compiled they showed a story so different from Dick's as to excite a certain awed incredulity in the staff. Dick had, as he said, been born in a small town in Colorado, and he had, as he said, sung in a choir; these were the only two points of agreement, and the latter point was susceptible of differing interpretations, since his singing in the church choir had lasted precisely two Sundays, due to an unfortunate alcoholic enthusiasm for carrying the melody. He was the fourth child in a large family. His parents were respectable people of slightly above marginal economic status. The other children had been unqualified successes in various undertakings. Two of them had completed college, one becoming a newspaperman, the other going on to professional training in dentistry. The other sibling, a sister, had completed high school and had married a steady young farmer in the vicinity. Dick had managed to play truant enough in grade school to convince his father that high school would be a waste of time, and after completing the freshman year, Dick had been allowed to withdraw and go to work. He had held a number of menial jobs around town, had followed several harvests, apparently earning his living from gambling but certainly never from working in the fields. The longest period he had held a job was for eleven months when he was a minor clerk in the local grain elevator. He was fired from this job for pilfering petty cash and stamps. His weakness for drink had given him a long record with the police, but no offence more serious than disturbing the peace was entered against him until the year before his entrance into the army, when he began to show more expansiveness in his psychopathy. He had appeared at three Denver banks, dressed in the manner of a wealthy cattleman, and made identical applications for loans to buy stock for a ranch he claimed he had bought. His talk was so convincing that all three banks sent men to the supposed site of the ranch to investigate, thus crippling Dick's plan. With the lack of foresight usual to psychopaths, he had imagined that the money would be paid over at once. His final brush with the law had occurred over a seeming reluctance to visit the army induction center when his appointment required. He had, as a matter of fact, been escorted to the rendezvous by the police, who appeared to have an understandable eagerness to help him leave town.

When the patient was confronted with this material, he showed no evidence of being disturbed nor did he indicate any willingness to change his own story. When questioning showed that he had no knowledge of either opera or electrical engineering above that of any person who had attended a Grace Moore movie or read *Tom Swift and His Electrical Laboratory,* he became irritated and claimed that he was being "persecuted" and wouldn't discuss the matter further unless he could "talk to his lawyer." He was eventually discharged from the army, and when last seen was being driven off in a car by a young woman who worked in one of the restaurants on the post.

It should be evident from the review of symptoms and from the case study just presented that psychopaths are not infrequent in our population. As a psychiatric classification, "constitutional psychopathic state" has been such a waste-basket term, used to label all types of queer or anti-social behavior, that most statistics on the incidence of this condition mean little (see Preu, 1944). However, if the term *psychopathic personality* is used to refer to the particular sort of person we have been describing, the diagnosis can be made with more precision. Cleckley, who has most definitively studied psychopaths, gives us some statistics from his own experience that may indicate something of their frequency. In the hospital where he did his research, of 857 patients who were admitted and presented in staff conference, 266 of them fit his classificatory criteria. If this incidence is typical of the country at large, then there must be a vast number of psychopaths among us. Army experience tends to bear out this impression, as do the daily newspaper reports of criminal and anti-social activities.

The question of etiology is not clear. Cleckley argued convincingly that the psychopath should be considered as psychotic, with his disorder being the consequence of a "semantic dementia," the individual failing to learn the emotional implications of language. He is a person whose appreciation of the meaning of "honesty," "beauty," "love," "trust," and other words that express abstract relationships with an emotional aspect is limited to what might be called the "dictionary" definitions of the terms. Because, through some reason or reasons, he does not learn the appropriate emotional reactions to such words, he can only be baffled at other people who seem to find an affective value in them. But he observes that, when such words are used, people react to them in certain rather standardized ways. He learns that *"I promise to pay you back"* helps him to get money from others, that *"I am sorry"* helps him avoid punishment, and that *"I love you"* helps him attain sexual satisfactions. The words are as blind and meaningless a formula to him as are the words "red," "green," "yellow," and so forth to a person who has been totally blind from birth. Since our society is so definitely held together by emotional unities, by conventional agreement, as it were, concerning the emotional reactions given to conventional symbols, the psychopath is a stranger in a strange land. He never develops the majority of social motives, the "superego," because he is never able to develop the emotional reactions necessary for inhibitory training. This is essentially Cleckley's position, and it seems the most plausible statement of etiology, as far as it goes.

Is there any way to go further in explaining the psychopath? How does the semantic dementia arise? What is the source of this inability to deal with emotional abstractions? Although this is still a question for research, there is a little evidence. As we have seen already, organic defects of the brain may produce a variety of aphasias and other less specific alterations of personality, some of which bear at least a little resemblance to the behavior of the psychopath. The psychopath perseverates, is irritable, is impulsive and unpredictable, is affected easily by small amounts of alcohol, and, most important, shows deficiencies in his ability to perceive abstractions. Even more important as evidence is the finding of Jasper and his associates (1938) and other investigators that between 70 and 90 per cent of children with behavior problems, in the groups studied, had electroencephalographic abnormalities of some kind. Studies of adult patients diagnosed as psychopathic personalities have also shown a higher percentage of EEG abnormalities than would be expected in a normal population. We have also seen that epileptic equivalent states may take the form of behavior similar to that of the psychopath. Therefore, as a research possibility, it would seem that a tentative hypothesis could be offered that psychopathic personality is a combination of symptoms accompanying particular types of organic brain defect, possibly occurring either in fetal life or during early infancy in the majority of cases.

General Summary

The concept of "constitution" has a broad usefulness in psychopathology. As we have seen, it is an integration of hereditary and acquired characteristics that give the organism a physical and psychological individuality. Much of the predictability of behavior comes from a knowledge of the constitutional characteristics of the individual. Of particular interest to us is the possibility that all persons have thresholds of resistance to environmental stress of various kinds, and that resistance is fundamentally a constitutional variable. One difference between our concept of constitution and that of many other writers should be noted. We have suggested the possibility that constitution is an integration of *both* genetic and environmental factors. Consequently, the constitution of the individual is susceptible to change in its overt manifestations under various environmental conditions. However, the outcome of environmental stimulation depends to a great extent upon constitutional factors. Thus, individual differences in behavior are a function of constitution.

DISCUSSION QUESTIONS

1. Can you give alternative definitions of "constitution"?
2. Is there a relationship between body type and personality type?
3. How does Sheldon's approach differ from preceding investigators?
4. Can you outline an experimental program for the investigation of constitutional factors in psychopathology?
5. How important a factor is individuality in the behavior disorders?
6. Can you give further examples of individual differences in behavior under stress?
7. Have you seen or heard of other examples of psychopathic personalities?
8. When you say of a trait that "it runs in the family," are you making a statement about heredity or about constitution?
9. Is there any real difference between "personality" and "constitution" in the way we have used these terms?
10. If your parents and grandparents all died of cardiac disorders, should this make any difference in the way you would manage your own life?

SUGGESTED READINGS

H. Cleckley (1950), *The Mask of Sanity* (2nd Ed.). St. Louis: C. V. Mosby Company.

D. W. MacKinnon (1944), "The structure of personality," in J. McV. Hunt, ed. (1944), *Personality and the Behavior Disorders,* pp. 3-48. New York: The Ronald Press Company.

W. H. Sheldon (1944), "Constitutional factors in personality," in J. McV. Hunt, ed., *ibid.,* pp. 526-549.

BIBLIOGRAPHIC SOURCES

It is somewhat difficult to obtain general discussions of constitutional factors in psychopathology. Harris (1948) has a chapter similar to our own. Harrison (1950) is good, but hard to get. Snodgrasse (1951), in a long and brilliant article, reviews the literature on the relationship between constitution and crime. Most of the constitutional literature may be found described succulently in that paper. Winthrop (1947) has developed a detailed outline for a generalized constitutional theory.

The major contributions of Sheldon and his associates have been published in three large volumes. The first (Sheldon and Stevens, 1940), *Varieties of Human Physique,* contains the basic somatotypes. The second (Sheldon, Stevens, and Tucker, 1942), *Varieties of Temperament,* developed the basic temperament correlates. This work is summarized by Sheldon (1944) in the article from which we quoted in this chapter. In 1948, Wittman and Sheldon introduced a new classificatory scheme for the extreme behavior disorders consisting of three fundamental types: (1) affective exaggerations, (2) paranoid projection, and (3) heboid regression. Wittman, Sheldon, and Katz (1948) found high correlations between the somatotypes, temperament types, and these behavior classes. The third major work (Sheldon, Hartl, and McDermott, 1949), *Varieties of Delinquent Youth,* was an extension of this approach to the study of 200 young delinquents. As we noted in the text, few have attempted to validate experimentally Sheldon's work. Two studies that tend to support Sheldon are Seltzer (1946) and Seltzer, Wells, and McTerman (1948). The study of Bellak and Holt (1948) failed to distinguish two types of extreme behavior disorder on the basis of the somatotypes, but did show rather clear differences between these patients and normal controls. Another research issue has been the relationship between the somatotypes and temperament types and performance on psychological tests (Child and Sheldon, 1941). Smith's (1949) study showed some slender confirmation of a relationship. A serious criticism has been raised by Adcock (1948) and Lubin (1950) to the effect that some of the intercorrelations (like those in Table 18) are internally inconsistent.

Parenthetically, the measurement of somatotypes by Sheldon's technique is a rather involved matter. For a discussion of Sheldon's method and further independent work, see Tanner (1951).

Indicative of the resistance that has been built up by the long succession of negative results in relation to morphological correlation, several widely used textbooks in the field of abnormal psychology give little space to Sheldon's studies. Maslow and Mittleman (1951) mention his work in a footnote. Cameron (1947) does not consider it. Thorpe and Katz (1948) and Cameron and Magaret (1951) devote one page to the topic. An excellent psychiatric text, Masserman's, *Principles of Dynamic Psychiatry*, describes Sheldon's work briefly, and then criticizes it on three points, one of which is undoubtedly valid, the others of which appear grossly unfair. Whatever future experimental decision is made, Sheldon's work stands, at the present, as the first systematic and quantitative investigation of constitutional types.

For introductions to the general area of typological study, MacKinnon's chapter in Hunt (1944) relates the history of typology in personality. Sheldon's chapter, as mentioned, pertains to historical approaches to constitutional typology. As a further supplement, Ekman (1951) is excellent.

On the psychopathic personality, the standard source is Kahn's (1931) *Psychopathic Personalities*, which, however, tries to encompass all the types of behavior disorders. Our section has drawn heavily on Cleckley's (1941) *The Mask of Sanity*, which could serve as a literary model for all writers in psychopathology. A second edition appeared in 1950. Somewhat selective bibliographies may be found in Cleckley's book, Gurvitz (1951), Maughs (1941, 1949), and Preu (1944). Gurvitz (1951) gives a scholarly history of the development of the concept. There is a growing literature that tends to criticize strongly the concept of psychopathic personality as signifying a real entity. Examples, varying in degree of condemnation, are Cruvant and Yochelson (1950), Karpman (1948), and Thornton (1951). Excellent introductions to the problem of psychopathic behavior in children are three symposia conducted by Karpman (1950, 1951, 1952). The extent of relationship between EEG recordings and psychopathic personality is somewhat controversial; we suggest the papers by Gurvitz (1951), Maughs (1949), and especially Hill (1952). For case material on the psychopath, Cleckley's book is a splendid source; there are many others available in the literature. One rather interesting case report is that by Gilbert (1948), who had an opportunity to make psychological examinations of the more important Nazi war prisoners before and during the Nuremberg trials. More complete case discussions may be found in Gilbert (1947, 1950).

XIII

Maturational Factors in Psychopathology

A life cycle is a time-space phenomenon . . . The progressive organization of this vast concatenation of cells in time and space constitutes the most intricate of all cycles.

—A. GESELL

Definition of Maturation

The organism is a growing, changing organization. From the time of conception and the first cell-division, the organism is constantly expressing changing potentialities of behavior. It is responsive to changes in its environment and reflects many of those changes in its developing structural pattern. During the uterine stage of its existence, the mammalian individual, due to the constancy of its environment, shows little apparent divergence from a normal developmental schedule. As its structure grows and changes, its behavior also grows more complex. *Maturation* has been defined as the changes in behavior attributable to anatomical and physiological development of the organism and has frequently been sharply differentiated from *learning*, which is defined as environmental modification of behavior, as an adaptive reaction to stimulation. Such a distinction has become increasingly unsatisfactory as we have learned more about the factors of development. It was once thought that structural (and much of behavioral) growth was simply the unfolding of potentialities hidden inside the specific genes in the germ plasm of the individual. As investigators in experimental em-

429

bryology have become more familiar with the complexities of embryonic development, they have come to stress the interdependence of organism and milieu and have recognized that even simple cell-division is as dependent upon appropriate environmental conditions as it is upon genetic potentialities. When extrinsic factors interfere with the normal interdependence, abnormal structure and function is often the result. Gross deviation in fetal interdependence results in the formation of individuals whose structures are poorly formed, distorted or absent. Such development failures are termed "monsters." It is probable that many other alterations in fetal environment, although not as dramatic as the monsters, in the long run produce a structural basis for equally pathological behavior. Fortunately the great majority of monsters do not survive until birth, and hence we do not know what their behavioral possibilities might be. If the developmental anomaly is of such a nature that a relatively normal biological adjustment is still possible, there may be relatively little reflection of defect in behavior. The so-called "Siamese Twins," a result of incomplete separation of two individuals, may often live to maturity and in some recorded instances have made normal marital and other social adjustments.

Experimental Evidence

Experimental and observational studies of maturation are abundant in the literature of psychology. The purpose of such studies has been to describe the developmental schedule of behavior as a function of increasing chronological age and to separate the changes in behavior due to such growth from those contributed by the individual's opportunities to learn.

A representative experiment is that of Carmichael (1927) with developing amphibia. Using the eggs of frogs and salamanders, both of which hatch into a swimming aquatic form, Carmichael kept one group of developing embryos in an anesthetic solution that did not interfere with normal growth but did effectively limit their movements. Another group of animals was allowed to develop normally. After a period of growth the small tadpoles of the normal group developed adequate swimming behavior. The anesthetized group at this state of development were still immobilized and thus had no swimming practice. After a further period of anesthetization, the experimental group were allowed to recover by being placed in fresh water. It was observed that they swam almost immediately and as well as the control group, in spite of their lack of opportunity gradually to practice swimming movements. Carmichael concluded that swimming behavior appeared as a result of the growth or maturation of the physical and neural structures used in the performance and was not a learned response in those particular organisms.

A study with similar purpose was carried out by McGraw (1935). Using a pair of twin boys, an experimental program of systematic training was applied to one of the pair, the other being left to his own resources during the daily training periods. The experimental twin was given extensive practice in such motor skills as climbing, walking, and so forth. Observations indicated only slight advantages accrued to training given before the period when these types of behavior ordinarily make their appearance in the untutored individual. McGraw concluded:

"The extent to which exercise of an activity may alter the development of a particular behavior course in infancy is contingent upon the following conditions: (1) the neuro-structural level at which the activity is controlled; (2) the state of plasticity or fixity of the behavior course at the time increased exercise or use is introduced; (3) the state of fixity attained by the behavior pattern at the time the factor of special exercise is withdrawn; and (4) the phylogenetic origin and importance of the behavior pattern." [1]

Observations of the time of appearance of given structures and organs have been correlated with similar observations of the appearance of patterns of behavior. In every case, of course, the development of the structure is a limiting factor on the development of the behavior. Until legs are strong and neuromuscular control is established, the child cannot walk. If this physical development and integration is delayed, there will be consequent changes in the time of appearance of behavior patterns. Factors that produce delayed or changed rates of maturation are therefore of importance to psychopathology.

Maturational Defects

CLASSIFICATION

The types of physical and physiological defects that alter normal maturation in such a way as to produce pathological behavior are usually due to defects that are minor, in comparison with the teratological cases cited above. Their importance lies in the influence they have upon (1) rate of maturation, and (2) upon the possible upper

[1] M. B. McGraw (1935), *Growth: A Study of Johnny and Jimmy*. New York: Appleton-Century-Crofts, Inc.

limits of maturation for particular functions. A review of the types of development defect that strongly influence behavior shows that most of them involve the nervous system, either directly or indirectly. These defects act to distort the normal maturational schedule and to make the individual less efficient in the learning that accompanies maturation.

Although no attempt will be made to consider comprehensively all such defects that may exist, the following pages will illustrate several of the most common. A convenient partial classification of such conditions is as follows:

1. Congenital defects (syphilis, mongolian idiocy, micro- and hydrocephalus, etc.)
2. Birth injuries
3. Diseases of childhood
4. Endocrine disturbances

CONGENITAL DEFECTS

Congenital simply means a condition that is present before or at the time of birth. It is usually used to distinguish certain disorders from others that are hereditary or that are acquired later in life. Thus, Huntington's chorea was called a "hereditary disorder," and encephalitis usually is acquired at some time after birth and is not termed "congenital." Actually, of course, the distinction is more convenience than reality since many conditions may start before birth but not show their most serious manifestations until some time after birth.

CONGENITAL SYPHILIS

It is possible for a mother to infect her child with syphilis either before or during birth. There has been some controversy over the possibility of syphilis infecting the germ plasm, and thus causing the disease to appear in subsequent generations, *i.e.*, to become hereditable. The possibility that syphilis in the parent might injure the germ plasm has afforded some comfort to moralists who have seen a verification of the Biblical threat of sin being "visited even unto the fourth generation." As recently as 1934, Sherbon stated:

> The toxins of syphilis in the blood of an infected mother or father may actually injure parts of the germ cells before or after fertilization, and the child which develops from such an ovum will be a defective child, but may not have an active infection; or he may be both defective and diseased.

. . . In rare cases it is possible that the sex chomosomes of the fertilized injured ovum may also be injured, and defects accordingly may appear in the "third and fourth generation." [2]

There has never been acceptable verification of this belief. Actually, congenital syphilis is a contact infection, and the spirochete that causes the disease must pass from the mother to the child through contact; in other words, the mother must have syphilis in an infectious form at the time she is bearing the child, or the child will not have congenital syphilis.

Congenital syphilis affects a child in various ways. Like the acquired syphilis of later years, it attacks almost any organ system. Skin eruptions, involvement of mucous surfaces of nose and throat, maldevelopment of bones, liver, heart ailments, and nutritional disturbances may all be found. A frequently found diagnostic sign is a moon or crescent shaped notching of the second or permanent teeth, particularly the central incisors. This sign is termed "Hutchinson's teeth." The effects of congenital syphilis may not be manifest in general behavior until some later time in the child's life. The chief behavioral defect is feeblemindedness (Young and Pilts, 1951). Various investigators have found that from 3 to 10 per cent of the patients hospitalized for mental deficiency have congenital syphilis. The mode of action of the spirochete varies in its specific attack on the central nervous system, but usually the result is a destruction of essential cortical pathways.

MENTAL DEFICIENCY

Although there are instances of children developing normally for as much as six to ten years of their life span and then seemingly coming to a halt insofar as intelligence is concerned, such cases are rare. In far the larger number of mentally defective persons the disorder is apparent almost from birth or would be if the infant were observed by competent examiners. Most anecdotes concerning the "late" type of feeblemindedness come from parents who have no adequate basis for evaluating the speed of their child's intellectual growth. Very often retarded intelligence is explained by parents as due to a head injury, "a fall from his high chair," perhaps. This, too, is rare. Falls from every

[2] By permission from *The Child, His Origin, Development, and Care*, by F. B. Sherbon. Copyrighted 1934. McGraw-Hill Book Co., Inc.

conceivable object and through a wide range of distances are experienced by almost every human being through his period of infancy and childhood. Whatever the etiological causes, and in this chapter we consider only a few of the many already known or suspected, mental deficiency is usually a congenital, if not an inherited, defect.

Another fact about the mental defective should be clearly recognized. The defective is not lacking simply in intelligence. He is retarded as an individual, and his slow development produces a qualitative difference as well. When the defective attains a mental age of four years, he is not equivalent to a normal child of four chronological years. In past years there was a tendency to put an extremely literal interpretation on mental age test scores. What was overlooked was the fact that the feebleminded person whose mental age was four might also have a chronological age of ten, twelve, or twenty. The chronological age helps point the clinical picture. The patient has grown physically more than the four years implied in the mental age, although perhaps not as fast nor as well as the normal twenty-year-old. Nevertheless, he has a physical and physiological maturation that must be reckoned with. He has also had the larger variety and sheer number of experiences conferred by his longer existence. These experiences have usually included a larger number of frustrations and humiliations than would confront the normal person in a lifetime, and they have been evaluated poorly. All these factors help to determine his personality.

A person is called "feebleminded" if his score on a standardized intelligence test is below certain more or less arbitrary limits. There are two intelligence tests most commonly used as measuring instruments, the Stanford-Binet and the Wechsler-Bellevue. Intelligence is classified on a slightly different basis in the two tests. Table 21 gives the Stanford-

TABLE 21

THE TERMAN CLASSIFICATION OF DEGREES OF INTELLIGENCE*

I. Q. Range	*Classification*
Below 70	Definite feeblemindedness
70-80	Borderline deficiency
80-90	Dullness
90-110	Normal or average intelligence
110-120	Superior intelligence
120-140	Very superior intelligence
140 and above	Genius or near genius

* Source: David Wechsler (1944), *The Measurement of Adult Intelligence* (3rd Ed.), p. 37. Baltimore: The Williams & Wilkins Company.

TABLE 22

THE WECHSLER CLASSIFICATION OF DEGREES OF INTELLIGENCE*

I. Q. Range	Per Cent of Population Included	Classification
65 and below......................	2.2	Defective
66-79.............................	6.7	Borderline
80-90.............................	16.1	Dull normal
91-110............................	50.0	Average
111-119...........................	16.1	Bright normal
120-127...........................	6.7	Superior
128 and over......................	2.2	Very superior

* Source: David Wechsler (1944), *The Measurement of Adult Intelligence* (3rd Ed.), p. 40. Baltimore: The Williams & Wilkins Company.

Binet classification and Table 22, the Wechsler classification. In both cases I. Q. stands for Intelligence Quotient and the basic notion is expressed by the formula:

$$\text{I. Q.} = \frac{\text{Mental Age}}{\text{Chronological Age}} \times 100$$

TABLE 23

CLASSIFICATION OF MENTAL DEFICIENCY*

Mental Age	Industrial Classification	Grade	
Under 1 year.........	Helpless	Low	⎫
1 year.........	Feeds self	Middle	⎬ Idiot
2 years........	Discriminates food from non-food	High	⎭
3 years........	No work; plays a little	Low	⎫
4 years........	Tries to help	Low	
5 years........	Only simplest tasks	Middle	⎬ Imbecile
6 years........	Tasks of short duration; washes dishes	High	
7 years........	Little errands; dusting.........	High	⎭
8 years........	Errands; light work; makes beds	Low	⎫
9 years........	Heavier work; scrubs, mends, lays brick	Low	
10 years........	Good institutional helpers; routine	Middle	⎬ Moron
11 years........	Fairly complicated work with occasional oversight	High	
12 years........	Uses machinery, cares for animals, cannot plan	High	⎭

* Source: H. H. Goddard, *Feeblemindedness: Its Causes and Its Consequences*, p. 581. Copyright 1914 by The Macmillan Company.

Thus, if a person develops mentally at the same rate he ages chronologically, his I. Q. should be a constant quantity over a wide range of age. Actually, the growth in mental age seems to slow up and finally stop in the first half of the life span. Accordingly, for adults, a chronological age of 16 is used as the divisor in determining I. Q.

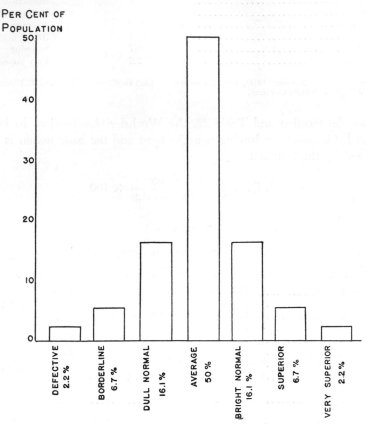

FIGURE 23. *Distribution of intelligence quotients in the population.*

As can be seen from the classification tables there are many degrees of mental deficiency, intelligence gradually shading into the normal zone. Table 23 further subdivides the defectives into roughly defined categories. In order to gain some idea of the proportion of the population that falls into these various groups, Figure 23 should be examined. It will be noticed that only about 2 per cent of the population can properly be called defective, from a statistical point of view. However, as Wechsler (1944) cautions, mental deficiency is to some extent a social concept, and defect is not completely described by the numerical index of mental age. The following case history from Wechsler illustrates this point:

> *Case 53.* J. M., 26 years old, native white, was arrested on a charge of impairing the morals of a minor (a girl of 10 years). He is reported to have made similar attempts on several previous occasions and had, for some years, been a persistent problem on this account. The family states: "We have always kept an eye on him because we felt he would get into trouble."
>
> *Physical examination:* Unattractive-looking youth who appears to be younger than he is. General physical and neurological examination as well as blood Wasserman is negative.
>
> *Psychiatric examination:* Appears dull and indifferent and childish. General reactions, immature. Is careless about person, but able to take care of himself. Diagnosis: mental defective, moron.
>
> *Psychological examination:* Stanford-Binet, 13 years 8 months, I. Q. (15 years) 91. . . .
>
> *Work history:* Patient was never able to find work for himself but a number of jobs were procured for him by his father. These he was unable to hold for any length of time.[3]

This patient, although scoring well above the level usually considered to indicate feeblemindedness, acted and appeared socially to be defective in intelligence.

Also illustrative of the complexities of the problem of feeblemindedness are those apparently contradictory individuals who appear mentally defective by almost all social standards, but who excel in some particular trait or aptitude. They are usually called *idiot savants*. In an earlier period of our study of mental deficiency many cases were described, with all sorts of marvelous capabilities. However, this was before the days of intelligence tests, and there was no objective way of establishing the authenticity of their mental handicap. At present the prevalent attitude toward the idiot-savant is somewhat more critical. More intensive study of their personalities and their intelligence ratings indicates that many are well within the normal range of intelligence, but are suffering from some other personality disorder that gives them the general appearance of deficiency. Pintner (1931) found only three cases in which intelligence tests had been utilized, and only one of these ap-

[3] David Wechsler (1944), *The Measurement of Adult Intelligence* (3rd Ed.), p. 51. Baltimore: The Williams & Wilkins Company.

peared to be defective. A study by Rothstein (1942) showed that the talented feebleminded person did poorly in aptitude tests of that talent, concluding that the talented behavior only appeared outside the rigid requirements of the test situation, and that the tests failed to tap the abilities because the latter were too highly specific. Scheerer, Rothmann, and Goldstein (1945) exhaustively studied the personality organization of a talented defective. The following is an abstract of their case history:

Case 54. L. became a problem child at age 2. His mother, a former school teacher, made careful written notes of his behavior. He was seen by several psychologists and psychiatrists during his 7th and 10th years, and the authors [Scheerer, Rothmann, and Goldstein] examined him at intervals from his 11th to his 17th year. His family history was negative for feeblemindedness. He was born in December, 1926, and his medical history was essentially without incident. "The only abnormality noted during L.'s first years is that he kicks more with his feet than other children and makes an unusual amount of movements with his extremities." Retardation was first suspected at 18 months, since his vocabulary had increased but little over the "dada" and "mama" of 6 months. He also began to show restlessness, fright, and insomnia. In his third year he showed signs of a remarkable interest and ability in music, rhythm, and counting. He knew the names of numerous phonograph records, recognized melodies, liked to count things, and began to develop a preference for calling off numbers quickly.

In his fourth and fifth year it was noted that his motor coordination was poor. He could not turn a door knob, catch a ball, steer a baby carriage, go to the bathroom alone, ride a tricycle, or hold a knife and fork correctly. Up to his tenth year he could still not put on or take off shoes and stockings by himself. Intellectually he manifested no idea of causation, never asking "why?" questions. "He is unable to understand or create an imaginary situation. He does not play with toys . . . nor does he show any conception of make-believe games. He cannot converse in a give-and-take use of language. He hardly ever volunteers factual information. He often fails to answer a question to the point and many times merely repeats it. He uses 'you' instead of 'I' and often says 'yes' instead of 'no.' His social development is similarly retarded. He is indifferent to other children, and will not listen to adults, save for his mother. She is the only person he cannot bear being separated from. Emotionally, he displays many tantrums, often for no apparent reason. Emotions are shallow and of short duration. Aside from his consistent love of music and his dependency on his mother, there is little emotionality of normal depth and coherence. He has a number of fears: he reacts with intense terror to a chiming clock, thunder, musical horns in cars, the drip of water from a faucet, the rattle of milk carts at night, plumbing sounds, steps overhead, the sight of lightning, a cat, a dog, a bird in a cage. For a long period he wakens regularly at night awaiting the sounds customary at this hour, and then begins his usual screaming." He never went outdoors alone until age 12. Food habits were rigid, he was distractible and restless and would not obey simple commands. "He grasps things indiscriminately, puts them into his mouth or holds them exaggeratedly tight in his grip. At the same time, L.'s propensity for numbers, melodies, and rhythm increases strikingly: so does his rote memory in these fields and spelling which he enjoys. Only while spelling, counting, or listening to musical recordings does he become quiet and sometimes restful. When music is played, he will eat anything, even things he dislikes, and sleeplessness is easily banished." He learned his alphabet easily and could spell about a hundred words by age 5. He learned numbers and before his fifth birthday could count by 2's, 4's, 8's and 16's. He could multiply (before his eleventh year) by adding the multiplicand number with great speed. In music he carried a tune, connected lyrics with melodies, tapped out tunes, and had an accurate melodic memory. Although most of these skills were apparent by his sixth year, he could not learn by instruction. At the end of a term and a half he left school at the teachers' request. "He does not respond to verbal directions. He refuses to participate in class activities, is uncooperative, unsociable, babyish, stubborn and willfully disobedient. He likes to be annoying, interrupting and mimicking; puts his fingers in his ears in an effort not to listen, and shows many childish mannerisms. His conversation is still in the first developmental stages"—so ran the school report.[4]

The authors concluded that L. lacked a capacity for abstraction and that this capacity was essential for the normal development of intelligence. When the individual lacks the capacity for abstracting, he "will cling tenaciously to those aspects of a situation and those features of material which make concrete palpable sense to him, *i.e.*, with which he can deal successfully" (page 61). Thus, the remarkable but senseless memory that idiot savants often display, indiscriminately remembering railroad timetables, almanac data, and so forth, constitutes an attempt on the part of the defective to make an adequate adjustment to a bewildering environment.

The many emotional complications that enter the life of the feeble-minded person are well shown in this case:

Case 55. S. R. is a single, white, saw-mill laborer who was inducted for army service at age 24. He has had a number of physical complaints for the past five years, including "chest pains," "head pains," "weakness," and vague pains in the arms and legs. He described these pains as continuous

[4] M. Scheerer, Eva Rothmann and K. Goldstein (1945), "A case of 'idiot savant': an experimental study of personality organization." *Psych. Mono., 58,* No. 4, American Psychological Association, Inc.

and "drawing." He also stated that he had been "nervous" and had difficulty in concentrating or learning. It is interesting to note that all his complaints became much worse following a quarrel with his drill sergeant.

S. R. comes from a poor farming family who have "been living off grandma's relief money" for years. The father is considered to be a chronic invalid who has "spells with his back" and tremors. He has been arrested with charges of bootlegging and drinking many times. The mother is "so nervous she can hardly hold a cup still." S. R. is the youngest of a family of five children.

S. R.'s past history showed that he wet the bed until age 17 and had many morbid fears since early childhood, being afraid of the dark, snakes, spiders, high places, and water. He left school at the age 15, after completing the eighth grade on his third attempt. Before entering the army he would get drunk about three times a month, but since his induction he has averaged three drinking bouts a week. Since he is a very religious member of a strict religious group, he has felt much guilt concerning his drinking. He has many religious conflicts over masturbation.

In appearance S. R. was untidy, slouched, slow, and apathetic. He talked with a whining, complaining air and frequently interrupted his remarks with sighs. He told of "feeling funny in his mind," and he was conscious of his inability to learn as rapidly or remember as long as other people.

Psychological tests showed poor attention, inability to perform simple arithmetic problems, poor power of abstraction, and a rashly impulsive satisfaction with inadequate solutions to test problems. The Rorschach test showed poor intellectual efficiency and a threatening anxiety.

Physical and neurological examinations were within normal limits.

The mental age, as shown by the Stanford-Binet Intelligence Test, was 8 years, 2 months. The I. Q. was 54.

In general, mentally defective patients show as many emotional problems as those of higher intelligence. This is one of the most effective arguments for the early hospitalization of severe grades of mental deficiency and provision of wise vocational guidance for the higher level defectives. Frequently, parents are reluctant to place the feeble-minded child in an institution. Such sentimental attachment very often results in a cruelly traumatic situation for the patient. Since the defective must live in a world dominated by people of higher intelligence, he is always at a disadvantage, even in his early childhood. The well-run institution, however, provides an environment where the patient does not receive constant frustration due to his low abilities, and it provides situations in which he can make a successful adjustment and even, on occasion, excel. Since most of the causes of mental deficiency are apparently buried in the developmental history of the patient, there is little to offer in the way of effective "cure" of the condition. Wise training, however, will develop the defective's abilities to an extent that could never occur in the patient's own home.

MONGOLIAN IDIOCY

This is a form of mental deficiency that usually becomes apparent in retarted behavior shortly after the birth of the patient. The name, *mongolian*, comes from a supposed resemblance to Oriental features, particularly the round face and narrowed appearance of the eyelids. Their range of mental ability actually seldom extends as low as the term *idiocy* would imply, and a few of them approach a low border-line normal intelligence. A more correct designation for their average range of intelligence would be "imbecile." Most of them are unable to make adequate adjustment outside an institution. About 10 per cent of all hospitalized defectives are mongoloid.

TABLE 24

ROLE OF AGE OF MOTHER ON INCIDENCE OF MONGOLOID IMBECILES.
ANALYSIS OF 217 FAMILIES INCLUDING ONE OR MORE MONGOLOIDS*

Mother's Age	Total Births	Per Cent Mongols
17-19	13	23
20-24	128	10
25-29	213	7
30-34	255	11
35-39	234	27
40-44	151	54
45-48	37	59

* Source: L. S. Penrose (1934), *Proc. Roy. Soc.*, B, *115*.

The causative factors in mongolian idiocy are still largely obscure. There does not appear to be a direct hereditary factor, since these patients are usually conceived of parents who are of normal intelligence and with a negative history for mental deficiency. Recent work has demonstrated that a significant relationship exists between the age of the mother and the number of mongolian offspring. Apparently the majority of mongolian children come from very young or very old mothers (see Table 24). Inadequate uterine environment has been suggested as a major direct causative factor.

There is no close agreement among various investigators as to the clinical appearances of mongoloid behavior. This is rather remarkable, considering the ease with which the condition can be recognized and diagnosed from the superficial physical appearance. Most observers agree that the mongoloid's social competence is even less than his mental test results would indicate, that most of them are of a cheerful disposition, and that most of them die at a relatively early age, few living beyond forty years. They seem to have an abnormally high incidence of respiratory, circulatory, and gastrointestinal disorders (Doll, 1946).

MICROCEPHALY

This is a relatively rare condition (less than one per cent of defective patients) in which the cranial volume is abnormally small. The condition is easily recognized, since the small brain is associated with a small, markedly receding head. The fontanelles close prematurely, due to inadequate brain development. It was formerly held that the small skull was the causative factor, and occasionally attempts were made to allow for greater brain growth by surgical removal of portions of the skull. However, the hypoplasia (under-growth) of the brain is the primary feature, and the skull growth is secondary.

Behaviorally, these patients range in intelligence from high-grade idiocy to low-grade imbecility. The Binet mental age runs from two to four years. As a rule microcephalics have few motor defects, but show only a primitive stereotyped language development. Emotionally they are generally euphoric and alert. Doll states: "They resemble the highest anthropoids in physical alertness, and 'little monkey' is a term as appropriate as it may be affectionate" (Doll, 1946, page 859).

Little is known of the etiology of the condition. There is no evidence of consistent familial patterns, and it is apparently due to strictly developmental anomalies. According to Doll, there is some relation between X-ray irradiation of the mother during pregnancy and the later production of microcephalics.

HYDROCEPHALUS

This is a condition in which the most apparent external feature is the unusually large head size. Pathologically the condition is characterized by a blocking of the circulation of cerebrospinal fluid with a consequent increase in intercranial pressure. The ventricles of the brain increase enormously in size at the expense of the neural tissue surrounding them, particularly in the cortex. As a result the cortex is thinned and atrophied. There are cases where this condition exists without increase in head size, and there is a type of hydrocephalus in which the fluid accumulation is in the sub-arachnoid space (external hydrocephalus). In many instances the diagnosis can be made with certainty only at the autopsy table.

Hydrocephalus usually results in mental deficiency, although the range of intelligence found in these patients varies from idiocy to normal ability. There are no specific characteristics of the hydrocephalic defective, although Doll states that their language ability is a little better than the mental age would indicate. The condition has about the same small incidence as is found in microcephaly.

BIRTH INJURIES

There are many ways in which the brain can be injured during the process of birth. Most common are trauma due to mechanical factors, and trauma due to physiochemical factors. The former are caused by difficult birth, in which the birth canal is of inadequate size, or where the infant's orientation is such that obstetrical forceps or other means of mechanical intervention must be used. Since the skull of the newborn is relatively pliable and easily distorted, the opportunities for injury are many. The locus of injury is usually the cerebral cortex or the basal ganglia. Injury may also result from *prenatal asphyxiation,* in which the brain is exposed to a degree of anoxia after the infant is deprived of placental oxygen and before normal breathing can be established.

Although birth injuries produce a wide variety of symptoms, there is almost always a retardation in mental development. The most distressing type of reaction following birth injury is *cerebral palsy.* This term is used to cover a large number of motor difficulties, the most frequent of which are *spasticity* and *athetosis.* Spasticity refers to a type of involuntary muscular contraction, a spastic paralysis being one in which the muscles of a limb are in a state of increased tonicity and contraction. Athetosis is characterized by slow, irregular, continuous worm-like movements, most marked in the fingers and wrists. The almost complete lack of motor coordination and the difficulty in normal locomotion and manipulation are in themselves grave obstacles to normal adjustment, and if special educational facilities are lacking, there is almost sure to be a functional retardation in behavioral development. In addition, the extent of cortical injury is sufficiently extensive in about one third of these cases to result in serious mental deficiency.

Within the past few years another possible manifestation of birth injury has been recognized. If the past histories of unstable, irritable, or delinquent problem children are analyzed, there is a significantly high percentage of difficult births, indicating the possibility of undetected cerebral injury at that time. In this same group of children is found a high percentage of abnormal electroencephalograms, again indicating disturbed cortical functioning. The percentage of abnormal EEG records runs, for various groups investigated, from 70 per cent to 90 per cent of all cases (Jasper, *et al.*, 1938; Lindsley and Cutts, 1940, 1941; Strauss, *et al.*, 1940; Brill, *et al.*, 1942; Brown and Solomon, 1942; Secunda and Finley, 1942).

DISEASES OF CHILDHOOD AND THEIR EFFECT ON MATURATION

The maturational schedule can be altered by the aftereffects of disease. Infants and children are subject to a number of serious disease conditions that in one way or another attack the central nervous system and cause permanent changes in development. This developmental handicap is a continuing obstacle to successful social adjustment because of the disabilities it imposes and also because of the psychological situation of overprotection that is likely to occur.

Epidemic encephalitis may be taken as an example of such a disease vector in abnormal behavior. Encephalitis is an infectious disease, caused apparently by a filterable virus. The symptoms of the active disease process are similar to those of influenza, and the two conditions are often confused. Mild cases of encephalitis often pass unnoticed by parents and medical aid is not requested. Following the acute phase of the disease, however, there are a number of sequelae that are markedly different from the normal convalescence of the influenza patient. In older children and adults there is the likely appearance of motor symptoms, usually the so-called *Parkinson's syndrome*. This condition is characterized by:

(1) Rigidity of the whole body with increased muscle tonus.

(2) Posture—stooped, with head forward and elbows flexed.

(3) Facial expression—mask-like, with lack of emotional expression.

(4) Gait—short shuffling steps, with patient leaning forward. The arms do not show associated swinging movements.

(5) Tremor—"pill-rolling" movements of the fingers; the head may

show a coarse, shaking tremor. Tremors tend to disappear when patient is executing voluntary movements.

There are few basic alterations in intellect or personality in the Parkinson syndrome. Pathological studies show that the disease affects all parts of the brain, but has its greatest effect on the sub-cortical centers of the thalamus and mid-brain. The residual symptom-complex may not be manifested for several years after the acute illness. In younger children up to about 5 years mental deterioration is frequent, and the end results are similar to the mental deficiencies found following birth injury. As the age of onset advances, obvious mental deterioration is reduced, but equally serious personality changes occur. These changes are primarily emotional in character, the patient becoming more irritable, excitable and aggressive, or, as sometimes happens, the changes are to the other extreme of excessive passivity, apathy, and semi-stupor. Because of these emotional changes, normal school, home, and general social adjustments become difficult. The following case is illustrative of the influence that encephalitis may have on general behavioral development:

Case 56. The mother of an eight-year-old girl came to a social welfare office in great perturbation. The police, she said, had just called her to say that they could no longer afford to spend 10 to 12 hours a day, two, three, or even four times a week, as they had been doing, to hunt her child. The mother reported that the child's running off had become so serious that she, in desperation, had resorted to tying the child in a rocking chair on the third floor. Usually when the child was finally found after her escapes, she would be roaming through the woods on the hills back of the river along which the family lived. There were other serious behavior disorders that came to light as investigation continued. The child would, on every possible occasion, empty into a common vessel all containers of salt and pepper. She would mix these two ingredients and then refill the shakers with the mixture. Very frequently she would go to wade in the creek which flowed past the house. As soon as her feet were wet, she would sit down in the water, take off her shoes and stockings, and watch them float down the creek and on into the river. All of this irrational behavior occurred in spite of an intelligence quotient of 108.

Past medical history showed that the child had been ill with "a high fever" when about three months of age, and had been hospitalized. The physician who had attended her at that time stated that her symptoms were compatible with a diagnosis of encephalitis. The behavioral consequences of encephalitis were presented to the mother and she was urged to admit her child to the hospital for further study. This the mother refused to do, and the agency heard nothing more of the case for about ten years. At that time, the physician of a city agency called to get information on the case. The girl, then almost 20, had been found wandering around the bedroom floors of downtown hotels and spending the nights in railroad stations. She had finally been institutionalized because of her inability to adjust to life in a city environment and because of very manifest deterioration.[5]

Because of the many different forms that maladjustive behavior may assume, diagnosis, of course, cannot be made solely on the basis of disturbed behavior. There is some evidence (Lindsley and Cutts, 1941) that encephalitis produces abnormal brain waves and that improvement in behavior is accompanied by increasingly normal electroencephalograms.

The differential effects of encephalitis on adults and children emphasize the importance of the developmental period for normal personality integration. As we have seen, adults who develop chronic encephalitis most frequently show the Parkinson syndrome, but have few basic personality changes. They remain alert and beneath their frozen facial mask they experience a normal appropriate degree and range of emotional experience. The difference in behavioral reaction to the disease may be explained by assuming a greater stability in the adult personality (and nervous system), of such an order that the adult has more resistance to the psychological stresses arising from the defect. The child, still maturing, with basic habits only poorly established, shows changed reactions to meet the stresses of the disease.

Treatment of this developmental disorder is not promising. Bond and Appel (1931) found that constant supervision and a constant program of activities designed to effect desirable habit-training were essential. This should be done in an institutional setting. After ten years they report that 20 out of 76 cases that were so treated had improved sufficiently to make an adequate social adjustment. The necessity for close supervision and the inadvisability of allowing such children to remain in either their own or foster homes create a serious problem for large communities. Juvenile delinquents should be given thorough medical and psychological examinations, since recidivism is to be anticipated from chronic encephalitics if the usual casual probation or social work supervision are the only measures taken.

[5] Florence M. Teagarden (1940, 1946), *Child Psychology for Professional Workers*, p. 499. New York: Prentice-Hall, Inc.

There are many other diseases with as grave developmental aspects as encephalitis. Sydenham's chorea, associated with rheumatic fever, is characterized by jerky, restless movements. The onset is usually gradual and may begin with a behavioral disturbance, such as temper tantrums, irritability, and restlessness. The motor symptoms may be indicated by clumsiness, motor incoordinations, and bizarre facial grimacing. With adequate medical treatment and care the patient usually recovers. However, there is often a residue of maladjustment, due to the long period of invalidism and absolute rest that has been forced upon the child by the demands of treatment.

Case 57. One such study was that of a twenty-two-year-old soldier who had been admitted to the psychiatric section of a large army hospital with a diagnosis of Sydenham's chorea. When observed in the ward his hands were engaged in an endless twisting movement, and his face would periodically be distorted by pronounced unilateral muscular spasms. The only features of this case that did not appear typical were the completely normal reports of laboratory examinations of the blood, and the cardiologist's report that no heart defect could be found. Although such evidence was not conclusively against the diagnosis of chorea, it suggested other possibilities. Accordingly, the patient was placed in a private room and unobtrusively kept under observation by attendants. They reported that he often completely relaxed and ceased to show the choreiform movements. In subsequent discussion with the patient, when these observations were mentioned to him, he admitted that he had feigned the symptoms in order to escape a disagreeable assignment. As a child he had had chorea and, as he said, spent the most wonderful three months of his life. His parents had taken him to Florida and had given him attentions more profusely than at any other time in his life. When placed under stress in the army, the adjustmental features of the old chorea had prompted him to fall back into as many as possible of the symptoms that had given him satisfaction before.

ENDOCRINE DISTURBANCES

Another large class of pathological conditions that have an effect on development are the malfunctionings of the endocrine system. The endocrine or ductless glands play a particularly important role in regulating growth and development, and their disorders are sometimes dramatically reflected in structure and behavior. So powerful an influence do the endocrines have on life and behavior that many physiologists and psychologists at one time tended to overemphasize their importance. Dr. L. Berman (1922), for example, wrote a book called *The Glands Regulating Personality,* in which he claimed that all personality was determined by the relative influence of various individual glands. Our more recent knowledge of the autonomic nervous system and of psychosomatic medicine has shown that, in quite another way, the endocrines do play an important part in behavior. But our principal interest now is in the part endocrine malfunctions play in maturation and development.

The endocrine glands are small organizations of secretory tissue, innervated by the autonomic nervous system, that pass their secretions directly into the bloodstream. There are at least eight types of endocrine; their location and function are given in Table 25. In order to appreciate the significance of glandular disorders, two general principles concerning their function should be understood. (1) The glands do not work independently, but all are supplemental in their function; the activities of each gland act to stimulate or inhibit the others. Thus a defect or disease that attacks one gland has bodily repercussions attributable to other glands in the system. (2) There are four bodily functions that are most directly dependent upon the endocrines: (*a*) growth, (*b*) nutrition, (*c*) sex, and (*d*) the coordination of smooth muscle activity, in conjunction with the autonomic nervous system.

We shall limit our discussion of the endocrine factors in psychopathology to two conditions: cretinism and pituitary dysfunctions.

Cretinism is a generalized developmental disorder that has as its cause an insufficiency of the thyroid gland. The thyroid normally secretes a small but constant amount of a chemical substance, thyroxin. Its function is to maintain a general optimal level of metabolism or energy exchange. If a child is born with rudimentary or absent thyroid gland, he fails to develop beyond an infantile level. The proportions between extremities and trunk are upset, and the cretin has short arms and legs. The skin is thick, dry, and often wrinkled; the hair is coarse and dry. There is a characteristic facial appearance, with a broad nose, thick lips and poorly developed teeth. The infant appears listless and apathetic and fails to show a development in intelligence with increasing chronological age. Because of their superficial resemblance to mongolian idiots, there is sometimes a confusion in diagnosis. This is important because cretinism, if treatment is started at an early age, may be improved. The treatment is life-long daily administration of thyroid. When cretins are given thyroid, symptoms disappear and the physical development approaches normal. Although most authorities are conservative in their estimates of the degree of recovery in intel-

TABLE 25

THE ENDOCRINE GLANDS AND THEIR FUNCTIONS

Gland	Location	Function	Disorders
1. Pineal	Under surface of cerebrum	Unknown	Sexual development disturbed in pineal gland tumors
2. Pituitary	Under surface of cerebrum	Controls growth and development (ant. lobe) Influences on blood pressure and water regulation (post. lobe)	Hypofunction: retarded development; diabetes insipidus Hyperfunction: giantism or acromegaly.
3. Thyroid	Front of trachea	Regulation of metabolism	Hypofunction in infancy: cretinism; adult: myxedema Hyperfunction: Goitre, increased metabolism
4. Parathyroid	On surface of thyroid glands	Regulation of calcium metabolism	Hypofunction: tetany, death
5. Thymus	Anterior mediastinum	Inhibitory effect on sexual development. Atrophies in adult	Hypofunction: Precocious sexual development
6. Adrenal cortex	Over kidneys	Influences sodium and water metabolism. Sexual glands	Hypofunction: Addison's disease Hyperfunction: Accelerated sexual development
7. Adrenal medulla	Over kidneys	Autonomic nervous stimulation (adrenalin production)	Hypofunction: No disease entities. Hyperfunction: none
8. Islets of Langerhans	In pancreas	Carbohydrate metabolism	Hypofunction: diabetes mellitus Hyperfunction: none
9. Gonads	Pelvis in female Testicles in male	Growth and reproduction	Hyperfunction: Sexual precocity Hypofunction: Under-development of secondary sex characteristics

ligence, the gains are large, and a condition of normal intellectual efficiency may be obtained.

A very similar condition may occur during adolescence or adulthood, if thyroid secretion diminishes. The disease is termed *myxedema*. The structural changes of skin, hair, and so forth are like those found in cretinism. The behavior of the myxedemic patient is altered in the direction of lethargy. Thinking is slowed, and the patient loses ability to initiate activity. Treatment of myxedema is more successful than in the case of cretinism, and as long as the patient continues to take his thyroid extract or his thyroxin he is able to maintain normal activity.

Disorders of the pituitary gland produce the most radical changes in external structure, but probably interfere much less with most behavioral variables than any other of the conditions we have reviewed. The pituitary gland, which consists of an anterior and posterior lobe lying deep in the brain, exercises an influence on assimilation, growth, and reproduction of all the cells in the body. The posterior lobe secretes hormones having metabolic regulatory functions. The anterior lobe of the gland produces at least two distinct hormones, (1) a growth or "somatotropic" substance, and (2) a gonad hormone. The pituitary substances apparently act as regulators of other endocrine glands, and through them control many sexual and growth functions.

Hypofunction of the pituitary in children results in several types of developmental abnormality. The *Lorain-Levi syndrome,* due to underdevelopment of the anterior lobe, is manifested by a complete dwarfism. The patient appears to be a very small adult; there is usually a retardation of primary and secondary sexual characteristics. Most of the midgets seen in the circus and in the motion pictures are dwarfs of this type. There is usually no defect of intelligence, and the only behavioral abnormalities are those connected with attempting a social adjustment in a world not ordered to their diminutive size. Another type of hypofunction is represented in *Froehlich's syndrome.* The chief characteristic is increased fat deposits, which localizes around the breasts and in an abdominal girdle. There is also an under-development of the genitalia. The behavioral consequences lie chiefly in the difficulty of adequate social adjustment. There is usually no certain knowledge of the etiology of either of these conditions. Froehlich's syndrome is sometimes due to a tumor of the pituitary, and operative intervention or X-ray therapy is beneficial. Success with administration of pituitary extracts has been variable.

Over-functioning of the pituitary is usually due to the development of tumors associated with the pituitary body. The symptoms of hyper-pituitarism, like the hypothyroidism previously discussed, depend upon the age of the patient at the time of the disorder. If the disease occurs before puberty, the patient develops symmetrically, but there is an overgrowth of all tissues. There are no specific behavioral symptoms, and the pituitary giant is usually free of intellectual defect. If the condition occurs after puberty, the overgrowth of tissue takes a different form, termed *acromegaly*. There is a disproportionate over-development of the short bones of the face, hands, and feet, the skull enlarges, and the lips protrude. The patient sometimes shows apathy, slowness in thinking and diminution of ability to concentrate and remember. Treatment is usually of little value, though occasional cases are aided by surgical removal of tumors or by X-ray therapy.

General Summary

We have now reviewed a host of biological factors that seem to influence the efficiency of an animal's adjustment. The biological substrata of behavior show a complex interweaving of genetic and developmental phenomena. It would be a mistake, however, to attempt a separation of these facts from the more purely psychological aspects of behavior. In a sense we can think of the organism making use of genetic, constitutional, and maturational structures and events as tools or techniques in its adjustment. From the evolutionary point of view the structures, the sequences of development of their interrelations are the result of natural selective processes. Much of psychopathology deals with the poor or faulty physique, the unintegrated constitution, and the impaired maturation. If natural selection operated in a social vacuum, most of the individuals so afflicted would fail to survive. Since, however, our cultural environment allows for great variability in all these factors and operates to preserve many of them, a potent vector is directed toward maladjustment. In a society where strong ethical and moral forces influence its members to protect the weak and ineffective, and where active attempts to combat disease by artificial means are encouraged, we must place an increasing emphasis on the study of the subject matter we have been discussing. Social control of mental disease undoubtedly depends upon the effectiveness of education and training of individuals, both from a therapeutic and prophylactic standpoint. But until we have more knowledge of genetic and developmental factors in psychopathology, we have no firm basis for planning effective use of our educational weapons. We must know the manner in which heredity operates and the extent to which it can be modified by environmental means. We must puzzle over the admitted interrelationships between the two until we can express such relationships with precision. As we have seen, poor heredity often implies poor environment, making the relative contribution of each difficult to assess. If, as some investigators indicate, there are significant genetic determiners for mental disease, it would be important to perfect ways of detecting individuals so affected and regulate their training in such a way that a maximum of preventive care would be afforded them. If body-build is correlated with personality type and with increased susceptibility to specific disorders, differing types of emotional and intellectual training should be available. It is not too absurd to suppose that a time will come when schools will recognize that "special classes" are as imperative for all those with genetic, constitutional, or maturational defects as they are now for the intellectually retarded and for those children with obviously recognizable physical defects. Such a mental hygiene or public health utopia, however, depends upon a great increase over our present knowledge of these factors. As we have indicated throughout the chapter, our knowledge is still sparse, and few positive statements can be made. At best we can only say that a fair weighing of the evidence yields a conviction that heredity cannot be discarded as a factor in psychopathology, that constitution is a basic variable in personality disorders, and that effective adult adjustment depends on a rather close adherence to a normal adjustmental schedule. Further, we can conclude that individual variability is great, but that all these factors resolve themselves into sources of adjustmental stress and into the determination of thresholds of resistance to stress.

DISCUSSION QUESTIONS

1. On the basis of present knowledge, what sort of social control of behavior disorders is suggested?
2. What are the facilities for defective children in your state?

3. Can you give examples of individuals who have overcome maturational defects to achieve successful adaptation?

4. What are some of the possible circumstances surrounding birth and the first few days of life that may have lasting effects on behavior?

5. Given two children with the "same" maturational defect, why might one be normal and the other mentally defective?

6. In light of the past three chapters, how important is a biological approach to psychopathology?

7. Could attempts to force learning in a child before he is maturationally equipped for such learning be considered as frustration? Give some examples of this type of situation.

8. In what way does the study of maturational influences on behavior help you understand the changes in behavior that are present in old age?

9. Why is it probably incorrect to ask such questions as: "When is the person mature"?

10. In learning the same task, what will be some possible differences between habits that result in people of different maturational levels?

SUGGESTED READINGS

C. E. Benda (1954), "Psychopathology of childhood," in L. Carmichael, ed., *Manual of Child Psychology,* pp. 1115-1161. New York: John Wiley & Sons, Inc.

C. P. Stone (1951), "Maturation and 'instinctive' functions," in C. P. Stone, ed., *Comparative Psychology* (3rd Ed.), pp. 30-61. New York: Prentice-Hall, Inc.

J. E. W. Wallin (1949), *Children with Mental and Physical Handicaps.* New York: Prentice-Hall, Inc.

BIBLIOGRAPHIC SOURCES

On maturation, if the reader wishes to start from conception in his readings, Needham's (1931) *Chemical Embryology,* Coghill's (1929) *Anatomy and the Problem of Behavior,* Child's (1924) *Physiological Foundations of Behavior,* Gesell's (1945) *Embryology of Behavior,* Corner's (1944) *Ourselves Unborn,* and Carmichael's (1954) article in the *Manual of Child Psychology* cover the earliest periods of life. The many publications of Arnold Gesell and his students (1925, 1928, 1934, 1946) offer one of the best descriptions of the human maturational process available at the present time.

Young and Pilts (1951) have presented experimental results illustrating the intellectual problems of the congenital syphilitic. With their sample of 40 syphilitic children compared with 40 control children, these authors demonstrated reliable differences in performance on the Wechsler Intelligence Scale for Children. They conclude (p. 242): "Congenital syphilis in the children in the present study is associated with significantly inferior intelligence and with selective impairment of mental functions."

There are many fine texts in the field of mental deficiency. Tredgold's (1947) *A Textbook of Mental Deficiency,* is a classic. Another excellent source is Penrose's (1949) *The Biology of Mental Defect.* Shorter, but equally comprehensive, is Doll's (1946) chapter in the first edition of Carmichael's (1946) handbook. In the second edition (Carmichael, 1954), Benda (1954) should be consulted. In addition, Wallin (1949) and Sarason (1953) are very helpful introductions to this area. The student will find most of the literature in the periodical, *American Journal of Mental Deficiency.* We have not stressed in the text one of the most crucial problems in mental deficiency, that is, acceptable criteria for the definition and classification of mental defect. Among many authors, Benda, Farrell, and Chipman (1951) and Heiser (1952) may be consulted. The legal problems in this connection are discussed in detail in the interesting article by Porteus and Corbett (1953). Finally, the student will find that some of the older literature is of more than historic interest. Goddard's (1919) *Psychology of the Normal and Subnormal* contains good descriptions of these patients. Healy's (1915) *The Individual Delinquent* is a classical contribution to the social aspects of mental deficiency, and Wembridge's (1931) *Life Among the Lowbrows* is a realistic description of the difficulties of the defective in a too complex society.

As an introduction, Ingall's (1952) semi-popular article on mongolism is excellent. In addition, however, the student should read the more extensive texts by Benda (1949), Engler (1949), and Penrose (1949). Statistical incidence data on mongolism are available in Böök and Reed (1950), Malzberg (1950), and Oliver (1950); all three should be consulted. Ingall's (1947) paper is an excellent technical review of the literature on the physiological and anatomical pathology of mongolism.

Extensive and intensive study of cerebral palsy is quite recent, but the literature is growing rapidly. Benda's (1952) monograph is highly recommended, although the student may find less technical papers are necessary for introductory material. Egel (1948) and Pohl (1950) may be read, but perhaps the best introduction for the student is the symposium on cerebral palsy published in the April, 1949, issue of *The Nervous Child.* There are 15 excellent papers on many of the problems in this area. Although all the papers should be read, Burgemeister and Blum (1949), Josephy (1949), Phelps (1949), and Putnam (1949) are specifically suggested. The paper by Phelps and a short article by Fay (1950) contain a suggested classificatory scheme for the palsy disorders.

Supplementary material on encephalitis may be obtained from the detailed observations of Fairweather (1947) on 275 adults diagnosed as encephalitic. Parkinson's syndrome is specifically discussed. A far more extensive report is by Neal, *et al.* (1942) *Encephalitis, a Clinical Study.* Added information on acromegaly may be found in Blueler (1951) based on a study of 28 acromegalics and 1,430 relatives. Blueler reports an extended case study of a mild case of acromegaly.

The amount of literature available on the various disorders mentioned in this chapter is highly variable, and the student should read one of the many fine general sources for added information. For a more complete picture of the neurological disorders described in this chapter, the standard texts of Grinker (1943), Wechsler (1943), or Brock (1938) may be read. Penrose (1949) and Benda (1952) are particularly useful for many more disorders than have been mentioned here. Perhaps the best single supplement to this chapter is the text by Wallin (1949). For an introduction to endocrinology, Hoskins (1950) is suggested.

XIV

Structure and Physiological Function in Psychopathology

So careful of the type she seems
So careless of the single life.
—TENNYSON, *In Memoriam*

The Role of Structure and Physiological Function in Adjustment

EVOLUTION AND BODY STRUCTURE

The anatomical structure of any organism has a long history. Except in the simplest types of unicellular creatures, we are able to glimpse some of the stages in the evolutionary history of animal life by studying the changes in the pattern of organ systems as we move along the phylogenetic scale. From such study we may conclude that, in a strictly biological sense, the body structure of any organism has developed in the direction of better adaptation of one kind or another. We note, for example, that the whale and the seal, both mammals, have developed an anatomical specialization for aquatic existence that any Olympic swimmer might envy. Zoological classification of morphological types gives a general confirmation of this principle. Variations of structure between the species have fitted them for more adequate adaptation to the type of environment in which they must exist.[1] As one instance we may cite the development of protective coloration as it is known in

[1] This statement avoids the question of whether environment did the selecting or whether variant species tended to seek out the environment best suited for their structural pattern. For psychopathology, this question is not of immediate importance.

456

many types of insects and vertebrates. Ptarmigan and rabbits become whiter in winter; the chameleon and many species of fish show pigment patterns that blend into the backgrounds of their habitats; some insects appear like twigs and others like leaves. As Wallace pointed out in his original communication on "natural selection" (1858), pigment patterns may work in many ways as adaptive media. Birds will not feed on brightly colored caterpillars, but will rarely refuse to eat the type of caterpillar that blends into its surroundings; in other words, color is adaptive either as a warning or as a concealment.

EVOLUTION AND BODILY FUNCTIONS

Function, as well as structure, is influenced by evolutionary processes. As structures become specialized, there is an accompanying specialization of function. As we view the phylogenetic scale, from the one-celled animals to the complex mammals, we see that separate organ systems of many kinds have developed. Whereas the amoeba performs all vital functions within its single cell, the higher animals have separated and delegated functions in a bewildering variety of ways. Man has one structural equipment-complex for digestion, another for respiration, another for reproduction, and so on. Not only have the organ systems been developed, but within and between these systems has grown an hierarchy of interrelated operations that have broadened the scope of adaptation tremendously. The development of receptor systems that are anatomically separate from the effectors but that may activate the effectors is an instance, giving the organism a flexibility of movement in its environment that is worlds in advance of the slow streaming progression of the amoeba. The survival of the individual animal and the propagation of its kind have come more and more to depend upon the smoothly integrated function of this multitude of specialized organ systems. Decreased opportunity for survival may result from interference with the integration, either through destruction of a part of the chain of organs or through circumstances that interfere with their harmonious operations.

ECOLOGICAL FACTORS IN BEHAVIOR

Our picture of adaptive evolution has thus far been drawn at a distance, in the perspective of knowledge given us by the geologists, paleontologists, and zoologists. If we come closer to a given species, if we follow an individual animal through his own lifetime, the optimistic picture of development toward perfection of adaptation is rudely disturbed. The structural and functional specialization has not been a guarantee of utopia. Along with the assets of effective species adjustment there are some liabilities, and as psychopathologists, these attract our interest. Even though, in the great realm of biology as a whole, animals strive, in structure and function, toward ever better adaptation, the over-all goals of nature are accomplished at a rather stiff price in individual effectiveness. This becomes quite evident when we study the social interactions of animals, a topic coming under the heading of *ecology*. The ecologist assures us that, for the natural economy as a whole, it is best and fitting that animals prey on other animals, that the weaker members of overabundant litters starve to death, that the grasses be eaten by the mouse, who is eaten by the owl, who is eaten by the wolves, who eat each other and are in turn attacked by bacteria or, indirectly, by drouth that kills the grass and starves the mouse, and the owl, and finally the wolf. All living things exist in a state of checks and balances; the ledger of nature must always balance, as humans have sometimes found to their great inconvenience. When game laws protect the deer and when cattlemen lobby for bounties on wolves, coyotes, and other predators, soon man finds that the number of deer are so great that he must either deprive cattle of feed and upset his own ecological scheme, or he must find some way of replacing the predatory animals that once held the deer in check. The recurrent plea of western ranchers that the elk are crowding the cattle off their ranges is a case in point.

Returning to our individual animal, existing in this all-inclusive, supra-human accounting system, we may recognize that the rabbit is caught by the coyote because it doesn't run as fast, or because it has a shorter memory, or because it hasn't a sufficiently keen sense of smell. We might add that the contribution made by these animals to the over-all ecological balance is probably a source of greater satisfaction to the coyote than to the rabbit. Evolutionary adaptation has not completely protected the animal in its individual social or ecological relationships. That the same generalization is true of man no one would seriously question. Evolution, it might be said, is a relatively blind development as far as social relationships are concerned. Many times the very characteristics that lead to success in some aspects of adjustment loom as disadvantages in other respects. Protective devices and adaptive structures may boomerang. The seal can escape almost any enemy in the water, but if the race be run on land, even man is able to catch and kill the seal. This is an important fact: *An animal's structure is relatively fixed and permanent and is incapable of the rapid modifications that may be demanded by environmental situations.* How often, for example, it would benefit the ground animal if he could fly as easily as the bird or could swim like a fish. Fixity of structure, however, sets definite limits on adjustment and confines the animal to a relatively limited range of environmental conditions. One of the problems of military biological research is that of fitting men for life at pressure-altitudes of from forty to eighty thousand feet above sea level and against speeds of over one thousand miles an hour. Many thousands of years ago the dinosaur became extinct because of a structural (and hence behavioral) pattern that made him dependent upon a particular type of semi-aquatic environment. When geological changes occurred, making deserts of his swamp-land habitat, the dinosaur was doomed because of his limited range of adaptation. We shall find that this limitation of behavior by structural patterns and their relative inflexibility is still playing a part in contemporary human psychopathology.

Evolution, then, affects behavior through structural patterns and contributes both adaptive and maladaptive factors to life. Evolution never seems to be *ahead* of the demands of the social environment in which the individual lives. To take another subhuman example and thus emphasize the general biological basis for the problem, let us consider that most human of birds, the penguin. It has become admirably suited to laying and hatching its eggs in the cold and darkness of Antarctic beaches and ice-foots. If each penguin mother and father could carry on the family nursery activities in a social vacuum they would have achieved a biological paradise, and we should be forced to recognize the all-pervading success of evolutionary processes. But, since penguins share a common breeding ground, secondary social complications frequently develop. Ponting (1923) has related observations of Adelie penguins' nest-building. Their nests are constructed of small, rounded pebbles, which must be gathered together off the beach and transported to the chosen nest location. While industrious couples are laboriously carrying stones, other penguins, just as industriously but not as honestly, are stealing the accumulation. The consequence is usually a great deal of confusion and intense inter-penguin rivalry. Ponting says:

Suspicion of their neighbors engenders in the hen penguins violent hatred, and is the cause of constant brawling and dissensions. It was quite common to see hens, on adjacent nests, with outstretched beaks, pecking savagely at one another. Sometimes their beaks would be interlocked for minutes, and the heads of many were swollen and bleeding from such conflicts. During these squabbles, the neighbors in the rear of the brawlers would regard the opportunity as favorable to purloin stones from the nests of the quarrelsome ones—and embrace it.[2]

It is not hard to see analogies with many aspects of human life in this scene. The penguin's structural and functional adaptation is well worked out, *for the species,* but, as Tennyson said so well, is ". . . careless of the single life." In other species we can see that much disordered behavior arises from the "struggle for existence," from all those factors that create problems out of such circumstances as being the smallest animal in the litter, being short of wind, being conspicuously colored, and lacking in or having weaker organs than do those with whom the competition takes place. We shall see the same factors emerging in critical importance for disordered behavior of humans.

Compensation for Defect

A study of the reactions of animals to injury and physical defect demonstrates a remarkable range of functional adaptation. Protoplasm makes, in every case, the best adjustment possible under the circumstances. The integrative pattern of organismic structure has contributed to this ability in several ways.

SYMMETRY AS AN AID IN ADJUSTMENT

Most animals show some kind of definite symmetry of structural organization. Although the amoeba has a flexibility of shape that allows it to assume almost any pattern, slightly more complex unicellular animals show the beginnings of structural design. There is a primitive symmetry in the paramecium and other protozoa; it is possible to distinguish to some extent "right-side, left-side," "top-bottom" and "front-back" relationships. In the metazoa we find two primary organizations

[2] H. G. Ponting (1923), *The Great White South,* p. 245. New York: Robert M. McBride & Company.

of symmetry, the radial (exemplified in the starfish) and the bilateral (as in insects, vertebrates, etc.). Both of these forms of symmetry are aids in adaptation. Because a symmetrical organism has duplication of parts, whether it be around a common center or on opposite sides of a central axis, it can still make partial adjustive movements if it loses the use of one side or the other. The dog injured in one leg manages to get around with amazing speed and agility on the three remaining. The bird with a wing injury can still run, the man with one eye can still see. This applies to internal organs as well as to the sensory and motor structures. Two lungs, two kidneys, symmetrical branching in the vascular system, two hemispheres in the brain—any one of these bilaterally symmetrical organs may, when diseased or injured, be removed and life yet go on.

STRUCTURAL COMPENSATION

Besides the advantage of having more than one of most structural features participating in adjustment, animals have shown themselves capable of making many compensatory *changes* in structure and function following injury or disease. In lower organisms and in the embryological stages of the higher organisms we find that the potentiality for regeneration of lost parts is developed to a high degree. If a flatworm is divided into two pieces, one piece may regenerate a head, the other a caudal section, and two well-adjusted worms exist in the place of the single mangled "parent." In the higher vertebrates the regenerative capacity has been largely exchanged for higher specificity of structure, but even in man we find partial regenerative processes at work. If the surface of the body is lacerated, the wound is closed by the production of scar tissue, making a patch stronger and more resistant to damage than the original tissues that were destroyed. The same process may take place in almost every organ system of the body. It is true that these regenerative processes have bad as well as good aspects for human adjustment, since the scar tissue is a patch and nothing more; it holds together the tissues on either side, but does not constitute a replacement. Somewhat dependent on the site of the injury, scars may cause more or less profound alterations of function. The scars of burns may contract a body surface or hollow viscera so much that normal function is impossible; the scars of brain injury may act as foci of irritative stimulation and produce convulsive seizures. In certain circumstances, which are not well understood, injury and chronic irritation appear to stimulate cell growth in wild and uncontrolled abandon and tumors of various types result.

A type of compensation for defect that is unique in man is the application of various physical appliances as remedies. A wide range of visual defects are helped by spectacles, poorly functioning organs of locomotion by crutches and motor vehicles, missing limbs by prosthetic substitutes, hearing defects by devices for amplifying the sound waves, and so on. Viewed biologically, this is a more remarkable technique than regeneration in the flatworms, since it demonstrates that the loss of adaptive flexibility at the level of cellular multiplication has been more than remedied by the development of structures (primarily the brain and hands) that give flexibility at another level. The fact that we can write and read books whose subject is *maladaptation* is an even better example of the type of compensation for defect available to the human species.

FUNCTIONAL COMPENSATION

The number of functional compensations for defect is incalculable. Much of the study of internal medicine is concerned with understanding and with aiding or interfering with these biological adjustments to defect. A few examples will suffice. When the body is attacked by bacteria, a cooperative protective mechanism is called into action. The rate of production of white blood cells increases; there is a concentration of these cells at the site of the infection. Attempts are made to wall off and destroy the invaders. Body temperature rises, the chemical composition of the bloodstream changes, and the complex process of immunity reaction is initiated. These are all physiological adjustments to stress. If they were absent, the organism would certainly perish. This very adaptive process, however, may play a role in behavior disorganization. As we remarked in Chapter II, efforts to maintain an equilibrium at this cellular level may proceed so vigorously and demand so much of the available bodily resources that adequate adjustment on other levels becomes impossible. The efforts of a man to conquer a bacterial enemy may render him so fatigued and possibly delirious that he is unable to meet the simplest of personal or social emergencies.

HOMEOSTATIC MECHANISMS

Less dramatic but just as important are the normal regulatory functions of the body, those adaptive devices that Cannon first called *homeostatic mechanisms.* For normal physiological functioning a wide variety of conditions within the body must be kept constant within small limits of permissible variation. The acidity-alkalinity balance for body fluids cannot vary greatly; the salt concentration and specific gravity of the blood and lymph and cellular contents must be quite constant; the nutritional state of the billions of body cells must be nicely regulated; the osmotic pressure at the cell-membranes must be maintained at correct levels; excretion must be regulated as to amount and chemical content; metabolic exchange with the environment must achieve a balance between intake and expenditure. All these precise adjustments play their role in maintenance of successful living. When circumstances interfere with one of these mechanisms, readjustments may take place in all the rest; again, the best possible equilibrium will be maintained. We have already seen what shifts may take place in the regulatory mechanisms under conditions of emotional stress.

BEHAVIOR ORGANIZATION AND COMPENSATION

The organism has another potent weapon in its attempt to keep on even terms with the world. From the standpoint of the psychopathologist by far the most important of the adjustments to defect is represented in the integrated behavior of the total organism. Psychologically speaking, there are many ways of performing the same task; if one structure is deficient, another can take over. If the right arm is broken or amputated, writing can be done with the left. If the arms are lost, mechanical contrivances permit the person to write by movements of his shoulders and trunk. In the "freak shows," we see that people have mastered writing with their toes substituting for fingers. As children we used to trace our names, with the letters three feet high, in fresh snow by tramping movements involving our whole bodies.

Many symptoms of organic behavior disorders are really attempts of the organism to adjust to the stresses brought on by defective structure and function. The "memory" of old people, who many times remember things that never happened, is a mechanism of this sort. Their failing memory and their loss of observational powers is compensated for by a process of filling in the gaps with imaginary material. This has the virtue of maintaining the continuity of personal experience necessary for an individual's sense of his integrity.

Another example of disordered behavior that appears very obviously as an attempt to avoid painful stimulation is observed in the actions of a dog with distemper. One frequent symptom is a wild running behavior that alternates with a savage growling crouch, as if the animal were first trying to run away from his pain and then attack it. It is plausible to think of the dog as acting out, in an overt and direct way, the basic avoidance response we discussed as part of the developmental history of anxiety. Intense pain often provokes such unreasoning attempts at escape in the human subject. The man with a toothache paces the floor, the person crazed with thirst attempts to throw himself off the life-raft, the man disappointed in love runs to "join the Foreign Legion." We have seen how the catatonic, in his excited phase, may be completely heedless of his safety in attempts to escape the conflicts that haunt him. At the heart of all escape behavior is this organic pain reaction. Pain, as a sensory phenomenon, apparently is an accompaniment of widespread sensory nerve discharge that has equally widespread motor effects.

Another type of compensation for defect has already been mentioned. This is the motivating influence that defect has on behavior. The short man, sensitive because of his stature, manages to act in a way that impresses people with his toughness or his athletic prowess. The socially unsuccessful college student redoubles his efforts to gain scholastic recognition. In some boyhood communities the minister's son is almost forced to lead in mischief. One of our friends said he owed his fistic ability to a kindly intentioned mother who named him "Percy" but forgot that he would grow old enough to go to school. Our war-injured patients in many instances have found their lives completely changed and a whole new set of problems facing them. In the ward for paraplegic[3] patients at one army hospital was a former mail-carrier. He had worked hard to pass his postal examinations and, before the war and his injury, had looked forward to a life of walking around the pleasant town in which he lived. Now, unable to move from his wheel-chair, he had acquired a new interest; almost by accident he found that he had considerable artistic ability and was engrossed in learning to decorate greeting cards, paint signs and do similar kinds of commercial art work. The initial circumstance behind the change in his life occupation was a destructive injury to his spinal cord. The injury did not

---

[3] Paraplegia—a condition of paralysis of the legs and lower part of the body, usually due to injury that lacerates or concusses the spinal cord. These cases are among the most convincing of arguments for the biological stupidity of war.

determine the form of the adaptation but it provided a necessary part of the motivation.

HIGHER LEVELS OF THE NERVOUS SYSTEM ARE INVOLVED IN MOST ORGANIC REACTIONS

Because the nervous system, and particularly the brain, is functionally connected to every organ of the body, the state of health or disease of all organ systems has its effect on brain function. This influence is not only by means of the nerve tracts that come into and go away from the brain, but also through the bloodstream. By this latter means endocrine secretions, nourishment, toxic byproducts of infection or exertion elsewhere in the body, roaming cells, blood clots, and gases all pass through the brain. Few organs have as high a metabolic rate as does the brain. These factors produce changes in brain function and thus changes in behavior. Since apparently most of our learned and habitual ways of behaving depend upon cerebral integration, the brain is ultimately a causal factor in all disordered behavior.

Pathological Reactions to Altered Organic Conditions

ANATOMICAL AND PHYSIOLOGICAL DEFECTS AS A SOURCE OF STRESS

In Chapter X we have already considered in some detail many behavioral reactions to altered organic conditions. Our concern in that chapter was chiefly with changes in the brain and central nervous system. However, continuing the discussion of Chapter X, we should be able to extend our analysis to all types of altered organic conditions even though organic brain changes are of paramount importance. Any defect is a hindrance to effective adjustment, and if the defect is of sufficient severity, adjustment may be impossible. As we saw in Chapter X, organic injury adds to the usual problems of the organism and may be thought of as a cause of stress, acting in opposition to the animal's attempts to maintain its equilibrium. The responses of the animal to this type of stress differ in no essential ways from his trial-and-error techniques for reducing other types of stress or solving any other problematic situation that hinders goal attainment. *For any organic defect, as for other forms of stress, there exists, for any individual, a* stress threshold beyond which continued stress will produce pathological reactions.

EPILEPSY

One disorder, which we have mentioned previously in the text, illustrates the part that factors of stress threshold may play. The behavior is *epilepsy*. This term refers to a condition whose major symptoms are convulsive seizures, which are mass muscular contractions, usually of the whole body and usually accompanied by partial or complete loss of consciousness. Epilepsy may have many precipitating causes. Abnormalities of structure within the brain, such as tumors, scar tissue, abscess, or abnormally high cerebrospinal pressure, may give rise to seizures. Conditions producing toxins in other parts of the body may, due to bloodstream transportation, affect the brain. In many instances the causative factors cannot be identified, and the symptoms cannot be attributed to a specific cause. Such cases are termed *idiopathic epilepsy*, as distinguished from the *symptomatic* and *focal* epilepsies whose causes we have indicated above. In all convulsive seizures the symptoms are remarkably similar, irrespective of the causative factors. The motor attack, the convulsion itself, is reaction to a stress that exceeds the threshold of the patient concerned.

The evidence for this statement, and indeed much of our present knowledge of epilepsy, is derived from electroencephalographic (EEG) studies. Hans Berger, a German psychiatrist and neurologist, discovered that the brain has a "spontaneous" electrical activity of small magnitude, which can be measured and recorded if suitably amplified. Using a laboratory galvanometer, he was able to describe many of the basic EEG phenomena. In recent years higher and more dependable amplification and recording have been achieved with the use of electronic devices, and the EEG is rapidly becoming a standard instrument for the clinical and experimental study of brain activity.

It has been well established that the normal resting brain gives off a rhythmic potential with a frequency of between eight and twelve cycles per second in the more anterior regions. The voltage of this discharge normally varies between about fifteen and seventy-five microvolts (millionths of a volt) when recordings are made with electrodes attached to the scalp. The basic eight- to twelve-cycles-per-second rhythm Berger termed *alpha activity,* and the faster rhythm he called *beta activity.* Figure 24 illustrates the placement of the electrodes and some typical normal tracings from various parts of the brain. It should be remembered that alpha activity is typical of the resting brain. Any type of stimulation of sense organs dampens the alpha, as does the effort involved in mental problem-solving. EEG tracings are usually taken with the subject in either a comfortably reclined position in a darkened room with eyes shut, or less usually, with the subject sitting upright in a relaxed position. Because of the great sensitivity of the amplifying device, great precaution must be taken to eliminate extra-cortical sources of electrical potential, whether from the subject in the form of muscular electrical discharges or from static and power appliances in his immediate environment.

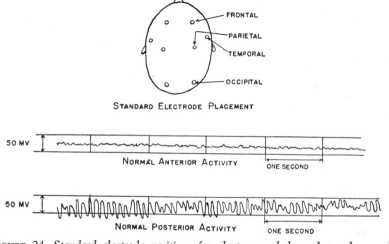

FRONTAL
PARIETAL
TEMPORAL
OCCIPITAL

STANDARD ELECTRODE PLACEMENT

50 MV

NORMAL ANTERIOR ACTIVITY   ONE SECOND

50 MV

NORMAL POSTERIOR ACTIVITY   ONE SECOND

FIGURE 24. *Standard electrode positions for electroencephalography and normal anterior and posterior recordings.*

When epileptics are examined by EEG methods, it is found that they produce a type of wave form not seen in the normal subject. This rhythm, illustrated in some of its variants in Figure 25, varies from one-half cycle per second to four or five cycles per second and has a greatly increased voltage, running commonly at one hundred microvolts and attaining three or four hundred microvolts on occasion. The slow activity is frequently accompanied by high-voltage, fast waves, which may be sinusoidal in form and of a frequency of about twenty per second or may be spike-like and of varying frequencies of occurrence. The slow, high-voltage waves are called *delta activity*. Epileptics may show these patterns both while having a seizure and in the intervals between seizures. In idiopathic epilepsy the delta activity is usually generalized in its manifestations, the high-voltage waves coming from all parts of the cerebral cortex. In the symptomatic epilepsies, particularly the focal group, the abnormal waves may come from only a restricted location in

RECORD FROM PATIENT IN GRAND MAL SEIZURE |← ONE SECOND →|

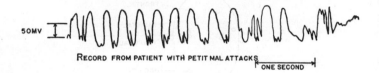

RECORD FROM PATIENT WITH PETIT MAL ATTACKS |← ONE SECOND →|

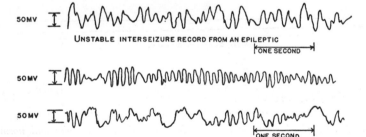

UNSTABLE INTERSEIZURE RECORD FROM AN EPILEPTIC |← ONE SECOND →|

RIGHT (ABOVE) AND LEFT (BELOW) OCCIPITAL RECORDS IN PATIENT
WITH A LEFT OCCIPITAL TUMOR

FIGURE 25. *Illustrations of abnormal EEG records.*

the cortex, indicating that the electrode is over or near the source of the disturbance.

If EEGs are taken of patients suffering from other forms of brain damage, it will be found that they also show a high percentage of delta activity. Similarly, the blood relatives of epileptics, many of whom have never shown overt symptoms of epilepsy, will have EEG records with high percentages of delta activity. Finally, if a large number of individuals are selected at random from a population of persons who are not epileptic, do not have epileptic relatives, and have no other obvious type of cortical disturbance, the EEGs of about 15 per cent of this group will show some delta activity. If this random sample were all exposed to conditions placing increased stress on their brains, the percentage of the group showing delta activity would increase. The usual stress test in the EEG examination is to require the patient to breathe very deeply and rapidly for at least three minutes. This procedure drives off carbon dioxide and changes the acidity of the blood supply of the brain.

What do these facts about the occurrence of the abnormal delta activity suggest? A reasonable conclusion might be that most, and possibly all, people are potentially liable to convulsive seizures, and that the seizures will occur if certain threshold stress values are exceeded. This conclusion is of great practical value in understanding convulsive phenomena. In idiopathic epilepsy, for example, attacks can be minimized by medication that raises the stress threshold. It has also been noted that emotion, conflict, fatigue, or concurrent disease processes may act as precipitants of seizures. Various types of brain injury appear to lower the convulsive threshold. It is a well-established clinical precept that the brain-injured person exposes himself to grave risks of convulsion or other disordered behavior if he ingests what would otherwise be minor amounts of alcohol or allows himself to become even a little fatigued. The following case illustrates this concept:

Case 58. Lieutenant S. J. was admitted to the neuropsychiatric section of an Army hospital from a nearby airfield with a diagnosis of "convulsive seizures, cause unknown." The previous day, while piloting a B-24 bomber on a routine training flight, S. J. had felt slightly nauseated and giddy. He attributed this to moderately turbulent air conditions that existed at the time. He asked his copilot to take the controls, stating that he wished to close his eyes and relax a moment. The copilot reported that S. J. then started to loosen his seat-belt, and almost immediately stiffened and jerked convulsively. Since his feet were still on the rudder pedals, and his movements threw his legs and trunk against the control column, the copilot maintained control of the plane only by vigorous exertion. The engineer and radio operator removed S. J. to the waist of the ship and sat on him while he continued his convulsive movements for a period of almost five minutes. The plane was over an hour away from its base, and before it returned, S. J. had regained consciousness but had no memory of the attack.

In the hospital a complete physical and neurological examination revealed no abnormality. The patient's previous medical history was entirely negative. Not only had he never had a convulsion before, but as far as he knew no member of his family had ever had an epileptic disorder. Psychiatric and psychological examinations showed only a very well adjusted, intelligent young man who appeared free of conflicts or emotional disorders. There was no indication of organic impairment of thinking. EEG studies were the only source of positive information. He had a pronounced dysrhythmia, with a large proportion of delta waves coming from all parts of the brain. It was apparent that S. J. could not be returned to duty, but it was difficult to find grounds for medical retirement from the service. A further review of the circumstances leading up to the training flight on which the attack occurred showed that S. J. had just returned from his last leave before a scheduled departure to an overseas assignment. He had prolonged the leave until the last moment and then had driven 36 hours continuously in order to get from his home to the airfield. In that 36 hours he had eaten only two sandwiches and one quart thermos of coffee. When he arrived at the field he found his name posted for a four-hour training flight, due to take off within the hour. Substituting two cups of coffee without sugar for a meal, he had then started on the flight and shortly after had his attack.

These circumstances seemed to indicate that S. J. was a person with relatively low tolerance for stress, whose carbohydrate intake had been severely limited at the same time that his expenditure and need for energy increased. The dysbalance afforded by this proved excessive, and the convulsions resulted. It was pointed out to the patient that the convulsions might not appear again in his life as long as he did not expose himself to comparable stresses. Although S. J. was extremely disappointed in his retirement, the explanation, coupled with his vivid realization of the danger to which he exposed himself and others, reconciled him to the disposition.

In this case, fatigue, lowered carbohydrate intake, and increased energy demands resulted in a seizure.

The same resistance factor may be shown in diseases other than epilepsy. In internal medicine it is well known that acute attacks of infectious disease are more likely if the patient has been weakened by other diseases, by overexertion, by malnourishment, and so on. Before patients are subjected to serious or protracted surgery, they are placed on a regimen calculated to improve their general health and resistance to shock. In the psychoneuroses and psychoses and in the borderline conditions of the usual individual, it is easily recognized that the amount of conflict, frustration, or anxiety that can be tolerated is partially dependent upon the factors of bodily condition and health.

Reciprocally, it is also true that the amount of organic damage that can be assimilated or tolerated by the patient varies with many factors.

This principle holds for the reactions of people to intoxication or poisoning, to infections, and to all other types of traumatic circumstances.

Returning to epilepsy, we find that the generalized convulsive seizure, the *grand mal* attack, as it is known, is not the only way that this disorder may be manifested. The chief variants in the epileptic pattern are the *petit mal* and *Jacksonian* attacks. The petit mal attacks are typically short lapses of consciousness without convulsive movements. The duration of a single attack may range from one or two seconds to as long as a minute or more, and they may occur with extreme frequency, ranging as high as ten or fifteen distinct attacks in a five-minute period. The patient rarely is aware of the disturbance unless he notes the disparity between his experience and the actual lapse of temporal intervals. The petit mal attack is accompanied by a fairly distinctive type of EEG, as shown in Figure 25. The discharge is usually generalized from all cortical areas, but it may start or be predominant in the frontal regions. Occasional individuals are found with the *spike-wave* EEG pattern and no history of petit mal seizures. These seizure patterns occur most frequently in children, tending to disappear or be replaced by more generalized convulsive activity in the adult.

The *Jacksonian seizure,* named after Hughlings Jackson, the great English neurologist, is a convulsive attack limited to a restricted group of muscles, or as is sometimes the case, a seizure that starts in a definite muscle group and then progressively involves a larger and larger proportion of the total musculature. The Jacksonian type of attack is rare in the idiopathic epilepsies and is usually indicative of an irritative focal lesion in a part of the motor area of the cortex corresponding to the locus of the seizure.

In addition to the grand mal, petit mal, and Jacksonian attacks, other behavioral phenomena have been observed as epileptic symptoms. *Automatisms* are confused periods when the patient is not aware of his behavior. They may follow major seizures or occur suddenly as a substitute or equivalent of a seizure. The football player who sustains a concussion and yet completes a game with no memory for events following his injury is showing a comparable phenomenon. In the epileptic automatism, the patient may become violent or dangerous, indulging in unprovoked attacks on others around him. In these automatic activities, however, we frequently see that they mirror the adaptive strivings of the patient. Penfield and Erickson (1941) tell of a patient who suddenly jumped out of his bed, threw the bed casters about, and shouted that he "wanted to help his mother"; he further stated, as he was being restrained, that he wanted to be a man, a hero, and intelligent. As the attack subsided the patient had little memory for the incident. Prominent as a factor in these confusional states seems to be a release of cortical inhibitions.

There has been, for many years, a controversy among psychopathologists over whether or not a distinctive *epileptic personality* exists. Many clinicians have believed that epileptics as a group showed certain personality traits related to their illness. The epileptic is described as an extremely sensitive and egotistic person, given to temper tantrums and rages. He is supposed to be more irritable, selfish, cruel, and asocial than the nonepileptic, with frequent anti-social and criminal behavior. Harrower-Erickson (Penfield and Erickson, 1941) concluded, after a review of the experimental and clinical literature and a consideration of her own experience in the Montreal clinic, that the evidence militated "against the existence of a specific and unique constellation of personality traits to be found invariably in all persons with seizures" (page 574). On the related matter of whether or not the epileptic presents a lowered intellectual capacity or is subject to deterioration of intellectual status, the answer is a qualified negative. Some patients do, with the passage of years, show a marked decline in intelligence; others may have seizures for equally long intervals and show no reduction. Further, there is no correlation between the severity of the seizure symptoms and the lowering of intelligence.

It is true, however, that the epileptic may show a variety of emotional difficulties and may have severe disturbance of personality functions. Epilepsy, when considered from a social point of view, constitutes a serious frustration for the patient. Never knowing when he will suffer an attack, he is ridden by a constant sense of insecurity and danger. The frightened and horrified reactions that many people still have toward the epileptic increase his sense of social isolation. Because of his illness, he must restrict his activity in many ways that handicap him in his adjustment to social living. He should not drive a car, swim, climb, or otherwise expose himself to situations where his unpredictable loss of consciousness would endanger him; his relations with other people are always threatened by the seizures. It is small wonder that many epileptics respond by narrowing their environment, appearing irritable, rejecting normal social satisfactions. But all epileptics do not have this personality, and there are many of them who have given every evidence of great accomplishment and of emotional and intellectual maturity. We see again that disordered behavior is the attempt of the person to make an adjustment to unusual and stressful conditions.

THE EPILEPTIC PSYCHOSES

Only a small percentage of epileptics develop psychotic reactions or show sufficient deterioration in their general social adjustment to require hospitalization. In 1949 there were only 1,397 admissions of psychotics with convulsive disorders to state mental hospitals and an additional 406 patients with epilepsy but without psychosis, a percentage of the total hospital admissions of about 1.7 per cent (Federal Security Agency, 1952).

Epileptics are hospitalized either because the factors producing the convulsions have also produced sufficient brain damage to lower drastically their adaptive efficiency or because their personality reaction to their illness (including the physiological impairment) has taken the form of psychotic behavior. Some patients, first admitted as epileptics, are later found to have had convulsions as early symptoms of other pathological brain processes, such as tumors.

We have discussed the symptoms of epilepsy as such and have described the so-called *equivalent states,* in which the individual may act in a wild and uncontrolled manner, inflicting damage on himself and others. Whether these equivalent states are substitutes for seizures or whether they are simply violent emotional protests against the patient's condition has never been satisfactorily decided. One point is sure, and that is the aggressive nature of the behavior. That this aggression may occur with limited objectives that have little social significance is shown in the following history:

Case 59. The patient, a corporal in the Air Forces, was sent to the hospital by direction of the president of a courtmartial, following testimony by medical officers that the offence of which the patient stood accused could have been an epileptic manifestation. He had been apprehended leaving a house that stood near the air field at which he was stationed. While in this house he had entered a bedroom in which a woman was sleeping, put one hand over her mouth, and with the other hand pulled her hair so violently that a great many hairs were pulled out. In the three months preceding this incident similar night attacks had been reported in the town. In each case the approach was similar, and the assailant seemed content to pull his victim's hair and then flee.

When the patient was caught, he had acted confused and would not account for his actions. When he awakened the next morning in the guardhouse, he asked why he was locked up and claimed he had no memory of the actions with which he had been charged. Before he was brought to trial, he told his defense counsel that he had "spells" occasionally, although the last ones had taken place two or three years before he volunteered for military service. He had concealed his defect from the induction medical examiners and had had no trouble in the army until the present difficulty. In the hospital he was given an EEG, which showed a decided dysrhythmia of a type characteristic of epilepsy. Although it was impossible to make a definite statement that his assaultive behavior was epileptic in origin, the senseless and perseverative nature of it, coupled with the excellent military record of the patient, lent credence to the possibility that he was not "responsible" for his actions.

The actual epileptic psychoses show most of the characteristics with which we are already familiar, including the preoccupation with personal problems, the anxiety, and the nonsocial attempts to reduce their anxiety. The following case, taken from Noyes (1934), is an extremely clear example:

Case 60. T. C. was admitted to the State Hospital at the age of thirty-one. He was described by his family as having a rather bad temper, being somewhat stubborn and inclined to boast. At seventeen he began to suffer from mild seizures with loss of consciousness but without generalized convulsive movements. Not until twenty-seven did seizures occur more than two or three times a year. At that age they began to occur once or twice a month. At twenty-nine the seizures became more severe with marked convulsive movements and longer periods of unconsciousness. Because of a seizure at his place of employment he lost his position in an ice factory. Unable to find other employment the patient became somewhat depressed, worried, irritable and "hard to get along with." His seizures became more frequent and severe. One day following a period of moody preoccupation during which he seemed unaware of his wife's presence he said to her, "Catherine, I've done good today. I've made my fortune." He then added, "Call the doctor and the priest. I'm afraid I'm going to die." That night he walked about all night, talking constantly about becoming rich, quoted passages from the salesmanship instructions issued by a concern for which he had recently attempted to canvass, and paid little heed to his environment. The following night he became so uncontrollable that at his family's request he was taken to the police station and on the following day committed to the State Hospital. He was brought to the institution in straps and in the admission office shouted in a loud tone, "I drank a lot. I don't need that fellow. I thought an awful lot of that fellow. I think an awful lot of my mother. I told them plenty. I said No! No!" At intervals he struggled violently to escape from the two officers who were holding him. When asked any questions he would shout, "None of your business."

On examination at the hospital he was noted to be a tall, ungainly individual, his ears standing out prominently at nearly a right angle to his skull and the conformation of his facies suggesting that he was a biological variant. He remained clouded for about six weeks, at times apparently hallucinated, sometimes preoccupied, mute and having to be tube-fed, again talking in a loud angry tone. When not in the continuous bath he was usually found in his room, frequently with his prayer beads hanging from his mouth, often nude, and when approached would spontaneously make such remarks as: "I'm—I'm trying to solve the problem. I am trying to find the solution Irish! Irish! Capital I, and eye for an eye, and a tooth for a tooth. I've tried to save my soul." After this prolonged clouded state the patient remained clear for two months, occasionally suffering from a convulsion. Four months after admission he again became cloudy. At times he was stuporous, at times excited, and on several occasions attempted suicide. Nine months after admission he was paroled to his family and for seven months remained well except for occasional light convulsions. At the end of that period while attending church he suddenly arose during services and began to pray loudly. He held a crucifix high above his head, and when led from the building seemed much confused. The patient was then returned to the hospital where the clinical course was much like that of the first residence.[4]

In this history the relationship between the disorder and environmental factors appears clear. Whether the psychosis would have taken place in this individual if he had not been epileptic cannot, of course, be answered. A general impression remains, however, that the small percentage of epileptics who become psychotic do so because of other factors than the brain pathology, which is such a significant vector in epilepsy as such. In other words, the malfunction of the patient's brain operates more as an adjustmental problem than as a direct cause of the psychosis. In this case the epilepsy precipitated social problems, such as difficulty in gaining employment, and the emotional outbursts were directed as much against the patient's social incapacities as against his epilepsy.

[4] A. P. Noyes (1934), *Modern Clinical Psychiatry* (3rd Ed.), p. 227. Philadelphia: W. B. Saunders Company.

CATASTROPHIC BEHAVIOR AS EXEMPLIFIED
IN ORGANIC DEFECTS

Suppose, in any situation and with any individual, we would be able to increase the difficulty of his adaptation by degrees and then observe his attempts to adjust, compensate, or assimilate the forces directed against him. We would find that different ways of reacting were characteristic of the differing degrees of stress. As we varied the stress in a continuous manner we would find that the reactions would show discrete qualitative changes, the adjustmental effort changing more or less abruptly at various points along our stress continuum. Low and moderate degrees of stress that are within the limits of any organism's usual experience would be met with behavior more or less successful in stress reduction. If we continue to increase the stress, however, we will always reach an intensity[5] that is too much to be reduced by the organism's normal repertoire of response. This state of affairs elicits initially a greater variability in reaction, which may result in the development of completely new techniques of adjustment, some of which are unqualified successes and some others of which are momentarily stress-reducing but become pathological if applied over a longer period of time. If we relentlessly continue to increase the stress on our subject and go beyond this region of increased variability, we finally come to an intensity that will completely overwhelm him; adjustment by an act in his repertoire of previously learned responses or by any new stratagem is impossible. The behavior then changes radically and a new type of action emerges, the *catastrophic response* we spoke of in our discussion of basic concepts. Up to this critical level of stress, although many of the responses have had undesirable aspects or have failed to reduce the stress completely, nevertheless, as Goldstein says:

. . . responses appear to be constant, correct, adequate to the species and to the individuality of the organism, as well as to the respective cir-

---

[5] Or, in many instances, a *duration* of time of application. A long duration of a relatively small stress that cannot be adequately handled at once may become equivalent to a stronger stress operating for a shorter period of time, as the relatively minor annoyance of a fly buzzing around when we are so busy we cannot brush it off, or the old torture technique of dropping water slowly on the forehead of the victim. This is an example of a rather generally observed relationship in biological energy exchanges and can be expressed as a formula: $It = k$, I symbolizing intensity, t standing for time, and k indicating that the product of intensity and time is a constant.

cumstances . . . the course of behavior has a *definite order*, a total pattern in which all involved organismic factors—the mental and somatic down to the physico-chemical processes—participate in a fashion appropriate to the performance in question.[6]

The catastrophic response, however, is entirely different in type from all that went before:

The "catastrophic" reactions, on the other hand, are not only "inadequate" but also disordered, inconstant, inconsistent, and embedded in physical and mental *shock*. In these situations the individual feels himself unfree, buffeted and vacillating. He experiences a shock affecting not only his own person, but the surrounding world as well . . . his reactivity is likely to be impaired . . . he becomes more or less unresponsive and fails even in those tasks which he could easily meet under other circumstances.[7]

This type of behavior is what we often refer to in common parlance as "nervous breakdown," "crack-up," and so forth and is back of the familiar statement that "every man has his breaking point."

Since the injured organism meets its environment with impaired resources, it must limit its behavior if catastrophic response is to be avoided. The crippled person does not attempt feats of locomotion beyond his reduced abilities, and the patient with cardiac or tubercular trouble drastically reduces his activity. Goldstein has described many instances of this simplification of behavior in patients with brain injuries. He noted that they attempt to avoid catastrophic situations by, among other things, a tendency toward orderliness.

Suppose a patient has just finished writing on a piece of paper. The examination is over. I take the pencil and place it carelessly on the sheet of paper which happens to lie obliquely on the table. As he gets up, the patient removes the pencil, puts the paper in line with the edge of the table, and then sets the pencil down, as parallel as possible, to the border of the paper. If, without comment, I again set the pencil obliquely on the paper, the patient, provided he has been watching, may once more place it in the same way as before. This game can be repeated several times, until he is either distracted by something else, or is told explicitly that I

[6] Kurt Goldstein (1939), *The Organism: A Holistic Approach to Biology Derived from Pathological Data in Man*, pp. 37-38. New York: American Book Company.
[7] *Ibid.*, p. 37.

want it this and this way. In this case the patient resigns himself to the situation, though usually with an expression of marked discomfort.[8]

We have met with this same general technique before in the behavior of the rigid obsessive-compulsive personality who must have a neat desk, pictures straight on the wall, and be on time for appointments. The same purpose would seem to be served in both instances. Patients whose cortical injuries have drastically reduced their use of symbolic language sometimes experience intense emotional conflicts over being expected to participate in therapeutic sessions designed to re-educate them in language functions. They resist the possibility of being placed in a situation that reveals their inadequacies. It is clear that these reactions are, in a broad sense, adjustive.

The catastrophic behavior itself, if it cannot be avoided, is almost completely unadaptive. We saw, in our discussion of emotional reactions, how socially destructive such emotional behavior could be. The person who has "lost his head" in the throes of a rage reaction is showing a type of catastrophic response similar to that shown by one who has received severe physical trauma.

Case 61. At the scene of a highway accident, a man staggered out of his car (which had just collided at high speed with a truck that had pulled unexpectedly out of a side road), blood streaming down his face, his lower lip torn and hanging, saying only, "My God, what is it? What is it?" While witnesses were examining the other occupants of the car, this man kept trying to pull them away, still mumbling, "What is it?" He was finally led to a car and prevailed upon to sit back and relax until an ambulance arrived. Within two minutes he was again staggering around the scene of the wreck, still asking his monotonous question. By the time he had reached the hospital and had been given the minor surgical treatment indicated, he had somewhat recovered from his shock, and his behavior became better organized. He was then able to describe the accident from his point of view and to ask intelligent questions. The sudden terrific nature of the impact and the complete change in his situation brought about by the accident had deprived him for the time of all capacity for adjustment. He was manifesting catastrophic behavior.

The behavior of low-grade mental defectives, of the hyperacute manic, and of severely demented schizophrenics present many of these same features of complete nonrelevance to the demands being made on the organism.

[8] *Ibid.*, p. 43.

Many types of stress then may each be enough to call forth catastrophic behavior. Injury to the central nervous system is a particularly frequent source of such maladaptation because of its strategic position as an integrating device essential to all types and kinds of behavior. Relatively slight cortical injuries can produce massive sensory and motor defects or hamper many other central integrative processes.

Personality and Organic Defect

ROLE OF THE PERSONALITY IN REACTION TO DEFECT

Many psychopathological conditions are precipitated by injury. A person who has reacted adequately to most life situations in the past can be changed through injury or disease to such an extent that he can no longer effectively adjust to the simplest sort of problem. War creates many such cases; that of the paraplegic mailman mentioned previously is an example. Disease of the pituitary gland can change a person's appearance and behavior so greatly that his most intimate friends might fail to recognize him. Hemorrhage into certain parts of the brain may reduce a mature, sagacious, and socially responsible adult into a state of whining, crying incompetence.

In the vast majority of pathological reactions having an organic basis, however, the pre-traumatic personality can be seen as one of the determinants of the post-traumatic symptomatology. The personality structure is crucial in two, certainly, and possibly three, respects:

(*a*) Determination of the level of resistance to breakdown.

(*b*) Determination of the content of the pathological behavior.

(*c*) In many instances the organic condition itself is the result of adjustmental strivings.

We have already discussed the level of resistance to breakdown as a general concept and have indicated the part it plays in determining subsequent behavior.

CONTENT OF ABNORMAL BEHAVIOR

By the *content* of abnormal behavior we mean simply the particular ideas or patterns that appear in the patient's actions. If a person dreams of dogs, the dogs are the content; if a person, after a blow on the head, becomes concerned about his skull, the worry over his skull is the content. The previous personality of the patient is crucial in providing content. His past experiences and his constitutional makeup determine the composition of the symptoms. This is as true for cases of organic injury as it was for the functional psychoses discussed in Chapter IX. Just as no two schizophrenic patients have the same delusions or hallucinations, so no two cases of brain injury behave in precisely the same manner, even if injured in exactly the same brain areas. No two delirious people say the same things or produce the same actions. No two people handle the minor discomfort of a headache in the same way. This fact should be borne in mind with respect to the various types of organically caused psychoses listed in Chapter X. It is easy to slip into the error of believing that a common organic causative agent evokes specific common behavioral reactions.

"ACCIDENTS" AND ADJUSTMENTAL STRIVINGS

Many studies have shown that accidents are not always accidental, and that a relatively small part of the population has a relatively large proportion of the accidents. Misfortune, like fortune, seems to come to the person who has prepared for it, or who is looking for it, or who has "grown used to" it. On the level of physical disease this was called "predisposition," and we saw evidence for it in the families of peptic ulcer cases. In an earlier chapter we talked about Freud's observations concerning the "psychopathology of everyday life" and noted with him that a strong purposive element seems hidden in even the most "accidental" happening. Although sometimes people get into circumstances producing physical injury through no fault of their own, in probably just as many instances the person who gets hurt is, in the vernacular, "asking for it."

A slightly more indirect way of seeking injury may be seen in the behavior of poorly adjusted people who discover what might be termed "dangerous" techniques of adjustment. Alcoholism, drug addiction, attempts at suicide, irritability or pugnaciousness leading to fights, all these and hundreds more of similar circumstances can be part of the pattern of factors leading up to the injury itself. A man may be insecure to such a painful extent that he finds excessive use of alcohol his only apparently satisfactory means of tension reduction. In his drinking he renders himself liable to physical injury through accidents or through the pathological effects of the alcohol on his bodily organs. If he is run over by an automobile and secures a paralyzing head injury, the alcohol and the insecurity back of the alcohol addiction are just as real etiological factors in the paralysis as was the cranial injury itself. If the man's liver cells break down under the impact of his alcohol intake, the responsible physician's treatment cannot content itself with removing the alcohol; the treatment must go back to the personality factors producing the need for an alcoholic technique of adjustment.

Thus, it is a matter of concern for the psychopathologist to inquire not only into the symptoms following injury but into the conditions antecedent to the injury. The post-traumatic behavior may often be better understood if the events leading up to the accident or illness are carefully reviewed. The following case illustrates this emphasis:

Case 62. John A., a 25-year-old Air Corps officer, was admitted to the hospital following an automobile accident in which he sustained multiple fractures of the skull and an undetermined amount of cortical damage. Although his injuries received immediate attention, including extensive removal of spicules of bone from the cortex, John lay unconscious for six days. Investigation of the accident showed that he had been alone in the car and had been travelling at a speed estimated by police to be in excess of eighty miles an hour. Further than that no reason could be given for the accident, which happened on a straight stretch of road. The car had turned into the barrow pit and had then rolled over many times. When John recovered consciousness, he had no memory of the incident and for several days was disoriented as to where he was, the month or season of the year, and as to his personal identity. When his wife called, he failed to recognize her.

Within two more weeks he gradually regained a portion of his memories. He re-established his identity, recalled his wife, and was able to talk intelligibly and correctly about most of his past life, including his year and a half of Army service. He still had an amnesia for the accident itself, however. In addition he showed many alarming changes of personality. His wife told the medical officers that her husband was a "changed man." She described him as a quiet, serious, intense person whose greatest interest was in flying. Since his injury he had become frivolous, coarse, and noisy, an individual who manifested no great interest in anything. As an example of his changed behavior she told of an incident that had happened that day. She had gone with him to the post barber shop, and while he was sitting in the chair, he asked her to tie his shoe. As she bent over to comply with his request, he drew back his other foot and kicked her rather violently, laughing uproariously to see her sprawling on the floor. On another occasion he had made amorous proposals to her in the post exchange, in a loud voice, and completely unconcerned by onlookers. X-ray studies of John's brain showed that a considerable area of the cortex, particularly in the frontal lobes, was atrophied. Psychological tests of intelligence were performed poorly. The psychologist reported that attention was easily diverted and that the patient "did not take the testing situation seriously." The Rorschach test showed an extreme impulsivity, a loss of intellectual efficiency, and an abandonment of popular or stereotyped approach to problematical situations. A psychiatric interview with the patient disclosed little pertinent information. The psychiatrist reported that John showed a loss of inhibitory control over his instinctive drives and an unrepressed hostility toward his wife and her parents.

An interview with the wife finally yielded a key to the understanding of his behavior. She said that on the night of the accident he had told her he would soon be sent overseas and proposed that she accompany him to a large town near what he thought would be the overseas staging area. She made a counter suggestion that she return to her parents and stay with them while he was away. He had at first accepted this and agreed that it would be a sensible course of action. Later in the evening, however, after several stiff drinks, he renewed his arguments against her plan and expressed a deep hostility toward her parents, even to the extent of accusing them of having forced him to marry her. She said that he had never given evidence of such feelings before, but that he had at various times shown resentment when she expressed concern over his safety while flying. Following the quarrel, he had started back to the field and had the accident. The interpretation of his behavior appeared to be that the head injury had released deep-seated but inhibited resentment against his wife, who appeared to him as an obstacle to the attainment of his ambition to excel as a flier.

Although most people who sustain head injuries show a certain measure of lost inhibition, the particular inhibitions that are lost depend on the personality of the patient, and the resulting behavior is a complex function of pre-traumatic needs, wishes, and experiences acting upon a sick individual who is also attempting to adjust to the handicaps imposed by the trauma.

Our consideration of pathological behavior following trauma would not be complete without mentioning again the reactions of the patient after the injury has healed and he is again structurally intact. The behavioral after-effects of injury, as we saw when we discussed the traumatic neuroses, often endure long after the physical effects have subsided.

REACTION TO ORGANIC DEFECT A FUNCTION OF MANY VARIABLES: A SUMMARY

Although our point of view toward the organic factors in psychopathology has been inherent in the selection of subject matter for discussion in this chapter, it may be well to make a few explicit statements concerning it.

According to an older, but still somewhat accepted point of view, the disordered behavior is *caused* by the action of a definite traumatizing agent. There are many types of such agent, bacteria, protozoan parasites, drugs, injury and destruction of tissues by physical forces, and so forth, and, within certain limits, these have been looked upon as capable of producing mental disorder in an individual irrespective of his pre-traumatic personality pattern. The form of the illness is thought of as being identified with the traumatizing agent.

Our approach, on the other hand, looks upon the traumatizing agent as only one of many factors whose combined action serves to bring about disturbed behavior *under certain conditions and in certain personalities.* If this is a correct way of looking at the problem, then it follows that all individuals exposed to the same objective extent of trauma will not inevitably develop the same symptoms. The traumatizing agent acts upon specific individuals, and the resultant is equally individual. Hallucinations are not found made to order in bottles of drugs, and delirium is not a simple function of body temperature elevation in fever. The action of alcohol on the human organism is an excellent example of the limitations of assuming an uncomplicated direct relationship between an injurious chemical and behavior. Common cocktail lounge lore and laboratory results agree that the amount of alcohol a person must consume before becoming drunk is a most variable quantity, not only from person to person, but for the same individual at different times. A host of physiological and psychological variables act together to determine the "drunkenness threshold." This is equally true of the other agents of trauma we have mentioned. For this reason we cannot speak as confidently even of the syphilitic "general paralysis of the insane," as Kraepelin once thought, since we must look not only at the patient who has this psychosis, but also at the other people with tertiary syphilis who are not thus affected. A part of the complete knowledge of any disease process is an explanation of the negative instances—of those cases in the population that, exposed to the same risks, do not show the same outcome.

In summary: *Traumatic situations cannot be explained solely in terms of the traumatizing agent. By itself no traumatic circumstance has· properties of causing any kind of behavior. The behavior that actually occurs is a resultant of the mutual interaction of many factors, the majority of which are not directly attributable to the injury.*

DISCUSSION QUESTIONS

1. How flexible is the human body in compensation for structural defect?
2. Can you cite from your own experience examples of catastrophic behavior?
3. What are some of the physiological and psychological problems facing man in his attempts at high-altitude and high-speed flight?
4. Is there evidence for the operation of homeostasis on the psychological level?
5. What are the implications to behavior of the discovery of spontaneous electrical activity of the brain?
6. How does the pre-traumatic personality structure determine the behavioral response to injury?
7. How "accidental" are many accidents?
8. Why is the approach of "environment-organism-behavior" preferable to study of environment and behavior alone? Or is it?
9. Does the obvious ecological devastation produced by man, such as in the wholesale destruction of the buffalo or the carrier pigeon, have any bearing on your understanding of the psychopathology of individual persons?
10. Is it possible to say that one organ system is more important than some other organ system in determining abnormalities of behavior?

SUGGESTED READINGS

S. Cobb (1944), "Personality as affected by lesions of the brain," in J. McV. Hunt, ed. (1944), *Personality and the Behavior Disorders*, pp. 550-582. New York: The Ronald Press Company.

J. F. Fulton (1951), *Frontal Lobotomy and Affective Behavior*. New York: W. W. Norton & Company, Inc.

K. Goldstein (1939), *The Organism*. New York: American Book Company.

BIBLIOGRAPHIC SOURCES

For a delightfully written introduction to the historical background of nineteenth century biology out of which the concept of adaptation emerged, the reader is referred to Drachman's (1930) *Studies in the Literature of Natural Science,* where the whole problem of evolutionary doctrine is traced through the various stages of development. The effect of evolutionary thought on American work has been examined in detail in the work edited by Persons (1950). The first chapter—by R. Scoon—is an excellent account of the historical background of the concept of evolution. A grandson of one of the great early evolutionary biologists has written a monograph on the status of our knowledge of organic evolution: Julian Huxley (1943) and *Evolution, The Modern Synthesis.* On protective coloration two very interesting books are Hingston's (1933) *The Meaning of Animal Color and Adornment,* and Cott's (1940) *Adaptive Coloration in Animals.*

The structural and functional changes along the phylogenetic scale from amoeba to mammal are amply documented by books of interest to the general reader. Allee (1938) discusses the first beginnings of social life in aggregations of unicellular animals and traces steps toward mammalian society. The book by Maier and Schneirla (1935) is both a text and a systematic treatment of animal psychology that is organized according to principles of phylogenesis, assembling the structural-functional correlations in a very useful manner.

On the important field of animal ecology, the text by Pearse (1947) is a good introduction. Russell's (1934) *The Behavior of Animals* has a chapter on the relationship between ecology and behavior. An early important symposium on *Organic Adaptation to Environment* was edited by M. R. Thorpe (1924). Of special interest to the psychopathologist is the chapter by Lull on "Dinosaurian climatic response." A recent development in ecological study has been the investigation of human ecology. Three excellent introductions are the texts by Hawley (1950), Quinn (1950), and the critical article by Hare (1952).

For the advantages and defects in the highly specialized type of functional and structural adaptation of the social insects, the collection of essays by W. W. Wheeler (1928), *Foibles of Insects and Men,* should prove stimulating. On structural pattern as a factor in adaptation, the classic works are Loeb (1918), Child (1924), Herrick (1924), and Coghill (1929). On regeneration and other aspects of the structural compensations for defect, see J. Huxley (1932), W. D'Arcy Thompson (1917), Stockard (1932), and Le Comte Du Nouy (1937).

In modern times, the notion of homeostatic mechanisms may be traced to the great nineteenth century physiologist, Claude Bernard. It was during the present century, however, that Walter Cannon stated most explicitly and in great detail the operation of these processes. We strongly suggest his already classic *The Wisdom of the Human Body* (Cannon, 1932). A recent broad survey of the concept may be found in Dempsey (1951). Due to the influence of N. Weiner's (1948) *Cybernetics,* there have been attempts to apply the notation and concepts of servo-mechanisms to homeostatic mechanisms. Outlines of this approach may be seen in Weiner's book and in Kreezer (1949).

The role played by the central nervous system is discussed at length by Tilney in *The Brain from Ape to Man* (1928) and *The Master of Destiny* (1930).

From the large literature on epilepsy, two books still serve as effective introductions. Lennox's (1941) *Science and Seizures* is designed to give the layman a survey of modern knowledge about epilepsy. Penfield and Erickson's (1941) *Epilepsy and Cerebral Localization,* presents an encyclopedic monograph on all phases of the subject. The photographs of the exposed brains in focal epilepsies and the chapter by Jasper on electroencephalography are two of the special features that make this book valuable to the student. More recent and equally excellent are Penfield and Kristiansen (1951) and Penfield and Jasper (1954). Penfield's (1948) paper discusses in detail the classification of epilepsy. The symposium papers edited by Hoch and Knight (1947) contain a variety of useful information. Historical discussions of epilepsy may be found in Bunker (1947) and Tempkin (1945).

On the use of the EEG, Gibbs and Gibbs' (1950) *Atlas of Electroencephalography* has a wide variety of illustrative EEG tracings, and it has a simple and understandable discussion of modern recording techniques in EEG work. In addition, there are many widely used texts: Cohn (1949), Ogilvie (1949), Hill and Parr (1950), and Schwab (1951). The student may find that the thorough review of the EEG literature by D. B. Lindsley in Hunt (1944) is a good place to start further study of the EEG. An excellent example of the use of the EEG as an experimental tool in the investigation of epilepsy is the study by Marshall, Walter, and Livingston (1953). As the major source of periodical literature, the journal *EEG and Clinical Neurophysiology* is suggested.

That there is no "typical" epileptic personality is generally agreed by most authorities and investigators (Piotrowski, 1947; Lisansky, 1948). Far more controversial is the issue of intellectual defect or lack of it suffered by epileptics. One major methodological problem appears to be the sample tested, whether private patients (Sheps, 1947; Collins, 1951) or institutionalized individuals (Belinson and Cowie, 1947; Reed, 1951). No conclusive answer is at present available; there is no reason to expect that it will be a simple one.

On the epileptic psychoses, Levin (1952) has a detailed review of 52 cases and their symptomatology. For extensive neurological investigations of traumatic epilepsy, Russell (1947) and Whitby (1947) are suggested.

The best single source for the concept of "catastrophic behavior" is Goldstein (1939). Grinker and Spiegel (1945) discuss reactions to stress from a different point of view and with functional rather than organic case material. Cobb's chapter in Hunt (1944) contains observations on the modifying effect of personality variables in the reaction to the stress of brain injury.

Finally, in a splendid article, Lashley (1947) has examined in clear detail the problem of the relationship between behavior and structural variation in the nervous system.

Social Factors in Psychopathology

Man is moved to effort, not under an immediate physio-
logical drive, but instructed by traditional rules, moved by
learned motive and controlled by value.

—MALINOWSKI

Culture and Psychopathology

"NORMAL" AND "ABNORMAL" ARE COVARIANT
WITH CULTURAL PATTERNS

As has been emphasized many times in this text, it is almost impossible to arrive at an understanding of pathological behavior without
taking account of the social setting in which it occurs. The old ad-
monition, "when in Rome do as the Romans," was a recognition of the
fact that evaluations of adjustmental adequacy depend on social variables. As anthropologists have extended our knowledge of the intimate
day-to-day lives of the members of cultures other than our own, we
have come to recognize that human social behavior has wide variety and
variability. Julia S. Brown (1952) has shown that a wide latitude exists
in attitudes toward and punishment of sexual deviations. Whereas most
of the societies in her sample universally banned incest, rape, and
adultery, there were considerable differences in attitude toward such
behavior as male and female homosexuality and pre-marital relations.
Under special conditions behavior was tolerated that is under severe
restriction in our own culture. Brown notes:

Sixteen societies of the sample reported instances of relaxation in the
form of general ceremonial license, and three societies reported instances
of highly immoral acts permitted under special circumstances to particular

individuals. Thus, the Thonga or Lamba father may commit incest with his daughter before embarking on an elephant hunt, in order to achieve great courage.[1]

Furthermore, Benedict (1934) and DuBois (1937) have demonstrated with comparisons of the behavior of differing cultures that many acts considered normal in one group may be the *usual* (or even obligatory) modes of adjustment in other groups. Since modern biology has failed to substantiate the thesis of inherent racial determinants between human beings, the conclusion is forced upon us that differences in behavior from culture to culture arise from learning and habit formation within a given social setting. If normal behavior differences can be accounted for in this way, then it is logical to assume that the varieties of pathological behavior may have a similar explanation. It is the purpose of this chapter to explore a few of the many conditions of human social living that have causative significance for psychopathology.

SOCIAL DETERMINATION OF EVALUATIVE ATTITUDES

To illustrate the role of society in psychopathology, it is necessary to understand certain factors in social behavior. We must realize that most individuals are completely immersed in their own cultural patterns, and that their point of view is limited by the standards and customs of their particular group. People are said to be *ethnocentric*. "Ethnocentrism may be defined as the tendency of persons to judge other cultures by the standards of judgment prevailing in their own" (Cuber, 1947, p. 82). Because of this tendency, it was assumed for many years that the Western European culture of which we are a part provided all the material needed for a complete study of psychopathology. A consequence of this assumption was a conviction that the factors that determined abnormal behavior here were universal factors, applicable to all people everywhere. Although there is a certain amount of truth in this belief, on the whole it led to erroneous conclusions, chiefly because the first and easiest approach to the study of psychopathology is through an analysis of *symptoms*. Now, symptoms are the means by which disorders are expressed and recognized by outside observers. They are, for the most part, overt ways of behaving, and thus take place in a

[1] Julia S. Brown (1952), "A comparative study of deviations from sexual mores." *Amer. Sociol. Rev.,* 17, footnote p. 136.

social setting. Inevitably, in our culture, symptoms are evaluated in terms of their social consequences; *bad* and *pathological* come to be identified with each other. If the same behavior pattern is seen in a person living in another culture, we make the ethnocentric mistake of judging it on the basis of our own cultural standards. It is obvious that culture is a factor in our evaluations of behavior, just as any type of partisan group membership is a significant variable. A home run or touchdown, when made by your team, is infinitely more to be desired and is more glorious when it happens than the same feat would be if scored by the opponents. The same situation is evident in war with far more serious implications. But war—and baseball—are social phenomena, and they produce but an exaggeration of the usual ethnocentric attitudes.

Ethnocentrism is directly related to the personality mechanism of *egocentrism*, and the transformation from the latter to the former is accomplished by that other mechanism of *identification*. As an individual grows up in a given cultural setting, many of the characteristic attributes of that culture become internalized and thus become a part of the personality. Egocentricity works to produce *my* country, *my* people, *my* way of doing things, resulting in the ethnocentric attitude we have described. If our viewpoint were completely without emotional determinants, it would not be necessary to spend so much time and energy in disparaging an enemy for the same type of activities that are praised when they occur within our own group. Ethnocentrism is itself a defense mechanism of sorts, and could almost be said to be a social version of egocentrism.

Why is social evaluation of behavior important to psychopathology? Having recognized that there is a relativity in the matter, and that behavior that is *good* and *acceptable* in one culture may be *bad* and *unacceptable* in another, is there anything to be gained by further elaboration of this fact? The answer is emphatically in the affirmative. As we have said, behavior takes place in a social setting. The organism, in its adjustmental strivings, can behave in a wide variety of ways. The attitudes of approval and disapproval prevalent in the society determine to a large extent what particular behaviors will be acceptable, and these attitudes will also determine what the effect of behaving in various ways will be upon an individual raised in such a society.

One's culture, then, has a dual influence on his behavior. First, it creates certain specific learning opportunities and establishes goals toward which its members strive. Second, it acts to limit the individual to a certain range of behavior and to punish him in various ways when that range is exceeded. From this point of view the usual major criterion of "normality" reduces to the ethnocentric judgments of the social group. Extending this line of thought, we might conclude that any behavior pattern that does not conflict with social standards is normal and of no interest to the psychopathologist. Such is never really the case, but might be true if there were a perfectly uniform and consistent body of social mores, laws, and traditions never at variance with man's biological nature and obligations. As we shall see, much human maladjustment stems from inconsistencies in social regulation, and from conflict between social expectation and biological urgency.

TRAINING FOR CONFLICT

Using our own culture as an example, we have already noted that children are generally taught to conform to a rather strict ethical system in which honesty, consideration for others, obedience to authority, and some variety of the "golden rule" are held up as the most desirable goals. They are also given oversimplified versions of history in which strongly nationalistic values are stressed and in which few of the realities of social conflict are mentioned. At the same time the goals of social living are dominated by an emphasis on material success and "reaching the top," with little regard for the realities of our competitive culture. This results in poor preparation for adequate adult adjustment. Competition in business and the professions often produces strong modifications in our working ideas of honesty. The child finds out that national and international affairs are not conducted in the simple straightforward way of elementary history and civics texts. Material success is difficult to achieve, and there is room for only a few at the top. Painfully the adult must come to the realization that his early teachings were statements of ideal goals. Since, however, childhood training is difficult to eradicate, most adults now have a greater or lesser measure of internalized conflict between what we have been taught to expect and the social realities of mature life. That a realistic type of training could be incorporated into the educational system without sacrificing any of the real values that are prized in our culture has been suggested by Steckle (1949), and there is no doubt that efforts along that line should be regarded as a public health obligation.

One example of conflicting values in our society has been suggested by Komarovsky (1946) in a study of women college seniors. From auto-biographical documents it was evident that many of the women were torn between two roles each of which they were expected to fulfill. The first role was that of the future wife and mother, and the second role was the "modern" or career woman. Conflict between these some-what incompatible situations was further increased by differential sup-port for one or the other from various relatives. As one senior put it:

How am I to pursue any course single-mindedly when some way along the line a person I respect is sure to say, "You are on the wrong track and are wasting your time." Uncle John telephones every Sunday morning. His first question is: "Did you go out last night?" He would think me a "grind" if I were to stay home Saturday night to finish a term paper. My father expects me to get an "A" in every subject and is disappointed with a "B." He says I have plenty of time for social life. Mother says, "That 'A' in Philosophy is very nice, dear. But please don't become so deep that no man is good enough for you." And, finally, Aunt Mary's line is careers for women. "Prepare yourself for some profession. This is the only way to insure yourself independence and an interesting life. You have plenty of time to marry." [2]

In our culture where the adult roles of women are becoming in-creasingly less defined, conflict is the expected result.

Suggestions of a direct relationship between contradictory aspects of childhood training and the development of psychosis come from Hunt (1938).[3] The patient was manic-depressive, depressed type. As a child, living in a marginal economic area, he had been taught two strongly contradictory practices. With several of his friends, he was introduced to bestiality and overt homosexual practices even before puberty. At the same time, he regularly attended a nearby church which stressed highly emotional revival meetings that had a strong effect on the patient. Coincidentally, the patient reported that several of the boys who had had similar experiences were also at one time or another committed as mental patients. Examination of the patient and unfortunately incom-plete hospital records provided sufficient evidence for Hunt to conclude that these contradictory sexual and religious practices had a strong effect in the development of adult psychoses.

[2] Mirra Komarovsky (1946), "Cultural contradictions and sex roles." *Amer. J. Sociol.*, 52, 184-189.
[3] J. McV. Hunt (1938), "An instance of the social origin of conflict resulting in psychoses." *Amer. J. Orthopsychiat.*, 8, 158-164.

Social or cultural conditions, then, are variables in eliciting pathological behavior. Our own culture, with its basic inconsistencies, forces confusion and conflict upon a great many people.

A BIOLOGICAL EVALUATION OF SOCIAL STRUCTURE

How can we evaluate these social factors from a biological point of view? We started our discussion of psychopathology by assuming that all behavior is fundamentally adaptive in its inception, even when the results of that behavior turn out actually to be maladaptive. The biological analysis of social behavior starts in a simple manner with the interactive influences of one individual upon another, or of a group upon an individual, and so on. However, the behavior of human individuals in their social groups has produced so many complex and relatively permanent behavior patterns, such as institutions, customs, mores, and so forth, that the original role of individuals in social interaction appears less and less to be a significant factor. As an example, political institutions seem almost independent of the people who live under them, and we often talk and act as if that were the case. Ethical systems are described as if they originated outside the influence of human individuals and as if they were supra-biological codes of action. Economics appears as a cosmic force, an institution acting upon but not part of mankind. Religion is often discussed as if it were an arrival from inter-stellar space, directed *at* mankind but not a part *of* mankind.

Starting from our biological point of view, it is at once apparent that all these activities are *human* activities, and that *they all have their origin in our efforts to adapt ourselves to the situations of life.* When men began to live in groups many modifications of individual life became necessary. New discoveries, new institutions, new ways of gaining the old ends of biological equilibrium emerged in group life. New motives, new goals, and new values resulted.

The basic criterion of the success of social institutions must be a biological criterion no different from that which we have applied throughout this book. Any social behavior, having as it does the ultimate purpose of maintaining the organism, must be evaluated in terms of the extent to which it fulfills that purpose. It is obvious that much of what we call social behavior seems only dimly to have biological utility. It would be an over-simplification to demand that each and every social act directly results in satisfaction of organic needs, or that every social act that did not result in such satisfactions be termed *pathological*. Social evolution has resulted in the emergence of a host of *secondary* needs and as many secondary and indirect techniques of satisfying those needs. On the whole, these emergent desires are of direct utility. They have resulted in a superior type of biological adjustment for mankind. In general, these secondary needs have been mechanisms for the utilization of cultural interrelationships in the struggle for survival. However, a clear distinction must be made between those aspects of social behavior that achieve adequate biological goals by *indirection*, and those forms of social behavior that directly or otherwise *interfere* with adequate biological adaptation (Howells, 1940). In our discussion of heredity and other organic factors in psychopathology we noted the variety of circumstances that were called pathological because they acted as obstacles to adjustment. Applying the same criterion to social phenomena, it seems an inescapable conclusion that many aspects of society represent pathological situations not only for the individual, but for the society itself.

Pathological trends in the culture will be reflected in the behavior of the individual. In this fact lies the greatest significance, not only for our theory of abnormal behavior, but for our attempt to arrive at a rational point of view with respect to therapy and mental hygiene. If our thesis is correct, the pathology of the society will induce disturbed behavior in the individual in his attempts to come to terms with his social environment.

TRAINING FOR ADJUSTMENT

Should we, then, direct our primary emphasis in preventing disease toward the faulty social scene, or should we attempt to erect defenses within the individual in order that he might withstand the threats of a disordered society? The former alternative has been the province of the social reformer, the latter is the traditional approach of the psychiatrist and clinical psychologist. It is admittedly easier to attempt the education of an individual than it is to change social trends. Yet, will the therapeutic and preventive efforts of the clinician ever be anything but temporary expedients as long as the society remains disordered?

We must not make the mistake of regarding society as being completely independent of the individuals who compose it. If *enough* people are convinced of anything, and if *enough* people are changed in their basic outlook toward reality, social change has been produced. It is true that social changes do not exactly parallel majority opinions, if only because any social situation is dependent upon such a multiplicity of variables that majority opinion may be in fundamental conflict over the respective variables. If we may refer to war again, it is undoubtedly true that a public opinion poll of the world at the present moment would reveal that a strong attitude exists in favor of peace among all men; if the poll concerned attitudes toward variables entering into the etiology of war, however, the conflict would be revealed. People do not agree on distribution of wealth, on territorial boundaries, on spheres of national interest, on tariff and other trade barriers, on the equality of races, on forms of government, and so on. The social changes, however, do take place, and when they do, individuals are involved as causes as well as effects.

A situation analogous to the problem of mental public health existed in the field of internal medicine with respect to typhoid fever. The incidence of this disease had among its most important vectors the contamination of drinking water by human excreta. The physician who treated individual cases of typhoid fever as they occurred performed a useful function, but did not materially lessen the incidence of the disease. Prevention was accomplished only after social factors were manipulated in such a way that contamination of drinking water was controlled. Here the individual citizen, of course, had to accept the sanitation program. To gain public health legislation in a democracy, recourse must be had to public opinion. Legislation, as public health officials have always found, must go hand in hand with education of individuals.

It is probable that the control of mental disease will ultimately stem from social changes, but the social changes themselves can come about only by means of the same type of procedure used in the control of typhoid fever or any other health menace. The recent work of public health services in fighting venereal disease illustrates this very well. But the very dependence of social change on opinions and attitudes of the individuals composing the society emphasizes the immense circularity of the problem. *Disordered society produces disordered members of that society who in turn perpetuate the disordered society of which they are a part.*

If our society evolves in the direction of biological utility, we have no cause for alarm. If it does not, there will inevitably come a time when the stress factor in social relationships will exceed the resistance thresholds of so many members of the society that disordered behavior will become pandemic, and the culture will be completely pathological. There are already warning signs of such a crisis in our culture. Vogt (1947) has shown that we have decreased the natural resources of the world to a point where it would be difficult to support a much greater population than is alive on the surface of this globe at the present time. Burch and Pendell (1947) have shown that our population increase is one of the greatest of threats to our survival. Some of the recent advances in techniques of biological warfare give promise of making the problem even more acute by rendering enemy lands infertile for long periods of time. We are reminded of the examples of ecology we discussed in Chapter XIV, but instead of coyotes, rabbits, and lemmings, whose ecological cycles are subject to other minor fluctuation, we have the human being who is apparently on the way to finding that the laws of ecology apply also to him.

PATHOLOGICAL BEHAVIOR OF CULTURAL GROUPS

Thus far we have spoken more or less in generalities about the pathology of cultures. Specific instances are not hard to find. There was a time when *war* as social behavior found some support among biologists as a manifestation of Darwinian struggle for survival, in which both victor and vanquished emerged shorn of their weak and ineffective elements. To advocate such an argument about modern war would be folly. It is possibly true that there was a time when direct struggle between two individuals resulted in victory for the one most adequately endowed for survival. It is even possible that the best interests of humanity were served by the death of the inferior, in that he could no longer reproduce his kind. But since the beginning of organized warfare this has not been the case. In the exercise of human group aggression, the demands of army organizations for more effective fighting have led to the evolution of ever more adequate ways of selecting from the general population the best and most well-adjusted individuals. The likelihood of being killed in war is, even in these days of holiday death tolls, considerably greater for the soldier than for the civilian. From the strictly human point of view, war has been biologically a destructive process, antithetical to the genetic improvement of mankind. Applying our criterion of *adjustment,* there is little that can be said in defense of war as a way of behaving. Our test question then is: does warfare as a pathological condition of society induce pathological behavior in the individual immersed in it? The answer may be found in the statistics of casualties in World War II. (Much of these data may be seen in Table 1, Chapter 1.)

We inducted an armed strength of over seven million men. There was a rigid examination of these men at the time of induction. All obviously mentally diseased persons were rejected. Although the efficiency of draft-board physical and psychiatric examinations has been questioned, it is a fact that much concern was manifested by induction officials because so many men were rejected. Of 16,000,000 men between the ages 18 and 38 years examined, 30% or 4,828,000 were rejected. About 12%, or 1,846,000 were rejected for reasons of mental illness. We can suppose, then, that at least the great majority of the seven million who were accepted were individuals who had made reasonably adequate adjustment to civilian life before the war, and, as far as could be predicted at the time of their induction, were good risks for withstanding the rigors of military service. It is reasonable to suppose, further, that military life in time of war would be at least a factor in the subsequent breakdown of those who passed the initial induction screening. By the end of the war in September 1945, the discharge rate for neuropsychiatric cases stood at roughly 6 per cent of the total inducted strength of the army. This meant that the war had been a factor in the incidence of mental illness of one kind or another in about 445,000 men. Since there were one million psychiatric admissions to army hospitals during the war, this is a truly expensive demonstration of the effect of a disordered culture on its members.

Since war is supposed to occur when no other method of adjusting differences will work, it is a confession of man's inability to control the social processes and institutions he has created. Since social institutions are ways of achieving biological equilibrium, those institutions that lead to, or at least do not prevent, war have the appearance of being pathological. The loyalties man have to such institutions, in the face of their revealed failure to promote adjustment, are pathological attachments. Historians tell us that the causes of war are manifold, usually reaching far back into the behavior of preceding generations. The War Between the States, as an instance, grew out of differences between agricultural and manufacturing economies and was hastened by a perseverative inability of both sides to work out a solution that would give the most adequate expression to all our resources. The great debates and discussions that took place in the fifty years before the War Between the States show the irrational and pathological nature of much of the behavior of individuals caught in this cultural conflict.

Thus socially approved behavior, characteristic of a large proportion of the members of a society, may still be pathological if the society itself expresses pathological trends. *This is the limitation we must place on the social concept of abnormality.* When the social definitions of acceptable or desirable behavior themselves transcend the limitations set by biological adjustment and survival, the psychopathologist cannot be guided by them. Although a person may behave in accordance with the dictates of a sick society and escape many tensions arising from his relationship to the group, at some level of his personality he is making a poor adjustment.

The convinced and accepted member of the Nazi state who believed the erroneous statements about racial differences, political philosophies, lives of people in other countries, and so forth and acted upon them, sooner or later found that the social concept of reality that he had been given was false to the facts. Shirer (1947) gives us a vivid reflection on this existing condition in the following quotation, written when he returned to Berlin for the first time after the war:

How many times had I stood opposite on the curb and watched the comings and goings of the great! They would drive up in their black Super-Mercedes cars: the fat, bemedaled Goering; the snake-like little Goebbels, though he lived just across the street; the arrogant, stupid Ribbentrop, though he lived a mere 100 yards down the street—these and Hess and the drunkard Ley and the debauched-looking little Funk with the small eyes of a pig, and the sadist Himmler (though he looked like a mild schoolmaster), and the other swashbuckling party hacks, and then the generals, their necks stiff even when they dismounted from a car, one eye inevitably squeezing a monocle, their uniforms immaculately pressed. They would come, be saluted by the guard of honor, and pass within this building to plot their conquests.

Today, I reflected, standing there in front of the Chancellery's ruins, they are all dead or in jail. This building in whose stately rooms they worked out so confidently and cold-bloodedly their obscene designs is, like them, smashed forever. Germany, their land, which they wanted to rule the world, is smashed too. It will not recover for a long time, and perhaps never.

And yet, what suffering they caused on this planet, these German men, before an aroused world turned them back and fought through to hunt them out and kill them or capture them. How many millions dead, killed, and murdered? How many maimed and broken? How many homes in ashes? Even though the fighting has stopped, the peoples of Europe this winter are hungry and cold, and a million or so of them probably will die all because of what these evil, stupid little men—in this building before it was smashed—did.

And do not forget either that these criminal men with their brutal, inhuman designs were—when last I stood before this building less than five years ago—heroes of this weird and tragic land. Crowds cheered them in the streets. The workers cheered them in the factories. The whole German nation followed them not only obediently but with enthusiasm. And the German people toiled like beavers so that these men might succeed in their plans to destroy and enslave the rest of the world. So many of our own people forget this as they pity the dazed and broken Germans hauling wood on their backs through the rubble of the German cities today.[4,5]

It is as deadly to the organism to be part of a pathological social process of such a kind as it would be for a person to be taught that he could step out of a tenth-story window without injury. In either case the ultimate physical or biological realities are there, and act as a limit to social or psychological conditions. When we discussed the "adjustment mechanisms," our principal criticism of them was their lack of ultimate biological utility. The criterion of utility is equally applicable to social behavior. Cultures are not immortal, and their decline and death come from their inability to meet the needs of the living creatures who compose them.

Other pathological behavior patterns in culture could be similarly examined. Benedict (1934) tells of the Kwakiutl Indians of Vancouver Island, whose cultural pattern was grandiose and paranoid; in this cultural milieu, acceptance and compliance with the socially accepted ways of life could lead a man to starvation and death. But this material of social pathology has been well treated in specific studies of the economic and political behavior of people in its pathological implications; the specific subject matter is beyond the scope of our text. What is important to emphasize, however, is that the psychopathologist must turn to the social sciences for a large part of his evidence on etiological factors in the behavior disorders. As we have seen, the "abnormal" is not only a concept partially defined by social evaluations, but also many of the *causes* of maladaptive behavior are of social origin.

[4] Author's italics.

[5] William L. Shirer (1947), "End of a Berlin diary." *Atlantic Monthly, 179,* 111.

Language Factors in Pathological Behavior

LANGUAGE AS A HUMAN TOOL

Although there are many significant ways in which man differs from other mammals and even from other primates, probably none of his properties has been as influential in determining his peculiar history as has been his development of language. As Mowrer and Kluckhohn (1944) have said, "Without the capacity to use and understand words, or their equivalents, the transmission of culture . . . would be impossible—as would probably also be the common neuroses and 'functional' psychoses as we know them." In the Greek legend Prometheus is represented as receiving the gift of fire from the gods, and thus unalterably changing the destiny of mankind. The gift of language could have been used as appropriately. To be able to talk meaningfully is to project your influence around corners, to control others in the dark or over great distances, to bring the intelligence of your sense organs to those who did not have your experience. Language enables a person to solve problems by trial and error without suffering the consequences of error, because the alternative solutions can be talked about and "tried" in words instead of in actions. Written language makes possible a continuously growing body of knowledge that has been accumulated over long periods of time, thus giving a person some aspects of experiences and situations that occurred long before he was born. Language, in short, transforms man into a creature who can exercise some control over space and over time, and who can, by so doing, exceed his physiological limitations.

In order to understand how language can be of etiological importance in psychopathology, let us review a few of the aspects of language behavior in human beings. First, language is primarily a bearer of meanings. Words stand for, represent, or are in some other way connected with specific aspects of persons and their environments. When the child first learns to speak, the words refer primarily to objects around him. The language of childhood consists, for the most part, of nouns, with a few words denoting actions, generalizations, connectives, or abstractions. In this the child is similar to primitive peoples, whose languages may contain, for example, a dozen words for different species of parrots but no term that means "parrot" in a generalized sense (see Werner, 1940,

p. 267). These specific word meanings are presumably learned by some type of associative process, in which the object (or some representation of it, such as a picture) is paired with the written or spoken word. Most of us have seen this process in action as a child and its mother go through a picture book; the mother shows the child a picture of a cat and says, "See the *kitty*." Later the child learns additional and subsidiary meanings for words, as "What is it that goes 'moo'?" and later still, when it can read a dictionary, it finds out that "cow" can be a verb, and then has another meaning. But by that time the language process has achieved a surface sophistication. The individual has acquired a large vocabulary of nouns referring to objects, of verbs referring to real actions, of words that have a technical value to communication by making speech shorter or smoother, as the connective words, and is beginning to learn a variety of words that have ambiguous or subtle distinctions of meaning. These latter words generally do not refer to real objects or real actions, but to imagined, idealized, or generalized concepts, such as "beauty," "evil," "ignorance," "theory," and so forth.

GENERALIZATION AND ABSTRACTION

Generalizing and *abstracting* are not only late in their appearance, they are also more complex psychological functions. When the small child uses the word "cat," the meaning is specific to one observed animal. More experience is necessary before "cat" is correctly generalized. Faulty generalizations from "cat" are frequently made, as when the child refers to any small animal as "kitty." Only gradually do appropriate generalizations emerge. This is as true in the cultural development of language as in the individual case. A generalization that included whales with "fish" was not corrected until scientific description identified the whale as a mammal. From the viewpoint of practical behavior, great importance attaches to correct generalization, that is, to generalizations that are congruent with reality. The old comedy standby of the man who acted toward "the pretty little animal with black and white stripes down its back" as if it were a cat is a case in point.

It is possible that many of the instances of *generalization* seen in the behavior disorders spring from the operation of defense mechanisms. Given an emotional state of the patient that colors his perceptions in anything that bears on his preoccupations, it is easy to see how words may be used to express generalizations that exist only for the patient. The paranoid who says "*All* men are against me" or the child who

builds up a negativistic attitude toward doctors because of a single unpleasant experience illustrate the tendency. Because of feelings of insecurity that, basically, have nothing to do with Jews or Negroes, but
which have some chance superficial connection with some individual of
a minority group, a person may generalize in such statements as *"All
Negroes are . . ."* or *"All* Jews are . . ."* Our language contains many
words that make such reactions easy; such words as "never," "every,"
"everyone," "nobody," and so forth are a part of the language technique
of generalization and are perfectly adapted to expressing the attitudes
and convictions of the person who sees the source of his emotional
disturbance in every aspect of his environment. Once a generalization
of this kind is made the patient has placed himself in a position from
which there seems little possible chance of escape. As Hayakawa (1941)
put it, ". . . notice the difference between what happens when a man
says to himself, 'I have failed three times,' and what happens when he
says, 'I am a failure!' It is the difference between sanity and self-destruction" (page 145). This emphasizes the difference between the generalizations that come from a common emotional attitude of the patient
toward a variety of objects, and the generalizations that are made on
the basis of characteristics of the objects themselves. The latter type of
generalization is closely related to that aspect of language behavior we
call abstracting.

Abstracting is another language process containing many potential
dangers. Since there are a definite and limited number of words with
which to represent the infinity of objects and events in the world around
us, we can only talk or write about a limited and selected aspect of this
infinitude. Any object has thousands of obvious properties or characteristics. An apple, for example, is a complex geometric solid; it has
selective refraction and reflection of light rays that give it a varying
appearance of color; it has the other physical properties of weight,
specific gravity, and so forth. It is a part of a living thing, which has a
definite place in the botanical classification of plants. It is an economic
force for the farmer and the consumer. In a more detailed scrutiny of
the apple other properties will appear. It has a definite chemical composition, being composed of complex substances with ramified but describ-
able properties. It has a molecular, atomic, and subatomic structure.
No two apples are alike, and small wonder. To be alike they would
have to have *all* of the properties to a common degree. The apples we
talk about when we ask the grocer to give us five pounds of them are of

necessity somewhat abstracted from the complex apple of reality. We can handle, weigh, and eat the real, unique apples, but we can only *talk* about them with varying degrees of abstraction. And so it is with all aspects of reality. There are levels of interaction with our environment that cannot easily be dealt with completely by language. Korzybski (1941) has termed this the "unspeakable" level. Our communications involve sacrifice of the infinite aspects of this unspeakable level by abstracting whatever limited number of properties we need or know at a given time. Now, this is simply an observed relationship between language and reality and grows out of our statement that a finite number of words must be used to cope with an infinite number of its aspects. If the principle were generally recognized, it is probable that language would not be the factor in psychopathology that it evidently is. But our training in language seldom emphasizes this, and language is often used as if it were a complete point-for-point representation of reality and not merely a symbolic map that abstracts selected aspects of reality.

LANGUAGE ACQUISITION

The way in which we learn language is of some importance in the development of false conceptions of the inclusiveness of words. Language learning is primarily an associative process, in which the word is paired with an object that it symbolizes. This process bears a close resemblance to (and is probably an example of) the conditioned response. In Pavlovian conditioning experiments, a hungry dog is exposed to the ringing of a bell and the sight of food. The immediate response to sight of food is salivation, but after several paired presentations of food and the bell, salivation will occur to the ringing of the bell alone. To put the results another way, the animal now reacts to the symbol (bell) as it had previously reacted to the food. There are a few small differences between the new conditioned response and the older unconditioned salivation to food itself, but in general the animal seems to act *as though* the sound of the bell were now an article of diet. *This possibility of transferring to the symbol the reactions originally made to the object is a major factor in the psychopathology of language.* Reality can never be completely expressed by words, and the verbal symbols of any object represent an abstraction from the infinite aspects of that object. If the person acts toward the symbol as he would toward the object, it is evident that a small part of the total situation is precipitating the response.

SYMBOL AND REALITY

This tendency to assume an identity between the word and the object can have serious consequences. Among primitive peoples there are many words that are thought to have magical properties and can only be used under highly regulated circumstances by a few selected individuals. There are some survivals of this in our own culture, notably with respect to religion and other similar institutions. The attitude toward profanity in "polite society" derives from the same feeling of identity between symbol and object. Frazer (1917) gives some excellent examples of this practice:

> The Cherokee Indians regard the rattlesnake as a superior being and take great pains not to offend him. They never say that a man has been bitten by a snake but that he has been "scratched by a briar." In like manner, when an eagle has been shot for a ceremonial dance, it is announced that "a snowbird has been killed" [page 399]. At certain seasons of the year parties of Jakuns and Binuas go out to seek for camphor in the luxuriant forest of their native country. . . . They are absent for 3 or 4 months together, and during the whole of this time the use of the ordinary Malay language is forbidden to them, and they have to speak a special language called by them the *bassa kapor* (camphor language). . . . Indeed, not only have the searchers to employ this peculiar language, but even the men and women who stay at home in the villages are obliged to speak it while the others are away looking for the camphor. They believe that a spirit presides over the camphor trees, and that without propitiating him they could not obtain the precious gum. . . . If they failed to employ the camphor language, they think they would have great difficulty in finding the camphor trees, and that even when they did find them the camphor would not yield itself to the collector [page 405].[6]

As long as the identity reactions do not lead to an actual conflict between reality and symbol they form merely a distinctive but not harmful aspect of our language behavior. But the habits established under such conditions operate in circumstances where the relation between language symbol and the world of reality becomes tenuous or breaks down. Since *the symbol is not the object*, it is possible to produce symbols (words) when no corresponding object is present. From the earliest times for which we have records of language, this phenomenon

[6] J. G. Frazer (1917), *The Golden Bough* (3rd Ed.). Vol. 3: "Taboo and the Perils of the Soul," pp. 399, 405. London and New York· The Macmillan Company.

has been prevalent in human cultures. In one of its most prosaic forms we call it a "falsehood," that is, a verbal statement that cannot be verified in reality. It is very easy for us to say, for example, that we possess a million dollars, even though we most certainly do not. If we have a taste for gossip, we can say that someone of our acquaintance drinks to excess, beats his wife, and habitually forges checks. Verbally, we can erect a picture of his personality that may be untrue in every particular. If everyone who heard us say these things knew the actual facts sufficiently well to be critical, they would reject our statement. If, however, we were writing this misinformation as a reference intended for people who had no other source of knowledge of the individual, the symbols might be accepted as representative of reality and become effective stimuli for the behavior, say, of refusing him employment.

Since, obviously, all men's knowledge of reality is imperfect, there will be countless instances when the recipient of language stimulation will not have the necessary data for correct evaluation of the symbol-reality relationship. The manner of reacting to the stimulation will then depend upon many other factors, such as the prestige of the speaker, the wishes and desires of the auditor, the apparent relationships with known facts, and, as important as the rest, the previous training of the auditor (including his whole set of social attitudes). In the course of human history, the amount of factual data about the world has increased with each generation, and it becomes more and more possible to evaluate the correctness of symbol-reality pairings. Primitive peoples with limited knowledge of the universe reflect the state of their knowledge by the degree of confusion that exists in their differentiation of symbols and the things they stand for. Even as short a time ago as the medieval period of our own culture, there existed many verbal descriptions of geographical regions that had never been seen. They were world-maps with almost no corresponding reality. Yet they exercised a very real influence on the thinking and actions of the people of that time. Columbus sailed west from Europe believing that he could reach the Asiatic continent most directly in that way; his actions were based on the maps of the time. James Harvey Robinson (1926) quotes the following from a thirteenth century treatise on animals:

> There is a little beast made like a lizard and such is its nature that it will extinguish fire should it fall into it. The beast is so cold and of such quality that fire is not able to burn it, nor will troubles happen in the place where it shall be. This beast signifies the holy man who lives by

faith, who will never be hurt from fire, nor will hell burn him. This beast we name also by another name, salamander. It is accustomed to mount into apple-trees, poison the apples, and in a well where it falls it poisons the water.[7]

Although no present-day zoologist would accept the words above as a representation of reality, it is probable that many people lacking zoo-logical training would believe at least some part of the description even today. Language as a vector in psychopathology depends to a large extent upon the education and training of the individual in symbol-evaluation. This in turn is related to the knowledge a person has of the world around him. In our culture the diffusion of knowledge is relatively great in such fields as geography and quite meager in most of the biological and social fields. It is not unusual to find supposedly "well-educated" people holding utterly erroneous beliefs about their bodily functions or about the relationships between their own culture patterns and those of other nations. A study of the delusory beliefs of psychotics would probably show that the great majority of those beliefs were in fields where the individual had little real knowledge for testing the relationships between his symbolic maps and reality. The large number of instances of bizarre delusions centering around fancied dis-orders of the internal organs and the equally fantastic introduction of radio into the delusions of control by outside forces seem to suggest such a language disorder.

LANGUAGE AND THE UNKNOWN

However, we should not make the mistake of implying that language plays a completely *causal* role in the development of psychopathology. Rather, language is a vehicle for conveying symbolically our under-standing of the environment and a major part of our actions in the environment. Words become stimuli to action, and if the words are in-adequate to portray the aspect of reality toward which we are respond-ing (through the words), then the adjustive nature of the response may well suffer. Since no person possesses all the available knowledge of his own time, all people inevitably will on occasion respond to false symbols. This is particularly true in those areas of human interest where there exists the combination of little available knowledge and great motivation, as in religious and political behavior. It is in such fields

[7] J. H. Robinson (1926), *The Ordeal of Civilization*, p. 202. New York: Harper and Brothers.

that we note the immense importance of *belief* and *faith* as prerequisites to institutionally accepted behavior. The word-map must be accepted uncritically, since there is no easy way to perform the tests of its correspondence with reality. Language being what it is, this is no barrier to the erection of further and more complex language structures on the basis of faith. Probably more paper and printer's ink has been devoted to writing about matters of faith than to all the aspects of science.

The same process of creating new worlds out of words is not confined to religion and politics. Most of the world's literature—drama, poetry, fiction—consists of word-maps with no direct and first-order correspondence to the unspeakable real nature of the world. Should we say that all this human verbal activity is undesirable and pathological? Superficially, there seems to be little difference between such a fictional product as Sinclair Lewis' *Main Street* and the elaborate systems of delusion produced by a psychotic patient. Both of them use words to create images that do not mirror actual people, places, or events. But superficial similarity ends the comparison. *The distinction between "normal" fantasy and literary creativity on the one hand and delusory belief on the other lies in the amount of insight that both producer and audience have for the degree to which the production represents reality.* The psychotic believes that his delusory system is a completely true and exact statement of reality, and he acts upon this belief. The writer and reader of fiction recognize that the truths of the production are on a higher level of abstraction, and that they only approximate reality in a very general way. It is said that George Barr McCutcheon, who wrote a series of romances based on the activities of nobility in a mythical country of his own creation, Graustark, received thousands of letters from readers who wanted to visit the country. They asked about travel routes, custom and passport information, names of hotels and points of interest, the best time of year to visit, and so on. Producers of various serial comic strips are in constant receipt of letters from readers, expressing anxiety about the characters of the strip or sending gifts to the characters. Obviously these people are behaving toward the symbols as if they stood in some way for a directly existing reality. People who habitually fail to distinguish between levels of abstraction in language expose themselves to the danger of making maladaptive responses to verbal stimulation. Ideally, education in our culture should be directed toward the training of people in the correct use and understanding of language. Unfortunately most of the language training in school is concerned with *form* and not *function*. We receive tuition in grammar and syntax, in spelling, and to some extent in the aesthetics of language, but rarely do language courses emphasize the role of language in culture or the ways in which language may be used or misused in thinking and action.

LANGUAGE PROPERTIES AND PSYCHOPATHOLOGY

Now that we have reviewed some of the aspects of language as behavior, let us turn to a consideration of the ways in which it concerns psychopathology. Specifically there are at least three properties of language behavior that have a direct bearing on abnormal behavior, namely: (1) time-binding, (2) identification, and (3) "counterfeit language." Although we consider each of these separately, they probably all blend into each other and are constantly present to some extent in the behavior of well-adjusted individuals.

TIME-BINDING

By *time-binding* we mean the property of language that permits a person to reconstruct through words many of the aspects of situations and experiences that occurred at another time or to construct in anticipation experiences or situations that have not yet occurred but that are expected to occur. Humans do not differ from other higher mammals with respect to being modified by past experience. The memory of a dog or an ape is quite good, and many aspects of previous stimulation will leave traces that influence further reaction. The great difference between man and the other animals lies in the *range* of stimuli that serve to build up these traces or to revive them. Language enormously extends the range of stimulation and memory. As was pointed out previously, this generally is an enormous advantage, making it possible for mankind to profit from the experience of the thousands of generations before him and to build the distinctively human attributes of culture and society. In the behavior of the individual, however, it is possible for this asset to assume undesirable forms under certain circumstances. Although all animals may be exposed to traumatic situations that induce catastrophic responses, the general memorial after-effects of such stimulation are relatively small. In the experimental neurosis, a removal of the animal from the general laboratory situation in which the conflict was induced is often a sufficient therapeutic device. If the animal is brought back to the specific situation, it will commonly again develop symptoms of disordered behavior. It is true that a small part of the original stimulus situation can revive the same type of response that was formerly given to the whole. In this respect both man and the lower animals seem to conform in their behavior to Hollingworth's principle of redintegration.

In man, a simple geographic change is usually ineffective in decreasing his neurotic symptoms, because a very important part of the original traumatic situation goes along with him, namely his *language reactions*. Because words give us a way of talking to ourselves as well as to other people, we can constantly rehearse or revive the situation on a verbal level. Since we are well trained to react to the symbol as we would to the object, the words describing the situation can often be as potent stimuli for emotional reaction as the original experience. There is thus built up a means of perpetuating the disordered behavior characteristic of the original traumatic event. Evidence on this point seems clear. In the experimental neurosis an animal is presented with punishment and with symbols of punishment. When the response of leg withdrawal is conditioned to the sound of a buzzer, the animal has acquired a symbol of punishment and has also learned a technique of avoiding punishment. If the experimenter varies the tone of the buzzer in such a way that some tones now signify punishment and others do not, the animal will build up selective reactions that break down only when discrimination of slight tonal differences becomes impossible. It continues to react to the symbol of punishment, but is no longer able to apply its technique for avoiding punishment. The animal's behavior becomes "neurotic," that is, it shows random emotional responses that are poorly organized with respect to the experimental situation and that meet our criterion of catastrophic behavior. As its ability to discriminate breaks down, the symbolic meaning that formerly was attached to a few specific stimuli irradiates in such a way that the symbol is generalized to *all stimuli*.

An even more vivid example of the power of verbal symbols to touch off emotional responses comes from psychotherapy with human patients. In the technique of *narcosynthesis,* a patient is given small amounts of a sedative drug, sodium pentothal and sodium amytal being the most common. While the patient is under the influence of the drug, the therapist gives a verbal description of a scene that the patient has been through, but for which he has shown an amnesia or a panic reaction when attempts have been made to discuss it. The therapist's words are frequently sufficient to elicit a rather full account of the traumatic experience from the patient, who reacts to the verbal picture of the traumatic scene as if the symbols were the reality. The effect is sometimes startling. A soldier who has taken part in a fierce battle will tell of the events he has experienced, go through all his emotional reactions to them, and even act out his memories with a compelling appearance of reality. In the following description of such a treatment session, note carefully how potent the verbal symbols of reality are for eliciting emotional behavior:

Case 63. The first patient was an Infantry officer. . . . Pentothal narcosynthesis was administered in the afternoon of the third day of hospitalization. The patient seemed to understand that the injection was designed to help him and although he trembled violently during its administration, he attempted to cooperate and control himself. Because he could not count, the narcosis was estimated to be sufficient after the injection of 0.5 grams. The patient lay quietly on the bed, without tremor. He was then told that he was in the Kairouan Pass, and the mortar shells were dropping about him. At the mention of the word "shells," he shuddered. He then sat up in the bed, and holding up two fingers, said, "Two people hurt . . . or killed?" He spoke fairly well, with a slight stutter, and seemed to be trying to recall the situation. He then spit on the floor— i.e., battlefield—and got out of bed, crying, "Steve! Steve, are you all right?" He knelt on the floor and passed his hands over it, as if examining a body. Standing up suddenly, he looked as if he were going to cry, and buried his face in his hands. He then clenched his fists and, assuming a belligerent attitude, he smiled grimly and said, "Never mind, I'll get even with those bastards. Those bastards! I'll kill them!" He began pacing up and down and then suddenly looked up and said, "Got to find Steve. Got to find Steve and Davey." He then lurched about the room looking for something; from time to time he cowered, as if hearing an approaching shell; and then trembling with fear, crouched on the ground, as he might in his foxhole. He did not appear to find what he was looking for, and eventually began the whole scene over again with the "two-people killed" episode.

The therapist remained in the background during this performance, allowing the patient a free rein. But when the patient, after several repetitions, made no further progress, the therapist stepped forward and said, "Steve isn't here now. How are you? What's happening to you?" The patient shook his head sadly and said, "I'm all right." Then he suddenly looked up with an expression of alarm, and for the first time coming into contact with the real environment said, "Where am I? Who are you?" He was told that he was in a hospital with a Medical Officer. He seemed partly to grasp this, but immediately returned to the problem of finding Steve and Davey. He was so dominated by this episode that contact with him was difficult to maintain. In the effort to maintain contact, the therapist kept talking to the patient, who appeared bewildered by the failure to find his friends. Finally, making an extreme effort to concentrate, he said, "There's a hole, a big hole. But I can't get to it in time." Since it was clear that no further progress could be made at this time, the patient was taken back to the wards, still puzzled. The narcosynthesis had been only partially successful. Speech had been recovered, and anxiety reduced to the point where the patient could make an effort to deal with the traumatic episode. However, the amnesia had only partly lifted, and contact with the present environment was slight. It was determined to repeat the pentothal the following day.

Twenty-four hours later considerable improvement was manifested. The patient was in fairly good contact. He remembered and cheerfully greeted the Medical Officer. He talked with much stuttering, and displayed considerable anxiety and apprehension. He remembered the substance of the material recalled the day before, but nothing about his previous life except the fact that he was worried about his wife. What it was that worried him, he did not know, nor did he know his wife's or his own first name. He was very anxious to get over his amnesia and kept asking to be told who he was. He eagerly agreed to another pentothal injection.

When adequate narcosis was obtained, the patient was told that he was at home, with his wife, but that something was wrong. He immediately sat up and said, "She's going to have a baby. I've been so worried about her." He paused, and said, "But I can't remember my Mother and Father. I know we come from Pennsylvania, but where?" He pondered for a long time without success. Suddenly he began to speak of his battle experience, now in the past tense, aware that he was telling the therapist a story: "We'd been pinned down in our foxholes all day. Jerry had us spotted, and was throwing mortars at us. I was terribly frightened, but I tried not to show it in front of the men. I had trouble keeping them in their foxholes. They wanted to get out and stretch every few hours. When anyone stood up, five or six mortar shells came over in a few seconds. We didn't know where the German batteries were located, couldn't find out. The shells came from nowhere; not a sign of a gun, not even a flash. I saw two men standing up out of their foxhole. I climbed out of mine to order them back into their hole. Just then a mortar came over and landed in a foxhole near me. Oh, that explosion! It knocked me down, but I got right up, and went over to the hole. Two men were in there, our first sergeant and a staff sergeant. I could hardly look at them. The first sergeant was on top. He was dead, with his head blown open. There wasn't any top to his head. The other man was underneath. He was still alive, but the side of his chest was open, and I could see part of the lung. He was crying; God, I can still hear him crying. I felt sick, and my mind was funny; I couldn't think. I was shaking so I could hardly move. I don't know how I did it, but I helped to take care of them. I told myself I had to hang on. I tried to get a grip on myself. The shells were falling all around us. Then I saw a gunflash. I knew where the German batteries were by the gunflash. Stevie was at the Command Post. I had to go find him, to tell him about the position so he could phone the Artillery. I went down the road to look for him. But I had to keep ducking down on the ground because the shells kept falling near me; I think the Germans could see me going down the road. But I couldn't find Steve. I never got to the Command Post. What happened to me? I remember: While I was going down the road, I heard three shells coming. I jumped into the ditch; it was a good ditch. One of the shells, the first one, landed on the road. I can still hear the sound of the shells: whirrr . . . Don't you hear it? Oh, what a sound! I don't want to ever hear that sound again. I remember the second shell landing behind me, off the side of the road. I don't remember the third. I don't remember what happened after that. Oh, those shells! They weren't mortars: you can hear mortars tumbling over and over. This was a whirr." At this point the patient covered his eyes with his hands, and buried his head on the Medical Officer's shoulder. Then he suddenly smiled and said, "I remember my name: it's F . . . I remember where I live. God, what a miracle that I can talk. I thought I'd never be able to, but I tried. I tried right along to talk and remember, but I couldn't. They must think I'm an awful baby. I am a baby to be like this." [8]

Significant for the present purpose is the apparent equivalence of the verbal symbols and the event itself. Given a background of traumatic experience, a few of the symbols of that experience are capable of inducing again the reaction to the original stimuli. Since we are constantly surrounded by a world of words, the chances of forgetting a traumatic situation after it has occurred are slight. As Freud (1920) has pointed out, psychological traumata consist of the repeated small occurrences of conflict or frustration that continually occur in the sick individual and have a cumulative effect in arousing emotional response. Language as an associative medium provides a richness of symbolic ties with all aspects of experience, and a chance verbalism, occurring in almost any context, has the effect of reviving painful memories. As far as basic dynamics are concerned, language introduces no new principle, but does provide a means of extending the redintegrative function. Through the power of constant symbolic rehearsal of painful experience, the human being minimizes the temporal aspect of memory, and forgetting proceeds at so much slower a rate that the phenomenon of time-binding becomes a serious etiological factor in disordered behavior. Because the verbal (and symbolical) aspects of experience are retained, words provide the most abundant source of redintegrative stimuli.

[8] R. R. Grinker and J. P. Spiegel (1945), *War Neuroses*. Philadelphia: The Blakiston Company.

IDENTIFICATION

Identification as a process in language behavior serves to make more understandable the role of time-binding. We defined identification in the present sense as the reactions that have the same form toward the symbol as toward the real object that is symbolized. In a highly verbal culture most such identification reactions are necessary, and refusal to make them would be maladaptive. Here again, however, the role of insight is paramount. When a hungry man salivates at a verbal description of tempting food, the identification he is making is only maladaptive if he is convinced that he has taken in nourishment.

Just such a process occurs in the language usage of the schizophrenic. One patient referred to in our discussion of the psychoses, it will be recalled, preceded every word of every sentence uttered by "what." A sample would go like this: "What-who what-is what-going what-to what-take what-me what-for what-my what-exercise?" or "What-I'm what-hungry." Long practice with this peculiar formula had made the patient extremely dextrous at its use, and gave, as may be imagined, a strange sound to his utterances. Study of the patient showed that "what" was a protective device. The patient was convinced that his words had a magic potency to direct energy of a destructive kind unless he interjected an element of doubt into his usage of them. "What" was such a word, and he used it in the same way a physicist would use a screen of lead to protect bystanders from the emanations of radium. Another patient described by Storch (1926) was unable to go through doors without intense panic and consistently refused to use the word "door." Inquiry revealed that the patient (a German) reacted to the German word for door (*tier*) as if it stood for animal (*tierre*) and stated that doors ate one up, the door being like the mouth of animals. The general reaction of large portions of our culture to verbal references to sex has at times been of almost the same pathological nature, and for many years was effective in preventing adequate public education on the problems of venereal disease. Only recently has the word "syphilis" been allowed to see the black and white of print in newspaper copy. Identification reactions reflect the recognition of the enormous power of word symbols in influencing behavior. Pornographic verbal descriptions of sexual episodes can serve to arouse sexual desires; vivid descriptions of bloodshed and cruelty can be as potent in arousing indignation as the actual sight of the incidents. Language has the property of stimulating behavior in many directions.

COUNTERFEIT LANGUAGE

Counterfeit language consists of all those linguistic formulae in which there is symbolized no basic reality. It is helpful to think of language as we do of money. When we use coins or paper money in our dealings with other people, we are employing a medium of exchange. There is no intrinsic value in the piece of paper that has the words "One Dollar" written on it; its value depends upon its role as a medium of exchange. Both parties to a transaction accept the money as a symbol of wealth, by means of which goods or services may be obtained. Counterfeit money resembles the real money that symbolizes wealth, but the imitation is a false symbol, since there is no direct reality behind it. If the counterfeit resembles the original with sufficient fidelity, however, people may be induced to act toward it as if it were real money.

The use of language similarly may involve the creation of counterfeit situations, in which the combination of symbols presented to the person may have no representation in reality. If the person acts toward these as if they meant something, the end result might well be maladaptive. Concrete illustrations are not hard to find. The practice of parents to discipline children by threatening them with the "Boogey Man" has given many of them a needless emotional reaction—toward a counterfeit symbol. In the various mental disease syndromes we find the tendency of patients similarly to create a completely verbal world and to behave as if it were real. The catatonic girl described in Chapter IX, who believed that her father was attempting to have her killed, the depressed woman who believed that she had committed the unpardonable sin toward her sister, the paranoid soldier who believed the islanders were in league with the Japanese are all examples of this reaction. The following letter, received by a colleague, is a particularly good instance of the formation of what Cameron (1948) has called the "pseudo-community" of the psychotic.

Dear Sirs:
    If you remember I was very ill at the beginning of May. I came out of it and was getting along fine. At first I was very exhausted but I have

done all my own work. Then something happened to my real husband and some way or other while I was ill you helped me. Then something happened to my husband and he was not ill or insane, but for a week he was almost out of his head. He broke the emergency brake on the car and almost choked me one night. He was that way for a week and it took real courage and love to bring him out of it. Something has happened to me this summer and I can explain all of it in my natural voice or write it down just as I am writing this.

Is there an experiment being conducted or did someone decide to have a perfect show and put me in that show. Is there any connection with certain radio vibrations or wave lengths. I have been rued very strongly since I was well and I have never believed in perfect fool way and I never believed in any of there perfect lines, but they have had many perfect mortgages on my house and they have made it a perfect house and they seem to be doing it by means of the telephone and the electricity and someone gave me the horrible power to see certain things and as long as they must have started another perfect show in and as long as it is real to me, for I hear them and they are evidently charged with so much electricity that every bone in my body is sore and they have put all different colored lights in my eyes until I can scarcely see and he wanted to carry me away to some place and he showed me all those horrid pictures. That didn't bother me so much except that I have been afraid for my own life and the life of my baby and then he has started in the last few days on my normal head and normal mind and he seems to want to make an instrument of some kind of me and he has made pin pricks or something in my head to last few days and I have been so exhausted that haven't been able to bring myself out of it the way I did before. They have been doing it for over three months and I have kept bringing myself out of it each time and I came up here to receive intelligent help and kindness. Really and truly it has been real horry and real rueing. They have had priests and nuns in my house and been putting Christ childs as they call them in my body and perfect marriages and sending them all up there to my home and they have been trying to make a perfect nun out of me and they have been going through my real body and been yelling about perfect brains and I tried to get help in and couldn't. They have even put helmets over my real normal head, and really and truly they are in the house all the time and don't give me a minutes rest. They go in me and I try to get different contacts in my normal head and they have taken away my normal breath time and time again and have some way closed up the passages in my nose and made passages into my ears and the last day they seem to be vibrating my ears and even putting those charges into my bones and the last few days and into my skull and naturally no intelligent woman wants to lose their normal intelligent brain in that way. They have black snake whips and one was their with a black hood and white body and black feet and one all in black with sort of a hood and one they called black mist and one with a white hood and black body and eels and ools and some are gray and some are black and they have little wires they wrap around the inside of the ear drum and one they call a perfect hoe and a perfect horror and they are terrible (really and truly). Some of the colors are white and green, red, yellow, light green, dark green, light blue and dark blue and one that is a young boy and tall ones in black and one they call hist and white horse and black horse and perfect ool and they seem to make some contact with the ground.

Would you please help me if you know anything about this, would you please help me. I can explain most of it to you if you wish me to do so. There seems to be a group of them and they seem to have had my normal mind all summer and I would like to have all the intelligent help and real Christian help I can get and they seem to have one old priest with them. I can explain this to you if you wish me to do so. This is not written very well, but I can come up tomorrow if you wish.

Sincerely yours,

In the field of social pathology we find diplomats drawing up and signing treaties that promise "eternal peace" or "complete disarmament" and in which, as we have learned in our own generation, there is little substance behind the words.

One of the dangers inherent in counterfeit language is the strongly negative reaction toward language symbols in general that may be established in the person. In folklore we have this trend illustrated by the story of the "Boy Who Cried Wolf." It is probable that this phenomenon has much in common with the "experimental extinction" that takes place in conditioned response experiments in the laboratory. If a dog builds up a conditioned salivary response to a bell because it has been associated with the sight and odor of meat, frequent presentation of the bell alone will result in a gradual decrease in conditioned salivation. The learned reaction can be revived if meat is again associated with the bell. Continuous exposure to counterfeit language stimuli may have the same effect. In those instances where it does not, and the verbal formulae continue to bring forth behavioral reactions, it is because of emotional factors in the reaction that themselves have strong reinforcement value. Thus, although everything the Nazis said about the Jews fits our definition of counterfeit stimuli, the reactions of all good Germans continued to be in the direction desired by the leaders. This was because, as we have pointed out before, the social situation was so structured that deep emotional satisfactions could be secured by conformity to Nazi concepts. The rational meanings were false, but the emotional reactions were satisfying and so reinforced the response to the false words.

LANGUAGE AND EMOTION

The relationship of language to emotional behavior is of especial importance to us. It seems evident that the emotional significance of words is not directly correlated with their rational symbolism. This is shown by the large number of euphemistic expressions we have for various aspects of our environment. Throughout our process of language acquisition we are constantly building up emotional reactions that become fixed parts of our general response to words. That the emotional reaction is not directly connected with the dictionary meanings of words is shown by the fact that we have "good" and "bad" words that have exactly the same general meaning. In Victorian times "limb" was a polite word for the nether extremities, and "leg" was indelicate and vulgar. We have a variety of short Anglo-Saxon terms for various excretory and sexual functions, none of which are admitted into polite usage, although all of them are probably a part of our vocabularies by the time we reach adolescence. In terms of specificity of meaning and economy of verbiage, the vulgar words are probably preferable to the longer Latin and Greek derivations that our mores compel us to use in most public circumstances. Unfortunately there is a paucity of experimental studies of the development of euphemisms and of the reasons why certain words are preferred to others having the same rational significance.

Much of the *individual* significance of words, as opposed to their communication value, stems from emotional connotations. Each person acquires his vocabulary in an individual setting, and the meaning complex associated with his vocabulary is peculiarly his own. Due to the leveling effect of culture, there are many words that also acquire more or less conventionalized emotional significance. To such words the term "stereotype" has been applied (Lippmann, 1922). It signifies that the members of a social group will react with uniform and predictable emotionally toned behavior to certain verbal concepts. Lippmann said, "In the great blooming, buzzing confusion of the outer world we pick out what our culture has already defined for us, and we tend to perceive that which we have picked out in the form stereotyped for us by our culture." [9] Expanding, he added a few pages later, "We are told about the world before we see it. We imagine most things before we

[9] From *Public Opinion*, p. 61. Copyright 1922 by Walter Lippman. Used by permission of The Macmillan Company.

experience them. And those preconceptions, unless education has made us acutely aware, govern deeply the whole process of perception. They mark out certain objects as familiar or strange, emphasizing the difference, so that the slightly familiar is seen as very familiar, and the somewhat strange as sharply alien. They are aroused by small signs, which may vary from a true index to a vague analogy." [10]

The effect of stereotypes was shown in a study by Heyer and O'Kelly (1948), in which scales were constructed to measure people's attitude toward Russia and their attitude toward the communistic political and economic philosophy maintained by the Russians. Half of the items in the scale mentioned Russia by name, and the other half consisted of statements of communistic and anti-communistic political or economic beliefs, none of which contained the words "communism" or "Russia." The results, when tallied separately for the "Russian" and for the "'communism" items, showed a uniformly greater acceptance of the communistic position than of the "Russian" position. This was true of a wide variety of socio-economic groups, including labor unions, service clubs, chambers of commerce, university and secondary school faculties, various religious groups, and high school and college students. Inclusion of the word "Russia" in an item aroused a stereotyped emotional response of disapproval that bore little connection with the meaning implied in the statement.

We have seen this tendency at work in the "allness" type of verbal reaction discussed a few pages back. Again, the pathological significance of this type of verbal reaction discussed is the way language reflects and stimulates behavior oriented to the emotional life of the individual and not to the external realities of the situation. Britt (1941) has remarked on the socially maladaptive significance of streotyped reactions as follows:

If men were entirely logical animals, all that would be necessary to control human behavior would be to discover what the "facts" on any issue are, and people would behave in rational ways. However, the experiences of politicians, courtroom lawyers, reformers, advertisers, radio men, newspaper men, all indicate that it is not necessarily the correct argument which wins, but rather the emotionally toned stereotypes and the ways in which they are presented. Nearly every president of the United States has realized the advantage of stereotyped phases. Theodore Roosevelt waged war on "big business," "the Yellow Peril," "race suicide," "standpatters," "mollycoddles," "pussyfooters," "hyphenated Americans," and "pacifists." Woodrow Wilson came along with attacks on "special privilege," "dollar diplomacy,"

[10] *Ibid.*, p. 67.

"war mongers," and "lowbrows." More currently Franklin D. Roosevelt condemned "monopolists," "unscrupulous money changers," "rugged individualists," "manipulators," "unethical competitors," "prophets of evil," the "overprivileged," and "economic royalists." [11]

The chief importance of words as emotional stimuli lies in the relative lack of control we have over this aspect of our language behavior. Both in using words and in responding to them we are influenced by largely unconscious emotional determinants that have little, if any, relevance to the situations to which we must adapt.

Technics and Psychopathology

The adjustmental problems of any individual are influenced by the culture in which he has membership. Culture has its origin in adaptive behavior, but cultural products are emergent realities that often provide new difficulties for the person who must deal with them. In this section we will consider some aspects of our own culture that are important to the theory of psychopathology.

The history of Western European culture has been marked by at least two trends that distinguish it from others. One is the development of scientific method and its application to a wide variety of subject matters. The other is an extensive application of mechanical and chemical principles to the production of goods and the satisfaction of human needs. There is a degree of interrelationship between these two trends, in that most of the advances in engineering and other practical technologies have depended upon the increase in knowledge brought about by the scientist. It has often been assumed that the correlation was perfect and that credit for the present state of the world, for good or bad, may be given to the scientist. Accordingly, depending upon the times, science has been viewed as the savior of mankind or as the source of mankind's ultimate destruction. During the depression of 1929-1939, many writers, believing that unemployment was due to the increased productivity of the machines, proposed a "moratorium" on scientific discoveries, implying that man already knew too much for his own good. In direct contrast to this attitude was the feeling many people had after the disclosure of the atomic bomb, that the only thing necessary to con-

[11] S. H. Britt (1941), *Social Psychology of Modern Life,* p. 200. New York: Rinehart and Company, Inc.

quer the remaining frontiers of ignorance was appropriation of money for the establishment of scientific laboratories. Cancer, war, unemployment, and all the rest of our ills seemed to them easily susceptible to organized mass research. Few scientists shared this conviction. They increasingly recognized the inadequacy of the old proverb, "Knowledge is power," when applied to the workings of a total society. It is true that there has never been a time in the history of the world when so much was known about the universe in which we live, and in which that knowledge has been applied to such a variety of technical problems. In manufacturing, communication, and transportation, our advances over other ages are clearly evident. We can produce more, talk over longer distances, and travel faster than men ever could before. In spite of this we have apparently advanced little if at all over primitive man in many crucial aspects of social relations. We have great cycles of economic instability, we have ever more destructive wars, we have imperfect correlation of production with need, and we are now approaching a stage in world history when our scientists assure us that the complete application of our knowledge to these maladjusted processes of warfare can easily destroy the entire culture. Evidently our knowledge *alone* does not prevent maladjusted behavior.

WHO KNOWS WHAT?

The reasons for this discrepancy between our knowledge and our actions are various. Some of them illustrate principles of psychopathology and are etiological factors in the development of mental illness. Some of the reasons, of course, are beyond the scope of a discussion of this kind and are the concern of other social sciences. Our interest in the struggles of the human creature to adapt and in his frequent failures leads us to identify certain aspects of this social pathology as pertinent to our inquiry.

One of the first things to consider is the degree to which the average person in our culture is influenced by its scientific and technical advances. It is an illuminating experience to stroll through the stacks of a large university library. Here, classified and catalogued, is the substance of the knowledge of our time. From "agronomy" to "zoology," we have at our disposal a multitude of facts. But who *knows* these things? Certainly no one person. Not in the last hundred years has it been possible to be a universal scholar. Our knowledge has accumulated too rapidly and is too diversified. On the faculty of a great university will be found individuals who are acquainted with the major discoveries in one small part of the whole field of knowledge. But even here we find specialization. The following quotation from F. M. Colby's *Trials of an Encyclopedist* illustrates the point:

> It may be merely an accident, but somehow I have always fared the worst among zoologists and botanists. Naturally, an editor of an encyclopedia cannot have a sub-editor for every animal, but that is what the zoologist apparently expected of me. Matters are far worse than in the days of Dr. Holmes' naturalist who flew into a rage because someone called him a Coleopterist. He was no smatterer, he said, trying to spread himself over the Coleoptera; he was a Scarabeist. Nowadays a zoologist seeks out his animal in early life and henceforth stays with it. Often the intimacy between them is so great that it seems indelicate to intrude. I have known a bivalve and a man to develop interests in common so exclusively molluscous or bivalvular that no human being dared break in.[12]

But these are the experts, the individuals whose professional lifework has been the mastery of their small share of our cultural attainment. In their fields they are capable of reasoned opinion and exact judgment. What of the vast majority of us? What is the state of our knowledge in any given field? Do we know a great deal more than we did a hundred years ago? Probably not. Ask the next few people you meet to explain to you the principles behind radio, the internal combustion engine, or vaccination. Quiz them on the theory of flight, on the complexities of international finance, on the role of the cerebral cortex in behavior. The answers will be revealing. We utilize a vast quantity of technical apparatus and methods without a true understanding of their working or significance.

In itself this is often of great importance for understanding maladjustment. Ignorance of the nature of barriers hampers our attempts to overcome them. For hundreds of years smallpox was a major disease threat, yet even to the present time there has been a determined resistance on the part of many people to vaccination. Their reasons show ignorance of the processes of immunization. When such opposition appeared in 1800, shortly after Jenner's original discovery, it could be explained as due to a lack of opportunity to learn. Many physicians were still unconvinced. When the same resistance appeared in 1926, however, the experts were agreed, and the basic principles of immunity

[12] F. M. Colby, *The Trials of an Encyclopedist*. Reprinted by permission of Dodd, Mead & Company, Inc., New York.

had been sufficiently understood that interpretation to the layman was easy and intelligible. Still many people refused to be vaccinated and refused to accept the facts as they then stood.

Even more remarkable as a pathological process is the continued existence of racial prejudices, supported by a mass of myth and folklore that has been disproven experimentally time and time again. During World War II, well over a million Jewish people were murdered in the cause of "racism." In a large part of our country the citizens manifest an unreasoned prejudice against the minorities in their midst. Yet at no time in the history of the world have we known more about the physical characteristics, the aptitudes, and abilities of various peoples, and at no time have we been able to give a more unequivocal answer to the myth of racial differences. Even now people in the United States repeat the same prejudices, refusing again to accept the factual data available to them.

It is alleged that something called "race" is the prime determiner of all the important traits of body and soul, of character and personality, of human beings and nations. And it is further alleged that this something called "race" is a fixed and unchangeable part of the germ plasm, which, transmitted from generation to generation, unfolds in each people as a typical expression of personality and culture. . . . Such a conception of "race" has no basis in scientific fact or in any other kind of demonstrable fact. It is a pure myth, and it is the tragic myth of our tragic era. Tragic, because it is believed and made the basis for action, in one way or another, by so many people in our time.[13]

To the psychopathologist this means that his evaluation of the cultural factors in mental disease cannot be made in terms of what is "known" in the sense of the highest attainments of the culture as a whole. He must reckon with the state of knowledge of the maladjusted individual. We have every reason for believing that people's actions are determined on the basis of emotional needs as old as man himself and with the help of factual information that is only slightly in advance of that possessed a hundred years ago. Otherwise, how could we explain the many pathological aspects of our culture? Individuals and groups in our civilization are handling technical forces of great complexity on the basis of age-old emotions and antiquated knowledge. We rightfully have laws against very young children driving powerful automobiles,

[13] M. F. Ashley Montague (1945), *Man's Most Dangerous Myth: The Fallacy of Race* (2nd Ed.), pp. 7-8. New York: Columbia University Press.

but we have the spectacle of nations trying to handle the terrifying social implications of nuclear fission in a framework of political action that has changed little from the time of the Congress of Vienna in 1814. In the perennial debates and accusations concerning the secrecy factors of nuclear fission, scientists have time and time again attempted to point out that there are no secrets about the basic physical principles of the atom bomb, and that security regulations should be completely concerned with technical details of manufacture and with stockpiling information. Yet, as we know, one of the reasons that scientists have shown reluctance to enter federal research positions has been the hampering restriction on free exchange of knowledge with other scientists.

Our present state of scientific sophistication rests on the power of what we call "the scientific method." Reduced to its most elementary terms, scientific method is a process of the successive construction of hypotheses, their empirical test, and correction of hypothesis on the basis of test. *The method depends completely upon the willingness to alter hypotheses that do not adequately conform with the experimental facts.* This process has led to those advances in knowledge and technique that distinguish our culture. But is the scientific method a way of thinking that is widespread among participants in the culture it made possible? Obviously not. Scientists have always been a distinct minority in our population, and even the scientists have not always carried their methodology into their own thoughts and actions outside their own particular province. Documentation of these points reveals, indeed, how small a part the scientific method plays in discussion and action on many of our most important problems.

We have seen throughout our discussion of pathological behavior the importance of actions that are correctly oriented to the nature of the frustrating agency. We analyzed the inadequacies of most defense mechanisms on this basis and concluded that the mechanisms did not work because they did not have as utilitarian a value as the person who adopted them believed. Applying our analysis to social problems, we may tentatively conclude *that behavior in the social field must be congruent with the properties of the barriers that exist in that particular field.* In a culture whose technology and knowledge are based on scientific method, adequate social adjustment can only be made by individuals who use scientific method in attacking their own social problems. This means essentially that the essence of scientific thinking should be commonly and universally used by anyone who hopes successfully to adapt himself to a world of machines. Control of a mechanized world can only be achieved by a closer approximation to behavior of the type that created the machine in the first place.

CULTURAL LAG

The sociological concept of *cultural lag* applies to this problem. Cultural lag is the delay between the rise of new ideas or techniques and their absorption into the general behavior of the society. The Industrial Revolution produced a host of new forces and problems for our civilization, many of which have not yet been adequately solved. The impact of scientific discoveries and technological inventions is being felt in many vital areas of our culture. The society as a whole is in a state of constant change. It is small wonder, then, that individuals find social adjustment difficult. In a stable society, where conditions remain constant for generation after generation, successful adjustmental techniques are accumulated and made integral parts of the mores and traditions of the culture. Western European civilization has not presented such dependability for some time. The increasing incidence of mental disease is a reflection of social instability. Adjustmental techniques lag behind the current structure of our society. Much of our fundamental training in social living is derived from the generation of our parents. School curricula, for example, are often established to meet problems of a world that has already changed. The rapid alteration in science, technology, world affairs, and social mores from year to year makes the usual school textbook inadequate by the time it is written. This is particularly true in the social sciences, where an attempt must be made to keep abreast of major social changes that take place ever more rapidly. As Kardiner (1945) has pointed out, the increasing emphasis on success as the dominant life goal has resulted in vastly more anxiety among people than in the days when achievement of heavenly bliss after death was the paramount aim. The net result of all this is that people become less and less secure in their environment. The expansion of our world, by means of radio, airplane, automobile, and so forth, has been accompanied by a contraction of a person's ability to adjust as an individual, unaided by others. At every point in his life he becomes increasingly dependent upon his society. Rarely do we find a person who is as independent of others as the pioneer and frontiersman of a few generations ago. For every detail of existence we find our unaided efforts counting for less. Much of our dependence on others is in ways that are indirect and not susceptible to personal control or intervention. The price of commodities is regulated by vast and complex interactions of many factors; our wages are similarly determined. Our frustrations arise from factors over which little personal control seems possible. All these circumstances are factors in the etiology of mental illness.

CORRECTIVE SOCIAL ACTION

Although we must defer a detailed consideration of therapy to Chapter XVII, we should indicate the major line of defense against the maladaptive influences in our social environment. In the first place we should recognize that culture is *man-made,* and that we are reasonably certain of the psychological properties of human beings that have made his cultural activities possible. By utilizing these factors in a rational manner, the pathological consequences of social life may be largely averted. Man's ability to learn and to devise adjustmental techniques has not been sufficiently exploited in the interests of social harmony. Our school curricula have placed too little emphasis in the past on the type of mental hygiene education that would encourage rational behavior and discourage mechanisms of defense. More needs to be done to train people in the techniques of successful group interaction in which the easy dependence on stereotypes is replaced by a mature reliance on cooperation in the solution of mutual problems. There should be a wider dissemination of the type of knowledge that would enable people to pass adequate judgment on important problems of world and national policy. Running through the whole educational life of the individual should be a constant emphasis on personal application of the scientific method to the point that assertions by public figures or in printed matter for public distribution would be accepted as a basis for action only when supported by evidence, or as an hypothesis for experimental test.

Such a program sounds impractical and inordinately ambitious. Yet, there is nothing of what we know about human psychology that would indicate such measures to be impossible. It is true that the emotional reactions against this type of education would be vociferously great, since too many cherished stereotypes, too many easy "articles of faith" would be disrupted. Yet the alternatives that face our world civilization show the folly of refusing to modify a social structure that contains so many factors that produce disordered behavior. The more we understand about pathological aspects of psychology the more clearly do we recognize the value of intelligent training in reality. This training must be applied to both parents and children, and should start very early in life. Much experimental work remains to be done on training techniques, particularly for the very young and for the adult who has been a product of an earlier type of management. We must frankly recognize the limitations of our knowledge, but we should also have the scientific temper that accepts ignorance only as a challenge to fresh experimentation.

DISCUSSION QUESTIONS

1. What are some of the specific inconsistencies that occur in the ideals of our culture?
2. What are the constructive and detrimental elements found in the cultural training of our children?
3. If we assume that some military training seems inevitable for almost every male for the next few years, what effects do you think this might have on future cultural mores?
4. Are there any present social institutions that appear to have little or no adaptational significance?
5. Do we ever possess sufficient knowledge to advocate or to institute social changes?
6. Can you suggest any changes that might be made in present methods of language-training?
7. What is the role of scientific knowledge in social change?
8. What difficulties might one run into if he tried to apply the scientific method exhaustively to his everyday life?
9. Is the application of science the responsibility of the scientist or the layman?
10. Is the greater social good achieved by increasing facilities for care of the mentally ill or by attempting to change the cultural vectors of abnormal behavior?

SUGGESTED READINGS

H. Cantril, ed. (1950), *Tensions That Cause Wars.* Urbana, Ill.: University of Illinois Press.

S. Freud (1930), *Civilization and Its Discontents.* London: Hogarth Press, Ltd.

I. J. Lee (1941), *Language Habits in Human Affairs*. New York: Harper and Brothers.

K. Lewin (1948), *Resolving Social Conflicts*. New York: Harper and Brothers.

BIBLIOGRAPHIC SOURCES

The major study of ethnocentrism is Adorno, Frenkel-Brunswick, Levinson, and Sanford (1950), *The Authoritarian Personality*. No short summary can describe the many facets of this investigation, and the book should be read completely. An excellent introduction is Levinson's (1949) preliminary report which clearly discussed the concept and describes the scale developed for the measurement of ethnocentrism. The central notion of these authors is that ethnocentrism is a set of basic opinions, attitudes, and values which the individual expresses both toward the groups with which he identifies and toward the groups to which he is negative. Further, these attitudes are characteristic of the individual and find expression throughout the context of his personality. For further experimental evidence, see Block and Block (1951), Prothro (1952), and O'Connor (1952).

On the discordant elements in our pattern of cultural training see Horney (1935), a short journal article that contains many of the points elaborated in her (1937) *The Neurotic Personality of Our Time*, in which Horney develops the idea of the child's "basic anxiety," the "feeling a child has of being isolated and helpless. in a potentially hostile world," and in *Our Inner Conflicts* (1945). Another fine article is by Ruth Benedict (1938), in which she discussed the continuities and discontinuities of cultural training in a number of societies.

A major interest of sociologists and social psychologists has been the investigation of social pathology. Any of the following texts will be useful: Bloch (1952), Cuber and Harper (1951), Elliot and Merrill (1950), Faris (1948), Gillin (1946), and Lemert (1951). All these texts discuss the pathology of the group and the individual. In addition, for general discussions of the adaptive and maladaptive features of social life, the student should consult Freud's *The Future of an Illusion* (1928) and *Civilization and Its Discontents* (1930). The latter book particularly occupies itself with the dilemma of reconciling reason and emotion in an adaptive manner. Flugel's (1921) *The Psychoanalytic Study of the Family* is a classic in psychoanalytic contributions to social psychology. The book by Waller (1938) is also useful. Aldous Huxley's (1932) *Brave New World* combines good reading with a thoughtfully satirical criticism of the type of idealistic social planning that fails to recognize the emotional aspects of personality among humans. Much the same may be said for George Orwell's (1951) splendid *1984*. Howells' (1940) *Hunger for Wholeness* is an extremely good presentation of the distinctions between adaptive and maladaptive social behavior; his section on the development of personality should be read in this connection. Evans' (1946) *The Natural History of Nonsense* is full of illustrations of the irrationality of much of our cultural pattern. As Evans says, "Until about a hundred years ago rational men lived like spies in an enemy country . . . to have revealed their true selves would have been fatal."

Of the many fine general books on specific cultural influences on behavior we suggest Kardiner (1935), Hallowell (1936, 1938), Lasswell's (1930) *Psychopathology of Politics,* Veblen's (1899) classic *The Theory of the Leisure Class,* Landis and Page's (1938) *Modern Society and Mental Disease,* Aichorn's (1935) *Wayward Youth,* Alexander and Healy's (1935) *Roots of Crime,* and Brown's (1933) *Immigration, Cultural Conflict and Social Adjustments.* Perhaps no authority has written more brilliantly on this topic than the late Kurt Lewin. Several of his papers have been collected in *Resolving Social Conflicts* (1948). Publications on specific variables are numerous and always provocative. Davis (1940) reports on the effect of severe cultural isolation on the personality of a child. Dickinson and Beam (1933) is a study of *The Single Woman.* Dunham (1937) and Faris and Dunham (1939) have produced extensive (and controversial) studies on the distribution of psychotic disorders in the various socio-economic districts of Chicago. For a review of this literature and other pertinent topics, Hare (1952) is suggested. Hovland and Sears (1940) demonstrated a relationship between lynching and certain economic factors in the social environment. Menninger and Chidester (1933) is a discussion of the role of financial loss in precipitating behavior disorders. Queen (1949) describes the possibility of measuring the relationship between social participation and social disorganization. On the subject of social roles in this context, Warren (1949), Stouffer and Toby (1951), and Ort (1952) are suggested. In addition, Cameron (1950) presents a specific and strong account of the relation of social roles to abnormal behavior. Cameron (1947) and Cameron and Magaret (1951) are also recommended.

The effect of social variables on personality has been discussed in so many places that the problem of selection is difficult. However, the following may be helpful: Dollard (1937), Linton (1938, 1945), Maslow (1937, 1951), Mead (1937), Murdock (1949), Plant (1937), Sargent and Smith (1949), Schilder (1938), Weinberg (1952), Witmer (1939), and Woodward (1938). But this literature is, to say the least, controversial, as may be seen from the following critical papers: Cantril (1947), Green (1948), and Lindesmith and Strauss (1950).

Much of the evidence that we have mentioned here has come from anthropologists. Chapter 3 in Sargent (1950) will introduce the student to this type of investigation. A fine introduction to the anthropological point of view with respect to pathological behavior is Benedict's (1934) *Patterns of Culture,* now available in the Penguin Book Series. A great deal of this literature is discussed in Yap (1951). As basic source books, Sumner's (1906) *Folkways* and Frazer's (1917) *The Golden Bough* should be examined by every student.

For a general introduction to the study of language, we suggest the text by Miller (1951). On language factors in psychopathology, Wendell Johnson's (1946) *People in Quandaries* is a good introduction, as is Hayakawa's (1941) *Language in Action.* Korzybski's (1941) *Science and Sanity* is harder reading and remains obstinately obscure in many spots, but contains the basic framework for the "general semantics" approach to psychopathology. From another point of view, the treatment by Cameron (1947) is strongly suggested. In addition, the paper by Goodstein (1951) presents the evidence and theories concerning the language of the schizophrenic. Lippmann's (1922) *Public Opinion* remains one of the best treatments of stereotypes and is easily available in a Penguin Book reprint. A book by Lee (1941), *Language Habits in Human Affairs,* presents a practical approach to semantically correct language usages. Osgood (1953) presents a behavioristic account of language development similiar to the one given here but in much more specific detail. An additional source that requires some sophistication is the monograph edited by C. E. Osgood and T. A. Sebeok (1954), *Psycholinguistics, A Survey of Theory and Research Problems.*

On war, see Britt's (1941) chapter on "Nationalism and war," Cantril's (1950) *Tensions That Cause Wars,* Hitler's (1939) *Mein Kampf,* Fay's (1930) *The Origins of the World War,* Mock and Larsen's (1939) *Words That Won the War,* Toynbees's *A Study of History* (1947, Somervell's abridgment), and Millis' (1931) *The Martial Spirit.*

On the relations between technical features of our culture and psychopathology, Lynd's (1939) *Knowledge for What?* presents a good "what to do about it" discussion. Mumford's (1934) *Technics and Civilization,* (1938) *The Culture of Cities,* and (1944) *The Conditions of Man* are thoughtful reviews of the technical roots of our culture. Köhler (1938) discusses the problem of establishing values in a cultural setting dominated in so many aspects by the scientific method and by technological data. Thurman Arnold's (1937) *The Folklore of Capitalism* combines an analysis of several current stereotypes about our economic system with an authoritative presentation of some of the legal aspects of our technical civilization. Bridgeman's (1938) *The Intelligent Individual and Society,* and Hilgard's article in Hartmann and Newcomb's (1939) *Industrial Conflict: A Psychological Interpretation* discuss the role of the rational man in our culture and give some suggestions for ways of overcoming irrational forces.

Theories and Treatment
of Disordered Behavior

*No scientist really knows what are the data he is dealing
with until he has the system in which they are integrated.
An isolated datum is a fragment. It becomes precise and
significant only when it is brought into a coherent system
and connected with other data.*

— s. c. pepper, *World Hypotheses*

Introduction

We now come to the last section of our work in psychopathology. Now that we have learned some of the basic psychological concepts, have become acquainted with some of the varieties of abnormal behavior, and have discussed some of the kinds of evidence bearing on causation, we are ready to take a look at theories of disordered behavior, and to learn a little about the ways that psychiatrists and clinical psychologists go about treating these disturbances.

Until now, what little theoretical material we have discussed has been largely implicit in the selection of material and in the choice of emphasis in its presentation. In this section we will describe, although very briefly, a number of the guesses that have been made concerning the origin and meaning of pathological behavior. Although we call these hypotheses and speculations "theories," they fall far short of the explicit, quantified, and testable theories that, to the scientist, represent peaks of elegance, and are best exemplified in matters that concern the physicist. Whether the science of psychopathology will ever attain even the foothills of this aspiration is difficult to say. As you have seen, the diversity of phenomena in this field can be almost overwhelming, and the very fact that most of the phenomena are deviations from the normal and expected makes for confusion.

Nevertheless, in spite of the difficulties, or perhaps just because of them, psychopathology has bred theoretical proposals in abundance. Many of them are broad, sweeping attempts to explain all behavior, normal or deviant; one of them, Sigmund Freud's theory, has been termed an intellectual influence on a par with Copernicus' theory of the solar system or Darwin's theory of evolution. Yet even the

531

broadest of them is unsatisfactory. None of them really succeeds, even for the short time or within the limited space that the best of theories may hope to attain adequacy. Yet, the first step for the student who may someday be the one to make a better theory is an introduction to the guesses that have been hazarded by his predecessors. Although none of the theories is completely right, all of them have something of the truth. They were constructed as the best way, for the particular theorist, of explaining his observations, and all the theorists we will present were observers, all of them saw patients by the hundreds, and all of them have managed to capture some fragment of insight for the problems their patients posed.

This suggests the sort of attitude that we should adopt toward theoretical proposals in psychopathology. We should regard theories as devices that teach us the relationships among the variables we are observing. We should use them to sharpen our own critical techniques, as exercises in scientific logic. We should regard them as historical landmarks on the way to man's understanding of himself. And, finally, we should regard them as challenges to experimentation and, if it lies within us, to better theory-making of our own.

When we come to a consideration of treatment we are really leaving the specific concerns of psychopathology, although anyone who has stayed with us this far should have a rather great curiosity about "what can be done about these things." As far back in the history of mankind as we have been able to trace, we find attempts to cure or ameliorate disorders of behavior. The reason we have put the chapter on treatment after the theories of psychopathology is that most of these therapeutic efforts have grown out of convictions as to the causes and nature of the disease. In a sense one might say that therapy in mental disease has always been more rational than therapy in any other branch of medicine. From the distant days when medicine men trephined holes in skulls for the avowed purpose of giving avenues for the escape of devils, down to the superficially similar operation of frontal lobotomy, the therapies have been indicated by the theories.

Because behavior disorders are a serious social problem, treatment of them has never been able to wait for certainties to be established. This may give the student the impression that therapy in this field is random, hit-and-miss, or, at best, enthusiastically muddled. Although this impression is in part a reflection of the true state of affairs, it is an odd fact that actually therapy is much more successful than a critical evaluation of the theory on which it is based would give anyone the right to expect. In addition, as we know more and more about the basic variables operating in the creation of pathological behavior, and are able to construct increasingly valid theories, we will be able to provide more effective treatment.

XVI

The Theories of Psychopathology

Men are ever engaged in the dual activity of making observations and then seeking explanations of the resulting observations.

—CLARK HULL, *Principles of Behavior*

THEORETICAL APPROACHES IN PSYCHOPATHOLOGY

It is generally conceded that a major function of science is to tell us "why" phenomena occur. Scientists have excluded most of the obvious metaphysical meanings of "why" and have pointed out that most questions that begin with "why" are more easily answerable if "how" is substituted. The scientist may then proceed to a description of the occurrence of phenomena in such a way that cause-and-effect relationships appear. In psychopathology aberrant behavior is the effect, and the second part of this text has been devoted to a detailed consideration of such effects. The causes, or at least a number of them, have been discussed in the chapters immediately preceding this one. In this chapter we will briefly describe some of the current concepts of the causation of disordered behavior and tie some of the ideas introduced in previous chapters to their theoretical parents.

The present state of theoretical psychopathology should be frankly recognized as immature. In the whole field there has been but one attempt to deal systematically with all the problems of behavior pathology, and thus there is really only one theory.[1] This, the psychoanalytic theory of Freud, is itself so unsystematic, when regarded by the cold

[1] Of the many theoretical approaches to behavior, a few have seriously tried to explain some aspects of psychopathology, but these have realistically avoided pushing their generalizations too far. It is perhaps one of the greatest weaknesses of Freud's theory that he tried to explain too much with too few concepts.

and logical eye of the psychological systematist, that we may truly say that a unified theory is still a matter for future scholars. Yet there are many hypotheses in the field, tentative explanations of this or that restricted group of occurrences. One person offers a theory of psycho-neuroses, another of behavior following brain injuries, still another a theory of delusion formation in paranoid schizophrenia. It is a situation that every young science has gone through, a time of classification and fact-gathering, of partial explanations refined by further observation, and of emphasis on now one and then another of the varied types of maladaptive behavior. Freud may have been, as some have said, the Darwin of psychopathology, and the future may justify the claim. *At present, however, no theoretical position has achieved the goal of providing an explanatory framework for all types of behavior deviations.* There are probably many reasons for this state of affairs, but two of them would seem to be (1) the fact that psychology as a whole is just beginning its task of systematic theorizing, an undertaking that will automatically include deviant as well as "normal" behavior, and (2) there have been few people of a systematizing temperament (or motivation) in the field. It is to those few that we owe most of the theoretical subject-matter to be presented in the following pages.

A classification of theoretical approaches to psychopathology shows that they may be roughly reduced to three: (1) the *organic-structural,* (2) the *functional-life history,* and (3) the *Gestalt* or *field-theoretical.* The organic approach is the oldest in point of time and is probably the one most consonant with the general systematic approach of medical biology, although the discoveries of psychosomatic medicine have tended to erase the sharp boundaries between this approach and the functional. The functional approach may be said to be the most popular in the field at the present time. The majority of psychiatrists and clinical psychologists could be placed within this category in their theoretical leanings. The Gestalt approach has been, in the vernacular of the track, a slow starter, and has spread more by piecemeal acceptance than by overwhelming domination.

The Organic-Structural Approach

According to this view, there are two types of etiological agents in the behavior disorders: (1) hereditary defects or predilections, and (2) acquired organic diseases. Essential to this point of view is a conviction that behavior is determined to a large extent by the structural potentialities of the organism. If the germ plasm is defective, or if disease or injury cripple the organism, the structural changes so induced will alter behavior.

Although we have said that the organic theory is the oldest, the statement is true only of its scientific status. The old ideas of spirit-possession and extra-corporeal influences were essentially nonorganic and were accepted even by men of great learning for many years. The swing of the pendulum toward an organic interpretation started in the early nineteenth century, with the discovery of the true significance of the nervous system in behavior. By 1860 Forbes Winslow in England had written a 576-page book, *On Obscure Diseases of the Brain and Disorders of the Mind,* in which he asserted that the etiology of the latter depended on abnormal states of the former. A short time later another English physician, Maudsley, stated:

No one now-a-days who is engaged in the treatment of mental disease doubts that he had to do with the disordered function of a bodily organ—of the brain. Whatever opinion may be held concerning the essential nature of mind, and its independence of matter, it is admitted on all sides that its manifestations take place through the nervous system, and are affected by the conditions of the nervous parts which minister to them. If these are healthy, they are sound; if these are diseased, they are unsound. Insanity is, in fact, disorder of brain producing disorder of mind; or, to define its nature in greater detail, it is a disorder of the supreme nerve-centres of the brain—the special organs of the mind—producing derangement of thought, feeling and action, together or separately, of such degree or kind as to incapacitate the individual for the relations of life.[2]

Their evidence came, of course, primarily from those individuals with organic lesions of the brain whose bizarre behavior combined with post-mortem findings gave the assurance for their assertions.

EMIL KRAEPELIN

However free of doubts the physician may have been concerning the organic basis for mental disease, the organic position remained merely a plausible hypothesis until research workers demonstrated that paresis was undoubtedly associated with syphilis. Anticipating this discovery

[2] Henry Maudsley (1875), *Responsibility in Mental Disease,* p. 15. New York: D. Appleton & Company.

to some extent, Emil Kraepelin, the German psychiatrist who had labored in the new science of experimental psychology under Wundt, published a classification of mental diseases in which each condition was regarded as being as specific a disease entity as paresis. Thus dementia praecox and the cyclothymic disorders were attributed to definite (but still unknown) organic causes, were thought to have a definite course, a definite symptomatic picture, a definite (but still undescribed) organic pathology, and a definite and predictable outcome. Kraepelin's classification did an immense amount of good in bringing terminological order into the field and in stimulating a great deal of research directed toward finding the responsible etiological agents. Kraepelin's theoretical approach has been scrutinized by Adolf Meyer, whose systematic rebellion against the Kraepelinian position we will describe shortly, in the following words:

Kraepelin bends the facts of psychiatric observation to the concept of disease processes. His psychiatry works with the postulate that each case presents one of a relatively small number of disease entities with definite cause, course and outcome. . . . Each disease has its specific lesion; and a true clinical entity has its unity of cause, course and outcome, and is necessarily the clinical picture of a unitary and specific histological process or condition, with general paralysis as the paradigm.[3]

TYPES OF CAUSES

The organic causes of mental disorder may be, according to the theory: (1) exogenous disease processes, such as bacterial or parasitical infections; (2) endogenous malfunctions of metabolism, digestion, respiration, cardiac action, or internal accidents, such as cerebral hemorrhage, embolism, and so forth, or faulty heredity; (3) traumatic destruction of structure, such as head injuries, poisoning, and so forth. In general, anything that interferes with adequate physiological function may be suspected as a causative agent for behavior disorders. Most organic theorists would add the proviso that the disturbance must influence brain function, since their position in this respect has not changed —the behavior disorders must be eventually reduced to symptoms of brain malfunction.

[3] Adolf Meyer (1910-1911), "Dementia praecox." *Journal of Abnormal Psychology*, 5, 274-285. By permission of the American Psychological Association, Inc.

EXPERIMENTAL EVIDENCE

What justification is advanced for this point of view? The evidence comes primarily from clinical observation. Paresis, Korsakow's psychosis, drug psychoses, disordered behavior associated with brain tumor, certain types of feeblemindedness, Huntington's chorea, and a whole host of similar conditions are cited. In each of these disorders some circumstance can be identified which, by acting on the body tissues, has been followed by deviant behavior. We have reviewed most of the pertinent facts in Chapters X and XIV. Underlying the facts, however, is a particular manner of interpreting them. A quotation from a once influential psychiatric monograph, which played a part in the theoretical controversy of organic versus functional, is indicative of the argument:

Biologists say there can be no function without structure. Therefore, there can be no abnormal function without abnormal structure. . . . If we could conceive of a mental state independent of the brain—and all known facts refute such a belief—then we could believe that certain forms of insanity were diseases of the mind and not diseases of the brain . . . success in treatment and prevention . . . depends upon establishment of a definite relation between mental symptoms and pathological conditions in the brain tissue; sufficient data are at hand to prove that such a relation does exist and that, when abnormal brain conditions are corrected, abnormal mental symptoms disappear.[4]

This statement contains at least two of the assumptions basic to the organic theories: (1) that abnormal function depends upon abnormal structure, and (2) that mental disorders are disease entities. Neither of these points is established beyond doubt. The first we have already evaluated at several points in the text. Suffice it to summarize here by saying that the experimental evidence shows that "bad" as well as "good" habits may be learned with precisely the same well-functioning physiological mechanism, and that the psychophysiology of emotion shows how disorganized social behavior may be under conditions where the body is working in a high state of physiological efficiency. The second assumption may be doubtfully regarded if it can be shown that disordered behavior develops along a continuum, with no sharp dividing

[4] H. Cotton (1921), *The Defective Delinquent and Insane: The Relation of Focal Infections to Their Causation, Treatment and Prevention*, pp. 14-15. Princeton: Princeton University Press.

lines between the symptomatic manifestations of the various disorders. In Part Two we learned that the same symptoms could be seen in many conditions that occupied different places in the classification, and that the resemblances sometimes greatly outweighed the differences, in spite of great differences in the "causal" backgrounds of the specific cases.

In the meantime, the organic theory has stimulated a host of research workers to explore the bacteriology, biochemistry, and pathological anatomy of the mentally ill. The vast majority of psychopathological conditions have withstood the onslaught, and the promise of revelation given by the identification of syphilis with paresis has not as yet been fulfilled. Out of research from the organic point of view have come some therapeutic techniques whose results have been sufficiently encouraging to keep the theory alive. The discovery that surgical injury to the frontal lobes may result in improvement in some psychotic conditions, the effect of shock and fever therapies, and the observations of reaction to drugs by patients have raised more theoretical questions than they have solved, however, as we shall see in the next chapter.

Within the past ten years there has been a resurgence of research interest in the organic approach to behavior. From neurophysiology, endocrinology, and physiological psychology have come new attacks on the functioning of the regulatory systems of the body as they relate to the gross patterns of observable behavior. Enough progress has been made to encourage tentative statements of new "organic" theoretical positions. Although none of these is sufficiently directed toward the problems of psychopathology to warrant its presentation here, the student is urged to inspect some of the offerings that are listed at the end of this chapter.

The Functional Theories

All functional theories, in one way or another, have their origin in the well-tested belief that the human organism shows an unusual capacity to learn. The organism is regarded, moreover, as capable of learning bad or maladaptive habits. The principal difference between the various functional theories lies (1) in the relative emphasis given to particular environmental factors in the production of disorders, (2) in the interpretation given to the role the organism plays in utilizing the poor habits it has learned, or (3) in the manner of habit acquisition and retention. It is no exaggeration of the facts to say that the functional approach has resulted in a detailed study of every conceivable aspect of the lives of human individuals and has produced a share of our knowledge of the general principles of behavior.

Historically, the functional theories are derivatives of associationism, itself a part of the empirical orientation in psychology that goes back a very long way. It is rather strange that empiricism was not seriously applied to psychopathology until the very last part of the nineteenth century, but it remains a matter of fact that Adolf Meyer's proposal to regard the psychoses as a consequence of experience was revolutionary in 1910, and that Freud was not able to give up completely the idea that some neuroses were directly attributable to an exhaustion of nerve fibers for some time after his original formulation of the functional origin of hysteria. As we look back, we can see that the idea of mental disease being a cumulative effect of past experience would be perfectly logical as part of a psychology that believed in the primacy of experience. But to trace these historical threads is a task for another time.

We will describe briefly a few of the more important functional approaches to psychopathology, without respect for chronological sequence. Actually, functional explanations appeared almost simultaneously in several different countries and as outgrowths of quite different types of research. The four countries that were the most active were France, Austria, Russia, and the United States. We turn first to the French.

THE FRENCH SCHOOL

As Boring (1950) has remarked, French psychology has always been oriented toward physiological and pathological problems. It was Flourens, who lived from 1794 to 1867, who first laid down the experimental design for studies of brain function and who first proposed a theory of equipotentiality of the cortical regions. It was Broca who, in 1861, advanced the notion of a speech center and who gave a localization for it. Françoise Magendie shares the honors with Charles Bell for differentiating between sensory and motor nerves. At a much later date Alfred Binet devised the first generally accepted intelligence test.

It is to be expected, then, that the French theoretical work in psychopathology would come from the hospitals and the medical clinics. From about 1870 there have been many contributors to a functional interpretation in the French tradition, but the two outstanding men of this group were Jean Martin Charcot (1825-1893) and Pierre Janet (1859-1947).

Charcot was in charge of the neurological service of the Salpêtrière and, as in any such large institution, had the opportunity of examining a large number of psychoneurotic patients. Hysteria was of special interest to Charcot. From the time of Hippocrates this baffling condition had been thought a disease of women, with an organic causation based probably on some malfunction of the female reproductive system. Charcot demonstrated that hysteria is no respecter of sex differences and is found in many male patients. This was, of course, a fatal blow to any notion about its uterine origin. Charcot was able to show that many individuals, when hypnotized, could develop hysterical symptoms (anesthesias, amnesias, etc.) in response to suggestions from the hypnotist. Since these symptoms could be manifested even after the subject had been awakened, and since the subjects claimed amnesia for the suggestions, Charcot assumed that the idea given during hypnosis could have an independent existence without being present in consciousness. Charcot believed hypnosis and hysteria to be either identical or closely related, and he suggested that unconscious ideas might be at the heart of the hysterical symptoms. However, he did not break completely from a conviction that the individual who could be hypnotized (and was hence hysterical) was essentially possessed of an hereditary and constitutional degeneracy.

Janet, a student of Charcot's, made intensive inquiries into the past history of many hysterics. He showed that hysterical symptoms could be accounted for by events in the patient's life. The following case is typical of his findings:

Case 64. A young woman who was a patient of Janet's had a complaint of feeling inexpressible panic and fear whenever she heard the ringing of church bells. When interviewed, she professed to have no knowledge of the origin of this fear. However, inquiry into her past history showed that, when she was a child, she had lived alone with her mother, an invalid who was critically ill with tuberculosis. One Sunday morning her mother had a severe hemorrhage, bleeding profusely from her mouth. The child was panic-stricken and, although terrified, held her mother's head in her lap and called vainly for aid. The mother died while she was in this position. The patient had no memory of hearing the church bells during this traumatic episode, but subsequently developed the panic symptoms whenever exposed to their sound.

Janet pointed out the decisive role of past associations in the production of symptoms and then went on to develop an hypothesis to explain
why past experiences result in mental illness in some people, and why
others are able to avoid such disorders. He postulated a normal level of
"nerve energy" or vitality, which serves to hold ideas in an integrated
associative pattern. The level of nerve energy may be depleted by many
circumstances of illness, injury, and most especially by emotional strain.
The normal integration of ideas in consciousness suffers when this takes
place, and the various systems of ideas tend to fly apart, to become
"dissociated," some ideas becoming unconscious. Thus the hysteric may
have difficulty in recalling emotional experiences, manifest multiple
personalities, develop anesthesias, functional paralyses, blindness, and
so forth. Substantially the same type of explanation was offered for the
other neuroses. In Janet's conception, it will be noted, the basic disorder
is a relative "disintegration" of the personality; the lowered psychic
tensions are not characteristic of just a single idea or of a small group
of associated ideas, but of the entire psychic system. Under circumstances that destroy the total integrative pattern, ideas will achieve an
organization in smaller units that operate in relative independence of
each other.

The evidence for this theoretical position, which was supported by
Binet and by Morton Prince in America, comes primarily from the
hysterical patients themselves. In cases of multiple personality it seemed
obvious that two systems of ideas could exist side by side in the same
individual, and yet show no mutual recognition or awareness of each
other's existence. Binet (1886, 1891) studied automatic writing and
hypnotic symptoms, with results that were interpreted as confirming
Janet's position. In automatic writing a person may be completely
occupied with conversation and yet rapidly write material on some entirely different topic. Binet showed that hysterics with symptoms of
anesthesia in a hand will repeat movements that the experimenter has
imposed on the passive hand, meanwhile carrying out other activities
with the nonanesthetic hand. Similar experiments have been performed
by many investigators since with confirmatory results. The interpretation that the French School made was that the execution of two or
more tasks simultaneously pointed to the dissociated existence of two or
more systems of ideas. The criticism of this statement most frequently
made is that no one has been able sufficiently to control attention to
make absolutely certain that the subject does not merely switch his at-

tention rapidly back and forth between the tasks. If this possibility is true, it points, not to a state of disintegration, but to a very high level of organization within the personality. As Murphy and Jensen (1933) have pointed out, even if the dissociative hypothesis were completely true, one would still have the task of explaining why the antagonism between various aspects of the personality existed. There is little room provided in Janet's theory for the motivational factors.

The concept of "lowered nerve energy," however, remains intriguing, particularly if we divorce it from its narrowly neurological connotations. We have seen that some such concept almost forces itself on us, and we have talked in detail about "stress thresholds" that influence the actual incidence of disturbed behavior. It is quite possible that the two concepts are based on a common observational background. We know that long-continued emotional strain, disease, illness, and so forth all play a part in determining resistance to stress (see Selye, 1950).

The contribution of Charcot, Janet, Binet, and Prince was to open the past life of the patient as a legitimate and pertinent aspect of research. Their clinical descriptions of psychoneurotic symptoms have become classics. They paved the way for theorists who added other concepts. One of these, Freud, may be said to have received his primary inspiration from the French School.

THE PSYCHOANALYTIC MOVEMENT

Although the functional approach to the study of mental disease depends basically on the notion of learning, another concept was needed to round out what we would now call a "modern point of view." The psychopathology of Janet, like the association psychology from which it derived, attempted an explanation of what was supposed to happen to the ideas that a patient possessed, but failed to give a convincing explanation of how the process took place. The missing concept was "motivation," and the man who, more than any other, gave it status in psychology was Sigmund Freud (1856-1939). It is possibly too early to take an historical attitude toward his contributions, but the inclination is great to call him the most significant figure in modern psychopathology.

It is impossible to give an adequate account of Freud's theory in the space we have. The interested student should follow the bibliographic leads at the end of the chapter. Freud's contribution was more than a theory of psychopathology; it was an entire system of psychology, by means of which he hoped to account for all types of behavior. Although his interests were originally in psychoneurotic patients, he soon found that his generalizations appeared to have validity for other disease conditions and for people who did not have problems sufficiently severe to bring them to his consulting rooms. Further, as Puner (1947) has said, Freud found much of the evidence for his theories in the workings of his own personality.

Freud was an Austrian Jew who had, in his childhood, seen some evidence of anti-Semitic feeling, and who was to be, in the last years of his life, possibly the most distinguished victim of the Nazi racial persecution. He studied medicine, became interested in neuropathology, and gave promise of becoming an outstanding research worker. However, a combination of personality difficulties and discrimination against his religious background led him into private practice and an interest in the psychoneuroses. He spent a year studying in Charcot's clinic and was impressed by the problems of hysterical patients. He was influenced in his thinking by a chance remark of Charcot's that there is always a sexual factor in the background of the hysteric. Returning to Vienna, he was associated with an older psychiatrist, Breuer, and began to treat hysterics by the use of hypnosis. He found himself more and more intrigued by the accounts of past history given by his patients under hypnosis and soon devised other ways of recovering past memories. The conviction that sexual factors were basic to the etiology of these conditions grew upon Freud and led eventually to the slow growth of a theory of behavior that we will now describe in brief outline.

Freud assumed that all behavior is motivated by a basic biological drive, the *libido*. This drive is essentially sexual in nature, and all other forms of motivation are secondary derivatives. The human personality is thought of as having three aspects, the *id*, the *ego*, and the *superego*. The id represents the primitive quest for satisfaction of the libidinous drive; it is raw, primordial, and animal-like. It is solely concerned with satisfaction, manifesting only the *pleasure-principle*. Its influences on personality are far-reaching, but unconscious. The adult is not directly aware of the id forces. The ego represents most of what we conventionally refer to as personality. It is the essential *I*, the consciously experiencing and experienced self. Id desires are translated into forms that will be acceptable to the person's ego. When the id strivings are not acceptable (and in our culture most of them are not), they are *repressed* or transformed into more socially suitable forms. The super-ego represents the moral and ethical standards that the person has acquired as the result of his experience in a given familial and cultural setting. It corresponds roughly to the everyday concept of "conscience," but is based upon the child's experience with parental prohibitions and standards. The superego is therefore the influence determining what wishes, desires, and strivings will attain conscious recognition and what will remain repressed.

Essential to the Freudian system, and indeed to most present-day psychopathology, is the concept of "unconscious motives." Although no psychologist or philosopher has ever seriously contended that all a man's wishes, ideas, or memories were present to his awareness at any one time, few scholars had attempted to postulate an active existence for such processes while they were unconscious. We have seen that Janet was forced to such a conclusion, but gave no satisfactory explanation of how the process worked. Freud claimed that many of the important wishes and memories were unconscious because they were *actively inhibited,* and only became conscious under the special circumstances of psychoanalytic interview, or in a disguised form in dreams, or still disguised, as symptoms of mental disorder.

From the time of birth or even before birth, the personality is being formed by the dynamic interaction of id, ego, and superego. To Freud the first few years of the child's life are of major and crucial importance. It is during this time that the superego is shaped and the ego is developed. Depending on the kind of experiences the child may have, the personality will be essentially healthy or will be sick. In all children, according to the theory, the sexual drive normally goes through the stages we have outlined in Chapter IV: (1) the autoerotic, in which *narcissism* or self-love is dominant. The person is completely satisfied by his own bodily processes. It is from this stage that enduring patterns of satisfaction from eating and excretory processes are derived; according to the theory, many later activities are expressions of the *oral* and *anal eroticism* acquired during this period; (2) a period of latency, lying between infancy and puberty, in which the early narcissism is widened to include pleasure outlets apart from the person, and in which sexual drive may be turned in the direction of parents and other authority figures in the environment. Because of the stern social taboos against incest, and because of the internalization of these inhibitory factors as superego, direct sexual expression is minimal. It is during this stage that unisexual outlets are approved by society (neighborhood gangs, girls' clubs, etc.); (3) the emergence of mature sexuality, with libido directed toward members of the opposite sex. Often circumstances arise that *fixate* the developmental process at a stage earlier than the heterosexual, thus leading to such forms of aberrant behavior as homosexuality, failure to emancipate oneself from parents, egocentrism, and so forth. Or, as we have seen, other circumstances may produce a *regression* from a later to an earlier level of adjustment. Even when the sexual evolution is normal, no one can be entirely free from frustration or repression. The constant striving of the id against the barriers to free expression results in the development of devious means of compromising with the inhibiting tendencies of the superego. We have described many of these devices in Chapter V as *behavior mechanisms* and have pointed out the part they play in reducing tension and resolving conflict. In *rationalization* for example, reasons acceptable to the superego are consciously advanced for a course of action that may have quite another real source of motivation. *Sublimation* would be the substitution of some socially acceptable form of behavior as a means of gratifying the libido indirectly. It has been described as a way of drafting sexual energy into socially worth-while channels. *Projection* is considered as a process of perceiving one's own id-strivings in the actions of others.

Of great importance to the analytic theory is the idea of *infantile sexuality* and of its influence on the problem of emancipating oneself from parents. The assumption that infants have sexual motives met with great resistance at the time Freud introduced it and is still frowned upon by casual readers of the theory. Freud claimed that the infant develops an attachment to parents that has all of the dynamic characteristics of love at any age, in that it is a sexual outlet, is subject to frustration, and that the behavioral consequences of that frustration are apparent in the later personality structure. Since society exerts such strong taboos on incest, the child is placed in a strong conflict situation, and *ambivalent* aggressive and submissive tendencies are developed. To this general emotional situation, with all its implications of trauma and disturbance, Freud gave the name *Oedipus complex,* after the Greek myth of the son who murdered his father and married his mother.

Psychoneurosis was basically an expression of the person's attempt to avoid those expressions of id-drive that society condemned as perverse, but that were actually the usual mode of sexual expression at an early level of development. As Freud says (1938):

> I must repeat what I have said in other publications, that these psycho-neuroses, as far as my experience goes, are based on motive powers of the sexual instinct. I do not mean that the energy of the sexual instinct merely contributes to the forces supporting the morbid manifestations (symptoms), but I advisedly maintain that this contribution supplies the only constant and most important source of energy in the neurosis . . . in all neurotics we find without exception, in the unconscious psychic life, feelings of inversion and fixation of libido in persons of the same sex.[5]

The conflict that results over these fixated manifestations of sex-drive are the source of the behavior mechanisms and thus of the neuroses themselves.

We have already seen the Freudian point of view with respect to the unconscious, to errors, and to dreams, in other chapters. In the following chapter we will discuss the therapeutic techniques that have grown out of the psychoanalytic theory.

Freud had many students, although he did not have professorial status in the Viennese medical world. Some of the students have modified his theory (and have been disowned by Freud in the process). Alfred Adler, with his substitution of a general "drive for superiority" for the libido, we have met in another chapter. Karl Jung, whom we have also met in connection with introversion and extraversion (Chapter XII), broadened the concept of the libido to include all forms of striving and modified the idea of the unconscious to include a somewhat mystical racial memory, handed down in the germ plasm, which exerted influence on behavior. In recent years the *Chicago group* of analysts (Alexander, French, Benedek, etc.) have been actively engaged in integrating the analytic approach with other trends in modern biology. Karen Horney and Erich Fromm have called attention to the great importance of social and cultural factors in the development of personality.

In summary, the analysts have contributed an emphasis on motivation and the role of unconscious factors to the structure of psychopathology. Of all the functional approaches the psychoanalytic has

---

[5] S. Freud, "Three contributions to the theory of sex." *Nervous and Mental Disease Monograph,* No. 7, pp. 26, 29, as cited in Freud (1938).

broken the most sharply with tradition and has come the closest to being a complete theory of behavior. The criticisms against it are numerous. It is not a rigorous system; it has logical incongruities; it is based in many instances on a type of circularity that defies the possibility of designing critical experimental tests of its propositions. For details of evaluation the student should refer to Sears (1943, 1944).

PSYCHOBIOLOGY

If we were to characterize the different theoretical approaches to psychopathology by countries of origin or major influence, we would have covered England (the organicists), France (Charcot and Janet), and Austria (Freud). Psychobiology is chiefly an American product. Its guiding figure was Adolf Meyer. He developed his theoretical approach in the general atmosphere of psychological functionalism and behaviorism; if we would summarize his theory in a phrase, we could say he applied the functionalist-behavioristic tenets to psychiatry. The result was a practical working technique that lies at the heart of the major part of contemporary American psychiatry. Meyer, for most of his academic life, was professor of psychiatry at Johns Hopkins Medical School. His personal influence has spread through his students to a dozen other great medical training centers. Meyer published little, but by his teaching and stimulation to others to research and writing, his ideas had a great influence on the American psychiatric scene.

Psychobiology is a deliberately coined word. Meyer used it to express his dissatisfaction with the academic *psychology* of the period (1900-1910). He felt (in common with Dewey and Angell of Chicago, although he rarely acknowledged it) that behavior was primarily an adaptive process, that the most striking manifestation of life was the unceasing attempt to adjust to environmental circumstances. Both normal and abnormal behavior could be accounted for in terms of the past experience of the organism. "Every mental activity or reaction leaves its engram and has a certain dynamic value in the after life of the individual and his general economy" (1911, p. 11). The study of mentally ill patients should not be confined to an examination of their present symptoms, but should be predominantly an inquiry into their past history. "It was possible to formulate the main facts of most cases in terms of a natural chain of cause and effect, utilizing the psychobiological material at hand" (1911, p. 10). He felt that the emphasis should be placed upon the individual and not on a "disease." Since the proposal was made at a time when Kraepelinian concepts were dominant, it was a novel concept. Among its values was the implication that classifications of mental disease and diagnostic labels often obscured the unique facts of the individual case. We have seen this same emphasis in Freud, and to a lesser extent, in Janet.

Psychobiology has never exerted the influence on academic psychology that the analytic systems have. This may appear strange, since psychobiology is an American product originating in the same rebellion against the Wundtian and Titchenerian type of psychology. There are several reasons for the lack of interaction. One very important reason was the rebellion itself. Meyer for many years identified all psychology with the narrow introspective approach of Titchener, as may be inferred by the criticisms of psychology that appeared in the survey of psychiatric education in America, prepared by his most famous student, Ebaugh (Ebaugh and Rymer, 1942). Therefore he boldly struck out to formulate a science of behavior that would be independent of what seemed to him to be the sterile psychology of the laboratory. This new science he called "ergasiology," from the Greek word *ergasia*, work or labor, emphasizing the activity of the total organism, including both the implicit processes of thinking and feeling, and the overt behavior, the "effective performances" that may be observed by others. The self-sufficiency of Meyer's conceptions, the restriction of their presentation to the curricula of medical schools, and their almost exclusive application to the problems of the mental diseases, all tended to limit their influence on psychology. Another reason, and one that attests to the scope of Meyer's thinking, was that psychobiology or ergasiology was developing parallel to very similar movements in academic psychology. Meyer's attempt to view the human organism realistically in its biological and social setting was being shared, quite independently, by a variety of psychologists during the period from 1910 to the present. The subject-matter, allowing for a few terminological differences, of Meyer's courses in psychobiology and the curriculum of the average undergraduate psychology major of the twenties or thirties was remarkably similar. Influences one way or the other, therefore, would be obscured. A third reason, again stemming from Adolf Meyer himself, is the fact that he has entered into few polemics. Even within the field of psychiatry itself, there have been remarkably few controversies over theoretical points of psychobiological doctrine. The theory is too eminently practical to provoke argument over details and is too well integrated with the biology and sociology being taught currently to present features for disagreement. In this it has been greatly different from psychoanalysis, which has stimulated some of the most pungent critical writing that "objective" scientists have permitted themselves since the anatomist Owen and Thomas Huxley exchanged verbal blows over Darwin's theory of evolution.

Psychobiology takes as its program a systematic attempt to understand the individual's struggle to adapt to his environment. Its method of investigation is the life history of the person. The reasonable assumption is made that the present condition of a patient is dependent upon what that patient has experienced in the past. A person's life is to be viewed as a dramatic production, a play whose plot unfolds as his history is followed from birth to death. The elements in this drama have been given by Muncie (1939) as follows:

> Psychobiological functions deal with a number of items: (1) native assets, in (*a*) instinctual drives or performances, (*b*) the fundamental organismal rhythms of waking and sleeping, and variations in fitness and efficiency, and (*c*) intellectual differentiations or endowment; (2) acquired skills; (3) basic mood and its variations; (4) habits; (5) memories; (6) ambitions and visions of opportunities and anticipations; (7) imagination and fancy; and (8) reasoning. These are variously organized into an individual constitution, or organization of basic tendencies. The more or less stable and dependable constitutional structure is modified through growth and by the more plastic situational, life experience factors. In such a way the individual's life record unfolds. It may be sampled at any time for purposes of cross-section examination, giving a momentary symptomatological picture, completely understandable only in connection with the dynamics of the time-bound longitudinal view. . . . Medical men, dealing with both personality functions and the workings of organ systems, have a unique opportunity to observe human behavior, living out the events of a biography with their personal and social implications. When this biography is attended with a degree of orderly operation and satisfaction from life, it is called "normal." [6]

This quotation shows how thoroughly "common-sense" is the psychobiological approach and how well it covers the main fields of contemporary psychological interest. As Meyer himself has frequently said, the psychobiologist wishes to study the individual from every aspect,

[6] W. Muncie (1939), *Psychobiology and Psychiatry*, p. 29. St. Louis: The C. V. Mosby Company.

but to do it in a way that is objective, concrete, and independent of mere analogical thinking.

The working technique of psychobiology lies in meticulous compilation of the personal history of the patient. At each stage of his life external events are listed in one column, personal items of health and disease in another, and reactions in another. Systematic comparison of the columns shows the evolution of abnormal behavior as an attempt to adjust to environmental stresses. Thus the symptoms of the patient assume meaning in terms of his past experiences. Therapy consists of an attempt to demonstrate these meanings to the patient, to give him insight for the causation of his symptoms.

THE SOCIOLOGICAL ORIENTATION

With the development of anthropology and the other social sciences, there came a realization that abnormality must be viewed in relation to the culture in which it occurs. A host of field studies of other societies showed that many types of behavior that we looked upon as pathological were the norm in other cultures. This led to some questioning of the definitions of abnormality currently used. Although it has been recognized for centuries that the "abnormal" person is one who does not make an adequate social adjustment, the analogical linking of mental and physical disease prevented much serious thought over the possibility of *defining* psychopathology as a cultural phenomenon. It is undeniable that personality is formed in a social matrix, and it is quite possible that the determinants of at least a portion of our mental ills are to be found in this same matrix.

Such is the position of the sociologically oriented theorist. In some way the causes of mental disease arise out of the interaction of the person with his society, and the type of society in which he lives will determine the level of his adjustment or maladjustment. There are many hypotheses that grow out of this basic proposition. We will review briefly only a few of them, as a supplement to the material presented in the preceding chapter.

The work in cultural anthropology of Franz Boas and his students, particularly Margaret Mead and Ruth Benedict, has furnished a fruitful source of material for psychopathological theory. They emphasized the relationship between the amount and kind of security furnished by a culture and the frequency of mental disorder. The more complex and loosely integrated the culture, the more difficult is adequate adjustment. Balancing this, to a small extent, they show that the definition of abnormality tends itself to be culturally determined.

The following quotation from Benedict summarizes something of the position of the cultural anthropologist toward the social relativity of the concept of abnormality and, still more fundamental, the dependence of the socialized human being on his culture for criteria of good and bad adaptation.

It is clear that culture may value and make socially available even highly unstable human types. If it chooses to treat their pecularities as the most valued variants of human behavior, the individuals in question will rise to the occasion and perform their social roles without reference to our usual ideas of the types who can make social adjustments and those who cannot. Those who function inadequately in any society are not those with certain fixed "abnormal" traits, but may well be those whose responses have received no support in the institutions of their culture. The weakness of these aberrants is in great measure illusory. It springs, not from the fact that they are lacking in necessary vigor, but that they are individuals whose native responses are not reaffirmed by society. They are, as Sapir phrases it, "alienated from an impossible world." . . . We must be willing to take account of changing normalities even when the question is of the morality in which we were bred. Just as we are handicapped in dealing with ethical problems so long as we hold to an absolute definition of morality, so we are handicapped in dealing with human society so long as we identify our local normalities with the inevitable necessities of existence.[7]

Of particular value has been the emphasis on a need for *comparative* psychopathology, that is, for a study of the disordered individual in the cultural setting of his illness and a consequent attempt to elucidate principles applying to aberrant behavior in all cultures and to work out the cultural influences that make the behavior appear abnormal. Coincident with this emphasis has been a criticism of the type of conventional approach to psychopathology that starts with a fixed list of symptoms and attempts to describe a disease instead of a person. This is the same objection raised by Freud and by Adolf Meyer.

The point of view expressed by the anthropologists and sociologists is essentially a plea for a more naturalistic consideration of the aberrant personality. One great temptation luring the theorist in psychopathology is the danger of reducing etiological hypotheses to a simplicity that

[7] Ruth Benedict (1934), *Patterns of Culture* (Pelican Books edition), pp. 249, 250, 251. Boston: Houghton Mifflin Company.

disregards the factual elements of the situation he is trying to explain. Most theories of behavior fall because they attempt to build on such a restricted number of variables that the theory loses predictive scope. An historical study of Freudian writings shows that the simple hypothesis with which Freud launched his ideas had to be constantly modified, extended, and complicated in an effort to account for the bewildering variety of facts that any behavior theory must eventually account for. Since human behavior cannot be separated from one cultural setting or another, the anthropological point of view cannot be lightly dismissed, but must be a factor in any future theory of psychopathology that aims at inclusiveness and validity.

An interesting variant on the social theme is given by Trigant Burrow (1937). Although his phyloanalysis has something of a tinge of mysticism, he is quite correct in stressing the role of social relationships in producing conflict and neurosis. Burrow believed that psychoneurotic difficulties arose because people were unable to give adequate outlet to their aggressive and submissive trends and still stay within their own version of "polite" relations with other people. The social structure of our culture, according to Burrow, forces neurosis upon the person. As Galt puts it:

> . . . normal society presents socially the same dissociations and image-substitutions as are represented in the neurotic personality; he finds that the prevailing "normal" social structure is not basic or fundamental in nature but on the contrary represents a secondary and substitutive fabric, which, like the fabrications of the neurotic, is without direct biological or organic foundations. His investigations show that the present social order is in large measure built upon proprietary thought-processes within each of us which do not rest upon a biological matrix embodying the phyletic experiences of the species as a whole. These processes are constructed rather upon the arbitrary mental concept or *social image* which each individual holds privately in respect to himself and others.[8]

We see here a reiteration of the James-Mead concept of the dual aspects of the socially developing personality. The "social image," as Burrow stresses, may develop in ways that are biologically maladaptive, since the society shields and approves such development. Accordingly, Burrow instituted a method of therapy that has been probably his most

---

[8] William Galt (1933), *Phyloanalysis: A Study in the Group or Phyletic Method of Behavior-Analysis,* pp. 40-41. London: Routledge and Kegan Paul Ltd.

significant contribution. He assembled groups of patients, and by the use of free and informal conversation between them, accompanied by analysis of the social interchange, he reported that the patients were better able to understand and control the types of maladjusted behavior that social situations in the past had forced upon them. We will discuss group therapy in more detail in the next chapter; Burrow was only one of several people to develop the technique, although he was one of the first.

Another analysis of the genesis of abnormality in our cultural setting was advanced by Karen Horney, a psychoanalyst. Although subscribing in general to the Freudian viewpoint, Horney nevertheless felt that the most significant factor in the development of mental illness is an inability of the individual to achieve the goals that are set for him by our society. She spoke of the "basic conflict" that is involved—incompatible attitudes toward other people, a disturbance in human relations, a confusion of the realistic relationship between goals and the ability to attain them. Her approach bears some similarities to that of Burrow. She also called attention to the fact that "the discrepancy between a neurotic's actual behavior and his idealized picture of himself can be so blatant that one wonders how he himself can help seeing it" (Horney, 1945, page 132). The *idealized image* is socially developed, and the discrepancy between that image and the real personality as it must face the problems of reality-adjustment is the basic conflict that calls forth the defense reactions that are the symptoms of psychoneurosis. Thus sexual conflicts are only a part of a more inclusive picture of a person who is out of harmony with his environment. Therapy must aim at resolving these conflicts, giving the person a more realistic insight concerning his potentialities and the incapacitating nature of his neurotic defenses, helping him to assume responsibility and to achieve a genuine feeling of independence from the supports that he has erected.

THE SEMANTICS APPROACH

A socially oriented theory of psychopathology, which we have drawn on in our analysis of language function, is that of *general semantics*. Semantics is the study of language as a means of symbolic communication; as a theory of psychopathology, general semantics is concerned with the relationships between language structure and usage on the one hand and personality and behavior on the other. A. Korzybski and his students have advanced the hypothesis that uncritical use of language is responsible for social and personal maladjustment by means of a faulty understanding and unrealistic manipulation of a social environment that is so overwhelmingly verbal in nature. If there is confusion in the symbolic interchanges between persons, imperfect understanding and discord are inevitable. The ease with which words can serve as redintegrative stimuli sharpens the danger. Falsehood, faulty generalizations, sensitivity to stereotypes, and many other forms of aberrant behavior may grow out of the way we use language. The use of semantics in therapy will be discussed later, although we may say here that the primary therapeutic goal of the general semanticist is similar to that of all socially oriented therapists, namely to sharpen the patient's evaluations and insights with respect to the social realities with which he must deal to achieve successful adaptation.

Configurational or Gestalt Theories

SOME GENERAL GESTALT PRINCIPLES

Within the broad framework of Gestalt psychology there are two somewhat different theoretical attacks on the problems of abnormal behavior. A quite strictly psychological approach is that of Kurt Lewin's topology. A more general biological theory is advanced by Kurt Goldstein, whose ideas we have presented in our discussion of stress and the catastrophic response. Our review of aspects of these positions will be, therefore, somewhat repetitive, but will also act to some extent as a summary of one of the viewpoints emphasized throughout the text.

To begin with, let us give a brief description of some of the background of Gestalt psychology. Gestalt theory arose as a reaction to the narrowly analytical psychology of Wundt, who had said that the task of psychology is to analyze mind into its elements. The Gestaltists objected that the results of such analysis are artificial and bear little resemblance to actual psychological happenings. The initial starting point of psychology should be with phenomena as such, with naive experience. We perceive objects, forms, and patterns, and only secondarily, as the result of learning, do we perceive simple sensory elements. Furthermore, it was claimed that the old psychology could not explain the real experience in terms of elements, since the critical factor in perception was the *organization* of stimuli, and not the actual stimuli themselves. For example, a melody is an experience that remains greatly similar when transposed into a different key; a wheel looks circular and a table top looks rectangular from almost all angles of regard, in spite of the fact that the retina seldom receives a projected light pattern corresponding to the physical shape of the object. Parts have no existence save as components of the total experience. Also, it follows that extracting a portion of any totality changes the whole from which it comes, and the part extracted becomes a new whole itself.

What then will be the materials of study? How will the laws of behavior be stated? If analysis is futile, what will be the method of investigation? Answering these questions in order, the subject matter of psychology is naive experience, total behavior. The laws of psychology are the laws of dynamic relationship, of psychological forces that operate to maintain the whole. Investigation alone does not change much. Fundamentally, the Gestaltist does about the same type of experiments as any other psychologist. Guided by his principles, he probably more often designs experiments in which the organism is less constrained by experimental conditions and in which the whole organism is under observation.

The fruits of Gestalt psychology have been most abundant in the fields of perception and learning, where they have arrived at certain principles concerning the manner in which an individual organizes the environmental field of his behavior. These principles, most easily demonstrated in perceptual experience, are assumed to be of general applicability to all phases of behavior, of being organismic in character. (For a presentation of these concepts the student is referred to the references given in the bibliographic section at the end of the chapter.)

KURT LEWIN AND TOPOLOGICAL PSYCHOLOGY

The specific contributions of Lewin and his students to theoretical psychopathology have been most outstanding in the area of motivation. Their experimental work has been on the consequences of reward and punishment, on the influence of various social settings, on the organization of personality traits, on an analysis of conflict situations, on the factors that produce emotional experiences and the effects of such experiences on behavior, and in general, on an exploration of the factors that unify the person and his environment. Theoretically, Lewin has attempted to develop a consistent theory of personality organized around the concept of motivation. Using the framework of the *psychological environment,* as we have described it previously, the person is seen as acted upon by forces that correspond to his needs and motives. Objects in the psychological environment have *positive* or *negative valences,* in accordance with their observed properties of attraction or repulsion of the person. The valences are congruent with the motives; to a hungry person a beefsteak or a restaurant door may have a strong positive valence; to a person suffering from nausea the valence would be as decidedly negative. The *life-space* of the person is thus a force-field, and his behavior will be determined by the pattern of forces and valences in this life-space. The life-space is viewed as containing within its boundaries many regions, some of which are more accessible and can be more freely traveled through than others, depending upon the state of fluidity or permeability of the internal boundaries. For example, an animal whose life is spent in seeking dark or confined spaces but who is confronted with a situation where food may be secured by traversing a brilliantly illuminated open space or by a longer route through a dark narrow alley would, from a Lewinian point of view, have two regions in his life-space differing in the ease with which locomotion could be made through them. The person who is faced with a difficult problem may be in a similar psychological situation to the animal. He may have, as the two regions in his life-space, a locus of logical solution procedures and a locus of rationalization. Ease of locomotion to the goal of problem solution may, for a given person, lie through logical thought, for another through rationalization.

Since the behavioral field of any person will contain more than one goal for most motives, and since many motives will be in existence at any given time, the field will present a complicated dynamic picture, with many forces acting upon the person simultaneously. Lewin's greatest contribution has been in his analysis of the conflict situations that result and of the manner in which they may be treated by the individual. His emphasis on the *uniqueness* of behavior situations has grown out of this type of approach, and he has attempted to formulate the laws of psychology on the basis of dynamic interrelationships of forces, using the same method of approach that has worked so well in the physical sciences. In physics, as Lewin has pointed out, no attempt is made to seek the laws of falling bodies in the specific case. No two objects fall at the same speeds, show the same accelerations, or terminate their fall in exactly the same manner, and no statement could be made that would completely describe a single unique case. The laws of falling bodies deal with the dynamic force relationship that obtains only under ideal conditions; each case must be dealt with by modifying the basic law to suit the given circumstances. In the ideal law of falling bodies, the fall is assumed to occur in a vacuum. When the fall occurs in air, modifications must be made in the formula. In psychology, laws of conflict may be discovered, but the application of those laws must always contain the proper corrections for the unique case.

In this connection Lewin is critical of one of the basic elements of the other functional approaches we have considered, namely, the importance of the past history of the organism in accounting for his present behavior. Although Lewin does not deny that the person is modified by experience, he doubts whether these modifications are relevant considerations in formulating principles of behavior. To return to our analogy with the laws of falling bodies, the geological and metallurgical history of a stone or a piece of metal is not considered in the statement of the fundamental law. All that is taken into account is the patterning of forces that act upon the object. The laws of falling bodies, as is true of most laws in the physical sciences, are *a-historical*.

Lewin would formulate the principles of psychology in the same way. The past experiences are of importance only in creating the unique situation. Aspects of that situation may be described in terms of universal, a-historical laws. For example, if it is established that a person is in a conflict over whether or not to cheat on an examination, the description of that conflict must be made in terms of the alternative regions in his life-space, of the various motivational forces, and of the various valences in his psychological environment. The history of the person may be instrumental in shaping the psychological environment in such a way that it contains a cheat-or-not-to-cheat conflict, but the psychologist, according to Lewin, will arrive at his laws of behavior by studying the situation *as it is given*. Derived from this same line of reasoning is Lewin's objection to statistical criteria of lawfulness. As he says, after citing typical results of statistical studies based on the average performance of children in various situations:

Valuable and indispensable as these facts are, they can rarely offer more than hints toward the problem of the forces of the environment. For, in the investigation of the fundamental dynamic relations between the individual and the environment, it is essential to keep constantly in mind the actual total situation in its concrete individuality. The statistical method is usually compelled to define its groups on the basis not of purely psychological characteristics but of more or less extrinsic ones (such as number of siblings), so that particular cases having quite different or even opposed psychological structure may be included in the same group. Especially to be emphasized, however, is the following consideration: the calculation of an average (e.g., of "the one-year-old child") is designed to eliminate the "accidents" of the environment; the determination of the "average situation" (e.g., of the average effect of the situation of being an only child) is to exclude individual variations. But the very relation that is decisive for the investigation of dynamics—namely, that of the position of the actual individual child in the actual, concrete, total situation—is thereby abstracted. An inference from the average to the concrete particular case is hence impossible. The concepts of the average child and of the average situation are abstractions which have no utility whatever for the investigation of dynamics.[9]

The significance of this systematic attack on motivational problems lies in the possibilities it gives for seeing the whole array of behavior disorders as subject to the same dynamic principles instead of as specific and nonrelated diseases. Throughout the text we have tried to show how the same type of symptom may be seen in many syndromes, and that in each it appears to be fulfilling the same dynamic purpose. Lewin is not alone, of course, in this basic outlook. In many respects his general approach is similar to that of Freud, as J. F. Brown (1940) has recognized in a book that combines the two in an explanation of pathological behavior. Both are convinced that there is a fundamental dynamics underlying all behavior, and that motivational striving toward goals is the basis of that dynamics. They further agree that disordered behavior appears when the goalward progress is blocked or frustrated.

KURT GOLDSTEIN

For the Gestalt approach to frustration we may turn to Kurt Goldstein. Goldstein is a neurologist who was in charge of a German hospital for the care of ex-soldiers who had incurred neurological injuries during World War I. His studies of brain-injured patients led him to adopt an organismic or Gestalt point of view. In 1934 Dr. Goldstein was forced to leave Germany by the Nazi regime, and in the enforced leisure of exile, produced a general summary of his theoretical interpretation of

[9] By permission from *A Dynamic Theory of Personality,* p. 68, by Kurt Lewin. Copyrighted 1935 by McGraw-Hill Book Company, Inc.

biology. This book, *The Organism,* contains several concepts that are important to etiology. Foremost is his discussion of the reaction of organisms to stress. He argues that all animals have one basic drive, underlying all others (as did Freud). This drive is the need for integrity, for maintaining the particular organization of protoplasm that constitutes the particular animal. It is not difficult to see how the need for food, water, mate, shelter, and so forth function to gratify this need. Without these things the organism could not maintain life. The need for integrity also extends into every phase of social life; an obvious example is the earnestness with which we strive to avoid appearing "stupid" or mistaken, the great lengths we are willing to go to for social approval and success. But the need for integrity is not satisfied without difficulty. As we discussed in Chapter III, motives are satiated only against resistance. The psychological environment of the organism, its "milieu," contains many stresses that sometimes tax adjustmental efforts severely. As the stresses increase in severity, more and more extreme adjustments are required of the animal. For any individual there is a severity of stress beyond which it cannot continue to adjust. If stress continues beyond this point, the organism resorts to a completely "disordered," relatively nonintegrated type of behavior. Goldstein, as we have seen, has termed this the "catastrophic response."

Another pertinent concept is his idea of post-traumatic behavior. To Goldstein the alterations in behavior following injury are a part of the organism's attempt to maintain its integrity. Since the organism meets the environment with impaired resources it must limit its behavior if catastrophic response is to be avoided. "A defective organism achieves ordered behavior only by a shrinkage of its environment in proportion to the defect" (Goldstein, 1939, page 46). This is an important principle that has been at least partially verified in patients with brain injury and can be observed by anyone in patients with locomotor difficulties. We have presented evidence for the possibility that the principle applies to psychological trauma as well as it seems to apply to the physical.

Goldstein, however, does not equate the basic need for integrity with the mere effort for self-preservation. The latter, he claims, is not an *essential* trait of the organism, but "the tendency towards self-preservation is a phenomenon of disease" (Goldstein, 1939, page 443). It is a conservative trend that may actually limit and cripple the organism in its attempt to secure optimal adaptation. Thus, the person who adopts various avoidance techniques in his attempt to deal with anxiety is, as we have seen, limiting his penetration of the environment and is creating new adaptational troubles in his efforts at solving the old.

SUMMARY OF GESTALT VIEWPOINTS

To summarize the Gestalt point of view, it is concerned more with the development of concepts and ways of thinking about behavior in general than it is with formulating a specific theory of some phase of psychopathology. Yet, as we remarked at the start of our discussion of etiology, the only successful and valid theory of the behavior disorders will be but a component part of such a general psychological theory. Freud started from the pathological and worked his way toward the normal; the Gestaltists, in general, started from the other end of the continuum, and both groups have arrived at the same point in this respect. The Gestaltists have emphasized motivation, analysis of the environment-person interrelationships, and the formulation of laws based on situations and not on persons. This has led to a relative disregard or devaluation of the "disease entity" concept of psychopathology and has put in its place an interest in the *processes* underlying all pathological behavior.

A General Summary of the Problems of Theory in Psychopathology

We have surveyed a variety of attempts to account for abnormal behavior. As a thoughtful consideration of these theories will show, some important insight is present in each approach. These theories reflect the observations of their sponsors; since they were all talking of the same type of material, it is plausible to assume that many of the divergences came about because of differences in emphasis. We are not saying, it should be noted, that there is no error in these theories. Theories combine observation with conjecture, and guesses are not always correct. In practice, the clinician frequently demonstrates that sometimes diagnosis and therapy are aided now by one theory, now by another. The psychiatric and psychological literature is full of the more or less eclectic amalgamation of differing theories. From a strictly scientific point of view, such eclecticism is in bad repute. Science is obliged to test hypotheses and to modify them in accordance with such trials. Ultimately, so the scientist believes, there will be but *one* theory that will adequately account for the phenomena, all others being either in error or redundant. However, the clinician performs a real service by his selective approach. He uses the concepts that fit the particular case, and as time goes on he finds that some concepts are more adequate than others. Thus there is a never-ending trial of concepts, which results in gradual selection of the correct and a gradual rejection of the erroneous. At the present time we are in a stage of rapid evolution with respect to etiological theories. It is not too much to expect that new and more adequate theories will emerge as laboratory and clinic converge on these problems.

The basic etiological problem, as it appears now, is the question of how the factors of heredity, past history, structure, and situational conditions mutually operate to produce a given type of behavior in a given person. In the last analysis each personality is unique. The older ideas of "diseases," which had a definite causation, a definite symptomatology, a definite treatment and course, and a definite prognosis have all but disappeared in all realms of medicine. Much of the credit for changes in medical thinking can be taken by the psychopathologist. As we saw in Chapter VI it must inevitably be recognized that psychological factors play a part in *all* disease processes. Understanding of the sick person is a many-sided task, involving all of science. So, fundamentally, we are seeking to answer the question: What, in any given patient, is the equation of all factors that will enable us to describe him as he is?

Etiology is important enough for its own sake; it represents our scientific curiosity and is our answer to the question of "How did he get that way?" But a knowledge of etiology is important for two other reasons: *prediction* and *treatment*. We must be able to make predictions in order to devise practical hospitalization plans, in order to integrate therapeutic efforts with the life pattern of the patient, and, most urgently, to institute good mental hygiene prophylaxis. Treatment is usually influenced by the therapist's concept of causation. Other things being equal, a "good" idea of specific etiology goes hand in hand with a successful plan of therapy. There are occasional exceptions in all fields of medicine, but empirical therapies have always been vastly improved when adequate background for their use was discovered.

DISCUSSION QUESTIONS

1. How important to progress in psychopathology are general theoretical approaches such as those mentioned in the text as opposed to limited conclusions based strictly on existing evidence?
2. Can we expect a theoretical system based on study of one particular disorder to successfully explain all other disorders?
3. Why is the constant re-evaluation of existing theoretical systems necessary?
4. In what way could the organic-structural dichotomy conceivably be fundamental to psychopathology?
5. By what criteria should we evaluate a theoretical system?
6. Which theoretical approach mentioned in the text appears most adequate on the basis of these criteria?
7. What difficulties of experimental test and verification seem to be particularly obtrusive in psychopathology?
8. Would it be possible for a theory such as Freud's to be quite correct for Vienna in the nineteenth century and be completely inadequate for Chicago in the twentieth century?
9. Is there an *organic* basis for *functional* disorders? That is to ask, is there a class of events in behavior that do not have an organic basis?
10. What is the point of Lewin's insistence that *laws* of behavior are a-historical? Does he really discount all the evidence we have cited that people are changed by their past experiences?

SUGGESTED READINGS

F. Alexander and Helen Ross, eds. (1952), *Dynamic Psychiatry*. Chicago: University of Chicago Press.

J. Dollard and N. E. Miller (1950), *Personality and Psychotherapy*. New York: McGraw-Hill Book Company, Inc.

S. Freud (1949), *An Outline of Psychoanalysis* (trans. by James Strachey). New York: W. W. Norton & Company, Inc.

G. Hartmann (1935), *Gestalt Psychology,* Chapter 14. New York: The Ronald Press Company.

W. Muncie (1948), *Psychobiology and Psychiatry*. St. Louis: C. V. Mosby Company.

BIBLIOGRAPHIC SOURCES

Since a full discussion of any theoretical approach could not possibly be included in a text of this size, the interested student is advised to consult at least one reference for each of the theories we have mentioned. In evaluating scientific theories of any kind, there is no substitute for the original writings of the individuals who propound the theories. Any secondary presentation almost automatically becomes an evaluation, both by virtue of the selection of material that is made and by the restatement of the original theorists' position in words chosen by the secondary writer. In some instances primary sources are difficult to obtain, either because of language hazards or because of the obscurity or prolixity of the theorist. In such instances, if the theory is important, condensations and secondary presentations are usually available.

For the development of theoretical trends in psychopathology, Zilboorg's (1941) *History of Medical Psychology* is excellent. For discussions of psychological theorizing in general, see Chapter I of Hull's (1943) *Principles of Behavior,* from which the quotation at the head of this chapter was taken, and also Chapters I and II of Lewin's (1935) *A Dynamic Theory of Personality.* That there are many varieties of psychological theory may be seen from the collection of papers presented in Marx (1951).

The organic approach to psychopathology is rarely presented in as direct and unmodified a way as was customary in writings of the last century. Hoskins' (1946) *The Biology of Schizophrenia,* Cobb's (1943) *The Borderlands of Psychiatry* and Gellhorn's (1953) *Physiological Foundations of Neurology and Psychiatry* are pertinent. Cooperative research on a very large scale has been increasing; these studies involve psychiatrists, neurologists, anatomists, physiologists, and psychologists in intensive study of a selected sample of disordered individuals. One of these is edited by F. A. Mettler (1949), *Selective Partial Ablation of the Frontal Cortex,* more commonly known as the Columbia-Greystone study. On the same scale is the study directed by R. G. Heath (1954), *Studies in Schizophrenia.* For an indication of just how much research is being done on the organic basis of behavior disorders, we strongly suggest the 38 papers published from the Milbank Memorial Fund Conference (1952) entitled *The Biology of Mental Health and Disease.* Finally, Cobb's article in Hunt (1944) has a very reasonable discussion of the fallacies involved in an exclusively organic approach.

On French psychology and psychopathology in general read, in addition to Zilboorg, Boring's (1950) erudite *History of Experimental Psychology.* Murphy's (1922) *An Historical Introduction to Modern Psychology* and Murphy and Jensen's (1933) *Approaches to Personality* also give some background to the French school. The best introduction to Janet is his *Major Symptoms of Hysteria* (1920), one of the most interesting books in the field of psychopathology. His other major works, which have been translated into English, are *Principles of Psychotherapy* (1924) and *Psychological Healing* (1926). On Prince's contributions, see his *The Dissociation of a Personality* (1906) and *Clinical and Experimental Studies in Personality* (1938).

The literature on psychoanalysis is of staggering dimensions. A complete annotated bibliography would make many interesting and thick volumes. There is no better source for psychoanalysis than Freud himself whose writings may be seen in the Modern Library Giant, which has been referred to throughout the text, and in his *A General Introduction to Psychoanalysis* (1943), and in *New Introductory Lectures on Psychoanalysis* (1933). Perhaps the most interesting of all Freud's works is his last, *An Outline of Psychoanalysis* (1949). The content is indicated in the introductory note: "The aim of this brief work is to bring together the doctrines of psychoanalysis and to state them, as it were, dogmatically—in the most concise form and in the most positive terms." In a discipline where the obscurities, metaphorical flights, and complexities of terminology make one occasionally wonder whether it is worth-while to read any of this work (Snyder, 1947), Freud's little book is a model of clarity. As his last statement of the principles of psychoanalysis, the book is of considerable theoretical interest. Of the many secondary sources available, Hendrik (1947), Brown (1940), Healy, Bronner, and Brower (1930), and Fenichel (1945) may be useful. Of the many criticisms of psychoanalysis, Jastrow's (1940) *Freud, His Dream and Sex Theories,* and Shaffer's (1936) *Psychology of Adjustment* still contain the most temperate and judicious statements of the considerable scientific antagonism toward psychoanalysis. Again, perhaps no single source surpasses Sear's (1943, 1944) papers examining in detail many of the psychoanalytic concepts. There are many biographies of Freud available: Puner (1947) gives a great deal of insight into the degree that his theoretical writings were autobiographical; Zilboorg (1951) presents a discussion somewhat more directly oriented toward his work. It appears, however, that the definitive biography of Freud will be found in Jones (1953), the first volume of which was available at the time this was written.

One of the few presentations of Jung's analytic system is given in Jacobi's (1943) *The Psychology of Jung.* The collected works of Jung are being published by Pantheon Books in the Bollingen Series; four volumes are in print at this writing.

Alexander, as the leader of the Chicago School, has written a great deal, and has had a very great influence on American psychiatry. Possibly the best single source would be his *The Medical Value of Psychoanalysis* (1936). A text edited by Alexander and Helen Ross (1952) contains a number of papers written by leading figures of the Chicago School with the implicit point of view of that group. A long and very critical examination of this movement has been published by Eissler (1950) representing the more classical point of view.

The substance of Adolf Meyer's writings has now been published in four volumes of *Collected Papers* (1950, 1951a, 1951b, 1952), edited by Eunice Winters, reproducing his work on neurology, psychiatry, medical teaching, and mental hygiene. For theoretical writings alone, there is the shorter volume of *Collected Papers* (1948). Lief's (1948) *The Commonsense Psychiatry of Dr. Adolf Meyer* combines biographical and interpretive material with 52 selected papers to provide probably the best primary source introduction to Meyer's system. Muncie's (1948) *Psychobiology and Psychiatry,* and Billings' *Handbook of Elementary Psychobiology and Psychiatry* are useful secondary sources. An interesting personal account of contacts with Meyer is given by Ebaugh (1937). In addition, for quite sophisticated implicit elaboration of the psychobiological point of view, see Cameron (1947) and Cameron and Magaret (1951).

The anthropological point of view has been documented throughout the text. In addition to the works of Benedict and Mead already cited, the book edited by Kluckhohn, Murray, and Schnieder (1953), *Personality in Nature, Society and Culture,* is a valuable repository of papers by a variety of authors.

Burrow's point of view is given in his *Biology of Human Conflict* (1937), *The Neurosis of Man* (1949), and in Galt's (1933) *Phyloanalysis.*

Horney's writing on psychoneurosis may be found in *The Neurotic Personality of Our Time* (1937), *New Ways in Psychoanalysis* (1939), *Self-Analysis* (1942), *Our Inner Conflicts* (1945), and *Neurosis and Human Growth* (1950).

For an excellent historical introduction to Gestalt psychology, see Chapter 23 in Boring (1950). Still the best introduction to Gestalt concepts and findings is Hartmann's (1935) *Gestalt Psychology.* The Gestalt movement was primarily founded by the work of three men: Max Wertheimer, Wolfgang Köhler, and Kurt Koffka. Wertheimer is best represented in English by his small and excellent book, *Productive Thinking* (1945). The best works of Koffka are perhaps *The Growth of Mind* (1924) and *Principles of Gestalt Psychology* (1935). Well-known works of Koehler are *The Mentality of Apes* (1925), *Gestalt Psychology* (1929), *The Place of Value in a World of Facts* (1938), and *Dynamics in Psychology* (1940). Perhaps the most widely influential in America of the Gestalt psychologists was the late Kurt Lewin. His work may be seen in Lewin (1935, 1936, 1938, 1948, and 1951). His article entitled, "Behavior and development as a function of the total situation," published in the first edition of Carmichael's (1946) *Manual of Child Psychology,* has been reprinted in the second edition (1954), followed by a thoughtful evaluation of the influence of the work of Lewin and his associates on child psychology by Escalona (1954). A valuable guide and criticism of Lewin's approach is Leeper's (1943) *Lewin's Topological and Vector Psychology.*

The work of Kurt Goldstein extends back to 1903. A bibliography of his work may be found in Goldstein (1952). To supplement this text, his book *The Organism* (1939) is recommended.

We have not specifically discussed in the text one of the fastest growing theoretical approaches to psychopathology, and it seems advisable that at least some mention should be made of it. We refer to the theoretical systems developed by academic psychologists using basic learning theory as a model. The assumption is that disordered behavior is fundamentally a problem in learning, and, accordingly, systematic applications and extensions of learning theory to psychopathology may provide fruitful insights into the understanding of abnormal behavior. Perhaps the first attempt of this sort was by Pavlov, but his notions about psychopathology depended less upon his classical experiments in conditioning than on his conceptions of the neurophysiology of the central nervous system. In 1936, one of the leading learning theorists, E. R. Guthrie, published a small but systematic book, *The Psychology of Human Conflict,* which attempted to explain disordered behavior by reference to the principles of Guthrie's theory of learning. Since then the learning theory models have multiplied rapidly. Under the impetus of Hull's (1943) learning theory, several investigators have published extensive accounts of psychopathology. One name which we have mentioned many times before is O. H. Mowrer, whose views are perhaps best seen in *Learning Theory and Personality Dynamics* (1950). Another systematic presentation is Dollard and Miller's (1950) *Personality and Psychotherapy.* The dedication of the latter book to Freud, Pavlov, and their students offers an insight into the intellectual background of this approach. It is Pavlov's conditioning experiments that lead most directly to Hullian learning theory. These authors have attempted to apply Hullian principles (or modifications of it) to Freudian concepts in an effort to construct a scientifically more acceptable system. The approach is new, the controversies numerous, and we have attempted no textual presentation. That many of the ideas are implicit in this text may be seen by referring again to Chapter III or Chapter VIII. But whether or not any learning theory approach alone will result in a successful understanding of psychopathology is an issue for future work to decide.

XVII

Treatment and Prophylaxis

> Doctor: *Not so sick, my lord,*
> *As she is troubled with thick-coming fancies,*
> *That keep her from her rest.*
> Macbeth: *Cure her of that:*
> *Canst thou not minister to a mind diseased,*
> *Pluck from the memory a rooted sorrow,*
> *Raze out the written troubles of the brain,*
> *And with some sweet oblivious antidote*
> *Cleanse the stuff'd bosom of that perilous stuff*
> *Which weighs upon the heart?*
> Doctor: *Therein the patient*
> *Must minister to himself.*
> —SHAKESPEARE, *Macbeth*

Introduction to Therapy

PSYCHOPATHOLOGY AND TREATMENT

Strictly speaking, the subject of therapy is not a part of psychopathology as such, since our interest is in a scientific description of disordered behavior and not in the process of treatment. It is possible and it is current practice, in the field of tissue pathology, to concentrate attention on the pathological conditions, leaving considerations of therapy to others. Psychopathology, however, is in a somewhat different position, since it is a fact that a great deal of what we know about the pathological process has been discovered and is made available to observation only in the course of therapy. Freud, for example, gained his first insight for neurotic behavior mechanisms while attempting to treat hysterics. The symptoms of behavior disorders do not leave relatively permanent traces in bodily tissues as is the case with physical diseases,

568

and the psychopathologist cannot depend upon post-mortem examination of his material for knowledge of behavioral disease processes. Behavioral observations during therapy, then, yield evidence aiding in our effort to describe the psychopathological processes. For this reason, we will briefly survey the major treatment techniques in use by psychiatrists, clinical psychologists, and social workers.

Since disordered behavior has been considered throughout most of history to be an illness or disease, it has been studied primarily by persons with a medical or at least a therapeutic orientation. For this reason we find that treatment has been carried on as far back as our history takes us. The physician, or his surrogate, has very properly refused to allow ignorance to be a plea for suspending remedial action. Thus, a great deal of the therapy in mental disorders has been overtly or implicitly experimental in character, since even at the present time we know much less than we would like to about the basic causative factors in these conditions. These therapeutic experiments are grist for our mill; they afford us data on a wide variety of aberrant reactions to unusual situations. As a minor example, the medieval "treatment" of hysterics by means of torture showed us that the hysteric was not motivated by superficial desires to escape or avoid situational punishment. Observation of the "fatherly advice" approach to emotional problems demonstrated the need of the frustrated person for security and protection. Many of the current therapeutic procedures are of at least as much benefit to the psychopathologist as to the patient. It should almost go without saying, of course, that effective therapy is related to increase in our scientific knowledge of behavior, and that each patient who undergoes therapy at any stage in the development of our science is contributing in some small way to the welfare of future patients. Our present concern, however, is with the therapeutic procedures as sources of information relevant to our main problem of understanding pathological behavior.

EMPIRICAL AND RATIONAL THERAPIES

A distinction may be made between *rational* and *empirical* therapies. In the former, the therapeutic efforts are based on a known relationship between the forces brought to bear on the patient and the disease condition from which he suffers. The use of penicillin in bacterial infections or of dilantin in epilepsy are illustrations. In the latter the therapy is based on past trial and error, and little is known about the actual process at work. The use of quinine in malaria for many years before the cause of the disease was known or before the action of quinine on that cause was understood is a good example of an empirical therapy. In dealing with disordered behavior, both types of therapy are used. As part of the experimental aspect of therapy, it is often the case that, with increasing knowledge, the erstwhile empirical method is established on a rational basis; there is nothing finalistic or absolute in the empirical-rational distinction.

TYPES OF TREATMENT AVAILABLE

At the present time the person with a behavior disorder finds available to him three main classes of therapeutic procedure, any or all of which may be applied to his particular case, depending on his problems, the type of therapist he consults, the facilities afforded by his social community, his economic and social status and a host of other variables, such as his age, general health, prejudices and attitudes, past interests and abilities, and so forth. The three classes into which all the behavior therapies fall are: (*a*) physical, surgical and chemical therapies; (*b*) psychotherapy and re-education; and (*c*) "adjunctive" therapies, such as bibliotherapy, music therapy, occupational therapy, drama therapy, and so forth. In the well-planned attack on a mental disorder all three therapeutic groups are utilized. Together they constitute the "armamentarium" of the psychotherapist; the art of treatment lies in the selection of weapons and the timing in their use. We will consider each of them in turn but the student should remember that they do not, in general, constitute alternative procedures. They are simply the analytical breakdown of a total therapeutic program.

THE GOALS OF THERAPY

The psychotherapist is interested in restoring to a patient the integration of personality resources that will give him personal happiness and social adaptability. These two goals are implicit in all therapeutic procedures and do not differ materially from the general aims of all therapy, whether it be for pneumonia and infantile paralysis or for economic and social insolvency. The word "restoration," as we have remarked previously, should not be taken too literally. Most behavior disorders have a long history and more than "restoration" is usually implied in therapy. Possibly some such term as "creation" would be better, since few patients would be much better off if they were merely restored to a previous level of happiness and efficiency. Therapy may best be understood as a process of *learning*, of acquiring new techniques of adaptation, and all the therapeutic devices we will discuss should be evaluated in terms of this criterion: *Does the therapy aid the patient to acquire new and more successful ways of adaptation?* As a part of the process of learning new habits, the patient must break off old habitual ways of trying to solve his problems. Some therapies seem more suited to the former, some to the latter. But no matter in what classificatory group, as above, the therapy falls, it is of value only in relationship to its effect on the learning process all patients must undergo.

Many troublesome problems should be recognized in connection with therapeutic goals. One that is often raised is the question of the extent to which a therapist should seek to modify the personality of the patient. For example, a patient may have a deep and serious emotional attitude of acceptance of some ethical, religious, or moral teaching that has little or no rational basis. Should the therapist attempt to change this attitude? Since this is not a treatise on therapeutic techniques, we will not attempt to give an answer, except to state that the therapist's decision should always be made within the framework of the criterion just advanced. If the patient's belief or attitude is seriously interfering with his adaptive efficiency, then the therapist must further evaluate whether or not removal of this belief would improve the situation. It may be added parenthetically that such questions indicate that the task of therapy in behavior disorders is not a field for amateurs, and that even the longest period of training and experience will not bestow omniscience on the therapist. The same question comes up in a different form, as we shall see in a moment, in connection with certain surgical procedures that interfere permanently with aspects of higher neural integration. The decision as to whether or not to operate is a weighty matter that cannot be disposed of easily.

Related problems center around the degree to which the therapist as a human being enters into the determination of therapeutic goals. The personality of the therapist is an important factor in therapy. If he has prejudices, they will influence his judgment, hence his therapeutic practices. If he feels himself that sex is sinful and should be repressed completely from consciousness, will he be able to deal with patients who feel the same way and are emotionally disturbed over the resulting conflicts? If he is a reactionary in politics, will he be able to aid a patient who is a left-wing socialist? From what we have seen of the way motives may manifest themselves in subtle and unconscious ways, we must expect that the therapist's personality will be a variable in therapy. This is another reason why psychotherapy is not a field for the untrained, no matter how excellent his intentions and how strong his motivation to help others. Modern training in psychotherapy, whether it be within the framework of psychobiology, psychoanalysis, or ordinary clinical psychology, always includes considerable effort on the part of the student therapist to understand his own personality. This is necessary if he is to avoid confusing the patient's problems and situation with his own and, in his attempts to aid the patient, find that he is really trying to treat himself.

Finally, there are problems of even a more basic nature. To what extent should the therapist attempt to aid a patient in conforming to a society that itself is irrational and disordered? Should the therapist attempt to make his patient an island of reason in a sea of emotionality, or should he be satisfied if the patient comes to conform with reasonable contentment to the social situation as it is? This is another of the problems that interest the psychopathologist but do not strictly concern him as a scientist. It emphasizes the fact that therapy itself is not a part of science, but is an art or a technology. As we suggested in Chapter XV, however, the psychopathologist may be allowed to say that one of the roads to a more adaptive human *society* would be the cumulative therapeutic effort to make more *individuals* capable of effective adjustment.

Chemical, Physical, and Surgical Therapies

CHEMOTHERAPY IN SEDATION

There is nothing the patient or the physician would like better than to have "some sweet oblivious antidote" that could be administered in small and accurately measured dosages, to work "cures" in the mentally ill. Unfortunately, as Macbeth's doctor so wisely said, "Therein the patient must minister to himself." Those words are as true today as they were in Elizabethan England, and there is no drug that can perform the dual function of wiping out old habit patterns and replacing them with new and better ones. Nevertheless, drugs have an important part to play in psychiatric therapy.

The first and major use of drugs is in *sedation*. A number of chemical substances are known that act on the nervous system in such a way as to produce muscular relaxation, drowsiness, and sleep. One of the threats to physical health in psychiatric patients is the exhaustion that can occur when the patient's preoccupations disturb his sleep, induce over-activity, or prevent adequate attention to nourishment. There is hardly a psychiatric condition in which the patient does not show some difficulty of this kind. The anxious person may have insomnia, a heightened tonicity of muscles, poor digestion, and so on. The manic patient, as we have noticed, may wear himself out with his ceaseless over-activity. The alcoholic may have no time for either sleep or nourishment. In all these cases the sedative effect of various drugs enables the physician better to control the patient and to build up an exhausted body while he is dealing in other ways with the emotional problems themselves. Sedation aids also by breaking up the vicious cycle that results when emotional factors produce fatigue and lowered competency to meet everyday problems, thus resulting in still further emotional reaction leading to more fatigue, and so on.

Two classes of drugs, the *barbiturates* and the *bromides,* are most frequently used. The bromides are used less commonly because of undesirable toxic effects that appear when they are continued over long periods of time or are given in large quantities. Among the barbiturates, sodium amytal (sodium isoamyl ethyl barbiturate) and sodium pentothal (sodium ethyl-methyl-butyl thiobarbiturate) are the ones customarily employed, although there are over sixty other similar substances having approximately the same type of physiological reaction. (Among those with which the student may have come in contact are Luminal, Dial, Nembutal, and Seconal.) The advantages to be sought for in any type of drug for sedative purposes are: (1) the ease with which the substance is eliminated from the system, together with a freedom from accumulation or "storing" of the drug in the body; (2) freedom from toxic "side-effects," such as disturbance of function of vital organs, skin rashes, etc.; and (3) rapidity of action, other things being equal, the drug that takes effect the more quickly after its administration being preferred.

Other sedative drugs used in psychiatric practice are *paraldehyde,* a not too distant cousin of ethyl alcohol, which has a rapid action, is of low toxicity, and produces relatively untroubled sleep, and *chloral hydrate,* another relatively simple organic compound, which has a soporific effect in very small doses.

Any of these drugs may turn from a therapeutic aid to a therapeutic problem if used improperly. The number of suicides that occur through the use of sedative drugs is only the most immediately dramatic type of problem that drugs may introduce. If sedation becomes, either with or without the aid of a physician, just another technique for escaping anxiety without doing anything about it, then the sedative drugs fulfill no useful purpose. For these reasons the practice of filling large prescriptions and allowing the patient to regulate his own drug intake is frowned upon by every responsible physician. Another type of danger inherent in sedative drugs is particularly threatening in the institutional management of patients, where constant over-sedation may be resorted to as a substitute for the chains and strait-jackets of another day or as a means of supplementing a staff of attendants, nurses, and doctors insufficient for the number of patients in the case load. The drugged patient is not disturbing to ward routine and hospital management, but he is being denied the opportunity of progressing toward whatever chances he may have for recovery.

Psychologically, the role of sedation in treatment would appear to be primarily as a means of giving the person respite from his adaptive struggles. To the emotionally disturbed patient, a night of dreamless sleep or a few hours without the torment of delusory threats is a positive aid in recruiting his strength for further struggle, much as a two-week vacation has value in aiding us to face the ordinary problems of life. The dangers of this escape have been mentioned above, but with suitable medical management and with suitable interpretation of the need for sedation to the patient, the mechanism-formation aspect may be largely eliminated. The need for interpretation is psychologically obvious but is frequently overlooked in practice. This is illustrated most vividly in the case of some depressed patients and even more paranoids, where the sedative drug prescription is incorporated into their delusional systems and acts as further evidence to them that they are being persecuted, threatened, done away with, and so forth. Further, since it is a common belief among uninformed people that a physician always cures by giving drugs, the doctor's directions to "take two of these pills at bedtime," unaccompanied by a discussion of the reasons for prescribing the medicine, may lead the patient quite naturally to assume that his recovery is inherent in the pills. The rapid way in which patients can develop dependence on drugs is simply a laboratory illustration of the formation of a new behavior mechanism which, like all the others, ministers to a need without fulfilling it.

SLEEP THERAPY

Growing out of the use of depressant drugs, such as sedatives, is a more definitely therapeutically oriented technique known as *prolonged narcosis, sleep therapy*, or more rarely, as *continuous sedation*. In this technique the patient is maintained for periods up to a week in a state of sleep, which may be lightened for feeding, or in which feeding may be done by artificial means such as intravenous injections, and so forth. The method was introduced by Klaesi (1922) and was applied by Bleckwenn (1930) to psychotic patients, using sodium amytal for producing the narcosis. The results were encouraging (Palmer and Braceland, 1937), although the amount of nursing and medical care involved makes the treatment prohibitive in understaffed institutions. During World War II, Sargant and Slater (1940), faced with the problem of treating a large number of exhausted and emotionally disturbed individuals who had been evacuated from Dunkirk, found that immediate and heavy narcosis for periods of from 48 hours to a week yielded good recoveries. Similar experiences have been reported in our army for emergency treatment of soldiers with acute panic reactions, the treatment often being carried out in advanced areas immediately behind the lines.

The psychological effects of prolonged narcosis, in addition to those involved in simple sedation, seem to be in the nature of an interruption of a traumatic process, preventing it from continuing and at the same time allowing the person to regain a measure of physical health. This effect is more easily realized in the sudden panic and exhaustion states that occur in times of greatly increased external stress and danger than in the slower and more chronic disorders. In preventing the development of traumatic neuroses, prolonged narcosis has apparently the best rational basis. When the person has been overcome by accident or threat of great danger, the immediate excitement and panic, if left untreated, frequently develops into the harrowing insecurity we have seen in the traumatic neuroses. If the escape from danger is quickly followed by relatively long periods of rest and sleep in a reassuring environment, it is observed that the memories of the time of stress lose a great deal of their emotionally disturbing quality. As Hastings, Wright, and Glueck (1944) remark, "It is apparently much easier to adjust to a terrifying experience with the attitude 'it happened two days ago' than to have to immediately face the situation with all its recent memories and impressions" (page 181).

Although this all may be true and seems to be abundantly demonstrated clinically, certain discrepancies in the results of experimental investigations of learning and retention should be subjected to research. Jenkins and Dallenbach (1924) found that subjects who slept in the interim between learning a list of nonsense syllables and recalling them retained more than a group engaged in other activities, results that have been confirmed by Dahl (1928) and Van Ormer (1932). It is possible that the traumatized person would spend the interim period in a more or less constant rehearsal of his memories, and that emotional aspects of memory are less easily subjected to distraction. The lack of superficial correspondence in these results, however, brings to mind Kempf's statement in his monograph on autonomic functions and personality (1918) that it is not unlikely that the laws of learning in the field of autonomic activity may be somewhat different from those which apply to the skeletal nervous system.

NARCOANALYSIS AND NARCOSYNTHESIS

In using the barbiturates in psychotherapy advantage is taken of the fact that the depressant drugs act on higher levels of the nervous system before acting on lower levels. We have seen in Chapter X how alcohol could be used to release cortical inhibitions, and in Chapter XV we presented a protocol of a patient's actions and conversation under the influence of sodium pentothal. This approach to producing the inhibited material in the patient's past experience is known as *narcoanalysis,* and when combined with attempts by the therapist to interpret the information so released, it is called *narcosynthesis.* The example given in Chapter VIII of the use of sodium amytal in aiding the therapist to suggest the removal of an hysterical paralysis is a variation of narcosynthesis, but is distinctly inferior as far as any real therapeutic gain to the patient is concerned.

Under the influence of amounts of barbiturates less than the dose required for sleep, the patient acts very much like the moderately intoxicated person. He loses his grasp on reality, talks more freely, expresses emotions in a manner that would be inhibited in a waking state, and can often produce a stream of recollections that would otherwise be unavailable. Similar effects may be produced by hypnosis unaided by drugs; some therapists combine the two techniques, finding that the process of inducing the hypnotic trance is made easier if the person's conscious defenses are blunted by the sedative.

Narcoanalysis is used to recover memories that the patient cannot or will not give in ordinary interviews. Because the patient does not edit and select his memories to the same extent as in a waking state, the popular press has called the substances used by such names as "truth serum." Hysterical amnesia victims may often "remember" their identity and the events occurring during their period of memory loss. In traumatic neurosis and in the agitated panic states seen during combat the patient may develop an amnesia for the traumatizing circumstances. However, this method is far from being what the name "truth serum" might imply. Some emotional resistances are too deep-seated to be unhorsed by such simple means. Occasionally the release of inhibitions brings behavior of a kind not anticipated by the therapist. One hysterical patient, in the course of an amytal interview, manifested such strong hostility toward the interviewer that he had to be forcibly restrained from a murderous attack. Just as in drunkenness from alcohol, the narcotic effect on higher levels of the nervous system will result in release of inhibited personality trends, whatever they may be. A patient is as capable of revealing fantasy as he is of stating objective facts, and his inability to differentiate between the two often results in the production of material that is very meaningful psychologically, but that would hardly meet a legal test as evidence. The therapeutic benefit in narcoanalysis comes to some extent from the very act of "unburdening," of getting tension release out of verbalizing, and sharing problems and emotions with another person. The narcosis permits the patient to release somewhat more repressed material than would be the case in a direct interview situation, and his relief may be proportional. In some people, however, the sudden cascade of inhibited memories and impulses may itself be traumatic, and narcoanalysis, unaided, may be a source of harm rather than benefit, although as Horsley (1936) has shown, even catatonic schizophrenics may be aided by judicious interviewing under the influence of barbiturates.

More therapeutic gain may be accomplished if the narcoanalysis is accompanied by an active attempt on the part of the therapist to abandon his passive role as a listener. As the patient relives his experiences, the therapist may take an active part in the situation, using the momentary release of the patient's inhibitions to better his rapport, to make suggestions concerning improvement, and to help the patient

connect his memories into a meaningful sequence that will give him a
real insight for the causes of his condition. As Glueck (1946) has emphasized, narcosynthesis calls for the same skill as any other form of
intensive psychotherapy, and under no conditions is the method to be
thought of as a simple and easy chemical route to psychotherapy.

SYSTEMIC AND "BODY-BUILDING" THERAPIES

The patient whose behavior is disordered usually shows his mal-
adaptations at the cellular and physiological levels as well as at the
social level. Sedation may be used to aid in the elimination of fatigue
and in preventing further exhaustion. In addition, it is necessary, in a
well-rounded therapeutic program, to give attention to the physiological
depletions. Aside from suitable diets, whose importance should not be
overlooked, other chemical techniques may play a part. In these days of
multiple vitamin preparations whose excellence and necessity form a
background to much of our radio entertainment, we need not spend
much time in describing their nature or the part they play in health
and disease. A fact that emerges from the study of all people who are
prevented from eating freely and abundantly shows that vitamin deficiencies frequently accompany the general lowering of nutritional adequacy. Alcoholism furnishes a good example. The person who has
entered on a long spree does not have the time, the inclination, or,
usually, the unencumbered finances, to eat a well-rounded diet. Two
or three weeks of subsisting on whiskey and on an occasional ham-
burger or hot dog may seriously deplete the bodily vitamin supply.
When the patient is admitted to a hospital, vitamin therapy should
accompany dietary changes, sedation, and attention to his psychological
problems. The vitamin B complex is particularly important because of
the relationship between lack of this vitamin and neurological disorders
such as neuritis and pellagra.

Emotional preoccupation interferes with appetite, as anyone who has
tried to eat while stricken with grief or while very angry can testify.
This presents a challenge to the hospital dietician and to the physician.
Attractive meals, variety in foods, and high nutritional value are important. To increase appetite many measures are available. Occupational
therapy, with regulated exercise, helps, as does a variety of "tonics" that
fill an appropriate section of the materia medica. Small dosages of
insulin have been found helpful in this respect, combining a mildly
sedative action with an increase in appetite. (Spies, *et al.*, 1938.)

The purpose of catering to the ailing physiological organism is to put it in better shape for the task of re-education that is psychotherapy. The "healthy mind in the healthy body" motto that adorns college gymnasiums the country over, is a sound psychiatric commandment, and, as the psychologist can verify, learning is influenced to greater or lesser degree by any condition of the learning organism. There is enough of a somatic basis for the organic complaints of the neurotic or psychotic patient to warrant serious attention to this principle. A number of years ago, S. Wier Mitchell, the fiction-writing American psychiatrist, achieved not a little success through a treatment that consisted almost entirely of putting the patient to bed in a comfortable room, feeding him the best foods, permitting him light amusement and otherwise letting him alone. While such a plan is not enough, it has some of the basic ingredients of good therapy.

THE SHOCK THERAPIES

Throughout the centuries that psychotic people have been observed, there have occurred remissions or improvements in the patient's condition as a result of exposure to severe stress of one kind or another. As Ward said in preface to her personal account of a schizophrenic episode, "Long ago they lowered insane persons into snake pits; they thought that an experience which might drive a sane person out of his wits might send an insane person back into sanity" (1946). A few of the physiological stresses on the schizophrenic that have been accompanied by improvement in their behavior are appendicitis (Ernst, 1918), injection of isotonic salt solution (L. V. Guthrie, 1918; W. C. Miller, 1919), treatment for thyroid condition (Hoskins and Sleeper, 1929), dysentery (K. Menninger and Kubitschilk, 1930), reaction to nonspecific proteins (Raphael and Gregg, 1921), and influenza (K. Menninger, 1925). The last, it should be noted, is balanced by another investigator's report of schizophrenia reactions *following* influenza (Kanman, 1930).

Modern shock therapies have been empirical in nature, and there is no acceptable theoretical explanation to account for their effect. In 1931 Solomon, Kaufman, and D'Elseaux noted that catatonic patients forced to inhale mixtures of oxygen and carbon dioxide (from 30 to 40 per cent CO_2) often emerged from their stupors, in contact, talked in a sensible manner, and, in general, seemed greatly improved. After a short time, as the effects of the treatment diminish, the patient gradually slips back into his inaccessible negativism. The use of this method is limited by the short-lived nature of its effect.

In 1935, a Viennese psychiatrist, Sakel (1935), announced a new treatment for schizophrenia that involved the production of a hypoglycemic shock in the patient, induced by large dosages of *insulin*. Insulin is an endocrine preparation, derived from the secretions of the islets of Langerhans in the pancreas, which is necessary for adequate sugar metabolism. In diabetes, insulin is used to supplement an inadequate natural production of the substance by the pancreas. If the dosage of insulin is greater than necessary for the amount of sugar to be metabolized, the patient develops "insulin shock," whose symptoms are loss of consciousness, often with convulsions. If the patient is given sugar, he recovers promptly from the shock. In the treatment of psychotics, the patient is given insulin intramuscularly to the point of inducing unconsciousness, a symptom that appears within one to four hours after the injection. After a variable period of time in the coma, from fifteen to forty-five minutes usually, sugar is administered, and the patient revived. Treatments are given usually on succeeding days until at least 15 have been experienced. The number of insulin shocks given will depend upon the improvement shown by the patient, as many as 50 or 60 separate shocks sometimes being administered. Sakel reported a recovery rate of 88 per cent of the patients treated. Glueck (1946) reports that the present statistics show that immediate improvement is to be expected in about 55 per cent of all patients treated and notes that Sakel's higher figures reflect the fact that his patients were treated in the first six months of their illness. If treatment is instituted during the first year of illness, from 60 per cent to 75 per cent remission rates are reported. The spontaneous remission rate in schizophrenia is between 15 per cent and 25 per cent. Follow-up studies of patients treated with insulin show that from 31 per cent to 41 per cent of the group originally treated maintain their recovery at the end of six years.

Contemporaneously with Sakel's development of insulin shock came a report by Meduna (1935) of successful treatment of psychotics by the use of drugs whose action on the nervous system was of such a nature as to produce convulsive seizures. Using first camphor, and then *metrazol,* a camphor derivative, Meduna and others have demonstrated improvement in the behavior of schizophrenics following a series of drug-induced convulsions. Within a minute or so of the time the drug is injected, the patient has a typical grand mal seizure, with tonic and clonic movements, followed by a period of relaxed unconsciousness. Not more than one convulsion is indicated in any one day, and the spacing of seizures is variable, depending on such factors as the patient's physical condition and the rapidity of improvement in behavior.

Metrazol shock is something of an ordeal. The convulsions introduce such strenuous muscular activity that at best the patient complains of muscular soreness and at worst he may contract muscles so vigorously that broken bones result. Not a few patients have been killed or seriously injured with vertebral fractures. In order to minimize this factor somewhat, the metrazol has been combined with small amounts of curare, a paralyzing agent, and the violence of the convulsion is abated with no apparent difference in the efficacy of the treatment. Another disadvantage of metrazol is the intense fear-response patients have reported in connection with the treatments. The period of time between injection and seizure is extremely unpleasant, with an emotional tone of dread and apprehension. Many patients become emotionally upset if they are forced to continue receiving shocks of this kind.

As compared to insulin, metrazol is not as satisfactory with schizophrenics (Pollock, 1939), although fewer metrazol seizures are required for depressed patients (Jessner and Ryan, 1941). As with insulin, there is no satisfactory rational explanation of the mechanism of the recovery. The convulsion itself does not seem to be necessary, since the results are no different when curare eliminates or reduces the seizures.

Because of the disadvantages to metrazol shock that have been noted, a different method of inducing seizures has all but replaced metrazol as a convulsive agent. This technique is electroshock. If electrodes are placed on either side of the head, and a brief duration of electric current is allowed to flow through the head between the electrodes, a grand mal seizure will result. The care of the patient before and after the convulsion is the same as in metrazol therapy. Electroshock treatments have the advantages of generally producing less protracted convulsions and having, accordingly, fewer injuries, and of giving the patient a much less unpleasant emotional experience.

The results of electroshock therapy, like metrazol, are better with the affective disorders. With the schizophrenics electroshock shows better results than metrazol but poorer than insulin (Malzberg, 1943, 1946).

Kris (1946) reports that catatonics are the best treatment risks among the schizophrenics, with hebephrenics and paranoids being decidedly inferior.

SURGICAL THERAPIES

Among the earliest human remnants discovered by the archeologist are human skulls with neat round trephine openings in them, suggesting that the primitive medicine man may well have occasionally decided on a direct attack at what he possibly regarded as the seat of the behavioral or physical disturbances. Some have speculated that the operation was performed for relief of "infantile convulsions, cerebral tension, cranial injuries, headaches, epilepsy, and blindness" (Robinson, 1931). In recent years we have returned somewhat to the prehistoric technique and have devised methods for treating psychiatric patients through surgical procedures.

We have already mentioned the attempt made by Cotton (1921) to treat psychotic patients by a systematic campaign against sources of focal infection in their bodies. Teeth were pulled, appendices removed, gall bladders taken out, and so forth. Cotton reported distinct improvement in remission rate following these routine surgical procedures. His results were not confirmed by subsequent investigators (see Kopeloff and Kirby, 1923) and, although it is freely admitted that surgery should not be denied the mental patient, the removal of focal infections is not looked upon as a major vector in securing remission of their behavioral ailments.

More drastic as a surgical therapy is the comparatively recent technique of *pre-frontal lobotomy,* first used by Moniz, a Portuguese neurosurgeon, in which the skull is entered by small trephine holes and a scalpel is inserted to make an arc-like cut that separates tracts of the frontal lobe from the rest of the brain. A variant procedure is to produce a similar lesion, but to enter the brain through the orbit of the eye. This method is termed *transorbital lobotomy.* Partial ablation of the cerebral cortex of the frontal lobe has also been done (Mettler, 1949). These treatments are used primarily on psychotics who have not responded to less severe therapies, although operations have been performed on severely anxious neurotics. Depressions of the senile, involutional, and cyclothymic types have shown the best results, schizophrenics somewhat poorer results, and alcoholics no benefit. Following the operation the patient usually shows very little impairment of intellectual functions. The personality, however, shows many of the changes we have associated with the brain-injured patients in Chapter X. They are more impulsive, have poor control of emotional expression, show a lack of inhibition of socially unacceptable behavior, and are less able to carry on sustained activities. On the positive side, they no longer seem capable of sustaining the persistent emotional tone characteristic of depression or acute anxiety. Their sadness becomes more situationally oriented and is usually gone even sooner after a disappointment than is the case with a normal person.

The decision to employ this type of treatment is a grave one to make; the interference with brain function is irreversible. Should the possibility of remission through other means remain, lobotomy should not be undertaken. Although the surgical danger is relatively slight, the personality changes appear desirable only in relation to the symptoms the patient is manifesting before operation. *Psychosurgery does not solve the essential problems that face the organism, but merely creates a defective organism whose problems are not really less serious.* Psychosurgery is too often an admission of failure in therapeutics; in such cases the production of brain defect is only a means of lessening the management and custodial problems of society.

FEVER THERAPY

One of the authentic revolutionists in therapeutics was Julius Wagner-Jauregg (1857-1940). He had observed that some psychotics appeared to improve after their recovery from diseases accompanied by a high fever, and he boldly proposed giving psychotic patients febrile diseases. After trying tuberculin and typhoid vaccine, he turned to malaria. By 1922 he had treated two hundred cases of paresis, a disease in which the mortality had been a sure 100 per cent, and had found that fifty of the cases had recovered to such an extent that they could leave the hospital and resume work. In 1927 Wagner-Jauregg received the Nobel Prize in Medicine for his achievement. Fever therapy is one of the best methods for treating all types of cerebro-spinal syphilis, and the recovery rate is about 30 per cent complete remissions at the end of two years, with an additional 25 per cent to 30 per cent showing a partial remission and a lack of progression of their symptoms. Malaria is still widely used, but in recent years two other devices have been employed to raise the patient's temperature to the desired level. The first of these, the Kettering hyperthem, is an air-conditioned cabinet in which radiant heat acts in a high humidity to produce the temperature elevation. The other is a high frequency electrical current, within the field of which the patient is placed. The current induces the desired rise in temperature. Except in persons who have definite pathology in some vital organ system, the fever therapy seems to have no deleterious effects on behavior or on general physical condition. It is unfortunate that fever therapy is of benefit only in neurosyphilis. A recent development in the treatment of neurosyphilis has been the use of massive dosages of the antibiotic penicillin (Moore, 1946). This technique appears to be as successful as the fever therapies (see Dattner, 1948).

Psychotherapy and Re-education

With all the treatments we have just reviewed, there has been a limit to their usefulness. Acting through various types of disturbance of organismic functions, they have constituted forces in the patient's environment and, in many instances, have had beneficial effects. But all psychiatric writers have emphasized that these therapies are most effective when they are accompanied by a re-educative process directed at giving the patient (*a*) an insight for the nature of his problems and (*b*) new and effective techniques for handling them. Even in paresis, that most "organic" of the psychopathological conditions, the fact that a patient manifested delusions of grandeur, for example, shows that the nervous system defect was matched by feelings of behavioral inadequacy. Psychotherapy would be necessary for such a person irrespective of whether the inadequacy of personality existed before the syphilitic infection or was a by-product of the infection. In either case, the person stands in need of ways of adjusting to the demands of society and his own ego after the fever therapy has given him respite from the infectious attack on his nervous system.

It is beyond the scope of this chapter to attempt a review of all the various forms of psychotherapy that are practiced at the present time. As one goes through a listing of them, the thought occurs that they differ only slightly in technique and very little at all in purpose or basic methodology. As we have said, *all* psychotherapy is an artificially contrived learning situation of one kind or another. In most of the milder psychoneurotic conditions psychotherapy may be used with only minimal assistance from other techniques; in the psychoses a combination of methods gives the best results.

DIRECTIVE INTERVIEWING

Techniques for aiding the person in understanding his own difficulties depend on the therapist and the patient jointly producing enough information about the circumstances of the patient's life experiences to piece together a developmental history of his personality development and an idea of the dynamics of his illness. This may be done in a number of ways. The simplest is the *directive interview,* in which the therapist asks questions about the patient's past, and in which the therapist guides the interview in a logical or chronological manner. The ordinary medical or social history is often taken in this fashion. Starting with "Name?" "Age?" "Year of birth?" and proceeding through questions about parents and relatives, circumstances of the patient's early life, schooling, diseases and accidents, love life and marriage, to an account of the patient's present situation, the therapist seeks to build up a dossier that will give him an understanding of the personality of the patient and the forces that have influenced his life and illness.

The therapeutic benefits from such procedures are slight. The patient may feel some relief from unburdening himself, and the therapist may derive a substantial amount of information. More often, the patient experiences a negative emotional reaction to a procedure of this kind. He is forced to face problems at a rate that may be faster than he can assimilate the emotional implications of the information he gives. The steady interrogation, covering every aspect of the person's life in a short time, provides so many redintegrating stimuli as to often cause an actual increase in the patient's symptoms. Another objection to this overly directive approach is that the information secured is *selected by the therapist,* and the patient is not given a chance to tell his story in a way that would emphasize those points that the patient feels to be important. When the therapist guides the interview, he loses the opportunity to observe the differential emotional reactions of the patient to events out of his past. Finally, having secured the information, the therapist is quite likely to find that the patient's insight is no better than when the interview started, since the patient has only passively responded to questions and has not been given the optimal conditions for making spontaneous and emotionally convincing connections between the various parts of the story. The objective chronological progression of anyone's life does not correspond to the way it is seen in retrospect by the experiencing person. If the reader looks back on his own life, he will see that any attempt to give another person a concept of that life necessitates following first one train of events, then another, with constant pauses for "flash-backs" and for developing the interrelations between one aspect and another. These personal patterns of life-history are disrupted in the directive interview and close the door on many otherwise useful sources of information and chances to gain understanding of the meaning of the history for the present difficulties.

NONDIRECTIVE APPROACHES TO THERAPY

Most therapeutic interviews are, accordingly, conducted on a *nondirective* basis, in which the therapist is more content to let the patient tell his story in his own way, exercising only such guidance as seems necessary to clear up a vague point, to bring out or emphasize a significant relationship, or to round out information on some topic. This method has as advantages the reverse of the criticisms of the directive approach. The patient develops relationships of past experiences in a way that already has some meaning for him, and which, as the interviews progress, develop new meanings. We all know how "talking things over" tends to clarify and reveal new aspects of problems that trouble us. This reorganization of experiences is vital to successful psychotherapy. Too, if the patient is determining the direction of the interview, the therapist is protected against subjectively introducing his own preconceived notions into selection of the patient's biographical material. The patient, in a nondirective approach, may produce material as slowly or rapidly as he pleases. As long as he sets the pace, there is some assurance that traumatic memories will not be produced until the patient is prepared to face them. Lastly, in this approach, the patient gains more of a feeling that he is working out his own problems and is not passively placing his dependence on an all-wise and all-powerful therapist.

FREE ASSOCIATION

As an example of nondirective therapy, let us take the conventional psychoanalytic treatment technique of *free association*. Freud, it will be remembered, first used hypnosis to recover memories of his patients, but recognized that such a technique contained many of the dangers we have seen as characteristic of a directive interview. In addition, since the patient's recollection of the information given during the trance was somewhat hazy, the development of insight was slower, and emphasis was necessarily placed on a directive therapeutic recourse to hypnotic suggestions. Freud's dissatisfaction with hypnosis led him to develop a new technique, in which the patient took over almost completely the determination of what information would be given to the therapist. In free association, the patient is instructed to talk about whatever comes into his mind, relaxing and allowing nothing that occurs to him to go unsaid, no matter how trivial, illogical, painful, obscene, or embarrassing the thoughts might be. In this way the therapist slowly, over a period sometimes of months or years, gains a knowledge of the patient, and the patient a knowledge of himself, which could not be secured in any other way. In free association, the patient expresses his dreams, his fantasies, his wishes, and his emotional reactions as well as the "facts" of his life. Freud felt that the use of this method ultimately resulted in the patient bringing into consciousness material that was of etiological significance but that had been repressed and was unavailable except by this technique. In the course of the free association sessions, the patient "lives through" the repressed but conflictual material, faces its emotional implications, and is able to view it in its connections with his contemporary real-life situation. The "fear of the unknown" becomes a "concern over the known." Most sources of anxiety go back to such early stages of the person's history that he is able to recognize the infantile nature of them when he becomes aware of what they are and the relation they have to his symptoms.

Illustrating how complex therapy is for a patient is the relationship that grows between the patient and the therapist. As the patient shares his life experiences and his intimate thoughts with the therapist, it has been observed that he gradually comes to act toward the therapist in much the same way he had acted toward the various significant people in his past. The patient relives his neurotic conflicts in this relationship. The phenomenon was described by Freud as *transference,* and he recognized it as an important factor in therapy. The patient shifts to the therapist the affectionate and hostile attitudes that he had developed in the past toward other people; the therapist, by suitable manipulations of this "transference neurosis," is able to bring these submerged attitudinal difficulties into the open. The therapist is then able to help the patient deal with them on a conscious, controllable level.

CLIENT-CENTERED THERAPY

Another type of nondirective approach to therapy has been developed by Carl Rogers (1942, 1951). Although bearing certain similarities to the psychoanalytic technique, Rogers' *client-centered therapy* goes to even greater extremes to assure noninterference with the patient. Rogers assumes that most people with psychological problems are able to develop their own solutions if the problems are discussed in the proper setting, and that a deep exploration of their early past is not necessary for these patients. Rogers agrees with the analysts in affirming that the emotional aspects of adjustment are the most important material for therapy. He further feels that all people possess a basic motivation toward optimal adjustment, and that they will seek out treatment and remain in the therapeutic situation as long as their need remains unsatisfied.

One of Rogers' most important contributions to psychopathology has been his careful analysis of the therapist's function. By means of recordings of therapy sessions, study of detailed protocols of the interchange between patient and therapist showed the extent to which each contributed to the interview. Rogers, in line with his assumptions about adjustment, attempted to make the therapist's function as nondirective as possible. He felt that the therapist should not ask questions, give advice, criticize, offer interpretations or attempt to reassure the patient. The role of the therapist should be a simple recognition of the emotional attitudes and expressions of the patient and an acceptance of the patient as a person. The therapist's contributions to the interview, then, consist primarily of restatements of information or attitudes expressed by the patient, and an attempt to show the patient that his expressions are being accepted. The following is an excerpt from a nondirective interview:

SUBJECT: Everything gets to going so badly that finally you end up by not going to class. You get sort of nonchalant. But you know damn well that you wanta get the work. You're lying to yourself.

COUNSELOR: You want to use some kind of defense when things are going so badly.

SUBJECT: Yes. It didn't happen so much this summer.

COUNSELOR: That kind of defeating situation makes you feel the best thing to do is just to give up and admit defeat.

SUBJECT: I want to give up, but there are too many other factors—too many people depending on me. It makes the idea of being alone in the world attractive.

COUNSELOR: You feel you have other people expecting a good bit of you, and it's a disturbing sensation.

SUBJECT: Right.[1]

In these interviews the entire responsibility for problem-solution is directly placed on the patient. As therapy proceeds, usually by a series of hour-long interviews in which the patient talks as freely and in whatever direction he may choose, alternate solutions of problems occur, and may be explored verbally. The decisions as to which of several alternate ways of acting should be taken are left strictly to the patient.

Rogers' nondirective therapy has proved to be of most value with college students and with the solution of marital and other adjustmental difficulties among people whose problems are not on a deeply neurotic or psychotic basis. The method is most applicable to people who are of at least average intelligence, who have some motivation toward managing their own affairs, who verbalize with some facility and who are willing to enter upon and maintain a therapeutic relationship with minimal assurance from the therapist. As a research technique, it has proven of value in contributing understanding of all therapy relationships.

HYPNOSIS AND CONDITIONING

Many other forms of psychotherapy are used. Hypnosis has been applied in many ways to treatment of behavior disorders, either as direct suggestive interference with symptoms or in combination with other techniques, as in *hypnoanalysis,* where it is blended with the psychoanalytic techniques in a way that has proven effective in some types of cases that would not have been suitable for other types of therapy (Lindner, 1946). The laboratory method of conditioning has been applied to a number of therapeutic problems. Alcoholics have been treated by pairing alcoholic beverages with chemical substances producing nausea and vomiting (Voegtlin, 1940). The object was to establish a conditioned response of distaste to the odor, sight, and taste of alcoholic beverages. Voegtlin reported an average of 64 per cent cures. Thimann

[1] William U. Snyder (1948), "Client-centered therapy," in L. A. Pennington and Irwin A. Berg, eds., *An Introduction to Clinical Psychology,* p. 466. Copyright 1948, The Ronald Press Company.

(1946) secured similar results, about 50 per cent of his treatments resulting in abstinence for the two- to four-year period of his follow-up
study. He emphasized a need for psychotherapy of other kinds as an
accompaniment of the conditioning procedure.

THE SEMANTIC APPROACH

Growing out of *general semantics,* which we reviewed in Chapter
XV, is a method of re-education that aims to achieve in the patient a
more intelligent use of language, avoiding the confusion and emotional
disturbances that people are subject to when they labor under misap-
prehensions about language structure and meaning. Korzybski (1941)
has laid down the following which semantic re-education seeks to
establish in its reorientation of the patient: (1) The word is not the
object it symbolizes, and therefore reactions to words should not be
made on the same basis as to the object. (2) Word symbols are not universal or all-inclusive in their meaning, since the word is merely a
symbolic representation of the object. (3) Words should be related to
specific instances and moments in time, since everything is constantly
changing, and word-symbols may give an appearance of permanence to
traits or objects which is misleading. (4) Because of this specificity of
meaning in word-object relationships, words should be indexed to avoid
the appearance of generality, as in restricting the meaning of a phrase
to the specific situation to which it applies. Education in general semantics is a useful therapy when combined with other approaches; it is
more useful as a prophylactic device, aiding in logical and realistic
thinking, and helping the individual avoid many of the traps of conflict engendered or carried by verbal symbols.

GROUP THERAPY

Since human beings live in groups and since many of their troubles
grow out of features of their group life, it is inevitable that some attempt should be made to administer psychotherapy to groups of patients.
In the last chapter we referred to Trigant Burrow and his belief that
neurosis had its inception in the person's inability to behave toward
other people in a biologically and emotionally satisfactory manner.
Burrow accordingly used the group as his therapeutic unit and attempted to re-educate his patients in techniques of group emotional
interchange. Many other workers have independently worked out ways
of carrying on psychotherapy in both small and large groups of patients.

During World War II, when large numbers of emotionally disturbed patients exceeded the facilities for individual treatment, group methods were adopted with fair amounts of success.

In group therapy the patients gather in an atmosphere of freedom from constraint and are encouraged to talk about their problems. The group therapist plays a role similar to the nondirective therapist, guiding the conversation on occasion, clarifying or summarizing issues, drawing out the more silent members of the group, sometimes raising important issues for discussion, but in general leaving the flow of interpersonal contacts to the patients. As a patient describes his symptoms, other patients add details of their own cases, suggest the purposes served by the symptoms, criticize each other's attitudes, and so forth. Hostilities that arise are settled within the group and by the group. In the course of several of these sessions, which usually last about an hour, each patient is able to observe how his illness is viewed by others and is able to consider other patients' illnesses in an increasingly objective manner. The method has an advantage over individual therapy in that the patient is modifying his behavior in a social situation resembling the life environment in which he must make his complete adjustment. The therapy group is society in microcosmos; the acceptance of his own and other people's difficulties gives him tolerance and a new freedom from the anxieties of social insecurity. He learns that his problems are not unique, and he finds that his own abilities and resources are as good as those of most of his fellows. These dynamics are described by Slavson (1947) as follows:

Generally, Activity Group Therapy provides spontaneous discharge of drives, diminution of tension and reduction of anxiety through physical and emotional activity in a group setting that permits unimpeded acting out within the boundaries of personal safety, and through free interaction with fellow-members that lead to a variety of relationships. Interpersonal and social situations constantly arise through which each discharges tensions, expresses emotions, discovers limitations, builds ego strength, finds some status for himself, develops relationships and a limited degree of derivative insight. The total situation is designed to supply substitute gratifications, give vent to aggression, reinforce the ego, particularly in regard to feelings of failure and inadequacy, counteract deflated self-evaluation, release blockings to expression in some, and build self-restraint in others.[2]

[2] R. Salvson, ed. (1947), *The Practice of Group Therapy*, pp. 33-34. New York: International Universities Press.

Although it is hard to evaluate the results of group therapy, in general it may be said that, when the groups are selected carefully, and when individual therapy is used as a supplement, this method is one of the most hopeful developments in the history of psychotherapy. In a civilization such as our own, where the abundance of psychiatric problems dwarf the efforts of the relatively few therapists, the extended benefits of psychotherapy given by group techniques are of great value. Since group methods are most applicable to young people and to those whose problems are still in a formative stage, group therapy also is a mental hygiene device that should be used even more than it is today. In primary and secondary education, the group techniques should be applied to emotional training as well as they are now applied to intellectual training.

Therapeutic Adjuncts

As the reader may have gathered in the introductory portion of this chapter, almost everything from the air a patient breathes to the clothes he wears may have an effect on his recovery. A few of these miscellaneous variables have been harnessed by the therapist and are turned to a controlled usage in promoting the welfare of patients.

BIBLIOTHERAPY

Bibliotherapy is a field in which relatively little research has been done. Considering the ocean of books in which the average child plunges when he first starts school, we do not know enough about the potentialities of controlled reading for either mental hygiene or therapy. Moore (1946) has used a graded list of children's books prepared by Kircher (1945), classified under headings relating to various aspects of young people's problems, as "honesty," "duty," and so forth. In working with children, he supplements his therapeutic interviews by recommending the reading of appropriate books. Other workers have utilized similar techniques, and there are a number of books on various problems of adjustment that are written specifically for people who are interested in finding nontechnical information about personality. Bibliotherapy may be used to impart general information and, of equal importance, particularly with young people, may be used to give material for identification and role-playing activity.

PSYCHODRAMA

Psychodrama is a technique, developed by Moreno (1944), that is somewhat similar to group therapy. The patients, assisted sometimes by the therapeutic staff, enact dramatic scenes of their own spontaneous devising, and thereby are able to portray their problems and their emotional reactions to others. As a means of allowing fantasy and "trial-and-error" to operate in the patient's search for knowledge and help, the technique is very useful. It has been applied more recently to instruction in many types of life situations and gives promise of being an effective instrument in mental hygiene.

FINGER-PAINTING

Finger-painting is a technique for exploring personality and, in conjunction with psychotherapy, is a valuable means of allowing outlet for fantasy and for gauging the progress of the patient's condition. Finger-painting was devised by Shaw (1934) and makes use of bright-colored pigments dissolved in a medium that may be freely daubed and stroked on paper. Mosse (1940) has shown how it may be applied in the treatment of adult neurotics. Finger-painting is only one form of the use of artistic expression as an aid in therapy, and most occupational therapists utilize any interest the patient may develop in the graphic arts. One of the best of such techniques is reported by Harms (1941), who had children draw lines portraying emotions, feelings, and their own preoccupations. Their productions proved extremely informative and a real help in psychotherapy.

MUSIC THERAPY

Music therapy provides a way of stimulating associations and revery and of promoting relaxation. We have already alluded to the potency of the words and music of popular songs in stirring up old memories and old emotions. Altshuler (1939, 1941) gives the following therapeutic values of music: (1) the capacity to produce physiological changes in metabolism, blood pressure, etc.; (2) the ability to influence the span of attention; (3) the power of diverting patients and substituting healthy for morbid preoccupations; (4) the ability to change the mood of patients; (5) the capacity to stimulate patients intellectually and emotionally. Similar use of music is reported by Harrington (1939).

OCCUPATIONAL THERAPY

Occupational therapy may be defined broadly as all the activities that patients may be given in an attempt to keep them occupied and to distract them from their emotional preoccupations. All well-run institutions for the treatment of behavior disorders maintain occupational therapy facilities in which patients may engage in such activities as basket and rug making, leather-work, wood-work, painting, sculping, stamp-collecting, and so forth. As Muncie (1939) says, work gives the sense of time passing at a normal pace rather than dragging interminably, and it also gives the patient a feeling of accomplishment by stimulating those assets that the patient still retains. Occupational therapy should be done in group situations as far as possible. Group projects are especially useful, since they enable patients to cooperate on relatively long-term mutual goals and encourage friendly interpersonal relationships.

The Mental Hygiene Movement

That an ounce of prevention is a good investment is nowhere any truer than in the personality disorders. Long years of maladaptive habits and the accumulation of daily traumatic experiences are necessary to produce a full-blown disturbance. In most cases therapy is almost equally protracted, entailing even further waste of time and human effort. Since sound habit systems and effective ways of dealing with problems are as easy to develop as are the bad ways, mental hygiene should not only be practiced from economic foresightedness but also because of the desirable positive effects of healthy adjustment. Yet, when Clifford Beers was released from the mental institution in which he had been hospitalized for an affective disorder, he found that practically no interest existed in preventive aspects of psychiatry and that facilities for mental hygiene were unheard of. Beers threw himself into stimulating mental hygiene work and was instrumental in founding the National Committee for Mental Hygiene in 1909. The mental hygiene movement spread over the world, and in 1930 there was held the first International Congress of Mental Hygiene, a meeting whose successors have become focal gatherings for the presentation of information on prophylaxis and psychopathology. At least part of the credit for the present inclusion of courses in mental hygiene in college curricula is due to Beers and the work that he started. The creation of out-patient clinics and the increasing number of psychiatrists and clinical psychologists whose services are devoted to schools, industrial establishments, municipal courts, and penal institutions are important factors in preventing mental illness, and again, they owe much to the emphasis started by Beers.

Although these facilities are excellent, they are still primarily efforts to catch patients at earlier stages of their illness, and the preventive aspects of their function are purely relative. *Preventive* mental hygiene, of a type comparable to other aspects of preventive medicine, where the causative factors in a disease condition are sought out and eliminated, still can hardly be said to exist. The federal government has recognized the need, and has passed a Mental Health Act, establishing an Institute, under the direction of the Public Health Service. From what we have seen in this text of the deep involvement of etiological factors in the social structure, we can predict that measures designed to eliminate these roots will be highly unpopular. The Public Health Service is accustomed to resistance in its efforts to protect the well-being of the American people, and it has had to fight hard for stream sanitation to control typhoid fever and for vaccination to control smallpox. Compulsory blood tests have been fought as an unwarranted interference with freedom of the individual. But these protests would be as nothing when compared to the resistance that would develop if the Public Health Service actually set out to eliminate some of the conditions in our social environment that contribute significantly to mental illness. Imagine the protests that would occur if a concerted attack were made on those irrational aspects of our culture that have been shown by verified observation to breed conflict and maladjustment. Think of the pressure that would be placed on our national legislators if the Public Health Service proposed an exclusively rational approach to problems of politics and religion. Vogt (1948) pointed out in cold statistics the impossible state of ecological disharmony that exists in our country, and his principal plea is for a rational consideration of his facts. Yet the measures he proposes are such as have been opposed by a wide variety of "special interests" in our country. Until we can begin to apply the basic lesson of mental hygiene, that adjustmental efforts must be based on an orientation to reality, then all "mental hygiene" will be more palliative than preventive. If it is true, as we believe, that many of the most significant factors in the development of disordered behavior are woven inextricably into our social pattern, the task of mental hygiene is indeed difficult.

There is an urgency today about problems of mental hygiene. Each year the control that man exerts over destructive forces becomes greater and yet he changes little in his basic mental health. The very fact that the technical achievement of nuclear fission was heralded to the world by news that one hundred thousand people had been killed by a single bomb speaks of a culture lacking in sanity. As the average American pondered that news, he was forced into the behavior mechanism of rationalization if he was to maintain his morale and his faith in his country. But there is no need to repeat what we have tried to say throughout this text. It should be obvious that correction of pathological behavior requires sweeping changes in those factors of the personal history of the patient that can be shown to play a part in the genesis of such behavior. The presence of possible hereditary and constitutional factors makes these changes even more vitally needed. Factors of genetically lowered resistance in an individual limit the amount of environmentally produced conflict he will be able to tolerate.

Conservative measures in mental hygiene must be directed toward strengthening the person's resistance to stresses that are inevitable in the environment that forms his habitat. Tolerance of frustration, as has been shown experimentally, can be influenced by factors of training, and many people may avoid catastrophic behavior if they have available techniques for meeting the emotional problems to which they are exposed. Here, within the present cultural setting, is an opportunity for the mental hygienist to see that parents and children receive training in these minimal techniques. Next best to eliminating sources of conflict and frustration is facilitating insight for the nature of the threats that surround us. If we cannot have the myth of "the rational man" made reality, at least we can hope that people know it is a myth. As our good friend Dr. Lynde Steckle has said, man's troubles come somewhat from mistaking his *emotional* conviction that he is acting reasonably for reasonable action.

DISCUSSION QUESTIONS

1. If you were a patient in psychotherapy would you prefer to be treated by a rational or empirical therapy?

2. Why is psychotherapy considered a learning process?

3. How important in psychotherapy is the personality structure of the therapist?

4. What are some of the goals toward which therapy should direct the patient?

5. Should psychotherapy be aimed at making the patients more like the average person or should the aim be to help the individual patient to fully realize his talents and potentialities even when the latter might make him more of a social deviate?

6. If it is the psychotherapist who decides when the patient has recovered, what sort of influences would you expect him to exert on the patient?

7. What are the main therapeutic functions of chemical, physical, and surgical treatment?

8. Does it appear rationally probable that we will ever find a simple chemical treatment, a "pill," that will cure behavior disorders?

9. If you were a neurosurgeon, what sort of questions would you want answered about a patient before you recommended a frontal lobotomy?

10. How important to society is the Mental Hygiene Movement?

SUGGESTED READINGS

F. Alexander and T. French, *et al.* (1946), *Psychoanalytic Therapy*. New York: The Ronald Press Company.

D. Brower and L. E. Abt, eds. (1952), *Progress in Clinical Psychology*. New York: Grume & Stratton.

O. H. Mowrer, ed. (1953), *Psychotherapy, Theory and Research*. New York: The Ronald Press Company.

C. Rogers (1951), *Client-Centered Therapy*. Boston: Houghton Mifflin Company.

C. Rogers and Rosalind F. Dymond, eds. (1954), *Psychotherapy and Personality Change*. Chicago: University of Chicago Press.

F. C. Thorne (1950), *Principles of Personality Counseling*. Brandon, Vt.: Journal of Clinical Psychology.

BIBLIOGRAPHIC SOURCES

For the difference between the attitudes of the tissue pathologist and the behavior pathologist in his textbooks, examine any of the standard works on tissue pathology. For a more extended discussion of treatment from the psychological point of view, the student may consult any of a number of texts from the area of clinical psychology: Pennington and Berg (1948,

1954), Richards (1946), Shaffer and Lazarus (1952), Thorpe and Katz (1948), and Watson (1949, 1951). An additional source is the two-volume set edited by Brower and Abt (1952) on *Progress in Clinical Psychology*. There is perhaps no single source more appropriate to a broad introduction to what clinical psychologists do than Brower and Abt.

The uses and misuses of sedation are discussed in Muncie (1948) and Strecker, Ebaugh, and Ewalt (1951). An example of the use of Nembutal is Bellak (1949). Amytal is discussed in Lipton (1950). On the variations in narcosis techniques, see Gillespie (1939), Glueck (1946), and Hastings, Wright, and Glueck (1944b).

An extended report on insulin shock therapy may be found in Sikes (1952). Bustamante (1951) reports that small doses of insulin combined with psychotherapy may be successful. Interest in carbon dioxide therapy has recently been revived following the publication of Meduna's (1950) *Carbon Dioxide Therapy*. Later experiments record positive results in the treatment of psychoneurosis (Jackman and Scharr, 1952; Milligan, 1951; Moriarity, combined with psychotherapy, 1952) and in schizophrenia (Lorenz, 1952). There seems to be little lasting benefit in the psychoses, but, as Lorenz points out, it at least appears to allow some communication with patients where none had been possible. The long-range efficacy in psychoneuroses seems still unknown; some partial information may be found in Silver (1953). For a sensibly critical review of this approach, see Freeman (1952). On electro-shock therapy, Osborne and Holmquist (1944) and Pacella (1949) give presentations of the various techniques. One immediate question that arises concerning the shock therapies in general is their effect on brain tissue. For an introduction to this type of investigation, see Himwich (1952). That there is little agreement on mechanisms involved in the shock therapies is splendidly illustrated by the paper of Gordon (1948) that lists 50 postulated theoretical conceptions, 23 of them psychological and the rest somatic. Another somewhat ignored problem is the fact that there is little solid experimental evidence that the shock therapies are indeed as successful in treatment as they are said to be. Much of the experimental literature on shock therapies may be found in the *Journal of Clinical and Experimental Psychopathology*.

Current interest in psychosurgery dates to Freeman and Watts' (1942) *Psychosurgery*, although attempts at this technique have been made for at least two thousand years (Ramsey, 1952). There have been many recent large-scale, cross-disciplinary studies such as those of Mettler (1949, 1952) and Greenblatt, Arnot, and Solomon (1950). These studies have already yielded a prodigious amount of intriguing neurophysiological information, but, as treatment, psychosurgery is somewhat less documented. For psychological changes from psychosurgery, Landis (1951) and Wittenborn and Mettler (1951) are suggested. One of the best introductions to the entire field is the small and sympathetic book by the great physiologist John F. Fulton (1951), *Frontal Lobotomy and Affective Behavior*. Despite all this activity, the statement by Birch (1952, p. 493) seems quite justified: ". . . the status of psychosurgery is epitomized by the fact that no adequate physiological or psychological rationale has been advanced to justify its practice."

The problem of therapy with children was not specifically mentioned in the text although interest has been extensive. For further information, Moustakas (1953), Slavson (1952), and Woltman (1952) are suggested.

Any student interested in psychotherapy should be familiar with at least these four journals: *Journal of Clinical Psychology, Journal of Consulting Psychology, American Journal of Psychotherapy,* and the *Journal of Abnormal and Social Psychology.* The most systematic—and outspoken— proponent of the directive interview has been Thorne whose views may be seen in a series of articles (Andrews, 1945; Thorne, 1945, *et seq.*) or in the text (Thorne, 1950), *Principles of Personality Counseling.* Two other writers stressing the directive approach are E. G. Williamson and J. G. Darley (see their reprinted articles in Brayfield, 1950; or Williamson's text, 1939). One of the best accounts of the goals and techniques of classical psychoanalytic therapy is again Freud's (1949) posthumous volume. *Psychoanalytic Therapy* by Alexander and French (1946) is probably the best source of information about trends in modern techniques in the psychoanalytic field. The principal sources for Rogerian methods are the book referred to in the text and *Client-Centered Therapy* (Rogers, 1951). Lindner (1944), Rosen (1953), and Watkins (1950) are examples of the use of hypnosis in treatment. On group therapy, two long bibliographic sources are available in Kotkov (1947, 1950). One of the best examples of group therapy in operation is Powdermaker, Frank, *et al.* (1953).

The case for bibliotherapy is presented by Gottschalk (1948), and a reference list has been prepared by the U.S. Veteran's Administration (1952). On the use of music in therapy, see Browne (1952) and Wenger (1952). Students interested in occupational therapy should be familiar with the *American Journal of Occupational Therapy.*

As we have mentioned before, the mental hygiene movement may be traced to Beers' (1908) *The Mind That Found Itself* and the tremendous effort that Beers put into the movement. There are many fine texts available. Any of the following may be useful: Bernard (1952), Carroll (1951), Crow and Crow (1951), and Wallin (1949).

Glossary

Glossary

Aberrant. Deviant.

Abnormal. See Chapter II.

Abreaction. A psychoanalytic concept signifying the release of suppressed emotion during therapy.

Abscess. A collection of dead white corpuscles generally due to bacterial infection.

Abstraction. As used here, refers to the process of describing an object in terms of a few essential qualities generally characteristic of the class of these objects.

Abulia. "Loss of will power." Marked difficulty in making decisions.

Acidosis. Hypoalkalinity of blood and tissues.

Acromegaly. Disorder characterized by overdevelopment of short bones of face, hands, and feet with enlargement of the skull. Due to overfunctioning of pituitary after onset of puberty.

Acrophobia. Excessive fear of high places.

Acute alcoholic hallucinosis. After heavy and prolonged drinking, individuals hear accusatory and threatening voices. These hallucinations seldom last long, but when present cause extreme anxiety.

Acute intoxication. Extreme intoxication to point of unconsciousness or lack of response to reality.

Acute mania. A psychotic state characterized by constant and exaggerated excitement but with little intellectual deficit or dissociation.

Acute retarded depression. A psychotic condition generally showing extreme sluggishness; activity only with great difficulty.

Adaptation. The physiological and psychological responses of the organism designed to achieve an optimum relationship with the environment.

Addison's disease. An emaciated condition due to hypofunction of suprarenal glands.

Adjunctive therapies. Supportive therapies designed to supplement therapy; for example, bibliotherapy, occupational therapy, etc.

Adjustment. As used here, synonymous with adaptation.

Adrenal glands. Paired endocrine glands resting above the kidneys.

Adrenalin. A stimulant extracted from and the secretion of the medulla of the adrenal gland.

Aelurophobia. Excessive fear of cats.

Affect. All the general types of phenomena commonly referred to as feelings and emotions.

Affective disorders. Psychotic disorders with major symptoms of emotional expression.

Affective exaggerations. Exaggerated emotional states.

Afferent nerves. Those which receive, encode, and transmit incoming stimulus signals.

Aggression. Overt hostility toward a potential or actual source of frustration.

Agitated depression. Psychotic syndrome characterized by deep emotional depression and heightened activity.

Agnosia. Inability to recognize objects.

Agoraphobia. Excessive fear of open places.

Agraphia. A form of aphasia characterized by an inability to write.

Agronomy. The study of soil management and crop production.

Aichmophobia. Excessive fear of sharp objects.

Alexia. A type of aphasia showing inability to read.

Algesia. Excessive pain sensitivity.

Algophobia. Excessive fear of pain.

Alienist. Psychiatrist (legal terminology).

Allergy. Physiological disease symptoms due, in part at least, to a heightened sensitivity to a variety of environmental objects.

Alpha rhythm. An eight to twelve cycles per second brain wave.

Alzheimer's disease. A progressive mental deterioration thought to be due to abnormal proliferation of threadlike cellular growths around the cortical neurons.

Amaurotic idiocy. A possibly inherited neurological disorder resulting in serious mental deficiency.

Ambivalence. Conflicting desires of approach and avoidance toward the same object or person.

Amblyopia. A deficit in vision without any apparent structural pathology.

Amentia. Synonymous with mental deficiency.

Amnesia. Loss of memory.

Anal eroticism. Psychoanalytic term describing desire to obtain gratification through anal stimulation. In psychoanalytic theory, it pertains to the anal stage of child sexual development.

Analgesia. Loss of pain sensitivity.

Analytic psychology. Theoretical point of view developed by Jung.

Andromania. Synonymous with nymphomania.

Anesthesia. Loss of sensitivity generally due to chemical depressants acting on the nervous system.

Anomia. Inability to name objects or persons.

Anorexia nervosa. Extreme loss of appetite.

Anosmia. Loss of sense of smell.

Anoxia. Oxygen deficit in the body tissues.

Anterograde amnesia. Inability to recall events following an injury.

Anthropoids. The higher species of mammals that most closely resemble man.

Anthropology. The study of man, his societies, and his artifacts.

Anthropomorphism. The tendency to ascribe human characteristics to either inanimate objects or lower animals.

Anthropophobia. Excessive fear of other humans.

Anxiety. Fear and apprehension usually with the object of fear unknown.

Anxiety neurosis. A disorder characterized primarily by chronic anxiety and/or anxiety states.

Anxiety state. A sudden and severe attack of anxiety, almost to the point of panic.

Apathy. Apparent lack of emotion, general indifference. Synonymous with blunting of the affect.

Aphasia. Loss of some language function ordinarily due to impaired cortical functioning.

Aphemia. Inability to speak due to organic damage.

Aphonia. Inability to speak without apparent organic damage.

Apoplectic habitus. DeGiovanni's body type consisting of a large trunk and a short body.

Argyll Robertson pupillary disturbance. A neurological sign of cerebral impairment where pupil of the eye does not react to changes in light intensity but continues to react in accommodation. Characteristic of general paresis.

Arterioles. Capillaries of the artery system.

Arteriosclerosis. A thickening or hardening of the artery walls resulting in a diminished blood supply.

Asocial. Pertaining to hostility toward social contacts.

Association. As used here, a concept in learning and personality theory which assumes that thoughts, ideas, or behavior patterns are linked together by their contiguity in space and time.

Astasia-abasia. An hysterical symptom of lack of muscular coordination without demonstrable organic impairment.

Astereognosis. Inability to identify objects by touch.

Asthenic. Kretschmer's body type of slender individuals with long bones and slight muscular development.

Asthma. A bronchial disease characterized by extreme coughing, wheezing, and difficult breathing in general.

Astrophobia. Excessive fear of astronomical objects and/or events.

Ataxia. Inability to coordinate muscles.

Athethosis. A cerebral palsy condition characterized by slow, irregular, continuous worm-like movements, most marked in the fingers and wrists.

Athletic. Kretschmer's body type of individuals with wide shoulders, sturdy, well-developed musculature, and good strength.

Atrophy. Progressive degeneration of tissue or organ systems.

Aura. Sensory hallucinations said to precede and signal the onset of epileptic attacks.

Autistic. Ego-centered; inward interest predominating over contact with reality.

Autoeroticism. Solitary sexual gratification, e.g., masturbation.

Automatisms. Activities carried out with little conscious awareness.

Autonomic nervous system. Visceral efferent part of the peripheral nervous system. See Chapter VI.

Avitaminosis. Vitamin deficiency.

Avoidance. As used here, pertains to withdrawal responses from uncomfortable or painful stimulation.

Babinski reflex. Spreading of toes resulting from touching sole of foot.

Barbiturates. A class of chemical anesthetics, the most common being sodium amytal and sodium pentothal.

Basedow's disease. Disease associated with hyperthyroidism.

Behavior. As used here, refers to overt muscular movement including language.

Behavior mechanism. A sequence of learned responses to frustration or stress that occur without consideration of rational or realistic evaluation of the problems they are intended to solve.

Behaviorism. The American school of psychology founded by J. B. Watson which feels that the only acceptable data for psychology are overt behavior.

Benign. Mild; opposed to malignant.

Bestiality. Sexual relations with lower animals.

Beta rhythm. Rapid frequency brain waves.

Bibliotherapy. Therapy involving controlled and planned reading for patients.

Bilateral symmetry. Having two complementary sides such as most animal bodies.

Blastophoric theory. Myerson's view that behavior disorders are caused by weak, defective, or abnormal germ plasm as a result of environmental injury.

Blunting of affect. General apathy or lack of emotion.

Body-building therapy. Restoration of optimal physiological functioning by means of diet and exercise. Synonymous with systemic therapies.

Brachycephalic. Having a short, broad head.

Broca's area. Speech center located in the second and third convolutions of the frontal lobes of the brain; precise location is in doubt.

Bromides. A class of chemical anesthetics.

Camphor. A crystalline derivative of terpene once used for shock therapy.

Carcinoma. A malignant tumor or cancer.

Cardiovascular diseases. Disorders of the circulatory system.

Castration complex. Psychoanalytic concept connotating excessive and irrational fear of castration or injury to the sex organs.

Catalepsy. A psychotic symptom characterized by the ability to maintain an imposed body position for long periods of time. See also *Cerea flexibilitas* and *Waxy flexibility.*

Catastrophic response. Adjustive reactions to demands beyond the limits of tolerance; generally disorganized and seemingly chaotic.

Catatonia. A form of schizophrenia chiefly characterized by (1) opposing extremes of movement inhibition and muscular aggression and (2) active aggression toward society.

Catharsis. Emotional release occurring during therapy.

Central nervous system. Brain and spinal cord.

Cerea flexibilitas. The cataleptic reaction where arms or legs may be placed in positions that will be maintained for long periods of time.

Cerebral arteriosclerosis. Hardening of cerebral arteries.

Cerebral cortex. The outer covering of the brain.

Cerebral dominance. The tendency of one hemisphere of the brain to be functionally predominant.

Cerebral palsy. A class of motor disorders probably due to brain injury at birth.

Cerebrotonia. One of Sheldon's temperament types. See Chapter XII.

Chemoreceptors. Receptors stimulated by chemical substances.

Chemotherapy sedation. The use of chemical sedatives as a therapeutic device.

Chloral hydrate. A sedative used in chemotherapy.

Chorea. A neurological disorder characterized by violent spasmodic muscular movement. Synonymous with St. Vitus's Dance.

Choreiform. Like chorea.

Claustrophobia. Excessive fear of enclosed places.

Client-centered therapy. The nondirective technique developed by C. Rogers. See Chapter XVII.

Climacteric period. The period preceding old age characterized by physiological and sometimes psychological change.

Coitus. Sexual intercourse.

Coma. Complete loss of consciousness with no response to sensory stimulation.

Compensation. A defense mechanism whereby deficit in one area of personality is substituted by development of another area.

Compensation for organic defect. As used here, a reaction to injury and physical defect, such as regeneration in lower animals or use of prosthetic devices by men. No basic dichotomy between this and preceding definition is intended.

Complex. An integrated pattern of repressed ideas having a strong emotional context.

Compulsion. Acts that the individual must carry out in spite of recognition on his part of their unreasonableness.

Concept. A thought, idea, or belief.

Concomitant. Accompanying.

Confabulation. In psychopathology, a stream of ideas or stories given by a patient with little factual content.

Conflict. Contradictory motives and needs within the same individual.

Confused states. Disorientation varying from uncertainty to loss of contact with the environment.

Congenital defects. Disorders caused by conditions present before or at the time of birth.

Congenital syphilis. The transmission of syphilis from mother to child, generally in utero.

Constitution. As used here, refers to body structure and physiological function.

Contiguity. As used in learning, refers to proximity in space and/or time of elements to be learned.

Conversion hysteria. A psychoneurotic condition characterized by the transformation of anxiety into physiological symptoms. Synonymous with conversion reaction.

Consciousness. As used here, awareness of the environment and a capacity to deal with it in a discriminatory manner. See Chapter III.

Corpus striatum. Part of the basal ganglia or gray matter of the telencephalon or endbrain.

Cortex. The outer covering of the cerebral hemispheres. Synonymous with cerebral cortex.

Counterfeit language. Words or phrases in which no basic reality is symbolized.

Cranial. Pertaining to the skull.

Cretinism. A developmental disorder caused by an insufficiency of the thyroid gland secretion, thyroxin.

Cultural lag. The delay between the rise of new ideas and techniques and their absorption into the general behavior of the society.

Cunnilingus. Oral stimulation of the female sexual organs.

Curare. A chemical depressant sometimes used in conjunction with shock therapies.

Cutaneous. Pertaining to the skin.

Cutaneous anesthesia. The psychoneurotic symptom of lack of skin sensation with little or contradictory relationship to physiological function.

Cyclothymia. Kretschmer's name for the psychosis characterized by alternating depression and excitement.

Decerebrate rigidity. Muscular state resulting when functional connections between cerebrum and lower parts of the central nervous systems are severed.

Decrement symptoms. As used here, responses to organic brain injury such as loss of consciousness, loss of muscular power, loss of speech functions, etc.

Delirium. A temporary state of confusion and disorientation generally accompanied by hallucinations and excitement.

Delirium tremens. A delirium state resulting from chronic alcoholism chiefly characterized by vivid and violent hallucinations.

Delta rhythm. Slow frequency, high-voltage brain waves.

Delusions. A belief or conviction that is firmly held irrespective of and with immunity to objective evidence as to its truth or falsity.

Dementia paralytica. Archaic name for general paresis.

Dementia praecox. Older term for psychotic disorders now more commonly named schizophrenia.

Dereistic thinking. Thought processes marked by their disregard for reality and conventional logical rules of discourse.

Deterioration. Progressive impairment of ability.

Diagnosis. Investigation, identification, and description of a disorder.

Dichotomous. Pertaining to separation into two categories.

Diffuse dissociated states. In general, conditions showing confusion and disorientation, for example, amnesia, hysterical fugues, sleep-walking, etc.

Diplopia. Double vision.

Dipsomania. Excessive desire to drink.

Directive interview. A psychotherapeutic technique that takes its name from the active role played by the therapist and the somewhat passive role of the patient. See Chapter XVII.

Disorientation. A state of confusion concerning the immediate environment, particularly with reference to spatial orientation and time.

Dissociation. Any gross disparity between the usually integrated psychological components of personality, such as between emotion and thought, thought and action, or emotion and action.

Dissociative reaction. As used here, a type of the psychoneurosis termed conversion hysteria or conversion reactions. May be treated as a separate class. Examples are the amnesias and multiple personality.

Dizygotic twins. Twins originating from two separate eggs.

Drama therapy. The therapeutic use of dramatic productions with patients as actors. The best example of this technique is psychodrama, developed by Moreno (1944).

Drives. The basic motivating forces directing behavior. Synonymous, here, with physiological needs and social motives.

Drug therapy. The use of chemical agents in therapy either as sedation (the barbiturates) or shock (insulin, metrazol).

Ductless glands. See endocrine glands.

Dwarfism. A retardation of growth probably due to hypofunction of the pituitary. See also *Lorain-Levi syndrome* and *Froehlich's syndrome.*

Dysfunction. Impaired function.

Dysphoric. Pertaining to a feeling of unrest, displeasure, and vague dissatisfaction.

Dysplatic. Kretschmer's body type of individuals showing endocrine disturbances resulting in disproportionate development.

Dysrhythmia. Inconsistent rhythm, generally applied to brain wave functions.

Echolalia. The tendency among some patients to repeat everything said to them apparently with little regard to content or meaning.

Echopraxia. The tendency of some patients to repeat the movements and gestures of individuals around them.

Ecology. The study of the relationship between organisms and their environment.

Ectomorphy. One of Sheldon's body types characterized in part by slight and delicate development. See Chapter XII.

Ego. The person's conception of himself as an individual. Sometimes synonymous with self. In psychoanalytic terminology, the conscious part of the structure of personality.

Egocentric. Pertaining to self-centeredness.

Egocentrism. A defense mechanism that involves exaggerated enhancement of the self.

Egomania. Intense and exaggerated preoccupation with self.

Electra complex. A psychoanalytic concept expressing a supposed sexual attachment of daughter to father with associated hostility toward the mother as a sexual rival.

Electroencephalogram. A technique for recording electrical activity of the brain.

Electromyographic technique. A method of recording muscular activity

Electroshock. A therapeutical technique involving the application of electric current to the head.

Embolism. The obstruction of a vessel, such as an artery or vein, by foreign matter.

Emotion. Behavior that appears when the motivated organism is blocked or thwarted while carrying out those activities that are necessary for the achievement of a goal. Subjectively, the behavior is manifested by strong feelings under a number of names, such as fear, anger, etc.

Empiricism. Either (1) observation and experiment or (2) the philosophical school asserting that knowledge is based only on experience.

Empirical therapies. Therapy based on trial and error when little is known about the actual disease process at work.

Encephalitis. An infectious disease causing inflammation of the brain.

Endocrine glands. Small organizations of secretory tissue, innervated by the automatic nervous system, that pass their secretions directly into the bloodstream.

Endogenous. Originating from within.

Endomorphy. One of Sheldon's body types characterized in part by heavy visceral development. See Chapter XII.

Engender. To cause.

Enuresis. "Bed-wetting"; urine elimination during sleep.

Epidemic encephalitis. See *Encephalitis.*

Epilepsy. A condition with major symptoms of convulsive seizures and partial or complete loss of consciousness. Cause frequently unknown.

Epileptic psychoses. Psychotic behavior due primarily to an underlying epileptic condition.

Equipotentiality. Of equal power or capability. Technically, the term is used to express the notion that various parts of the brain may perform identical functions.

Ergasiology. Adolf Meyer's term for the science of behavior.

Erogenous zones. Body parts which, when stimulated, are associated with sexual sensations.

Erotic. Pertaining to arousal of sexual feelings.

Ethnocentrism. The identification of an individual with his own culture, sub-culture, or race and his subsequent evaluations of other groups in terms of his own.

Etiology. Study of cause.

Eugenics. The study of techniques for the control of inherited characteristics.

Eunuch. Castrated male.

Euphoria. A feeling of elation and intense happiness.

Exhibitionism. Exposure of the sexual organs in order to achieve sexual satisfaction.

Exogenous. Originating from external causes.

Expansive. Out-going, unrestrained.

Extravert. An out-going, socially conscious, socially expressive individual.

Extrapyramidal tracts. A series of descending pathways from the cerebral cortex to various subcortical levels.

Fabrication. As used here, synonymous with confabulation.

Familial amaurotic idiocy. An apparently inherited neurological disease with serious mental deficiency. Synonymous with amaurotic idiocy.

Fantasy. Flights of imagination.

Fear. The intense desire to withdraw from or avoid a threatening object, person, or environment.

Feeblemindedness. The term generally applied to the mentally deficient.

Fellatio. Oral stimulation of the male sex organ.

Fetal curl. The psychoanalytic term for the patient who assumes a position reminiscent of that taken by the fetus in the womb.

Fetichism. A sexual aberration where any object may attain the potency of a sexual object in eliciting sexual satisfaction.

Fever therapy. The treatment of syphilis by a high fever.

Finger-painting. A therapeutic technique used primarily with children.

Fixation. A psychoanalytic term signifying delayed psychosexual development.

Focal epilepsy. Epilepsy caused by specifiable structural damage.

Folie à deux. Literally, "madness of two," where relatives or close associates of a patient identify strongly with the patient and become as ill as the patient himself.

Foreconscious. Thoughts just outside the threshold of awareness but readily recalled.

Fraternal twins. Twins developing from two separate eggs. Synonymous with dizygotic twins and contrasted with monozygotic or identical twins.

Free association. The process in therapy where the patient is instructed to verbalize at random without attempting to control the sequence of recollection.

Frigidity. Lack of sexual desire.

Froehlich's syndrome. A disorder presumably due to hypofunction of the pituitary characterized by heavy fat deposits and underdeveloped genitalia.

Frustration tolerance. The ability of the individual to adapt to frustrating situations.

Fugue state. An amnesic condition where the individual may travel or leave his environment without any subsequent memory. Synonymous here with hysterical amnesia.

Functional decortication. The apparent loss of cortical control without any organic damage. Perhaps common in emotional behavior.

Functional psychosis. A type of serious behavior disorder characterized by a disruption of the integrated adaptation to stress at all levels. The term "functional" refers to the fact that no organic agent or defect has been identified.

Ganser syndrome. A psychoneurotic condition characterized by a grotesque simulation of psychotic behavior.

Gastroptosis. "Dropped stomach." A condition in which the stomach is abnormally depressed from its normal position in the abdominal cavity.

Generalization. The process of deriving the nature of a class from a knowledge of the particulars of the class.

General paresis. Psychotic disorder caused by a syphilitic infection of the meninges and cerebral structures.

Genetic. Hereditary.

Gerontology. The systematic study of the aged.

Glove anesthesia. Paralysis of the hand and wrist areas with no reasonable physiological basis. A psychoneurotic symptom.

Glycogen. A carbohydrate related to starch.

Grand mal. The generalized convulsive seizures of epilepsy.

Gynophobia. Excessive fear of women.

Habits. Learned patterns of behavior.

Hallucinations. Sensory experiences for which no adequate sensory stimulation can be discovered.

Hebephrenia. A type of schizophrenia characterized by silliness, fragmentation of affective and intellectual processes, and the formation of extremely bizarre delusional and hallucinatory experiences.

Hedonistic. Pertaining to gratification primarily by pleasure-seeking activities.

Hematophobia. Excessive fear of blood.

Hermaphrodite. An individual possessing both male and female sexual organs.

Heterosexual. Desiring or achieving sexual gratification from the opposite sex.

Histochemical. Pertaining to chemical analysis of the tissues.

Homeostasis. The tendency for physiological functioning to achieve an optimal equilibrium. May be extended to psychological phenomena.

Homeostatic mechanisms. Refers to the variety of physiological techniques of achieving homeostasis.

Homosexuality. Obtaining sexual gratification from the same sex.

Homo sapiens. Genus and species name for man.

Huntington's chorea. Disease characterized by massive atrophy of the convolutions of the cerebral cortex and the corpus striatum.

Hutchinson's teeth. Moon- or crescent-shaped notching of the second or permanent teeth, particularly the central incisors; diagnostic sign of congenital syphilis.

Hydrocephalus. A disorder characterized by a blocking of the circulation of cerebrospinal fluid with a consequent increase in intercranial pressure resulting in unusually large head size.

Hydrophobia. Excessive fear of water.

Hydrotherapy. Treatment technique involving submersion in hot and cold water.

Hyper-. Prefix signifying excess, greater than normal.

Hyperactive. Excessively active.

Hyperacute mania. A psychotic syndrome where the patient becomes violently active and often completely uncontrollable.

Hyperacute retarded depression. A psychotic syndrome characterized by almost complete immobility and stupor; responsiveness to environmental stimulation of any kind is minimal.

Hyperalgesia. Excessive pain sensitivity.

Hyperpituitarism. Overactivity of the pituitary.

Hypertension. High blood pressure.

Hyperthyroidism. Excessive action of the thyroid.

Hypnoanalysis. The use of hypnosis in combination with psychoanalytic procedures.

Hypo-. Prefix signifying deficit, activity below normal.

Hypochondriasis. Intense, persistent, and exaggerated preoccupation and worry over bodily processes, usually associating the experience of these processes as symptomatic of disease.

Hypokinesis. Low level of muscular activity.

Hysteria. A solution to the problems of anxiety in which the patient develops physical and/or behavioral symptoms that enable him to avoid the anxiety-producing situation and effectively reduce his anxiety to a level of acceptable tolerance; a class of psychoneuroses, synonymous with conversion reaction.

Hysterical amnesia. See *Fugue state.*

Id. A psychoanalytic concept referring to basic unconscious instinctual drives.

Identical twins. Twins developed from a single egg. Synonymous with monozygotic twins and contrasted with fraternal or dizygotic twins.

Idiopathic. In general denotes that the causative factors cannot be identified.

Idiopathic epilepsy. Epileptic disorders where no specific cause can be discovered.

Idiot. A class of mental deficiency usually specified by I.Q. scores of less than 25.

Idiot savants. Individuals who appear mentally defective by almost any social standard, but who excel in some particular trait or aptitude.

Illusion. Faulty or mistaken interpretations of sensory stimulation.

Imbecile. A class of mental deficiency usually specified by I.Q. scores of from 25 to 50.

Impotence. Apparent lack of sexual ability.

Incest. Sexual intercourse between closely related individuals such as brother and sister, father and daughter, etc.

Inferiority complex. An exaggerated and chronic feeling of personal mediocrity and unworthiness.

Inhibit. To block or restrain.

Innervation. Stimulation or excitation.

Insanity. A legal term specifying either that the individual cannot discriminate between "right" and "wrong" or that he cannot exercise control over his actions.

Insight. A reasonably correct personal understanding of an individual's past and present situation and his motives, habits, and personality.

Instinct. Complex, unlearned behavior patterns.

Insulin. The secretion of the Isles of Langerhans in the pancreas involved normally in sugar metabolism. Used in shock therapy.

Intelligence Quotient. The ratio between mental age (as determined by intelligence tests) and chronological age.

Interference symptoms. As used here, refers to class of responses to organic damage. Synonymous with decrement symptoms.

Introspection. Critical and careful observation of the contents of consciousness.

Introvert. An individual characterized by self-centered interests and withdrawal from social contacts. Opposed to extravert.

Invert. Synonymous with homosexual.

Involutional melancholia. A psychotic disorder supposedly associated with the climacteric period.

Jacksonian seizure. A convulsive epileptic attack limited to a restricted group of muscles; or a seizure starting from a definite muscle group and progressing throughout the total musculature.

Juvenile paresis. General paresis in children.

Kettering hyperthem. A device for the induction of high fever, used in the treatment of syphilis.

Kleptomania. Excessive desire to steal.

Korsakoff's psychosis. A psychotic syndrome characterized by amnesia, disorientation in space and time, and marked confabulation; probably caused by a combination of chronic alcoholism and vitamin deficiency.

Latent. Pertaining to the hidden potential.

Leucotomy. Psychosurgical technique involving transorbital entry to the brain with purpose of cutting association pathways from the frontal lobes to the rest of the brain.

Lesbianism. Female homosexuality.

Libido. Psychoanalytic concept connotating basic biological drive.

Lobectomy. Psychosurgical technique involving removal of part of frontal lobes of the brain.

Lobotomy. The psychosurgical technique by which the frontal lobes are severed from the rest of the brain.

Localized dissociations. Refers to psychoneurotic symptoms such as the hysterical anesthesias and paralyses.

Lorain-Levi syndrome. Syndrome overtly characterized by complete dwarfism; due to underdevelopment of the anterior lobe of the pituitary and the resultant hypofunction of that gland.

Lues. Archaic for syphilis.

Luminal. A barbiturate used as an anesthetic.

Lunacy. Somewhat archaic legal term for insanity.

Lymphocytes. A type of amoeboid cell found in the lymph fluid.

Macrocephalic. A disorder overtly characterized by an excessive enlargement of the head.

Macrosplanchnic. Viola and Naccarati's body type of stout individuals.

Maladaptive. Poor or inadequate adaptation.

Maladjustment. As used here, poor or inadequate adaptation.

Malingerer. An individual who pretends to be ill.

Mania. A psychotic syndrome characterized by exaggerated and violent excitement.

Manic-depressive psychosis. A psychotic syndrome characterized either by pathological depression or excitement or alternating periods of both.

Masochism. Obtaining sexual satisfaction from experiencing pain or abuse.

Masturbation. Obtaining sexual gratification by self-manipulation of sexual organs.

Maturation. Changes in behavior attributable to anatomical and physiological development of the organism.

Megalomania. Delusions of grandeur.

Melancholia. Deep, exaggerated depression.

Menopause. Period of physiological change in women in later middle age, the major overt symptom being the end of ovulation and menstruation.

Mental deficiency. The class of individuals retarded both intellectually and socially.

Mental hygiene movement. The study and promotion of techniques for the prevention of the behavior disorders.

Mesomorphy. One of Sheldon's body types characterized in part by excellent structural development. See Chapter XII.

Messianic complex. The delusion of God-like superiority.

Metabolism. The total chemical processes involved in cellular life.

Metrazol. A camphor derivative and stimulant used to induce convulsion as a technique of shock therapy.

Microcephaly. A disorder characterized overtly by an exceptionally small head; the central causative factor is the underdevelopment of the brain due to restricted cranial volume.

Microsplanchnic. Viola and Naccarati's body type of thin, tall individuals.

Mongolian idiocy. A disorder characterized physically by a supposed resemblance to Oriental features; psychologically these individuals are much more often imbeciles rather than idiots.

Monozygotic twins. Twins developed from a single egg. Synonymous with identical twins.

Morbid. Archaic for diseased, pathological.

Moron. A class of mental deficiency usually arbitrarily specified by I.Q. scores from 50 to 70.

Morphology. The study of the structure and forms of organisms.

Mosaic. Pattern.

Motivation. The basic causal forces directing behavior.

Motives. The specific motivational forces, either physiological needs and/or social motives.

Multiple personality. Individuals showing two or more completely different and autonomous personalities. The classic fictional example is Stevenson's Dr. Jekyll and Mr. Hyde.

Music therapy. A therapeutic adjunct designed to provide a way of promoting relaxation.

Mutism. Lack of ability to speak.

Myxedema. A lethargic disorder caused by hypofunction of the thyroid gland.

Narcissistic. Exaggerated love of self; sexual satisfaction obtained through self-admiration.

Narcoanalysis. The use of drugs to produce repressed material from the patient's past experience.

Narcolepsy. A chronic irresistible tendency to fall asleep while going about daily activities.

Narcosynthesis. Narcoanalysis combined with attempts by the therapist to interpret the information released during narcoanalysis.

Necrophilia. Sexual relations with dead bodies.

Necrophobia. Excessive fear of dead bodies.

Negativism. A persistent opposition against attempts made to guide or direct the individual's conduct.

Nembutal. A barbiturate used as an anesthetic.

Neologisms. Literally, new words. Characteristic of schizophrenic language, usually with no obvious meaning.

Neuresthenia. A psychoneurotic condition showing a predominance of fatigue feelings, sometimes known as "college student's syndrome." This term is not used in our terminology.

Neuron. A nerve cell.

Neuropsychiatry. Branch of medicine concerned with the behavior disorders. Synonymous with psychiatry.

Neurosis. That type of behavior disorder in which the disturbances of behavior do not affect the individual sufficiently to terminate completely the possibility of at least some social adjustment. Synonymous with psychoneurosis.

Neurosyphilis. Syphilitic infection of the nervous system.

Neurotic-depressive reaction. Condition characterized by overwhelming feelings of sadness, sorrow, grief, and self-depreciation. Synonymous with reactive depression.

Nihilistic delusion. The belief that nothing is real.

Normal. See Chapter II.

Normosphlanchnic. Viola and Naccarati's body type of individuals with constant proportion between vertical and horizontal body diameters.

Nosology. The study and application of the process of systematic classification.

Nyctophobia. Excessive fear of darkness.

Nymphomania. Exaggerataed sexual desire by female.

Nystagmus. A rhythmic, involuntary, oscillation of the eyes.

Objectless fear. Anxiety.

Obsession. A persistent, unavoidable, and often irrational idea (or complex of ideas).

Obsessive-compulsive neurosis. A class of psychoneurosis characterized by obsessions and compulsions that serve to reduce anxiety.

Ochlophobia. Excessive fear of large crowds.

Oedipus complex. The psychoanalytic concept connotating sexual attraction of the son for the mother and hatred toward the father as a sexual rival.

Olfactory hallucinations. The perception of generally unpleasant odors without any adequate stimulus being present.

Operational fatigue. Psychosomatic symptoms of general lethargy and apathy found frequently among combat personnel after long periods of combat; these symptoms develop in previously well-adjusted individuals. Synonymous with battle fatigue.

Optimal. Pertaining to best or most favorable.

Oral eroticism. A psychoanalytic concept referring to pleasurable sensations elicited by stimulation of mouth regions, presumably a stage in the psychosexual development of the child.

Organic psychosis. The psychotic disorders that may be attributed to definite bodily causes.

Ortopsychiatry. Investigation and treatment of children's behavior disorders.

Overcompensation. Excessive use of compensation to the point where behavior is no longer adaptive. One ability may be overemphasized to overcome deficits in other areas to the point where none of the behavior is appropriate.

Paraldehyde. A colorless chemical used as a sedative.

Paramnesia. "Recall" of fictitious events.

Paranoia. A disorder characterized by little loss of intellectual efficiency but by an elaborate, rigid, and usually superficially logical set of delusional beliefs. Not to be confused with paranoid schizophrenia.

Paranoid. As frequently used, pertains to an individual suffering from either (1) paranoia or (2) paranoid schizophrenia.

Paranoid schizophrenia. A psychotic disorder characterized by fairly well-organized delusional systems, usually of a persecutory or grandiose nature. Differs from paranoia in far greater loss of contact with reality and loss of intellectual efficiency. Not to be confused with paranoia.

Paranoid state. A minor, transitory, form of paranoia where the patient develops delusional beliefs, usually of a persecutory nature, arising from situational inadequacies or frustration.

Paresis. Psychotic disorder presumably caused by syphilitic infection of the central nervous system. Also termed "general paresis."

Parkinson's syndrome. Serious motor malfunctioning as a result of encephalitic infection of the brain.

Pathogenic. Disease-causing.

Pathological. Diseased or disease-causing.

Pathological intoxication. An allergic-like reaction to alcohol, in that small amounts may precipitate violent behavior, the intensity of which has no relation to the amount of alcohol drunk. Usually transitory.

Pederasty. Sexual intercourse involving the anus.

Pedophilia. Sexual relations between adult and child.

Penis-envy. Psychoanalytic concept connotating a desire by a female child for possession of male sexual organs.

Peripheral nervous system. Generally all the nervous system excluding the central nervous system and in particular that part extending to the outer surfaces of the body.

Perseveration. As used here, refers to the tendency of the patient with organic damage to show less behavior potentiality and correspondingly increased repetition of a small reduced set of habits.

Perseverative reactions. Continual repetition of unsuccessful behavior.

Personality. The expression of the organism's unique potentialities in any given situation.

Pervert. Archaic term for sexual deviant.

Petit mal. A type of epileptic behavior generally consisting of short lapses of consciousness with or without mild convulsive movements.

Phallic symbol. Psychoanalytic term connotating objects symbolizing male sex organ.

Phlegmatic. Pertaining to a sluggish or apathetic personality type which was said to be due to an overabundance of the humor, phlegm.

Phobia. Strong, unreasonable fears, usually directed at some specific environmental object.

Photophobia. Excessive fear of light.

Phthisic habitus. DeGiovanni's body type consisting of short trunk and long body.

Phylogenetic. Pertaining to the history of the species.

Phyloanalysis. The theory of psychopathology developed by Trigant Burrow stressing the role of social relationships in producing conflict and neurosis.

Pick's disease. A progressive presenile disorder possibly caused by neurological degeneration in the brain.

Pleasure principle. A psychoanalytic concept connotating the basic motivation of the id.

Polemic. Pertaining to controversial and/or pedantic argument.

Pons. A mass of transverse nerve fibers on the ventral surface of the hind brain consisting largely of white matter.

Post-hypnotic suggestion. Instructions given during hypnosis to be carried out by the subject after hypnosis.

Pragmatics. The study of the relationship between words and their objects.

Pre-frontal lobotomy. The psychosurgical technique involving surgical separation of the frontal pole from the rest of the brain.

Prenatal asphyxiation. Exposure of the brain to oxygen deprivation after the infant has lost placental oxygen and before normal breathing can be established.

Prognosis. The prediction of the future course of a disease.

Projection. The individual ascribes to others wishes, motives, and fears that are his own but of which he is usually unaware.

Projective techniques. Testing devices with loosely structured stimuli designed to elicit verbal behavior reflecting a projection of some of the inner content of personality structure.

Prophylaxis. In general, pertaining to prevention of disease.

Prosthenic device. An artificial part added to the body usually to replace a missing member.

Pseudocyesis. Imagined pregnancy.

Psychiatrist. A physician who has specialized in the area of psychiatry.

Psychiatry. The division of medicine that studies and treats the behavior disorders.

Psyche. Synonymous with mind.

Psychic processes. Mental functions.

Psychoanalysis. The general body of theory and treatment techniques originated by Sigmund Freud.

Psychoanalyst. In the United States, a physician who is specifically trained in psychoanalytic theory and technique. Psychoanalysts in other countries are not always medically trained.

Psychobiology. The general theory of psychopathology originated and developed by the American psychiatrist, Adolf Meyer.

Psychodrama. The therapeutic technique developed by Moreno involving a dramatic production with patients as actors. The plays are generally specifically designed in reference to the patient's background and problems.

Psychodynamics. A general term signifying the study of personality and psychopathology with special reference to basic motivation, and possibly applicable to all theories in these areas.

Psychology. To some, the study of behavior; to others, the study of mind and mental processes.

Psychoneurosis. That behavior disorder in which the disturbances of behavior do not affect the individual sufficiently to terminate completely the possibility of at least some social adjustment. Synonymous with neurosis.

Psychopathic personality. A type of disorder showing few of the characteristics of psychosis or psychoneurosis but rather a complete lack of ability in making an adjustment to society. Synonyms are "constitutional psychopathic inferiority," "constitutional psychopathic state," or simply "psychopath."

Psychopathology. The study of defective, inefficient, or maladjusted behavior. Synonymous with abnormal psychology.

Psychosis. The class of serious behavior disorders of such intensity that any sort of social adjustment is impossible; the behavior is characterized by a disruption of adaptation at all life levels.

Psychosomatics. The study of the relation between emotional expression and the physiological correlates of emotion with special reference to bodily health and disease.

Psychosurgery. The therapeutic technique utilizing surgical insult, generally to the brain.

Psychotherapy. The therapeutic techniques dependent primarily on psychological methods as contrasted with somatic techniques such as chemotherapy, etc. The relationship between patient and therapist is entirely a verbal one.

Pyknik. Kretschmer's body type of stocky, plump, rounded individuals.

Pyromania. Excessive desire to start fires.

Radial symmetry. Refers to those animal forms characterized by outward development from a center, for example, the starfish. Contrasted with bilateral symmetry.

Rapport. A favorable emotional relationship between therapist and patient.

Rationalization. The process of consciously explaining or justifying a thought, feeling, attitude, or action on what are meant to appear as logical and rational grounds, irrespective of the actual underlying motivation, which may be unconscious and unknown to the individual.

Rational therapy. Therapeutic efforts are based on a known relationship between the therapeutic devices and the disease condition. Contrasted with empirical therapies.

Reactive depression. A psychoneurotic condition characterized by overwhelming feelings of sadness, sorrow, grief and self-depreciation. Synonymous with neurotic-depressive reaction.

Redintegration. The elicitation of a complex response to only part of a complex stimulus, the whole of the stimulus having previously been associated with the response.

Regression. Having achieved a more mature state of adjustment, the individual, faced with stress, relinquishes later-learned techniques and returns to an immature and infantile level of adjustment.

Remission. Loss of symptoms, apparent recovery.

Repression. The unconscious rejection from awareness of those aspects of past experience that have either immediate or remote potentialities for causing pain.

Resistance. In psychoanalytic therapy, an emotional rejection of the therapist by the patient (usually motivated by an unconscious unwillingness to examine and verbalize repressed material).

Retarded depression. A psychotic syndrome showing lowered general activity, a depressed mood, a loss of spontaneity, and heightened susceptibility to fatigue.

Retrograde amnesia. Failure of recall for events preceding traumatic injury.

Rorschach test. A projective technique composed of standardized stimulus cards with vaguely outlined ambiguous figures. Commonly known as the "Ink-Blot" test.

Sadism. Obtaining sexual satisfaction from imposing pain on others.

Sapphism. Female homosexuality. Synonymous with lesbianism.

Satyriasis. Pathological sexual desire in male.

Schizophrenia. A group of psychotic disorders characterized by fundamental disturbances in reality-relationships and concept formations, with consequent affective and intellectual disturbances in varying degrees and mixtures.

Scotophilia. Sexual gratification from viewing sexual acts of others.

Seconal. A chemical used as an anesthetic.

Self. As used here, synonymous with ego.

Semantics. The theoretical framework developed by A. Korzybski concerning the study of language.

Senile pyschosis. A psychotic syndrome characterized by progressive intellectual, emotional, and social disintegration. A disorder of the aged often caused by neurological or cardiovascular changes.

Septicemia. Blood poisoning.

Servo-mechanism. A type of self-correcting machine.

Sexual deviate. An individual not conforming to sexual techniques or behavior approved by the culture.

Sham rage. Sherrington's name for the behavior of decorticate animals, shown in response to completely neutral stimuli.

Shock therapy. Treatment techniques involving drugs or electrical stimulation and usually inducing convulsive behavior.

Sicklemia. A deformation of the red blood cells due primarily to oxygen deprivation; this disease may possibly be racially determined.

Siguad types. A body type system with four categories of individuals; respiratory, digestive, muscular, and cerebral.

Sleep therapy. A technique where the patient is maintained for periods up to a week in a state of sleep.

Sodomy. Anal intercourse.

Somatic. Pertaining to the body.

Somatotonia. One of Sheldon's temperament types characterized in part by vigorous muscular activity. See Chapter XII.

Somatotype. Body type.

Somnambulism. Sleep-walking.

Somnambulistic wanderings. Sleep-walking.

Spasticity. As used here, applies to cerebral palsy: a type of involuntary muscular contraction, a spastic paralysis being one in which the muscles of a limb are in a state of increased tonicity and contraction.

Stereotype. A uniform and predictable emotionally toned response given by members of a particular social group to certain objects or concepts.

Stress. The wide variety of circumstances that renders adaptation difficult or which calls forth increased effort on the part of the organism.

Stylus maze. An apparatus widely used for the study of learning. It consists of a revolving turntable on which there is a small spot. The subject attempts to keep a pointer (stylus) in contact with the spot.

Subacute mania. All those emotional deviations in the direction of mania from a mild euphoria to a relatively uninhibited excitement in which contact with reality is still predominantly retained.

Subconscious. See Chapter III. Perhaps that part of personality which cannot be readily verbalized.

Sublimation. The individual changes from a frustrated or disapproved activity to one that promises the same rewards or goal attainments but that can be carried out more easily.

Superego. A psychoanalytic concept connotating that part of personality signifying the social and cultural mores.

Sydenham's syndrome. A disorder characterized by jerky, restless movements; probably a result of rheumatic fever.

Sympathism. The person contrives to put himself into a position where others will notice him and express their concern over his difficulties.

Symptomatic epilepsy. Epilepsy due to toxins affecting the brain.

Synapse. The connecting point between two nerve cells.

Syncope. Loss of consciousness due to cerebral anoxia.

Syndactilism. A hereditary condition in which the digits of the hands and feet are fused together.

Syndrome. Group of apparently related symptoms.

Tetany. Physiologically intermittent muscular spasm of arms or legs, characteristic of parathyroid disturbances; also one of Jaensch's morphological types.

Thanatophobia. Excessive fear of death.

Thematic Apperception Test. A projective technique, developed by Murray and Morgan, using a set of ambiguous pictures about which the patient constructs a story.

Thyroxin. The secretion of the thyroid gland.

Tic. A localized twitching, spasm or jerking of muscles without organic cause.

Time binding. Korzybski's term for the property of language that permits a person to reconstruct through words many of the aspects of situations and experiences that occurred at another time or to construct in anticipation situations that have not yet occurred.

Topectomy. Psychosurgical technique involving removal of brain tissue.

Trance. Hypnotic-like state.

Transference. The affectionate or hostile attitudes that the patient expresses toward the therapist based on past identifications of the patient.

Traumatic. Pertaining to injury or shock.

Traumatic neuroses. The psychoneurotic conditions precipitated by either bodily harm or strong threat of injury.

Tremor. A localized involuntary muscle spasm.

Trephination. Perforation of the skull.

Trichotomous. Pertaining to division into three classes.

Tubular vision. An hysterical symptom involving a concentric constriction of the visual field. Sometimes called "tunnel vision."

Unconscious. See Chapter III.

Unicellular. Pertaining to one-celled organisms.

Valences. Forces.

Vasoconstriction. Constriction of the blood vessels.

Vasodilation. Dilation of the blood vessels.

Vertigo. A feeling of dizziness.

Viscera. The internal organs, particularly those of the abdomen.

Viscerotonia. One of Sheldon's temperament types. See Chapter XII.

Waxy flexibility. A symptom of catatonic schizophrenia where the patient can maintain rigid muscular extensions for long periods of time. Synonymous with cerea flexibilitas.

Wechsler-Bellevue. An adult intelligence test developed by Wechsler.

Word-salad. A characteristic of much schizophrenic language particularly of the hebephrenic; there is seldom any meaningful content, many new words are coined, and sound-association is substituted for meaning-association.

Zoophilia. Excessive love of animals.

Zoophobia. Excessive fear of animals.

Bibliography

Bibliography

Abramson, H. A. (1948), "Psychosomatic aspects of hay fever and asthma prior to 1900." *Ann. Allergy. 6,* 110-121: 147.

Abse, D. W. (1950), *The Diagnosis of Hysteria.* Baltimore: The Williams & Wilkins Company.

Adams, D. K. (1931), "A restatement of the problem of learning." *Brit. J. Psychol.* 22, 150-178.

Adcock, C. J. (1948), "A factorial examination of Sheldon's types." *J. Pers., 16,* 312-319.

Adler, A. (1917a), *The Neurotic Constitution.* New York: Dodd, Mead & Company, Inc.

—— (1917b), "Study of organ inferiority and its psychical compensation." *Nervous and Mental Disease Monograph Series, No. 24.*

—— (1927), *Understanding Human Nature.* New York: Greenberg, Publisher, Inc.

—— (1931), *What Life Should Mean to You.* Boston: Little, Brown & Company.

Adorno, T. W., Else Frenkel-Brunswick, D. J. Levinson, and R. N. Sanford (1950), *The Authoritarian Personality.* New York: Harper and Brothers.

Agar, W. E. (1938), "The concept of purpose in Biology." *Quart. Rev. Biol., 13,* 255-273.

Aichhorn, A. (1935), *Wayward Youth.* New York: Viking Press, Inc.

Albee, G. W. (1951), "The prognostic importance of delusions in schizophrenia." *J. abnorm. soc. Psychol., 46,* 208-212.

Alexander, F. (1936), *The Medical Value of Psychoanalysis.* New York: W. W. Norton & Company, Inc.

—— (1950), *Psychosomatic Medicine.* New York: W. W. Norton & Company, Inc.

——, and T. M. French (1946), *Psychoanalytic Therapy: Principles and Application.* New York: The Ronald Press Company.

——, ——, et al. (1948), *Studies in Psychosomatic Medicine.* New York: The Ronald Press Company.

————, and W. Healy (1935), *Roots of Crime*. New York: Alfred A. Knopf, Inc.

————, and Helen Ross, eds. (1952), *Dynamic Psychiatry*. Chicago: University of Chicago Press.

Allee, W. C. (1938), *The Social Life of Animals*. New York: W. W. Norton & Company, Inc.

Allport, G. W. (1937), *Personality, A Psychological Interpretation*. New York: Henry Holt & Company, Inc.

———— (1953), "The trend of motivational theory." *Amer. J. Orthopsychiat., 23*, 107-119.

Altschuler, I. M. (1939), "Rational music-therapy of the mentally ill." *Music Teach. Nat. Ass. Proc.*, 153-157.

———— (1941), "The part of music in resocialization of mental patients." *Occup. Ther., 20*, 75-86.

Altschule, M. D. (1951), "Effects of factors that modify cerebral blood flow on hallucinations in schizophrenia." *J. clin. exp. Psychopath., 12*, 123-129.

———— (1953), *Bodily Physiology in Mental and Emotional Disorders*. New York: Grune & Stratton.

Ames, L. B., and J. Learned (1946), "Imaginary companions and related phenomena." *J. genet. Psychol., 69*, 147-167.

Anastasi, Anne, and J. P. Foley, Jr. (1948), "A proposed reorientation in the heredity-environment controversy." *Psychol. Rev., 55*, 239-249.

Anderson, E. E. (1938a), "The interrelationship of drives in the male albino rat. II. Intercorrelations between 47 measures of drives and of learning." *Comp. Psychol. Monog., 14*, No. 6.

———— (1938b), "The interrelationship of drives in the male albino rat. III. Interrelations among measures of emotional, sexual, and exploratory behavior." *J. genet. Psychol., 53*, 335-352.

Andrews, Jean S. (1945), "Directive psychotherapy. 1. Re-assurance." *J. clin. Psychol., 1*, 52-66.

Angyal, A. (1951), "A theoretical model for personality studies." *J. Pers., 20*, 131-142.

Antonitis, J. J., and A. J. Sher (1952), "Social regression in the white rat." *J. Psychol., 33*, 99-111.

Appel, J. W. (1946), "Incidence of neuropsychiatric disorders in the United States Army in World War II." *Amer. J. Psychiat., 102*, 433-436.

Arestad, F. H., and Mary A. McGovern (1953), "Hospital service in the United States." *J. Amer. Med. Assoc., 152*, 143-163.

Arnold, Thurman, W. (1937), *The Folklore of Capitalism*. New Haven, Conn.: Yale University Press.

Arnow, A. J. (1952), "Verbal hallucinations: a restitutional symptom." *Bull. Menninger Clin., 16,* 178-183.

Ascher, E. (1952), "A criticism of the concept of neurotic depression." *Amer. J. Psychiat., 108,* 901-908.

Atkin, I. (1953), "Difficult delusions." *Lancet, 264,* 213-215.

Ausubel, D. P. (1950), "Negativism as a phase of ego development." *Amer. J. Orthopsychiat., 20,* 796-805.

—————— (1952), *Ego Development and the Personality Disorders.* New York: Grune & Stratton.

Babcock, H. (1930), "An experiment in the measurement of mental deterioration." *Arch. Psychol.,* No. 117.

Babinski, J., and J. Froment (1917), *Hysteria or Pithiatism and Reflex Nervous Disorders of War.* London: University of London Press.

Bard, P. (1934), "Emotion. I. The neuro-humoral basis of emotional reactions," in C. Murchison, (1934), *A Handbook of General Experimental Psychology,* pp. 264-311. Worcester, Mass.: Clark University Press.

——————, and V. B. Mountcastle (1948), "Some forebrain mechanisms involved in expression of rage with special reference to suppression of angry behavior." *Res. Publ. Assn. nerv. ment. Dis., 27,* 362-404.

Barker, R., T. Dembo, and K. Lewin (1941), "Frustration and regression: An experiment with young children," in *Studies in Topological and Vector Psychology, II.* University of Iowa *Stud. Child Welf., 18,* No. 1, 1-314.

Barnacle, C. H. (1949), "Psychosomatic aspects of gastro-intestinal disorders." *Rocky Mtn. Med. J., 46,* 642-647.

Bartlett, F. C. (1932), *Remembering.* London: Cambridge University Press.

Bauer, J. (1945), *Constitution and Disease* (2nd Ed.). New York: Grune & Stratton.

Bevelas, A. (1942), "Morale and the training of leaders," in G. Watson, ed. (1942), *Civilian Morale.* Second yearbook of S.P.S.S.I. Boston: Published for Reynal and Hitchcock by the Houghton Mifflin Company.

Beach, F. A., and J. Jaynes (1954), "Effects of early experience upon the behavior of animals." *Psychol. Bull., 51,* 239-263.

Becker, H. (1933), "The sorrow of bereavement." *J. abnorm. soc. Psychol., 27,* 391-410.

Beebe-Center, C. G. (1932), *Pleasantness and Unpleasantness.* New York: D. Van Nostrand Company, Inc.

Beers, C. (1908), *The Mind That Found Itself.* New York: Longmans, Green & Company.

Beier, E. G. (1951a), "The effect of induced anxiety on the flexibility of intellectual functioning." *Psychol. Monogr.*, 65 (No. 365.)

—————— (1951b), "The problem of anxiety in client-centered therapy." *J. consult. Psychol.*, 15, 359-362.

Belinson, L., and W. S. Cowie (1947), "Electroencephalographic characteristics of institutionalized epileptics." *Amer. J. ment. Def.*, 52, 9-15.

Bellak, L. (1948), *Dementia Praecox*. New York: Grune & Stratton.

—————— (1949a), "A multiple-factor psychosomatic theory of schizophrenia." *Psychiat. Quart.*, 23, 738-755.

—————— (1949b), "The use of oral barbiturates in psychotherapy." *Amer. J. Psychiat.*, 105, 849-850.

——————, and Elizabeth Willson (1947), "On the etiology of dementia praecox; a partial review of the literature, 1939 to 1945, and an attempt at conceptualization." *J. nerv. ment. Dis.*, 105, 1-24.

Benda, C. E. (1949), *Mongolism and Cretinism* (2nd Ed.). New York: Grune & Stratton.

—————— (1952), *Developmental Disorders of Mentation and Cerebral Palsies*. New York: Grune & Stratton.

—————— (1954), "Psychopathology of childhood," in L. Carmichael, ed. (1954), *Manual of Child Psychology* (2nd Ed.), pp. 1115-1161. New York: John Wiley & Sons, Inc.

——————, M. J. Farrell, and C. E. Chipman (1951), "The inadequacy of present day concepts of mental deficiency and mental illness in child psychiatry." *Amer. J. Psychiat.*, 107, 721-729.

Bender, L., and F. Vogel (1941), "Imaginary companions of children." *Amer. J. Orthopsychiat.*, 11, 56-66.

Benedek, Therese (1946), *Insight and Personality Adjustment: A Study of the Psychological Effects of War*. New York: The Ronald Press Company.

Benedict, Ruth (1934a), "Anthropology and the abnormal." *J. Gen. Psychol.*, 10, 50-82.

—————— (1934b), *Patterns of Culture*. Boston: Houghton Mifflin Company.

—————— (1938), "Continuities and discontinuities in cultural conditioning." *Psychiatry*, 1, 161-167.

Bentley, M., and E. V. Cowdry, eds. (1934), *The Problem of Mental Disorder*. New York: McGraw-Hill Book Company, Inc.

Bergman, P. (1947), "Analysis of an unusual case of fetishism." *Bull. Menninger Clin.*, 11, 67-75.

Berman, L. (1922), *The Glands Regulating Personality. A Study of the Glands of Internal Secretion in Relation to the Types of Human Nature*. New York: The Macmillan Company.

Bernard, H. W. (1952), *Mental Hygiene for Classroom Teachers*. New York: McGraw-Hill Book Company, Inc.

Berndt, R. M., and Catherine H. Berndt (1951), "The concept of abnormality in an Australian aboriginal society," in G. B. Wilbur and W. Muensterberger (1951), *Psychoanalysis and Culture.* New York: International Universities Press.

Berry, M., and J. Eisenson (1942), *The Defective in Speech.* New York: Appleton-Century-Crofts, Inc.

Bettelheim, B. (1943), "Individual and mass behavior in extreme situations." *J. abnorm. soc. Psychol., 38,* 417-452.

Beverly, B. I. (1942), "Anxieties of children; their causes and implications." *Amer. J. Dis. Child., 64,* 585-593.

Biel, W. C. (1939), "The effect of early inanition upon maze learning in the albino rat." *Comp. Psychol. Monog., 15,* No. 74.

———— (1940), "Early age differences in maze performance in the albino rat." *J. Gen. Psychol., 56,* 439-453.

————, and L. I. O'Kelly (1940), "The effect of cortical lesions on emotional and regressive behavior in the rat. I. Emotional behavior." *J. Comp. Psychol., 30,* 221-240.

Bigelow, N. (1953), "Considerations in the differential diagnosis of schizophrenia." *Psychiat. Quart., 27,* 382-389.

Billings, E. G., F. G. Ebaugh, D. W. Morgan, L. I. O'Kelly, Genevieve B. Short, and F. C. Golding (1943), "Comparisons of one hundred army psychiatric patients and one hundred enlisted men." *War. Med., 4,* 283-298.

Billingslea, F. Y. (1941), "The relationship between emotionality and various other salients of behavior in the rat." *J. Comp. Psychol., 31,* 69-77.

Binet, A. (1886), *La psychologie du raisonnement.*

———— (1891), *Les alterations de la personnalité.*

Birch, H. G. (1952), "Psychosurgery," in D. Brower and L. E. Abt, eds. (1952), *Progress in Clinical Psychology* (Vol. II, Sec. 1), pp. 312-323. New York: Grune & Stratton.

Bitterman, M. E., and W. H. Holtzman (1932), "Development of psychiatric screening of flying personnel. III. Conditioning and extinction of the galvanic skin response in relation to clinical evidence of anxiety." USAF, *Sch. Aviat. Med.,* Prog. No. 21-37-002, Rep. No. 3.

Blackwenn, W. J. (1930), "Production of sleep and rest in psychotic cases." *Arch. Neurol. and Psychiat., 24,* 365.

Blair, G. M. (1950), "Personality and social development." *Rev. educ. Res., 20,* 375-389.

Bleuler, E. (1924), *Textbook of Psychiatry.* New York: The Macmillan Company.

Bloch, H. A. (1952), *Disorganization: Personal and Social.* New York: Alfred A. Knopf, Inc.

Block, J., and Jeanne Block (1951), "An investigation of the relationship between intolerance of ambiguity and ethnocentrism." *J. Pers., 19,* 303-311.

Blueler, M. (1951), "The psychopathology of acromegaly." *J. nerv. ment. Dis., 113,* 497-511.

Bluhm, Hilde O. (1948), "How did they survive? Mechanisms of defense in Nazi Concentration Camps." *Amer. J. Psychother., 2,* 3-32.

Blum, G. S. (1953), *Psychoanalytic Theories of Personality.* New York: McGraw-Hill Book Company, Inc.

Boisen, A. T. (1936), *The Exploration of the Inner World.* Chicago: Willett, Clark & Company.

Bolles, M. (1937), "The basis of pertinence." *Arch. Psychol.,* No. 212.

―――, and D. Goldstein (1938), "A study of the impairment of 'abstract behavior' in schizophrenic patients." *Psychiat. Quart., 12,* 42-65.

Bond, E. D., and K. E. Appel (1931), *The Treatment of Behavior Disorders Following Encephalitis: An Experiment in Reeducation.* New York: The Commonwealth Fund.

Bonner, H. (1951), "The problem of diagnosis in paranoic disorders." *Amer. J. Psychiat., 107,* 677-683.

Böök, J. A., and S. C. Reed (1950), "Empiric risk figures in mongolism." *J. Amer. Med. Assn., 143,* 730-732.

Boring, E. G. (1933), *The Physical Dimensions of Consciousness.* New York: Appleton-Century-Crofts, Inc.

――― (1950), *A History of Experimental Psychology* (2nd Ed.). New York: Appleton-Century-Crofts, Inc.

Botwinick, J., and J. E. Birren (1951), "The measurement of intellectual decline in the senile psychoses." *J. consult. Psychol., 15,* 145-150.

Bowman, K. M., and E. M. Jellinek (1941), "Alcoholic mental disorders." *Quart. J. Studies of Alcohol, 2,* 312-390.

―――, and M. A. Rose (1952), "Criticism of the terms 'psychosis,' 'psychoneurosis' and 'neurosis.'" *Amer. J. Psychiat., 108,* 161-166.

Bradley, C. (1941), *Schizophrenia in Childhood.* New York: The Macmillan Company.

Bradley, J. H. (1952), *Patterns of Survival.* New York: Grune & Stratton.

Brayfield, A. H., ed. (1950), *Readings in Modern Methods of Counseling.* New York: Appleton-Century-Crofts, Inc.

Brecher, Sylvia (1946), "The value of diagnostic signs for schizophrenia on the Wechsler-Bellevue adult intelligence test." *Psychiat. Quart. Suppl., 20,* 58-64.

Bridgeman, P. W. (1938), *The Intelligent Individual and Society.* New York: The Macmillan Company.

Brill, N. Q., and G. W. Beebe (1951), "Follow-up study of psychoneuroses. preliminary report." *Amer. J. Psychiat., 108,* 417-425.

Brock, S. (1938), *The Basis of Clinical Neurology*. Baltimore: William Wood & Company.

Brogden, W. J. (1951), "Animal studies of learning," in S. S. Stevens, ed. (1951), *Handbook of Experimental Psychology*, pp. 568-612. New York: John Wiley & Sons, Inc.

Brower, D., and L. E. Abt, eds. (1952), *Progress in Clinical Psychology* (2 vols.). New York: Grune & Stratton.

Brown, G. G. (1952), "Culture, society and personality: a restatement." *Amer. J. Psychiat., 108*, 173-175.

Brown, J. F. (1940), *Psychodynamics of Abnormal Behavior*. New York: McGraw-Hill Book Company, Inc.

Brown, J. S., and I. E. Farber (1951), "Emotions conceptualized as intervening variables—with suggestions toward a theory of frustration." *Psychol. Bull., 48*, 465-495.

Brown, L. G. (1933), *Immigration, Cultural Conflicts and Social Adjustment*. New York: Longmans, Green & Company.

Brown, W. T., and C. I. Solomon (1942), "Delinquency and the electroencephalogram." *Amer. J. Psychiat., 98*, 499-503.

Browne, Hermina E. (1952), "The use of music as a therapy." *Ment. Hyg., 36*, 90-103.

Buhler, C. (1930), *The First Year of Life*. New York: The John Day Company, Inc.

Bunker, H. A. (1947), "Epilepsy: a brief historical sketch," in P. H. Hoch, and R. P. Knight, eds. (1947), *Epilepsy: Psychiatric Aspects of Convulsive Disorders*. New York: Grune & Stratton.

Burch, G. I., and E. Pendell (1947), *Human Breeding and Survival: Population Roads to Peace or War*. New York: Penguin Books Ltd.

Burgemeister, Bessie B., and Lucille H. Blum (1949), "Intellectual evaluation of a group of cerebral palsied children." *Nerv. Child, 8*, 177-180.

Burks, Barbara S. (1942), "A study of identical twins reared apart under different types of family relationship," in Q. McNemar and M. A. Merrill, eds. (1942), *Studies in Personality*. New York: McGraw-Hill Book Company, Inc.

——, and Anne Roe (1949), "Studies of identical twins raised apart." *Psychol. Monogr., 63*(5), Whole No. 300.

Burlingame, C. C. (1947), "If child guidance clinics—why not Parentoriums?" *Conn. Med. J., 11*, 829-832.

Burrow, T. (1937), *The Biology of Human Conflict*. New York: The Macmillan Company.

—— (1949), *The Neurosis of Man*. New York: Harcourt, Brace & Company, Inc.

Burton, A., and R. E. Harris (1947), *Case Histories in Clinical and Abnormal Psychology*. New York: Harper and Brothers.

Burtt, H. E. (1948), *Applied Psychology*. New York: Prentice-Hall, Inc.

Bustamante, J. A. (1951), "The use of insulin in small doses as a method to facilitate the action of psychotherapy in some psychoneurotic disorders." *Amer. J. Psychother.*, 5, 425-433.

Byrd, R. E. (1938), *Alone*. New York: G. P. Putnam's Sons.

Cameron, D. E. (1945), "Some relationships between excitement, depression, and anxiety." *Amer. J. Psychiat.*, 102, 385-394.

―― (1948), "Anxiety states." *Canad. med. assoc. J.*, 59, 307-310.

Cameron, N. (1938a), "A study of thinking in senile deterioration and schizophrenic disorganization." *Amer. J. Psychol.*, 51, 650-665.

―― (1938b), "Reasoning, regression, and communication in schizophrenics." *Psychol. Monog.*, 50, No. 1.

―― (1943), "The development of paranoiac thinking." *Psychol. Rev.*, 50, 219-233.

―― (1944), "The functional psychoses," in J. McV. Hunt, ed. (1944), *Personality and the Behavior Disorders* (2 vols.). New York: The Ronald Press Company.

―― (1947), *The Psychology of Behavior Disorders*. Boston: Houghton Mifflin Company.

―― (1950), "Role concepts in behavior pathology." *Amer. J. Sociol.*, 55, 464-467.

―― (1951), "Perceptual organization and behavior pathology," in R. R. Blake, and G. V. Ramsey, eds. (1951), *Perception, an Approach to Personality*. New York: The Ronald Press Company.

――, and Ann Magaret (1951), *Behavior Pathology*. Boston: Houghton Mifflin Company.

Campbell, J. D. (1950), "Mild manic depressive psychosis, depressive type: Psychiatric and clinical significance." *J. nerv. ment. Dis.*, 112, 206-236.

Campos, F. A. deM., W. B. Cannon, H. Lundin, and T. T. Walker (1929), "Some conditions affecting the capacity for prolonged muscular work." *Amer. J. Physiol.*, 87, 680-701.

Cannicott, R. G., and J. P. Umberger (1950), "An investigation of the psychoanalytic 'mechanism' of repression: The retention of verbal material associated with noxious stimulation." *Proc. Okla. Acad. Sci.*, 31, 176-178.

Cannon, W. B. (1932), *Wisdom of the Body*. New York: W. W. Norton & Company, Inc.

―― (1936), *Bodily Changes in Pain, Hunger, Fear, and Rage*. New York: Appleton-Century-Crofts, Inc.

――, H. Newton, E. M. Bright, V. Menkin, and R. M. Moore (1929), "Some aspects of the physiology of animals surviving complete exclusion of sympathetic nerve impulses." *Amer. J. Physiol.*, 89, 84-107.

Cantril, H. (1947), "The place of personality in social psychology." *J. Psychol., 24,* 19-56.

———, ed. (1950), *Tensions that Cause Wars.* Urbana, Ill.: University of Illinois Press.

Cares, R. M. (1951), "Juvenile amaurotic family idiocy: features suggestive of precocious senility." *Psychiat. Quart., 25,* 445-457.

Carmichael, L. (1927), "A further study of the development of behavior in vertebrates experimentally removed from the influence of external stimulation." *Psychol. Rev., 34,* 34-47.

——— (1954), "The onset and early development of behavior," in L. Carmichael, ed. (1954), *Manual of Child Psychology,* pp. 60-185. New York: John Wiley & Sons, Inc.

Carroll, H. A. (1951), *Mental Hygiene* (2nd Ed.). New York: Prentice-Hall, Inc.

Cattell, R. B. (1950a), *An Introduction to Personality Study.* New York: Longmans, Green and Company.

——— (1950b), *Personality: A Systematic Theoretical and Factual Study.* New York: McGraw-Hill Book Company, Inc.

Cherry-Garrard, A. (1930), *The Worst Journey in the World.* New York: Dial Press, Inc.

Child, C. M. (1924), *Physiological Foundations of Behavior.* New York: Henry Holt & Company, Inc.

Child, I. L., and W. H. Sheldon (1941), "The correlation between components of physique and scores on certain psychological tests." *Char. and Person., 10,* 23-24.

Clark, L. C., Jr. (1948), "The chemistry of human behavior." *Amer. J. Orthopsychiat., 18,* 140-152.

Cleckley, H. (1950), *The Mask of Sanity* (2nd Ed.). St. Louis, Mo.: C. V. Mosby Company.

Cleghorn, R. A. (1952), "The interaction of physiological and psychological processes in adaptation." *Psychiat. Quart., 26,* 1-20.

Cleugh, J. (1952), *The Marquis and the Chevalier.* New York: Duell, Sloan & Pearce.

Cobb, S. (1943), *Borderland of Psychiatry,* Cambridge: Harvard University Press.

——— (1944), "Personality as affected by lesions of the brain," in J. McV. Hunt, ed. (1944), *Personality and the Behavior Disorders* (2 vols.). New York: The Ronald Press Company.

——— (1950), *Emotions and Clinical Medicine.* New York: W. W. Norton & Company, Inc.

——— (1952), *Foundations of Neuropsychiatry* (Rev. Ed.). Baltimore: The William & Wilkins Company.

Coburn, C. A. (1922), "Heredity of wildness and savageness in mice." *Behav. Monog., 4,* 1-71.

Coghill, G. E. (1929), *Anatomy and the Problem of Behavior.* New York: The Macmillan Company.

Cohen, M. E., and P. D. White (1950), "Life situations, emotions, and neurocirculatory asthenia (anxiety neurosis, neurasthenia, effort syndrome)." *Res. Publ. Assn. nerv. ment. Dis., 29,* 832-869.

―――― and ―――― (1951), "Life situations, emotions, and neurocirculatory asthenia (anxiety neurosis, neurasthenia, effort syndrome)." *Psychosom. Med., 13,* 335-357.

Cohn, R. (1949), *Clinical Electroencephalography.* New York: McGraw-Hill Book Company, Inc.

Collier, R. M. (1953), "The case study of an hysterical fugue." *J. abnorm. soc. Psychol., 48,* 433-442.

Collins, A. Louise (1951), "Epileptic intelligence." *J. consult. Psychol., 15,* 392-399.

Cooke, E. D. (1946), *All but Me and Thee.* Washington: Infantry Journal Press.

Corner, G. W. (1944), *Ourselves Unborn, Natural History of the Human Embryo.* New Haven, Conn.: Yale University Press.

Cott, H. B. (1940), *Adaptive Coloration in Animals.* London: Cambridge University Press.

Cotton, H. (1921), *The Defective Delinquent and Insane: The Relation of Focal Infections to Their Causation, Treatment, and Prevention.* Princeton: Princeton University Press.

Crede, R. H., N. C. Chivers, and A. P. Shapiro (1951), "Electrocardiographic abnormalities associated with emotional disturbances." *Psychosom. Med. 13,* 277-288.

Crow, L. D., and Alice Crow (1951), *Mental Hygiene* (2nd Ed.). New York: McGraw-Hill Book Company, Inc.

Cruvant, B. A., and L. Yochelson (1950), "The psychiatrist and the psychotic psychopath; a study in interpersonal relations." *Amer. J. Psychiat., 106,* 594-598.

Cuber, J. F. (1947), *Sociology, A Synopsis of Principles.* New York: Appleton-Century-Crofts, Inc.

―――――, and R. A. Harper (1951), *Problems of American Society: Values in Conflict* (Rev. Ed.). New York: Henry Holt and Company, Inc.

Dahl, A. (1928), "Über den Einflus des Schlafens auf das Wiederkennen." *Psychol. Forsch., 11,* 290-301.

Dakin, E. (1930), *Mrs. Eddy, The Biography of a Virginal Mind.* New York: Charles Scribner's Sons.

Darkey, Margaret, and Elizabeth W. Amen (1947), "A continuation study of anxiety reactions in young children by means of a projective technique." *Genet. Psychol. Monogr.*, 35, 139-183.

Dattner, B. (1948), "Neurosyphilis and the latest methods of treatment." *Med. Clin. No. Am.*, New York Number, 707-719.

Davidson, Audrey, and Judith Fay (1953), *Phantasy in Childhood*. New York: Philosophical Library.

Davidson, M. (1937), "A study of schizophrenic performance on the Stanford-Binet Scale." *Brit. J. Med. Psychol.*, 17, 93-97.

Davies, R., and E. F. Gale, eds. (1953), *Adaptation in Micro-organisms*. New York: Cambridge University Press.

Davis, K. (1940), "Extreme social isolation of a child." *Amer. J. Sociol.*, 45, 554-565.

Dayton, N. A. (1940), *New Facts on Mental Disorder. Study of 89,190 Cases*. Springfield, Ill.: Charles C. Thomas, Publisher.

Deese, J. (1952), *The Psychology of Learning*. New York: McGraw-Hill Book Company, Inc.

Dempsey, E. W. (1951), "Homeostasis," in S. S. Steven, ed. (1951), *Handbook of Experimental Psychology*. New York: John Wiley & Sons, Inc.

Despert, J. Louise (1948), "Delusional and hallucinatory experience in children." *Amer. J. Psychiat.*, 104, 528-537.

Deutsch, A. (1938), *The Mentally Ill in America*. New York: Doubleday & Company, Inc.

Deutsch, Helene (1944), *The Psychology of Women*. New York: Grune & Stratton.

Dickinson, R. L., and L. Beam (1933), *The Single Woman*. Baltimore: The Williams & Wilkins Company.

Deithelm, O., and M. R. Jones (1947), "Influence of anxiety on attention, learning, retention and thinking." *Arch. Neurol. Psychiat. Chicago*, 58, 325-336.

Dockeray, F., and G. G. Lane (1950), *Psychology* (2nd Ed.). New York: Prentice-Hall, Inc.

Doll, E. A. (1946), "The feeble-minded child," in L. Carmichael, ed. (1946), *Manual of Child Psychology*. New York: John Wiley & Sons, Inc.

———, W. M. Phelps, and R. T. Melcher (1932), *Mental Deficiency Due to Birth Injuries*. New York: The Macmillan Company.

Dollard, J. (1937), *Caste and Class in a Southern Town*. New Haven, Conn.: Yale University Press.

———, L. Doob, N. Miller, O. Mowrer, and R. Sears (1939), *Frustration and Aggression*. New Haven, Conn.: Yale University Press.

────, and N. E. Miller (1950), *Personality and Psychotherapy*. New York: McGraw-Hill Book Company, Inc.

────, and O. H. Mowrer (1947), "A method for measuring tension in written documents." *J. abnorm. soc. Psychol.*, 42, 3-32.

Drachman, J. M. (1930), *Studies in the Literature of Natural Science*. New York: The Macmillan Company.

Drever, J. (1952), *A Dictionary of Psychology*. Baltimore: Penguin Books.

DuBois, C. (1937), "Some anthropological perspectives on psychoanalysis." *Psychoanal. Rev.*, 24, 246-263.

Dunbar, H. F. (1943), *Psychosomatic Diagnosis*. New York: Paul B. Hoeber, Inc.

──── (1947a), *Emotions and Bodily Changes* (3rd. Ed.). New York: Columbia University Press.

──── (1947b), *Mind and Body: Psychosomatic Medicine*. New York: Random House.

──── (1948), *Synopsis of Psychosomatic Diagnosis and Treatment*. St. Louis, Mo.: C. V. Mosby.

Dunham, H. W. (1937), "Ecology of the functional psychoses in Chicago." *Amer. Sociol. Rev.*, 2, 467-477.

Dunn, L. C. (1947), "The effects of isolates on the frequency of a rare human gene." *Proc. nat. Acad. Sci., Wash.*, 33, 359-363.

Du Nouy, P. L. (1937), *Biological Time*. New York: The Macmillan Company.

Dusser de Barenne, J. G., and Y. D. Koskoff (1932), "Flexor rigidity of the hind legs and priapism in the 'secondary' spinal preparation of the male cat." *Amer. J. Physiol.*, 102, 75-86.

Ebaugh, F. (1937), "Adolf Meyer, the Teacher." *Arch. Neurol. Psychiat., Chicago*, 37, 732-741.

Egan, J. R., L. Jackson, and R. H. Eanes. (1951), "A study of neuropsychiatric rejectees." *J. Amer. Med. Assn.*, 145, 466-469.

Egel, Paula F. (1948), *Technique of Treatment for the Cerebral Palsy Child*. St. Louis, Mo.: C. V. Mosby.

Eglash, A. (1952), "The dilemma of fear as a motivating force." *Psychol. Rev.*, 59, 376-379.

Eichler, R. M. (1951), "Experimental stress and alleged Rorschach indices of anxiety." *J. abnorm. soc. Psychol.*, 46, 344-355.

Eichorn, Dorothy H., and H. E. Jones (1952), "Development of mental functions." *Rev. educ. Res.*, 22, 421-438.

Eissler, K. R. (1950), "The Chicago Institute of Psychoanalysis and the sixth period of development of psychoanalytic technique." *J. gen. Psychol.*, 42, 103-157.

Ekman, G. (1951), "On typological and dimensional systems of reference in describing personality—studies in constitutional psychology." *Acta Psychol., 8,* 1-24.

Elizur, A. (1949), "Content analysis of the Rorschach with regard to anxiety and hostility." *Rorsch. Res. Exch., 13,* 247-284.

Elliot, Mabel A., and Francis E. Merrill (1950), *Social Disorganization* 3rd Ed.). New York: Harper and Brothers.

Ellis, H. (1942), *Studies in the Psychology of Sex* (Modern Library Edition). New York: Random House, Inc.

England, A. O. (1946), "Non-structured approach to the study of children's fears." *J. clin. Psychol., 2,* 364-368.

Engler, M. (1949), *Mongolism (Peristatic Amentia).* Baltimore: The Williams & Wilkins Company.

Erickson, M. A. (1938a), "A study of clinical and experimental findings on hypnotic deafness. I. Clinical experimentation and findings." *J. Gen. Psychol., 19,* 27-150.

—— (1938b), "A study of clinical and experimental findings on hypnotic deafness. II. Experimental findings with a conditioned response technique." *J. Gen. Psychol., 19,* 151-167.

—— (1939a), "An experimental investigation of the possible anti-social use of hypnosis." *Psychiatry, 2,* 391-414.

—— (1939b), "Experimental demonstrations of the psychopathology of everyday life." *Psychoanal. Quart., 8,* 338-353.

—— (1939c), "The induction of color blindness by a technique of hypnotic suggestion." *J. Gen. Psychol., 20,* 61-89.

Ernst, J. R. (1918), "Catatonic dementia praecox: Report of a case showing marked remission following appendicostomy with colonic irrigation." *Studies of Dementia Praecox, 1,* 27-29.

Escalona, Sibylle (1954), "The influence of topological and vector psychology upon current research in child development: an addendum," in L. C. Carmichael, ed. (1954), *Manual of Child Psychology* (2nd Ed.), pp. 971-983. New York: John Wiley & Sons, Inc.

Evans, B. (1946), *The Natural History of Nonsense.* New York: Alfred A. Knopf, Inc.

Eysenck, H. J. (1947), *Dimensions of Personality.* London: Kegan, Paul.

—— (1951), "The organization of personality." *J. Pers., 20,* 101-118.

—— (1952), *The Scientific Study of Personality.* New York: The Macmillan Company.

Fairweather, D. S. (1947), "Psychiatric aspects of the post-encephalitic syndrome." *J. ment. Sci., 93,* 201-254.

Farber, I. E., and K. W. Spence (1953), "Complex learning and conditioning as a function of anxiety." *J. exp. Psychol., 45,* 120-125.

Faris, R. E. L. (1948), *Social Disorganization.* New York: The Ronald Press Company.

———, and W. H. Dunham (1939), *Mental Disorders in Urban Areas.* Chicago: University of Chicago Press.

Fay, S. B. (1930), *The Origins of the World War.* New York: The Macmillan Company.

Fay, Temple (1950), "Cerebral palsy: Medical considerations and classification." *Amer. J. Psychiat., 107,* 180-183.

Federal Security Agency. (1952), Public Health Service. *Patients in Mental Institutions, 1949.* Washington: U. S. Government Printing Office.

Felix, R. H. (1953), Testimony given at Hearings before the Committee of Interstate and Foreign Commerce, pp. 1087. House of Representatives, Eighty-third Congress. Washington, D. C.: U. S. Government Printing Office.

———, and M. Kramer (1953), "Extent of the problem of mental disorders." *Annals of the American Academy of Political and Social Science, 286,* 5-14.

Fenichel, Otto (1945), *The Psychoanalytic Theory of Neurosis.* New York: W. W. Norton & Company, Inc.

Flugel, J. C. (1921), *The Psychoanalytic Study of the Family.* London: International Psychoanalytic Press.

Foder, N., and F. Gaynor, eds. (1950), *Freud: Dictionary of Psychoanalysis.* New York: Philosophical Library.

Ford, C. S., and F. A. Beach (1951), *Patterns of Sexual Behavior.* New York: Harper and Brothers.

Forster, F. M. (1953), Testimony given at Hearings before the Committee of Interstate and Foreign Commerce. House of Representatives. Eighty-third Congress. Washington: U. S. Government Printing Office.

François M. (1927), "Contribution à l'étude du sens du temp. La temperature interne, comme facteur de variation de l'appréciation subjective des durées." *Année psychol., 28,* 186-204.

Franklin, J. C., B. C. Schiele, J. Brozek, and A. Keys (1948), "Observations on human behavior in experimental semi-starvation and rehabilitation." *J. clin. Psychol., 4,* 28-44.

Frazer, J. G. (1917), *The Golden Bough* (3rd Ed.). London: The Macmillan Company.

Freed, H., E. Spiegel, and H. T. Wycis (1949), "Somatic procedures for the relief of anxiety: a review." *Psychiat. Quart., 23,* 227-235.

Freeman, M. J. (1953), "The development of a test for the measurement of anxiety: a study of its reliability and validity." *Psychol. Monogr., 67*(3), No. 353.

Freeman, T. (1952), "Some comments on views underlying the use of ether and carbon dioxide in psychotherapy." *Brit. J. med. Psychol.,* 25, 148-155.

Freeman, W., and J. W. Watts (1942), *Psychosurgery.* Springfield, Ill.: Charles C. Thomas, Publisher.

Fremont-Smith, F. (1934), "The influence of emotion in precipitating convulsions." *Amer. J. Psychiat.,* 13, 717.

Freud, Anna (1937), *The Ego and Mechanisms of Defense.* New York: Stechert & Company.

Freud, E. D. (1951), "Speech rehabilitation in a case of organic aphasis." *Case Rep. Clin. Psychol.,* 2(3), 23-25.

Freud, S. (1920), *A General Introduction to Psychoanalysis.* New York: Liveright Publishing Corporation.

——— (1924), *Collected Papers.* London: Hogarth Press, Ltd.

——— (1927), *The Ego and the Id.* London: Hogarth Press, Ltd.

——— (1928), *The Future of an Illusion.* London: Woolf.

——— (1930), *Civilization and Its Discontents.* London: Hogarth Press, Ltd.

——— (1933), *New Introductory Lectures on Psychoanalysis.* New York: W. W. Norton & Company, Inc.

——— (1938), "Psychopathology of everyday life," in A. A. Brill (trans.), *The Basic Writing of Sigmund Freud.* New York: Random House, Inc.

——— (1943), *A General Introduction to Psychoanalysis.* New York: Garden City Publishing Company.

——— (1949), *An Outline of Psychoanalysis* (trans. by James Strachey). New York: W. W. Norton & Company, Inc.

Frink, H. W. (1921), *Morbid Fears and Compulsions.* New York: Moffat, Yard & Company.

Fry, C. C. (1951), "A study of the rejection causes, success, and subsequent performance of special groups," in L. Carmichael, and L. C. Mind, eds. (1951), *The Selection of Military Manpower: A Symposium.* Washington, D. C.: Natural Academy Science—Natural Resources Council.

Fryer, D. H., and E. R. Henry, eds. (1950), *Handbook of Applied Psychology.* New York: Rinehart & Company, Inc.

Fulton, J. F. (1949), *Physiology of the Nervous System* (3rd Ed.). New York: Oxford University Press.

——— (1951), *Frontal Lobotomy and Affective Behavior.* New York: W. W. Norton & Company, Inc.

Futterman, S., and E. Pumpian-Mindin (1951), "Traumatic war neuroses five years later." *Amer J. Psychiat.,* 108, 401-408.

Galt, W. (1933), *Phyloanalysis. A Study in the Group or Phyletic Method of Behavior-Analysis.* London: Routledge & Kegan Paul, Ltd.

Galton, F. (1914), *Hereditary Genius.* New York: The Macmillan Company.

Garfield, S. L. (1949), "An evaluation of Wechsler-Bellevue patterns in schizophrenia." *J. consult. Psychol., 13,* 279-287.

Garlow, L., C. N. Zimet, and H. J. Fine (1952), "The validity of anxiety and hostility Rorschach content scores among adolescents." *J. consult. Psychol., 16,* 73-75.

Gaskell, W. H. (1921), *The Involuntary Nervous System.* New York: Longmans, Green & Company.

Gates, R. R. (1946), *Human Genetics.* New York: The Macmillan Company.

—— (1952), "Genetics and normal mental differences," in Milbank Memorial Fund Conference (1952), *The Biology of Mental Health and Disease,* pp. 277-282. New York: Paul B. Hoeber, Inc.

Gellhorn, E. (1950), in P. H. Hoch, and J. Zubin, eds. (1950), *Anxiety,* pp. 205-217. New York: Grune & Stratton.

—— (1953), *Physiological Foundations of Neurology and Psychiatry.* Minneapolis: The University of Minnesota Press.

Gesell, A. (1925), *The Mental Growth of the Pre-School Child.* New York: The Macmillan Company.

—— (1928), *Infancy and Human Growth.* New York: The Macmillan Company.

—— (1934), *Infant Behavior: Its Genesis and Growth.* New York: McGraw-Hill Book Company, Inc.

—— (1945), *The Embryology of Behavior.* New York: Harper and Brothers.

—— (1946), "The ontogenesis of infant behavior," in L. Carmichael, ed. (1946), *Manual of Child Psychology.* New York: John Wiley & Sons, Inc.

Gibbs, F. A., and E. L. Gibbs (1950), *Atlas of Electroencephalography. Vol. I. Methodology and Control* (2nd Ed.). Cambridge, Mass.: Addison-Wesley Press.

Gilbert, G. M. (1947), *Nuremberg Diary.* New York: Farrar, Straus and Company.

—— (1948), "Herman Goering, amiable psychopath." *J. abnorm. soc. Psychol., 43,* 211-229.

—— (1950), *The Psychology of Dictatorship.* New York: The Ronald Press Company.

Gill, M. M. (1948), "Spontaneous regression on the induction of hypnosis." *Bull. Menninger Clin., 12,* 41-48.

Gillespie, R. D. (1939), "Narcosis therapy." *J. Neurol. and Psychiat.*, 2, p. 45.

Gillin, J. L. (1946), *Social Pathology* (3rd Ed.). New York: Appleton-Century-Crofts, Inc.

Ginzberg, E., J. L. Herma, and S. W. Ginsburg, eds. (1953), *Psychiatry and Military Manpower Policy: A Reappraisal of the Experience in World War II*, New York: Kings Crown Press.

Gleser, G., and G. Ulett (1952), "The Saslow Screening Test as a measure of anxiety proneness." *J. clin. Psychol.* 8, 279-283.

Glixman, A. (1948), "An analysis of the use of the interruption-technique in experimental studies of 'repression.'" *Psychol. Bull.* 45, 491-506.

Glueck, B. C., Jr. (1946), "Pharmacological therapies in psychiatric practice," in B. Glueck, ed. (1946), *Current Therapies of Personality Disorders*. New York: Grune & Stratton.

Goddard, H. H. (1914), *Feeblemindedness: Its Causes and Its Consequences*. New York: The Macmillan Company.

———— (1919), *Psychology of the Normal and Sub-normal*. New York: Dodd, Mead & Company, Inc.

Goldschmidt, R. B. (1952), *Understanding Heredity*. New York: John Wiley & Sons, Inc.

Goldstein, K. (1924), "Das Wesen der amnestischen Aphasie." *Schweiz. Arch. Neurol. Psychiat.*, 15, 163-175.

———— (1939), *The Organism: A Holistic Approach to Biology Derived from Pathological Data in Man*. New York: American Book Company.

———— (1942), *Aftereffects of Brain Injuries in War*. New York: Grune & Stratton.

———— (1943), "On so-called war neuroses." *Psychomat. Med.*, 4, 376-383.

————, and M. Scheerer (1941), "Abstract and concrete behavior: An experimental study with special tests." *Psychol. Monog.*, 53, No. 2.

———— (1948), *Language and Language Disturbances*. New York: Grune & Stratton.

———— (1952), "The effect of brain damage on personality." *Psychiatry*, 15, 245-260.

Goodstein, L. D. (1951), "The language of schizophrenia," *J. gen. Psychol.*, 45, 95-104.

Gordon, H. L. (1948), "Fifty shock therapy theories." *Milit. Surg.*, 103, 397-401.

Gottschalk, L. A. (1948), "Bibliotherapy as an adjuvant in psychotherapy." *Amer. J. Psychiat.*, 104, 632-637.

Grace, W. J., S. Wolf, and H. G. Wolff (1951), *The Human Colon*. New York: Paul B. Hoeber, Inc.

Green, A. W. (1948), "Culture, normality and personality conflict. *"Amer. Anthrop., 50,* 225-237.

Green, M. D. (1944), "Proof of mental incompetency and the unexpressed major premise." *Yale Law Journal, 53,* 271-311.

Greenberg, Pearl (1951), "A case of pronounced fetishism." *Case Rep. clin. Psychol.* 2(3), 32-41.

Greenblatt, M., R. Arnot, and H. C. Solomon, eds. (1950), *Studies in Lobotomy.* New York: Grune & Stratton.

Griffith, Coleman R. (1943), *Principles of Systematic Psychology,* Urbana, Ill.: University of Illinois Press.

Grinker, R. R. (1943), *Neurology.* Springfield, Ill.: Charles C. Thomas, Publisher.

———, and J. P. Spiegel (1945a), *Men Under Stress.* Philadelphia: The Blakiston Company.

———, and ——— (1945b), *War Neuroses in North Africa.* Philadelphia: The Blakiston Company.

Gronich, L., and G. W. Pangle (1949), *Aphasia, A Guide to Retraining.* New York: Grune & Stratton.

Gurvitz, M. (1951), "Developments in the concept of psychopathic personality." *Brit. J. Delinquency, 2,* 88-102.

Guthrie, E. R. (1938), *The Psychology of Human Conflict.* New York: Harper and Brothers.

——— (1944), "Personality in terms of associative learning," in J. McV. Hunt, ed. (1944), *Personality and the Behavior Disorders* (2 vols.). New York: The Ronald Press Company.

——— (1952), *The Psychology of Learning* (Rev. Ed.). New York: Harper and Brothers.

Guthrie, L. V. (1918), "Condensed notes on history of fifteen cases of dementia praecox treated by isotonic salt solution, administered intravenously or by hypodermoclysis." *Studies in Dementia Praecox, 1,* 61-72.

Haldane, J. B. S. (1948), "The formal genetics of man." *Proc. roy. Soc., Sec. B., 135,* 147-170.

Hall, C. S. (1938), "The inheritance of emotionality." *Sigma Xi Quarterly, 26,* 17-27.

——— (1951a), "Individual differences," in C. P. Stone, ed. (1951), *Comparative Psychology* (3rd Ed.), pp. 363-387. New York: Prentice-Hall, Inc.

——— (1951b), "The genetics of behavior," in S. S. Stevens, ed. (1951), *Handbook of Experimental Psychology,* pp. 304-329. New York: John Wiley & Sons, Inc.

Hall, K. R. L., and T. G. Crookes (1952), "Studies in learning impairment. II. Psychoneurotic patients." *J. ment. Sci.*, 98, 273-279.

Hallowell, A. I. (1936), "Psychic stress and culture patterns." *Amer. J. Psychiat.*, 92, 1291-1310.

———— (1938), "Fear and anxiety as cultural and individual variables in a primitive society." *J. soc. Psychol. 9*, 25-47.

Halstead, W. C. (1947), *Brain and Intelligence: A Quantitive Study of the Frontal Lobes*. Chicago: University of Chicago Press.

———— (1951), "Biological intelligence." *J. Pers.*, 20, 118-130.

Hambling, J. (1951), 'Emotions and symptoms in essential hypertension." *Brit. J. Med. Psychol.*, 24, 242-253.

———— (1952), "Psychosomatic aspects of arterial hypertension." *Brit. J. Med. Psychol.*, 25, 39-47.

Hamilton, J. A., and W. D. Ellis (1933a), "Behavior constancy in rats." *J. genet. Psychol.*, 42, 120-139.

————, and I. Krechevsky (1933b), "Studies in the effect of shock on behavior platicity in the rat." *J. Comp. Psych.*, 16, 237-253.

Hammond, K. R. (1948), *Social Effects on Psychiatric Hospitalization*. Unpublished Ph.D. Thesis, University of California, Berkeley.

Hampton, P. J. (1947), "A descriptive portrait of the drinker. III. The psychotic drinker." *J. soc. Psychol.*, 25, 101-117.

Hanfmann, E. (1950), "Psychological approaches to the study of anxiety," in P. H. Hoch and J. Zubin, eds. (1950), *Anxiety*, pp. 51-69. New York: Grune & Stratton.

Hanson, F. B., and Z. Cooper (1930), "The effects of ten generations of alcoholic ancestry upon learning ability in the albino rat." *J. Exper. Zool.*, 56, 369-392.

Hanson, G. C. (1950), "The normal and abnormal in behavior," in W. H. Mikesell, ed. (1950), *Modern Abnormal Psychology*, pp. 3-21. New York: Philosophical Library.

Hare, E. H. (1952), "The ecology of mental disease. A dissertation of the influence of environmental factors in the distribution, development and variation of mental disease." *J. Ment. Sci.*, 98, 579-594.

Harms, E. (1941), "Child art as aid in the diagnosis of juvenile neuroses." *Amer. J. Orthopsychiat.*, 11, 191-209.

Harriman, P. L. (1947), *The New Dictionary of Psychology*. New York: Philosophical Library.

Harris, I. D. (1951), "Characterological significances of the typical anxiety dreams." *Psychiatry*, 14, 279-294.

Harris, J. (1948), "Observations concerning typical anxiety dreams." *Psychiatry*, 11, 301-309.

Harris, N. G. (1948), "The importance of constitutional factors," in N. G. Harris, ed. (1948), *Modern Trends in Psychological Medicine,* pp. 51-68. New York: Paul B. Hoeber, Inc.

Harrison, F. M. (1950), "Personality, physique and disease." *Delaware St. Med. J.,* 22, 191-195.

Harsh, C. M., and H. G. Schrickel (1950), *Personality: Development and Assessment.* New York: The Ronald Press Company.

Hart, B. (1931), *The Psychology of Insanity.* New York: The Macmillan Company.

Hart, H. H. (1948), "Sublimation and aggression." *Psychiat. Quart.,* 22, 389-412.

Hartmann, G. (1935), *Gestalt Psychology: A Survey of Facts and Principles.* New York: The Ronald Press Company.

Hasting, D. W., D. G. Wright, and B. C. Glueck (1944a), *Psychiatric Experiences of the Eighth Air Force.* New York: Josiah Macy, Jr., Foundation.

———, ———, and ——— (1944b), "Sodium amytal narcosis in treatment of operational fatigue in combat aircrews." *War. Med.,* 5, 368.

Hawley, A. H. (1950), *Human Ecology.* New York: The Ronald Press Company.

Hayakawa, S. I. (1941), *Language in Action.* New York: Harcourt, Brace & Company, Inc.

Head, H. (1920), *Studies in Neurology* (2 vols). London: Oxford University Press.

——— (1926), *Aphasia and Kindred Disorders of Speech.* New York: The Macmillan Company.

Healy, W. (1915), *The Individual Delinquent.* Boston: Little, Brown & Company.

———, A. F. Bronner, and A. M. Bowers (1930), *The Structure and Meaning of Psychoanalysis.* New York: Alfred A. Knopf, Inc.

Heath, R. G., Chm. (1954), *Studies in Schizophrenia.* Cambridge, Mass.: Harvard University Press.

Hebb, D. O. (1949), *The Organization of Behavior.* New York: John Wiley & Sons, Inc.

——— (1951), "The place of neurological ideas in psychology." *J. Pers.,* 20, 39-55.

Heinicke, C., and Beatrice B. Whiting, comp. (1953), "Bibliography on personality and social development of the child, and selected ethnographic sources on child training." *Soc. Sci. Res. Coun. Pamph.,* No. 10.

Heiser, K. F. (1952), "Applications of clinical psychology of mental deficiency," in D. Brower, and L. E. Abt, eds. (1952), *Progress in Clinical Psychology* (Vol. 1, Sec. 2), pp. 450-458. New York: Grune & Stratton.

Henderson, D. K. (1939), *Psychopathic States*. New York: W. W. Norton & Company, Inc.

———, and R. D. Gillespie (1940), *A Textbook of Psychiatry*. London: Oxford University Press.

Hendrick, Ives (1947), *Facts and Theories of Psychoanalysis* (2nd Ed.). New York: Alfred A. Knopf, Inc.

Henry, G. W. (1948), *Sex Variants: A Study of Homosexual Patterns*. New York: Paul B. Hoeber, Inc.

Herrick, C. J. (1924), *Neurological Foundations of Animal Behavior*. New York: Henry Holt & Company, Inc.

Heyer, A. W., Jr. (1949), " 'Scatter Analysis' techniques applied to anxiety neurotics from a restricted culture—educational environment." *J. Gen. Psychol., 40,* 155-166.

Higginson, G. D. (1950), "Legal and scientific concepts of mental illness," in W. H. Mikesell, ed. (1950), *Modern Abnormal Psychology,* pp. 261-318. New York: Philosophical Library.

Hilgard, E. R. (1939), "Social psychology and public policy," in G. W. Hartmann, and I. Newcomb, eds., *Industrial Conflict: A Psychological Interpretation*. New York: The Cordon Company, Inc.

——— (1948), *Theories of Learning*. New York: Appleton-Century-Crofts, Inc.

——— (1949), "Human motives and the concept of the self." *Amer. Psychol., 4,* 374-382.

——— (1951), "Methods and procedures in the study of learning," in S. S. Stevens, ed. (1951), *Handbook of Experimental Psychology,* pp. 517-567. New York: John Wiley & Sons, Inc.

———, and D. M. Marquis (1940), *Conditioning and Learning*. New York: Appleton-Century-Crofts, Inc.

———, L. V. Jones, and S. J. Kaplan (1951), "Conditioned discrimination as related to anxiety." *J. exp. Psychol., 42,* 94-99.

Hill, D. (1952), "EEG in episodic psychotic and psychopathic behavior." *EEG clin. Neurophysiol., 4,* 419-422.

———, and G. Parr, eds. (1950), *Electroencephalography: A Symposium on Its Various Aspects*. London: Macdonald.

Himler, L. E. (1951), "Psychiatric aspects of aging." *J. Amer. Med. Assn., 147,* 1330-1331.

Himwich, H. E. (1952), "Effect of shock therapies on the brain." in Milbank Memorial Fund Conference (1952), *The Biology of Mental Health and Disease, pp.* 548-567. New York: Paul B. Hoeber, Inc.

Hingston, R. W. G. (1933), *The Meaning of Animal Color and Adornment*. London: Cambridge University Press.

Hitler, A. (1939), *Mein Kampf*. New York: Reynal & Hitchcock.

Hoagland, H. (1933), "The physiological control of judgments of duration: Evidence for a chemical clock." *J. gen. Psychol., 9,* 267-287.

Hoch, P. H. (1950), "Biosocial aspects of anxiety," in P. H. Hoch, and J. Zubin, eds. (1950), *Anxiety*, pp. 105-118. New York: Grune & Stratton.

—— (1951), "Experimentally produced psychoses." *Amer. J. Psychiat.*, 107, 607-611.

—— (1952a), "Experimental induction of psychoses," in Milbank Memorial Fund Conference (1952), *The Biology of Mental Health and Disease*, pp. 539-547. New York: Paul B. Hoeber, Inc.

—— (1952b), "Psychosomatic problems: methodology, research material and concepts." *Psychoanal. Rev.*, 39, 213-221.

——, and R. P. Knight, eds. (1947), *Epilepsy; Psychiatric Aspects of Convulsive Disorders*. New York: Grune & Stratton.

——, and J. Zubin, eds. (1950), *Anxiety*. New York: Grune & Stratton.

——, J. P. Cattell, and H. H. Pennes (1952a), "Effects of drugs; theoretical considerations from a psychological viewpoint." *Amer. J. Psychiat.*, 108, 585-589.

——, J. P. Cattell, and H. H. Pennes. (1952b), "Effects of mescaline and lysergic acid (d-LSD-25)." *Amer. J. Psychiat.*, 108, 579-584.

Hoerr, N. L., A. Osol, *et al.*, eds. (1952), *Blakiston's Illustrated Pocket Medical Dictionary*. New York: The Blakiston Company.

Hollingworth, H. L. (1920), *The Psychology of Functional Neuroses*. New York: Appleton-Century-Crofts, Inc.

—— (1930), *Abnormal Psychology*. New York: The Ronald Press Company.

Holloman, L. L. (1943), "On the supremacy of the Negro athlete in white athletic competition." *Psychoanal. Rev.*, 30, 157-162.

Holt, E. G. (1931), *Animal Drive and the Learning Process*. New York: Henry Holt & Company, Inc.

Holtzman, W. H., and M. E. Bitterman (1952), "Psychiatric screening of flying personnel. VI. Anxiety and reactions to stress." USAF, *Sch. Aviat. Med.*, Proj. Rep. No. 21-37-002, Rep. No. 6.

Holzberg, J. D., and J. R. Wittenborn (1953), "The quantified multiple diagnostic procedure in psychiatric classification." *J. clin. Psychol.*, 9, 145-148.

Horney, Karen (1935), "Culture and neurosis," *Amer. Sociol. Rev.*, 1, 221-230.

—— (1937), *The Neurotic Personality of Our Time*. New York: W. W. Norton & Company, Inc.

—— (1939), *New Ways in Psychoanalysis*. New York: W. W. Norton & Company, Inc.

—— (1942), *Self-Analysis*. New York: W. W. Norton & Company, Inc.

—— (1945), *Our Inner Conflicts: A Constructive Theory of Neurosis*. New York: W. W. Norton & Company, Inc.

—— (1950), *Neurosis and Human Growth*. New York: W. W. Norton & Company, Inc.

Horsley, J. S. (1936), "Pentothal sodium in mental hospital practice." *Brit. J. Med., 1,* 938.

Hoskins, R. G. (1946), *The Biology of Schizophrenia*. New York: W. W. Norton & Company, Inc.

—— (1950), *Endocrinology* (Rev. Ed.). New York: W. W. Norton & Company, Inc.

——, and F. H. Sleeper (1929), "A case of hebephrenic dementia praecox with marked improvement under thyroid treatment." *Endocrinology, 13,* 245-262.

Hovland, C. I. (1951), "Human learning and retention," in S. S. Stevens, ed. (1951), *Handbooks of Experimental Psychology*. New York: John Wiley & Sons, Inc.

——, and R. R. Sears (1940), "Minor studies of aggression. VI. Correlation of lynchings with economic indices." *J. Psychol., 9,* 301-310.

Howells, T. H. (1940), *Hunger of Wholeness*. Denver: World Press, Inc.

—— (1945), "The obsolete dogmas of heredity." *Psychol. Rev., 52,* 23-24.

Huddleson, J. H. (1932), *Accidents, Neurosis and Compensation*. Baltimore: The Williams & Wilkins Company.

Hulett, J. E., Jr., and R. Stagner, eds. (1951), *Problems in Social Psychology*. Urbana, Ill.: University of Illinois Press.

Hull, C. L. (1943), *Principle of Behavior*. New York: Appleton-Century-Crofts, Inc.

—— (1951), *Essentials of Behavior*. New Haven: Yale University Press.

—— (1952), *A Behavior System*. New Haven: Yale University Press.

Hunt, H. F., A. Carp, W. A. Cass, Jr., C. L. Winder, and R. E. Kantor, (1948), "A study of the differential diagnostic efficiency of the Minnesota Multiphasic Personality Inventory." *J. consult. Psychol., 12,* 331-336.

Hunt, J. McV. (1941), "The effect of infant feeding-frustration upon adult hoarding in the albino rat." *J. abnorm. soc. Psychol., 36,* 338-360.

——, ed. (1944), *Personality and the Behavior Disorders*. New York: The Ronald Press Company.

——, and C. N. Cofer (1944), "Psychological deficit," in J. McV. Hunt, ed. (1944), *Personality and the Behavior Disorders*, pp. 971-1032. New York: The Ronald Press Company.

——, H. Schlosberg, R. L. Soloman, and E. Stellar (1947), "Studies of the effects of infantile experience on adult behavior in rats. I. Effects of infantile feeding-frustration on adult hoarding." *J. Comp. Physiol. Psychol., 40,* 291-304.

Hunt, W. A., and C. L. Wittson (1948), "Some sources of error in the neuropsychiatric statistics of World War II." *J. clin. Psychol.*, 5, 350-358.

——, ——, and E. B. Hunt (1952), "Military performance of a group of marginal neuropsychiatric cases." *Amer. J. Psychiat.*, 109, 168-171.

Hunter, W. S. (1947), "Summary comments on the heredity-environment symposium." *Psychol. Rev.*, 54, 348-352.

Huntington, E. (1924), *Civilization and Climate* (3rd Ed.). New Haven: Yale University Press.

Hurst, L. A. (1951), "Genetics of schizophrenia: reply to Pastore." *Psychol. Bull.*, 48, 402-412.

—— (1952), "Research in genetics and psychiatry: New York State Psychiatric Institute." *Eugen. News*, 37, 86-91.

Huxley, A. (1932), *Brave New World*. New York: Doubleday & Company, Inc.

—— (1954), *The Doors of Perception*. New York: Harper and Brothers.

Huxley, J. S. (1932), *Problems of Relative Growth*. New York: Dial Press, Inc.

—— (1943), *Evolution, The Modern Synthesis*. New York: Harper and Brothers.

—— (1953), *Evolution in Action*. New York: Harper and Brothers.

Ingalls, T. H. (1947), "Pathogenesis of mongolism." *Amer. J. Dis. Child*, 73, 279-292.

—— (1952), "Mongolism." *Scientific Amer.*, 186(2), 60-66.

Jackman, A. J., and C. A. Scharr (1952), "Evaluation of carbon dioxide therapy of the neuroses." *J. clin. exper. Psychopath.* 13, 17-30.

Jackson, J. H. (1931), *Selected Writings of John Hughlings Jackson. Vol. I. On Epilepsy and Epileptiform Convulsions* (Edited by James Taylor). London: Hodder & Stoughton, Ltd.

Jacobi, J. (1943), *The Psychology of Jung*. New Haven: Yale University Press.

Jameison, G., and J. Wall (1932), "Mental reactions at the climacterium." *Amer. J. Psychiat.*, 88, 895-909.

James, W. (1890), *The Principles of Psychology* (2 vols.). New York: Henry Holt & Company, Inc.

Janet, P. (1920), *The Major Symptoms of Hysteria*. New York: The Macmillan Company.

—— (1924), *Principles of Psychotherapy*. New York: The Macmillan Company.

—— (1926), *Psychological Healing*. London: George Allen & Unwin, Ltd.

Jasper, H. H., P. Solomon, and C. Bradley (1938), "Electro-encephalographic analyses of behavior problem children." *Amer. J. Psychiat.*, 95, 641-658.

Jastrow, J. (1940), *Freud, His Dream and Sex Theories*. Cleveland: The World Publishing Company.

Jellinek, E. M. (1942), *Alcohol Addiction and Chronic Alcoholism*. New Haven, Conn.: Yale University Press.

Jenkins, J. G., and K. M. Dallenbach (1924), "Oblivescence during sleep and waking." *Amer. J. Psychol.*, 35, 605-612.

Jennings, H. S. (1930), *The Biological Basis of Human Nature*. New York: W. W. Norton & Company, Inc.

Jersild, A. T. (1954), *Child Psychology* (4th Ed.). New York: Prentice-Hall, Inc.

———— (1948), "Children's fears." *J. Nat. educ. Assn.* 37, 212-213.

Jessner, L., and V. G. Ryan (1941), *Shock Treatment in Psychiatry*. New York: Grune & Stratton.

Johnson, W. (1946), *People in Quandaries: The Semantics of Personal Adjustment*. New York: Harper and Brothers.

Josephy, H. (1949), "The brain in cerebral palsy. A neuropathological review." *Nerv. Child*, 8, 152-169.

———— (1953), "Pick's disease." *Arch. Neurol. Psychiat., Chicago*, 69, 637-638.

Kahn, E. (1931), *Psychopathic Personalities*. New Haven, Conn.: Yale University Press.

Kalinowsky, L. B. (1950), "Problems of war neuroses in the light of experience in other countries." *Amer. J. Psychiat.*, 107, 340-346.

Kallmann, F. J. (1938), *The Genetics of Schizophrenia*. New York: J. J. Augustin.

———— (1946), "The genetic theory of schizophrenia: an analysis of 691 schizophrenic twin index families." *Amer. J. Psychiat.*, 103, 309-322.

———— (1950), "The genetics of psychoses: analysis of 1,232 twin index families." *Amer. J. Hum. Genet.*, 2, 385-390.

Kanman, G. R. (1930), "Schizophrenic reaction following influenza." *J. Amer. Med. Assn.* 94, 1286-1288.

Kantor, J. R. (1947), *Problems of Physiological Psychology*. Bloomington, Indiana: The Principia Press, Inc.

Kaplan, O. S. (1945), *Mental Disorders in Later Life*. Stanford University, Calif.: Stanford University Press.

Kardiner, A. (1935), "A role of economic security in the adaptation of the individual." *The Family*, 187-197.

———— (1939), *The Individual and His Society*. New York: Columbia University Press.

—— (1941), *The Traumatic Neuroses of War.* New York: Paul B. Hoeber Inc.

——, and Associates (1945), *The Psychological Frontiers of Society.* New York: Columbia University Press.

Karpman, B. (1948), "The myth of the psychopathic personality.' *Amer. J. Psychiat., 104,* 523-534.

——, chm. (1950), "The psychopathic delinquent child. Round table, 1949." *Amer. J. Orthopsychiat., 20,* 223-265.

——, chm., *et al.* (1951), "Psychopathic behavior in infants and children: a critical survey of the existing concepts. Round table." *Amer. J. Orthopsychiat., 21,* 223-272.

——, L. W. Sontag, R. D. Robinovitch, H. S. Lippman, and R. S. Laurie (1952), "A differential study of psychopathic behavior in infants and children. Round table, 1951." *Amer. J. Orthopsychiat., 22,* 223-267.

Kasanin, J. S., ed. (1944), *Language and Thought in Schizophrenia.* Berkeley, Calif.: University of California Press.

Kates, S. L. (1950), "Objective Rorschach response patterns differentiating anxiety reactions from obsessive-compulsive reactions." *J. consult. Psychol., 14,* 226-229.

Kempf, E. (1918), *The Autonomic Functions and the Personality.* Washington, D. C.: Nervous and Mental Disease Publishing Company.

Kendig, L., and W. Richmond (1940), *Psychological Studies in Dementia Praecox.* Ann Arbor, Mich.: Edwards Brothers, Inc.

Keys, A., J. Brozek, A. Henshel, O. Mickelson, and H. L. Taylor; assisted by E. Simonson, A. S. Skinner, and S. M. Wells (1950), *The Biology of Human Starvation* (2 vols.). Minneapolis, Minnesota: University of Minnesota Press.

Kinsey, A. C., W. B. Pomeroy, and C. E. Martin (1947), *Sexual Behavior in the Human Male.* Philadelphia: W. B. Saunders Company.

——, ——, ——, and P. H. Gebhard, *et al.* (1953), *Sexual Behavior in the Human Female.* Philadelphia: W. B. Saunders Company.

Kircher, Clara (1945), *Character Formation Through Books: A Bibliography* (2nd Ed.). Washington, D. C.: Catholic University of America Press.

Klaesi, J. (1922), "Über die Therapeutische anwendung der 'Davernarkose' mittles somnifens bei schizophrenen." *Zeitschrif. f. d. ges. Neurol. u. Psychiat., 74,* 557.

Klee, J. B. (1944), "The relation of frustration and motivation to the production of abnormal fixations in the rat." *Psychol. Monc g., 56,* 1-45.

Klein, G. S., and D. Krech (1951), "The problem of personality and its theory." *J. Pers., 20,* 2-23.

Kleitman, N., F. J. Mullins, N. R. Cooperman, and S. Titelbaum (1937), *Sleep Characteristics*. Chicago: University of Chicago Press.

Kluckhohn, C., (1949), "The limitations of adaptation and adjustment as concepts for understanding cultural behavior," in J. Romano, ed. *Adaptation*, pp. 96-113. Ithaca, N. Y.: Cornell University Press.

Koch, S. (1951), "The current status of motivational psychology." *Psychol. Rev.*, 58, 147-154.

Koffka, K. (1924), *The Growth of the Mind*. New York: Harcourt, Brace & Company, Inc.

—— (1935), *Principles of Gestalt Psychology*. New York: Harcourt, Brace & Company, Inc.

Köhler, W. (1925), *The Mentality of Apes*. New York: Harcourt, Brace & Company, Inc.

—— (1929), *Gestalt Psychology*. New York: Liveright Publishing Corporation.

—— (1938), *The Place of Values in a World of Facts*. New York: Liveright Publishing Corporation.

—— (1940), *Dynamics in Psychology*. New York: Liveright Publishing Corporation.

Koontz, A. R. (1948), "Psychiatry in the next war: Shall we again waste manpower?" *Milit. Surg.*, 103, 197-202.

Kopeloff, N., and G. H. Kirby (1923), "Focal infection and mental disease." *Amer. J. Psychiat.*, 3, 149-192.

Korzybski A. (1941), *Science and Sanity*. Lancaster, Pa., and New York: The International Non-Artistotelian Library Publishing Company; The Science Press Printing Company, distributors.

Kotkov, B. (1947), *A Bibliography for the Student of Group Therapy*. Boston: Veterans Administration, Boston Regional Office.

—— (1950), "A bibliography for the student of group therapy." *J. clin. Psychol.*, 6, 77-91.

Krafft-Ebing, R. (von) (1904), *Psychopathia Sexualis*. New York: Rebman.

Kraepelin, E. (1919), *Dementia Praecox*. Edinburgh: E. & S. Livingstone, Ltd.

Krasner, L. (1953), "Personality differences between patients classified as psychosomatic and as nonpsychosomatic." *J. abnorm. soc. Psychol.*, 48, 190-198.

Krech, D., and G. S. Klein (1952), *Theoretical Models and Personality Theory*. Durham, N. C.: Duke University Press.

Kreezer, G. L. (1949), "The derivation of the transfer functions of homeostatic systems from experimental response curves." *J. Psychol.*, 28, 487-493.

Kretschmer, E. (1925), *Physique and Character*. New York: Harcourt, Brace & Company, Inc.

Kubie, L. S. (1949), "The neurotic potential and human adaptation," in J. Romano, ed. (1949), *Adaptation*, pp. 77-96. Ithaca, N. Y.: Cornell University Press.

Landis, C. (1951), "Psychological observations on psychosurgery patients." *Psychiat. Quart.*, 25, 409-417.

——, and M. Bolles (1946), *Textbook of Abnormal Psychology*. New York: The Macmillan Company.

——, and W. A. Hunt (1939), *The Startle Pattern*. New York: Rinehart & Company, Inc.

——, T. Forbes, L. Mays, P. Dubois, W. Shipley, and Z. Piotrowski (1934), "Studies of catatonia." *Psychiat. Quart.*, 8, 535-552, 722-744.

Langley, J. N. (1921), *The Autonomic Nervous System*. Cambridge, England: W. Heffer & Sons, Ltd.

Lashley, K., ed. (1932), *Studies in the Dynamics of Behavior*. Chicago: University of Chicago Press.

—— (1947), "Structural variation in the nervous system in relation to behavior." *Psychol. Rev.*, 54, 325-334.

Lasswell, H. D. (1930), *Psychopathology and Politics*. Chicago: University of Chicago Press.

Lazarus, R. S., J. Deese, and Sonia F. Osler (1952), "The effects of psychological stress upon performance." *Psychol. Bull.*, 49, 293-317.

Lee, I. J. (1941), *Language Habits in Human Affairs*. New York: Harper and Brothers.

Leeper, R. (1935), "The role of motivation in learning." *Ped. Sem.*, 46, 3-40.

—— (1943), *Lewin's Topological and Vector Psychology*. Eugene, Oregon: University of Oregon Press.

Leese, Stephanie M., D. A. Pond, and J. Shields (1952), "A pedigree of Huntington's chorea." *Ann. Eugen., Camb.*, 17, 92-112.

Lemert, E. M. (1951), *Social Pathology*. New York: McGraw-Hill Book Company, Inc.

Lennox, W. G. (1941), *Science and Seizures*. New York: Harper and Brothers.

—— (1947), "The genetics of epilepsy." *Amer. J. Psychiat.*, 103, 457-462.

——, E. L. Gibbs, and F. A. Gibbs (1939), "Inheritance of epilepsy as revealed by the electroencephalograph." *J. Amer. Med. Assn.*, 113, 1002-1003.

—— (1951), "The heredity of epilepsy as told by relatives and twins." *J. Amer. Med. Assn.*, 146, 529-536.

Leonard, W. E. (1927), *The Locomotive God.* New York: Appleton-Century-Crofts, Inc.

Leutenegger, R. R. (1951), "A bibliography on aphasia." *J. Speech Hearing Dis., 16,* 280-292.

Levin, M. (1948), "Bromide psychoses: four varieties." *Amer. J. Psychiat. 104,* 798-800.

—— (1950), "The frequency of drug psychoses." *Amer. J. Psychiat., 107,* 128-130.

Levin, S. (1952), "Epileptic clouded states." *J. nerv. ment. Dis., 116,* 215-225.

Levine, M. (1942), *Psychotherapy in Medical Practice.* New York: The Macmillan Company.

Levinson, D. J. (1949), "An approach to the theory and measurement of ethnocentric ideology." *J. Psychol., 28,* 19-39.

Levy, D. M. (1928), "Fingersucking and accessory movements in early infancy: An etiologic study." *Amer. J. Psychiat., 7,* 881-918.

—— (1934), "Experiments of the sucking reflex and social behavior of dogs." *Amer. J. Orthopsychiat., 4,* 203-224.

—— (1937), "Primary affect hunger." *Amer. J. Psychiat., 96,* 643-652.

—— (1939), "Release therapy." *Amer. J. Orthopsychiat., 9,* 713-736.

Levy, J., and Ruth Monroe (1938), *The Happy Family.* (Reprinted, 1948) New York: Alfred A. Knopf, Inc.

Lewin, K. (1935), *A Dynamic Theory of Personality.* New York: McGraw-Hill Book Company, Inc.

—— (1936), *Principles of Topological Psychology.* New York: McGraw-Hill Book Company, Inc.

—— (1938), "The conceptual representation and the measurement of psychological forces." *Cont. Psychol. Theor., 1,* No. 4, 1-266.

—— (1946), "Behavior and development as a function of the total situation," in L. Carmichael, ed. (1946), *Manual of Child Psychology.* New York: John Wiley & Sons, Inc.

—— (1948), *Resolving Social Conflicts.* New York: Harper and Brothers.

—— (1951), *Field Theory in Social Science* (Edited by Dorwin Cartwright). New York: Harper and Brothers.

Lewis, N. D. C. (1936), *Research in Dementia Praecox.* New York: National Committee for Mental Hygiene.

—— (1949), "Criteria for early differential diagnosis of psychoneurosis and schizophrenia." *Amer. J. Psychother., 3,* 4-18.

Lictenberg, P. (1949), "Sublimation." *Persona, 1*(2), 2-9.

Liddell, H. S. (1936), "Nervous strain in domesticated animals and man." *Cornell Veterinarian, 26,* 107-112.

—— (1949), "Adaptation of the threshold of intelligence," in J. Romano, ed. (1949), *Adaptation,* pp. 53-76. Ithaca, N. Y.: Cornell University.

—— (1950), "Animal origins of anxiety," in M. S. Reymert, ed. (1950), *Feelings and emotions: The Mooseheart Symposium.* New York: McGraw-Hill Book Company, Inc.

—— (1952), "Anxiety and other feelings." *Trans. N. Y. Acad. Sci., 14,* 276-278.

Lief, A. (1948), *The Commonsense Psychiatry of Dr. Adolf Meyer.* New York: McGraw-Hill Book Company, Inc.

Lindesmith, A., and A. Strauss (1950), "A critique of culture-personality writings." *Amer. sociol. Rev., 15,* 587-600.

Lindner, R. M. (1944), *Rebel Without a Cause: The Hypnoanalysis of a Criminal Psychopath.* New York: Grune & Stratton.

—— (1946), "An evaluation of Hypnoanalysis," in B. Glueck, ed. (1946), *Current Therapies of Personality Disorders.* New York: Grune & Stratton.

Lindsley, D. B. (1944), "Electroencephalography," in J. McV. Hunt, ed. (1944), *Personality and the Behavior Disorders* (2 vols.). New York: The Ronald Press Company.

—— (1951), "Emotion," in S. S. Stevens, ed. (1951), *Handbook of Experimental Psychology,* pp. 473-516. New York: John Wiley & Sons, Inc.

——, and K. K. Cutts (1940), "The electroencephalograms of 'constitutionally inferior' and behavior problem children: comparison with normal children and adults." *Arch. Neurol. & Psychiat., Chicago, 44,* 1199-1212.

——, and —— (1941), "Clinical and electroencephalographic changes in a child during recovery from encephalitis." *Arch. Neurol. & Psychiat., Chicago, 45,* 156-161.

Linton, R. (1938), "Culture, society and the individual." *J. abnorm. soc. Psychol., 33,* 425-436.

—— (1945), *The Cultural Background of Personality.* New York: Appleton-Century-Crofts, Inc.

Lippitt, R. (1940), "Studies in topological and vector psychology. I. An experimental study of the effect of democratic and authoritarian group atmospheres." *Univ. Iowa Stud. Child Welfare, 16,* No. 3, 45-195.

Lippmann, W. (1922), *Public Opinion.* New York: The Macmillan Company. Reprinted as P-1, Pelican Books, New York, 1946.

Lipton, E. L. (1950), "The amytal interview; a review." *Amer. Practit. & Dig. Treatmt. 1,* 148-163.

Lisansky, Edith S. (1948), "Convulsive disorder and personality." *J. abnorm. soc. Psychol., 43,* 29-37.

Liss, E. (1944), "Examination anxiety." *Amer. J. Orthopsychiat.*, *14*, 345-349.

Loeb, J. (1913), *Artificial Parthenogenesis and Fertilization*. Chicago: University of Chicago Press.

———— (1918), *Forced Movements, Tropisms and Animal Conduct*. Philadelphia: J. B. Lippincott Company.

Loevenhart, A. S., W. F. Lorenz, and R. M. Waters (1929), "Cerebral stimulation." *J. Amer. Med. Assn.*, *92*, 880-883.

Lorenz, Maria, and S. Cobb (1953), "Language behavior in psychoneurotic patients." *Arch. Neurol. Psychiat., Chicago, 69*, 684-694.

Lorenz, W. F. (1952), "Use of carbon dioxide in dementia praecox," in Milbank Memorial Fund Conference (1952), *The Biology of Mental Health and Disease*, pp. 568-581. New York: Paul H. Hoeber, Inc.

Lorr, M. (1954), "Rating scales and check lists for the evaluation of psychopathology." *Psychol. Bull., 51*, 119-127.

Louttit, C. M. (1947), *Clinical Psychology of Children's Behavior Problems*. New York: Harper and Brothers.

Lowenbach, H., and R. B. Suitt (1950), "Alterations of anxiety subsequent to physical treatment of psychiatric disorders, with observations for insulin sub-shock, electroshock, and neurosurgical procedures," in P. H. Hoch and J. Zubin, eds. (1950), *Anxiety*, pp. 218-242. New York: Grune & Stratton.

Lubin, A. (1950), "A note on Sheldon's table of correlations between temperamental traits." *Brit. J. Psychol. Statist. Sect., 3*, 186-189.

Lucas, J. D. (1952), "The interactive effects of anxiety, failure, and intraserial duplication." *Amer. J. Psychol., 65*, 59-66.

Luria, A. R. (1932), *The Nature of Human Conflicts* (Trans. by W. H. Gantt.). New York: Liveright Publishing Corporation.

Lynd, R. S. (1939), *Knowledge for What? The Place of Social Science in American Culture*. Princeton, N. J.: Princeton University Press.

Mace, N. C., S. A. Koff, J. Chelnek, and S. L. Garfield (1949), "Diagnostic problems in early schizophrenia." *J. nerv. ment. Dis., 110*, 336-346.

MacCurdy, J. I. (1918), *The War Neuroses and Shell Shock*. Cambridge, England: Cambridge University Press.

MacKinnon, D. W. (1953), "Fact and fancy in personality research." *Amer. Psychol., 8*, 138-145.

MacKinnon, Jane (1947), "The homosexual woman." *Amer. J. Psychiat., 103*, 661-664.

Maier, N. R. F. (1939), *Studies of Abnormal Behavior in the Rat*. New York: Harper and Brothers.

────── (1949), *Frustration, the Study of Behavior Without a Goal.* New York: McGraw-Hill Book Company, Inc.

──────, and T. C. Schneirla (1935), *Principles of Animal Psychology.* New York: McGraw-Hill Book Company, Inc.

Malmo, R. B., C. Shagass, and J. F. Davis (1947), "Pain as standardized stimulus for eliciting differential psychological responses in anxiety." *Amer. Psychol.,* 2, 344.

────── (1950), "Experimental studies of mental patients under stress," in M. S. Reymert, ed. (1950), *Feelings and Emotions: The Mooseheart Symposium,* pp. 169-180. New York: McGraw-Hill Book Company, Inc.

────── and A. Amsel (1948), "Anxiety-produced interference in serial rote learning with observations on rote learning after partial frontal lobotomy." *J. exp. Psychol.,* 38, 440-454.

──────, and C. Shagass (1949), "Physiologic studies of reaction to stress in anxiety and early schizophrenia." *Psychosom. Med.,* 11, 9-24.

Malzberg, B. (1943), "The outcome of electric shock therapy in the New York Civil State Hospitals." *Psychiat. Quart.,* 17, 154-163.

────── (1946), "Public Health aspects of insulin and other shock therapies," in B. Glueck, ed. (1946), *Current Therapies of Personality Disorders.* New York: Grune & Stratton.

────── (1948), "A statistical study of first admissions with involutional psychoses to hospitals for mental disease in New York state." *Psychiat. Quart. Suppl.,* 22, 141-155.

────── (1949), "A statistical study of psychoses due to drugs or other exogenous poisons." *Amer. J. Psychiat.,* 106, 99-106.

────── (1950), "Some statistical aspects of mongolism." *Amer. J. ment. Def.,* 54, 266-281.

Manus, G. I. (1949), "The behaviorial correlates of essential hypertension: a critical review of the literature." *J. intercollegiate Psychol. Assn.,* 1, 36-50.

Margetts, E. L. (1953), "The concept of the unconscious in the history of medical psychology." *Psychiat. Quart.,* 27, 115-138.

Marshall, C., E. A. Walter, and S. Livingston (1953), "Photogenic epilepsy: parameters of activation." *Arch. Neurol. Psychiat., Chicago,* 69, 760-765.

Martin, R. F. (1936), *An Attempt as the Experimental Demonstration of Regression in Hypotheses in Rats.* Unpublished M. A. thesis, University of Oregon (1936).

────── (1940), "Native traits and regression in rats." *J. Comp. Psychol.,* 30, 1-16.

————, and C. S. Hall (1941), "Emotional behavior in the rat. V. The incidence of behavior derangements resulting from air-blast stimulation in emotional and non-emotional strains of rats." *J. Comp. Psychol., 32*, 191-204.

Martin, R. T. (1952), "The notion of normality." *Aust. J. Psychol., 4*, 28-39.

Martin, W. E., and Celia B. Stendler (1953), *Child Development: The Process of Growing Up in Society.* New York: Harcourt, Brace & Company, Inc.

Marx, M. H. (1950), A stimulus-response analysis of the hoarding habit." *Psychol. Rev., 57*, 80-93.

———— (1951), *Psychological Theory.* New York: The Macmillan Company.

Maslow, A. H. (1937), "Personality and culture patterns," in R. Stagner (1937), *Psychology of Personality.* New York: McGraw-Hill Book Company, Inc.

————, ed. (1951), "American culture and personality." *J. Soc. Issues.* 7(4), 44 pages.

Masserman, J. H. (1946), *Principles of Dynamic Psychiatry.* Philadelphia: W. B. Saunders Company.

Maudsley, M. (1887), *Responsibility in Mental Disease.* New York: D. Appleton-Century Company.

Maughs, S. (1941), "A conception of the psychopathic personality." *J. Crim. Psychopath., 2*, 329-356.

———— (1949), "Psychopathic personality: A review of the literature, 1940-1947." *J. clin. Psychopath., 10*, 247-275.

May, R. (1950), *The Meaning of Anxiety.* New York: The Ronald Press Company.

———— (1950a), "Historical roots in modern anxiety theories," in P. H. Hoch, and J. Zubin, eds. (1950), *Anxiety,* pp. 3-16. New York: Grune & Stratton.

———— (1950b), "Toward an understanding of anxiety." *Pastoral. Psychol., 1*(2), 25-31.

May, P. R. A., and F. G. Ebaugh (1953), "Pathological intoxication, alcoholic hallucinosis, and other reactions to alcohol; A clinical study." *Quart. J. Stud. Alcohol., 14*, 200-227.

McClelland, D. C. (1951), *Personality.* New York: William Sloane Associates.

McCord, F (1941), "The effect of frustration on hoarding in rats." *J. Comp. Psychol., 32*, 531-541.

McDonald, W. (1915), "Mental disease and language." *J. Nerv. Ment Dis., 42*, 482-540.

McFarland, R. A. (1946), *Human Factors in Air Transport Design*. New York: McGraw-Hill Book Company, Inc.

McGill, V. J., and L. Welch (1947), "Hysteria as a conditioning process." *Amer. J. Psychother., 1,* 253-278.

McGeoch, J. A., and A. L. Irion (1952), *The Psychology of Human Learning* (2nd Ed.). New York: Longsman, Green & Company.

McKelvey, R. K., and M. H. Marx (1951), "Effects of infantile food and water deprivation on adult hoarding in the rat." *J. comp. physiol. Psychol., 44,* 423-430.

McLaughlin, J. T. (1950), "Normality and psychosomatic illness." *Ment. Hyg.* 34, 19-33.

McNemar, Q. (1940), "A critical examination of the University of Iowa studies of environmental influences upon the I. Q." *Psychol. Bull., 37,* 63-92.

Mead, G. H. (1934), *Mind, Self and Society*. Chicago: University of Chicago Press.

Mead, Margaret (1928), *Coming of Age in Samoa*. New York: William Morrow & Company.

—— (1935), *Sex and Temperament in Three Primitive Societies*. New York: William Morrow & Company.

—— (1937), *Competition and Cooperation Among Primitive Peoples*. New York: McGraw-Hill Book Company, Inc.

—— (1947), "The implications of cultural change for personality development." *Amer. J. Orthopsychiat., 17,* 633-646.

Meduna, L. (1935), "Die Konvulsiontherapie der Schizophrenie." *Psychiat. neurol. Wchnschr., 37,* 317.

—— (1950), *Carbon Dioxide Therapy*. Springfield, Ill.: Charles C. Thomas & Company, Publisher.

Meltzer, H. (1930), "The present status of experimental studies on the relationship of feeling to memory." *Psychol. Rev., 37,* 124-139.

Menninger, K. (1925), "Influenza and schizophrenia." *Amer. J. Psychiat., 5,* 469-529.

—— (1937), *The Human Mind* (2nd Ed.). New York: Alfred A. Knopf, Inc.

—— (1938), *Man Against Himself*. New York: Harcourt, Brace & Company, Inc.

——, and P. E. Kubitschilk (1930), "Amelioration of schizophrenia following dysentery." *J. Nerv. and Ment. Dis., 72,* 535-537.

Menninger, W. C. (1947), "Psychiatric experience in the war, "1941-1946." *Amer. J. Psychiat., 103,* 577-586.

—— (1949), "Emotional factors in organic disease." *Ann. Intern. Med., 31,* 207-215.

————, and L. Chidester (1933), "The role of financial loss in the precipitation of mental illness." *J. Amer. Med. Assn., 100,* 1398-1400.

Mettler, F. A., ed. (1949), *Selective Partial Ablation of the Frontal Cortex.* New York: Paul B. Hoeber, Inc.

————, ed. (1952), *Psychosurgical Problems.* Philadelphia: Blakiston.

Meyer, A. (1904), "The anatomical facts and clinical varieties of traumatic psychoses." *Amer. J. Insan. 60,* 373-441.

———— (1911), *Dementia Praecox.* Boston: Richard G. Badger.

———— (1948), *Collected Writings.* New York: McGraw-Hill Book Company, Inc.

———— (1950), *The Collected Papers of Adolf Meyer. Vol. I. Neurology* (Eunice E. Winters, ed.). Baltimore: Johns Hopkins Press.

———— (1951a), *The Collected Papers of Adolf Meyer. Vol. II. Psychiatry* (Eunice E. Winters, ed.). Baltimore: Johns Hopkins Press.

———— (1951b), *The Collected Papers of Adolf Meyer. Vol. III. Medical Teaching* (Eunice E. Winters, ed.). Baltimore: Johns Hopkins Press.

———— (1952), *The Collected Papers of Adolf Meyer. Vol. IV. Mental Hygiene* (Eunice E. Winters, ed.). Baltimore: Johns Hopkins Press.

Mikesell, W. H., ed. (1950), *Modern Abnormal Psychology.* New York: Philosophical Library.

Milbank Memorial Fund Conference (1952), *The Biology of Mental Health and Disease.* New York: Paul B. Hoeber, Inc.

Miles, H. H. W., S. Cobb, and H. C. Shands, eds. (1952), *Case Histories in Psychosomatic Medicine.* New York: W. W. Norton & Company.

Miller, G. A. (1951), *Language and Communication.* New York: McGraw-Hill Book Company, Inc.

Miller, J. G. (1942), *Unconsciousness.* New York: John Wiley & Sons, Inc.

———— (1950), "The experimental study of unconscious processes," in M. L. Reymert, ed. (1950), *Feelings and Emotions: The Mooseheart Symposium,* pp. 261-267. New York: McGraw-Hill Book Company, Inc.

Miller, N. E. (1941), "An experimental investigation of acquired drives." *Psychol. Bull., 38,* 534.

———— (1944), "Experimental studies of conflict," in J. McV. Hunt, ed. (1944) *Personality and the Behavior Disorders* (2 vols.). New York: The Ronald Press Company.

———— (1951a), "Comments on theoretical models. Illustrated by the development of a theory of conflict behavior." *J. Pers., 20,* 82-100.

———— (1951b), "Learnable drives and rewards," in S. S. Stevens, ed. (1951), *Handbook of Experimental Psychology,* pp. 435-472. New York: John Wiley & Sons, Inc.

—— (1952), "Comment of theoretical models: Illustrated by the development of a theory of conflict behavior," in G. S. Klein and D. Krech, eds. (1952), *Theoretical Models and Personality Theory,* pp. 82-100. Durham, N. C.: Duke University Press.

——, and W. R. Miles (1936), "Alcohol and removal of reward." *J. Comp. Psychol., 21,* 179-204.

——, and J. Dollard (1941), *Social Learning and Imitation.* New Haven: Yale University Press.

Miller, W. C. (1919), "Treatment of dementia praecox by intravenous injections of NaCl, together with studies of the Cl content of the blood." *Studies in Dementia Praecox, 2,* 147-149.

Milligan, W. L. (1951), "Treatment of psychoneurosis: modified CO_2 abreactive technique." *Brit. Med. J.,* No. 4720, 1426-1428.

Millis, W. (1931), *The Martial Spirit.* New York: Literary Guild of America.

Mock, J. R., and C. Larsens (1939), *Words that Won the War.* Princeton: Princeton University Press.

Moldawsky, S., and Patricia C. Moldawsky (1952), "Digit span as an anxiety indicator." *J. consult. Psychol., 16,* 115-118.

Money, J. (1948), "Delusion, belief, and fact." *Psychiatry, 11,* 33-38.

Montagu, M. F. A. (1945), *Man's Most Dangerous Myth: The Fallacy of Race* (2nd Ed.). New York: Columbia University Press.

Montague, E. R. (1953), "The role of anxiety in serial rote learning." *J. exp. Psychol., 45,* 91-96.

Moore, J. C. (1946), *Penicillin in Syphilis.* Springfield, Ill.: Charles C. Thomas, Publisher.

Moore, T. V. (1946), "Bibliotherapy in psychiatric practice," in B. Glueck, ed. (1946), *Current Therapies of Personality Disorders.* New York: Grune & Stratton.

—— (1951), *The Nature of Treatment of Mental Disorders* (2nd Ed.). New York: Grune & Stratton.

Morel, B. A. (1860), *Trate des Maladies Mentales.* Paris: Victor Mosson.

Moreno, J. D. (1944), "A case of paranoia treated through psychodrama." *Sociometry, 7,* 312-327.

Morgan, C. T. (1947), "The hoarding instinct." *Psychol. Rev., 54,* 335-341.

——, E. Stellar, and O. Johnson (1943), "Food-deprivation and hoarding in rats." *J. comp. Psychol., 35,* 275-295.

——, and E. Stellar (1950), *Physiological Psychology* (2nd Ed.). New York: McGraw-Hill Book Company, Inc.

Morgan, J. J. B., and G. D. Lovell (1948), *The Psychology of Abnormal People* (3rd Ed.). New York: Longmans, Green and Company.

Moriarty, J. D. (1952), "Carbon dioxide inhalation therapy of neuroses." *J. clin. exp. Psychopath., 13,* 181-194.

Morlan, G. K. (1948), "The statistical concept of normal: a criticism." *J. gen. Psychol., 38,* 51-56.

Mosse, E. P. (1940), "Painting-analysis in the treatment of neuroses." *Psychoanal. Rev., 27,* 68-82.

Moustakas, C. E. (1953), *Children in Play Therapy.* New York: McGraw-Hill Book Company, Inc.

Mowrer, O. H. (1939), "A stimulus-response analysis of anxiety and its role as a reinforcing agent." *Psychol. Rev., 46,* 553-565.

———— (1940), "An experimental analogue of 'Regression' with incidental observations on 'Reaction-Formation.' " *J. abnorm. soc. Psychol., 35,* 56-87.

———— (1948), "Learning theory and the neurotic paradox." *Amer. J. Orthopsychiat., 18,* 571-610.

———— (1954), "What is normal behavior?" in L. A. Pennington and I. A. Berg, eds. (1954), *An Introduction to Clinical Psychology* (2nd Ed.), pp. 58-88. New York: The Ronald Press.

———— (1950a), *Learning Theory and Personality Dynamics.* New York: The Ronald Press Company.

———— (1950b), "Pain, punishment, guilt, and anxiety," in P. H. Hoch and J. Zubin, eds. (1950), *Anxiety,* pp. 27-40. New York: Grune & Stratton.

———— (1952a), "Learning theory." *Rev. Educ. Res., 22,* 475-495.

———— (1952b), "Neurosis and its treatment as learning phenomena," in D. Brower and L. E. Abt, eds. (1952), *Progress in Clinical Psychology* (Vol. I, Sec. 1), pp. 312-323. New York: Grune & Stratton.

———— (1952c), "Symposium, 1952. The therapeutic process. III. Learning theory and the neurotic fallacy." *Amer. J. Orthopsychiat., 22,* 679-689.

———— (1953), *Psychotherapy, Theory and Research.* New York: The Ronald Press Company.

————, and C. Kluckhohn (1944), "Dynamic theory of personality," in J. McV. Hunt, ed. (1944), *Personality and the Behavior Disorders* (2 vols.). New York: The Ronald Press Company.

————, J. McV. Hunt, and L. S. Kogan (1953), "Further studies utilizing the discomfort-relief quotient," in O. H. Mowrer (1953), *Psychotherapy Theory and Research,* pp. 257-295. New York: The Ronald Press Company.

Muenzinger, K. (1942), *Psychology, The Science of Behavior.* New York: Harper and Brothers.

Mumford, L. (1934), *Technics and Civilization.* New York: Harcourt, Brace & Company, Inc.

—— (1938), *The Culture of Cities.* New York: Harcourt, Brace & Company, Inc.

—— (1944), *The Condition of Man.* New York: Harcourt, Brace & Company, Inc.

Muncie, W. (1948), *Psychobiology and Psychiatry.* St. Louis, Mo.: The C. V. Mosby Company.

Munn, N. L. (1950), *Handbook of Psychological Research on the Rat.* Boston: Houghton Mifflin Company.

Murdock, G. P. (1949), "The science of human learning, society, culture, and personality." *Sci. Mon., N. Y., 69,* 377-381.

Murphy, G. (1929), *An Historical Introduction to Modern Psychology.* New York: Harcourt, Brace & Company, Inc.

—— (1933), *Approaches to Personality.* New York: Coward-McCann, Inc.

—— (1947), *Personality, A Biosocial Approach to Origins and Structures.* New York: Harper and Brothers.

Murphy, Lois, B. (1944), "Childhood experience in relation to personality development," in J. McV. Hunt, ed. (1944), *Personality and the Behavior Disorders* (2 vols.). New York: The Ronald Press Company.

Myers, H. J., and S. Von Koch (1945), "Reactive depressions: a study of 100 consecutive cases." *War Med., Chicago, 8,* 358-364.

Myerson, A. (1925), *The Inheritance of Mental Diseases.* Baltimore: The Williams & Wilkins Company.

Nardini, J. E. (1952), "Survival factors in American prisoners of war of the Japanese." *Amer. J. Psychiat., 109,* 241-248.

Neal, Josephine, *et. al.* (1942), *Encephalitis: A Clinical Study.* New York: Grune & Stratton.

Needham, J. (1931), *Chemical Embryology.* Cambridge, England: Cambridge University Press.

Neilsen, J. M., and C. B. Courville (1951), "Role of birth injury and asphyxia in idiopathic epilepsy." *Neurology, 1,* 48-52.

Neumann, Meta A., and R. Cohn (1953), "Incidence of Alzheimer's disease in a large mental hospital: relation of senile psychosis and psychosis with cerebral arteriosclerosis." *Arch. Neurol. Psychiat., Chicago, 69,* 615-636.

Newman, H. H., F. N. Freeman, and K. J. Holzinger (1937), *Twins: A Study of Heredity and Environment.* Chicago: University of Chicago Press.

Newton, R. D. (1948), "The identity of Alzheimer's disease and senile dementia and their relationship to senility." *J. ment. Sci., 94,* 225-249.

Nichtenhauser, A., Marie L. Coleman, and D. S. Ruhe (1953), *Films in Psychiatry, Psychology, and Mental Health.* New York: Health Education Council.

O'Connor, Patricia (1952), "Ethnocentrism, 'intolerance of ambiguity,' and abstract reasoning ability." *J. abnorm. soc. Psychol.,* 47, 526-530.

Oedegaard, O. (1952), "The incidence of mental diseases as measured by census investigation versus admissions statistics." *Psychiat. Quart.,* 26, 212-218.

Oestlyngen, E. (1949), "Possibilities and limitation of twin research as a means of solving problems of heredity and environment." *Acta Psychol.,* 6, 59-90.

Ogilvie, R. S. (1949), *Handbook of Electroencephalography.* Cambridge, Mass.: Addison-Wesley Press.

O'Kelly, L. I. (1940a), "An experimental study of regression. I. Behavioral characteristics of the regressive response." *J. Comp. Psychol.,* 30, 41-53.

——— (1940b), "An experimental study of regression. II. Some motivational determinants of regression and perseveration." *J. Comp. Psychol.,* 30, 55-95.

——— (1940c), "The validity of defecation as a measure of emotionality in the rat." *J. Gen. Psychol.,* 23, 75-87.

——— (1953), "Physiological changes during psychotherapy," in O. H. Mowrer, ed. (1953), *Psychotherapy, Theory and Research,* pp. 641-656. New York: The Ronald Press Company.

———, and W. C. Biel (1940), "The effect of cortical lesions on emotional and regressive behavior in the rat. II. Regressive behavior." *J. Comp. Psychol.,* 30, 241-254.

———, and L. C. Steckle (1940), "The forgetting of pleasant and unpleasant experiences." *Amer. J. Psychol.,* 53, 432-434.

Oliver, C. P. (1950), "Mongolism: multiple occurrence in siblings." *Eugen. News,* 35, 35-39.

Orlansky, H. (1949), "Infant care and personality." *Psychol. Bull.,* 46, 1-48.

Ort, R. S. (1952), "A study of role-conflicts as related to class level." *J. abnorm. soc. Psychol.,* 47, 425-432.

Orwell, G. (1951), *1984.* New York: New American Library.

Osborne, S. L., and H. J. Holmquist (1944), *Technique of Electro-Therapy.* Springfield, Ill.: Charles C. Thomas, Publisher.

Osgood, C. E. (1953), *Method and Theory in Experimental Psychology.* New York: Oxford University Press.

————, and T. A. Sebeok, eds. (1954), *Psycholinguistics: A Survey of theory and research problems.* Supplement to *J. abnorm. soc. Psychol., 49,* No. 4, Part 2.

Pacella, B. L. (1949), "Varieties of electric shock therapy." *J. nerv. ment. Dis., 109,* 396-404.

Palmer, H. D., and F. J. Braceland (1937), "Six years' experience with narcosis therapy in psychiatry." *Amer. J. Psychiat., 94,* 37-52.

————, D. Hastings, and S. Sherman (1941), "Therapy in involutional melancholia." *Amer. J. Psychiat., 97,* 1086-1115.

Pastore, N. (1949a), *The Nature-Nurture Controversy.* New York: King's Crown Press.

———— (1949b), "The genetics of schizophrenia." *Psychol. Bull., 46,* 285-302.

———— (1952), "Genetics of schizophrenia: a rejoinder. *Psychol. Bull., 49,* 542-544.

Patrick, J. R. (1934a), "Studies in rational behavior and emotional excitement. I. Rational behavior in human subjects." *J. Comp. Psychol., 18,* 1-22.

———— (1934b), "Studies in rational behavior and emotional excitement. II. The effect of emotional excitement on rational behavior in human subjects." *J. Comp. Psychol., 18,* 153-195.

Pearl, R. (1940), *Introduction to Medical Biometry and Statistics* (3rd Ed.). Philadelphia: W. B. Saunders Company.

Pearse, A. S. (1947), *Animal Ecology.* New York: McGraw-Hill Book Company, Inc.

Penfield, W., and T. C. Erickson (1941), *Epilepsy and Cerebral Localization.* Springfield, Ill.: Charles C. Thomas, Publisher.

———— (1948), "Classification of the epilepsies." *Arch. Neurol. Psychiat.,* Chicago, *60,* 107-118.

————, and K. Kristiansen (1951), *Epileptic Seizure Patterns: A Study of the Localizing Value of Initial Phenomena in Focal Cortical Seizures.* Springfield, Ill.: Charles C. Thomas, Publisher.

————, and H. Jasper (1954), *Epilepsy and the Functional Anatomy of the Human Brain.* Boston: Little, Brown.

Pennington, L. A. and I. Berg, eds. (1954), *An Introduction to Clinical Psychology* (2nd Ed.). New York: The Ronald Press Company.

Penrose, L. S. (1944), "Heredity," in J. McV. Hunt, ed. (1944), *Personality and the Behavior Disorders* (2 vols.). New York: The Ronald Press Company.

———— (1949), *The Biology of Mental Defect.* New York: Grune & Stratton.

Persons, S., ed. (1950), *Evolutionary Thought in America.* New Haven, Conn.: Yale University Press.

Phelps, W. M. (1949), "Description and differentiation of types of cerebral palsy." *Nerv. Child.*, *8,* 107-127.

Phillips, J. (1912), "Note on wildness in ducklings." *Anim. Behav.*, *2,* 363-364.

Piaget, J. (1923), "La pensée symbolique et la pensée de l'enfant." *Arch. Psychol., Genève., 18,* 273-304.

Pincus, G. (1936), *The Eggs of Mammals.* New York: The Macmillan Company.

Pintner, R. (1931), *Intelligence Testing: Methods and Results.* New York: Henry Holt & Company, Inc.

Piotrowski, Z. (1937), "The Rorschach inkblot method of organic disturbances of the central nervous system." *J. nerv. ment. Dis., 86, 525-537.*

—— (1947), "The personality of the epileptic," in P. H. Hoch and R. P. Knight, eds. (1947), *Epilepsy: Psychiatric Aspects of Convulsive Disorders.* New York: Grune & Stratton.

Plant, J. (1937), *Personality and the Cultural Pattern.* New York: The Commonwealth Fund.

Pohl, J. F. (1950), *Cerebral Palsy.* St. Paul, Minn.: Bruce Publishing Company.

Polatin, P., P. H. Hoch, W. A. Horwitz, and L. Raizin (1948), "Presenile psychosis: Report of two cases with brain biopsy studies." *Amer. J. Psychiat., 105,* 97-101.

Pollock, H. M. (1939), "A statistical study of 1140 dementia praecox patients treated with metrazol." *Psychiat. Quart., 13,* 558-568.

—— (1945), "A statistical review of mental disorders in later life," in O. S. Kaplan (1945), *Mental Disorders in Later Life,* pp. 7-23. Stanford University. Calif.: Stanford University Press.

Porter, J. H., F. A. Webster, and J. C. R. Licklider (1951), "The influence of age and food deprivation upon the hoarding behavior of rats." *J. comp. physiol. Psychol., 44,* 300-309.

Porteus, S. D., and G. R. Corbett (1953), "Statuatory definitions of feebleminded in U. S. A." *J. Psychol., 35,* 81-105.

Powdermaker, Florence B., and J. D. Frank, *et al.* (1953), *Group Psychotherapy.* Cambridge, Mass.: Harvard University Press.

Prescott, D. A. (1938), *Emotion and the Educative Process.* Washington, D. C.: American Council on Education.

Preu, P. W. (1944), "The concept of psychopathic personality," in J. McV. Hunt, ed. (1944), *Personality and the Behavior Disorders* (2 vols.). New York: The Ronald Press Company.

Prince, M. (1906) *The Dissociation of a Personality,* New York: Long-mans, Green & Company, Inc.

—— (1938), *Clinical and Experimental Studies in Personality* (2nd Ed.). (A. A. Roback, ed.) Cambridge, Mass.: Sci-Art Publishers.

Prothro, E. T. (1952), "Ethnocentrism and anti-Negro attitudes in the deep south." *J. abnorm. soc. Psychol., 47,* 105-108.

Puner, Helen W. (1947), *Freud: His Life and His Mind.* New York: Howell, Soskin, Publishers, Inc.

Purcell, Clarie K., J. Drevdahl, and K. Purcell (1952), "The relationship between attitude I. Q. discrepancy and anxiety." *J. clin. Psychol., 8,* 82-85.

Purtell, J. J., E. Robins, and M. E. Cohen (1951), "Observations on clinical aspects of hysteria." *J. Amer. med. Assn., 146,* 902-909.

Putnam, T. J. (1949), "The neurology and neurosurgery of cerebral palsies and related disorder." *Nerv. child., 8,* 170-176.

Queen, S. A. (1949), "Social participation in relation to social disorganiza-tion." *Amer. sociol. Rev., 14,* 251-257.

Quinn, J. A. (1950), *Human Ecology.* New York: Prentice-Hall, Inc.

Rado, S. (1952), "On the psychoanalytic exploration of fear and other emotions." *Trans. N. Y. Acad. Sci., 14,* 280-283.

Raginsky, B. B. (1948), "Psychosomatic medicine: its history, development and teaching." *Amer. J. Med., 5,* 857-878.

Raines, G. N., and L. C. Kolb (1943), "Combat fatigue and war neurosis." *U. S. Nav. Med. Bull., 41,* Part I, pp. 923-936; Part II, pp. 1299-1309.

Ramsey, G. V., and F. A. Mettler (1951), "Some psychological changes following psychosurgery." *J. abnorm. soc. Psychol., 46,* 548-556.

Rank, O. (1929), *The Trauma of Birth.* New York: Harcourt, Brace & Company, Inc.

Ranson, S. W., H. Kabot, and H. W. Magoun (1934), "Autonomic re-sponses obtained by electric stimulation of the hypothalamus prioptic region and septum." *Arch. Neurol. Psychiat., Chicago, 33,* 467.

Rapaport, D. (1942), "Freudian mechanisms and frustration experiments." *Psychoanal. Quart., 11,* 503-511.

—— (1951), "The conceptual models of psychoanalysis." *J. Pers., 20,* 56-81.

Raphael, T., and S. Gregg (1921), "Reaction in dementia praecox to the intravenous administration of non-specific proteins." *Amer. J. Psychiat., 1,* 31-40.

Rashkis, H. A., and G. S. Welsh (1946), "Detection of anxiety by use of the Wechsler scale." *J. clin. Psychol., 2,* 354-357.

Raup, R. B. (1926), *Complacency: the Foundation of Human Behavior*. New York: The Macmillan Company.

Reed, H. R. (1951), "The intelligency of epileptics." *J. genet. Psychol.*, 78, 145-152.

Rees, J. R. (1945), *The Shaping of Psychiatry by War*, New York: W. W. Norton & Company, Inc.

Reider, N. (1950), "The concept of normality." *Psychoanal. Quart.*, 19, 43-51.

Reymert, M. L., ed. (1950), *Feelings and Emotions: The Mooseheart Symposium*. New York: McGraw-Hill Book Company, Inc.

Ribble, Margaret (1938), "Clinical studies of instinctive reactions in new babies." *Amer. J. Psychiat.*, 95, 149-158.

—— (1939), "The significance of infantile sucking for the psychic development of the individual." *J. nerv. ment. Dis.*, 90, 455-463.

Richards, T. W. (1946), *Modern Clinical Psychology*. New York: McGraw-Hill Book Company, Inc.

Richter, C. P. (1947), "Biology of drives." *J. comp. physiol. Psychol.*, 40, 129-134.

Riesenman, F. R. (1950), "Anxiety and tension in the pathogenesis of sleep disturbances." *J. clin. Psychopath.*, 11, 82-84.

Ripley, H., E. Shore, and G. Papanicolaou (1940), "The effect of treatment of depression in the menopause with estrogenic hormone." *Amer. J. Psychiat.*, 96, 905-914.

Ritter, W. E. (1919), *The Unity of the Organism of the Organismal Conception of Life*. Boston: Richard G. Badger.

Rivers, W. H. R. (1920), *Instinct and the Unconscious*. Cambridge, England: Cambridge University Press.

Roback, A. A., ed. (1938), *Clinical and Experimental Studies in Personality* (2nd Ed.). Cambridge, Mass.: Sci-Art Publishers.

—— (1952), *The Psychology of Character* (3rd Ed.). Cambridge, Mass.: Sci-Art Publishers.

Robinson, J. H. (1921), *Mind in the Making*. New York: Harper and Brothers.

Roethlisberger, F. J., and W. J. Dickson (1941), *Management and the Worker*. Cambridge: Harvard University Press.

Rogers, C. R. (1942), *Counseling and Psychotherapy*. Boston: Houghton Mifflin Company.

—— (1951), *Client-Centered Therapy*. Boston: Houghton Mifflin Company.

Romanes, G. J. (1892), *Darwin, and After Darwin*. Chicago: Open Court Publishing Company.

Romano, J., ed. (1949), *Adaptation*. Ithaca, N. Y.: Cornell University.

Rosanoff, A. J. (1935), "The etiology of manic-depressive syndromes, with special reference to its occurrence in twins." *Amer. J. Psychiat.*, *91*, 725-762.

—— (1938), *Manual of Psychiatry and Mental Hygiene*. New York: John Wiley & Sons, Inc.

——, *et al.* (1931), "The etiology of so-called schizophrenic psychoses, with special reference to their occurrence in twins." *Amer. J. Psychiat.*, *91*, 247-286.

Rosen, H. (1953), "Hypnodiagnostic and hypnotherapeutic fantasy-evaca- and acting-out techniques." *J. clin. exp. Hypnosis*, *1*, 54-66.

Rosenzweig, S. (1944), "An outline of frustration theory," in J. McV. Hunt, ed. (1944), *Personality and the Behavior Disorders* (2 vols.). New York: The Ronald Press Company.

Ross, Helen (1951), *Fears of Children*. Chicago: Science Research Associates.

Ross, T. A. (1937), *The Common Neuroses: Their Treatment by Psychotherapy*. Baltimore: William Wood & Company.

Rothstein, H. S. (1942), "A study of aments with special abilities." Unpublished Master's thesis, Columbia University.

Ruckmick, C. A. (1936), *The Psychology of Feeling and Emotion*. New York: McGraw-Hill Book Company, Inc.

Rupp, C., and G. Wilson (1949), "General pathologic findings associated with cases of so-called functional psychoses." *J. nerv. ment. Dis.*, *110*, 419-424.

Russell, E. S. (1934), *The Behavior of Animals*. London: Edward Arnold & Co.

Russell, W. R. (1947), "The anatomy of traumatic epilepsy." *Brain*, *70*, 225-233.

Sadger, J. (1920), *Sleep Walking and Moon Walking*. Washington, D. C.: Nervous and Mental Disease Publishing Company.

Sahs, A. L., and J. F. Fulton (1940), "Somatic and autonomic reflex in spinal monkeys." *J. Neurophysiol.*, *3*, 258-268.

Sanders, M. J. (1937), "An experimental demonstration of regression in the rat." *J. exp. Psychol.*, *21*, 493-510.

Sarason, S. B. (1953), *Psychological Problems in Mental Deficiency* (2nd Ed.). New York: Harper and Brothers.

Sarason, S. B., and G. Mandler (1952), "Some correlates of test anxiety." *J. abnorm. soc. Psychol.*, *47*, 810-817.

Sarbin, T. R. (1950), "Mental age changes in experimental regression." *J. Pers.*, *19*, 221-228.

Sargant, W., and E. Slater (1940), "Acute war neuroses." *Lancet*, *249* (July 6, 1940), 1-2.

Sargent, S. S. (1950), *Social Psychology*. New York: The Ronald Press Company.

Sargent, S. S., and Marian W. Smith, eds. (1949), *Culture and Personality*. New York: The Viking Fund.

Scheinfeld, A. (1949), *Women and Men*. New York: Harcourt, Brace & Company, Inc.

—— (1950), *The New You and Heredity*. Philadelphia: Lippincott.

Schiele, B. C. (1946), "Huntington's chorea in relation to the heredity of personality disorders." *Lancet, 66*, 393-396.

Schiff, E. C. Dugan and L. Welch (1949), "The conditioned PGR and the EEG as indicators of anxiety." *J. abnorm. soc. Psychol., 44*, 549-552.

Schilder, P. F. (1938), *Psychotherapy*. New York: W. W. Norton & Company, Inc.

—— (1941), "The psychogenesis of alcoholism." *Quart. J. Stud. Alcohol., 2*, 277-292.

Schlosberg, H. (1954), "Three dimensions of emotion." *Psychol. Rev. 61*, 81-88.

Schoenfeld, W. N. (1950), "An experimental approach to anxiety, escape, and avoidance behavior," in P. H. Hoch and J. Zubin, eds. (1950), *Anxiety*, pp. 70-99. New York: Grune & Stratton.

Schwab, R. S. (1951), *Electroencephalography in Clinical Practice*. Philadelphia: W. B. Saunders Company.

Schwab, R. S., and T. DeLorme (1953), "Psychiatric findings in fatigue." *Amer. J. Psychiat., 109*, 621-625.

Schwarz, R. (1933), "Measurement of mental deterioration in dementia praecox." *Amer. J. Psychiat., 89*, 555-560.

Scott, J. P. (1949), "Genetics as a tool in experimental psychological research." *Amer. Psychol., 4*, 526-530.

Searle, L. V. (1949), "The organization of hereditary maze-brightness and maze-dullness." *Genet. Psychol. Monogr., 39*, 279-325.

Sears, R. R. (1943), *Survey of Objective Studies of Psychoanalytic Concepts*. New York: Social Science Research Council, Bull. No. 51.

Sears, R. R. (1944), "Experimental analysis of psychoanalytic phenomena," in J. McV. Hunt, ed. (1944), *Personality and the Behavior Disorders*, pp. 306-332. New York: The Ronald Press Company.

Seashore, H. S., and A. Bavelas (1942), "A study of frustration in children." *J. genet. Psychol., 61*, 279-314.

Selye, H. (1950), *Stress*. Montreal: Acta, Inc.

—— (1952), *The Story of the Adaptation Syndrome*. Montreal: Acta, Inc.

—— (1953), "The general-adaptation-syndrome in its relationships to neurology, psychology and psychopathology," in A. Weider (1953), *Contributions Toward Medical Psychology* (Vol. I.), pp. 234-274. New York: The Ronald Press Company.

——, and C. Fortier (1950), "Adaptive reactions to stress." *Psychosom. Med.*, *12*, 149-157.

Secunda, L. and K. H. Finley (1942), "Electroencephalographic studies in children presenting behavior disorders." *New Engl. J. Med.*, *226*, 850-854.

Seltzer, C. C., F. L. Wells, and E. B. McTerman (1948), "A relationship between Sheldonian somatotype and psychotype." *J. Pers.*, *16*, 431-436.

Senn, M. J. E., ed. (1953), *Problems of Infancy and Childhood.* New York: Josiah Macy, Jr., Foundation.

Shaffer, G. W. and R. S. Lazarus (1952), *Fundamental Concepts in Clinical Psychology.* New York: McGraw-Hill Book Company, Inc.

Shaffer, L. F. (1936), *Psychology of Adjustment.* Boston: Houghton Mifflin Company.

—— (1947), "Fear and courage in aerial combat." *J. consult. Psychol.*, *11*, 22-37.

Shands, H. C., and J. E. Finesinger (1952), "A note on the significance of fatigue." *Psychosom. Med.*, *14*, 209-314.

Sharp, W. L. (1950), "Fate of 395 mild neuropsychiatric cases salvaged from training period and taken into combat." *Amer. J. Psychiat.*, *106*, 801-807.

Shaw, R. F. (1934), *Finger Painting.* Boston: Little, Brown & Company.

Sheldon, W. H., S. S. Stevens, and W. B. Tucker (1940), *The Varieties of Human Physique.* New York: Harper and Brothers.

——, and S. S. Stevens (1942), *The Varieties of Temperament.* New York: Harper and Brothers.

——, E. M. Hartl, and E. McDermott (1949), *Varieties of Delinquent Youth.* New York: Harper and Brothers.

Sheps, J. G. (1947), "Intelligence of male non-institutionalized epileptics of military age." *J. ment. Sci.*, *93*, 82-88.

Sherrington, C. S. (1900), "Experiments on the value of vascular and visceral factors for the genesis of emotion." *Proc. Roy. Soc.*, *66*, 390-403.

—— (1953), *Man on His Nature* (2nd Ed.). New York: Doubleday and Company, Inc.

Shoben, E. J., Jr. (1950), "The Wechsler-Bellevue in the detection of anxiety: a test of the Rashkis-Welch hypothesis." *J. consult. Psychol.*, *14*, 40-45.

Shulman, A. J. (1950), "The etiology of schizophrenia." *Psychiat. Quart.*, 24, 515-531.

Sikes, Z. S. (1952), "Insulin shock therapy." *Neurophychiatry*, 2, 1-17.

Silver, G. A. (1953), "Carbon dioxide therapy." *Psychiat. Quart.*, 27, 52-58.

Simon, W. (1949), "Schizophrenia: fundamental concepts of eight noted psychiatrists." *Milit. Surg.*, 105, 375-381.

Simpson, G. G. (1949), *The Meaning of Evolution.* New Haven: Yale University Press.

———— (1953), *The Major Features of Evolution.* New York: Columbia University Press.

Singer, K. (1949), "The meaning of conflict." *Aust. J. Psychol. Phil.*, 27, 145-170.

———— (1950), *The Idea of Conflict.* Melbourne, Australia: Melbourne University Press.

Skeels, H. M. (1940), "Some Iowa studies of the mental growth of children in relation to differentials of environment: A summary." *Year B. Nat. Soc. Stud. Educ.*, 89 (II), 281-308.

Skinner, B. F. (1938), *The Behavior of Organisms.* New York: Appleton-Century-Crofts, Inc.

Slade, W. G. (1933), "Earthquake psychology. II," *Australas. J. Psychol. and Phil.*, II, 123-133.

Slavson, S. R. (1947), *The Practice of Group Therapy.* New York: International Universities Press.

———— (1940), "Group therapy." *Ment. Hyg.*, 24, 36-49.

———— (1952), *Child Psychotherapy.* New York: Columbia University Press.

Slotkin, J. S. (1952), *Personality Development.* New York: Harper and Brothers.

Smith, H. C. (1949), "Psychometric checks on hypotheses derived from Sheldon's work on physique and temperament." *J. Pers.*, 17, 310-320.

Smith, H. W. (1949), "Organism and environment: dynamic oppositions," in J. Romano, ed. (1949), *Adaptation*, pp. 23-52. Ithaca, N. Y.: Cornell University.

Snodgrasse, R. M. (1951), "Crime and the human constitution: a survey." *J. crim. law Criminol.*, 42, 18-52.

Snyder, W. U. (1947), "The present status of psychotherapeutic counseling." *Psychol. Bull.*, 44, 297-386.

Spence, K. W. (1951), "Theoretical interpretations of learning," in S. S. Stevens, ed. (1951), *Handbook of Experimental Psychology*, pp. 690-729. New York: John Wiley & Sons, Inc.

―――― (1951), "Theoretical interpretations of learning," in C. P. Stone, ed. (1951), *Comparative Psychology* (3rd Ed.), pp. 239-291. New York: Prentice-Hall, Inc.

――――, and I. E. Farber (1953), "Conditioning and extinction as a function of anxiety." *J. exp. Psychol., 45,* 116-119.

――――, and Janet Taylor (1951), "Anxiety and strength of the UCS as determiners of the amount of eyelid conditioning." *J. exp. Psychol., 42,* 183-188.

Spies, T. E., C. D. Aring, J. Gelperin, and W. B. Bean (1938), "The mental symptoms of pellagra; their relief with nicotinic acid." *Amer. J. Med. Sci., 196,* 467.

Stagner, R. (1931), "The redintegration of pleasant and unpleasant experiences." *Am. J. Psych., 43,* 463-468.

―――― (1948), *Psychology of Personality* (2nd Ed.). New York: McGraw-Hill Book Company, Inc.

―――― (1951), "Homeostasis as a unifying concept in personality theory." *Psychol. Rev., 38,* 5-17.

―――― (1952), "Personality development." *Rev. educ. Res., 22,* 459-474.

Standish, C. T., J. Mann, and D. Menzer (1950), "Some aspects of the psychopathology of schizophrenia." *Psychiatry, 13,* 439-445.

Starling, E. H. (1933), *Principles of Human Physiology* (6th Ed.; ed. and rev. by C. Lovatt Evans). Philadelphia: Lea & Febiger.

Steckle, L. C. (1949), *Problems of Human Adjustment.* New York: Harper and Brothers.

――――, and L. I. O'Kelly (1940), "The effect of electric shock upon later learning and regression in the rat." *J. Psychol., 9,* 365-370.

――――, and ―――― (1941), "Persistence of response as a function of thirst in terms of early experience with electric shock." *J. Comp. Psychol., 32,* 1-9.

Stein, M. (1952), "Traumatic war neuroses: a survey or behavior disturbances under combat stress and their prophylaxis and treatment." *Neuropsychiatry, 2,* 18-42.

Stellar, E. (1954), "The physiology of motivation." *Psychol. Rev., 61,* 5-22.

Stewart, G. R. (1936), *Ordeal by Hunger.* New York: Henry Holt & Company, Inc.

Stolurow, L. M., ed. (1953), *Readings in Learning.* New York: Prentice-Hall, Inc.

Stone, C. P. (1949), *Case Histories in Abnormal Psychology.* Stanford University. Calif.: Stanford University Press.

Storch, A. (1926), *The Primitive Archaic Forms of Inner Experiences and Thoughts in Schizophrenia.* Washington, D. C.: Nervous and Mental Disease Publishing Company.

Stouffer, S. A., and J. Toby (1951), "Role conflict and personality." *Amer. J. Sociol., 56,* 395-406.

Strauss, H., W. E. Rahm, Jr., and S. E. Barrera (1940), "Studies on a group of children with psychiatric disorders. I. Electroencephalographic studies." *Psychosomat. Med., 2,* 34-42.

Strecker, E. A. (1941), "Chronic alcoholism: a psychological survey." *Quart. J. Stud. Alcohol., 2,* 12-17.

—— (1952), *Basic Psychiatry.* New York: Random House, Inc.

——, and F. T. Chambers (1945), *Alcohol, One Man's Meat.* New York: The Macmillan Company.

——, F. G. Ebaugh, and J. R. Ewalt (1951), *Practical Clinical Psychiatry* (7th Ed.). Philadelphia: Blakiston.

Sumner, W. G. (1906), *Folkways.* Boston: Ginn and Company.

Symonds, P. M. (1946), *The Dynamics of Human Adjustment.* New York: Appleton-Century-Crofts, Inc.

—— (1949a), *Dynamic Psychology.* New York: Appleton-Century-Crofts, Inc.

—— (1949b), *Adolescent Fantasy, an Investigation of the Picture-story Method of Personality Study.* New York: Columbia University Press.

—— (1951), *The Ego and the Self.* New York: Appleton-Century-Crofts, Inc.

Tait, C. D., Jr., and G. C. Burns (1951), "Involutional illness; a survey of 379 patients, including follow-up study of 114." *Amer. J. Psychiat., 108,* 27-36.

Tanner, J. M. (1951), "Current advances in the study of physique, photogrammetric anthropometry and an androgyny scale." *Lancet, 260,* 574-579.

Taylor, Janet A. (1951), "The relationship of anxiety to the conditioned eyelid response." *J. exp. Psychol., 41,* 81-92.

—— (1953), "A personality scale of manifest anxiety." *J. abnorm. soc. Psychol., 48,* 285-290.

——, and K. W. Spence (1952), "The relationship of anxiety level to performance in serial learning." *J. exp. Psychol., 44,* 61-64.

Temkin, O. (1945), *The Falling Sickness: A History of Epilepsy from the Greeks to the Beginnings of Modern Neurology.* Baltimore: Johns Hopkins University Press.

Terman, L. M., and C. C. Miles (1936), *Sex and Personality.* New York: McGraw-Hill Book Company, Inc.

Thetford, W. N. (1952), "Fantasy perceptions in the personality development of normal and deviant children." *Amer. J. Orthopsychiat., 22,* 545-550.

Thimann, J. (1946), "The conditioned reflex treatment for alcoholics," in B. Glueck, ed. (1946), *Current Therapies of Personality Disorders.* New York: Grune and Stratton.

Thompson, D'A. W. (1917), *Growth and Form.* Cambridge, England: Cambridge University Press.

Thompson, M. (1949), *The Cry and the Covenant.* New York: Doubleday & Co.

Thorndike, E. L. (1935), *The Psychology of Wants, Interests, and Attitudes.* New York: Appleton-Century-Crofts, Inc.

―――― (1940), *Human Nature and the Social Order.* New York: The Macmillan Company.

Thorndike, R. L. (1935), "Organization of behavior in the albino rat." *Genet. Psychol. Monog.,* 17, 1-70.

Thorne, F. C. (1945), "Directive psychotherapy. II. The theory of self-consistency." *J. clin. Psychol.,* 1, 155-162. (*Et. seq., J. clin. Psychol.,* 1945-1948.)

―――― (1950), *Principles of Personality Counseling.* Brandon, Vt.: Journal of Clinical Psychology.

Thornton, N. (1951), "The relation between crime and psychopathic personality." *J. crim. law Criminol.,* 42, 99-204.

Thorpe, L. P. (1938), *Psychological Foundations of Personality: A Guide for Students and Teachers.* New York: McGraw-Hill Book Company, Inc.

―――, and B. Katz (1948), *The Psychology of Abnormal Behavior: A Dynamic Approach.* New York: The Ronald Press Company.

Thorpe, M. R., ed. (1924), *Organic Adaptation to Environment.* New Haven, Conn.: Yale University Press.

Tichy, Fae Y. (1953), "Barbiturate intoxication." *Neurology,* 3, 58-67.

Tilney, F. (1928), *The Brain from Ape to Man* (2 vols.). New York: Paul B. Hoeber, Inc.

―――― (1930), *The Master of Destiny.* New York: Doubleday & Company, Inc.

Tillim, S. J. (1952), "Bromide intoxication." *Amer. J. Psychiat.,* 108, 109-202.

Tolman, E. C. (1942), *Drives Toward War.* New York: Appleton-Century-Crofts, Inc.

―――― (1949), *Purposive Behavior in Animals and Men.* (Reprint of 1932.) Berkeley: University of California Press.

Toynbee, A. J. (1947), *A Study of History.* (Abridgement by D. C. Somervell.) New York: Oxford University Press.

Trapp, C., and E. James (1937), "Comparative intelligence rating in the four types of dementia praecox." *J. nerv. ment. Dis.,* 86, 399-404.

Tredgold, A. L. (1947), *A Textbook of Mental Deficiency* (6th Ed.). Baltimore: The Williams and Wilkins Company.

Tryon, R. C. (1940), "Genetic differences in maze learning in rats." *Thirty-ninth Year Book of the National Society for the Study of Education,* Part I, 111-119.

Tweed, A. R. (1948), "Two cases of bromide psychosis simulating an involutional paranoid." *Amer. J. Psychother., 2,* 650-657.

Ulett, G. A., G. Gleser, Ann Lawler, and G. Winokur (1952), "Psychiatric screening personnel. IV. An experimental investigation of development of an EEG index of anxiety tolerance by means of photic stimulation—its validation by psychological and psychiatric criteria." USAF, *Sch. Aviat. Med.,* Proj. No. 21-37-002, Rep. No. 4.

Ulett, G. A., G. Gleser, G. Winokur, and Ann Lawler (1952), "The EEG as an index of anxiety-proneness." *EEG clin. Neurophysiol., 4,* 379-380.

Ullman, J. R. (1947), *Kingdom of Adventure: Everest.* New York: William Sloane Associates, Inc.

U. S. Veterans Administration (1952), Reference Library Division. *Bibliotherapy: A Bibliography.* Washington: U. S. Government Printing Office.

Van Ormer, E. B. (1932), "Retention after intervals of sleep and waking." *Arch. Psychol., 21,* No. 137.

Vaughn, C. L. (1937), "Factors in rat learning." *Comp. Psychol. Monog., 14,* No. 3.

Vaughn, W. F. (1928), *The Lure of Superiority.* New York: Henry Holt & Company, Inc.

Veblen, T. (1899), *The Theory of the Leisure Class.* New York: The Macmillan Company.

Vigotsky, L. (1934), "Thought in schizophrenia." *Arch. Neurol. Psychiat., Chicago. 31,* 1063-1077.

Voegtlin, W. L. (1940), "Treatment of alcoholism by establishing a conditioned reflex." *Amer. J. Med. Sci. 199,* 102.

Vogt, W. (1948), *Road to Survival.* New York: William Sloane Associates, Inc.

Von Bertalanffy, L. (1951), "Theoretical models in biology and psychology." *J. Pers., 20,* 24-38.

Wallenberg-Chermak, Marianne (1952), "Delusions of multiple pregnancy in psychotics." *Psychiat. Quart. Suppl. 26,* 244-247.

Waller, W. (1938), *The Family: A Dynamic Interpretation.* New York: The Dryden Press, Inc.

Wallin, J. E. W. (1949), *Personality Maladjustments and Mental Hygiene* (2nd Ed.). New York: McGraw-Hill Book Company, Inc.

———— (1949), *Children with Mental and Physical Handicaps*. New York: Prentice-Hall, Inc.

Ward, Mary Jane (1946), *The Snake Pit*. New York: Random House, Inc.

Warner, S. J. (1950), "The Wechsler-Bellevue psychometric pattern in anxiety neurosis." *J. Consult. Psychol., 14,* 297-304.

Warren, R. L. (1949), "Social disorganization and the interrelationship of cultural roles." *Amer. Sociol. Rev., 14,* 83-87.

Watkins, J. G. (1950), *Hypnotherapy of War Neurosis*. New York: The Ronald Press Company.

Watson, R. L., ed. (1949), *Readings in the Clinical Method in Psychology*. New York: Harper and Brothers.

———— (1951), *The Clinical Method in Psychology*. New York: Harper and Brothers.

Webster, A. P. (1950), "High altitude-high velocity flying with special reference to the human factors: I. Outline of human problems." *J. aviat. Med., 21,* 82-84, 89.

————, and O. E. Reynolds (1950), "High altitude, high velocity flying with special reference to the human factors. II. Time of consciousness during exposure to various pressure altitudes." *J. aviat. Med., 21,* 237-245.

Wechsler, I. (1929), *The Neuroses*. Philadelphia: W. B. Saunders Company.

———— (1943), *A Text Book of Clinical Neurology*. Philadelphia: W. B. Saunders Company.

Wegrocki, H. J. (1939), "A critique of cultural and statistical concepts of abnormality." *J. abnorm. soc. Psychol., 34,* 166-178.

Weider, A., ed. (1953), *Contributions Toward Medical Psychology* (Vol. I.), pp. 136-170. New York: The Ronald Press Company.

Weihofen, H. (1933), *Insanity as a Defense in Criminal Law*. New York: The Commonwealth Fund.

Weil, A. (1945), *Textbook of Neuropathology* (2nd Ed.). New York: Grune & Stratton.

Weinberg, S. K. (1952), *Society and Personality Disorders*. New York: Prentice-Hall, Inc.

Weiner, N. (1948), *Cybernetics*. New York: John Wiley & Sons, Inc.

Weisenburg, T., and K. E. McBride (1935), *Aphasia: A Clinical and Psychological Study*. New York: The Commonwealth Fund.

Weiss, E., and O. S. English (1949), *Psychosomatic Medicine* (2nd Ed.). Philadelphia: W. B. Saunders Company.

Weiss, P. (1949), "The biological basis of adaptation," in J. Romano, ed. (1949), *Adaptation*, pp. 1-22. Ithaca, N. Y.: Cornell University Press.

Welch, L. (1953), "Human conditioning and anxiety." *Ann. N. Y. Acad. Sci., 56,* 266-272.

———, and O. Diethelm (1950), "Effect of pathologic anxiety on inductive reasoning." *Arch. Neurol. Psychiat., Chicago, 63,* 87-101.

———, and J. F. Kubis (1947), "The effect of anxiety on the conditioning rate and stability of the PGR." *J. Psychol., 23,* 83-91.

———, and ——— (1947b), "Conditioned PGR (psychogalvanic response) in states of pathological anxiety." *J. nerv. ment. Dis., 105,* 372-381.

Wellman, B. L. (1934), "Growth in intelligence under differing school environments." *J. Exp. Ed., 3,* 59-83.

Wells, F. L. (1935), "Social maladjustments: Adaptive regression," in C. Murchison, ed. (1935), *Handbook of Social Psychology.* Worcester, Mass.: Clark University Press.

———, and W. L. Woods (1946), "Outstanding traits in a selected college group, with some reference to career interests and war records." *Genet. Psychol., Monogr., 33,* 127-149.

Wembridge, E. R. (1931), *Life Among the Lowbrows.* Boston: Houghton Mifflin Company.

Wenger, P. (1952), "The value of music in the successful psychotherapy of a schizophrenic patient." *Psychiat. Quart. Suppl., 26,* 202-209.

Wepman, J. M. (1951), *Recovery from Aphasia.* New York: The Ronald Press Company.

Werner, A., E. Hoctor, and C. Ault (1941), "Involutional melancholia: A review with additional cases." *Arch. Neurol. Psychiat., Chicago, 45,* 944-952.

Werner, H. (1940), *Comparative Psychology of Mental Development.* New York: Harper and Brothers.

Wertheimer, M. (1945), *Productive Thinking.* New York: Harper and Brothers.

Wesley, Elizabeth (1953), "Perseverative behavior in a concept formation task as a function of manifest anxiety and rigidity." *J. abnorm. soc. Psychol., 48,* 129-134.

Wexberg, L. E. (1949), "Insomnia as related to anxiety and ambition." *J. clin. Psychopath. 4,* 373-375.

Wheeler, W. M. (1928), *Foibles of Insects and Men.* New York: Alfred A. Knopf, Inc.

Whitby, C. W. M. (1947), "Early traumatic epilepsy." *Brain, 70,* 416-439.

Whitney, D. D. (1946), *Family Skeletons.* Lincoln: University of Nebraska Press.

White, A. D. (1896), A *History of the Warfare of Science with Theology in Christendom.* New York: D. Appleton.

White, R. W. (1948), *The Abnormal Personality.* New York: The Ronald Press Company.

Wilkins, W. L. (1952), "Applications of clinical psychology to addiction," in D. Brower and L. E. Abt, eds. (1952), *Progress in Clinical Psychology* (Vol. I, Sec. 2), pp. 481-490. New York: Grune & Stratton.

Williams, R. D. (1938), "Studies in contemporary psychological theory." *J. Psychol.*, 6, 69-79; 99-114.

Williamson, E. G. (1939), *How to Counsel Students.* New York: Mc-Graw-Hill Book Company, Inc.

Wilson, S. A. K. (1924), "Pathological laughing and crying." *J. Nerv. and Psychopathol.*, 4, 299–333.

——— (1929), *Modern Problems in Neurology.* Baltimore: William Wood & Company.

Winthrop, H. A. (1947), "A contribution toward a scientific program for a systematic constitutional psychology." *J. Gen. Psychol.*, 37, 139-157.

Witmer, H. (1939), "Some parallels between dynamic psychiatry and cultural anthropology." *Amer. J. Orthopsychiat.*, 9, 95-102.

Wittels, F. (1941), "The phantom of omnipotence." *Psychoanal. Rev.*, 28, 163-172.

Wittenborn, J. R., and J. D. Holzberg (1951), "The generality of psychiatric syndromes." *J. consult. Psychol.*, 15, 372-380.

———, and F. A. Mettler (1951), "Practical correlates of psychiatric symptoms." *J. consult. Psychol.*, 15, 505-510.

Wittman, M. (1933), "The Babcock deterioration test in state hospital practice." *J. Abnorm. Soc. Psychol.*, 28, 70-83.

Wittman, Phyllis (1939), "Diagnosis and analysis of temperament for a group of alcoholics compared with controls." *Elgin Papers*, 3, 94-99.

———, and W. Sheldon (1948), "A proposed classification of psychiatric behavior reactions." *Amer. J. Psychiat.*, 105, 124-128.

———, ———, and C. J. Katz (1948), "A study of the relationship between constitutional variations and fundamental psychotic behavior reactions." *J. nerv. ment. Dis.*, 108, 470-476.

Wolf, A., and D. Cowen (1952), "Histopathology of schizophrenia and other psychoses of unknown origin," in Milbank Memorial Fund Conference (1952), *The Biology of Mental Health and Disease*, pp. 469-497. New York: Paul B. Hoeber, Inc.

Wolf, S., and H. G. Wolff (1943), *Human Gastric Function.* Oxford: Oxford University Press.

Wolfe, J. B. (1939), "An exploratory study of food storing in rats." *J. Comp. Psychol.*, 28, 97-108.

Woltman, A. G. (1952), "Play and related techniques," in D. Brower and L. E. Abt, eds. (1952), *Progress in Clinical Psychology* (Vol. I, Sec. 1), pp. 312-323. New York: Grune & Stratton.

Woodard, J. W. (1938), "The relation of personality structure to the structure of culture." *Amer. Sociol. Rev.*, 3, 637-651.

Woods, F. A. (1906), *Mental and Moral Heredity in Royalty*. New York: Henry Holt & Company, Inc.

Woodworth, R. S., and H. Schlosberg (1954), *Experimental Psychology* (Rev. Ed.). New York: Henry Holt and Company.

Wortis, S. (1953), Testimony given at hearings before the Committee of Interstate and Foreign Commerce. House of Representatives, Eighty Third Congress. Washington: U. S. Government Printing Office.

Yap, P. M. (1951). "Mental diseases peculiar to certain cultures: a survey of comparative psychiatry." *J. ment. Sci.*, 97, 313-327.

Yerkes, A. W. (1916), "Comparisons of the behavior of stock and inbred albino rats." *J. Anim. Behav.*, 6, 267-296.

Yerkes, R. M. (1913), "The heredity of savageness and wildness in rats." *J. Anim. Behav.*, 3, 286-296.

Young, Florence, M., and Virginia A. Pilts (1951), "The performance of congenital syphilitics on the Wechsler Intelligence Scale for children." *J. consult. Psychol.*, 15, 239-242.

Young, K. (1952), *Personality and Problems of Adjustment* (2nd Ed.). New York: Appleton-Century-Crofts, Inc.

Young, P. T. (1936), *Motivation of Behavior*. New York: John Wiley & Sons, Inc.

—— (1943), *Emotion in Man and Animal*. New York: John Wiley & Sons, Inc.

—— (1951), "Motivation of animal behavior," in C. P. Stone, ed. (1951), *Comparative Psychology* (3rd Ed.). New York: Prentice-Hall, Inc.

Zachry, C. B. (1940), *Emotion and Conduct in Adolescence*. New York: D. Appleton-Century Company, Inc.

Zeller, A. F. (1950a), "An experimental analogue of repression. I. Historical summary." *Psychol. Bull.*, 47, 39-51.

—— (1950b), "An experimental analogue of repression. II. The effect of individual failure and success on memory measured by relearning." *J. exp. Psychol.*, 40, 411-422.

Zilboorg, G. (1941), *A History of Medical Psychology*. New York: W. W. Norton & Company, Inc.

—— (1935), *The Medical Man and the Witch During the Renaissance*. Baltimore: Johns Hopkins Press.

Zinsser, H. (1940), *As I Remember Him: The Biography of R. S.* Boston: Little, Brown & Company.

Index

A